Excavations alongside Roman Ermin
Gloucestershire and Wiltshire

The archaeology of the A419/A417
Swindon to Gloucester Road Scheme

Volume 2: Medieval and post-medieval activity,
finds and environmental evidence

By Andrew Mudd, Robert J. Williams and Alan Lupton

With major contributions by

T Allen, A Barclay, S Lawrence, S Mortimer,
J Muir, A Parkinson and J Timby

and contributions by

D Allen, L Allen, K Atherton, K Ayres, P Blinkhorn, P Bradley, A Boyle,
G Campbell, K M Clark, C Cropper, G B Dannel, J A Davies, B Dickinson,
T Durden, H Drake, M Henig, N Jeffries, G McDonnell, D Mackreth,
N Mitchell, W R G Moore, A Powell, R Pelling, M Robinson,
F Roe, R Scaife, I Scott, K Welsh and D Williams

Editor Angela Boyle

Illustrations by M Costello, R Goller, M Middleton, L Padilla and R Read

Oxford Archaeological Unit
1999

© Oxford Archaeological Unit
Volume 2 ISBN 0–904220–18–4
Series ISBN 0–904220–16–8

Printed in Great Britain by
UNiSKiLL Ltd
Eynsham, Oxfordshire

The publishers wish to acknowledge with gratitude
the funding by RMS Ltd
which made this publication possible.

Volume 1: Contents

Contents

Contents

Volume 2: Contents

Contents

Contents

Volume 1: List of figures

CHAPTER 4

CHAPTER 5

Volume 2: List of figures

CHAPTER 6

CHAPTER 7

CHAPTER 8

CHAPTER 9

Volume 1: List of tables

Volume 2: List of tables

CHAPTER 8

Volume 1: List of plates

Plate 4.11   Area A roundhouses. The earlier pair of entrance postholes under excavation
(structure 1463) lie inside the later pair (structure 1464). 162
Plate 4.12   Area A roundhouse. The picture shows the later entrance postholes and interior flooring. 164
Plate 4.13   Area C Oven 647. The latest in a series of ovens on this spot. 172
Plate 4.14   Area A interior of superimposed structures under excavation.
Stone wall footings 758 (structure 1452) in the foreground overlie
the earlier penannular ditches the later of which is filled with pitched
stone to the left. Hearth 756 (centre) lies close to the later wall. Patches of
stone flooring occupy the interior. 195
Plate 4.15   Area A. Sherds of Dressel 20 amphora, almost indistinguishable from
stone, lie in front of and under a large facing stone of wall 730 (structure 1452). 196
Plate 4.16   Area A. Squared grooved stone lying against wall 841 at the probable entrance
to structure 1452. 196
Plate 4.17   Area A structure 1452. Traces of the stone-footed circular or polygonal building.
The ditches and stone culvert of the earlier structures lie to the left. 197
Plate 4.18   Area D structure 1457. The building has been cut away by the medieval lynchet (top). 203
Plate 4.19   Corn dryer 42. 213
Plate 4.20   Area A. Structure 985 is defined by a semi-circular gully. The stone culvert of the
earlier penannular ditch lies in the foreground and sections through the
penannular ditches are being excavated in the background. 218
Plate 4.21   Period 2b Area A. Linear wall 36 butts curving wall 722 (structure 713).
The pitched stone to the left may have come from the collapse of 36. 220

CHAPTER 5

Volume 2: List of plates

CHAPTER 6

CHAPTER 8

Acknowledgements

The A419/A417 Design, Build, Finance and Operate (DBFO) contract was awarded to Road Management Services (Gloucester) Ltd (RMS) in January 1996 by the Secretary of State for Transport. The construction project was undertaken by RMS's sister company Road Management Group Construction Joint Venture (RMGJV), both companies are a consortium of four equal partners, AMEC, Alfred McAlpine, Brown and Root and Dragados. The Oxford Archaeological Unit (OAU) were contracted by RMGJV's environmental and landscape consultants, Chris Blandford Associates (CBA) to provide the total archaeological input. The Highways Agency's Department's Agent for the project was WSP Civils (formerly Frank Graham Consulting Engineers).

The successful integration of the civil engineering works with the archaeological excavations and watching briefs resulted from the close-co-operation of many individuals from the different companies involved. The following deserve special mention and thanks for all their help and assistance. Bob Golding (RMGJV – Project Director). John McGinty (RMGJV – Project Manager), Phil Smith (RMS – Agent) Mike Reid (RMS – Assistant Agent), Derek Parody (Parkman/ Howard Humphreys – Designers Principal), Peter Bigby (RMGJV – Chief Engineer), Tony Zandona and Dave Willis (WSP Civils Engineers – Department's Agent) and Philip Russell-Vick and Mark Holland (CBA).

Thanks are also due to other RMGJV staff and their sub-contractors for their unstinting help and patience in providing a variety of services, particularly include the following: Rob Ayres, Steve Ayres, Sue Barlow, Peter Bundell, Andy Bowyer, Dave Cox, Jeff Curry, Colin Edwards, Tony Fielden, Duncan Gibson, Ian Gillett, Keith Godson, Dave Ireland, John Kirby, John Nichols, Dave Pickering, Richard Pollard, Keith Titman, Dave Wooldridge, Richard Young, and last, but not least, Packie McGettigan, RMGJV's Plant Manager for never failing to get the right plant to the right place at the right time.

In addition grateful thanks must be expressed to Helen Glass and Dave Maynard of CBA, who acted as Project Archaeologists, for their support and enthusiasm during the setting up, execution and publication of the project. The Department's Agent's archaeological advisors (Jan Wills and Charles Parry of Gloucestershire County Council) monitored the archaeological work, and Jan Wills and Roy Canham (County Archaeologists for Gloucestershire and Wiltshire respectively) gave invaluable advice on the archaeology of the region.

We would like to acknowledge the co-operation of English Heritage who are responsible for the management of the Scheduled Ancient Monuments which were affected by the road scheme. Liaison was maintained throughout the project with the County Archaeologists for Gloucestershire and Wiltshire and with English Heritage.

An archaeological project the size and complexity of the A419/A417 DBFO Road scheme could not have been completed both within time and budget without the unstinting assistance of numerous staff of the Oxford Archaeological Unit. George Lambrick, OAU's Deputy Director, was the Project Director and was instrumental in both setting up the project and ensuring the intellectual coherence and credibility of what at first seemed to be a varied assortment of sites of different periods and types.

The principal Field Directors and Supervisors were Richard Brown, Sean Cook, Rob Early, Alan Lupton, Brian Matthews, Andrew Mudd, Jeff Muir, Paul Murray, Andrew Parkinson, Mick Parsons, Phil Piper, Mark Roberts, Ken Welsh and Duncan Wood, ably and professionally assisted by Assistant Supervisors and Field Technicians too numerous to mention by name. Suffice it to say they know who they are, and all must be congratulated on their enthusiasm and perseverance, especially those who worked at Birdlip Quarry, in deepest winter.

The core watching brief staff consisted of Sean Cook, Mark Gocher, Andy Mayes, James Mumford, Paul Murray and Mike Simms whose endurance must be congratulated given the long hours involved and the often tedious nature of the work. Leigh Allen (Finds Manager), Greg Campbell (Environmental Manager), Paul Hughes (Graphics Manager) and Nicky Scott (Archives Manager) all gave invaluable assistance and support at every stage of the project. Dr Mark Robinson provided the main environmental advice during both the fieldwork and post-excavation phases of the project. Other members of staff including Tim Allen, Alistair Barclay, Paul Booth, Theresa Durden and David Jennings have all given invaluable advice during the post-excavation stage. Dave Wilkinson provided Health and Safety advice. Particular mention must be made of Angela Boyle whose editing skills have ensured the seamless transition of draft texts into the finished publication. Dr Martin Henig and Dr Ann Woodward acted as academic referees. Roger Featherstone (RCHM[E]) provided OAU with some invaluable aerial photographs.

Mention must be given to those who lay behind the scenes, whose contribution to the project is difficult to describe or define precisely, but without whose efforts and assistance the work would have been so much more difficult, namely: Alison Gledhill, Simon Palmer, Kay Procter, David Stevens, Louise Waltham, Graham Walton and Ianto Wain.

We are grateful to Bryn Walters for permission to reproduce his aerial photograph of Latton 'Roman Pond' (Plate 4.7).

Fiona Roe would like to acknowledge the Department of Earth Sciences, University of Oxford, for the use of facilities, and Jeremy Hyde, who made the thin section. Roger Howell assisted with the necessary fieldwork. She would also like to thank Sue Byrne at Gloucester Museum, Robert Clary at Chedworth Roman Villa, Guy Kilminster at Cheltenham Museum and Judy Mills and John Paddock at Corinium Museum.

Adrienne Powell would like to thank Kate M. Clark for examining and reporting on the skeletal pathology within the animal bone assemblages at Duntisbourne Grove and Middle Duntisbourne, Kevin Rielly for

sharing unpublished data from Bagendon and Ditches and Dave Webb who provided photographs for the report.

Leigh Allen is grateful to Arthur MacGregor for his identification of the horn vessel from Cowley Underbridge Trench 6.

Angela Boyle would particularly like to thank Paul Hughes, Mike Middleton and Rob Reed for their advice and many long hours working on the final illustrations for the project at short notice.

Bob Williams
Project Manager
July 1999

Summary

The Oxford Archaeological Unit undertook a series of excavations along the line of the Swindon to Gloucester DBFO road improvement in 1996 and 1997. The road ran between Nettleton in the Gloucestershire Cotswolds and Cricklade on the Thames. The work was undertaken on behalf of the construction consortium Road Management Group (RMG). The work was carried out according to specifications approved and monitored by the Highways Agency, and included a range of mitigation strategies selected as appropriate archaeological responses. In addition a scheme-wide watching brief was undertaken along the 25 km route. The sites examined included both those identified from previous surveys and evaluations, and new discoveries.

The work entailed the excavation of around thirty-five sites, or parts of sites, of differing types and periods. These included two adjoining Bronze Age ring ditches near Preston, middle Iron Age settlements at Highgate House, Preston and Ermin Farm, late Iron Age enclosures at Duntisbourne Grove and Middle Duntisbourne, a Roman settlement at Birdlip Quarry, and a medieval kitchen block at Street Farm, Latton. In addition there were a number of other discoveries

relating particularly to Roman Ermin Street. These included a probable roadside funerary monument and trackway at Field's Farm, Roman trackway ditches and quarries at Court Farm, Latton and part of a late Roman midden at Weavers Bridge. Ermin Street itself was examined with seven trenches through the Roman and later roads. Burford Road (Akeman Street) was examined in two sections with less significant results.

Important environmental evidence was obtained from work at Latton 'Roman Pond' (within a Scheduled Ancient Monument) and in the Churn Valley. A programme of radiocarbon dating was also undertaken, both in relation to the environmental sequences and the earlier prehistoric and Iron Age sites.

A consistent theme of fieldwork was the coincidental discovery of small numbers of prehistoric features as a result of stripping large areas (such as at Birdlip Quarry, Duntisbourne Grove and Trinity Farm). Less surprisingly, numbers of Roman, medieval and post-medieval field boundaries were recorded as well as traces of ridge-and-furrow cultivation. The evidence for earlier boundaries and agriculture has been presented along with other miscellaneous features in summary form.

Chapter 6:   The Medieval and Post-Medieval Periods

INTRODUCTION

Evidence for medieval and post-medieval activity was scattered throughout the sites excavated on the project. This mostly consisted of boundaries, ridge and furrow, lynchets and other features reflecting agricultural land use. There was little evidence of settlement, and Street Farm was the only site where medieval and post-medieval buildings were examined. A post-medieval dewpond was excavated near Daglingworth Quarry. Quantities of medieval and later finds were recovered from superficial contexts at several sites where no other associated archaeological features were found. A few sherds of early Saxon pottery from two sites – Latton and Duntisbourne Leer - are significant for their rarity in this region, and are also mentioned in this chapter.

The persistence of Roman landscape features into medieval and later times is a characteristic of a number of sites. This most clearly applies to Ermin Street and also to other Roman roads and trackways. The post-Roman elements of the road investigations are more conveniently dealt with in Chapter 5, although a few minor trackways and cobbled surfaces are included in the present chapter. Post-Roman features on a number of the other sites are included in Chapter 4, either because they are very minor (such as the wheel ruts at Field's Farm, Birdlip Quarry and other sites) or because they develop from Roman ones and naturally take their place in the narrative of the Roman site. This particularly applies to the ditches and plough-soils at Latton 'Roman Pond' and the ditches at Exhibition Barn.

The archaeology at Street Farm comprises the bulk of this chapter. The evidence from the other sites forms a more miscellaneous collection and is considered under topics which include, among others, surface scatters of material, agricultural features (particularly ridge and furrow), boundaries, trackways, and the river channels at Weavers Bridge. The locations of all these sites are shown on Figure 6.1.

STREET FARM
By Ken Welsh, Paul Blinkhorn and Andrew Mudd

Introduction

The village of Latton, Wiltshire, lies on the first gravel terrace between the floodplains of the river Churn and Ampney Brook. The centre of the village is situated to the north-east of Ermin Street (A419) although cartographic evidence indicates that houses have existed at a distance from the village centre since at least the late 18th century, fronting the Cirencester Road on both sides (Figs 6.6–6.7).

The development corridor south-east of Street Farm passed through the land between the A419 and the backfilled Thames and Severn Canal, skirting behind the present properties on the south-western road frontage, and rejoining the line of the A419 south of

Latton (Figs 4.32 and 6.2). There was potentially some impact on archaeological remains relating to earlier buildings in this area. Evaluation in 1991, which was aimed at finding possible house platforms, revealed little except a possible Roman quarry pit and cobbled surfaces of probable post-medieval date which lay close to the modern road (CAT 1991, 61–3). For the stage 3 mitigation an area of 2.1 hectares was archaeologically stripped and a strategy of sample excavation adopted. Initially, a 6 m-wide corridor along the south-western edge of the site was stripped and recorded in advance of the construction of a haul road. This identified dense quarry pitting, some linear features and the foundations of a limestone building (building 164). The haul road was diverted to allow detailed excavation of this building. Building 164, which is the main subject of this chapter, proved to be a medieval kitchen which had undergone modifications and a probable change of use in the post-medieval period.

The quarry pits were examined by sample excavation. Two trenches positioned to examine the possible Roman quarrying are described in Chapter 5. A third trench lay within the backfilled Thames and Severn Canal and was abandoned.

In October 1996, following the main excavation, the line of a new water main was stripped under archaeological supervision. Several property boundaries were recorded, extending from the road towards the main excavation area. The boundaries overlay extensive quarry pitting, mostly of post-medieval date and probably associated with the maintenance of the road. A possible roadside ditch, or a continuation of the linear Roman quarry (Chapter 5), was also excavated.

Medieval and later quarrying

Throughout the site much of the natural gravel had been affected by small-scale quarrying. Very few of the quarry pits could be clearly defined due to later disturbance. The Roman pits are described in Chapter 5. Medieval quarrying was recorded underlying building 164 (see below) and the pitting extended to the north and north-east, towards the modern road. The pits displayed a great variability of size and shape but were generally shallow. In many instances the depth of the pits coincided with the level of the modern water table and this may have influenced the depth to which they were originally dug.

The main area of regular, closely cutting pits was recorded between boundaries 1 and 2 (Fig. 6.2). The upper fills of these pits were identical and the individual pits were roughly rectangular with an average width of *c.* 2 m and an average length of *c.* 3 m. Where excavated, the depth did not exceed 0.4 m. Much of the rest of the site had also been affected by

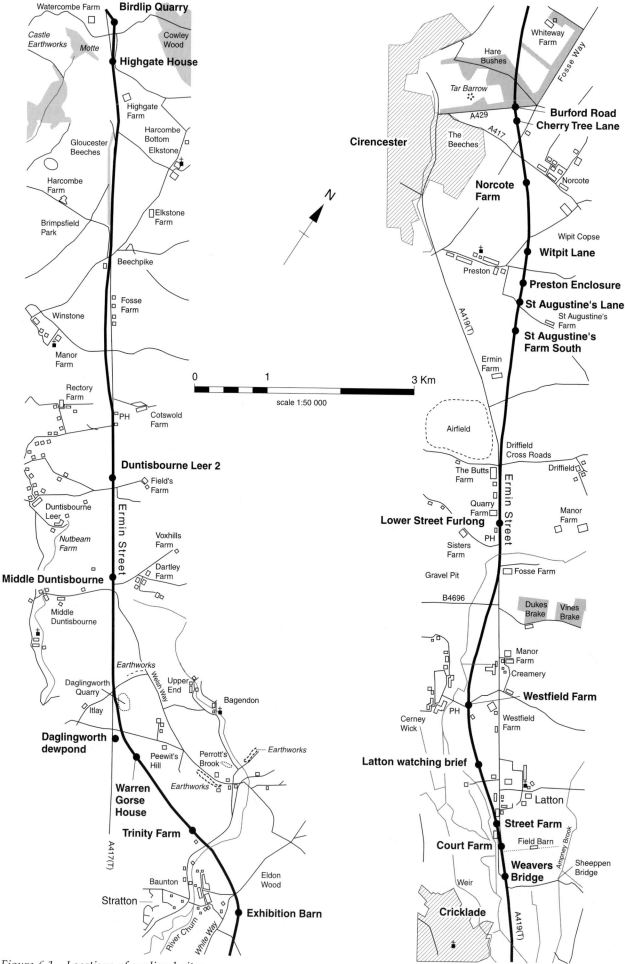

Figure 6.1   Locations of medieval sites.

quarrying, although regular, rectangular pitting was only clearly present in two areas, to the east and west of boundary 3 and two areas immediately to the east and west of boundary 7. The pits in these areas had similar dimensions to those found between boundaries 1 and 2. Post-medieval red earthenware pottery was recovered from pits in the eastern area of boundary 3 (contexts 540, 541 and 542). All of the areas of this later, regular quarry pitting appeared to respect the line of the post-medieval plot boundaries that stretched back from the road frontage.

Building 164

Summary

Building 164 was a rectangular stone-founded structure, located approximately 22 m from the present A419 and positioned roughly parallel to it. It appears to have served as a kitchen block in its earliest form, as it contained the remains of three ovens, two of which may have been in use simultaneously. A large range of grains, pulses and legumes were preserved in burnt deposits associated with their use (Table 8.58, see Pelling, Chapter 8). Artefactual evidence associated with the building was limited, but the pottery recovered suggests a construction date in the 13th-14th century. This construction phase (Phase 1) of the building showed a sequence of modifications to the structure and has therefore been divided into three sub-phases (Phase 1a, 1b and 1c – shown on Fig. 6.3). Little or no evidence was recovered of associated contemporary structures. This is most likely a reflection of the limited nature of the excavation as well as truncation by later features

It is not clear when the Phase 1 building fell out of use but there is a complete lack of the commoner later 16th- and 17th-century pottery types of the region, suggesting a hiatus in use at that time (see Blinkhorn and Jeffries, Chapter 7). The new building (Phase 2) was probably constructed in the early 18th century and seems to have had a different function, with a lack of occupation debris suggesting that it probably served as an outbuilding. Several major mod-ifications were made to this building and it has also been divided into three sub-phases (Phases 2a–c).

Phase 1a *(Fig. 6.3, Plate 6.1)*

The original rectangular building was oriented north-west – south-east and had external dimensions of 8.9 m by 5.2 m. Its foundations (265) survived to an average depth of 0.15 m and were bottomed onto underlying quarry pits (430, 505, 507, 508, 512, 571, 598, 624) and natural gravel. The walls, which did not survive above foundation level, were 0.7 m wide, of unbonded, roughly-dressed limestone blocks. Later rebuilding had removed the majority of the north-eastern wall. No direct evidence of a doorway survived but it may have been located at the most southerly point of the north-eastern wall, as the south-east wall shows no evidence of ever having been bonded to the

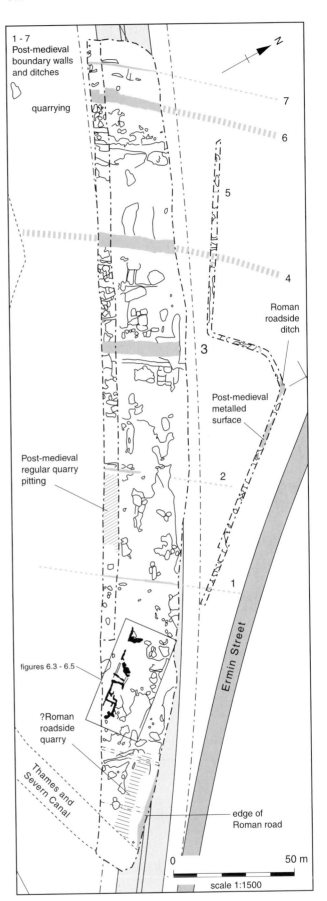

Figure 6.2   Street Farm, trench plan.

Plate 6.1 Street Farm. Building 164 under excavation. The 18th–century building (foreground) overlies the medieval kitchen.

missing section of the north-east wall. A small sherd of Brill/Boarstall ware pottery no earlier than the early 13th century was retrieved from the build of wall 265. A layer of compact silty clay and gravel (561) sealed the quarry pits beneath the structure. This layer was up to 0.08 m thick and probably formed the original floor of the building.

Two ovens (567 and 516) were associated with Phase 1a. A roughly circular flue, measuring 0.60 m by 0.50 m, was built into the northern corner of the original outer wall. The wall was increased to a thickness of 1.1 m in order to accommodate the flue, creating an external chimney (582), 1.2 m wide. The depth of the foundations was also increased to 0.4 m, with the flue extending to the full depth. This serviced a roughly circular oven (567), measuring 1.70 m by 1.75 m, with an internal chamber with a diameter of approximately 0.8 m. Very little of this survived apart from the foundations, which were constructed of roughly hewn limestone slabs showing traces of a pale sandy mortar (564), bedded within a shallow construction cut (581). Within the construction cut, a layer of compact, burnt orange sandy clay (579 = 577) up

to 0.09 m thick formed the original oven floor. The top of this layer (578) was of a similar composition but contained fragments of charcoal. Two charcoal layers within the oven (602 and 613) were sampled for environmental remains and found to contain a high proportion of chaff, which had probably been used as fuel (Table 8.58).

There were two cuts within the oven chamber, the earliest of which (573) was shallow and located within the entrance. This was filled with a mixed burnt deposit, probably derived from the clay base of the oven and resulting from the action of raking-out of the chamber. It was truncated by a roughly circular cut (575), 0.40 m by 0.37 m and 0.32 m deep, with a flat base. It coincided with the flue within the build of wall 265 and was probably cut in order to unblock it.

The other phase 1a oven (516) was located in the southern corner of the building against wall 265. It was roughly square, measuring 2.1 m by 2.0 m north-east - south-west, and was constructed of limestone rubble and was clay-faced with roughly dressed limestone slabs, of which up to four courses survived. The north-western half of the oven chamber contained two limestone hearth-stones (569) and both these slabs and the facing stones of this area of the chamber were burnt red. The surface of the floor layer (561) was also strongly affected by heat immediately in front of the oven. A thin spread of charcoal (503), probably raked-out from the oven, overlay the clay floor and the hearth stones and petered out by pit 596 (see below). Three sherds of pottery dating from the 13th century were recovered from this spread. There was also a thin layer of charcoal (517) within the oven chamber. The layer was overlain by a deposit of sandy loam (548) which contained burnt limestone fragments and probably derived from cleaning the sides of the flue.

A shallow pit (596), 1.2 m in diameter and 0.30 m deep, was cut through the clay floor adjacent to a gully (598), aligned north-west by south-east, and a posthole (594), 0.25 m in diameter and 0.24 m deep. The function of these features was not clear. Pit 596 was subsequently backfilled with limestone fragments and gravel in a matrix of silty clay (597) which contained two sherds of pottery dating from the early 13th century. A heavily truncated pit (617) was located towards the south-eastern end of the building. This feature contained a mixed compacted fill of gravel, limestone and clay and was probably associated with the initial construction of the building.

Phase 1b (Fig. 6.3)

At a later date, a layer of gravel (502) was deposited over charcoal layer 503, and formed a new floor surface in the south-eastern half of the building. The north-west limit of the layer was in a straight line, suggesting that it had once abutted a wall, so that the building had at that stage been divided into two rooms. The north-west room had internal dimensions of 3.6 m north–west to south-east and 4.1 m north-east to south-west. The south-east room measured 3.8 m north-west to south-east and 4.1 m north-east to south-west. Three layers of charcoal (472, 500 and 501), overlay the gravel layer (502) in the south-east room, implying the continued use of oven 516. Layer 500 produced sherds of Tudor Green Ware with a production span of *c.* 1380–1550 and Cistercian Ware datable to the period *c.* 1475–1550. New hearth-stones were laid in the oven that covered the earlier ones and partially overlay layer 503 (see above). The charcoal layers were cut by an oval feature (473) of uncertain function.

In the eastern corner of the building a new oven (563) was constructed of pitched limestone. The limestone slabs were rammed into firm clay (623) lining a shallow cut to form a hearth at least 1.5 m long and 1.1 m wide. The north-western half of the oven was destroyed by later modifications to the building but the surviving portion suggests that the hearth was originally circular. No burnt material was associated with the oven but the surface of the limestone forming the central part of the hearth was heat-reddened. The hearth had been contained by a curving wall (609) constructed of roughly hewn limestone and extending beyond the original line of the north-east wall (265) of the building. The external angle between the oven and the wall of the building was squared off with roughly coursed limestone (586), 0.28 m deep, which probably formed the foundation of an external chimney.

No evidence for a new floor surface was found in the north-western room, although a very mixed silty clay layer (558), with a maximum thickness of 0.03 m, probably represented occupation debris associated with its use. It did not extend over the base of oven 567 which suggests that the oven was still present, although, to judge by the absence of burnt material, not in use. A shallow circular pit (509), measuring 1.95 m in diameter,

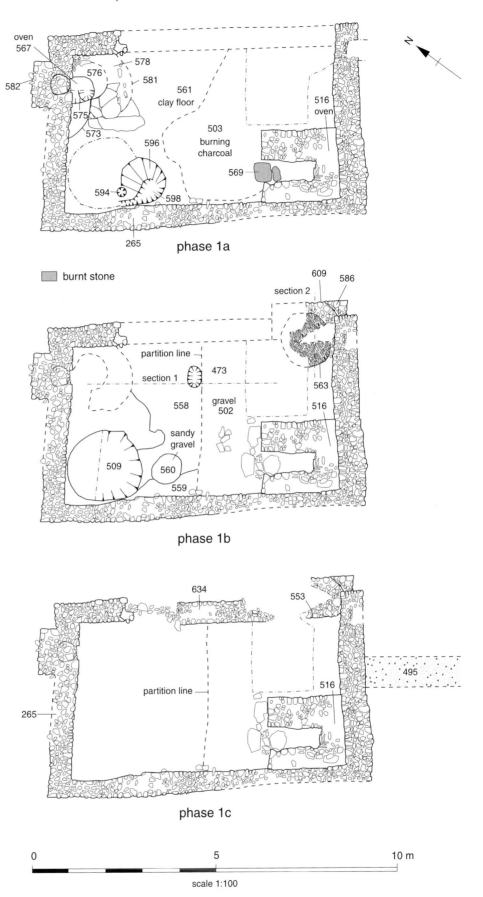

Figure 6.3   Street Farm, phase 1.

cut layer 559 in the western corner of the building. Its function is unknown but it was filled with a brown silty clay which did not contain charcoal or other burnt material. A layer of silty sand and limestone fragments (559) overlay 558 and was dumped against the south-west wall of the north-west room, probably to level the surface. A patch of sandy gravel (560) overlay 559.

Phase 1c (Fig. 6.3)

The building was re-ordered again when oven 563 was demolished and the flue was blocked with uncoursed limestone rubble (553) placed directly onto the hearthstones. Wall 265 was rebuilt to the north-west of the oven and a doorway into the north-west room was constructed. The new section of the wall (634) was 0.55 m wide and constructed of limestone facing stones with a rubble core. It was slightly offset to the south-west of the existing wall. The building probably remained partitioned during this phase but it is not certain if oven 516 remained in use.

Any deposits contemporary with the use of the building had been removed by later activity on the north-west, north-east, and south-east sides. However, to the south-west the Phase 2 extension had protected the underlying deposits. A layer of clay loam (621), 0.10 m thick and containing gravel and limestone fragments, had built up or was deposited against wall 265 on the south side. A compact layer of gravel and limestone fragments in a silty loam matrix overlay this and formed a metalled yard surface (495). Pottery from this layer includes sherds of later medieval and transitional wares of the mid-16th century or later.

Phase 2a (Fig. 6.4)

The building was rebuilt during this phase upon the foundations of the Phase 1 structure, except at the north-west gable end where the original wall may have been re-used. A slight realignment of the walls, however, meant that the south-west and north-east walls did not fully overlie the earlier foundations. The new building was extended by 4.7 m to the south-east and measured 13.4 m from north-west to south-east and 5.1 m from north-east to south-west. The north-west wall reused the foundations (265) of the earlier building but the flue of oven 567 was blocked with limestone rubble. The new walls (north-east wall 260, south-east wall 353 and the south-west wall 264) were constructed of roughly-hewn limestone rubble with no bonding material and survived to a maximum height of four courses (0.26 m). They were appreciably narrower than the earlier walls, with an average width of 0.5 m. Post-medieval pottery was recovered from the construction trench of wall 353. All of the internal structures of the earlier building and its south-west wall were levelled and the Phase 1 foundations were sealed by a compact, yellowish brown silty clay layer (262) that was up to 0.24 m thick. This deposit formed the floor, or floor make-up layer, of the new building. Layer 262 produced a pottery assemblage with a *terminus post quem* of the mid-16th century or later and included

medieval wares that were almost certainly redeposited. In the south-east part of the building, the layer was overlain by another of sandy gravel (423) which was perhaps the remnants of a floor. To the north-west, patches of limestone fragments (547) may have had a similar function.

The position of the original doorway is probably indicated by an alteration in the construction of wall 264, 4.5 m from its north-west corner, and suggests the doorway was originally *c.* 3 m wide. There was no evidence of an opposing doorway, although had one existed it would have been obscured by later modifications.

Phase 2b (Fig. 6.4)

The doorway was partly blocked with limestone rubble (263). The rubble narrowed the doorway to *c.* 1.75 m, with flat limestone slabs (456), up to 0.50 m across, forming the threshold. A new doorway was constructed in the north-east wall (260) at a similar date. A baffle entrance was formed by the construction of an internal L-shaped wall (261) with foundations of roughly-hewn, limestone fragments, six courses of which survived to a depth of 0.40 m. The building appears to have remained without division.

Phase 2c (Fig. 6.5)

A square pit (388) was cut into the entrance way up against wall 261. A stone-lined drain or gully (580) linked the pit to an external, stone-lined pit or tank (587=588). It was not clear whether these features were capped and it is possible they put this doorway out of use. The tank was *c.* 1.5 m wide and filled with a greyish brown sandy silt (591), which probably accumulated during use. It contained sherds of 19th-century pottery. The feature was not completely excavated. The doorway in the south-west wall, which had been reduced in size during Phase 2b, was blocked with further limestone rubble (570). It is unclear whether this was strictly contemporary with the modifications on the other side of the building.

Associated structures

The deposits outside building 164 were not extensively sampled. Later 19th- and 20th-century pitting affected much of the area and the earlier structural remains were very fragmentary. In addition, a water main that ran across the northern part of the area had completely destroyed a 2 m strip parallel to the street frontage. A limited number of small hand-excavated trenches were dug in order to establish the depth and date of deposits. All the traces of surviving structures are likely to be contemporary with, or later than, the latest phase of building 164.

The south-east wall of building 164 was robbed out by trench 429. A layer of limestone rubble (391) partially overlay the robber trench and extended to the south-east, forming an external surface. Further traces of the surface abutted the north-east wall (260)

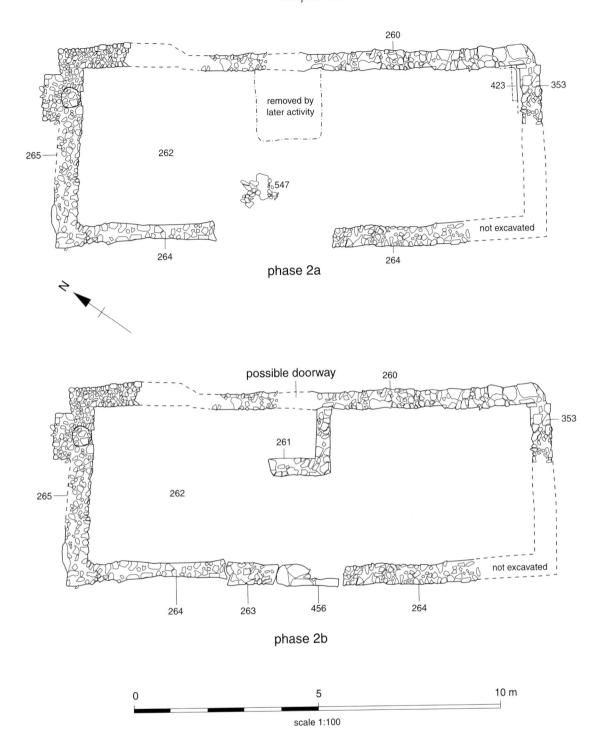

Figure 6.4   Street Farm, phases 2a and 2b

and extended at least 9 m to the north-east of it. Its full extent was not established within the excavated area. Several stone-packed postholes (321, 325, 327, 329) were recorded in the surface and it is probable that they were part of a wooden structure south-east of building 164 and stratigraphically later. A layer of brown silty clay (358) overlay surface 391 in places and may have accumulated during the use of the post-

built structure. A clay pipe bowl (cat. 737) dating to the late 17th century was recovered from 358 although this is residual. There was no relationship between the stone-lined tank (587) and surface 391, but since 391 did not overlie the tank it is possible that the surface was contemporary with it. To the east of the tank, a drain (290) ran east-west cutting surface 391. It was constructed of, and capped with, flat limestone slabs.

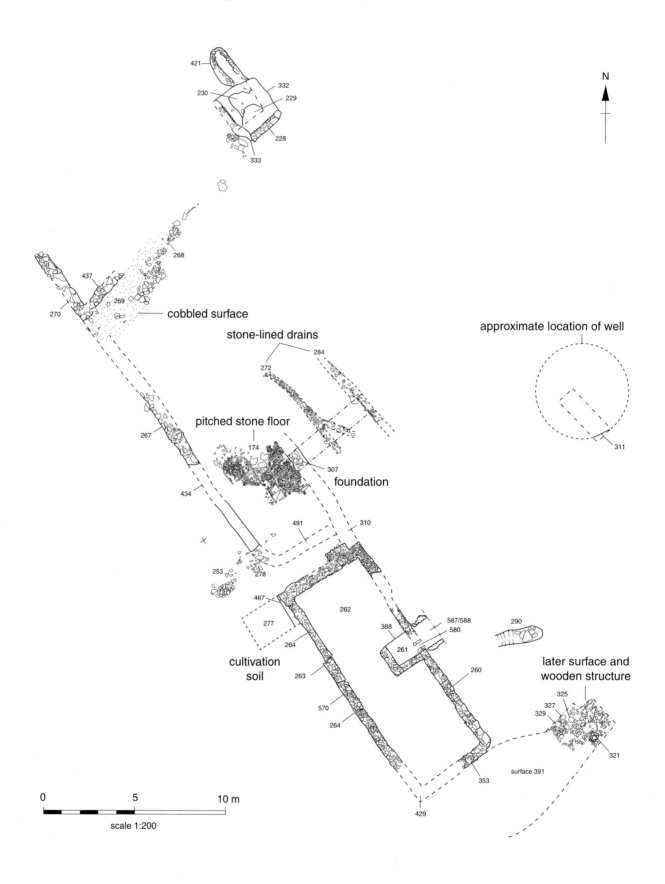

Figure 6.5   Street Farm, phase 2c.

Pottery dating to the 19th century was recovered from the build of the drain.

To the south-west of building 164, a vertical-sided cut (467) respected the line of wall 264. It was at least 15 m north-west to south-east and 0.3 m deep, and contained a dark grey-brown clay loam (277) which produced a single sherd of pottery with a *terminus post quem* of the mid-16th century. It is interpreted as a cultivation bed associated with Phase 2 of building 164.

Two parallel wall remnants (267 and 307) were located to the north-west of building 164 and were oriented from south-east to north-west. They were on the same alignment as building 164 and probably formed another structure. Robber trench 491 ran between the two walls on the south-eastern side, and a fragment of wall (253) continued this alignment to the south-west. An irregular limestone rubble layer (278) between the remnant of wall (253) and the robber trench (491) probably derived from the robbing of the wall. Wall 267 (= 270) extended the alignment of wall 264 (building 164) for at least 21 m. Where it survived, it was constructed of limestone rubble, of which only one course remained. The line of the rest of the wall was preserved by robber trench 434. Both pottery and a clay pipe bowl of 19th-century date were recovered from the build of 267. A short section of wall (437) abutting wall 267 at an approximate right-angle also yielded 19th-century pottery.

Wall 307, located 4.2 m from and opposite 267, had also been robbed. The robber trench (310) was up to 0.25 m deep and the footings of 307 survived in the base to a depth of 0.2 m, suggesting that they formed part of a more substantial wall than 267. Within the space bounded by walls 267 and 307 was a well-made surface of pitched limestone (174) with a central gutter. The surface extended for at least 4.0 m north-west by south-east and for 3.0 m north-east by south-west. The relationship between 174 and walls 267 and 307 had been removed by the wall robbing, but it is likely that the walls and floor were coeval. To the north, patches of rough cobbled surface (269) overlay robber trench 434 and appeared to respect wall 437. Nearby, a deposit of roughly squared limestone blocks (268) may represent collapse from wall 437.

To the east of wall 307 lay two drains or soakaways (272 and 284). Drain 284 was partially excavated and consisted of a vertical-sided cut, 0.45 m deep, the sides of which were lined with roughly dressed limestone slabs 0.06 m thick. Drain 272 was not excavated. A well (311) lay to the east of the drains although its extent was not determined. It was lined below a depth of 0.20 m with roughly-hewn limestone slabs (306) which formed a circular well shaft about 1 m across. This was filled with a waterlogged clay loam (305) containing 18th- and 19th-century pottery. The well was not excavated below the first course of the lining. A layer of clay gravel (304) overlay 305 and 306 and filled the upper 0.2 m of 311. It also contained 18th and 19th-century

pottery. This layer extended beyond the well cut, representing the disuse and backfilling of the well.

To the north, a short length of wall (228) formed the south-east side of a small structure which had external dimensions of 3.0 m north-west by south-east and 2.7 m north-east by south-west. The wall survived to a length of 2.1 m and had a width of 0.6 m. It was constructed of roughly-hewn limestone, one course of which survived to a height of 0.1 m. The south-west edge of the structure was formed by a narrow trench (333) lined on the north-west side with limestone slabs, probably packing stones for a wooden fence or wall. The other two sides of the structure probably remained open. The floor of the structure was made up from layers of compact clay (332= 229, 230). Immediately to the north-west of the clay floor, and contemporary with it, was a rectangular pit (421), 2.2 m long, 1.2 m wide and 0.5 m deep, that was lined with rough limestone fragments on three sides. The function of the structure is unknown. Pottery from the floor of the structure dated to the later 19th century.

Post-medieval property boundaries *(Fig. 6.2)*

The site was crossed by a number of property boundaries, extending from the street frontage (the modern A419) to the Thames and Severn Canal, all but one of which are shown on the 1805 Inclosure map. The 1805 map and the OS first edition map of 1875 also record several buildings located on and behind the street frontage (Figs 6.6–7).

Boundary 1 (wall 12) was of dry-stone construction and consisted of irregular blocks of limestone which survived to a maximum of six courses. Three sherds of post-medieval red earthenware pottery were recovered from the build of the wall. The continuation of this wall was recorded within the pipe trench investigations, immediately behind the street frontage. The boundary appeared on the 1805 Inclosure Award map but was not shown on the 1875 Ordnance Survey map.

Boundary 2 (wall 19) was parallel to boundary 1 and had a similar construction. It extended from the south-western edge of the excavation for a distance of 15 m but it had been removed by later activity to the north-east and was also not present within the pipe trench. Like boundary 1, boundary 2 appeared on the 1805 map but not on the 1875 map.

Boundary 3 (ditch 14) was 4.6 m wide, 0.5 m deep and extended from the south-western edge of the excavation for a distance of 35 m to the north-east edge of the site where it was overlain by structure 543. The ditch appeared on the 1805 Inclosure map but had apparently gone by 1875. However, a number of trees survive on the same alignment in the field to the south of the road corridor.

Boundary 4 (ditch 133) was at least 5 m wide and was visible as a ditch before the excavation began. It could not be excavated because of the high water table. Further to the north, within the pipe trench, the boundary was preserved as a limestone wall-footing

(918), of dry-stone construction. It appeared on both the 1805 and 1875 maps.

Boundary 5 (wall 875) was recorded within the pipe trench and was a limestone wall of dry-stone construction. Post-medieval and 19th-century pottery sherds were recovered from the build of the wall. The wall overlay a feature which may have been an earlier ditch on the same alignment, although it was not possible to establish this within the confines of the trench. Its fills produced similar pottery, indicating that it may have been backfilled to allow the construction of the wall. The boundary continued as a ditch to the south but this could not be excavated. The boundary appears on the 1805 Inclosure award map, extending from the street frontage back to the canal but by 1875 the boundary stopped short of the road corridor and did not reach the canal.

Boundary 6 (ditch 93) was at least 3.5 m wide and 1.2 m deep. It was revealed within a machine-excavated slot but could not be recorded fully because of the high water table. The ditch extended across the full width of the road corridor. This boundary appeared on both the 1805 and 1875 maps.

Boundary 7 (ditch 77) was 1 m wide and 0.5 m deep an also extended across the whole width of the road corridor. This boundary only appears on the 1875 Ordnance survey map subdividing a larger property shown in 1805.

Other structures

Two short lengths of wall (469 and 471) were recorded almost immediately to the north of boundary 1. They probably formed part of a small building with an uncertain function. Pottery indicates a 19th-century date which is contemporary with the latest phase of building 164 to the south-east.

Along the north-east edge of the site, behind the existing houses of Latton village, walls 543 and 458 were recorded crossing the ditch for boundary 3. Wall 543 may have been the foundation for a small structure with wall 458 perhaps forming the former property boundary of buildings fronting onto the A419.

Discussion of the site

Chronology

There were few datable finds from the Phase 1 structure but despite this, it is still possible to construct a tentative chronology. The quarry pits underlying the building produced very little pottery, with the exception of 430 and 512 which yielded a total of nine sherds (534 g) of medieval Cotswold wares. The relatively large size of the sherds would suggest that they are contemporary with the backfilling of the features. Such pottery was in production from the mid-12th century onwards and this corresponds reasonably well with the chronology of the ceramic assemblage from the building. The foundations (265) produced a single sherd of Brill/Boarstall ware with a *terminus post quem* of the earlier 13th

century. The rest of the pottery from this phase comprised four sherds of Minety-type wares in charcoal spreads 503 and 517 and two sherds from the fill 597 of pit 596. This would suggest that the building was occupied during the 13th-14th centuries in its earliest phase.

The dating evidence for Phase 1b, while similarly slight, suggests that the alterations to the structure took place during the 15th century. The assemblage comprises three small sherds of Tudor green and Cistercian ware, which occurred in floor layer 500, and a sherd of Minety-type ware, from the levelling deposit 559 (cat. 204). The Tudor Green and Cistercian types were tablewares which were current during the 15th and earlier 16th centuries. The other sherds include a fairly large fragment of a sooted Minety-type ware vessel with an internal glaze. This is likely to be of a similar date, as the internal glazing of vessels is a feature that was far more common in the later medieval period. Two sherds of the same material were found in the patch of gravel (560) that overlay the levelling deposit 559.

The final occupation of the building during Phase 1c is difficult to date because of the paucity of evidence. However, the presence of red earthenwares in yard deposit 495, coupled with the lack of Ashton Keynes redwares, suggests that the structure went out of use in the mid-16th century.

It is equally problematic to ascribe a chronology to the earliest occupation of the Phase 2 structure. It is likely that the medieval and early post-medieval material was redeposited but, as noted in the pottery report (see Blinkhorn and Jeffries, Chapter 7), the absence of locally produced Ashton Keynes ware at the site suggests that the second phase of the structure does not predate the later 17th century and that the structure was not occupied during the later 16th and 17th centuries. Early 18th-century pottery is present,

Figure 6.6   1805 Inclosure Map.

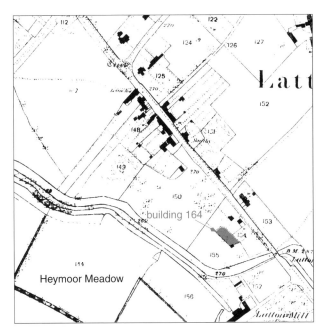

Figure 6.7   1875 OS 2" Map.

such as the Westerwald Stoneware mug-base of that date, and several types of wares were present that predate the mid-18th century. On ceramic grounds the structure appears to have been disused by the middle of the 19th century. This is confirmed by cartographic evidence which indicates that this building was standing in 1805, but had disappeared by 1875 (Figs 6.6–6.7).

Building 164 and associated structures

The Phase 1 building can be interpreted as a bake-house or kitchen block and appears typical of those which are known from the period. While the fact that it seems detached is partly due to the limited nature of the excavations, such buildings, because of their inherent fire risk, were often kept well apart from other buildings in a settlement (Platt 1978, 57–8). Examples of very similar buildings, dating from the 13th–16th century, have been excavated at Great Linford, Buckinghamshire (Mynard and Zeepvat 1992). Here, nearly all the crofts examined in the village contained bake-houses and/or brew-houses either as detached buildings or as blocks attached to the dwelling. Five were quite clearly identifiable as detached buildings, four of which were of a similar size and with the same range of features as building 164. The type therefore appears to have been common. Building 164 was undoubtedly associated with a dwelling to the east which may have had a frontage on the road. The dwelling need not have been of any great status, although it is not possible to infer status from the kitchen alone since it is clear from sites such as Great Linford and also Dean Court, Cumnor, Oxfordshire (Allen 1994), that both manor houses and

cottages had kitchen blocks of quite similar size and form.

It is uncertain whether building 164 would have been entirely stone-built, although it may be reasonable to assume that the chimney stacks were. The structural evidence, including the shallowness of the wall foundations, is very similar to that from the medieval buildings at Great Linford, all of which were considered likely to have been timber-framed on dwarf walls (Mynard and Zeepvat 1992, 50) although perhaps not fully timber-framed (Smith 1992). Even on the limestone uplands at Upton, Gloucestershire, the evidence suggests that the medieval buildings were timber-framed on walls about 2 ft (0.6 m) high (Hinton and Rahtz 1966, 102), so it appears that construction technique need not have been determined by the availability of local stone. At Dean Court, however, quite similar evidence for wall foundations, added to large amounts of rubble and roof tile, has suggested construction in stone (Allen 1994, 421). The lack of demolition rubble at Street Farm might suggest the use of timber framing, or alternatively the re-use of the stone in later periods. The deeper foundation of the north-west wall may be significant and indicate a different structural technique at this end of the building. The fact that this was the only wall which was not comprehensively rebuilt from the foundations in Phase 2 may also be taken to indicate that this wall had survived to be re-used – something which would not have been possible with full timber framing and may suggest stone. However, the use of combinations of materials in different walls is not unusual in medieval buildings (Smith 1992, 130), so that if the north-west end wall were stone-built it need not imply that the whole building was.

The interior ovens have close parallels at other sites. Circular oven 563, with a bordered, pitched stone floor, is similar to that in the possible bake-house complex in Croft G, Great Linford (Mynard and Zeepvat 1992, fig. 26, feature 71), and also at Dean Court (Allen 1994, fig. 48, feature 421), both also of 13th-15th century date. A number of circular oven features at Great Linford are interpreted as copper bases used in brewing, although it is not clear how this interpretation was reached. In the north-west corner of building 164, pit 509 (which may have replaced 596 in the earlier sub-phase) has quite a precise parallel with pit 1503 at Dean Court, the purpose of which was essentially unclear, but which may have been the site of a tank or vat for steeping grain in the brewing process (Allen 1994. 431, fig. 50). The association between a steeping tank or 'coble' and a malting kiln is known from sites such as Canal Street, Perth (Coleman 1996), where the coble was a square, plank-lined pit about 3 m across. Square, thick-walled ovens such as oven 516 are commonly interpreted as malting kilns, and this may be an indication that building 164 was used for brewing as well as baking, although there was no evidence for this from the charred remains. The abandonment of the building in the 16th century can be attributed to changes in the design of dwellings in the post-medieval period which led to kitchens being more closely integrated with the living area.

The rebuilding and extension of building 164 (Phase 2), which probably took place in the early 18th century, followed a period of disuse which appears to have lasted a century or more. During this time the original kitchen block probably collapsed, at least partly, but the fact that the new building used the earlier wall foundations on the long axes, resulting in the construction of a building of the same width as the earlier one, suggests that enough of the old building must have survived for its plan to be re-used. It has already been suggested that the north-west gable wall might have been standing to be incorporated into the new building.

The new structure had narrower walls than the medieval one and a timber-framed construction appears likely. There are few clues as to the function of the building in Phase 2. There is no suggestion that it was a dwelling and the 3 m-wide doorway on the south-west side in Phase 2a indicates that it was probably a barn. There may have been an opposed doorway as well, which would be typical of barns for crop storage, although, if this were present, the remaining wall indicates that it would not have been as wide. A single doorway, presumably facing away from the dwelling and the main arable fields, could be taken to indicate that the barn was used to store hay from the floodplain meadows (Heymoor Meadow on the 1805 Inclosure map, Fig. 6.6). It is likely that controlled rights to grazing and hay shares operated for the inhabitants of the parish, as they did for the inhabitants of Cricklade on North Meadow at this time (Whitehead 1982)

The main access to the Heymoor Meadow appears to have been via Street Farm to the north, but there is clear cartographic evidence from a slightly later period of a bridge across the Churn at Latton Mill, which is the obvious point of access to the meadows from the southern part of Latton, and this would have been very convenient for building 164 before the canal separated this plot of land from the mill, and the river itself, in the 1780s.

Changes to the building in Phases 2b and 2c are difficult to explain. A change in function is implied by the narrowing of the entrance in Phase 2b, unless the rubble wall 263 can be interpreted as a consolidation of the threshold rather than a blocking wall. Internally, the L-shaped baffle appears too small to have enclosed a functional room or alcove, and the slightly greater depth of its foundation suggests that it may have supported a stairway to a loft. Modifications to this area in Phase 2c, with the insertion of a drain and exterior tank are also not readily explained, particularly as the south-west entrance seems to have been blocked at the same time resulting in no clear point of access to the building. On stratigraphic grounds it is possible that the drain and tank were inserted after the building fell out of use.

The patchy remains to the north-west of building 164 are difficult to interpret but the main wall alignments, 307 and 267/270 with related robber

trenches, continuing the long axis of the building, would seem to indicate a range of farm buildings here. A long narrow building is shown here on the 1805 Inclosure map (Fig. 6.6). The shallower foundations of the south-west wall and the 19th–century date of its construction suggest that this building may have been modified from one which was initially open on this side. The pitched stone surface, 174, with associated drains appears to be contemporary with the building and suggests that it was for housing animals. It is possible that it was a cowhouse, although it is rather narrow and would not have housed many animals. It may have been for pigs. It is less likely to have been for sheep who would normally have been housed in the fields, if at all. In his survey of the agriculture of Gloucestershire, Turner noted that most farmers dairied a little for home consumption and kept their animals in stalls where they were fed hay, chaff, barley meal, oats and bran (1794, 8). The animal shelter would logically have been positioned next to the barn if the latter were used for storing and preparing fodder and straw, and such an arrangement of barn and cowhouse appears the most likely interpretation of this range. While the later transformations to building 164 are difficult to understand it need not have ceased being a barn. Some barns (such as chall barns in Cornwall and bank barns in the north) had storage space in lofts loaded through upper floor doors or pitching eyes (Barnwell and Giles 1997, 102–104, 129–131) and need not have had a wide entrance at ground level. Traditional barns were also adapted to various developments in the 19th century and it is possible, for instance, that the use of alternative animal feeds, particularly oil cake from around 1830 (ibid., 6), made an entrance for wagons redundant.

To the north-east the small square structure with attached trough would appear to be an emplacement for agricultural machinery of some sort. The well, lying to the east of the range, appears to have been filled in during the 19th century, although it is shown on the 1875 Ordnance Survey map.

Despite the extremely tentative nature of this interpretation it is possible to place it within the general context of agricultural developments from the early 18th century. The century saw an intensification of farming practices linked to, among other things, the breeding and care of livestock and the production of manure for the arable fields (Barnwell and Giles 1997, 4–5). There was also a tendency towards the improvement of farm buildings in the interests of greater efficiency, although this process may have come relatively late to Latton whose fields were not enclosed until 1805 and are uniquely and specifically labelled 'common fields' in Whitworth's 1783 survey for the Thames and Severn Canal. It was probably the re-organisation of land under enclosure which accounts for the demise of the farm buildings in this plot, although the canal may have had an earlier adverse effect on the suitability of the buildings for their purpose, particularly if access to Heymoor Meadow had been important. The ranges of buildings evident in 1805, and apparently enclosing a farmyard, had disappeared by 1875. It is interesting to note that a new building had sprung up on the other side of Ermin Street by this time, and, although there is no indication that it is a farmhouse, such a re-orientation of the farm towards the gravel terrace is something which may well have resulted from a rationalisation of landholding. The re-organisation of both land and farm buildings was commented on favourably by Turner during the time when enclosure was in progress in the region:

> Farm Houses and Offices in the old inclosures are frequently unhandy and inadequate to the farms annexed to them, which, doubtless, arises from the improvements in husbandry since their building. In the new inclosures, they are generally speaking very conveniently situated, with sufficient shed room for cattle and implements. (Turner 1794, 19).

MISCELLANEOUS EVIDENCE FROM OTHER SITES
By Helen Drake, Andrew Mudd and Kate Atherton

Summary

The evidence for medieval and later activity within the road corridor was widespread, but limited to miscellaneous features and finds which, on the whole, did not form coherent units for analysis. Most of the evidence recovered consisted of individual finds scatters, ditches, quarries, walls and plough furrows. There were no features related to settlement sites other than those already described at Street Farm. The evidence for road construction in the post-Roman period is for the most part contained in Chapter 5, although some other evidence of road surfaces appears below.

A thematic summary of these features and finds is presented below in a highly abstracted form. Detailed descriptions can be consulted in the archive.

Finds scatters

Early Saxon pottery from Latton and Duntisbourne Leer

Three sherds of early Saxon pottery were recovered during the scheme-wide watching brief just west of the lane running south from Street Farm (Fig. 4.32). One sherd came from a shallow ditch on a similar alignment to the ditches which contained Roman pottery, while two sherds came from the soil on the edge of the field which was interpreted as a headland. Early Saxon pottery, associated with burnt daub and animal bone, was discovered in a pit in this field in 1995 in an evaluation connected with the Esso Midline Project (Wilts. SMR SUNE400). This strongly suggests an early Saxon settlement in this area, although there is no clear evidence of one from the cropmarks.

Two small sherds of early Saxon pottery also came from the upper fill of a Roman trackway ditch at Duntisbourne Leer Area 2 (Chapter 4, Fig. 4.12). It is possible that these are associated with a nearby settlement although this must remain speculative on such limited evidence.

Witpit Lane

Although no trace of settlement was found at this site, which lay immediately to the south of Witpit Lane, large quantities of medieval material were collected during fieldwalking and evaluation. Three evaluation trenches in this area all recorded medieval finds from superficial layers with one (Trench 1991/530) yielding *c.* 45 sherds of pottery, mainly from the 11th–13th century, in addition to charcoal, slag, coke, iron nails and a silver halfpenny of Henry III (1218–42). However, no features were found. A geophysical survey of the area also proved negative.

The excavation of 70 x 25 m within the road corridor also failed to reveal any settlement-related features, medieval activity being represented only by a plough-reduced headland at the southern edge of the site which was respected by five plough-furrows. These and the later drains are described below (see ridge and furrow). Material from limited hand-excavation comprised around 40 sherds mostly of medieval green-glazed Minety Ware of the 12th–14th century. Some bone, fired clay and a horseshoe fragment were also recovered. The concentration of pottery and other finds appears high for a manuring scatter although there is little clue as to what else it might represent. The site lies about 0.5 km north-east of the village of Preston and a little further from a possible deserted medieval settlement north of Witpit Copse (Glos. SMR 7364) and the finds would be unlikely to represent dumps from that far away. It is possible that there was a settlement here, the evidence for which had been completely ploughed out, or that there was a nearby site of some sort. Gerrard (1994b, 118) has speculated that there may have been a nearby kiln producing green-glazed ware.

There is possible evidence of medieval crofts on the other side of Witpit Lane from the number of small, narrow fields running back from the lane which are shown on an estate map of 1687 as well as on the Inclosure map of 1770. These are of a very similar size to the properties within the village of Preston, and, although they may have originally been agricultural allotments rather than dwellings, the latter appears at least as likely on the cartographic evidence. The new road crossed this area cutting the corner of a block of woodland which appears to be a 19th-century plantation, but during the watching brief ground conditions were too wet for stripping and the area could not be examined.

Cherry Tree Lane

The excavation at Cherry Tree Lane (Fig. 3. 28) yielded two unusual items of interest in the assemblage of post-medieval material. The topsoil contained a fragment of a glass linen smoother or slick-stone (cat. 666), an item which can occur on glass manufacturing sites in the 16th century (see Cropper, Chapter 7). A possible 'melt' glass fragment was also recovered from the topsoil at a later stage, and there is therefore a slight suggestion of glass production somewhere in the area.

Two hearths or shallow ovens (4 and 15) discovered in the excavation are of unknown purpose and date. They cut the lower colluvium here and almost certainly post-date the Iron Age features on the site (Chapter 3). A medieval or later date is considered probable. They were of rectangular form, about 1 m by 0.6–0.8 m and 0.1–0.2 m deep. Both had been carefully constructed with near vertical sides although hearth 15 had more rounded corners than the square hearth, 4. Each contained a burnt fill of dark silt-clay containing charcoal and burnt limestone. The blocks of limestone were located in the upper half of the features and may be an indication that the rims of the hearths had been lined. There were clear indications of burning *in situ*. The hearths would seem unlikely to be connected with glass production, but perhaps indicate some other low-level industrial activity here in the medieval period or later.

Ridge and furrow

There was evidence for ridge and furrow cultivation at a number of sites, particularly in the parishes of Latton and Preston. This type of cultivation evidence is broadly placed in the medieval to early post-medieval period, and the excavations could add little more precision to dating the specific examples encountered. However, in some instances a relative chronology of cultivation and other agricultural features was evident and could be used to suggest a development of land use.

Latton

At Westfield Farm two distinct series of ridge and furrow were evident in Area 2 (Fig. 4.31) with three broad furrows oriented approximately east-west cutting a group of narrow furrows aligned approximately at right-angles. The broad furrows were 3–4 m wide and spaced 15–16 m apart (centre to centre). Only one yielded any finds in the form of a sherd of red earthenware of the 16th century or later. The furrows would therefore seem to be part of a post-medieval strip-farming system. These furrows were seen further east in Evaluation Trench VII and in the watching brief. They are also visible on air photographs (Plate 4.5). A broad furrow was also recorded in Area 1 west of the Cerney Wick road. This was aligned north to south at right angles to the post-medieval field boundary ditch. It appeared to stop about 20 m short of this ditch which may indicate the existence of a broad headland.

The narrow furrows were in some cases barely evident but appeared to form a pattern of furrows spaced about 7 m apart. Their alignment closely follows that of the Roman boundary ditch 31/32 (Chapter 4) and it is possible that they represent the medieval utilisation of a pre-existing field system.

East of Latton 'Roman Pond' broad ridge and furrow is clearly visible as cropmarks (Plate 4.5). Some of this was recorded in the watching brief (Fig. 4.32). Although dating evidence was not recovered from the furrows themselves, they were stratigraphically late. An interpretation of the air photograph indicates that they cut across the largest, and what appears to be the latest, of the field boundaries in this area towards the western side of the field. The furrows were about 16 m apart and up to 6 m wide. On the eastern side of the field was found a layer of soil (22), about 1 m deep and 20 m wide, which was interpreted as a headland. The chief interest of this feature is that three sherds of early Saxon pottery came from it and an adjacent ditch (see Finds Scatters, above).

Further south-east at Court Farm broad ridge and furrow is also evident on air photographs (Chapter 4 and Plate 4.3). A number of linear features were found truncating the Roman quarry pits in the excavated area although none were closely datable. A small amount of medieval coarseware came from features at the north-west end of the site (32 and 42, Fig. 4.15) but the others were without finds. Most of these features were interpreted as shallow ditches up to 0.3 m deep although a consideration of the air-photographic and geophysical evidence suggests a pattern of ridge and furrow is present with furrows spaced at approximately 15 m intervals. The clarity of the geophysical evidence in particular indicates that these furrows are quite substantial which may account for their ditch-like appearance.

Between Spine Road and Latton Creamery abundant ridge and furrow was recorded in the watching brief. This is clearly visible on air photographs and the evidence, which extends outside the road corridor, was plotted by the Royal Commission in 1993. The block of ridge and furrow recorded in the watching brief ran at right-angles to Ermin Street and appeared to be quite regular, with furrows spaced at 7 to 10 m intervals. Pottery of the late 12th to 14th centuries was recovered from two of them. The cropmarks show broader ridge and furrow in this field on a more or less perpendicular alignment and possibly another phase on a similar alignment. However, the relationship between these patterns is not clear. A single long furrow running parallel to Ermin Street was also recorded at the Spine Road junction (chainage 3500) further north-west.

Preston

All the sites in the parish of Preston had evidence for ridge and furrow with the exception of Ermin Farm. The large area stripped at St Augustine's Farm South and St Augustine's Lane revealed extensive traces of ploughing which had truncated the prehistoric features at those sites (Chapters 2 and 3). However, no dating evidence was obtained from any of them.

The densest pattern of furrows was seen on Site Na, St Augustine's Farm South, where two series of furrows, one broad and one narrow, formed a lattice pattern. Both series were spaced at approximately 9 m intervals and were aligned with the current field boundaries. It was not possible to discover the relationship between them. The broader series, aligned north-east to south-west, was found in Site O where eleven furrows were recorded. A single furrow on a roughly east-west alignment was found in Site Nb. At St Augustine's Lane traces of a system of furrows were found running north-west to south-east. They were spaced at intervals of about 9 m and roughly aligned with the lane to the south. The watching brief to the north of the site recorded ridge and furrow on the same alignment as far as Ampney Lane.

At Preston Enclosure broad ridge and furrow was recorded on the site and is also visible as a cropmark (Plate 3.1). The furrows were unevenly spaced at 8 m to 14 m intervals. Material recovered from the furrows included medieval wares and post-medieval sherds of the 16th-18th centuries.

The excavations just south of Witpit Lane revealed five furrows aligned north-south. These respected a headland which extended between 10 m and 20 m from the field boundary at the southern end of the site. The system of ridge and furrow was seen to continue in the watching brief as far as Witpit Lane. The furrows were 7–8 m apart and contained a single shallow fill of grey-brown silt-clay. Furrows 10 and 27 contained no dating evidence. Furrows 6 and 22 yielded solely medieval material in the form of three sherds of Cotswold type Oolitic ware, and a late 12th to 14th-century jug handle in addition to bone and fired clay. Furrow 4 contained a larger quantity of material, consisting of bone, flint, nails and 28 sherds of pottery, the majority of which was medieval. Two residual Roman fragments were also found along with one sherd of post-medieval red earthenware pottery. It is unclear whether this post-medieval sherd provides an approximate date for the ridge and furrow or whether it can be considered intrusive. The site was crossed by a series of five shallow post-medieval ditches which appeared to have been intended for drainage. They followed the alignment of the earlier furrows quite closely except two which ran at right-angles as feeders. However, they did not run in the bottoms of the furrows and, in contrast to the pattern of drains at Norcote Farm (below) may have been laid out without regard to the earlier topography.

At Norcote Farm a number of wide furrows ran across the site from north to south at 6–8 m intervals. They were up to 2 m wide. Medieval and post-medieval pottery and a piece of medieval floor tile were recovered from the fills. Land drains filled with limestone ran down the centre of each furrow, indicating that the furrows were visible until early modern drainage improvements.

Other sites

Two plough furrows (5 and 30) were noted in the excavations at Lower Street Furlong. The furrows were 13 m apart and were aligned east-west across the site. Both were 3 m wide and 0.30 m deep, with a flat base and each contained a single fill of light brown sandy-clay. Two post-medieval pottery sherds were found in the fill (6) of furrow 5.

A number of furrows aligned north-west to south-east were also recorded in the watching brief north of Itlay.

Lynchets at Birdlip Quarry *(Fig. 6.8)*

The Roman features uncovered at Birdlip Quarry, had been truncated by later ploughing. The extent and depth of this varied, appearing to have had a negligible or limited impact within the dry valley, but a relatively severe impact on the hill slope and at the western extension to the site. The most dramatic evidence for this was a series of five lynchets that were cut into the side of the hill but which had not been visible before the site was stripped. The lynchets were up to 5 m wide and 0.35 m deep although the upper lynchet was somewhat less substantial. They ran in relatively straight lines that formed terraces with moderately steep edges on the up-slope side and flat bases tapering into the lower hill slope. The bases of the lynchets were normally scored with plough marks and it is likely that they were created by ploughing along the contours over a long period rather than the deliberate, labour-intensive excavation of the terraces by hand. The plough marks tended to be lighter on the down-slope side of each lynchet, suggesting that the bedrock had, to some extent, been protected by a 'positive lynchet' in this area. The resulting terraces would have been between approximately 10–12 m wide.

There was no secure dating evidence for the lynchets although they were clearly post-Roman. They were filled by a mid brown or slightly reddish brown silt loam with abundant fine weathered fragments of limestone. This was similar to the pre-modern ploughsoil (4) from which a single sherd of green-glazed pottery, dated from the 13th to the 14th century, was retrieved.

Plough marks were common over most of the Birdlip Quarry excavation area that lay outside the dry valley except where limestone bedrock outcropped. Ploughing appears to have been deepest in the western extension to the site where scoring ran the length of this part of the site over 0.5 m below the modern ground surface. Curiously, deep ploughing was restricted to the southern part of this area leaving some earlier archaeological deposits intact on the northern edge of the site where the modern topsoil was actually shallowest, indicating probable differences in land use in post-Roman times. A fragment of clay tobacco pipe from the lower colluvial ploughsoil (20) suggests that ploughing continued into the post-medieval period. The plough marks were evident up to the stone rubble in Area A, ploughing presumably continuing at a shallower depth. Plough marks were again present at the east of Area A, cutting undisturbed silt within the dry valley itself. These are thought to belong to the same cultivation regime although there is no stratigraphic reason why they could not be Roman.

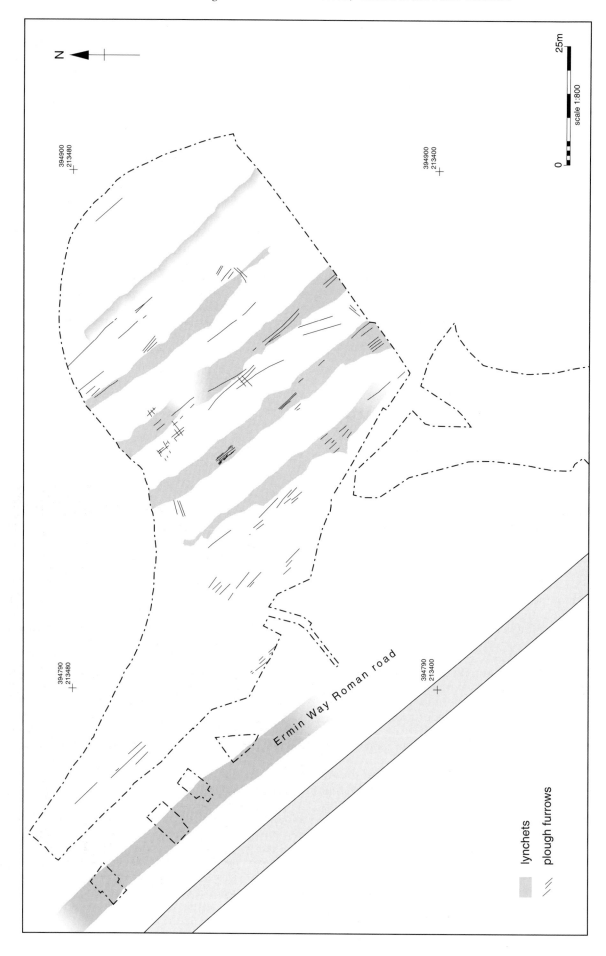

Figure 6.8 Birdlip Quarry, plan of lynchets.

Daglingworth Quarry Dewpond *(Fig. 6.9, Plate 6.2)*

A rectangular cropmark (RCHME ref. SP 0005/6) at Daglingworth Quarry proved to be a dewpond. The feature measured *c*. 7 m by 12 m and contained a rubble backfill that was removed by machine. The limestone below was hand-cleaned and a quadrant was removed to uncover a series of undated loose rubble fills from an earlier quarry cut.

Description

The lining of the dewpond was a tenacious blue-grey clay (122), 0.20 m thick, below a thin deposit of lime-based mortar (128), into which a stone surface (133) was set. The sides of the feature were constructed of courses of roughly-squared slabs (0.20 m by 0.10 m by 0.05 m), placed on edge. The sunken central area was made of large roughly-hewn limestone blocks (0.40 m by 0.40 m by 0.05 m). The clay lining extended beyond the edges of the limestone and was probably intended to prevent damage to the sides of the pond. The primary fill of the dewpond was a light grey-brown silt with frequent small limestone inclusions (120) which was up to 0.10 m thick. This layer extended over the entire area of the structure and was probably formed when the pond was in use. The thinness of the deposit suggests that the pond was either in use for a short period of time or that it was regularly cleaned. Deposit 120 contained a number of finds, including ten sherds of 19th- and 20th-century pottery and a base and body fragment from a 20th-century green-tinted mould-blown bottle.

A deposit of backfilled limestone rubble (124, 130, 131) lay over the silty layer and was mixed with clay towards the edges of the feature. The rubble consisted of stones that were mainly moderately flat and double-faced and therefore similar in appearance to stones used in drystone walls. Medieval and post-medieval pottery was recovered from this deposit during the evaluation phase. The fill was sealed by a thick (0.20 m) capping of a light grey-brown lime-based mortar (125) and this in turn was overlain by the ploughsoil horizon (126).

Discussion

The term dewpond is usually applied to ponds that are artificially constructed on land, part-icularly downs, where there is no adequate supply of water from springs or surface drainage (Pugsley 1939). They were either square or circular and were carefully constructed to capture rainfall and reduce evaporation because they were not fed by any external source of water (Rackham 1986). A few examples, such as this one, are found near roads on hillsides to collect the surface run-off from the road (Clutterbuck 1865). Most of the sources relating to dewponds date from the 19th and early 20th century when they were still in use and being built. An article published in *Farmer's Weekly* (8 April 1938) records photographically how a dewpond was constructed. A hollow was first excavated with the sides sloping at a gradient of 1:3, and then lined with puddled clay. Slaked lime in powder form was deposited to seal the clay, which in turn was covered with a layer of straw. The material removed during the creation of the hollow was then replaced, and rammed into the primary layers to create a hard surface. The Thorpe Downs dewpond, described by Slade (1877) in his treatise on dewponds, was similarly constructed with '...a layer of clay about 12 inches thick, mixed with lime to stay the progress of earthworms, and covered over with first a coating of straw (to prevent the sun cracking the clay), and finally with loose rubble......'. Other examples (Clutterbuck 1865; Martin 1915; Pugsley 1939) also describe this method, with only minor variations in the materials used and the sequence in which they were deposited. Straw was not always used and concrete or chalk puddle were occasionally used instead of clay to form the lining. This initial layer was essential in the construction of dewponds as it provided a firm impermeable base for the structure. Dewponds were always shallow, with

Plate 6.2 Daglingworth Quarry dewpond.

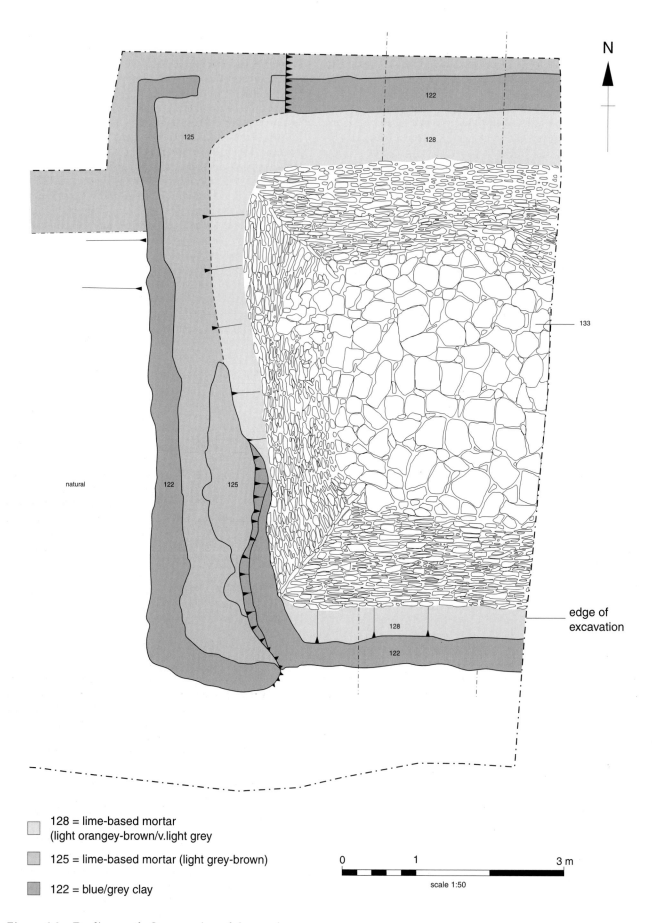

Figure 6.9   Daglingworth Quarry, plan of dewpond.

128 = lime-based mortar
(light orangey-brown/v.light grey

125 = lime-based mortar (light grey-brown)

122 = blue/grey clay

0   1   3 m

scale 1:50

none of the examples cited being more than two metres deep. Once constructed, water was usually introduced by either transporting it to the dewpond or, in the case of a bad winter, the pond was filled by snow (Clutterbuck 1865; Slade, 1877; Martin, 1915).

Only three other examples have been recorded in Gloucestershire. A circular dewpond, with an approximate diameter of 10 m and a lining of limestone blocks, was found at Coberley Cricket Ground. The latter was first recorded in 1863 and was apparently not present in 1838. The second dewpond, at Macaroni Farm in Eastleach, was built *c*. 1789 and only fell into disuse during the Second World War. The third example is situated in the parish of Minchinhampton but has not been excavated. The Daglingworth dewpond clearly represents one of the more carefully constructed examples recorded. No finds were recovered from or beneath the pond's lining and the date of its construction is not clear. It is probably safe to assume that, like other structures of this type, it was built in the 18th or 19th century, and from its position may have been associated with road improvement at this time, perhaps with the aim of collecting water draining off the road. The finds from fill 120 suggest an early 20th-century date for its last known use. The fact that it is not depicted on maps between 1816 and 1938 cannot be taken as evidence of its non-existence at this time.

Boundary ditches

Boundary ditches of medieval and later date were commonly encountered although their significance in terms of their contribution to an understanding of the landscape and its development was not normally clear. In some cases a relationship with Roman boundary ditches was apparent. These have generally been described in Chapter 4. Ditches relating to Ermin Street and Burford Road have been described with the sections through those roads in Chapter 5. The following is a brief summary of the remaining significant evidence.

The ditches at Exhibition Barn are one group which are particularly interesting as they seem to be showing a continuous development from Roman through to modern times. They have been described in Chapter 4 and are shown on Figures 4.33–34. The Roman roadside ditch at Birdlip Quarry also appears to have had a persistent influence on later land use (Chapter 4). The stratified sequence in Area 2A clearly showed that a medieval/post-medieval ditch (1310) followed precisely the same course as the Roman ditch (Figs. 4.98; Figs 4.98–99, sections 275 and 296). This also appears to have been the case in Ermin Street Trenches 1 and 2 to the north. In Ermin Street Trench 3, south of the settlement site, a minor Roman ditch was recut in the medieval and/or post-medieval period and the alignment was later followed by a drystone wall and a modern hedgerow (Fig. 4.101, section 302).

The field boundaries at Latton 'Roman Pond' have also been described (Chapter 4). The sequence of six intercutting ditches forming group 430 (Fig. 4.28,

sections 40, 1 and 26), almost certainly represents the continuous maintenance of this boundary since the Roman period although there was little supporting artefactual evidence.

Further west the post-Roman features (chiefly ridge and furrow) at Westfield Farm have been discussed above. The boundary ditches at this site and land as far as Latton Creamery are shown in Figure 4.31. In Westfield Farm Area 1 the re-cut east-west ditch represented a field boundary which was evident until at least 1875. To the north, ditch 5, found in the watching brief is also shown on the 1st edition OS map of 1875. The field boundaries in the Latton Creamery site and Evaluation Trench V are part of the post-medieval 'ladder' pattern of narrow fields which are evident from cropmarks. It is unclear whether this was a pre-enclosure pattern or one which resulted from the enclosure of a large field or fields.

Walls

Daglingworth Warren Gorse House (Area 2)

A small trench was opened up specifically to examine boundary features at the junction of the parishes of Bagendon, Baunton and Daglingworth. Three extant drystone walls (203, 204 and 207) were recorded in section. There was no dating evidence for any of them. Their foundations were built upon a colluvial soil directly under the modern topsoil. Wall 207, between Daglingworth and Baunton was the best construction and may have been repaired or rebuilt quite recently. It was 0.63 m wide and had been capped with concrete. Wall 203 between Daglingworth and Bagendon was the widest at 1.30 m, and wall 204, between Baunton and Bagendon was 0.8 m wide. The foundation for an earlier wall (202) was located parallel to wall 204 and 2.4 m to the north. It was visible as a linear spread of limestone rubble that measured 1.82 m wide by 0.22 m deep. No relationships between the drystone walls were established and there was no indication of boundary features earlier than the stone walls.

Burford Road and Ermin Street sections

Drystone walls were encountered in a number of the road sections where they formed field boundaries or revetments to the sides of the highway. None could be dated conclusively but (with the exception of one or two examples of probable Roman date, discussed in Chapter 5) all would appear to be post-medieval constructions.

The southern side of Burford Road was delimited by a substantial drystone revetment (Fig. 5.9, Trench 5, 566; Fig. 5.10, Trench 6, 605) which was intended to prevent road deposits from slipping in to the large quarries here. The wall was probably associated with the construction of the 'macadamised' road in the early 19th century, although modern repairs had clearly also been undertaken to 566. There was another drystone wall on the northern side of the road in Trench 3 (305). This appeared to be more or less contemporary with the early 19th-century road deposits, defining a road corridor about 20 m wide. However, it was built upon a thin layer of gravel and silt (306) which directly overlay a Roman quarry pit (319), and which contained a decorated medieval copper alloy stud from a horse harness (cat. 557), so it is possible that the wall was earlier than this.

A drystone wall was found alongside Ermin Street in Trench 3, at Birdlip Quarry, (Fig. 4.101, section 302) where it followed the line of a recent hedgerow. This may have been the same wall which was recorded at Cowley Underbridge (Trench 6, wall 639 – Fig. 5.3) which was probably early 19th century in date. At The Highwayman (Fig. 5.7) two stratigraphically late walls, 514 and 515, appear to have bounded the early modern road construction which would have been restricted to a narrow 4 m-wide corridor as a result. There was another boundary wall (546) on the northern side. At Dartley Bottom (Fig. 5.2) a boundary wall (870) on the northern side of the road may have been of turnpike or more recent date.

Quarry pits

Quarry pits were identified on a large number of sites on different geologies. It was of some importance to distinguish Roman quarry pits from later ones, but the features often yielded little artefactual material and were nowhere extensively sampled. As a result their dates are not always clear. Quarry pits demonstrated or thought to be of Roman date have been described and discussed in Chapters 4 and 5. Apart from any artefactual and stratigraphic dating evidence, the Roman pits appear to have been characteristically smaller and shallower than later ones. This may be because those encountered were primarily or exclusively dug to provide roadstone. Later, building stone became a more significant material (at least on limestone geology) and quarries appear to have been larger. Linear quarries also appear to have been dug to provide material for field walls.

Lower Street Furlong

Post-medieval quarrying had affected much of the south-east corner of the site. A large, irregular quarry pit (24) was identified measuring at least 20 m by 10 m. It was not fully excavated and its depth was therefore not established. Post-medieval pottery was recovered from the upper fill.

St Augustine's Farm South

Two linear quarry pits (3175 and 3177) were uncovered during the stripping of the southern end of Area O. Quarry pit 3175 was 5 m wide and 0.48 m deep with a flat base and stepped sides. It extended for 34 m within the excavation area and for an unknown distance beyond. The quarry followed the line of a standing drystone wall suggesting that it may have been dug to provide stone for the wall, although this lay 20 m away.

The pit appeared to have been left open to fill naturally. It is possible that the quarry served as a field boundary, although it was too broad to have been intended purely as a ditch.

Quarry pit 3177 had a similar profile and depth to quarry 3175 although only 4 m of the feature lay within the excavation area. It contained three fills of grey-brown silt-clay, which were banked up against the south-eastern edge of the cut. It appeared to have been deliberately backfilled from the south-eastern edge. Two sherds of red earthenware pottery, dating from the mid 16th century onwards, were recovered from the latest fill, 3176.

Exhibition Barn

Two quarry pits (6 and 14) were noted at this site. Pit 6 was in an isolated position in the southern part of the site. It was circular, 8 m in diameter and *c.* 2.5 m deep with a flat base and steeply sloping sides. The primary fill (5) yielded part of a yellow-green, mould-blown glass bottle dated to the 17th or 18th centuries. The small size of the pit suggests that it had served no more than a local need. The full extent of quarry pit 14 was not exposed and it may have been sub-rectangular or linear in plan (Fig. 4.34). It lay close to and parallel to the medieval ditch 22 and the quarry may have been for the construction or repair of a field wall, although none currently exists on this alignment. Alternatively, it may have been dug for another purpose at the edge of the field. A quadrant was sample-excavated to a depth of 1.20 m without its base being reached. The latest fill contained a single sherd of medieval pottery dating from the 13th century onwards (Table 7.32).

Burford Road

The quarry pits on both sides of Burford Road have been described in Chapter 5. The large quarry on the southern side appears to have been an important source of building stone in the post-medieval period. It was next to, but not the same feature as, Hare Bushes Quarry, which appears on the 1875 1st edition Ordnance Survey map and was a source of Great Oolite and finds of fossil eggs in the mid 19th century (Gerrard and Viner 1994, 137). A large area of quarrying was found extending further away from the road during the watching brief in this area. These features presumably relate to the expansion of Hare Bushes Quarry from the late 19th century.

Highgate House

A large linear quarry (266), flanking Ermin Street, was recorded during the excavation and the subsequent stripping of the road corridor. It was 10 m wide and 2.90 m deep and had a flat bottom. It contained no datable material, although its size and linearity strongly suggests that it was post-medieval and may have provided building material for the road, or for drystone walling alongside it. Three further (undated) quarry pits were observed to the north-west in the watching brief and four modern quarry pits in the length of road between Highgate House and Highgate Farm.

Trackways and cobbled surfaces

There was abundant evidence for road use in medieval, and particularly, post-medieval times. The road constructions relating to Ermin Street and Burford Road have been described and discussed in Chapter 5, as has the post-Roman development of The Lynches Trackway. The more inconclusive traces of cobbling at Sly's Wall South and Duntisbourne Leer, which may be post-Roman, are in Chapter 4. Wheel ruts were ubiquitous on all sites adjacent to Ermin Street and indicate that post-medieval traffic used a relatively wide corridor on both sides of the metalled road surface. Most of this evidence will not be described here, although the hollow way at Middle Duntisbourne represents an extreme effect of post-medieval road use and is of some interest for that reason. The post-medieval hollow way at the Trinity Farm site, Bagendon, is also described below.

Middle Duntisbourne hollow way

An irregular linear spread of soil was identified along the north-eastern limit of the investigated area and parallel to Ermin Street (Fig. 3.35). The spread, consisting of worn limestone fragments within a brown silty deposit, proved to be a series of deep ruts which converged into a single hollow way track towards the north-west. The hollow way had a width of 5 to 7 m and a depth of 0.40 m, with parallel ruts, 1.5 m apart, in the base.

The ruts and hollow way had formed more than 10 m to the side of Ermin Street indicating that the main highway had become unusable or at least inappropriate for the volume and nature of the traffic using it. The surface of worn limestone yielded a single sherd of Ashton Keynes pottery suggesting a date of mid 16th to late 18th century for the use of the route, which is entirely compatible with what is known of the state of the highways in the late medieval and early modern periods. Traffic-related objects recovered included over twenty horseshoe nails and several hobnails. A deposit (196) well within the rutting yielded, in addition to horseshoe nails, a fragment of a cast mould decorated rumbler bell, an object which was part of a horse harness and which dates from the early post-medieval period onwards. A similar object was recovered from the topsoil at the same site.

Trinity Farm hollow way

A series of linear features were recorded crossing the site south-east to north-west (Fig. 2.9). The profile through the features suggests that they represent the course of a shallow hollow way (42) and associated wheel ruts (features 40, 41 and 43). Feature 42 was a *c.* 2.5 m wide depression that was located between

features 41 and 43. It had a shallow U-shaped profile, 0.20 m deep. Finds dating to the late 19th or early 20th century indicate that the trackway had been in use until recently. Its course coincides with an existing footpath which also appears on the 1st edition Ordnance Survey map of 1875.

The Thames and Severn Canal *(Figs 6.6-7)*

Part of the disused and backfilled Thames and Severn Canal was located in the excavations at Court Farm and Street Farm in Latton although nowhere was it examined by excavation. The canal, finally completed in 1789, linked the Stroudwater Navigation at Stroud to the Thames at Inglesham and had originally been a wide canal with 44 locks. It was plagued by problems throughout its existence, caused by a shortage of water, poor workmanship and competition (Russell 1971, 20). Eventually it was abandoned and was backfilled between 1927 and 1933. The line of the canal is still visible in some sections of the modern landscape with an earthen bank along its north-eastern edge.

The canal appears on 19th-century maps closely following the River Churn south of Cirencester. East of Latton, the North Wiltshire Branch Canal was built in the early 19th century as a spur, joining the Thames and Severn Canal at Latton Lock and 'The Basin'. South of Latton the canal ran to the rear of properties fronting Ermin Street and narrowed to less than 15 m wide to pass under Ermin Street at Latton Bridge before turning to follow the edge of the turnpike road south to Cricklade Wharf (near Weavers Bridge).

In the current project the canal was located at the extreme south-east corner of the Street Farm excavations. At Court Farm the course of the canal was seen to turn roughly 45 degrees at the north-west end of the site and run along the edge of the excavation area. Its chief effect here was to truncate all the Roman deposits immediately fronting Ermin Street.

Weavers Bridge: river channels and water control ditches

At the northern end of the excavation area, which examined the late Roman site (Chapter 4), were a number of braided river channels cut by drainage ditches (Figs 4.38–39). The area was characterised by extensive floodplain activity with two main alluvial deposits also identified.

River channels

The major river channel (130) ran east-west truncating the late Roman midden. It was about 20 m wide and 0.4 m deep. A further six, smaller channels were identified on a more north-south or north-west – south-east alignment. All were shallow and, like channel 130, with flat bases. Finds were sparse but consistent with a medieval date. A group of sherds from a late 12th- to 14th-century vessel came from one of the fills (fill 45 of channel 44). An environmental sample from channel 120 (Tables 8.51–8.52, sample 6; see Pelling,

Chapter 8), contained waterlogged plant remains which were mostly of aquatic species characteristic of slow-flowing or stagnant water bordered by tall, dense vegetation. The charred assemblage, in contrast, contained a high percentage of free-threshing wheat rachis and some cereal grains typical of the medieval period.

A group of five *in situ* worked wooden stakes (105, 106, 107, 108 and 139) were grouped towards the southern edge of channel 130. All were made from oak heartwood and showed evidence of careful tooling. Their tips were slightly blunted and/or crumpled, which indicates that they had been driven into the ground see Mitchell, Chapter 7. Their function remains unclear but, since waterlogged material was present in the adjacent channel, they may well have been associated with the channel, serving as mooring posts or part of a bridge or jetty.

Alluvium

Two main deposits of alluvium (91 and 92), both overlying and cut by floodplain-related features, were identified at the northern end of the site. Both consisted of blue-grey silt-clays, with the later of the two deposits (91) being heavy mottled. A number of finds were recorded from the lower deposit (92), including horseshoes, animal bone fragments, and a human skull (see Boyle, Chapter 8). A column sample through the deposits recovered some charred plant remains from the base (Table 8.51, sample 8; see Pelling, Chapter 8). These were dominated by grain of free-threshing wheat with occasional other food plants of a medieval character, a date confirmed by the presence of a shell of the mollusc *Hellicellinae*, which is generally regarded as a medieval introduction. Like the charred remains from the river channel, the presence of economic plant species, probably from the dumping of processing waste, suggests settlement nearby.

Drainage ditches

Four ditches were identified which, where relationships could be established, were shown to cut the river channels. Three ran on approximately north-south alignments and were between 3–4 m wide and 0.22–0.5 m deep with regular U-shaped profiles. An environmental sample (Table 8.52, sample 7; see Pelling, Chapter 8) was taken from a clean deposit of blue grey clay in ditch 20. This contained a waterlogged plant assemblage indicative of a muddy ditch, with terrestrial species much more common than aquatic ones. The insect assemblage suggested lush vegetation as well as possible grazing land or hay meadow.

Discussion

Not many conclusions can be drawn concerning medieval activity on the site. Shifting river meanders clearly indicate intense and prolonged hydrological processes in the post-Roman period, the development and causes of which lie outside the scope of this investigation. However, a few observations can be made from cartographic and air-photographic evidence. The broadest river channel from the excavations can be seen to be following the general east-west alignment of one of the major river channels shown on the Andrews and Drury map of 1773 (although it is not the same channel depicted) which relates to the drainage pattern before the Thames and Severn Canal was completed in 1789. It is probable that the present channel lying immediately west of the site (and which is not shown on the Andrew's and Drury map) took most of the flow from the earlier channel which remained as a mere ditch. An earlier palaeochannel, which appears to have been a branch of Ampney Brook, is evident from cropmarks north-east of the site (shown on Fig. 4.37). This probably had a pre-Roman origin since it appears to have been crossed by a (presumably) Roman ditched trackway south of Sheeppen Bridge but was respected by another trackway to the east (RCHME NGR Index No. SU 1094/ 28 and 29). The palaeochannel ran on approximately the same alignment as the north-south channels and drainage ditches in the excavated area and it is possible, although this point is highly speculative, that this was an earlier natural alignment of the drainage system which retained some significance in the medieval period.

Human activity at this time is evident from the charred plant remains. These came from one of the river channels and also from the alluvium (Table 8.51, samples 6 and 8) and consisted of cereal remains which appear to indicate dumps of crop processing waste. This economic evidence, which contrasts with the evidence for the natural environment from waterlogged plants, must have derived from a nearby settlement. None is known from immediately adjacent to the site, although a scatter of 13th-14th century pottery has been recorded from a little over 200 m north of Weavers Bridge (Wilts. SMR SU09SE 455) (Fig. 4.39). The pottery scatter coincides with the location of Latton Lower Mill on the Andrews and Drury map which had ceased to exist by 1875. Material of 13th- to 14th-century date has also been imprecisely located in the area of Cricklade Wharf (also called Latton Wharf) (Johnson 1991, 10) and it is possible that a settlement existed closer to Weavers Bridge. The scatter may be related to (undated) features recorded in the watching brief just north of the old wharf on the other side of the A419.

Chapter 7:   Artefactual evidence

THE STRUCK FLINT
By Theresa Durden

Trinity Farm

Introduction

A total of 490 pieces of flint was recovered from this site, including 389 chips retained from sieved soil samples. All of the flintwork apart from 2 broken flakes came from the fills of three pits (7, 9 and 11) which contained Beaker sherds.

Raw material and condition

Flint is not native to most of the area under discussion and so chalk flint would have been imported from the downland to the south or east (Darvill 1987, 48). Drift flint from the gravels of the Upper Thames valley may also have been used in small quantities. The flint is in fresh condition and corticated grey/white. A few pieces had lighter blue/white speckled cortication.

The assemblage

Assemblage composition is summarised in Table 7.1. Pit fills 7 and 9 contained most of the material (414 pieces). Broad flakes dominate the assemblage, with blades and blade-like flakes almost absent. In fill 7 flakes were almost exclusively inner flakes, with only two pieces retaining some cortex. No completely cortical pieces were found in this context. Fill 9 only contained a few flakes with cortex, and one cortical flake. Fill 11 contained mostly tiny chips recovered from sieving. Hammer mode on the flakes was a mixture of soft and hard, with plain butts. A few narrow butted flakes were noted. Flakes from 9 and 11 are broadly comparable, although those from 9 may be slightly more irregular in shape.

Four cores were found; a small multi-platform flake core (9 g) and a core on a thick flake (4 g) from fill 7, and a small blade core (7 g) and another core on a flake (7 g) from fill 9 (Fig. 7.2.15–17). The cores on flakes showed only a few broad, squat removals. The blade core is probably residual and datable to the Mesolithic/earlier Neolithic. It is notable that all of the cores are small and not ideal for working down, which suggests raw material was at a premium.

Retouched material consisted of 14 scrapers (Fig. 7.1.1–14), 2 retouched flakes and 1 fragmentary retouched piece. Fill 7 contained three scrapers, a side scraper, end scraper and horseshoe scraper. The end scraper was steep but quite finely flaked. A retouched flake was also recovered from this context. Fill 9 contained 10 scrapers; 2 end-, 3 side-, 3 end-and-side, 1 discoidal and 1 thumbnail scraper. Some of these scrapers were quite steep, with some step-flaking, while others, notably the end-and-side scrapers and the discoidal scraper, were shallower and more finely flaked (Fig. 7.1.1). The thumbnail scraper, a typical find in Beaker assemblages, was steep but finely flaked. This context also contained a retouched flake and a fragmentary unidentifiable retouched piece. Fill 11 contained one end-and-side scraper which appears to have been used as a core, some flakes having been removed from its ventral surface (Fig. 7.1.6).

Discussion

The technological attributes of the debitage in the pits, and the presence of the thumbnail scraper, would accord with the Beaker date assigned to these features on the basis of pottery. The considerable quantity of retouched pieces in fill 9 is reminiscent of the Beaker pit 1260 from Roughground Farm, Lechlade (Allen *et al.* 1993, 18). Non-funerary Beaker sites are rare in the region (cf. Darvill 1987, 82) so this discovery adds to their number. The large number of chips (228) might suggest flint was knapped into or close to the pit; about a dozen of the chips may be retouch chips. Considerable numbers of chips were also found in the other pits. The relative lack of large cores and cortical flakes taken with the presence of these chips might suggest the later stages of flint knapping and possibly artefact manufacture in the vicinity. It is possible that the contents of these pits, especially contexts 7 and 9, represent a ritual deposit.

Birdlip Quarry *(Fig. 7.4.25–27)*

Introduction

A total of 152 pieces of flint was recovered from this site, including one piece of burnt unworked flint, and 34 chips and small flakes retained from sieved soil samples from contexts 81 and 89. Although a fairly

Table 7.1   Flint from Trinity Farm.

flakes	blades	blade-like flakes	chips	cores	retouched	total
77	1	2	389	4	17	490

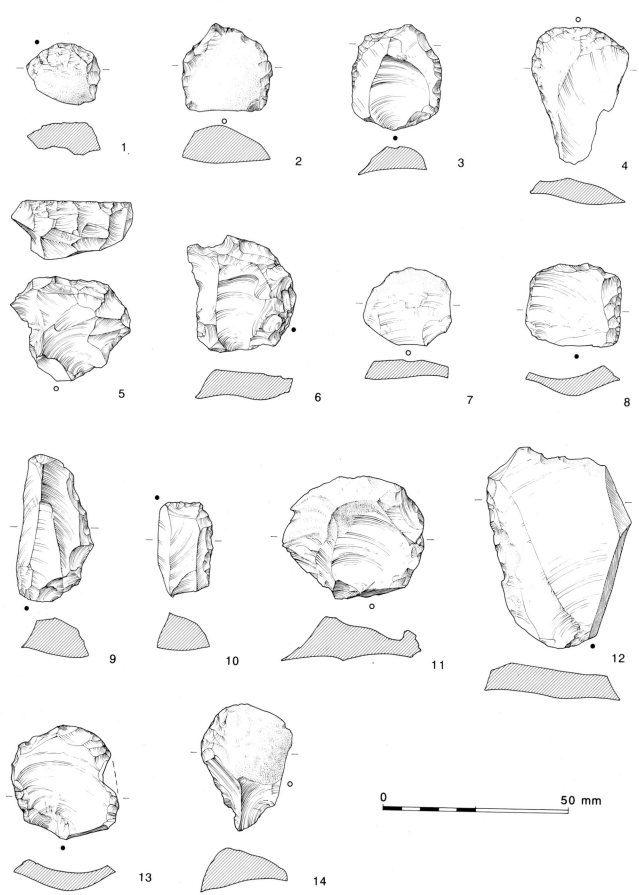

Figure 7.1   Worked flint from Trinity Farm, see catalogue for details.

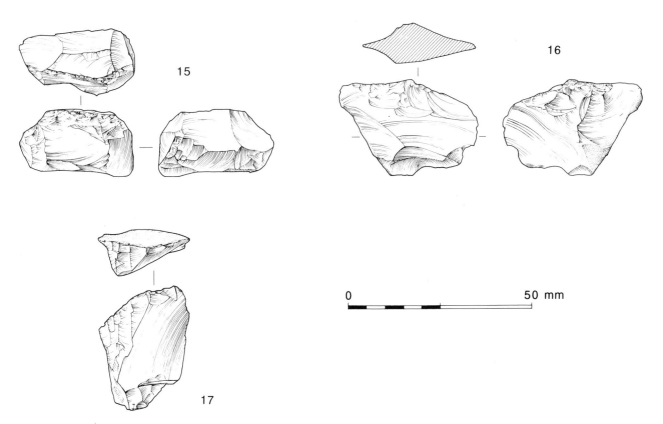

Figure 7.2   Worked flint from Trinity Farm, see catalogue for details.

large number of flints were recovered from this site, most contexts apart from 81 and 89 contained only a few pieces at most. There was no associated prehistoric pottery.

Raw material and condition

One flake of Bullhead flint was found in context 954. This is a distinctive flint recognisable by a thin orange band present under a dark grey or greenish cortex. This flint is often found in the London area, North Surrey and Kent (Shepherd 1972, 114), but it also occurs at the base of the Reading Beds (Dewey and Bromehead 1915, 2). It may also occur in a derived state in the river gravels of the Thames. Otherwise, the material was as at Trinity Farm (see above).

The assemblage

As no contexts stood out as containing a large assemblage of flintwork, the complete site assemblage is considered as a whole. The composition of the collection is shown in Table 7.2.

Broad flakes dominate the assemblage, though blade-like flakes and blades form 20% of all flake material (excluding chips). Morphologically the flakes

are a mixture, some pieces being quite irregular in outline and thickness and others relatively thin and more regularly-shaped. A mixture of hard and soft hammers were used and the majority of butts were plain. One retouched flake with a faceted butt was recovered from context 729.

Six cores were collected; these consisted of two multi-platformed flake cores, a keeled flake core, a struck nodule, a bladelet core (Fig. 7.4.27) and a blade core fragment. All of the cores were small, weighing 4-20 g, either because cores were well worked-down or because the starting piece of raw material was small; this would suggest raw material was at a premium, probably because it was imported into the area. The small size of cores was also noted at Trinity Farm. The flake cores showed little control over knapping, with flakes often ending in hinge fractures and the cores being poorly-maintained. The blade cores, however, were more carefully flaked.

A total of 18 retouched pieces were recovered, comprising 12 scrapers, 3 retouched flakes, 1 leaf arrowhead from context 1510 (Fig. 7.4.25), 1 serrated flake from context 329 and 1 miscellaneous retouched piece. The scrapers were mostly end, end-and-side types, and often on thick or irregular flakes, forming a fairly steep scraping angle. A horseshoe scraper

Table 7.2   Flint from Birdlip Quarry.

flakes	blades	blade-like flakes	cores	chips	retouched	waste	rejuvenations	total	broken	burnt
88	1	21	6	13	18	3	1	151	84	3

(Fig. 7.4.26) from context 1149 was on a thinner, more regular piece and was finely flaked. The leaf arrowhead, datable to the earlier Neolithic, was a small example, measuring 25 x 19 mm.

Discussion

It is difficult to place a date on the assemblage as the flintwork is thinly spread over a large number of contexts and may well be residual in many cases. The relatively high percentage of blade-like material, the presence of blade cores, a possible core rejuvenation tablet and the leaf arrowhead would point to a level of earlier Neolithic activity on the site. Serrated flakes are found in assemblages from the Mesolithic through to the early Bronze Age. The broad flakes, poorly-worked flake cores and thick scrapers may also point to later Neolithic/earlier Bronze Age domestic activity.

Duntisbourne Grove

Introduction

A total of 506 pieces of flint was recovered from this site, forming the largest lithic assemblage from any of the excavated sites. This total includes 2 pieces/2 g of burnt unworked flint. The bulk of the flintwork came from three prehistoric pits: 94 (fills 95, 111 and 113); 142 (fills 143 and 168); 144 (fill 145). Indeterminate prehistoric pottery and one possible earlier Neolithic rim were recovered from another pit containing flint (63) and possible middle Iron Age sherds from 113 in pit 94.

Raw material and condition

See Trinity Farm (above)

The assemblage

Assemblage composition is summarised in Tables 7.3–4.

Debitage

Flakes dominated the assemblage and these consisted mostly of broad, regular flakes. These were generally quite thin and struck with a mixture of hard and soft hammers, although soft hammers tended to dominate, especially in the pit contexts. Flake butts were a mixture of narrow or punctiform butts and broad butted flakes, with occasional faceted butts occurring in pit 94 (typology after Tixier *et al.* 1980). Five rejuvenation flakes were recovered; these were all from pit contexts (63, 95, 113 and 145) and included two crested flakes from context 113 (Fig. 7.5.35) a type of debitage which is also produced in the initial preparation of cores as well as rejuvenation. Crested flakes are typical of Mesolithic and earlier Neolithic industries, and rejuvenation is generally more common in these earlier industries than in the later Neolithic or Bronze Age.

Only four cores were recovered from the site; these consisted of a flake core fragment from context 95, a possible burnt and broken tortoise core from the same context, a partly discoidal core from context 111 and a multi-platformed flake core from context 113. These core types, the tortoise core in particular, are typical of later Neolithic industries, although the core fragment from 95 showed signs of platform abrasion, a practice which removes projections resulting from flake removal and strengthens the platform edge (Barton 1992) and is more commonly found in earlier industries.

Retouched pieces

A total of 26 retouched pieces were recovered, forming 5.2% of the struck flint assemblage. Most of the retouched pieces were found in pit contexts. The different retouched categories are shown in Table 7.4. Simple retouched flakes were the most common, and these were mostly on broad regular flakes, although an example from 143 was made on a blade-like flake. A cortical piece from 113 was retouched around all the edges and may have been a rejected arrowhead blank or perhaps a representation of an arrowhead. Two simple awls, made on a blade and a blade-like flake, were recovered from pit fill 63 and one piercer was present in fill 113. Only two scrapers were found, these comprised a small, well-flaked end and side scraper from context 46 and a long end scraper on a blade-like flake from 203.

A complete chisel arrowhead (Fig. 7.5.31) and two probable leaf arrowhead tips were recovered (Fig. 7.5.30); both tips, one of which was burnt, were from context 113, and the chisel arrowhead, which was quite crude but probably of Clark's type D (Clark 1934), was found in context 95. All three arrowheads, therefore, came from pit 94.

Seven serrated flakes were found in a number of different contexts, all from pit fills bar one possible broken example from a probable Roman ditch (87). Pit 142 contained four examples, one of these bore edge gloss (Fig. 7.5.33) and another was made on a blade. A burnt, fragmentary example was found in pit 144 and another from pit fill 191.

Dating and discussion

A broad Neolithic date can be assigned to the flintwork from the pits, possibly middle to later Neolithic. Earlier Neolithic industries tended to favour the use of soft hammers for the production of blades and blade-like flakes, and the presence of broad, regular flakes struck with soft hammers alongside a small blade-like component may indicate a crossover between typically earlier and later Neolithic technologies. The traits of many of the simple retouched pieces would also support this date. The possible tortoise core is of later Neolithic date. The long scraper, although not from a pit, would not be out of place in an earlier Neolithic assemblage. Serrated flakes are present in assemblages from the Mesolithic through to the early Bronze Age, although the example from pit 142 which was made on a blade is more likely to date to the earlier part of this range. The leaf arrow-heads are typically of earlier Neolithic date, while the

Table 7.3   Flint from Duntisbourne Grove

flakes	blades	blade-like flakes	cores	chips	retouched	waste	rejuvenations	total	broken	burnt
337	24	39	4	65	26	4	5	504	266	90

chisel arrowhead would date to the later Neolithic. The two types are from different fills, but little difference can be observed in the associated debitage, which might otherwise suggest that the chisel arrowhead is from a later fill. It is possible that this pit contained an assemblage of middle-later Neolithic date, in which leaf arrowheads may still have been current. It is notable that they are both fragmentary.

The assemblage from this site is interesting in that it derives mostly from a small number of pits, with very few other contexts containing struck flint. The pits contain a relatively high proportion of retouched material, a percentage that would be consistent with a domestic assemblage according to Wainwright (1972). There is, however, little other evidence for settlement and it may be that the contents of these pits formed a ritual deposit. There is little evidence for flint knapping in or around the pits, as cores were rare and relatively few chips were found in the sieved residue of samples from the pits. No obvious refits were found, although a flake which had been broken in two in antiquity (the break was slightly corticated) was found in pit 144. Interestingly, the flake was completely corticated, so the break may indicate later usage. This, together with the presence of the three arrowheads in pit 94, may suggest the deliberate selection of material for deposition in at least some of the pits rather than the haphazard dumping of rubbish. Evidence for similar acts of deliberate deposition is well documented for the whole country (Thomas 1991, 60–62).

Table 7.4   Retouched material from Duntisbourne Grove

retouched flake	arrowhead	serrated flake	scraper	awl	piercer	total
11	3	7	2	2	1	26

Early-middle Neolithic activity in the region appears to have concentrated on the Cotswold uplands (Darvill 1984a, 89, fig. 3; 1987, 46), most of the evidence in the form of long barrows. Apart from the causewayed enclosures of Crickley Hill and Peak Camp to the north-east of Duntisbourne, there is little documented settlement evidence for this period with which to compare the pits at Duntisbourne Grove. Evidence in the form of surface flint scatters has been found in the course of fieldwalking in the north Cotswolds (Marshall 1985) and finds are more abundant to the west in the Severn Valley (Darvill 1987, 46). The distribution of flint and stone axes concentrates on the Cotswold uplands (ibid. 47) in a similar pattern

to the long barrows, suggesting that further survey of this area might reveal more evidence like that from Duntisbourne Grove.

All sites with small lithic assemblages

Introduction

A total of 22 sites possessed very small assemblages of struck flint, the largest being Norcote Farm with 39 pieces. Owing to this scarcity, there is little to be said about much of the material; instead a basic catalogue of material is presented for each site, with more detailed comments where appropriate.

Duntisbourne Leer

A total of 6 pieces; 2 flakes, 1 blade-like flake, 1 burnt core fragment, 1 steep end scraper and 1 barbed and tanged arrowhead (Fig. 7.3.18). The latter piece was found in the ploughsoil and is of Beaker/early Bronze Age date.

Preston Enclosure

Flake material consisted mostly of broad flakes, some struck with a soft hammer. These include a possible rejuvenation flake which removes part of a striking platform, and a flake with a faceted butt which may have been struck from a tortoise core. Retouched material consisted of a fabricator of Mesolithic or early Bronze Age date (Fig. 7.3.20), a barbed and tanged arrowhead of Beaker/early Bronze Age date (Fig. 7.3.19), an earlier Neolithic laurel leaf (Fig. 7.3.21), a serrated flake, a retouched blade, a notched flake and an end-and-side scraper and scraper fragment. The collection appears to be of mixed date, with a possible range from the Mesolithic through to the early Bronze Age.

Middle Duntisbourne

Flakes were all broad, but of varying thicknesses, struck mostly with soft hammers. Undiagnostic. The arrowhead, however, was a leaf type, possibly unfinished, and datable to the earlier Neolithic (Fig. 7.3.22). Most pieces corticated blue/white.

Cherry Tree Lane

A total of 11 pieces; 7 flakes, 1 discoidal core, 2 scraper fragments and 1 microlith (Fig. 7.3.23) (obliquely blunted point). The flakes are broad, soft-hammer

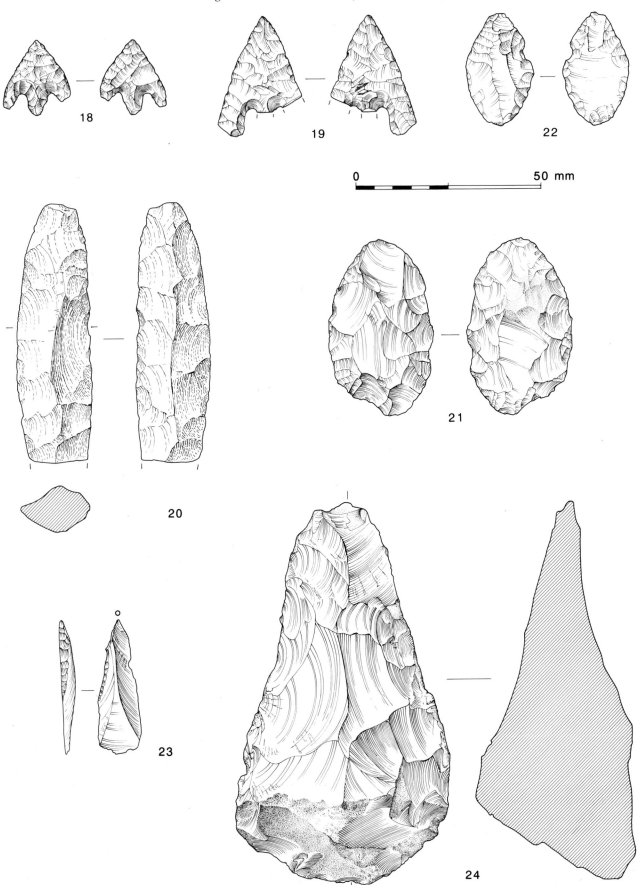

Figure 7.3   *Worked flint from Duntisbourne Leer, Preston Enclosure, Middle Duntisbourne, Cherry Tree Lane Compound and Latton Watching Brief, see catalogue for details.*

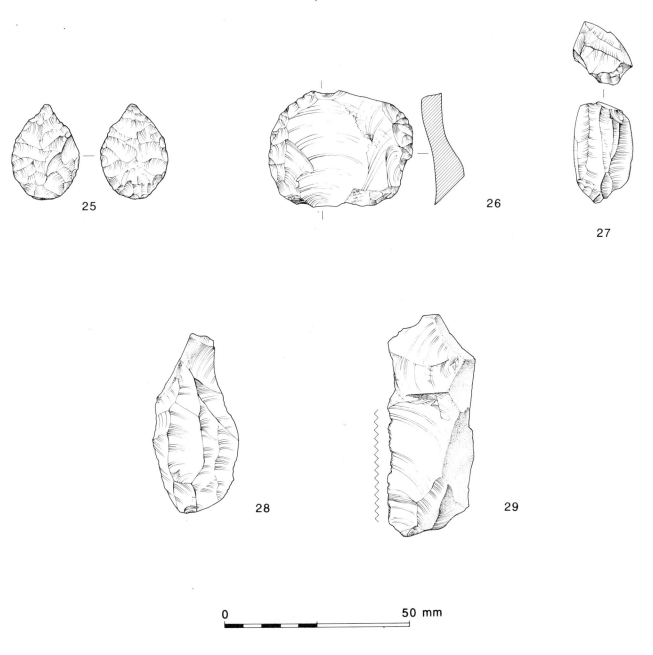

Figure 7.4   Worked flint from Hare Bushes North and Birdlip Quarry, see catalogue for details.

struck pieces; the discoidal core is quite small (19 g) with small, hinged flake removals and may be of later Neolithic date. The microlith is an earlier Mesolithic type.

Latton Watching Brief

A total of 7 pieces; 4 flakes, 1 retouched flake, a possible flake from a tortoise core and an Acheulian hand axe in rolled condition (Fig. 7.3.24), patinated orange-brown. The Acheulian tradition is thought to date broadly to the lower Palaeolithic period (Mellars 1974, 48–52; Saville 1984a, 61–66). Acheulian finds are very

rare in the area and mostly confined to the river gravels (Darvill 1987; 18–20).The tortoise core flake is of later Neolithic date.

Hare Bushes North

A total of 17 pieces; 7 flakes, 1 blade-like flake, 2 pieces irregular waste, 1 retouched flake (Fig. 7.4.28), 1 multi-platformed flake core, 1 core fragment and 2 serrated flakes (Fig. 7.4.29) (plus 2 more dubious examples). The complete core is quite small (18 g) with small flake removals, some of which are hinged. Removals on the core fragment are similar. Two of the serrated flakes

313

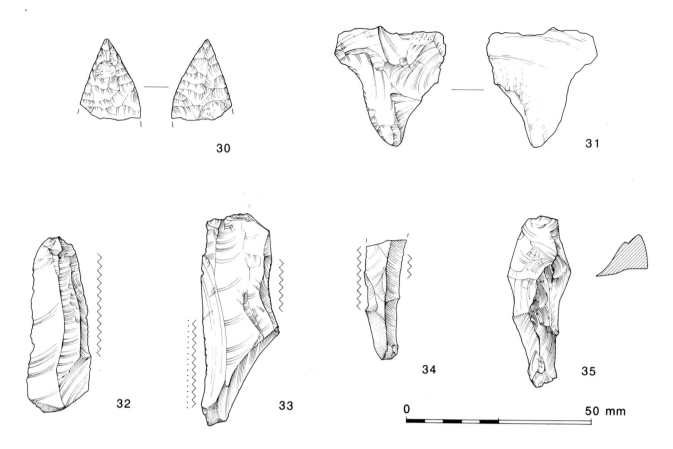

Figure 7.5   Worked flint from Duntisbourne Grove, see catalogue for details.

are dubious examples as the serrations are coarse but very small, and discontinuous along the flake edge. Serrated flakes have a date range from the Mesolithic to the early Bronze Age.

Street Farm

A total of seven pieces- four flakes (contexts 178, 252, 365, 737), one blade-like flake (context 220), 2 pieces burnt unworked flint (unstratified) weighing 24 g. Undiagnostic.

St Augustine's Farm South

Flakes were mostly broad, soft-hammer flakes. Of these, two were possible rejuvenation flakes, removing part of a platform edge. The core fragment was part of a broad flake core. The presence of rejuvenations, soft hammer struck flakes and blade-like pieces would suggest a Neolithic date, possibly middle Neolithic. Most pieces corticated blue/white.

Norcote Farm

Flakes were mostly broad and struck with soft hammers. Blade-like flakes were also struck with soft hammers and often had abraded platforms and dorsal blade scars. The cores comprised two flake core fragments, a single platformed blade core (broken), and

a small keeled flake core (7 g) made on a piece of dark grey chert. The chert is similar in appearance to Portland chert from Dorset on the south coast though this may not necessarily be the source. The retouched material consisted of one end scraper and two end-and-side scrapers, a serrated flake and a truncated flake.

The mix of broad and narrow flakes, the dominance of soft hammer flaking and the presence of the blade core could point to earlier Neolithic activity. It is possible, however, that the material is of mixed date; the flake cores could be later Neolithic, and the blade core and the truncated flake could equally date to the Mesolithic period. Serrated flakes are found in assemblages from the Mesolithic through to the early Bronze Age. The presence of dorsal blade scars on this piece, however, might suggest it was Mesolithic or earlier Neolithic in date.

Witpit Lane

A total of 6 pieces; 3 flakes, 1 piece irregular waste, 1 horseshoe scraper, 1 possible burnt scraper fragment. The horseshoe scraper may be Neolithic.

Cirencester Watching Brief

A probable barbed and tanged arrowhead, barbs and tangs broken off. Beaker/early Bronze Age date.

Westfield Farm

A single flake and a core on a flake (10 g) with a few small hinged removals.

Sly's Wall South

One notched flake.

Exhibition Barn

1 miniature multi-platformed flake core (2 g). Tiny flake removals, some hinged.

Catalogue of illustrated flint *(Figs 7.1–7.5)*

Trinity Farm (Figs 7.1–2)

1   Thumbnail scraper. Ctx 9.
2   Discoidal scraper (incomplete). Ctx 9.
3   End-and-side scraper. Ctx 9.
4   End-and-side scraper. Ctx 9.
5   End scraper. Ctx 9.
6   End-and-side scraper. Ctx 11.
7   End scraper. Ctx 9.
8   Side scraper. Ctx 9.
9   Side scraper. Ctx 9.
10   End-and-side scraper. Ctx 9.
11   Side scraper. Ctx 9.
12   Side scraper. Ctx 7.
13   Horseshoe scraper. Ctx 7.
14   End scraper. Ctx 7.
15   Core on a flake. Ctx 7.
16   Core on a flake. Ctx 9.
17   Blade core. Ctx 9.

Duntisbourne Leer (Fig. 7.3)

18   Barbed and tanged arrowhead. Ctx 1, sf 3.

Preston Enclosure (Fig. 7.3)

19   Barbed and tanged arrowhead (broken). Ctx 145, sf 4.
20   Fabricator (broken). U/S.
21   Laurel leaf. Ctx 8, sf 3.

Middle Duntisbourne (Fig. 7.3)

22   Leaf-shaped arrowhead (unfinished). Ctx 142.

Cherry Tree Lane (Fig. 7.3)

23   Microlith: obliquely blunted point. Ctx 23.

Latton Watching Brief (Fig. 7.3)

24   Acheulian handaxe. Ctx 5, sf 1.

Birdlip Quarry (Fig. 7.4)

25   Leaf-shaped arrowhead. Ctx 1150, sf 1510.
26   Horseshoe scraper. Ctx 1149, sf 1507.
27   Bladelet core. Ctx 64, sf 332.

Hare Bushes North (Fig. 7.4)

28   Retouched flake with dorsal blade scars. Ctx 1010.
29   Serrated flake. Ctx 1010.

Duntisbourne Grove (Fig. 7.5)

30   Arrowhead tip. Ctx 113, sf 289.
31   Chisel arrowhead, type D? Ctx 95, sf 256.
32   Serrated flake. Ctx 143, sf 333.
33   Serrated flake with edge gloss. Ctx 143, sf 331.
34   Serrated blade (broken). Ctx 168, sf 345.
35   Crested flake. Ctx 113, sf 263.

EARLIER PREHISTORIC POTTERY
By Alistair Barclay

Introduction

Ten of the excavated sites and part of the watching brief produced a total of 329 sherds (592 g) of Neolithic and Bronze Age pottery and a further four sites produced relatively small quantities of indeterminate prehistoric pottery (Table 7.5). The overall assemblage has a Neolithic to late Bronze Age date range and is characterised by mostly small and often abraded body sherds with a relatively small average sherd weight (<2 g). The recovery of albeit small quantities of Neolithic pottery from four sites is of some importance. The recovery of Beaker pottery from four of the sites is of some significance for this region; one of these produced a relatively large assemblage of Wessex/Middle Rhine Beaker pottery from a series of pit deposits.

Methodology

All of the material was recorded and quantified by sherd count and weight (Table 7.5). In the absence of featured sherds, dates were assigned on the basis of fabric analysis. A record was made of diagnostic forms and decoration and a selection of material is given in the catalogue below. The sherds were analysed using a binocular microscope (x 20) and were divided into fabric groups by principal inclusion type using the OAU alpha-numeric fabric recording system. OAU standard codes are used to denote inclusion types: A = sand (quartz and other mineral matter), F = flint, G = grog, C = calcareous matter excluding shell, S = shell, P = clay pellets, Q = quartzite. Size range for inclusions: 1 = <1 mm fine; 2 = 1-3 mm fine-medium and 3 = 3 mm < medium-coarse.

Fabrics

In total 15 fabrics were identified of which four are Neolithic, seven are Beaker, one is early Bronze Age, one is middle Bronze Age and two are of indeterminate prehistoric date. None of the identified fabrics can be considered as unusual. The three earlier Neolithic fabrics are similar to other fabrics found in the Cotswolds and on the Thames gravels (cf. Smith and Darvill 1990; Williams 1982). The use of unmodified clay or clay without added temper to manufacture Peterborough Ware can be paralleled from elsewhere within the Upper Thames Valley (Barclay in prep. a). Of the six identified Beaker fabrics five typically have grog as their principal inclusion. However, the remaining fabric which is principally calcite tempered is unusual. The single early Bronze Age fabric associated with a Collared Urn is typical. The shell fabric S2 is considered to be middle Bronze Age, although in the absence of featured sherds the date must remain uncertain.

Neolithic

F2/EN Hard fabric with medium angular flint. St Augustine's Lane, ctx 83.

FA2/EN Hard fabric with medium angular flint and sparse quartz sand. Court Farm, ctx 120; St Augustine's Farm South, ctx 3165.

S/L(S)2/EN Soft fabric with common, mostly leached, shell platelets. St Augustine's Farm South, context 3165.

VAP2/LN Soft fabric with sparse-common voids (?leached calcareous matter), rare quartz sand and rare clay pellets. Duntisbourne Grove, ctx 113.

Late Neolithic/early Bronze Age

GV2/LNEBA Soft slightly vesicular fabric with medium sized grog. Nettleton to Stratton Watching Brief, chainage 5200(2).

Beaker

Calcite-tempered: CVR2/EBA/BKR Soft fabric with common angular (rhombs) calcite inclusions, some lenticular voids and rare sub-rounded rock fragments. Trinity Farm, ctx 9.

Grog-tempered: G2/G?/EBA/BKR Soft fabric with medium sub-rounded grog. Preston Enclosure, ctxs 8 and 19; Trinity Farm, ctxs 7 and 9, St Augustine's Lane, ctx 6.

G3/EBA/BKR Soft fabric with large sub-angular grog. Trinity Farm, ctx 27.

GA2/EBA/BKR Soft fabric with medium subrounded grog and rare quartz sand. Court Farm, ctx 120.

Grog and calcareous-tempered: GC2/EBA/BKR Soft fabric with medium sub-rounded grog and sparse sub-rounded calcareous limestone fragments. Trinity Farm ctxs 7, 9 and 11.

GC3/EBA/BKR Soft fabric with medium sub-round grog and sparse small to large (over 3 mm) poorly sorted sub-rounded calcareous limestone fragments. Trinity Farm, ctxs 9 and 11.

Early Bronze Age

G2/EBA Soft fabric with medium sub-rounded grog. St Augustine's Lane, ctx 3017.

?Middle Bronze Age

L(S)2/- Soft fabric with moderate medium sized voids probably from leached shell. Cherry Tree Lane, ctxs 28 and 36; Highgate House, ctx 125; Court Farm, ctx 223; Latton 'Roman Pond' B1996/1 sf 72; St Augustine's Farm South, ctxs 3008 and 3121; St Augustine's Lane, ctxs 6, 12, 26, 47, 59 and 147.

Indeterminate and non-earlier prehistoric

L(S)/- and 2/- Soft fabric with moderate medium sized voids probably from leached shell, Birdlip Quarry, ctxs 89 and 253; St Augustine's Farm South, ctx 3102; Cherry Tree Lane Compound, ctx 36.

G?/- Soft fabric with grog inclusions St Augustine's Farm South, ctx 3102.

Discussion

Earlier Neolithic

Earlier Neolithic pottery was recovered from four of the excavated sites (see Table 7.5). This includes three rims and a small number of body sherds from simple Plain Bowls. A single context (63) from Duntisbourne Grove produced a rim and four body sherds (10 g) probably from a relatively small bowl (Fig. 7.6.36). Originally shell-tempered, this fabric is now vesicular with many lenticular voids. The simple and plain rim is thickened and out-turned. Similar rim forms are recorded from the Crickley Hill causewayed enclosure, some 11 km to the north-west (Dixon 1971, fig. 9.1 and 3). A body sherd from context 20 at Court Farm in a flint- and sand-tempered fabric may also be of this date. A fragment from a ?rolled rim in a sand and flint-tempered fabric was recovered from context 3165 at St Augustine's Farm South; and a shell-tempered body sherd from the same context could be of contemporary date. The rolled rim can also be paralleled amongst the pre-cairn pottery assemblage at Hazleton North (Smith and Darvill 1990, fig. 156. 1 and 7). Part of a simple rim from context 83 at St Augustine's Farm South is also likely to be of this date.

The earlier Neolithic pottery is likely to date to the middle centuries of the 4th millennium BC and is broadly contemporary with the use of both the causewayed enclosures and long cairns found in the adjacent areas of the Cotswolds (cf. Darvill 1987). Regionally these finds are important as very little of this material has been recovered from domestic rather than funerary or ceremonial contexts.

Later Neolithic and late Neolithic/early Bronze Age

Two sites produced material of this date (see Table 7.5). Context 113 (sf 117) from Duntisbourne Grove contained two refitting sherds that appear to come from the collar of a single small vessel (Fig. 7.6.37), most likely attributable to the Fengate Ware sub-style of the Peterborough Ware tradition (Smith 1976). The fabric (VAP2) is unusual and appears to contain no added temper. The short slightly convex collar appears to be plain and part of a possible neck-pit survives along the cavetto zone. In addition, a number

Table 7.5   A summary quantification and breakdown of the earlier prehistoric pottery assemblage by period and site.

Context	Earlier Neolithic	Later Neolithic (Peterborough Ware)	LNEBA	BKR	EBA	?MBA Preh	Indeter	Total
Watching brief (NOSNI)			4, 10 g					4, 10 g
Birdlip							34, 38 g	34, 38 g
Highgate House						1, 4 g		1, 4 g
Duntisbourne Grove	5, 10 g	2, 8 g						7, 18g
Trinity Farm				165, 255 g				165, 255 g
Cherry Tree Lane						36, 73 g		36, 73 g
Preston Enclosure				2, 3 g				2, 3 g
St Augustine's Lane	1, 3 g			1, 1 g		78, 104 g		80, 108 g
St Augustine's Farm South	2, 4 g				1, 5 g	12, 25 g	3, 2 g	18, 36 g
?Cirencester Road							2, 2 g	2, 2 g
Latton Roman Pond						5, 17 g		5, 17 g
Latton Court Farm	1, 1 g			1, 2 g		1, 12 g	2, 4 g	5, 19 g
Total	9, 18 g	2, 8 g	4, 10 g	169, 261 g	1, 5 g	133, 235 g	41, 46 g	359, 583 g

of indeterminate late Neolithic/early Bronze Age sherds including a simple rim were found during a watching brief of the north of Stratton to Nettleton improvement.

The possible collar from a Fengate Ware vessel from Duntisbourne Grove has a date range somewhere between the late 4th-early 3rd millennium BC (cf. Gibson and Kinnes 1997). Relatively little Peterborough Ware has been found in this region (Darvill 1987, 69) and the only significant find comes from Cam, some 20 km to the west (Smith 1968). Elsewhere within this region Peterborough Ware has sometimes been found in secondary deposits associated with the reuse or blocking of earlier Neolithic funerary monuments (Darvill 1987, 66–7).

Beaker

Beaker pottery was recovered from Trinity Farm, Preston Enclosure, St Augustine's Lane and Court Farm (see Table 7.6). However, only Trinity Farm produced a significant group of material.

A large assemblage of pottery was recovered from three pit deposits at Trinity Farm. In total these pits produced 164 sherds from a maximum of perhaps 14 vessels (Fig. 7.6.38–52) with a further sherd coming from context 27. Many of these vessels are represented by single sherds and in no case was it possible to reconstruct a complete vessel profile. The three pits (contexts 8, 10 and 12) occurred in a line and were spaced closely together. The pottery from the three pits is very similar and it is possible that some of the material recovered from the separate fills derives from the same vessels. It is interesting to note that the overall sherd size is relatively small which might indicate that the material was broken and collected in a midden-like deposit prior to burial. The total assemblage includes vessels with non-plastic finger-nail decoration and, to a lesser, extent, impressed combed lines. All of the vessels are relatively thin-walled and sherds from heavier 'domestic' Beakers are absent. The featured sherds indicate that the original profiles might have

been slight and sinuous. Typologically the material can be considered to be early within the Beaker sequence and this is supported by the two radiocarbon determinations from pits 7 and 9 (2476–2142 cal BC, NZA 3673, R24151/17, 3876±57BP; 2462–2130 cal BC, NZA 8674, R24151/18, 3836±58BP). The closest affinities are perhaps with the Wessex/Middle Rhine group as defined by Clarke (1970).

At Preston Enclosure contexts 8 and 19 produced two small and abraded sherds of Beaker pottery (3 g). Both occurred with other larger Iron Age sherds and are assumed to be residual/redeposited (see Timby below). The sherds are relatively thin-walled (5 mm), decorated with impressed comb motifs (bands and ?chevrons) and are manufactured from grog-tempered fabrics (the other sherds from contexts 19, 64/65, 74 and 160 are not thought to be Beaker and are considered to be Iron Age or later. A single sherd was recovered from a context that also produced Iron Age pottery at Court Farm and, therefore, can be considered to be residual.

Very little Beaker material has been recovered from the immediate area of the Upper Thames Valley that is crossed by the route of the A417/A419 (cf. Darvill 1987, 81–8). A significant deposit of Beaker material was recovered from a single pit at Roughground Farm, Lechlade which is approximately 13 km east of Preston (Darvill 1993) and Beaker pottery has also been found at Shorncote, 5 km to the south (Morris 1994b, 34–5; Barclay and Glass 1995, 42). The assemblage from Preston Enclosure is too small to suggest affinities with particular styles, apart from stating that the sherds all derive from fine vessels. However, it can be suggested that the relatively large group of material from the pits at Trinity Farm has affinities with the Wessex/Middle Rhine style. Similar material was recovered from Roughground Farm, Lechlade and from the Marlborough Downs (Cleal 1992; Darvill 1993). Stray finds include part of a fine Beaker from Crickley Hill (Darvill 1987), while Beaker associated burials occur at Shorncote and Lechlade (Barclay and Glass 1995; Timby 1998b).

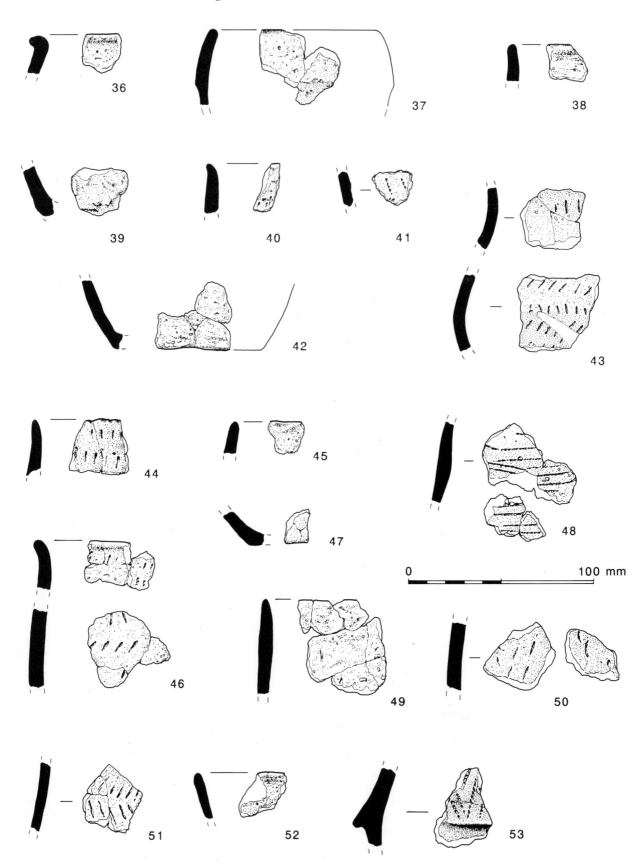

Figure 7.6   Neolithic and early Bronze Age pottery.

Table 7.6   Summary quantification (sherd number, weight) and breakdown of the Beaker assemblage from Trinity Farm by fabric and context.

Context	Fabric						Total
	C2/CVR2	G2	G3	GC2	GC3	GC + G -*	
7		4, 5 g	3, 8 g	11, 14 g		11, 9 g	29, 36 g
9	13, 10 g			19, 84 g	7, 36 g	83, 54g	122, 184 g
11	1, 1 g			6, 25 g		6, 2 g	13, 28 g
27			1, 8 g				1, 8 g
Total	14, 11 g	4, 5 g	4, 16 g	36, 123 g	7 ,36 g	100, 65 g	165, 256 g

* Sherds recovered mostly from sieving

However, none of these vessels have typologically affinities with the material from Trinity Farm. Only one funerary Beaker has affinities with this material from this region, the probable Wessex/Middle Rhine vessel from Sale's Lot, Withington (Darvill 1987, 86).

Early Bronze Age (excluding Beaker)

Early Bronze Age pottery was recovered from only one of the excavated sites (see Table 7.5), a single grog-tempered sherd from the fill of a ring ditch of an early Bronze Age barrow at St Augustine's Farm South. It probably derives from an early Bronze Age urn and is likely to be broadly contemporary with the construction and primary use of the monument. In addition, a rim fragment from a Collared Urn was found in the evaluation (1991.545, context 6, subsoil). The rim is grog-tempered and decorated with lines of impressed twisted cord (Fig. 7.6.53).

Longworth lists only seven Collared Urns from Gloucestershire, two of which are of uncertain provenance (1984, 199–200). The rim fragment is too small to place in either his Primary or Secondary series. However, the lack of an internal moulding and the concave collar form seem to favour Longworth's Secondary Series (1984, 5). Enough of the collar survives to suggest that the vessel was decorated with a zig-zag motif created from impressed twisted cord. This motif is not restricted to either Series and has no direct parallel within the small group of urns from Gloucestershire. However, more distant parallels can be found in the Oxfordshire part of the Upper Thames Valley, for example at Barrow Hills, Radley (Cleal 1999). In the Upper Thames region Collared Urns are almost exclusively from funerary deposits and, therefore, the sherd from context 6 (subsoil) at St Augustine's Farm South is more likely to derive from a disturbed funerary context.

?Middle Bronze Age

Possible middle Bronze Age pottery (133 sherds, 235 g) was recovered from six of the excavated sites (see Table 7.5). All of this material consisted of plain shell-tempered body sherds that, due to leaching, were in a generally poor condition. In the absence of featured sherds some doubt must remain regarding the attribution of the material to this period. Shell-tempered fabrics were also used in the Iron Age and it is certainly possible that at least some of this material could be of this date instead. Where possible, sherd thickness was measured and found to range between 5–12 mm. In general, the wall-thickness of middle Bronze Age pottery may be expected to fall within the range 10–20 mm. In contrast to these assemblages we might expect Iron Age pottery to include a significant proportion of thinner-walled vessels. Whilst this is a somewhat crude approach the suggestion is that the relatively low size range pottery would favour an Iron Age rather than a middle Bronze Age date for at least some of the material. In addition, the pottery from the evaluation at St Augustine's Farm South (Timby 1991) was re-examined and found to be of the same indeterminate later prehistoric character; again, wall thickness was measured and found not to exceed 10 mm.

Middle Bronze Age pottery is uncommon in this region and has only been found at a relatively small number of sites (Darvill 1987). Recent excavations at Shorncote have produced important assemblages from both funerary and domestic sites (Hearne and Heaton 1994; Barclay and Glass 1995), while an important group of Bucket Urns was recovered from a pit deposit at Roughground Farm, Lechlade (Hingley 1993). Whilst the material could be redeposited middle Bronze Age, the radiocarbon date of 409–193 cal BC (NZA 8766. R24151/13, 229±59BP, 95% confidence) could support an Iron Age date. This type of pottery can be found in association with early field systems and land divisions and, therefore, the association of possible middle Bronze Age sherds with the segmented ditches at St Augustine's Lane and St Augustine's Farm South is of significance.

Late Bronze Age

Late Bronze Age pottery was recovered from Court Farm. A single sherd manufactured in a flint, sand and grog tempered fabric is thought to be of this date, rather than early or middle Bronze Age. It is assumed to be residual within a later feature.

Indeterminate prehistoric

A total of 41 sherds (46 g) from Birdlip, St Augustine's Farm, Court Farm and Cirencester Road watching brief could not be assigned to a particular ceramic style. Most of this material was small and abraded, although mainly though to be handmade and, therefore, probably prehistoric.

Conclusion

The total assemblage recovered is of some importance despite its relatively small size. Very little earlier prehistoric pottery has been recovered from non-funerary sites in this region, perhaps because of the ephemeral nature of the settlement record. However, this type of project with its off-site approach provides an opportunity to recover such traces. The discovery of both earlier and later Neolithic pottery within pit deposits at Duntisbourne Grove provides evidence for the wider domestic landscape during this period. The recovery of Beaker pottery from four of the sites, with a notable concentration in the vicinity of Preston is of interest, especially given the paucity of Beaker associated sites in this area and in the region generally. Similarly, the traces of later Bronze Age material from a small number of sites and in one case in association with a system of land boundaries at St Augustine's Farm South is of importance for studying the wider chronological developments within the landscape.

Catalogue of illustrated sherds *(Fig. 7.6)*

Duntisbourne Grove

36 Earlier Neolithic. Rim and four body sherds. Fabric: LS2/EN. Colour: ext. brown: core black : int. brown. Condition: average-worn. Ctx 63.

37 Later Neolithic Peterborough Ware ?Fengate sub-style. Two refitting rim sherds. Fabric: VAP2/LN. Colour: ext. reddish-brown: core and int. yellowish-brown. Condition: worn. Ctx 113.

Trinity Farm

38 Beaker. Rim. Fabric: GC2/EBA. Colour: ext. yellowish-brown: core yellowish-brown: int. yellowish-brown. Condition: average. Ctx 7.

39 Beaker. Base angle. Fabric: GC2/EBA. Colour: ext. Yellowish-brown: core yellowish-brown: int. yellowish-brown. Condition: average. Ctx 7.

40 Beaker. Rim. Fabric: GC2/EBA. Colour: ext. yellowish-brown: core yellowish-brown: int. yellowish-brown. Condition: average. Ctx 7.

41 Beaker. Decorated body sherd with comb impressions. Fabric G2/EBA. Colour: ext. reddish-brown: core black: int. yellowish-brown. Condition average. Ctx 7.

42 Beaker. Three base sherds. Fabric GC3/EBA. Colour: ext. greyish brown: core and int. black. Condition average. Ctx 7.

43 Beaker. Neck, belly and base sherds with finger-nail decoration (10 sherds). Fabric GC2/EBA. Colour: ext. reddish-brown: core black : int. blackish brown.

Condition average-worn. Ctx 9.

44 Beaker. Rim sherd with impressed finger-tip decoration possibly from the same vessel as 43. Fabric GC2/EBA. Colour: ext. reddish-brown: core black: int. brown. Condition average. Ctx 9.

45 Beaker. Rim sherd. Fabric GC3/EBA. Colour: ext. yellowish-brown: core black: int. yellowish-brown. Condition average. Ctx 9.

46 Beaker. Finger-nail decorated rim and body sherd possibly the same as 45. Fabric GC3/EBA. Colour: ext. yellowish-brown: core black: int.yellowish-brown. Condition average. Ctx 9.

47 Beaker. Base sherd (3 g). Fabric: GC2/EBA. Colour: ext. reddish-brown: core black: int. yellowish-brown. Condition: average. Ctx 9.

48 Beaker. Four body sherds with all-over comb decoration. Fabric: GC2/EBA. Colour: ext. reddish-brown: core black: int. black. Condition: average. Ctx 9.

49 ?Beaker. Two rim sherds with possible impressed finger-nail decoration (15 g). Fabric: GC3/EBA. Colour: ext. yellowish-brown: core and int. grey. Condition: worn. Ctx 9.

50 Beaker. Two body sherds with impressed finger-nail decoration. Fabric GC2/EBA. Colour: ext. reddish-brown: core black grey: int. yellowish-brown. Condition average. Ctx 11.

51 Beaker. Body sherd with incised lines possibly made with a finger-nail to form a herring bone pattern. Fabric: GC2/EBA. Colour: ext. reddish-brown: core black: int. yellowish-brown. Condition: average. Ctx 11.

52 Beaker. Rim sherd. Fabric: GC2/EBA. Colour: ext. yellowish-brown: core black: int. yellowish-brown. Condition: average. Ctx 11.

St Augustine's Farm South

53 Collared Urn. Fragment from lower half of collar with impressed twisted cord decoration that appears to form part of a zig-zag motif. Fabric grog. Colour ext. reddish brown core and int. black. Condition fair to worn. Evaluation Site R, ring ditch, ctx 6, subsoil.

LATER PREHISTORIC AND ROMAN POTTERY
By Jane Timby

Introduction

Work along the route has resulted in the recovery of several new collections of pottery dating to the Iron Age and Roman periods. In total, 16 sites have yielded pottery of later prehistoric date and 27 sites have produced Roman pottery. The quantities range from just single sherds through to 151 kg for Birdlip Quarry. Of the 30 or so sites, eight have been selected for more detailed summaries or reports: one site of early-mid Iron Age date (Preston Enclosure), two middle Iron Age sites (Ermin Farm, Highgate House), and three sites dating to the 1st century AD (Duntisbourne Grove, Middle Duntisbourne, Court Farm) considerably augmenting the existing regional pottery database. In addition there are two Roman sites (Birdlip Quarry, Weavers Bridge).

Iron Age and Roman fabric descriptions

The following fabric descriptions represent a single series for the Iron Age and Roman sites with the exception of the material from Birdlip Quarry which is described separately and reference to this can be made for some fabrics. Each fabric description is followed by the forms, date and a list of the sites and contexts from which it has been recorded.

Iron Age

Shell-tempered

H1   Generally with a brown or brownish-orange exterior and a black, brown or dark grey interior surface with a grey-brown core. The paste contains a sparse frequency of coarse fossil shell fragments up to 6–8 mm in size, and variable quantities of finer limestone and fossiliferous fragments.

Forms: Slack-sided or vertical-walled jars with simple rims (Ermin Farm, ctxs 5, 57, 83, Fig. 7.7.60); barrel jars, or globular-bodied jars with thickened rim (Ermin Farm, ctx 4, Fig. 7.7.58–59, 62).

Date: EIA-MIA

Sites: Ermin Farm, Highgate House, Preston Enclosure

H2   A brown or grey fabric usually with a grey core containing a common frequency of crushed fossil shell up to 3 mm across. The fabric is moderately hard with a laminar fracture. Variable amounts of other calcareous matter is often present including fragments of bryozoa, but the shell is dominant creating a striated effect in fracture.

Forms: Beaded rim jar (Court Farm, ctx 333, Fig. 7.11.120).

Date: MIA

Sites: Ermin Farm, Highgate House, Preston Enclosure, Court Farm, Duntisbourne Grove

Limestone-tempered

L1   A black ware containing a scatter of fossil shell/ limestone up to 1 mm in size.

Forms: Simple undifferentiated rim jars with vertical walls (Court Farm, ctx 319).

Date: MIA

Sites: Court Farm, Ermin Farm, Highgate House, Preston Enclosure, Middle Duntisbourne, Duntisbourne Grove.

L2   Brown surfaces with a mid-grey core. The paste contains a moderate to common frequency of fine limestone including discrete ooliths and fossil shell

fragments. Rare inclusions up to 3 mm but generally finer. There is quite a variety in texture between vessels.

Forms: A large jar with an expanded rim in a coarser version of this fabric came from ditch 59 at Preston Enclosure (Fig. 7.7.54). Vessels in slightly finer fabric include slightly curved wall jars with simple undifferentiated rims (eg. Preston Enclosure, Fig. 7.7. 55–56). Globular bodied jars with slightly beaded rims (Court Farm, ctx 436; Highgate House, ctx 210, Fig 7.8.64). Some sherds show a smoothed finish whilst others are left matt.

Date range: EIA-MIA

Sites: Court Farm, Ermin Farm, Highgate House, Preston Enclosure, Middle Duntisbourne

L3(= MALVL2)

L4   A brown or black fabric predominantly tempered with a common to moderate density of crushed, angular crystalline calcite, fragments mainly less than 2 mm, occasionally larger.

Forms: No featured sherds, but mainly handmade jars.

Sites: Court Farm, Preston Enclosure, Duntisbourne Grove

L5   A brown ware containing a sparse/common/ moderate frequency of fine limestone, discrete oolites, oolitic conglomerates, and fossil fragments up to 2.5 mm across. Some pieces are very friable as a result of a high density of temper.
   Forms: A slightly beaded rim jar in a thin-walled fineware version of the fabric (Preston Enclosure, ctx 8, Fig. 7.7.57), bevelled rim jar (Court Farm, ctx 333, Fig. 7.11.120; Duntisbourne Grove, ditch group 9, Fig. 7.10.110).

Date: ?MIA-LIA

Sites: Court Farm, Ermin Farm, Preston Enclosure, Middle Duntisbourne, Duntisbourne Grove

L6   A reddish-brown ware with a mid-brown core. The paste contains a moderate to common frequency of fine limestone, shell, calcite and oolites. Particularly distinctive are fragments of bryozoa.

Forms: Simple undifferentiated jars with vertical sides (Court Farm, ctx 235, Fig. 7.11.119).

Date: MIA

Sites: Court Farm

L00   Variants of Jurassic limestone-tempered wares but not distinctive or frequent enough to warrant further classification.

Sites: Highgate House, Duntisbourne Grove

Limestone and iron

LI   A reddish brown ware with a dark brown core. The sandy texture shows at x20 magnification a sparse scatter of fossil shell and limestone fragments up to 3 mm accompanied by a scatter of rounded grains of quartz sand, less than 1 mm. Most distinctive, however, is a scatter of dark reddish-brown shiny, rounded or oval iron oolites 1–2 mm in size.

Forms: Flat base sherd from a jar (Ermin Farm, ctx 4).

Date: ?MIA

Sites: Ermin Farm, Highgate House

LSI A fabric showing a red-brown exterior and outer core and a black interior and inner core. The sandy texture contains sparse limestone/fossil shell up to 3 mm in size with a moderate frequency of rounded quartz (more than fabric LI). Some of the sand grains have fallen out from the surfaces leaving pock marks. Also present is a scatter of sub-angular to rounded, matt reddish-brown iron 1-2 mm across and finer.

Forms: No featured sherds.

Date: ?MIA

Sites: Ermin Farm, Highgate House

Sand and limestone

SL1 A hard reddish-brown ware with a fine sandy texture and a black core. At x20 a sparse scatter of rounded quartz grains are visible along with a few fragments of fossil shell and limestone up to 4 mm across.

Forms: Bodysherds with incised line decoration (Court Farm, ctx 223 and 242, Fig. 7.11.117–8).

Date: EIA

Sites: Court Farm, Highgate House

SL2 Other sand and limestone-tempered wares occasionally with distinctive iron grains.

Forms: Handmade and wheelmade everted rim jars (Court Farm, ctx 263).

Date: LIA

Sites: Court Farm, Highgate House

Sandy wares

S1 A black or brownish-black ware with a common to dense frequency of sub-angular, well-sorted, fine grained quartz sand, sparse iron and occasional grey rounded argillaceous inclusions (?clay pellets) up to 3 mm in size.

Forms: Unfeatured sherds, probably from bowls/jars. Saucepan pot (Ermin Farm, ctx 57, Fig. 7.7.61).

Date: ?MIA - ?LIA

Sites: Ermin Farm, Highgate House, Preston Enclosure, Court Farm

S2 A mid-brown ware with a reddish-orange core. The fabric contains a common to high frequency of fine quartz sand and fine mica.

Form: No featured sherds.
Date: ?MIA

Site: Preston Enclosure

SI A fine to medium sandy ware with distinctive grains of red-brown iron present.

Sites: Highgate House

Grog-tempered

GI Greyish-brown, slightly vesicular fabric containing fine grog, dark brown argillaceous fragments, red-brown iron and ?fine limestone/shell.

Form: Jar/bowl with an externally ribbed rim (Highgate House, ctx 229, Fig. 7.8.68).

Date: ?LIA

Sites: Highgate House

Flint-tempered

FL A black ware with a reddish-brown core containing a sparse to moderate frequency of angular calcined flint up to 2 mm in size. Sparse grains of red-brown iron are also visible in the fine sandy matrix.

Form: Handmade everted rim jar (Court Farm, ctx 288, Fig. 7.11.123).

Date: ?LIA

Site: Court Farm

Malvernian rock-tempered

MALVREA: GL TF18. Peacock (1968) fabric group A.

Form: No featured sherds.

Date: MIA-Roman

Site: Highgate House

Roman

Cross references are given where applicable to the Gloucester City Unit fabric series (GL) (cf Ireland 1983) and the Cirencester (CIR) fabric series (Rigby 1982). The codes are based on those developed for the national Roman fabric reference collection (Tomber and Dore 1996, 368–82).

Native wares

MALVL1: Malvernian limestone-tempered (GL TF33), Peacock (1968) group B1.

Forms: Handmade jars usually with everted rims and a burnished finish (Court Farm, ctx 325, Fig. 7.11.122; Highgate House, ctx 211, Fig. 7.8.66; Duntisbourne Grove, ctxs 215 and 83, Fig. 7.10.108-9), simple vertical undifferentiated rims (Court Farm, ctx 325; Highgate House, ctx 211), globular-bodied jar with short vertical rim (Highgate House, ctx 109, Fig. 7.8.63; Middle Duntisbourne, ctx 41 Fig. 7.9.88) and beaded-rim jars (Duntisbourne Grove, ctxs 83 and 9, Fig. 7.10.110). A sherd from Highgate House, ctx 211 (Fig. 7.8.67) is decorated with horizontal parallel tooled lines.

Date: M-LIA/early Roman

Sites: Court Farm, Highgate House, Middle Duntisbourne, Duntisbourne Grove

MALVL2: Malvernian limestone-tempered ware (GL TF216) (Spencer 1983).

Form: Large storage jars with hammer-head rims (Duntisbourne Grove, ctx 181).

Date: 1st century BC-1st century AD

Sites: Middle Duntisbourne, Duntisbourne Grove

GROG: Grog-tempered ware (GL TF2A–C).

Forms: Handmade and wheelmade everted rim jars, (eg. Court Farm, ctxs 110 and 363, platters (eg. Middle Duntisbourne, ctx 208, Fig. 7.9.91).

Date: 1st century AD

Sites: Court Farm, Middle Duntisbourne, Duntisbourne Grove

Local wares

SVWOX2: Severn Valley ware (GL TF11B) (Webster 1976).

Forms: Carinated bowl/cup (Middle Duntisbourne, ctx 288), jars (Weavers Bridge).

Sites: Court Farm, Preston Enclosure, Weavers Bridge, Middle Duntisbourne, Duntisbourne Grove, Birdlip Quarry

SVWEA1: Early SVW variant (grog).
A moderately soft, smooth soapy fabric containing sparse organic material, fine rounded to sub-angular grog/clay pellets, iron and very rarely, limestone fragments.

Forms: Mainly handmade but some wheel-turned/wheelmade vessels, occasionally with a burnished finish. Carinated cups/bowls and necked bowls (Duntisbourne Grove, ctxs 64, 50 and 9, Fig. 7.10. 111–113).

Sites: Court Farm, Middle Duntisbourne, Duntisbourne Grove

SVWEA2: Early Severn Valley ware (GL TF11D) (Timby 1990).

Forms: Wheelmade carinated cups/bowls (Court Farm, ctx 287; Duntisbourne Grove, ctx 43); bevelled rim beaker (Duntisbourne Grove, ctx 9, Fig. 7.10.114); necked bowls (eg. Duntisbourne Grove, ctx 73).

Sites: Court Farm, Middle Duntisbourne, Duntisbourne Grove

SVWEA3: Early Severn Valley ware (charcoal tempered) (GL TF17).

Forms: Carinated bowls (Middle Duntisbourne ctx 12), wheelmade necked bowl (Duntisbourne Grove, ctx 9, Fig. 7.10.115).

Sites: Middle Duntisbourne, Duntisbourne Grove

WMBBW: wheelmade black burnished ware (GL TF201; CIR TF5) (Rigby 1982, 152).

Forms: Wheelmade vessels including small jars with beaded or everted rims (Court Farm, ctxs 10, 288 and 486), bowls (Court Farm, ctx 10, Fig.7.11.124–125).

Date: Neronian-mid 2nd century

Sites: Court Farm, Middle Duntisbourne, Duntisbourne Grove

SWOX- South-west oxidised ware (GL TF15).

Sites: Court Farm, Birdlip Quarry

Foreign imports

Arretine (probably Lyons) (LYOSA).

Form: Cup, Haltern type 8 (Middle Duntisbourne, ctx 1, Fig. 7.9.69).

Site: Middle Duntisbourne

LGFSA: South Gaulish samian (La Graufesenque)

Forms: Drag 18 (Court Farm, ctx 176); ?24/5 (Court Farm, ctx 259); 27 (Duntisbourne Grove, ctx 15), 29 (Duntisbourne Grove, ctx 162, Fig. 7.10.96).

Sites: Court Farm, Preston Enclosure, Middle Duntisbourne, Duntisbourne Grove

LEZSA: Lezoux, Central Gaulish samian

Form: Drag 27 (early type) (Middle Duntisbourne ctx 154, Fig.7.9.71).

Site: Middle Duntisbourne

LMVSA/LEZSA: Central Gaulish samian.

Site: Weavers Bridge

GABTN1: Gallia Belgica *terra nigra*

Forms: Cups Cam type 56 (Middle Duntisbourne, ctxs 289, 56, 57, Fig.7.9.77); platters Cam type 12 (Middle Duntisbourne, ctx 7/246, Fig.7.9.78), Cam 12/13 (Middle Duntisbourne, ctx 210) and Cam 8 (Duntisbourne Grove, ctx 49, Fig. 7.10.98).

GABTR1A: Gallia Belgica *terra rubra* 1A

Form: Platter.

Site: Duntisbourne Grove, ctx 118.
GABTR3: Gallia Belgica *terra rubra* 3

Forms: Girth beaker (Middle Duntisbourne, ctx 55, Fig. 7.9.73) with combed decoration (Middle Duntisbourne, ctx 4).

NOGWH: North Gaulish fine whiteware

Form: Butt beaker, Cam. type 113 (Middle Duntisbourne, ctx 69, Fig. 7.9.79).

Sites: Middle Duntisbourne, Duntisbourne Grove

CGWSOX: ?Central Gaulish white-slipped oxidised ware (see petrological report by Williams below).

Form: ?Flagon (Duntisbourne Grove, ctxs 69 and 77).

MOSBS: Moselkeramick black-slip red ware (GL TF 12J)

Sites: Weavers Bridge, Birdlip Quarry

FWBLMI: Fine, black micaceous ware with no obvious inclusions. Probably a Gaulish import from its early date.

Forms: Small jar/beaker (Duntisbourne Grove, ctx 25, Fig. 7.10.100; Middle Duntisbourne, ctx 39, not illustrated).

Site: Middle Duntisbourne, Duntisbourne Grove

FWBUFF: Thin-walled buff, fine sandy ware. Probably beaker. ?North Gaulish.

Site: Middle Duntisbourne, ditch group 4, cat. 82, not illustrated.

FWOX/FWSLOX: Oxidised fine sandy wares/slipped oxidised fine sandy ware. Source unknown.

Site: Middle Duntisbourne.

Amphorae

BATAM1: Baetican amphorae (early). Cam 185A/Haltern 70 (Peacock and Williams 1986, class 15). (for petrological report see Williams below).

Sites: Middle Duntisbourne, Duntisbourne Grove

BATAM2: Baetican amphorae, Dressel 20 (Peacock and Williams 1986, class 25) (GL TF 10A).

Sites: Court Farm, Weavers Bridge

CAMAM1: Campanian black sand amphora, Dressel 2–4, (Peacock and Williams 1986, Class 10).

Site: Duntisbourne Grove

CAMAM2: Campanian volcanic amphora, Dressel 2–4, (Peacock and Williams 1986, Class 10).

Site: Middle Duntisbourne

Regional imports

SAVGT: Savernake ware (GL/CIR TF6) (Annable 1962; Swan 1975).

Forms: Beaded rim jars (Middle Duntisbourne, ctx 218) and large storage jars (Duntisbourne Grove, ctx 99, Fig. 7.10.116 and Middle Duntisbourne, ctx 218, Fig. 7.9.87), the latter with lightly incised diagonal line decoration.

Date: ?mid 1st–2nd century

Sites: Court Farm, Weavers Bridge, Middle Duntisbourne, Duntisbourne Grove, Birdlip Quarry

DORBB1 - Dorset black-burnished ware (GL TF4, CIR TF74) (Gillam 1976; Holbrook and Bidwell 1991).

Forms: Jars (eg. Weavers Bridge, ctx 57, Fig. 7.12.127), flanged conical bowls (Weavers Bridge, ctx 51), grooved rim bowls (Weavers Bridge, ctx 51), straight-sided dishes (Weavers Bridge, ctx 51).

Sites: Court Farm, Weavers Bridge, Duntisbourne Grove, Birdlip Quarry

MICGW: Micaceous greyware.
Forms: Jars imitating DORBB1 forms (Weavers Bridge, ctx 57, Fig. 7.12.128).

Date: Late 2nd–4th century

Sites: Weavers Bridge, Birdlip Quarry

LNVCC: Nene Valley colour-coated ware.

Forms: Straight-sided dish (Weavers Bridge, ctx 57, Fig. 7.12.136).

Date: Later 2nd–4th century

Site: Weavers Bridge

OXFRC: Oxfordshire colour-coated wares (GL TF12A, 9X; CIR

Forms: Beaker (Weavers Bridge ctx 57, Fig. 7.12.137), mortaria, dish Young type C45 (Weavers Bridge, ctxs 57 and 71), types C47, C83 (Weavers Bridge, ctx 51).

Sites: Weavers Bridge, Birdlip Quarry.

OXFWH: Oxfordshire whitewares (GL TF13, 9A)

Forms: Mortaria (Young 1977 forms M18, M20, M22) (Weavers Bridge, ctx 57, Fig. 7.12.133–134).

Sites: Weavers Bridge, Birdlip Quarry.

PNKGT: Midlands pink grog-tempered ware (Booth and Green 1989, 77–84).

Site: Weavers Bridge, Birdlip Quarry

Coarsewares, source unknown

GREY 1 (OXFORD R10): Miscellaneous fine, reduced sandy wares, probably mainly north Wiltshire products.

Forms: Jars, everted rim beakers (Court Farm, ctx 132), everted and expanded rim jars (Weavers Bridge, ctx 57).

Sites: Preston Enclosure, Court Farm, Weavers Bridge, Birdlip Quarry

GREY 2 (OXFORD R20): Miscellaneous medium grade, reduced sandy wares.

Forms: Wheelmade everted, expanded rim jars (Court Farm, ctx 132; Weavers Bridge, ctx 112), straight-sided dishes (Weavers Bridge, ctx 57), flanged bowls (Weavers Bridge, ctx 57), imitation moulded platter (Middle Duntisbourne, ctx 12).

Sites: Court Farm, Middle Duntisbourne, Birdlip Quarry

LOCGW3: A medium to fine, hard, grey sandy ware distinguished by a scatter of dark grey argillaceous rounded inclusions.

Forms: Wheelmade jars.

Sites: Court Farm, Birdlip Quarry

LOCGW8: A hard, black medium grade sandy ware (ie. macroscopically visible quartz grains) with a distinctive red core.

Date: ?LIA/early Roman

Sites: Court Farm

LOCOX1 (OXFORD 010): Miscellaneous fine, oxidised sandy wares.

Forms: Ring-necked flagon (Court Farm, Fig. 7.11.126),

rouletted sherds from a butt beaker (Court Farm, ctx 10).

Sites: Court Farm, Weavers Bridge, Duntisbourne Grove

LOCOX2 (OXFORD 015): Medium sandy ware.

Form: Rimsherd imitating imported cup form Cam. 56 (Middle Duntisbourne ctx 56).

Date: Pre-Flavian

Site: Middle Duntisbourne

Preston Enclosure

An assemblage of 477 sherds weighing 1988 g dating to the Iron Age and Roman periods was recovered from 26 contexts. Most of the sherds appear to date to the early-middle Iron Age with just 23 very small abraded sherds of Roman date.

Most of the later prehistoric sherds are in shell or limestone-tempered fabrics typical of the middle Iron Age. Although featured sherds are sparse, several pieces showed elements of form and/or decoration suggestive of an early Iron Age element to the site, for example, the earliest cut of the external gully 175, fill 176, produced both a carinated bodysherd, possibly a shouldered jar, in a coarse shell-tempered ware (fabric H1) and a sherd in a similar fabric with incised line decoration.

The main enclosure (1), comprising ditches 3, 59, 66, and 86 produced a total of 88 sherds, weighing 880 g. The group is dominated by limestone-tempered sherds, mainly fabric L2 with small amounts of L4 and L5 (Table 7.7). The pieces are relatively well-preserved with an average size of 10 g. Featured sherds were limited to a large, expanded rim jar (Fig. 7.7.54), in a limestone and shelly fabric (L2), from ditch 59, fill 64/5. Similar vessels were present in the early-middle Iron Age assemblage from Uley Bury (Saville 1983a, fig. 10). Three intrusive sherds in the form of one scrap of samian and two tiny pieces of Severn Valley ware were present amongst the material from ditch 3, fill 6.

Pottery from the internal features was sparse, the only fills to produce more than 10 sherds being the two rectangular pits 130 and 283 (Table 7.7). Again fabric L2 was dominant along with sherds of L5 in 130. Pit 283 was the only feature to produce the sandy fabric S2. The sherds from the latter two pits were particularly small, averaging around 2 g. Of the internal gullies, only gully 145, cuts 32 and 92, produced pottery, a total of 25 sherds of mainly fabric L2 with some fabric H2, some of the latter showing traces of internal carbonised residue.

One of the largest groups from the site came from tree-throw hole or pit 14 with 229 sherds although many of these were very fragmented, the average sherd size for the group being just 3 g. The fabrics are again dominated by fabric L2 although a greater range of other wares are present in the group, notably the very coarse shell-tempered ware H1 and a sandy ware (fabric S1) (see Table 7.7). Most of the material can be assigned to the middle Iron Age where rims are either plain undifferentiated (Fig. 7.7.55–56) or slightly beaded (Fig. 7.7.57).

The only pit from outside the enclosure to contain pottery was 280, which produced 65 sherds. Whilst fabric L2 was again dominant a significant number of coarser shell-tempered wares were present which might argue for a slightly earlier date. Of the four superimposed gullies to the west of the main enclosure, cut 175 (176) produced 10 sherds including the two with early Iron Age affinities mentioned above, all in coarse shell-tempered wares (H1). If the gully post-dates the enclosure all this material may be redeposited.

A few sherds of Roman date were recovered from surface cleaning, plough furrows and context 160, which also contained later material. The sherds are small and abraded, commensurate with material that has been in the ploughsoil for some time, and are not sufficiently common to indicate Roman occupation in the very immediate vicinity.

Catalogue of illustrated sherds (Fig. 7.7)

54 Large vessel with an expanded rim, red-brown in colour with a dark grey inner core. The paste contains moderate fossil shell and limestone, including discrete ooliths and bryozoa (fabric L2). Some fragments are very coarse, up to 18 mm in size. Ditch 59, fill 64/5.

55 Rim and bodysherd from a slightly curved wall jar with a simple undifferentiated rim. Dark grey mottled with red-brown patches with a red-brown core. The paste contains moderate shell and limestone, fragments up to 4 mm and finer. Fabric L2. Tree-throw hole/pit 14, fill 8.

56 Rim similar to 55. Dark grey-brown in colour with slightly denser shell and limestone. Fabric L2. Tree-throw hole/pit 14, fill 8.

57 Slightly beaded rim jar in a mid-brown, thin-walled, very friable, fabric containing common oolitic limestone. Fabric L5. Tree-throw hole/pit 14, fill 8.

Ermin Farm

An assemblage of 236 sherds of Iron Age pottery (1391 g) was recovered from ten contexts. The sherds were relatively poorly preserved with an average sherd weight of 6 g. The group appears to date to the middle Iron Age period. The fabrics were restricted to fossil shell (H1, H2), limestone (L1, L2, L5, LI) and sandy wares (S1). Looking at the assemblage as a whole (cf. Table 7.8), the shelly wares account for 21% by count (48% by weight), the limestone fabrics for 17% (21.5% by weight) and the sandy wares for 37% (26%). The remainder comprised unidentifiable crumbs.

Approximately one third of the pottery, some 80 sherds, came from the fill of ditch 6 with further material from ditches 10 and 54 which form part of the same enclosure (structure 49). Additional groups were recovered from the adjacent enclosure ditches 63 and 68 (structure 48), from the antenna ditch 85

Table 7.7   Preston Enclosure, distribution of fabrics in main features by sherd count and weight.

FABRICS	Enclosure 1		Gully 14		Tree-throw hole 14		Pit 130		Pit 280		Pit 283	
	no	wt	no	wt	no	wt	no	wt	no	wt	no	wt
H1	1	2			10	80			14	51		
H2	14	71	10	27			1	1			3	20
L1					6	28						
L2	60	788	15	70	94	381	11	56	50	58	9	10
L4	1	3										
L5	1	6			29	85	5	34	1	4		
S1					1	4						
S2											3	4
SVWOX	2	3										
Samian	1	2										
Unclass	7	2			88	60	1	12			4	3
E PREH	1	2			1	1						
TOTAL	88	880	25	97	229	639	18	103	65	113	19	37

and pit 59. Table 7.8 summarises the fabrics from each of these groups.

The pottery from enclosure 49 includes a number of sherds from coarseware jars with several sherds from a single vessel in fabric H1 (Fig. 7.7.58). A slightly more slack-sided vessel with a thickened rim (Fig. 7.7.59) also came from this ditch.

The pottery from enclosure 48 also includes a number of coarseware jars with simple rims (eg. Fig. 7.7.60) but of particular note are several sherds from a sandy vertical-sided vessel in the style of a saucepan pot from fill 57. The upper zone is decorated with simple incised curvilinear decoration in the form of arcs (Fig. 7.7.61). A further sherd from the same or a similar vessel and showing part of a curvilinear line came from 64, enclosure 49. The saucepan pot tradition is considered to cover a wide territory during the 4th-2nd centuries BC (Cunliffe 1991, 79), although the profile of this vessel is more typical of the Wessex region (cf. vessels from the Yarnbury-Highfield or St Catharine's Hill-Worthy Down style (Cunliffe 1991, figs A:15-6)). In fact Preston lies in a blank zone on the simplified distribution map of pottery styles in southern Britain (Cunliffe 1991, fig. 4.6) falling between the Croft Ambrey-Bredon Hill style to the north-west and the less coherent Southcote-Blewburton style to the south. The Preston example shows little similarity typologically with vessels from the Herefordshire-Cotswold region (Croft Ambrey-Bredon Hill style) which have slightly more curved profiles, stamped decoration and a distinct fabric reflecting their production sources in the Malvern hills.

Antennae ditch 85 produced a group of 18 sherds, mainly coarse shell or sandy wares with an absence of limestone-tempered ware. Pit 59 contained just four bodysherds in fabric L2.

A comparison of the assemblages between enclosures 48 and 49 do show some differences in terms of overall composition. Enclosure 49 has a higher proportion of limestone-tempered wares and less sandy ware, whereas enclosure 48 has negligible limestone-tempered ware and a higher proportion of sandy ware. Since most of the latter derives from a single vessel the figures may not have much significance and a larger sample may show a similar range between the two enclosures.

Catalogue of illustrated sherds (*Fig. 7.7*)

58 Rim, and joining bodysherds and a base (not directly joined) from a globular-sided simple rim jar. A dark brown fabric with a pale brown interior containing sparse coarse, fossil shell and other fragments of limestone detritus (fabric H1). Structure 49, ditch 6, (5).

59 Slightly slack-sided jar in a matt red-brown to brown fabric with a grey inner core. The fabric contains sparse, coarse, fossil shell and finer lime-stone/fossil detritus (fabric H1). Structure 49, ditch 6, (4).

60 A simple rim jar in a brownish-black ware with sparse coarse fossil shell in a sandy matrix (fabric H1). The interior surface has traces of blackened residue. Enclosure 48, ditch 63, (57).

61 Several fragmentary sherds from a saucepan pot with a slightly beaded rim marked with a tooled line just below the outer rim and incised curvilinear decoration. Black in colour with a burnished finish. The paste contains dense, fine, sand with occasional rounded argillaceous inclusions up to 3 mm in size (fabric S1). Enclosure 48, ditch 63, (57).

62 A simple rim probably from a more globular-bodied jar in a dark brown ware with a darker core containing sparse, coarse shell and mixed limestone/fossil detritus (fabric H1). Ditch 85, (83).

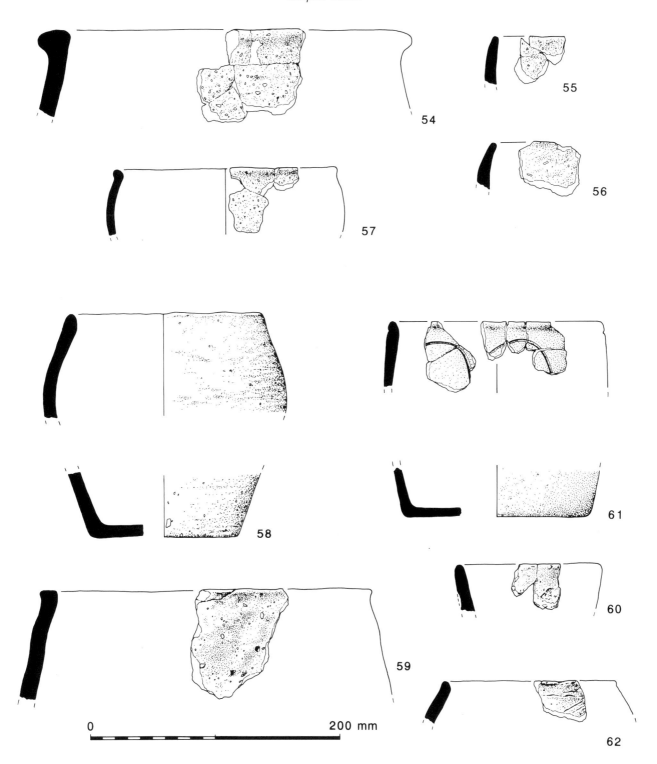

Figure 7.7   Pottery from Preston Enclosure and Ermin Farm.

Highgate House

A small assemblage of 293 sherds (1132 g) from 25 individual contexts was recovered. The pottery mainly dates to the later prehistoric period, in particular the mid-late Iron Age, with just two or three Roman sherds. The material was generally in poor condition with particularly small fragmentary sherds, the average weight being just 2.3 g. Featured sherds were rare and thus close dating is based on the fabric composition. The majority of the fabrics were fossil shell and/or limestone-tempered. Two main calcareous wares could be distinguished, those with Jurassic limestone, and therefore, of likely Cotswold origin (fabrics L2, LS, LI, LSI), and those with inclusions more typical of the Palaeozoic outcrops and

Table 7.8   Ermin Farm, distribution of fabrics by sherd count and weight across main features.

FABRIC	Structure 49 No	wt	Structure 48 no	wt	Ditch 85 no	wt	Pit 59 no	wt
H1	18	532	27	104	11	29		
H2	1	9						
L1	1	4						
L2	13	87					4	24
L5	20	168	3	4				
LI	1	20	0	0	2	5		
S1	4	12	85	311	5	42		
crumbs	41	40						
TOTAL	99	872	115	419	18	76	4	24

thus likely to come from the Malvern area (MALVL1). Decorated Malvernian limestone-tempered wares as defined by Peacock (1968) probably date from the 3rd-2nd century BC, the plain burnished wares typified by much of the material from Highgate House having a potentially longer timespan. The presence of at least one decorated sherd suggests this site may have been acquiring a small proportion of Malvernian material in the middle Iron Age, corresponding with the perceived chronology of the shell- and limestone-tempered wares. Other fabrics present include a small amount of sandy ware (fabric S1, SI) also typical of the middle Iron Age, Malvernian rock-tempered ware (MALVREA) (Peacock 1968, group A), and grog-tempered ware. The absence of early variants of the Severn Valley industry (SVWEA1–3) and the tiny proportion of grog-tempered ware (ie. one sherd) might suggest abandonment of the site by the 1st century BC.

Pottery was recovered from three ditch sections in Trench 1, ditch 144 (cuts 103, 112 and 131), and two from Trench 2, ditch 265 (cuts 212 and 223). Table 7.9 quantifies the fabrics from these two ditches. The sections belonging to the single enclosure 144/265 all produced Malvernian limestone-tempered ware mixed with various other sherds (fabrics H1, H2, L2, LSI, SI, LI, MALVREA, GLQ and GI). Of the 213 sherds from Ditches, Malvernian limestone wares account for 59% by sherd number. Vessels include burnished Malvernian jars (Fig. 7.8.66) and a sherd decorated with horizontal parallel tooled lines (Fig. 7.8.67). A single unusual rim sherd from (229) in a grog-tempered fabric (Fig. 7.8.68) may well be late Iron Age in date, although it is not typical of the area.

Small groups of pottery were recovered from five of the six pits in Trench 1 (116, 120, 122, ?133, 142) and two pits from Trench 2 (203 and 230). Of the pit assemblages, 120, 132, and 142 all include sherds

Table 7.9   Highgate House, distribution of pottery fabrics across main features.

FABRIC	Ditch 144 no	wt	Ditch 265 no	Wt	Pits No	wt	Colluvium no	wt
H1	1	2						
H2	1	21			6	8		
L2	8	43	5	54	5	36	14	12
LI	40	178			1	8		
LSI	22	205						
L00					1	2		
LS					1	3	1	2
S1							1	2
SI	1	15						
GI			1	29				
GLQ			3	15				
MALVREA	4	14						
MALVL1	42	147	83	232	13	34	31	53
SVWOX	2	11						
MISC OXID					2	6		
UNCLASS					3	7		
TOTAL	121	636	92	330	32	104	47	69

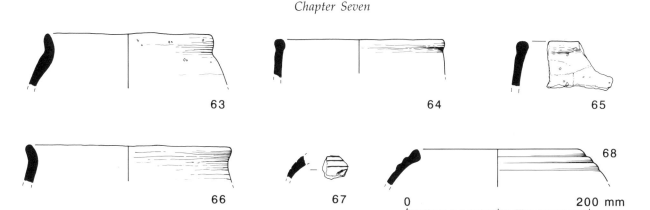

Figure 7.8 Pottery from Highgate House.

of Malvernian limestone-tempered ware and would thus appear to be contemporary with the enclosure. Pits 116 and 122 produced fabrics L2, H2 and SL only and could possibly be slightly earlier but the numbers are very low. Pits 203 and 230 both contained a single oxidised sherd each, that from 233, at less than 1 g in weight, could not be confidently assigned a date, although the piece from 203 would definitely appear to be Roman.

A single Roman sherd belonging to the Severn Valley ware tradition was recovered from the subsoil (101). In addition a few sherds came from the subsoil in Trench 1 and from the colluvial layers in Trench 3. The latter produced further mid-late Iron Age sherds and also one possible Roman or later scrap. Malvernian sherds came from 307 and 308, whilst 309 yielded sherds in fabric L2 only.

Catalogue of illustrated sherds (Fig. 7.8)

63   Handmade jar, fabric MALVL1, with a burnished finish. Ditch 112 (109).

64   Handmade jar with a slightly beaded rim, fabric L2. Ditch 212 (210).

65   Rim and joining bodysherds from a vertical walled, simple rim jar, fabric L2. Ditch 212 (211).

66   Everted rim and joining bodysherds from a handmade jar, fabric MALVL1. Burnished exterior. Ditch 212 (211).

67   Bodysherd from a jar, fabric MALVL1, decorated with horizontal parallel tooled lines. Ditch 212 (211).

68   Rim from a jar/bowl in a greyish-brown, slightly vesicular fabric containing fine grog, dark brown argillaceous fragments and fine ?limestone/shell. Fabric GI. Ditch 223 (229).

Middle Duntisbourne

The site at Middle Duntisbourne yielded a total of 888 sherds, 7511 g from *c.* 60 contexts from both the evaluation and subsequent excavation (Table 7.10). With the exception of four sherds (24 g) of post-medieval/modern date from the topsoil and trackway 130, the assemblage appears to date to a single relatively short phase of occupation in the 1st century AD. Although the average sherd weight is rather low at 8.6 g, there are several sherds present from individual vessels, with the substantial parts of complete vessels from ditches 40 and 51.

The assemblage comprises a mixture of local native handmade and wheelmade wares along with several exotic imports dating to the Tiberio-Claudian period. To date, such a complement of wares has only been recorded from the Bagendon complex (Clifford 1961) including the site at Ditches (Trow 1988) (cf. Duntisbourne Grove below). A full breakdown of the fabrics can be found in Table 7.10.

Imports

The imports to the site include fine tablewares from Gaul and amphora from Italy and Spain. The sigillata includes sherds of Arretine, South Gaulish and early Central Gaulish (Lezoux) wares. There are also several vessels from the North Gaulish industries, notably *terra nigra, terra rubra* and fine whitewares. In addition, there are sherds of a slipped fine orange ware (possibly Central Gaulish), a fine buff ware, and a black micaceous ware which, although of unknown origin, are also clearly Roman products and, as such, imports to the site at such an early date.

The Samian by G B Dannell (Fig. 7.9)

69   Arretine cup, Haltern 8. Tiberian? The rouletting is fairly coarse and paste a little pink possibly suggesting a Lyons source? (Fig. 7.9.69). Topsoil (1)

70   South Gaulish cup, Drag 24/5. Claudian? Ditch group 4.

71   An early example of a Lezoux cup Drag 27. Claudian? (Fig. 7.9.71). Ditch 260, fill 154.

Gallo-Belgic wares by Jane Timby (Fig. 7.9)

Nine sherds from a *terra nigra* (TN) platter were recovered from the evaluation (SMR 4678). The excavations produced a further six sherds of TN and three small pieces of terra rubra (TR3), along with 21 sherds of whiteware butt beaker, Camulodunum type 113 (Hawkes and Hull 1947, 238). Other possible

Table 7.10   Middle Duntisbourne: distribution of fabrics across main ditch groups.

FABRIC	group 4		group 310		group 121		other	
	No	wt	No	wt	no	wt	no	wt
Imports								
Arretine							1	4
CG sam	1	1						
SG sam	1	3						
GABTN	4	19	11	51				
GABTR3	3	4						
NOGWH	21	163						
FWBLMIC	24	262					2	7
FWSLOX	4	40						
FWOX	3	19					1	4
FWBUFF	5	10						
AMP	2	15					3	10
Native wares								
L1	1	10						
L2	1	1						
L5	1	6						
H2	2	12						
GROG	10	70			6	12	6	40
MALVL1	88	358	30	58			3	2
MALVL2	24	113						
Severn Valley wares								
SVWOX	46	297						
SVWEA1	14	70	2	14			12	34
SVWEA2	257	1291	9	33	17	23	28	43
SVWEA3	25	146					4	20
Wiltshire wares								
SAVGT	130	3874	3	31	1	18	21	191
WMBBW	6	18					5	13
Other								
reduced sandy	24	45					4	8
oxidised sandy	1	2					3	7
Unclassif	9	12			1	3		
TOTAL	707	6861	55	187	25	56	93	383

imports include a fine oxidised, slipped ware, probably a flagon, a fine buff sandy ware and a black micaceous ware. All of the group is likely to have arrived at the site in the Claudian period.

72   Two very small bodysherds from a TR3 beaker with combed decoration. Unstratified (4).

73   One small rimsherd from a TR3 girth beaker, Cam. type 82–4 (Fig. 7.9.73). Ditch 145, (55).

74–75   Two bodysherds from a TN cup, probably a Cam. type 56. Ditch 144, (56) and (57).

76   Platter rimsherd in TN, Cam. type 12/13. Ditch 139, (210).

77   Rim and basesherd from a TN cup, Cam. type 56 (Fig. 7.9.77). Ditch 254, (289).

78   Two rimsherds and seven bodysherds from a TN platter Cam. type 14 (Fig. 7.9.78). Glos. 4678 (7)= ditch 141, (246)

79   Three rimsherds and 15 bodysherds from a whiteware butt beaker with rouletted decoration, Camulodunum type 113. Ditch 40 (69). Further single bodysherds were recovered from ditch 40 (41), ditch 46 (45) and ditch 260 (154) (Fig. 7.9.79).

80   Base sherd in a fine orange ware with a white slip. (157) Two further small bodysherds from (69).

81   Black micaceous fineware. Represented by 24 bodysherds probably from a beaker or carinated jar. Ditch 40 (39)

82   A fine, buff sandy ware, probably from a beaker. Five sherds from ditch 18, (62) and (64).

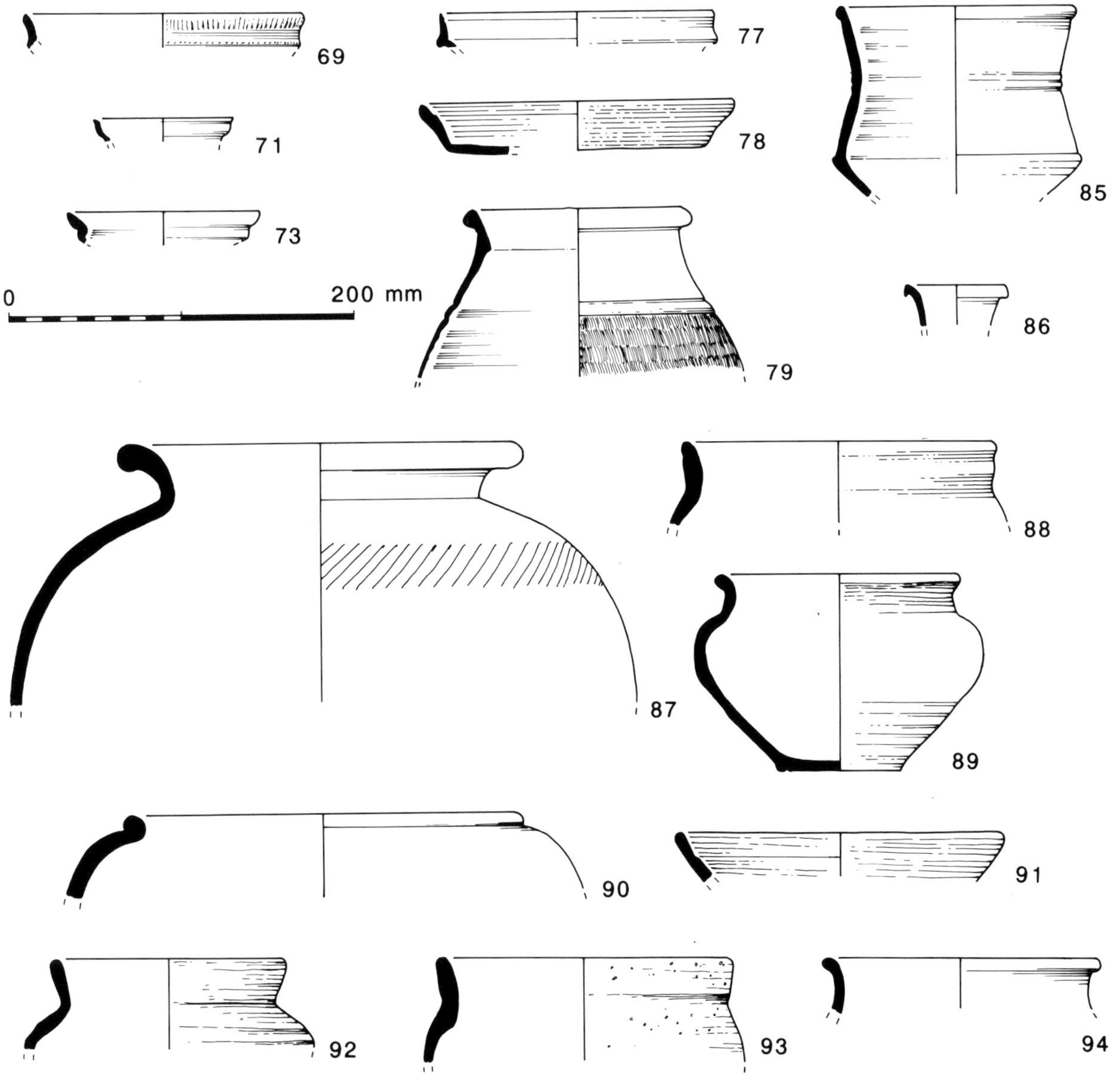

Figure 7.9   Pottery from Middle Duntisbourne.

The amphorae by David Williams

83   Two small friable bodysherds from a Camulodunum 185A/Haltern 70. Ditch 254, (256) and (288).

84   Three small bodysherds. Thin sectioning shows an assemblage which is dominated by small pieces of volcanic rock, potash felspar and green clinopyroxene. This fabric strongly suggests an origin somewhere along the volcanic tract of Italy. In all probability, the vessel represented here is a Dressel 2–4 amphora.U/S

Discussion

The bulk of the assemblage, 80.5% by count (92% by weight) came from ditch group 4 (see Table 7.10). The remaining material came from ditch groups 310, 121 and from quarry pits 167, 213, 237, ditch 111 and topsoil or unstratified finds.

The pottery from ditch 4 was dominated by sherds of early Severn Valley ware (SVWEA1–3) (42% by count) in both handmade and wheelmade forms, and Savernake ware jars (18.5%). Malvernian limestone-tempered wares were also quite well represented accounting for 12.5%. This ditch also produced the bulk of the imported wares. Although several of the fabrics could potentially date to the immediate pre- and post-conquest, the almost ubiquitous presence of Savernake ware, traditionally regarded as a post-conquest industry (cf. Swan 1975), would suggest that the main focus of activity dates to the post-conquest period. There is nothing, however, that indicates a date beyond the Flavian period, suggesting abandonment around AD 60/65. Many of the wares are typical of late Iron Age traditions in this area, in particular the Malvernian limestone-tempered handmade black jars (MALVL1), the large hammer-rim bowls (MALVL2), which were circulating from the 1st century BC until well into the 1st century AD, and a small number of shell- and limestone-tempered wares. The presence of imports of this calibre is rare in Gloucestershire as a whole but well-known from both Bagendon (Clifford 1961) and Ditches, North Cerney (Trow 1988).

Ditch group 121 produced far less material with only 25 sherds of largely early Severn Valley or grog-tempered ware. Only a single Savernake sherd was present and imported wares were absent. Although the low proportion of Savernake ware might be taken as an indication of a possibly earlier date of abandonment, perhaps around the mid 1st century AD, the absence of imports cannot be regarded as significant in such a small sample.

Ditch group 310 yielded slightly more material (55 sherds) which generally mirrors, on a smaller scale, the assemblage from ditch group 4. Imports in this case were limited to 11 sherds of TN.

None of the other features produced any imports, with the remaining sherds all coming from the topsoil or unstratified contexts. Of the other small groups, ditch 111 produced a single sherd of SVWEA3, quarry pit 213, 13 sherds, mainly SVWEA1–2, quarry pit 167, a single sherd of SAVGT and pit 281 six sherds of MALVL1 and SVWEA2.

Catalogue of illustrated sherds (coarsewares) (Fig.7.9.85–94)

85 Several joining sherds from a cordoned, carinated bowl in wheel-turned Severn Valley ware (SVW EA2). Ditch 219 (218).

86 A small necked beaker in a fine oxidised, sandy ware (fabric LOCOX1). Ditch 219 (218).

87 Savernake ware (SAVGT) storage jar decorated with a zone of lightly incised diagonal lines. Ditch 219 (218).

88 Handmade jar, MALVLI. Ditch 40 (43).

89 Wheelmade necked bowl, dark brown to black in colour with a mid brown interior and dark grey core. Fine sandy paste with moderate oolitic limestone, fine mica and rare iron (SVW variant). Ditch 51 (84)

90 Bead-rimmed jar. Savernake ware (SAVGT). Ditch 254 (255).

91 Handmade platter/shallow dish with burnished surfaces. Grog-tempered, GROG1. Quarry pit 213 (208).

92 Wheelmade jar with a burnished exterior surface. Dark brown-black with a dark grey core, grog-tempered, GROG1. Ditch 18 (24).
93 Handmade limestone-tempered jar, MALVL1. Ditch 40, (41).

94 Wheelmade necked bowl, SVWEA3. Ditch 40, (41).

Duntisbourne Grove

Duntisbourne Grove produced an assemblage of some 1890 sherds (10, 255g) from both the evaluation and subsequent excavation (Table 7.11). The material was well fragmented with a generally low overall average sherd weight of 5.4 g. In total, 81 contexts yielded pottery. The assemblage appears to belong to one relatively short period of occupation dating to the mid-1st century AD.

Imports

The Samian by G B Dannell

95 South Gaulish cup ?Drag 27. Pre-Flavian. Ditch 13, (15).

96 South Gaulish bowl, Drag 29. c. AD 60–75. Perhaps by a mould-maker to Medillus; he stamped a very similar design to the upper zone on another Drag 29 (Walters M 308). From a relatively new mould, very neat. Ditch 152, (162). Fig. 7.10.96.

Gallo-Belgic wares and other fineware imports by Jane Timby

97 A very small bodysherd from a TR1A platter. Ditch 117, (118).

98 Rim from a TN platter Cam. type 8. Ditch 48, (49). Fig. 7.10.98.

99 White ware butt beaker Cam. type 113. A total of 30 sherds mainly from ditch 45 (47, 64) with further pieces from ditch 13 (15), ditch 24 (25), and ditch 152 (162). Fig. 7.11.99.

100 Fine black micaceous ware. One rim from a jar, ditch 24 (25) and five plain bodysherds from ditch 51 (52) and ditch 55 (56). Fig. 7.11.100.

The amphorae by David Williams

Camulodunum 185A/Haltern 70 (not illustrated)

101 Small bodysherd and a sherd belonging to part of the neck. Ditch fill 13 (15).

102 Five small bodysherds and a handle stub with the beginnings of a median groove. Ditch fill 45 (47).

103 Small friable bodysherd. Ditch fill 45 (64).

104 Three bodysherds. Subsoil (46).

All of these sherds, along with two small friable pieces from Middle Duntisbourne, are in a very similar gritty fabric. Thin sectioning and petrological analysis show a heterogenous arrangement of rock and mineral inclusions which are commonly associated with the Dressel 20 amphora form (Peacock and Williams 1986, class 25). However, the handle stub with the beginnings of a median groove and the general thinness of the walls of the bodysherds, suggest that these particular amphorae (one or more from each site) are more likely to be a Camulodunum 185A/Haltern form (Peacock and Williams 1986, class 15).

This late Republican/early Imperial amphora type was made in the region of the River Guadalquivir in

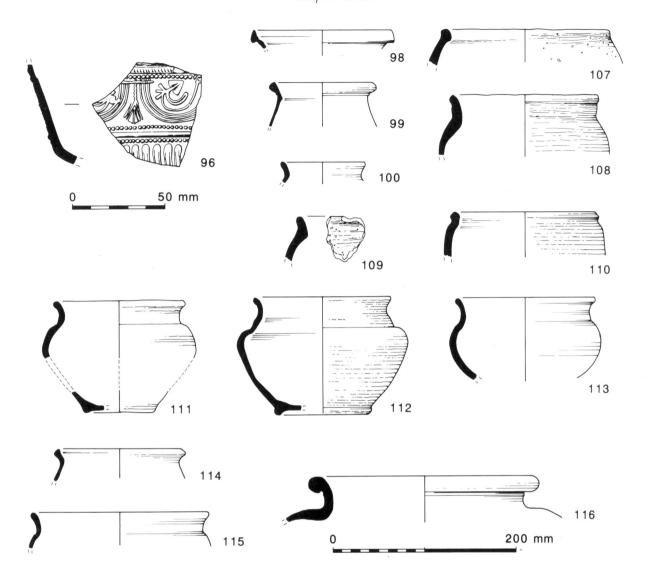

Figure 7.10   Pottery from Duntisbourne Grove

Baetica, southern Spain, and shares an identical fabric to the more commonly found olive-oil container Dressel 20. At times, amphorae of Camulodunum 185A/Haltern 70 seem to have carried olives, judging by the large quantity of olive stones discovered in a vessel of this form recovered from the Sud-Lavezzi II shipwreck (Liou 1982). However, inscriptions suggest that the main contents carried may have been *defrutum*. This has been interpreted by van der Werff (1984) as a liquid belonging to the *vins cuits*, while Sealey (1985) believes it was a non-alcoholic syrup used for sweetening or as a preservative. The date range is from about the middle of the 1st century BC to the Flavian period (Colls *et al.* 1977; Tchernia 1980; van der Werff 1984). Camulodunum 185A is found in late Iron Age contexts in the Wessex region and surrounding area (Williams and Peacock 1994) and also in the east of the country (Wickenden 1986).

Dressel 2–4

105   Two small 'black sand' bodysherds. Ditch 13 (15).

These two sherds are in the distinctive 'black sand' fabric that is normally associated with production within the Bay of Naples region of Campania (Peacock and Williams 1986, class 10). In all probability they belong to the bifid-handled Dressel 2-4 amphora, which was commonly used to transport wine (Peacock and Williams 1986, class 10). Italian forms of this type are well-known in the British late Iron Age as well as in Roman contexts (Williams 1986; Williams and Peacock 1994).

Flagon/Amphora

106   Sixteen bodysherds from a white-slipped, very micaceous orange ware, probably a flagon. Ditch 68 (69, 77).

Table 7.11   Duntisbourne Grove, distribution of fabrics across main feature groups.

FABRIC	Group 8 no	Group 8 wt	Group 9 no	Group 9 wt	Group 10 no	Group 10 wt	Group 11 no	Group 11 wt	Group 114 no	Group 114 wt	Other no	Other wt
Imports												
Samian	2	16	1	2								
GABTR1A									1	2		
GABTN			1	6								
NOGWH	2	2	28	124	1	4						
CGWSOX									16	63		
FWBLMI	2	3			1	6	3	4				
AMP			16	446							2	84
Native												
H2	1	6										
L1									1	9		
L5	4	45			2	33			1	4	10	37
L00	2	16			6	28					6	12
MALVL1	56	268	388	850	20	128			15	175	44	479
MALVL2	35	260									37	249
GROG	25	44	1	8	10	120			2	25	25	138
CALC	2	7	7	78								
Severn Valley wares												
SVWEA1	64	135	92	672	73	651			15	102	50	159
SVWEA2	36	183	148	562	2	16			2	18	14	67
SVWEA3	19	39	33	263	4	76					1	3
SVWOX	32	163	5	23							6	26
SVWvar	0	0	2	4								
Wiltshire wares												
SAVGT	210	861	46	774	18	575	1	12	15	175	38	479
WMBBW	24	46	11	38							11	36
Other												
LOCFGW	49	150	15	83					2	3	13	52
LOCOX	49	106										
DORBB1	1	1									3	10
unclass.	8	17	26	43					2	3	19	62
TOTAL	623	2368	820	3976	137	1637	4	16	72	579	279	1893

Due to the comparatively thin walls of this sherd, it is difficult to be certain whether it represents an amphora, in which case another Dressel 2–4, or a flagon. However, taking into account the petrology, it is more likely to be a flagon. In thin section biotite mica is common (clearly seen in hand specimen), together with pieces of volcanic rock, clinopyroxene, felspar, polycrystalline quartz and some argillaceous material. This assemblage is close to that of the fabric attributed to the Central Gaulish flagon from the late Iron Age burial at Dorton, Bucks., and a similar source (and ?type of vessel) appears possible for the Duntisbourne vessel (Rigby and Freestone 1983).

Discussion

The assemblage from Duntisbourne Grove shows a similar profile to that from Middle Duntisbourne with several native wares accompanied by early Roman wares, notably Savernake ware and Severn Valley ware and a small group of exotic imports of pre-Flavian date.

The largest groups of wares came from ditches 8 and 9 with 623 and 820 sherds respectively. The material from ditch group 8 included a small number of imported finewares; samian, whiteware and black micaceous ware. The samian sherds, the only examples from the site, apart from one core chip from context 15, are both of pre-Flavian date although one dated AD 60–75, is amongst the latest of any of the imports from either of the Duntisbourne sites. Savernake ware, early Severn Valley wares, wheel-made black burnished ware, various Roman reduced wares and Malvernian limestone wares are all well-represented. The increased number of greywares also emphasises the comparatively late date of abandonment for this group. At least one, possibly two sherds, of early DORBB1 is also present. Products of the Durotrigian industries have been documented from other sites in Gloucestershire in 1st-century contexts (Timby forthcoming c; unpub. a).

Ditch group 9 shows a slightly different complement of wares to that from ditch group 8. Imports are represented by TN, whiteware and amphora sherds. Malvernian wares account for 48% of the group compared to just 14% in ditch group 8, Severn Valley wares for 35% compared to 27% and Savernake wares for just 6% whereas they formed 32% of the ditch group 8 assemblage. This suggests an earlier date for ditch group 9, perhaps in the immediate post-conquest period.

Ditch group 10 produced 147 sherds, but this total includes imported finewares, with Savernake wares accounting for 12% by count emphasising a post-conquest terminus post quem. Ditch group 11 only produced four sherds and ditch group 114, a further 72 sherds including imports, this time GABTR1A and a Central Gaulish flagon, both potentially of pre-conquest date. However, Savernake wares at 21% indicate a similar post-conquest date of abandonment for group 114.

Other features to produce pottery include quarry pits 31, 121, 136, 150 and 151; pits 62 and 66, cobbled layer 181 and the subsoil. The only imports from this group of contexts were two amphorae sherds from the subsoil.

In contrast to Middle Duntisbourne, this assemblage contains a much higher proportion of later Iron Age fabrics, in particular Malvernian limestone-tempered wares (MALVL1-2) and proto- and early Severn Valley wares (SVWEA1-3) which might argue for a slightly earlier starting date of activity, or a distinctly different but broadly contemporary form of occupation. The samian from ditch group 8 implies a similar date of abandonment for the two sites. The differences between the two sites may therefore be the result of social, economic or functional factors.

Catalogue of illustrated sherds (Fig. 7.10)

107   Handmade jar in an oolitic limestone-tempered fabric (L5). Ditch 16, (19).

108   Handmade jar with a burnished exterior, MALVL1. Ditch 55 (215).

109   Handmade jar with a burnished exterior, MALVL1. Ditch 81 (83).

110   Beaded rim jar with a burnished exterior, MALVL1. Ditch group 9.

111   Wheel-turned necked bowl, SVWEA1. Ditch 45, (64).

112   Necked bowl, probably originally burnished. SVWEA1. Ditch 48, (50).

113   Several joining sherds from a necked bowl. SVWEA1. Ditch group 9.

114   Bevelled rim beaker. SVWEA2. Ditch group 9.

115   Wheelmade necked bowl, grey in colour. (SVWEA3). Ditch group 9.

116   Necked storage jar, Savernake ware (SAVGT). Ditch 55, (99).

Court Farm

A moderately small assemblage of 475 sherds (2558 g) mainly of Iron Age and Roman date was recovered from 72 contexts. Also present were a few sherds of earlier prehistoric date, many redeposited in later contexts (see Barclay above) and 25 sherds dating to the medieval and post-medieval periods (see Blinkhorn below). Although the pottery indicates a relatively long period of activity the extensive quarrying in the early Roman period has considerably mixed the artefact assemblage.

The later prehistoric and Roman pottery was sorted by fabric type and quantified by sherd count and weight for each excavated context. The data summarised on an Excel spreadsheet forms part of the site archive. Details of fabrics can be found above with a summary quantification in Table 7.12.

Iron Age

Approximately 109 sherds, (24% by count), weighing 578 g, date to the later prehistoric period, although most are redeposited in later contexts. The fabrics include flint-, grog-, limestone- and sand-tempered wares with several mixed temper types. The group also appears to contain a sherd of later Bronze Age/early Iron Age date (see Barclay above). Typical middle Iron Age forms include vertical-sided (Fig. 7.11.119), and beaded rim jars (Fig. 7.11.120). A collection of oolitic limestone-tempered sherds (fabric L5) from a large jar in 428 (Fig. 7.11.121) suggest a middle-late Iron Age date. Other contexts containing sherds of comparable date, both limestone- and sand-tempered examples, include 22 (pit 24), 83 (pit 82), 149 (furrow 167), 235 (ditch 232) and 436 (pit 467). The only features to exclusively contain middle Iron Age pottery are quarry pits 52, 141, and 262, and gully 427.

Roman

Most of the features contained pottery characteristic of the 1st century AD with a mixture of handmade native wares and more Romanised wheelmade types. Although wares typical of the later Iron Age are present in small quantities from the site, these could equally well date to the post-conquest period and there may have been a hiatus in activity at the site in the first half of the 1st century AD. Both trackway ditches (490 and 489) yielded small groups of pottery from their recuts. Several of the fabrics appear to be early/middle Iron Age or, in one case, of earlier prehistoric date, but the presence of several sherds from a well fragmented wheelmade black sandy ware jar (LOCGW8) from 218 (segment 217), and single sherds of Savernake ware (SAVGT) and wheelmade black burnished ware (WMBBW) from 242 (segment 243) indicate filling in the later 1st century or even early 2nd century AD. Pottery from the fills (234 and 235) of the recut feature

Table 7.12   Court Farm, distribution of pottery in the pits.

Pit	Fabric codes	Total no	Total wt
11	SAVGT,WMBBW,LOCOX,FL,L6,L00	17	53
24	L2	3	13
35	DORBB1,WMBBW,LOCGW	12	23
37	SVWEA2,LOCGW,LOCWSOX,L2,	9	14
39	SAVGT	1	13
52	GS, L2	6	25
82	GROG, SAVGT, LOCGW, L2	4	34
106	SAVGT,SAM,LOCGW	5	23
109	GROG	1	8
119	SAM, WMBBW, GROG, SF	4	5
141	L6	1	5
163	LOCOX	1	2
174	SAVGT,SAM,GROG,LOCGW,DORBB1,SVWOX	36	161
247	GROG, L6, SLG	3	16
259	SAM	1	1
262	SL	5	8
265	MALVL1, SVWEA2, LOCGW	5	29
285	MALVL1,SVWEA2,WMBBW,SAVGT,LOCGW,GROG,LOCOX,FL,L2,GS	54	265
312	SAVGT,BATAM,SVW,LOCGW,L1,L2,L5	29	243
315	LOCGW8,FL,L5	4	32
318	SVWEA2, SAVGT, LOCGW, GROG, L1, L5	11	66
326	MALVL1	1	10
328	GROG, WMBBW, SAVGT	41	208
332	GROG	1	10
334	FL, GROG, SL, H2	7	72
339	SVWOX	5	26
364	GROG	1	7
427	L5	22	120
437	WMBBW, SAVGT, GS, L2	5	38
440	SVWEA2, SL	5	46
467	GROG, LOCGW	3	31
TOTAL		303	1607

(segment 232) comprised two redeposited Iron Age sherds. Fill 402 (segment 401) produced four sherds including one scrap of South Gaulish samian and two fragments of probable intrusive medieval pottery, whilst 223 (segment 225) yielded two Iron Age sherds. The only fill to produce pottery from the trackway ditches 488 and 491 was 135 (segment 136), with four early Severn Valley ware sherds. The surface of the trackway produced a single Savernake ware sherd from repair 304.

Early Roman pottery was recovered from 19 of the quarry pits (Table 7.12), with pottery dating to the first half of the 1st century AD from seven pits (109, 247, 326, 332, 334, 364, 440) and exclusively Iron Age pottery from a further five pits (24, 52, 141, 262, 427) and ditch 427. Finds were generally sparse and only 8 pits yielded more than 10 sherds. The Roman pottery was relatively consistent across the pits, mainly types current from the late Neronian/Flavian period through to the early 2nd century AD, for example black wheelmade sandy wares (WMBBW), various local grey wares and Savernake ware. A number of sherds more typical of the later Iron Age, mainly limestone and grog-tempered wares, occurred alongside the Roman sherds, and may be residual, although they are a common feature on rural sites, and may still have been in use. The grog-tempered sherds probably first appeared in the first half of the 1st century AD but the limestone-tempered pieces could potentially date back to the 1st century BC. Continuation into the 2nd century is indicated by the material from pit 312 which includes Severn Valley wares, Dressel 20 amphora and south-west oxidised sandy ware. The same date could be given to pits 35 and 174, as both contained DORBB1 and grey sandy wares mixed in with earlier material. Several pits contained sherds of samian, of particular note a cup Drag 24/5 of pre-Flavian date from 259 and a dish Drag 18 from pit 176. Pit 11 contained a rouletted sherd from an orange sandy ware butt beaker. Other imports were restricted to Dressel 20 amphorae and Malvernian limestone-tempered jars. Whether the pits yielding pre-Roman wares can be regarded as earlier in the sequence, or simply a distortion due to the small assemblage sizes is difficult

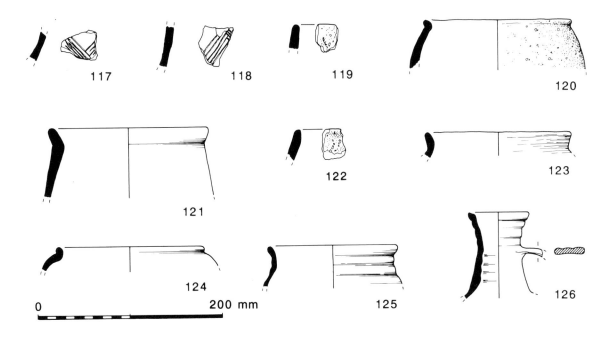

Figure 7.11   Pottery from Court Farm.

to determine. If the pitting is exclusively Roman it would imply the almost complete obliteration of an earlier phase of occupation.

Other features with early Roman pottery include ditches 341, 477, 480 and 483, gully 168, a post-medieval field-drain 49 and tree-throw hole 113. Pre-Roman pottery (ie. handmade ware of 1st century AD date) was associated with ditch 136 and pits 326, 332, 334, and 364 whilst middle Iron Age sherds were residual in the post-medieval field-drain (context 83) and ditches 225, 232 and 342.

Catalogue of illustrated sherds (Fig. 7.11.117-126)

117   Bodysherd decorated with incised lines. Hard fabric, red-brown in colour with a black core. Sandy texture with a sparse scatter of fossil shell and limestone. Fabric LS. Residual in ditch 243 (242).

118   Bodysherd similar to 1. Ditch 225 (223).

119   Rim sherd of vertical-sided jar with a simple rim. Reddish-brown in colour with a brown core. Fabric L6. Ditch 232 (235).

120   Beaded rim jar. Fine, shell-tempered ware, fabric H2. Quarry pit 334 (333).

121   Bevelled rim jar in oolitic limestone-tempered ware (L5). Ditch terminal 427 (428).

122   Rim from a Malvernian limestone-tempered jar, (MALVL1). Quarry pit 326 (325).

123   Handmade everted rim jar in a dark brown, flint-tempered fabric with a red-brown core, Fabric FL. Ditch 285 (288).

124   Wheel-turned beaded rim jar in a sandy ware (WMBBW). Quarry pit 285 (288). Quarry pit 285 (288).

125   Everted rim, wheelmade jar/bowl (WMBBW). Pit 11=123 (10).

126   Ring-necked flagon. Fine oxidised ware with dark orange, rounded, clay pellets. Fabric LOCOX. Ditch 477 (479).

Weavers Bridge

The assemblage from Weavers Bridge comprises 796 sherds, 7416 g from 11 contexts (Table 7.13). Particularly large groups of material were associated with buried soil 51 and midden 57, accounting for 95% of the total assemblage by weight. With the exception of a group of medieval material from the fill of the river channel 45, all the pottery dates to the later Roman period.

The range of Roman fabrics present are common for this locality in the later 2nd-4th centuries, namely samian (CGSAM), Dressel 20 amphora (BATAM); Dorset black burnished ware (DORBB1), products of the Oxfordshire industries, in particular colour-coated forms (Young 1977, forms C22, C83, C47, C45) and white ware mortaria (Young 1977, forms M18, M20, M22), grey micaceous ware (MICGW), Nene Valley colour-coated ware (LNVCC) and late grog-tempered storage jar (PNKGT). Various local grey wares are also present including vessels imitating DORBB1 forms. A summary of the different wares present can be found in Table 7.13.

Most of the pottery was recovered from the midden 57, accounting for some 68% by count, (65% by weight), of the total recovered assemblage. The average sherd weight, 9 g, is quite low for Roman material although typical of rubbish deposits. One might expect to find larger, better preserved sherds in an in-situ midden deposit, suggesting that this material has either been deliberately broken up or has been redeposited.

The midden contained a variety of wares and forms including cooking, storage, serving and drinking vessels; the sort of range to be expected from a typical domestic household. Cooking vessels include DORBB1 jars, grey ware jars and mortaria (OXFWH; OXFRS). Storage vessels are represented by Midlands grog-tempered large storage jars (PNKGT) and Savernake ware (SAVGT). Serving vessels might include the numerous straight-sided dishes/bowls in DORBB1 and local grey ware copies, alongside dishes and bowls in Oxfordshire red-slipped wares and samian, while drinking vessels are represented by beakers (OXFRS; MOSBS). Seven fragments of roofing tile (tegulae) also came from context 57 (see Allen below).

The presence of the small amount of samian and Savernake ware in the midden deposit could suggest occupation dating back to at least the later 2nd century although this might represent redeposited or curated material as it is in association with later vessels. Both tablewares and storage vessels tend to have longer survival rates than other domestic wares and the samian in particular is very worn and abraded.

The DORBB1 and the Oxfordshire colour-coated wares both indicate a date from the second half of the 3rd century. The absence of certain forms and fabrics, such as flanged bowls, parchment wares or late shelly wares, might suggest that the midden was abandoned in the later 3rd century.

Soil horizon 51 overlying the midden produced the second largest collection of wares, some 216 sherds (27% by count, 29% by weight). Again, the average sherd size is quite low at 10 g. Although many of the same wares are present as in the midden, for example, DORBB1, PNKGT, OXFRS, MICGW and local grey wares, the forms, in particular conical flanged bowls in DORBB1 and a stamped bowl (OXFRS) (Young 1977, form C83) indicate a *terminus post quem* well into the 4th century. The absence of any late Roman shell-tempered wares might suggest a mid-4th century *terminus ante quem*.

Catalogue of illustrated sherds from midden 57 (Fig. 7.12)

127 Jar, DORBB1 (Gillam 1976, type 11).

128 Jar, MICGW imitating DORBB1.

129 Necked jar, in a local grey, medium sandy ware (LOCGW).

130 Jar in a very fine, grey ware (LOCGW).

Table 7.13   Incidence of fabrics from Weavers Bridge.

Fabric common name	Code	Wt	%	No	%	EVE	%
FOREIGN IMPORTS							
Samian	SAMCG	27	*	6	*		
Moselkeramic	MOSBS	3	*	1	*		
Dressel 20 amphora	BATAM	127	2	3	*		
REGIONAL IMPORTS							
Savernake	SAVGT	120	1.5	1	*		
Dorset BB1	DORBB1	1156	15.5	102	13	217	32.5
Oxon white ware mortaria	OXFWH	198	2.5	7	*	50	7.5
Oxon white wares	OXFWH	106	1.5	14	2		
Oxon red-slip mortaria	OXFRS	18	*	3	*		
Oxon colour-coat	OXFRS	751	10	161	20.5	68	10
Midlands grog-tempered	PNKGT	674	9	21	2.5		
Nene Valley colour-coat	LNVCC	24	*	2	*	9	1
LOCAL/SOURCE UNKNOWN							
Severn Valley ware	SVWOX	14	*	1	*		
micaceous grey ware	MICGW	142	2	6	*	11	1.5
fine grey ware	LOCGW	929	12.5	105	13.5	94	14
medium sandy grey ware	LOCGW	375	5	7	*	35	5
coarse sandy grey ware	LOCGW	2398	32	239	30.5	178	26.5
fine oxidised ware	LOCOX	54	*	14	2		
sandy oxidised ware	LOCOX	4	*	1	*	6	1
Unclassified	OO	259	3.5	87	11		
TOTAL		7379	100	781	100	668	100

* = less than 1%

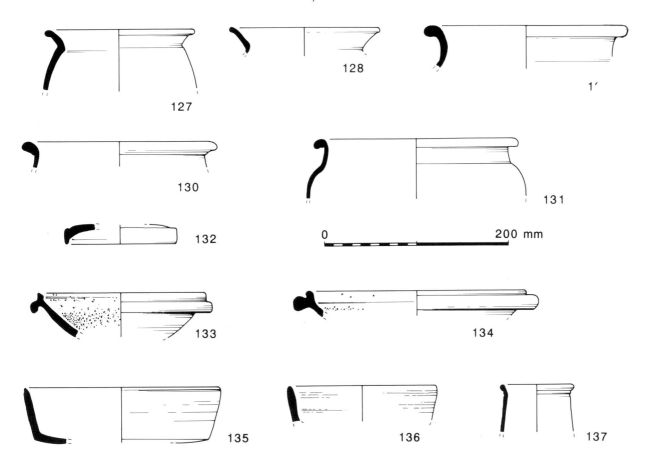

Figure 7.12   Pottery from Weavers Bridge.

131   Necked jar in fine sandy ware with blue-grey surfaces and a brick-red core (LOCGW).

132   Lid in a partially burnt, black, medium sandy ware (LOCGW).

133   Oxfordshire white ware mortarium (Young 1977, type M18) (OXFWH).

134   Oxfordshire white ware mortarium (Young 1977, type M22) (OXFWH).

135   Straight-sided dish in local grey sandy ware (LOCGW).

136   Straight-sided dish in Nene Valley black colour-coated ware (LNVCC).

137   Oxfordshire beaker, black colour-coat on buff fabric (OXFRS).

ROMAN POTTERY FROM BIRDLIP QUARRY, COWLEY
By Jane Timby with a report on the samian by Brenda Dickinson

Introduction

The excavations yielded *c.* 16,700 sherds of pottery, 151 kg by weight, 104.19 estimated vessel equivalents (eve). With the exception of a very small number of prehistoric, medieval and post-medieval wares, the assemblage dated to the Roman period, in particular the later 2nd through to the later 4th centuries. No sub-Roman material was recovered.

The following report is divided into three sections: the first presents a fabric and form description, the second a discussion of the pottery in relation to the site and the third an appraisal of the assemblage in its regional context. As a result of the character of the assemblage, in particular its lack of diversity and its poor preservation, only a small number of pieces were selected for illustration. The illustrated vessels reflect in essence the character of the assemblage depicting most of the most common types, as well as several pieces with graffiti.

Methodology

The pottery was sorted into fabrics and quantified by sherd count, weight and eve for each recorded context. The fabric codes originally designated were those of the Gloucester type fabric series (cf. Ireland 1983), although several wares were not represented. For the purposes of publication the wares have been coded according to the nomenclature proposed for National Roman Fabric Reference Collection (NRFRC) (Tomber and Dore 1996). As this at present only relates to regional types, the local wares have been coded using the same system, but are unique to this report. A concordance of the new codes with the Gloucester fabric series can be found in Table 7.14. Collections of very small sherds (less than 10 mm square) were allocated a miscellaneous code (OO) and merely counted and weighed.

Rim sherds were coded where possible according to vessel type: jar, bowl, dish, cup, tankard, beaker, flagon, jug, lid, mortarium and amphora, indicated by Roman numerals. Within each basic type, sub-types were created on the basis of rim/vessel morphology.

Condition

Although the quantity of pottery recovered was quite large, the sherds are in relatively poor condition and there are few reconstructible profiles. Much of the material is fairly abraded, with a low mean sherd weight of 9 g. Many of the colour-coated wares have lost their surfaces making identification difficult, especially in discriminating them from oxidised Severn Valley ware. The condition of the pottery is very typical of assemblages from Roman sites located on the Cotswolds, such as Uley (Leach 1993, 219), Frocester (Timby forthcoming) and Kingscote (Timby 1998a). The problem is exacerbated on other Roman Cotswold sites due to modern ploughing, a long history of disturbance and redeposition through successive periods of occupation, and the soft nature of many of the fabrics.

Fabrics and forms

Table 7.14 summarises the overall quantities of individual pottery fabrics from the site. From this it is immediately apparent that the assemblage is dominated by two coarseware fabrics, Severn Valley wares (SVWOX2) and Dorset black burnished ware (DORBB1). The former account for *c.* 30% of the assemblage by weight, 27% by sherd count, compared to 29% DORBB1 by weight, 39% by count. Continental imports to the site are limited to samian, Gaulish black-slipped ware and amphorae, mainly Dressel 20. Other regional imports include a few colour-coated vessels from the Nene Valley and New Forest industries, at least one vessel from the Alice Holt kilns, Mancetter-Hartshill mortaria, Midlands grog-tempered ware and Midlands late Roman shell-tempered ware. Products from both the North Wiltshire and Oxfordshire industries are well-represented. The general paucity of continental imports may to a certain extent be a reflection of the date of occupation. The samian, although generally of rather poor quality (see Dickinson below) comprises 2.5% by sherd count of the assemblage. Similarly the very presence of olive oil and wine amphorae suggest a certain modest level of sophistication.

Jars dominate the form types accounting for 58% of the assemblage by eve, with storage jar rims accounting for less than 1% of the overall jar assemblage, a relatively low proportion in view of the rural character of the site. The proportion of storage jars appears to be higher on other rural sites such as,

for example, Frocester Court (Timby forthcoming). The commonest rim forms are downward hooked triangular shapes which are common 3rd-4th century SVWOX2 types and simple everted flaring types reflecting the DORBB1 range. Bowls/dishes account for 27% of the assemblage by eve with the straight-sided dish being the commonest type (40% of the group) followed by flanged rim forms at 22%. Flat rim forms accounted for 4% and grooved rim bowls, 13.7%. The remaining 15% of the eves are made up of flagons (5%), mortaria (4%), tankards (2.4%), beakers (2%); with colanders, amphorae, lids and cups all contributing less than 1% each. Flagons and drinking vessels (beakers/tankards) are surprisingly low, and a paucity of cups was also noted in the samian assemblage (see Dickinson below).

Common names are followed by the NRFRC codes and the Gloucester type fabric (TF) codes (see Table 7.14 for overall quantities of individual fabrics).

Samian
By Brenda Dickinson

The excavation produced 397 sherds of samian, almost all of them unstratified or residual. The material represents a maximum of 314 vessels, of which 275 sherds, or a maximum of 199 vessels, are attributable to specific forms or vessel types (dishes, cups, etc.). Calculation by sherd and vessel count produces almost identical ratios of Central to East Gaulish ware, with 76% (sherd count) and 77% (vessel count) from Central Gaul and 24% and 23% respectively from East Gaul. Only three samian factories seem to have supplied the site, Lezoux in Central Gaul to *c.* AD 200, and the two large East Gaulish manufacturers of the late 2nd and 3rd centuries, Rheinzabern and Trier. As is normal in Britain, Rheinzabern ware pre-dominates, accounting for approximately 75% of the East Gaulish material.

The samian ranges from *c.* AD 125 to the 3rd century (before AD 260), but only three (decorated) vessels, two from Area A, the other without precise provenance, suggest activity on the site in the Hadrianic or early Antonine periods. Contemporary plain forms, such as Dr. 18/31, 27 and 42 are conspicuous by their absence. Typologically, the rest of the assignable samian forms date from after *c.* AD 160, the best represented vessels being Dr. 31 and 31R. There are twice as many examples of the latter, revealing a preference for bowls of wider diameter, in the later 2nd century at least. It is also worth noting that dishes and bowls account for 90% of the material, which highlights the relative unimportance of samian cups on the site. Drinking vessels of other materials must therefore have been used, presumably for drinks other than wine.

Although dating evidence for East Gaulish ware is still lamentably scarce, there are a few vessels here which can be assigned to the 3rd century on analogy with examples in dated contexts elsewhere. This, combined with the noticeably high proportion of East Gaulish ware, 24%, indicates that samian

Table 7.14 Overall quantities of individual pottery fabrics from Birdlip Quarry.

Fabrics: common name	Code/TF	Wt	%	No	%	eve	%
FOREIGN IMPORTS							
Samian	8	2504	1.5	397	2.5	351	3
Gaulish black-slipped ware	MOSBS, 12K	45	*	20	*	1	*
Dressel 20 amphora	BATAM, 10A	15027	10	149	1	64	*
Gallic	GALAM, 10B	680	*	72	*		
S Spanish	10E	304	*	6	*		
LOCAL WARES							
grog-tempered	GROG, 2	459	*	92	*	6	*
SVW	SVWOX2, 11B	44635	29.5	4018	24	2172	21
SVW variants	SVWOX2, 11v	209	*	41	*	23	*
SVW handmade	SVWOX2, 23	528	*	20	*		
Micaceous ware	5	3362	2	413	2.5	244	2
REGIONAL IMPORTS							
Savernake	SAVGT, 6	5344	3.5	110	*	56	*
Black-burnished	201	199	*	24	*	47	*
Wilts orange sandy	231	1765	*	231	1	147	1.5
Wilts grey sandy	232	1398	1	204	1	50	*
?Wilts colour-coat	12D	89	*	6	*	15	*
?Wilts/SW wslip	15A	557	*	91	*	425	4
?Wilts/SW no slip	15	290	*	73	*	32	*
REGIONAL IMPORTS							
Malvernian ware	MALREA, 18	10	*	1	*		
BB1	DORBB1, 4	43954	29	6541	39	4527	43
Oxon whiteware	OXFWH, 13	172	*	28	*		
Oxon ww mortaria	OXFWH, 9A	2870	2	110	*	290	*
Oxon wslip mortaria	OXFWS, 9W	39	*	2	*		
Oxon parchment ware	OXFPA, 1A	224	*	12	*	41	*
Oxon colour-coat	OXFRS, 12A	6021	4	1084	6.5	284	3
Oxon cc mortaria	OXFRS, 9X	980	*	75	*	142	*
Nene Valley cc	LNVCC, 12B	80	*	20	*	14	*
Nene Valley mortaria	LNVCC, 9E	107	*	2	*	10	*
New Forest cc	NFOCC, 12C	107	*	16	*	6	*
Mancetter-Hartshill	MAHWH, 9D	343	*	3	*	48	*
Late shelly ware	ROBSH, 22	332	*	62	*	86	*
late grog-tempered ware	PNKGT, 241	1190	*	32	*	28	*
Alice Holt greyware	ALHRE, 212	55	*	2	*	5	*
SOURCE UNKNOWN							
Misc colour-coats	12	138	*	20	*	10	*
Unknown mortaria	9	29	*	2	*		*
Greyware	LOCGW1	2418	1.5	280	1.5	309	3
Greyware	LOCGW2	121	*	6	*	2	*
Greyware	LOCGW3	6025	4	626	4	494	5
Greyware	LOCGW4	1709	1	301	2	174	*
Greyware	LOCGW5	289	*	22	*	33	*
Greyware	LOCGW6	430	*	65	*	13	*
Greyware	LOCGW7	218	*	13	*		
shell-tempered ware	SHEL	150	*	22	*		
Misc whiteware	WW	105	*	35	*		
misc limestone	LIME	8	*	4	*		
misc oxidised	OXID	894	*	249	1.5	37	*
misc reduced	GREY	3922	2.5	764	4.5	233	2.5
Less than 10 mm	00	539	*	275	1.5		
Prehistoric	PREH	33	*	34	*		
Medieval	MED	12	*	2	*		
Post-medieval	PMED	48	*	30	*		
TOTAL		150967	100	16707	100	10 419	100

* = less than 1%

continued to hold its own against other types of domestic pottery into the 3rd century. The range of forms is neither extensive nor unusual, and this, combined with the scarcity of moulded decorated bowls in the assemblage, suggests that this was a site of only modest status.

Decorated ware (not illustrated)

138 Form 37, Central Gaulish. A double-bordered medallion includes a scarf-dancer (O.361A). The figure-type was used at Lezoux in the Hadrianic-Antonine period. *c.* AD 130–160. U/S

139 Form 37, Central Gaulish. The double-bordered ovolo with rosette tongue (Rogers B18) and the wavy-line border below it (Rogers A23) are both on an unprovenanced bowl with a mould-signature of Drusus ii, in the Colchester and Essex Museum. *c.* AD 125–145. Ctx 731.

140 Form 37, Central Gaulish, featuring a small horse (D.908 = O.1976) and a zig-zag panel border. The latter was used by Servus iv and a few other Lezoux potters working in the period *c.* AD 160–200. Ctx 840.

Potters' stamps. Ligatured letters are underlined

141 BELSA(ARVE[F] on form 31R: Belsa Arve(rnicus?) of Lezoux, Die 1a (Dickinson 1986, 187, fig. 3.19). This stamp occurs in a group of late-Antonine wasters in a kiln at Lezoux and in another group of (plain) samian of the same date, recovered off Pudding Pan Rock, Kent. *c.* AD 170–200. Ctx 41.

142 NVMIDIMA on form 79 (R?) or Tg (R?): Iulius Numidus of Lezoux, Die 4a (Dickinson 1986, 190, fig. 3.68). Stamps from several of this potter's dies have been found at forts on Hadrian's Wall; this particular one is known from Benwell. His forms include some which were not introduced before the later 2nd century, such as Dr.31R, W.79 and W.80. *c.* AD 160–190. Ctx 867.

143 Form 31, Central Gaulish, stamped AT[. Mid- to late-Antonine. Burnt. Ctx 1229.

144 Form 31, stamped]VLIANVSF. The piece is slightly burnt, but the fabric seems most likely to belong to the Central Gaulish range. Although the form of the vessel appears to be Dr. 31, there is a circle round the stamp, as on rouletted dishes; there is perhaps also a faint band of rouletting on the base, close to its junction with the wall. The potter's name is beyond conjecture. Mid- to late-Antonine. Ctx 1335.

Imported wares

Gaulish (Moselle) black slipped ware (MOSBS, TF 12k)

Only twenty sherds of Gaulish colour-coated beaker were noted, probably all from the East Gaulish industry. This is generally dated to the period AD 180/90–250 in Britain (Richardson 1986, 119).

Amphorae

Amphora sherds accounted for 10.5% by weight of the total assemblage (1% by sherd count). Most of the sherds came from Dressel 20s; additional sherds came from Gallic and undesignated South Spanish types.

Dressel 20 (BATAM, TF10A) (Peacock and Williams 1986, class 25, 136–40).

The globular olive-oil amphora, Dressel 20 originating from the south Spanish province of Baetica is one of the commonest types to be found in Britain and is the most frequent amphora at Birdlip Quarry. Production commenced during the Tiberian period, and continued until at least the late 3rd century. Only one rim was present (ctx 318 (296) Area B, Phase 2) which approximated type 19 dating to the later 1st-early 2nd century (Peacock and Williams 1986, fig. 66, after Martin-Kilcher).

Gallic (GALAM, TF10B) (Peacock and Williams 1986, class 27)

Quite a high number of sherds of Gallic amphora, (72 in total) were present. The fabric is fine and buff in colour and is probably from the Gauloise 4 (Pélichet 47) flat-bottomed wine amphora, although no featured sherds are present. This is another long-lived form, predominantly made in southern France, where several kilns have been found in recent years (Laubenheimer 1985). It was the commonest wine amphora to be imported into Britain in the 2nd century. Sherds first occur in Area C, Phase 1 which produced the highest concentration of 28 sherds.

South Spanish (TF10E)

Six sherds, probably of south Spanish origin but types uncertain.

Coarsewares

A: Native wares
Grog-tempered ware (GROG, TF2)

Fabric: Moderately soft, slightly soapy ware of variable character but containing sparse to moderate sub-rounded grog fragments along with sand, iron and organic material.

Forms: Handmade vessels, mainly jars.

Date: The sherds are quite fragmentary and are possibly residual from 1st/early 2nd-century occupation in the general locality.

B: Local industries

B1 Severn Valley Ware (SVW) (SVWOX2; Glos TF11B, 11V and 23)

Severn Valley wares collectively account for 30% by weight (24% by sherd count) of the assemblage and is the commonest fabric by weight, second by sherd count. Sherds are present throughout the site.

SVWOX2, TF11B

Fabric: (*cf.* Webster 1976; Rawes 1982). Both oxidised and grey wares have been subsumed into this group within which there are a number of minor fabric variations. These were deemed insufficiently distinctive to redefine the group, but would suggest more than one production site or source of clay was being used.

Forms: A diverse range of mainly jar, bowl and tankard forms occurs. Rim forms include bifid, hooked, everted and triangular pendant, mainly types current in the 3rd and 4th centuries.

Date: The industry is a long-lived one dating from the 1st–4th centuries.

TF11

Fabric: Used for probable SVW ware variants.

TF23

Fabric: A coarse handmade SVW almost exclusively used for large storage-type jars. The fabric generally contains a large number of impurities in the clay body in the form of clay pellets and organic material.

B2: Highly Micaceous Wares (MICGW, TF5)

This fabric is very common in Gloucestershire, particularly on sites south of the Severn dating from the mid/late 2nd through to the 4th century. At Birdlip it accounts for just 2% by weight which may suggest the site is on the limit of the market for this product whose source is currently unknown (for further discussion see below).

Fabric: A generally light-textured, well-fired sandy ware, usually grey or black in colour, occasionally orange-brown. The sandy texture of the fabric varies considerably from moderately coarse to fine, but is always characterised by the prominent presence of fine white mica (muscovite). Sparse dark grey rounded clay pellets are also usually present. The group undoubtedly contains a number of sub-types but at present it is not possible to make any meaningful distinctions.

Forms: A particularly wide range of forms were made in this fabric including wheelmade copies of BB1 and SVW types, for example jars, plain-rimmed dishes, flat-rimmed dishes and flanged bowls. The imitation also extends to the use of burnished lattice decoration.

B3: Wiltshire Region (Fabrics SAVGT, TF6; WMBBW, TF201; WILCC, TF12D; WILRE, TF 231; WILOX, TF232)

Savernake ware (SAVGT, TF6)

Fabric: (*cf.* Annable 1962; Rigby 1982, 153).

Forms: Large handmade storage jars, mainly with everted, rounded rims and finer wheelmade vessels.

The industry, thought to date from around the mid-1st century AD, continues well into the 2nd century. The wheelmade wares are likely to date from the early 2nd century. Storage jars tend to be relatively long survivors and thus much of the material from the site may be curated from the later 1st- early 2nd century.

Wiltshire black-burnished ware (WMBBW, TF201)

Fabric: A fine grained, sandy ware with a black-burnished exterior. The core is usually brown, grey or black.

Forms: Wheelmade vessels including beakers, flat-rimmed dishes, small carinated jars, and lids. Burnished lattice decoration or barbotine dot decoration is frequently employed. The substantial part of a flat-rimmed bowl was recovered from well 891 (Fig. 7.15.193).

This ware is particularly well known on sites with 1st-century occupation, for example Kingsholm, Gloucester (Timby unpub.), Cirencester (Rigby 1982, fabric 5) and Bagendon (Fell 1961b, fig. 65, 116d). It is well represented at Frocester (Timby forthcoming) and Uley (Leach 1993). Whilst a specific source has yet to be identified for the ware, the character of the fabric and the pattern of occurrence would suggest a source in north Wiltshire. At Birdlip it is quite rare with just 24 sherds which is probably a reflection of the later chronology of the site.

Orange sandy ware (WILOX, TF231)

Fabric: A hard, pale orange ware, often with a grey inner core. The matrix contains abundant fine quartz sand and occasional iron.

Forms: Wheelmade jars and flagons.

This ware undoubtedly originates from one of the many north Wiltshire kiln sites in production from the early 2nd century (Anderson 1979). The fabrics closely resemble those from the Whitehill Farm kilns situated west of Swindon. It is well represented in assemblages both from Gloucester (cf. Ireland 1983, fig. 73, 278–85) and more particularly Cirencester (Cooper 1998, 329ff) in 2nd- and 3rd-century contexts.

Grey sandy ware (WILRE, TF232)

Fabric: Reduced version of above.

Forms: The form repertoire is slightly less varied than the oxidised forms and includes mainly jars.

North Wiltshire colour-coated ware (WILCC, TF12D) (Anderson 1978; 1979)

Fabric: A fine, orange, sandy ware with a grey core, and a red to light brown colour-coating. The entire colour range can extend from orange to black, and occasionally even plum-coloured resembling that found on later New Forest products. The colour-coat is invariably matt and thin.

Forms: Almost exclusively used for making beakers.

Production of this ware dates from the 2nd century, well before the other regional colour-coated industries. Where material has become very abraded it is frequently difficult to distinguish from other colour-coated ware and for this reason may well be under-represented. Only six sherds were identified.

C: Possible Wiltshire or Avon

South-west plain and white-slipped ware (SOWWS, TF15, 15a)

Fabric: A hard, generally oxidised, but frequently mottled grey-orange ware with a dense granular texture. The matrix contains a common frequency of medium to fine quartz sand and rare iron grains. Some vessels have a thin white slip (=15a). Occasionally vessels show a red burnished finish (SOWRB).

Forms: Mainly used for tablewares, in particular flagons and beakers. The white-slipped version mainly occurs as small flagons (cf. Fig. 7.13.157 and 162).

Production would appear to date from the 2nd into the 3rd century. The distribution points to a source in the south-west region and the north Wiltshire area is a possibility. However, a moderately heavy presence on sites in Avon could also suggest a source in this area. The fabric occurs on most sites of Roman date in the region and has been identified locally at Gloucester, Uley (Leach 1993, fabric 13), Frocester (Timby forthcoming, fabric 34) and Cirencester (Cooper 1998, fabric 88/95).

D: Regional Wares

D1:   Dorset Black-Burnished Ware (DORBB1, TF4)

Fabric: (Williams 1977; Holbrook and Bidwell 1991, 88–138)

Black-burnished ware is the second commonest fabric by weight at 29% but the commonest by count at 39%. The wares are present throughout, from Phases 1 to 6. Of particular note are two semi-complete vessels, one a flanged bowl from the corn dryer (Fig. 7.15.192); the other a jar from context 943. The former is likely to date from *c.* AD 270 onwards, the latter on the basis of its obtuse lattice from *c.* AD 220+. The jar which may well have been a foundation deposit no longer has its rim and is sooted. The vessel repertoire is dominated by jars, accounting for 58.5% of the total BB1 assemblage on eves. Decoration is exclusively of the burnished lattice type. The second commonest form type present is the plain-rimmed dish (Holbrook and Bidwell 1991, types 56, 57 and 59) accounting for 21% by eve. The flanged-rim bowl (Holbrook and Bidwell 1991, type 45) was also popular accounting for 11% by eve. This vessel form is more typical of the later stages of the industry dating from *c.* AD 270 onwards.

Flat grooved-rim bowls (Holbrook and Bidwell 1991, type 43) dating from *c.* AD 180/210–270 are slightly less common but considering their shorter duration well represented at 7.5%. The remaining vessels include examples of flat-rimmed dishes (Holbrook and Bidwell 1991, types 38–40, 49). Types 38 and 49 date from the early 2nd century, the other types from the late Antonine to the mid-3rd century. Together these vessels account for less than 1% by eve, again reflective of their earlier chronology. Other minority types present in small quantities include beaded-rim bowls, and oval, handled fish dishes. No lids or jugs were present.

At least nine DORBB1 vessels were recovered with simple graffito scratched into the vessel surfaces after firing Fig. 7.13.147, 150, 152, 153; Fig. 7.14.170; Fig. 7.15.190–191). These were mainly crosses found both on the rims and on the underside of the bases. One vessel had three parallel lines on the upper body, a dish has three parallel marks on the rim. No pattern could be determined for the occurrence of these vessels on the site and no similar graffiti were found on any other wares.

The emphasis is on types belonging to the later part of the industry, although wares are relatively well represented amongst the Phase 1 material.

D2:   Oxfordshire Industry

Vessels from the Oxfordshire industries are moderately well represented in the assemblage with examples of all the main products. In total these account for 7% by weight (8% by sherd count).

Whitewares (OXFWH, TF13) (Young 1977, 93–112)

Apart from a probable candlestick base with square rouletted decoration (Fig. 7.13.156) there were no featured sherds in this ware.

Whiteware mortaria (OXFWH, TF9A) (Young 1977, 56–79)

Types present include Young 1977, types M13, M17, M18, M20 and M22. The commonest forms were M17 dating to AD 240–300 and the later M22 produced AD 240–400+.

White-slipped mortaria (OXFWS, TF9W) (Young 1977, 117–22)

Flanged mortaria Young 1977 type WC7 were present in contexts 34 and 128.

Parchment ware (OXFPA, TF1A) (Young 1977, 80–92)

Mainly represented by bowls with red painted decoration, Young 1977, type P24, dating to AD 240–400. A single rim from a less common globular jar or bowl (Fig. 7.14.174) (Young 1977, form P34) came from context 128.

Red-slipped wares (OXFRS) (TF12A) (Young 1977, 123–84)

A diverse range of wares with beakers and dishes of Young type C45 particularly well represented. Owing to the poor condition of much of the material in this category, it is quite likely that products of other colour-coated industries may have been subsumed into the group or abraded OXFRS have been placed in the miscellaneous oxidised or SVWOX2 groups. Other forms present include various beakers, bowls (Young 1977, ?C48, C51, C81 and ?C89) and flasks (C8).

Colour-coated mortaria (TF9X) (Young 1977, 174–6)

Both the common forms Young types C97 and C100 are present, in production from AD 240 and AD 300 respectively.

D3:   Nene Valley Industry

Colour-coated ware (LNVCC, TF12B) (Howe *et al.* 1980)

Forms: Vessels present mainly comprised beakers.

Date: Late 2nd-4th century.

D4:   New Forest

Colour-coated ware (NFOCC/NFORS, TF12C) (Fulford 1975)

Forms: Sherds mainly from indented beakers including one with white painted decoration and one sherd with applied barbotine scales.

Date: Late 3rd/4th century.

D5:   Mancetter Hartshill

Two sherds of mortaria (MAHWH, TF9D) were recorded including a vessel with a hammer-head rim Fig. 7.14.169.

D7:   West Midlands

Shell-tempered ware (ROBSH, TF22)

Fabric: A fairly hard, mostly wheelmade ware with a smooth, soapy feel. The paste contains a moderate to common frequency of fossil shell up to 3 mm in size and sparse black shale/mudstone. Vessels are usually a pale reddish-brown to dark grey in colour. A much coarser shell-tempered fabric was also recorded (see SHEL below). It is unclear whether the two fabrics are related.

Forms: Mainly jars with triangular rims (Fig. 7.14.171), usually with characteristic rilling on the exterior surface.

The ware has a wide distribution across the Midlands from the later part of the 4th century.

Grog-tempered ware (PNKGT, TF241)

Fabric: (Booth and Green 1989, 77–84)

Forms: Large handmade storage jars.

This vessel type is being increasingly recognised over quite a wide area with a possible concentration in the south Northants./north Bucks. area. The large jars appear to be amongst the wider traded products and have been found at Uley (Leach 1993, 232), Frocester (Timby forthcoming), Barnsley Park (Webster and Smith 1982, fig. 50.76) and Gloucester (Timby unpub.). The vessels appear to date to the later 3rd/4th century.

D8:   Alice Holt, Surrey

Grey ware (ALHRE, TF 212) (Lyne and Jefferies 1979)

Form: Two sherds from a large storage jar were present in context 34, Phase 6.

Date: 4th century.

E: Unclassified. Probably local, sources unknown

Miscellaneous: A substantial quantity of unclassified grey and black wares were present. The more distinctive examples were allocated codes as described below; the remainder were subsumed into a general reduced ware (GREY) category. Unclassified oxidised wares are labelled OXID; colour-coated wares CC, whitewares (WW), limestone-tempered wares (LIME).

LOCGW1

Fabric: A hard grey ware with a dark brick-red core. A moderately fine sandy fabric with no macroscopically visible inclusions but a rough feel.

Forms: Mainly jars with bifid or simple everted rims, more rarely flanged bowls.

LOCGW2

Fabric: A hard grey sandy ware. The matrix contains sparse fine macroscopically visible, rounded, quartz grains set within a finer background scatter. Rare, black iron grains.

Forms: Everted rim jars.

LOCGW3

Fabric: A pale grey, very hard, ware characterised by a scatter of dark grey-black fine inclusion of iron, some of which have caused fine streaking to the vessel surface. The inner core is occasionally orange-brown in colour. Possibly a north Wiltshire product. A fine sandy texture with no visible grains.

Forms: Jars with triangular or everted rims. Other less common forms include beakers, flanged bowls and a flagon. The substantial part of a jar in this fabric was recovered from ctx 989 (987). One sherd from ctx 251 was decorated with impressed crescent-shaped motifs.

LOCGW4

Fabric: A black, medium sandy ware with a distinctive sandwich-effect core which is grey with red-brown margins. At x20 the matrix shows moderate to common frequency of well-sorted rounded quartz accompanied by sparse fine white specks, ?limestone.

Forms: Several vessels imitate BB1 forms, particularly everted rim jars some with burnished lattice decoration, straight-sided dishes, beaded rim dishes and flanged bowls.

LOCGW5

Fabric: A moderately hard, pale grey ware, with a white and dark grey speckled appearance. The fine textured paste contains fine sand and sparse fine, dark grey-black, iron and rounded discrete grains of oolitic limestone.

Forms: A small group which includes jars, a flanged bowl and a straight-sided dish.

LOCGW6

Fabric: A hard, medium grey sandy ware with a sparse scatter of sub-angular, white, limestone inclusions and a scatter of rounded dark grey ?clay pellets. The surfaces of some sherds have a pocked appearance where the latter have shrunk more than the surrounding clay body and fallen out.

Forms: The only two featured vessels in this fabric are a storage jar (1500) and a straight-sided dish (7).

LOCGW7

Fabric: A hard, very fine, compact grey fabric with distinctive dark grey streaking on the exterior surface. Apart from fine dark grey-black iron there are no other macroscopically visible inclusions.

Forms: Only represented by 13 sherds from closed forms, no featured sherds.

SHEL

Fabric: A slightly friable dark grey fabric with a red-brown surface. The paste contains a common frequency of fossil shell fragments up to 2–3 mm in size.

Forms: Handmade closed forms. No featured sherds.

Discussion

This is the first large quantified Roman assemblage to have been recovered from a site located between Cirencester and Gloucester. The group shows quite a short timespan in comparison to many other sites in the locality spanning just two centuries of occupation. The objective of the pottery analysis was threefold: to attempt to unravel the chronological history of the site, to look at the composition of the assemblage for any functional patterns which might give an insight into status and to place the assemblage in its regional context.

The pottery was dispersed over a large number of contexts across the site. This combined with the condition of the material and the high level of redeposition limits the feasibility of identifying functional changes across the excavated area. Because of the piecemeal nature of the archaeology and the necessity to individually phase the separate areas, it is not proposed to discuss every phase group, but to highlight the more significant assemblages. Table 7.15 summarises the quantities of pottery associated with each main area by phase to provide some insight into how the pottery was distributed across the site and how much reliance can be placed on material from individual phases. It is clear that Area A produced most material, 50% of the total site assemblage, followed by Area B (11%). Most of the other areas produced moderately small assemblages.

The main period of occupation of the site appears to lie in the later 2nd-mid/late 4th century, a period notoriously difficult to define with any great precision in the ceramic record. There are four problems with the assemblage here. First, it is dominated by products of long-lived industries, in particular SVW and DORBB1. Second, closely dateable diagnostic sherds are rare. Third, a high proportion of the contexts only contain a low number of sherds; the later dark soil accumulations produced the highest concentrations of wares. Finally, it is clear from the samian and other wares that there has been considerable redeposition.

Many of the contexts have been arranged into family groups and the contexts forming these are discussed as such. Any other useful or significant groups are briefly discussed by Area and phase. Further detailed information for specific contexts has been integrated into the stratigraphic narrative. A full breakdown can be found in the site archive. Table 7.16 summarises fabric types by phase across the site.

Area A (including Areas 2B and 2C)

Phase 1: occupation pre-dating structures

There are no cut features containing pottery allocated to this phase, the only sherds in Area A coming from 3 layers: 1139 with 10 sherds, 994 with 38 sherds and the colluvium 1140 with 55 sherds. The sherds from layer 994 are very scrappy with an average weight of just 4 g. The assemblage contained samian of late 2nd-mid 3rd-century date but the coarsewares were essentially the same as the overlying phase 2 material. Material from the colluvium was slightly better preserved at 8 g and contained several wares which potentially date to the first half of the 2nd century, such as Wiltshire grey and oxidised wares, Savernake ware and SVW. Layer 1283 above the colluvium produced seven sherds which were not closely dateable.

Phase 2: structures 1450 and 1451

Contexts associated with structure 1450 produced a total of 173 sherds (1302 g) (Table 7.17). Upcast from

Table 7.15 Summary of pottery associated with each main area by phase, Birdlip Quarry.

Area	Phase 1 No.	1 Wt.	2 No.	2 Wt.	3 No.	3 Wt.	4 No.	4 Wt.	5 No.	5 Wt.	6 No.	6 Wt.
A	179	1111	995	7709	757	13500	1369	11063	479	3532	2045	19518
B	9	72	120	851	164	1532	79	718	55	347	1288	9359
C	166	1228	30	188	1113	8305						
D	87	309	224	2098	113	843						
E	27	119	137	573	233	2084						
2A	4	5	126	2095	143	1017	185	1085				
2B	48	354	39	546	278	2587	506	4979	308	3933		
2C	0	0	97	467	560	4459						
3	156	1581	562	7813	201	1561	27	131				
5.1			18	459	1	1						
5.2			12	85	1	20						
5.3					4	27						
5.4					1	100						

the cutting of the ditch (807, 1128) produced very abraded small sherds. Pottery from stone surface 1128 produced several unfeatured sherds in fabrics probably dating to the 2nd century and very similar to the underlying 1139. Layer 1149, associated with the early building, contained sherds from a miscellaneous greyware jar which had joining sherds in the terminal of the penannular ditch 1002. There were few sherds associated with the primary fills of ditch 1067. The lowest fill 953, along with 851–2, all contained a small number of sherds, probably of mid-late 2nd-century currency. Layer 915 above 953 contained a grooved rim DORBB1 bowl indicating a date after AD 180/210. An equivalent layer 995 contained a straight-sided DORBB1 dish and a SVWOX2 tankard again suggesting a date from the later 2nd century. Layers 1050 and 929 on the other hand seem to contain very abraded fragments of OXFRS which must date after AD 240 along with a 4th-century coin perhaps indicating later disturbance (cat. 436).

Only one internal posthole, 1147, contained pottery and this included Antonine samian and a grooved rim DORBB1 bowl, which has to date after AD 180/210. Of the features at the entrance to 1450, only one context (819) contained more than ten sherds, which again included Antonine samian and a DORBB1 grooved rim bowl. This together with late 2nd/mid 3rd-century samian from pit 862 and gully 866 and a Mancetter-Hartshill mortarium from pit 820 confirm a late 2nd-/early 3rd-century *terminus post quem* for this phase.

Structure 1451 produced a broadly similar quantity of pottery although there are some subtle changes. The proportion of both DORBB1 and SVWOX2 increased (Table 7.17). The entrance postholes of the new structure contain sherds of an OXFWH mortarium, (Young 1977, type M17) dated to the period AD 240-300. Pottery from the ditch terminals (955 and 987) suggests a date of early-mid 3rd-century with DORBB1 jars (Gillam 1970, type G144), grooved rim bowls and straight-sided dishes and Gaulish black-slipped ware. The stone floor 802 of the structure produced similar

material to the gully 866=819 with a mid 2nd to mid 3rd-century range of wares.

Generally speaking, the internal layers and features yielded little pottery and most of this seems to date to the later 2nd to mid 3rd century. The presence of a later 3rd/4th-century flanged bowl may be due to later disturbance.

Other phase 2 contexts

Ditch group 1453 produced 18 sherds of SVWOX2 and DORBB1 indicative of a mid-late 3rd-century abandonment. Other features placed into Phase 2 include a cremation jar from pit 978 in a well-fragmented greyware (LOCGW3) decorated with lightly tooled wavy lines. The rim and neck zone were missing and dating cannot be precise. A second partially complete but again very fragmented vessel was recovered from pit 942. This was a DORBB1 jar decorated with an obtuse burnished line lattice indicating a date of manufacture after AD 220. The sherds were sooted and the rim missing.

A substantial quantity of material was recovered from the three layers (984, 803 and 780) which are thought to comprise midden deposits on floor 802. In total 331 sherds were recovered although the condition varies greatly. In 984, the average sherd weight was quite high, at 19.5 g, and perhaps suggestive of relatively *in situ* rubbish. This decreased to 15.5 g in 803 and to 8.5 g in 780 overlying 984, although all three layers contained essentially the same repertoire of wares. Possibly the upper layers of the midden had been exposed for some time causing degradation of material. The pottery includes mid-late Antonine samian, DORBB1 grooved rim bowls (AD 180/210–270) and Gaulish black-slipped ware suggesting perhaps a mid-later 3rd century *terminus post quem*.

The sequence of three ditches 1256 (group 698), 1258 (group 700) and 1255 all produced small collections of pottery. Ditch 1258, probably the earliest, produced three unfeatured sherds of SVWOX.

Table 7.16 Summary of fabric types by phase, Birdlip Quarry.

PHASE	1	1	1	2	2	2	3	3	3	4	4
FABRIC	No.	Wt.	Eve	No.	Wt.	Eve	No.	Wt.	Eve	No.	Wt.
IMPORTS											
SAMIAN	3	5		24	180	21	16	130	13	27	99
MOSBS				4	6					1	1
BATAM				12	1907		25	4354			
GALAM							1	80			
REGIONAL											
MALREA											
DORBBI	45	199	8	339	1659	144	286	1890	195	475	2305
OXFWH	1	3		1	20						
OXFWHMO				7	141	9	4	127	16	10	326
OXFRS				2	16		3	16		74	281
OXFRSMO										1	7
OXFPA				1	22						
OXFWS											
LNVCC							2	25		3	4
NFOCC											
MAHWH				2	75	12					
ROBSH											
PNKGT											
ALHRE											
WILTSHIRE											
SAVGT	2	14	7	13	43		3	95	5	11	365
WILBBW				3	42	10					
WILRE	21	71		4	33					12	29
WILOX	10	138		14	69	6	3	51	5	7	26
WILCC							3	22			
SOWWS/OX	10	50		8	27		16	107	100	15	103
LOCAL											
GROG											
SVWOX2	75	579	31	256	2448	90	115	922	35	179	2114
MICGW				21	112	3	28	142	11	82	484
LOCGW1				39	311	32	19	118	30	43	341
LOCGW2											
LOCGW3	1	2	5	108	1053	10	40	340	24	27	170
LOCGW4	2	9		7	23		44	152	7	11	60
LOCGW6							4	30		1	5
MISC.											
GREY	11	46	12	48	192	14	5	28	10	42	223
OXID				3	8		9	36		3	34
MORT	1	19									
CC										4	21
TOTAL	182	1135	63	916	8387	351	626	8665	451	1028	6998

Ditch 1255 contained mid-later Antonine samian, a DORBB1 early flanged rim dish and a DORBB1 jar with an incised X on the rim (*cf.* Fig. 7.13.152). Ditch 1256 had a smaller assemblage but it is essentially the same date suggesting that the ditches had fallen out of use by the end of the 3rd century. These were then followed by an accumulation of soil (1235–6 and 1253) which also contained wares of mainly 3rd-century date. Of note was another DORBB1 jar (Gillam 1970, type G144) with a graffito scratched onto the rim (*cf.* Fig. 7.13.153) from 1236.

Phase 3

Ditch group 1454 produced 102 sherds (2040 g) including much the same repertoire as seen above, for example, OXFWH mortarium (Young 1977, type M17), DORBB1 and SVWOX2. A slightly later date is intimated by the presence of a small number of DORBB1 flanged rim conical bowls of late 3rd/4th-century date. One DORBB1 jar from 738 had a scratched graffito (Fig. 7.13.150).

Ditch 1229/233 produced an assemblage amount-

4	5	5	5	6	6	6
Eve	No.	Wt.	Eve	No.	Wt.	Eve
23	15	66	3	29	207	8
	1	2		3	5	
	2	147		11	615	
				1	11	
				1	10	
173	188	886	55	597	5080	456
				1	1	
26	1	24		14	399	42
	24	153	9	248	1414	44
	6	63	5	19	395	53
				2	39	
	1	1		1	3	
	5	33		2	16	
	1	9		29	187	71
				5	265	10
				2	55	5
	2	69		14	273	11
				77	820	19
	1	3				
108	8	28		5	9	
	1	9		11	85	
55	137	1338	14	420	5338	273
40	10	49		64	605	52
16	7	36		67	752	108
				1	68	
10	20	255	13	83	1115	98
	2	4		61	422	72
	3	20		56	368	8
11	10	135		119	516	9
8	2	28		9	79	
	50	46		62	92	
5						
475	497	3404	99	2014	19244	1339

with OXFWH mortaria type M17 (Young 1977), and SVWOX2 bifid rim jars suggest these soils developed in the second half of the 3rd century. Colour-coated wares were limited to six or so sherds from 84. Of particular note were 22 large sherds of Dressel 20 oil amphora from 840.

Phase 4

Contexts allocated to Phase 4 yielded a total of 1032 sherds, of which 46% are DORBB1 and 17% SVWOX2 (by count). A marked increase of OXFRS to 7% suggests activity well into the 4th century. A single sherd of late Roman shell-tempered ware (ROBSH) dating to after *c.* AD 360 from 736 may well be intrusive.

The interior features of structure 1452 produced very little pottery with the exception of 729 which produced 99 sherds. These included Nene Valley colour-coated ware (LNVCC), and DORBB1 flanged rim conical bowls dating to the later 3rd/early 4th century.

Occupation layers from outside the structure were ceramically much richer with layers 735-6, 778 and 798 collectively producing 250 sherds. Layer 778 mainly contained mid-late 3rd-century sherds but nothing diagnostically 4th century. By contrast layer 736 with a very small average sherd weight and a coin of AD 388–95 (cat. 483) contained OXFRS, ROBSH and later DORBB1 types (nb. coin and late shell-tempered ware may be intrusive). Pit 1263, Area 2B, produced a good group of 77 sherds including a DORBB1 jar (Gillam 1970, type G145) and a OXFWH mortarium (Young 1977, type M18).

Phase 5

The general soil layer (704) associated with this phase produced 224 sherds, 1243 g including a SVWOX2 jar sherd with a scratched interior surface, presumably from use. The assemblage is again diverse with sherds ranging from the mid-late Antonine period through to the second half of the 4th century. A further reflection of its disturbed nature is indicated by the low average sherd weight of 5.5 g. Layer 815, the rubble collapse of structure 1452, produced the same range of 4th-century wares with, in addition, sherds of New Forest colour-coated ware (NFOCC) beaker and Midlands late grogged storage jar (PNKGT).

Occupation soil 1225, Area 2B, sealing pit 1263, also produced a good 3rd-century group, some 229 sherds with an average sherd weight of 12 g. Both flanged bowls and colour-coated wares were absent. A partly complete 3rd-century DORBB1 jar (1274) was associated with this layer.

Phase 6: groups 985, 713, 1460

Stake-wall structure 985 produced just seven sherds, probably 3rd-century types. The overlying stone structure 713 produced 4th-century pottery from 717 and 1224, apparently contemporary with the two 4th-century coins from the latter (cat. 439 and 464).

ing to some 97 sherds, although with a long diachronic range from the mid/late 2nd century (1230=primary fill) through to the later 3rd century for material from the upper layer (211) which includes an OXFRS flagon (Young 1977, type C8).

Soils 188, 840 and 848–9 collectively yielded 580 sherds of pottery. It is noticeable that material from 188 and 840 is better preserved with almost double the average sherd weight compared to 848–9. The presence of DORBB1 forms grooved rim bowls and flanged rim conical bowls (Gillam 1970, G145) along

Table 7.17   Birdlip Quarry, pottery from structures 1450 and 1451.

FABRIC	1450 NO	%	WT	%	EVE	%	1451 NO	%	WT	%	EVE	%
IMPORTS												
Samian	12	7	59	4.5	8	9	11	5	41	2.5	6	5
MOSBS							1	*	2	*		
BATAM	5	3	266	20.5			1	*	125	7.5		
REGIONAL IMPORTS												
DORBB1	63	36	306	23.5	26	30	93	45	514	30.5	69	56.5
LNVCC	2	1	3	*	8	9						
OXFWHMO							6	3	138	8	7	6
OXFRS	2	1	13	1			2	1	10	*		
WILTSHIRE WARES												
WMBBW							1	*	3	*		
WILOX/RE	2	1	6	*								
SAVGT	2	1	26	2			1	*	8	*		
SOWWS/OX	2	1	9	*								
LOCAL WARES												
SVWOX2	28	16	400	31	10	11.5	59	28	756	45	40	33
MICGW	3	1.5	43	3			1	*	8	*		
LOCGW1	7	4	37	3			3	1.5	7	*		
LOCGW2	1	*	9	*								
LOCGW3	12	7	38	3	5	6	9	4	28	1.5		
LOCGW4	7	4	13	1			2	1	4	*		
misc greyware	23	13	71	5.5	29	34	12	6	30	2		
misc oxidised	2	1	3	*	0	0	5	2.5	16	1	0	0
TOTAL	173	100	1302	100	86	100	207	100	1690	100	122	100

* = less than 1%

Layer 34, abutting structure 713, produced one of the larger assemblages of pottery from the site from a single context with 766 sherds, 7980 g. This predominantly dates to the 4th century with all the common late Oxfordshire mortaria types (Young 1977, types M20, M22, WC7, C97, C100), the only vessel of Alice Holt ware from the site, a storage jar and sherds of wheelmade late Roman shell-tempered ware all suggesting that the layer was still accumulating after AD 360/70. Layer 7, a general cleaning context from the same locality, also produced a large assemblage of some 719 sherds, 6966 g with a very similar composition but with 20 sherds of shelly ware, one of the highest concentrations from the site (see also Area D, Phase 3, layer 14 below).

Structure 1460 produced 25 sherds which included a mid-late 3rd century OXFWH mortarium and an OXFRS mortarium probably also of later 3rd-century date, associated with redeposited material. A late 3rd-century date might also be applicable to material associated with structure 1462 (Area A/2B).

A group of 4th-century pottery (205 sherds) was associated with soil layer 1244, Area 2B, and has an average sherd size of 15.5 g. Several colour-coated wares were present including both New Forest and OXFRS vessels.

Area B

Phase 1

Very little pottery came from deposits predating the main ditches, and none from sealed deposits that would provide reliable dating.

Phase 2

Ditch 701 only produced 10 sherds, none closely datable, and ditch 701 had no pottery. More material was recovered from the recut ditch 698, some 96 sherds suggesting abandonment by the 3rd century. Parallel ditch 699, with slightly less pottery, would appear to be contemporary.

Phases 3 and 4

The cobbled surface 307 creating the hollow way sealing ditch 699 contained sherds dating to the 3rd century. An absence of colour-coated wares might suggest it falls into the earlier part of the century, but surface 251, if part of the same episode of activity, pushes the date well into the later 3rd century with OXFRS beaker and dish sherds, a parchment ware bowl (Young 1977, P24) and a coin struck AD 270–84 (cat. 379). Accumulations 230 and 260 (Phase 4) above 307 only produced moderate quantities of pottery but with OXFRS suggesting a date after *c.* AD 250.

Phase 6

The final soil accumulations 128 and 31 both produced very large assemblages of pottery, 534 and 745 sherds respectively. Layer 128 with an average sherd weight of 9.4 g contained all the late Oxfordshire products but no late shell-tempered ware suggesting a *terminus ante quem* of AD 350/60. Layer 31 with a more fragmented assemblage (average 6 g) contained a similar repertoire and a single sherd of late shell-tempered ware. Oxfordshire industry forms include beakers and Young (1977) types C45, C89, C97, C100, WC7 and P24. The DORBB1 includes oval fish dishes, conical flanged rim bowls, straight-sided dishes and jars (Gillam 1970, G147/8). Sherds of New Forest colour-coated ware are also present.

Area C

Phase 1: oven structure 643 and associated gullies 696 and 697

The only oven structure to produce pottery was 643, with 19 sherds, probably all datable to the 2nd century, with DORBB1, SVWOX2 and local greyware. Sherds from gully 696 are probably of similar currency but again nothing very distinctive is present. Gully 697 produced a good group of 111 sherds from 228, 258 and 386, with a further 712 sherds from 18. Material from the former group suggests a late 2nd- to mid-3rd-century date whilst the latter indicates accumulation well into the mid-4th century. A sherd from a DORBB1 jar, (Gillam 1970, type G142), from 258 joins with a sherd in 18. Context 258 also produced the substantial part of a DORBB1 grooved rim dish. Ditch 1229/233, which cut the ovens, contained material dating to the 2nd/3rd centuries (see above).

Area D

Phase 1: structure 1456 (Table 7.18)

Ditch 269 contained several 2nd/3rd century wares including an unusual rouletted OXFWH candlestick base (Fig. 7.13.156). Material appears to have still been accumulating or disturbed in the later 3rd/4th century as indicated by a single DORBB1 conical flanged rim bowl from 270. The upper ditch fill 369 also contained a number of later 3rd/4th century sherds with a barbotine scale decorated OXFRS beaker (AD 270–400), flagon and mortarium.

The floor surface 268 produced part of a DORBB1 conical flanged bowl and sherds from a DORBB1 jar decorated with an oblique lattice (AD 220+) and with calcareous deposits on the interior surface from holding water.

Phase 2: structure 1457 (Table 7.18)

Ditch 271 only produced pottery finds from the upper fills which would indicate a mid to late 3rd-century date for abandonment. The two postholes, 434 and 275 both produced pottery. The material from 434 (435) includes an OXFRS flanged bowl (Young 1977, type C51) and 17 sherds of shell-tempered ware. At present the latter is difficult to identify closely. It is slightly coarser then the usual late Roman shell-tempered ware, but association of the colour-coat suggests it should also be of late Roman date. Further sherds of OXFRS (AD 240–400) were recovered from 275.

Phase 3

The spread of dark earth 14 produced 113 sherds (843 g) which included 20 sherds of ROBSH, one of the two highest concentrations on the site.

Area 3

Rectangular building

A single jar (1536) was found near the threshold stone. Unfortunately the rim and neck zone were missing but the vessel, in a North Wiltshire oxidised sandy fabric, could date from the mid/late 2nd century. Pottery from the fill of 1548 with sherds of DORBB1, SVWOX2, Savernake ware and micaceous greyware suggests a later 2nd century date. Pottery sealed by the pitched stone floor 1504 includes OXFRS and PNKGT which has to date to the second half of the 3rd century.

Pottery from the late floors 1512 and 1521 includes late 3rd/4th century colour-coated wares including a fragment of burnt OXFRS mortarium.

Corn dryer 42 (Table 7.19)

The corn dryer (33, 43, 81, 190) produced 233 sherds of pottery (1946 g). Of particular note is an almost complete DORBB1 conical flanged bowl from 190 (Fig. 7.15.192). The pottery suggests the structure was abandoned in the 4th century. The rubble backfill of the stokehole (81) contained later 2nd/3rd century samian, and a DORBB1 jar (Gillam 1970, type G142) perhaps suggesting deliberate infill with midden material reflected in a relatively low average sherd size of 8.4 g.

Wells 277, 299 and 891 (Table 7.20)

Well 277 contained a modest assemblage of 107 sherds mainly from the infill (368). This is dominated by sherds of SVWOX2 with a small amount of DORBB1 none of which need be later than the late 2nd-mid 3rd century.

Well 299 produced 209 sherds. Pottery associated with the Period 1 construction, use and collapse (335) includes one sherd of OXFRS (AD 240–400) possibly intrusive, SVWOX2 and LOCGW1. Similar sherds came from 366 whilst both 606 and 597 produced

Table 7.18   Birdlip Quarry, pottery from structures 1456 and 1457.

FABRIC	1456						1457					
	NO	%	WT	%	EVE	%	NO	%	WT	%	EVE	%
IMPORTS												
Samian	2	2	13	3								
MOSBS							1	*	2	*		
BATAM							5	3	53	3		
REGIONAL IMPORTS												
DORBB1	90	80	392	86	35	100	46	29	346	18	29	24
OXFWH	1	*	19	4								
OXFWHMO							3	2	83	4	10	8
OXFRSMO							1	*	15	*	2	1.5
OXFRS							1	*	2			
PNKGT							1	*	39	2		
ROBSH							1	*	6	*		
WILTSHIRE WARES												
WILOX/WILRE	1	*	1	*								
LOCAL WARES												
SVWOX	15	13	22	5			60	38	990	52	41	34
MICGW							4	2.5	87	4.5	29	24
LOCGW2							1	*	28	1.5		
LOCGW3	2	2	6	1			5	3	55	3	9	8
LOCGW4							5	3	45	2		
SHEL							17	10.5	117	6		
misc greyware							8	5	33	2		
misc oxidised	1	*	4	*								
TOTAL	112	100	457	100	35	100	159	100	1901	100	120	100

* = less than 1%

sherds of mid-late Antonine samian and Dressel 20 amphora. Apart from the single OXFRS none of the material need be later than AD 200/250. More material recovered from the Period 2 contexts represents rubbish accumulation in the weathering cone. This includes a number of typical 4th-century wares, notably colour-coats OXFRS, LNVCC, late DORBB1 forms such as G146 and late Roman shell-tempered ware, alongside sherds of later 2nd–3rd century date.

Well 891, again divided into two periods, produced a total of 366 sherds. A total of 242 sherds of pottery was recovered from the lower fills 1047, 895–7 and 880. The presence of OXFRS from 880 and a DORBB1 jar G143 suggests a date in the second half of the 3rd century. The material from the other contexts has more of an early to mid 3rd-century flavour with DORBB1 jars G133, G138, straight-sided dishes and grooved rim bowls. A balance might suggest AD 260/80. The upper fills produced less material but with OXFWH mortaria (Young 1977, type M17), OXFRS (type C45) and DORBB1 flanged rim conical bowls indicates a date in the later 3rd/early 4th century.

Boundary ditches

The three main boundary ditches associated with Area 3, namely 1680 Phase 1, 1681 Phase 2 and 1682

Phase 3, all produced pottery although the last-named only contained three sherds. The wares from 1680 and 1681 are summarised in Table 7.21. Ditch 1680, with a total of 64 sherds, included mid-late samian and 3rd century DORBB1. Ditch 1681 also with 64 sherds, but in a much better state of preservation, produced a number of 4th-century forms, for example a jar G147, OXFWH mortarium M22, OXFRS forms C51, C45 and shell-tempered ware (SHEL). The material from 1682 is redeposited, the dating deriving from the coins.

The Phase 1 ditches, group 690, gully 65 did not produce enough pottery to suggest a date other than Roman. Ditch group 683 (Table 7.21), Phase 1/2, yielded a total of 182 sherds which included several DORBB1 jars of G142–3 indicating a 3rd-century date. Colour-coated wares were absent. Of the phase, 2 ditches, group 689 with 96 sherds includes later 3rd/4th century OXFRS beakers, DORBB1 flanged rim conical bowls and PNKGT alongside 4th-century coins. An OXFWH mortarium (Young 1977, type M13) (?AD 180–240) was also present. Group 688 with 72 sherds contained several SAVGT sherds but a later Roman date is indicated by the presence of OXFRS mortaria and DORBB1 flanged rim conical bowl. Approximately two-thirds of a straight-sided DORBB1 dish with a slightly beaded rim marked with three small notches came from 73 (Fig. 7.15.191).

Table 7.19   Birdlip Quarry, pottery from corn dryer and associated boundary ditches.

Fabric	No	No%	WT	WT%	EVE	EVE%
IMPORT						
Samian	4	1	52	1.5		
REGIONAL IMPORTS						
DORBB1	226	69	1690	56	164	86
WILTSHIRE WARES						
WMBBW	13	4	32	1		
SOWOX	2	*	5	*		
LOCAL WARES						
SVWOX2	40	12	970	32	7	3.5
MICGW	5	1.5	22	*		
LOCGW3	16	5	128	4	19	10
LOCGW4	10	3	54	2		
MISCELLANEOUS						
Oxidised	5	1.5	18	*		
Reduced	6	2	43	1.5		
TOTAL	327	100	3014	100	190	100

Of the gullies, only 85 and 684 produced viable collections of pottery both of which indicate a late 3rd/4th-century date of abandonment.

The Birdlip Quarry pottery in its regional context

To summarise, the Birdlip pottery assemblage dates from around the middle of the 2nd century through to the later 4th century. Much of the earlier material appears as redeposited sherds in later contexts. Apart from the samian, earlier wares include products of the Wiltshire industries, in particular fabrics SAVGT, WILRE, WILOX and WMBBW, all of which were current in the 2nd century. The coarseware assemblage throughout is dominated by products of the Severn Valley industry and vessels from the Dorset black burnished industry. In the later 3rd–4th centuries samian tablewares are replaced by products of the large regional colour-coated industries, mainly Oxfordshire, but also a few New Forest and Nene Valley beakers. In the later 4th century, sherds of late Roman shell-tempered ware appear. There is no ceramic evidence to suggest the site continued beyond the later 4th century.

A number of Roman sites in the immediate locality that have recently been published or analysed are useful for comparison with this site. Birdlip Quarry is of particular interest with regard to ceramics as it lies on top of the Cotswold ridge between Cirencester and Gloucester. In the past the topographic divide between these two important Roman towns has been regarded as something of a ceramic watershed in that the character of the assemblages from the two centres, although similar in general composition, shows very different biases towards certain fabrics. It has been assumed that this is a simple product of market forces and the added difficulties of transporting goods up and down the escarpment. Birdlip however, demonstrates that this might not have been the case.

In addition, there has been recent work on three other large assemblages from the general locality and these can be compared with the Birdlip group (Table 7.22). These include Uley, the site of a Roman temple (Leach 1993); Frocester, a Roman villa with earlier settlement (Timby forthcoming), and Kingscote, a villa-like house with a mosaic and a wall painting set within what is provisionally interpreted as a villa estate (Timby 1998a). The same table includes data from an urban site in Gloucester. The site selected is Berkeley Street (site code 77/69) which has one of the largest assemblages from within the colonia and is one of the few sites where the entire Roman sequence has been excavated. Although the group is useful in terms of demonstrating a typical range from Gloucester, it is also unfortunately heavily biased by the presence of a pottery kiln on the site, whose concomitant debris dominates the pottery totals. To date there are no fully quantified assemblages available from Cirencester but work by Nicholas Cooper (1998) on Admiral's Walk illustrates the pattern of supply to the town.

Chronologically, Kingscote is closest to Birdlip in that occupation from the excavated site appears to date back to the early 2nd century. Both Uley and Frocester have pre-Roman occupation. All three rural sites were occupied in the 3rd and 4th centuries.

Urban centres such as Gloucester, and, to a much lesser extent, Cirencester, show more diverse assemblages compared to the rural sites, in that both were receiving a wider range of fineware imports, mortaria and amphorae. Samian ware at Gloucester accounted

Table 7.20 Birdlip Quarry, pottery from wells 277, 299 and 891.

FABRIC	Well 277 No.	%	Wt.	%	Eve	%	Well 299 No.	%	Wt.	%	Eve	%	Well 891 No.	%	Wt.	%	Eve	%
IMPORTS																		
samian							18	8.5	62	4			2	0.5	33	1		
BATAM	3	3	1667	38			6	3	280	17			1	*	23	0.5		
GALAM							10	5	9	0.5								
REGIONAL IMPORTS																		
DORBBI	7	6	40	1	15	12	80	38	549	33	77	55	179	49	1294	30.5	220	67
OXFRS							2	1	13	0.5			8	2	48	1	17	5
OXFRS MO													2	0.5	26	0.5		
OXFWH							2	1	13	0.5			1	*	3	*		
LNVCC							1	0.5	7	*								
ROBSH							1	0.5	15	1								
WILTSHIRE WARES																		
WMBBW							1	0.5	17	1			1	*	87	2	19	6
SAVGT													3	1	221	5	8	2
WILOX											1	*	5					
SWOX							2	1	2	*			10	3	84	2		
LOCAL WARES																		
SVWOX	95	89	2649	60	103	83	47	22.5	424	26	31	22	75	20	1386	33.5	39	12
micaceous gyware	2	2	39	1	6	5							6	1.5	106	2.5		
LOCGW1							15	7	128	8	32	23						
LOCGW2							1	0.5	6	*								
LOCGW3							11	5	54	3			36	10	339	8	23	7
LOCGW4							1	0.5	18	1			19	5	247	6	3	1
LOCGW7													10	3	160	4		
MISC.																		
GREY							10	5	45	3			12	3	62	1.5		
OXID							1	0.5	4	*								
TOTAL	107	100	4395	100	124	100	209	100	1646	100	140	100	366	100	4124	100	329	100

Table 7.21 Birdlip Quarry, total quantities of individual fabrics from ditches 1680, 1681, 683, 684, 688, 689 and 85.

DITCHES FABRIC	1680 No.	Wt.	Eve	1681 No.	Wt.	Eve	683 No.	Wt.	Eve	684 No.	Wt.	Eve	688 No.	Wt.	Eve	689 No.	Wt.	Eve	85 No.	Wt.	Eve
IMPORT																					
SAMIAN	1	10					1	1								1	4		1	4	
BATAM	2	40		1	70	5	2	293					1	370		5	227		4	521	22
REGIONAL																					
DORBBI	33	91	22	23	254	37	116	447	64	6	18		44	604	77	33	192	12	18	192	17
OXFWHMO				1	69	5	1	7	5	14	194	12				1	84	10			
OXFRS	1	5		3	67	5				7	15		4	10		10	24	1	10	36	
OXFRSMO													4	53	8						
PNKGT				2	39											1	20				
WILTSHIRE																					
SAVGT							1	29					12	144		5	58				
WILRE				2	15		2	8													
WILOX							2	2													
SOWWS										1	11										
LOCAL																					
SVWOX2	19	211	14	22	433	18	45	170	5				3	14		33	376	16	11	224	15
LOCGW1																2	20				
LOCGW3	3	98		5	75	20	3	18								5	30	12	1	44	
LOCGW4							6	18		1	1										
LOCGW7	3	58																			
MISC.																					
GREY							1	4		3	4		4	10					5	64	10
OXID	2	22		1	10		1	2		8	27										
CC							1	5													
SHEL				4	32																
TOTAL	64	535	36	64	1064	90	182	1004	74	40	270	12	72	1205	85	96	1035	51	50	1085	64

Table 7.22   Comparison of pottery fabrics from Birdlip Quarry, Kingscote, Uley, Gloucester and Frocester.

Fabrics	Birdlip		Kingscote		Uley		Gloucester[1]		Frocester	
	% WT	% EVE	% WT	% EVE	% WT	% EVE	% WT	% EVE	% WT	% EVE
pre-Roman native ware	np	np	np	np	13.8	8	1	*	17.6	9.4
IMPORTS										
Samian	2	3	1.2	2.4	*	5	6	10	*	1.8
Cologne colour-coat	np	np	*	*	np	np	*	*	np	np
Gaulish black-slipped ware	*	*	*	*	*	*	*	*	*	*
amphora (Dressel 20)	10	*	8.2	*	1	*	9.5	10	4.6	*
amphora (other)	*	*	*	*	np	np	7	*	*	*
mortaria (imported)	np	np	np	np	np	np	6	1.5	np	np
WILTSHIRE WARES										
wm black-burnished (201)	*	*	4.7	7.8	2	2.8	*	*	1.4	3.6
Savernake	3.5	*	4.7	*	5.6	1.5	*	*	5	1.4
Wilts oxid/reduc (231/231)	2	1.5	1.6	2.5	ni	ni	*	*	*	*
SW sandy/slipped (15/15a)	*	4	2.3	6	5.5	5.5	*	*	*	*
SW colour-coated ware	*	*	*	*	1.5	5	*	*	*	*
REGIONAL IMPORTS										
Dorset BB1	29	43	16.8	24.5	13.3	15	10	13.5	15	23
late shelly ware (22)	*	*	*	*	2	3.5	*	*	*	*
late grogged ware (241)	*	*	*	*	*	*	np	np	*	*
Nene Valley colour-coats	*	*	*	*	*	*	*	*	*	*
mortaria (various)	*	*	*	*	ni	ni	1	*	*	*
OXFORDSHIRE WARES										
whiteware incl mortaria	2	8	1.4	1	1	*	1	1	*	*
colour-coats incl mortaria	5	4	4.3	6.2	4.1	6.5	*	1	1.8	3
white-slipped mortaria	*	*	*	*	ni	ni	*	*	*	*
parchment ware	*	*	*	*	ni	ni	*	*	*	*
LOCAL WARES										
micaceous greyware (5)	2	2	35.6	24.5	32.8	32	1	*	21.8	26.5
Severn Valley wares	30	21	9.8	6.3	14.9	13.5	19.5	10.5	26.9	26.9
Gloucester kiln wares	np	np	np	np	np	np	30	41	np	np
OTHER WARES	9	15	4.5	12	0	0	5	6.5	1	1
SUB/POST ROMAN WARES	np	np	np	np	*	*	np	np	*	*
TOTAL EVES/WEIGHT	150967	10426	497406	46865	467000	ni	251 357	43669	479920	40186

Notes: The figures for Uley have been reworked from the published piecharts (Leach 1993, fig. 163); those for Frocester are based on Timby (forthcoming); Gloucester figures are based on assemblage from Berkeley Street (site code 77/69) stratified Roman levels only.

* = less than one percent; ni = not identified; np = not present

for 6% by weight, 10% by count compared to the 3% at Birdlip. Leaving aside the Gloucester kiln wares which account for 30% by weight of the Berkeley Street group, the commonest wares by far are Severn Valley ware followed by Dressel 20 amphorae and Dorset black burnished ware. There are nearly twice as many SVWOXs by weight reflecting the availability of these wares from the Severn Plain. Severn Valley wares are by contrast relatively rare at Cirencester where the assemblages tend to be dominated by products of the Wiltshire industries and DORBB1. The dominance of SVWOX at Birdlip therefore implies that it was drawing a considerable part of its pottery from the west. In terms of DORBB1, Birdlip would appear to be more comparable with Cirencester where in the later Roman period DORBB1 tended to dominate most assemblages. For example, in a typical early 3rd-century group (Admiral's Walk), it accounted for 25% by eve, whereas in mid-late 3rd- and early-mid 4th-century groups it accounted for between 41–5%, and in the later 4th century it dropped away to 25–8% (data taken from Cooper 1998). A recent survey by Allen and Fulford (1996) highlighted the Fosse Way as one route by which DORBB1 was distributed. It would seem that Cirencester may well have been drawing its supplies directly from the Poole harbour region rather than perhaps via any coastal routes through Gloucester.

Turning to the three 'rural' sites, one significant difference between Birdlip and Kingscote on the one hand and Uley and Frocester on the other is the almost complete absence of pre-Roman native ware reflecting a probable absence of any 1st-century occupation at the former two localities. The level of imported finewares is very similar at all the sites, the highest coming from Uley (5% by eve). Birdlip has a slightly higher proportion of amphora closely followed by Kingscote. Differences start to emerge for the Wiltshire products which are better represented at Kingscote and Uley, with both Frocester and Birdlip falling into the Gloucester pattern. Although DORBB1 is well represented at all the sites it does not reach the proportions seen at Birdlip. One of the greatest differences is seen in the proportions of SVWOX and micaceous greywares (TF5). Severn Valley wares form the commonest fabric type at Frocester accounting for some 27%, very close to the pattern at Birdlip. The proportions are considerably less at Kingscote and Uley where the commonest single fabric is micaceous greyware accounting for 35.6% and 32.8% by sherd count and weight respectively. Micaceous greyware is also well represented at Frocester where it is the second commonest ware at 22% (weight). At Birdlip, however, it only represents 2% of the total assemblage, and it is similarly poorly represented at both Gloucester and Cirencester. This strongly supports a southern source for this particular micaceous greyware fabric and a production centre in the general locality of Kingscote is a strong possibility. This is reinforced by an apparent absence of the ware from sites in the south Cotswolds / Avon area. The micaceous greyware found in Gloucester and other sites north of the Severn, particularly in the Forest of Dean / Chepstow area, although visually very similar, often appears slightly later in the 3rd–4th centuries, and may represent a separate industry.

Another site which shares many common features with Birdlip is Brockworth, situated in the Severn Valley between Gloucester and the Cotswold escarpment (Rawes 1981). The site, mainly comprising ditched paddocks associated with two roundhouses, produced a good assemblage of pottery. Although not quantified in detail this was dominated by sherds of SVWOX and DORBB1, with samian and products of the Oxfordshire industry also well in evidence.

In conclusion, therefore, it would appear that although the Birdlip Quarry assemblage shares features in common with Cirencester to the south-east and Gloucester to the north-west, it appears to be most similar to sites on the Severn Plain, reflected by the popularity of SVWOX2 at the site. Although the percentage of samian appears low, it is consistent with that from the other rural sites which superficially might appear to represent higher status establishments. It should be noted, however, that Birdlip Quarry was only part of what is clearly a much larger site and there may well be a higher status element elsewhere in the complex. The low proportion of large storage jars is also surprising as these tend to be better represented on rural sites; Frocester for example, has

a large number. Although the level of other Roman finewares also appears to be consistent across all these sites, the proportion of drinking vessels at Birdlip is markedly low compared with Kingscote, for example. The reason for this is not clear especially since the presence of Gallic amphora might be taken to indicate some wine consumption. Is a low number of drinking vessels and flagons, for example, a reflection of a lower status establishment?

The samian perhaps mitigates against this and one possibility is that the assemblage at Birdlip, much of which comprises midden material, partially derives from a higher status establishment in the immediate locality, the excavated structures being peripheral to the wider picture. It has been observed elsewhere that surface debris becomes much more frequent in the 3rd century with midden areas adjacent to buildings (Plouviez 1995, 73). Alternatively, this assemblage might be typical of any modest Roman settlement in the Cotswolds, the composition reflecting availability of wares and market forces rather than status. Assessment against other finds from the site may help clarify this

Catalogue of illustrated pottery *(Figs 7.13–15)*
Drawn by Lesley Collett

Period 1, Area A

Phase 1

145 Base from an oxidised sandy ware beaker, with circular hole drilled through. Fabric WILOX. Layer 1140.

Phase 2

146 Fine grey ware necked jar, fabric LOCGW. Ditch 1450, segment 1003, fill 1002.

147 Base from a DORBB1 jar with an X incised into the base. Ditch 1451, segment 955, fill 954.

148 SVWOX2 tankard with hole, ?accidental, through base. Ditch 1451, segment 987, fill 986.

Phase 3

149 DORBB1 flanged rim conical bowl. Ditch 1454, segment 737, fill 738.

150 DORBB1 jar with oblique burnished line lattice decoration. Three parallel, vertical lines have been incised on upper body after firing. Ditch 1453, segment 737, fill 738.

Period 1, Area 2C

Phase 2

151 DORBB1 flanged rim bowl. Ditch 1255, fill 1250.

152 DORBB1 jar with incised cross on inner rim face. Ditch 1255, fill 1250.

153 DORBB1 jar with oblique lattice decoration. Edge of incised graffito on inner rim face. Layer 1236.

Period 1, Area C

Phase 1

154 DORBB1 jar with oblique lattice decoration. Ditch 697, segment 259, fill 258. Joining sherd in layer 18.

155 DORBB1 flanged rim bowl. Ditch 697, segment 259, fill 258.

Period 1, Area D

Phase 1

156 Whiteware base with square rouletted decoration, possibly a candlestick. Fabric OXFWH. Ditch 697, fill 270.

Period 1, Area E

157 Disc-necked flagon. Fabric SOWWS. Ditch 322, fill 323.

Period 2, Area A and 2B

Phase 3

158 Disc-necked flagon. Fabric SOWRB. Area A, layer 849.

159 Fine greyware jar. Fabric LOCGW. Area A, layer 849.

160 Wheelmade black jar. Fabric SAVGT. Area A, layer 849.

161 Foot or handle. Fabric WILOX. Area A, layer 731.

Phase 3–4

162 Disc-necked flagon. Fabric SOWWS. Area 2B, layer 1277.

Phase 4

163 Bowl-shaped object with a notched rim. Soft, red-orange tile-like fabric. Area A, feature 755, fill 1022.

Phase 5

164 Wide-mouthed jar. SVWOX2. Area 2B, layer 1225.

165 Large hook-rimmed jar. SVWOX2. Area 2B, layer 1225.

166 Large hook-rimmed jar. SVWOX2. Area 2B, layer 1225.

167 Tankard. SVWOX2. Area 2B, layer 1225.

168 Everted rim jar. Fabric WILRE. Area 2B, ditch 1252, fill 1264.

Phase 6

169 Mancetter-Hartshill hammer-head mortarium,

with a slightly worn interior surface (MAHWH). Area A, wall 1460, segment 904, fill 905.

170 Base sherd from a straight-sided DORBB1 dish, with an incised X on the upper surface. Area A, layer 34.

171 Late shelly ware jar. Fabric ROBSH. Area A, layer 53.

Period 2, Area B

Phase 4

172 Large storage jar. Midlands grog-tempered ware PNKGT. Layer 260.

173 Flanged hemispherical bowl. SVWOX2. Layer 260.

Phase 6

174 Oxfordshire parchment ware (OXFPA) globular bowl or jar with traces of red paint (Young 1977, type P34), layer 128.

175 Everted rim jar. LOCGW. Layer 128.

176 Flanged rim bowl. LOCGW. Layer 128.

177 Straight-sided dish. MICGW. Layer 128.

178 Jar. SVWOX2. Layer 128.

179 Bifid rim jar. SVWOX2. Layer 128.

180 Wide-mouthed jar. SVWOX2. Layer 128.

181 Polygonal bowl-shaped object with stabbed dot decoration on the upper surface. Soft, orange tile-like fabric. Layer 250.

Period 2, Area C

Phase 3

182 Flanged, moulded rim jar. SVWOX2. Layer 18.

183 Flat-rimmed bowl. SVWOX2. Layer 18.

184 Wide-mouthed jar. SVWOX2. Layer 18.

Period 2, Area D

Phase 2

185 Rimsherd from an OXFRS cup/small bowl. Posthole 275, fill 411.

Period 2, Area 3

Phase 2

186 DORBB1 jar. Ditch 1502, fill 1501.

187 DORBB1 jar with oblique burnished lattice. Ditch 1502, fill 1501.

188 Tankard. SVWOX2. Ditch 1502, fill 1501.

189 Greyware jar. LOCGW. Ditch 1502, fill 1501.

Period 2, Area 2A

Phase 2

190 Base from a DORBB1 jar with an incised X on the base. Ditch 1330, fill 1328.

Other features

191 DORBB1 straight-sided dish with slight beading of the rim. Three equidistant small knicks have been incised into the rim edge after firing. Ditch 688, segment 67, fill 73.

192 DORBB1 flanged rim bowl with intersecting burnished line arc decoration. Corn dryer 44, fill 190.

193 DORBB1 Flat-rimmed bowl. Wheelmade black burnished ware, WMBBW. Well 891, fill 896.

194 DORBB1 straight-sided dish with a burnished wavy line. Well 891, fill 896.

195 DORBB1 straight-sided dish with beaded rim and intersecting arc decoration. Well 891, fill 896.

196 DORBB1 grooved rim bowl with intersecting arc decoration. Well 891, fill 896.

197 DORBB1 jar. Well 891, fill 896.

Discussion of the Iron Age and Roman pottery

Although pottery is one of the most abundant finds from sites dating to the Iron Age and early Roman periods in Gloucestershire, many of them were dug some years ago, for example, Bagendon (Clifford 1961), Salmonsbury (Dunning 1976) and Shenberrow (Fell 1961a). Others remain unpublished, for example the farmstead at Winson, the lower lying settlements at Claydon Pike and Coppice Corner, Kingsholm, Glos., and Beckford, Hereford and Worcester, or comprise moderately small groups such as those from Uley Bury and Norbury (Saville 1983a). Work on some of the more recently investigated sites is still in progress, for example Naunton (Timby in prep. b); Guiting Power (Marshall 1995) and Sherbourne House, Lechlade (Timby in prep. c.). The only sites to be published where large-scale modern excavations have taken place are Crickley Hill (Dixon 1994) and Birdlip Bypass, Cowley (Parry 1998). Other more recent smaller scale excavations with relevant pottery groups include Ditches, North Cerney (Trow 1988) and Roughground Farm, Lechlade (Darvill *et al.* 1986; Allen *et al.* 1993).

In the case of the Roadscheme, a number of similarly dated small assemblages were recovered from other sites along the road corridor. Although not warranting full publication, owing to its limited nature or poor preservation, this material may prove of greater significance in the future. These sites are therefore noted below.

Early-middle Iron Age

The earliest Iron Age assemblages recovered are probably those from Ermin Farm and Preston Enclosure with further odd sherds from other sites. Of note are several mainly residual early Iron Age sherds from Trinity Farm. Here, a notched rim in limestone-tempered ware (fabric L1) was associated with sherds in fabric L2 and H2. Two multiple-line incised decorated sherds also of early Iron Age date were recovered from Court Farm.

Most known assemblages of early Iron Age date from Gloucestershire come from the numerous hillforts to be found on the Cotswold ridge, such as Crickley Hill (Elsdon 1994), Burhill (Marshall 1989) and Shenberrow (Fell 1961a). Non-hillfort settlements are less common and few have been investigated. Amongst these are Ireley Farm, Stanway and Sandy Lane, Cheltenham (Saville 1984b, 154), and of particular note the extensive early and middle Iron Age occupation in and around Lechlade (Darvill *et al.* 1986; Allen *et al.* 1993; Bateman 1997). The absence of decorated wares, both of the finger-tipped and incised line varieties from both Ermin Farm and Preston Enclosure analogous with those from Lechlade, Crickley Hill or Sandy Lane (Purnell and Webb 1950), and an almost complete absence of carinated vessels would indicate that both the sites are later in date belonging to the early-middle Iron Age phase.

A comparison of the material from Ermin Farm and Preston Enclosure shows similarities in terms of fabric types but significant differences in terms of the proportions of the different wares present (Table 7.23). This mainly manifests itself in the percentage of limestone-tempered wares which is much lower at Ermin Farm being compensated for by a higher percentage of sandy wares. Coarse shelly wares are also slightly more common. Most of the sandy sherds belong to a vessel in the saucepan-pot tradition with curvilinear decoration that is likely to be of middle Iron Age date. The lack of any parallel for such a vessel in this region would strongly suggest it is imported. The moderately high proportion of shelly ware might imply a longer period of use at Ermin Farm, as such wares are common in the later Bronze and early Iron Ages. Alternatively the very different types of settlement represented by the two sites may be similarly manifested in the pottery assemblage.

Assemblages belonging to the middle Iron Age are better represented in Gloucestershire with significant groups known from the hillforts at Salmonsbury (Dunning 1976) and Uley Bury (Saville and Ellison 1983), the upland sites at Guiting Power (Saville 1979b), Birdlip Bypass (Parry 1998) and Huntsman Quarry, Naunton (Timby in prep. b) and the lowland domestic settlements at Claydon Pike in the Thames Valley and Frocester (Price forthcoming) and Eastington, near Stroud (Gardiner 1932) in the Severn Valley. Again many of the groups are small, inadequately published or unpublished. The large prehistoric assemblage recently excavated from Naunton spanned the later Bronze Age through to the middle Iron Age, and has a similar range of material to the Preston sites, with a high proportion of Jurassic limestone-tempered fabrics (64%) in the later period (Table 7.23). Shelly wares, well-represented at 25%, have been confirmed by radiocarbon dating to extend back into the 8th century BC (Foster pers. comm.).

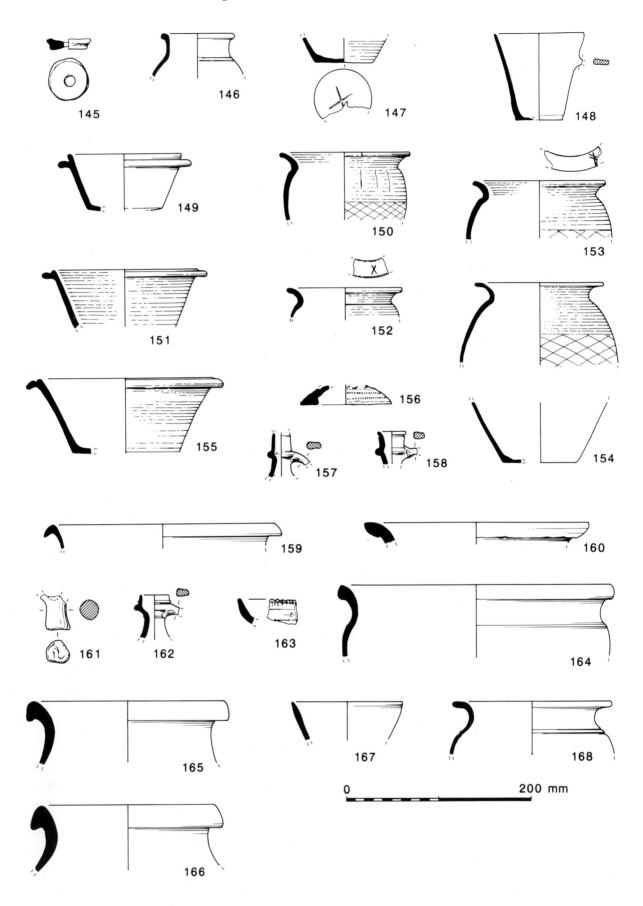

Figure 7.13   Pottery from Birdlip Quarry.

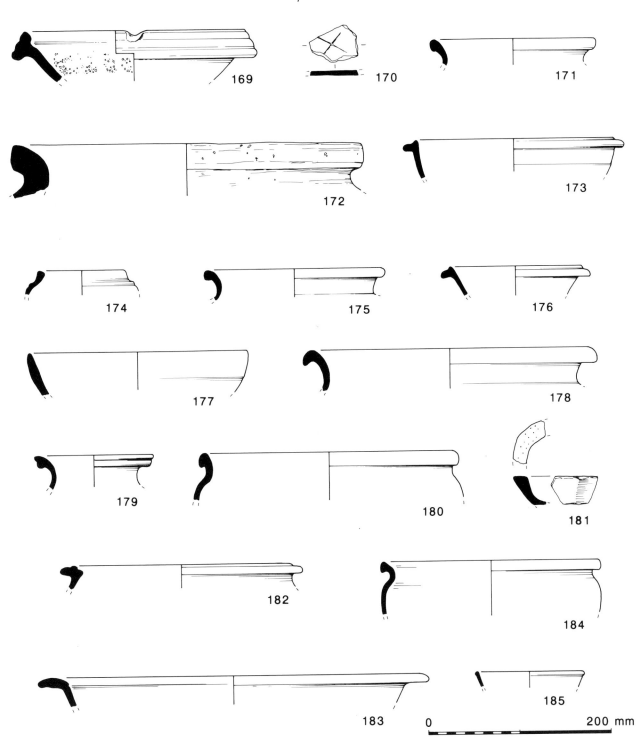

Figure 7.14   Pottery from Birdlip Quarry.

The assemblage from Highgate House would also appear to belong to the middle Iron Age but unlike the Preston sites, the fabric types appear to indicate that occupation may extend into the later Iron Age period (3rd–1st century BC). A comparison of the fabric range (Table 7.23) shows a much lower percentage of fossil shell-tempered ware, and a significant percentage of Jurassic limestone-tempered wares, but the commonest fabric is Malvernian limestone-tempered ware

accounting for 59% of the group. This contrasts with the recently published middle Iron Age assemblage from Birdlip which was mainly composed of wares of Jurassic limestone type with only 10% (by weight) of Malvernian limestone origin and no other types (Parry 1998, 74). This might point to a slightly later date of occupation at Highgate House.

Morris (1996), in reassessing pottery from western Britain, suggested that during the early Iron Age, most

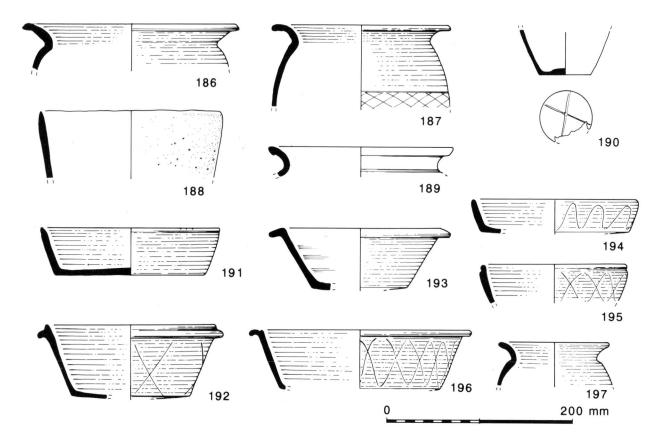

Figure 7.15 Pottery from Birdlip Quarry.

pottery tended to be made from clays local to the sites. Such a conclusion would be supported by the mainly limestone and fossil shell-tempered pottery from Preston, which is located on cornbrash, a hard fossiliferous limestone (Torrens 1982, 77). Detailed petrological analysis, however, would be required to determine whether the 'Jurassic limestone-tempered' group of wares can be provenanced more specifically. The group is a relatively large one, and occurs across quite a wide area of the Cotswolds. The presence of Malvernian rock-tempered ware dating to the mid-later Bronze Age from sites both in Herefordshire and a middle-late Bronze Age metalworking site at Sandy Lane, Cheltenham (Timby 1999), might indicate exchange/trade networks in operation at quite an early date and thus by implication the presence of semi-specialist potters. The Malvernian wares have the advantage in that the fabrics are particularly distinctive (*cf.* Peacock 1968). The more ubiquitous Jurassic limestone/fossil shell-tempered wares are less easy to provenance to a specific source.

Although comparative data is sparse, the assemblage from The Loders, Lechlade appears to have a particularly high proportion of finewares (Hingley 1986), suggesting marked differences in the assemblages. This is reinforced by the pottery recovered from Salmonsbury, which contains a complement of material unparalleled elsewhere in the region (Dunning 1976).

In the middle Iron Age, regionally distributed pottery became increasingly common, notably products from the Malvern region. These wares, first highlighted by Peacock (1968), have been taken to be products of semi-specialist manufacture. Around this time, briquetage (salt containers) from Droitwich begin to appear in assemblages, indicating the existence of exchange/trade networks, the two commodities presumably using the same routes. Briquetage has been found at a number of sites in the area, notably Naunton (Morris forthcoming), Salmonsbury, Oxenton, Lechlade, Uley Bury (Morris archive reports 1981–2, cited in Saville 1984b, 157) and Thornhill Farm (Timby in prep. a). The only site from the road scheme to produce sherds of Malvernian group A pottery was Highgate House which was also the only site to produce a piece of briquetage. No sites produced any of the classic stamped wares highlighted by Peacock (1968), although a sherd with tooled lines from Highgate House may belong to his B1 group.

Later Iron Age/early Roman

Three sites date to the later Iron Age-early Roman period; Duntisbourne Grove, Middle Duntisbourne and Court Farm. Street Farm produced a very small group of *c.* 10 sherds of 1st-century AD date including fabrics MALVL1, MALVRA and SVWEA.

Table 7.24 compares the individual fabrics from

Table 7.23   Comparison of sites with later prehistoric pottery expressed as a percentage by sherd number and weight of total later prehistoric assemblage.

FABRIC	Preston Enclosure		Ermin Farm		Highgate House		Court Farm		Middle Duntisbourne		Duntisbourne Grove		Naunton	
	no	wt	no	wt	No	wt	no	wt	No	wt	no	Wt	no	wt
Shell	14.7	15	24	48.5	3	2.4	2	7	1.6	2.5	0.1	0.25	25.4	32
Limestone	65.0	78.6	18.6	22.4	33.2	49	56	58.5	3	10.8	4.3	7.8	64.3	63.6
Sand	0.9	0.4	40	26.2	0.7	1.5	2.8	1.2					8.7	0.7
Unclass	19.4	5.9	17	3	1	0.6	12	2.8	1.6	1	10.8	5.1	5.9	0.9
MALVL1					59	41	7	5.1	93.7	85.6	83.6	83.3	1.3	0.8
MALVREA					1.4	1.2							0.4	0.5
Calcite	0.2	0.15					0.7	0.4					0.3	0.25
Grog					1.4	4.0	15.6	21.5			1.2	3.6	1.5	1.1
Total LP sherds	448	1959	236	1391	286	1108	141	685	127	471	750	2367	3058	36976
ROMAN	23	21			7	24	306	1851	640	6136	1060	7427	3207	26624
TOTAL	471	1980	236	1391	293	1132	447	2536	767	6607	1810	9794	6265	63600

these three sites. Court Farm has quite a different fabric composition compared with the Duntisbournes. Firstly, occupation appears to extend back into the middle Iron Age whereas the Duntisbourne sites only appear in the later part of the late Iron Age. Secondly, Court Farm was not receiving the same range of pre-conquest imports, the main imports being post-conquest samian and Dressel 20 amphora. The range of late Iron Age native wares seen at Middle Duntisbourne and Duntisbourne Grove are only poorly represented at Court Farm which may have been temporarily abandoned in the early 1st century AD or shifted in focus. A new phase of activity during the Flavian period is characterised by a more 'Romanised' assemblage. Wheelmade wares such as WMBBW and various grey and oxidised wares probably from the north Wiltshire industries are present. Unlike Middle Duntisbourne and Duntisbourne Grove the site was not abandoned in the pre-Flavian period but continued into the early 2nd century.

Material dating to the later Iron Age/early Roman period is rare in the county and for this reason defining the later Iron Age phase on ceramic grounds is extremely problematic. These groups considerably augment the database but again do not offer any independent dating evidence for the adduced ceramic sequence. Only three reasonably large groups of pottery dating to the later Iron Age and early Roman periods have been published from Gloucestershire: Salmonsbury (Dunning 1976), Bagendon (Fell 1961b) and Ditches (Trow 1988). Several smaller groups have been noted, for example, Roughground Farm, Lechlade (Green and Booth 1993) and Duntisbourne Abbots (Fell 1964) and Birdlip Bypass, Cowley (Parry 1998). To this material can be added Frocester Court on the Severn Plain (Timby forthcoming), Abbeydale and Saintbridge on the outskirts of Gloucester (Timby unpub. b), Thornhill Farm, near Fairford (Timby in prep), Wycomb, and Coppice Corner, Kingsholm, Gloucester (Timby unpub. b) and Claydon Pike.

The pottery from both Bagendon and Salmonsbury, although quite different in certain respects, includes a significant number of necked bowls and carinated, cordoned bowls in wheel-turned fabrics. Conventional dating would place such pottery in the second quarter of the 1st century AD (Saville 1984b, 159) although some authorities would prefer to see local wheelmade pottery as a post-conquest phenomenon in the west linked with the arrival of the Roman army (Rigby 1982, 199). At Ashville, near Abingdon similar 'Belgic' wheelmade wares from the Period 3 ditches were considered to date from the late 1st century BC (De Roche 1978, 73). A recent reappraisal of the associated finewares from these ditches suggests that this dating may be a little early and that the ditches fell out of use in the pre- or early Flavian periods (Timby, Booth and Allen 1997). The date of the appearance of wheelthrown pottery in the region is thus still not certain, although the fact that both handmade and wheelthrown vessels occur in the Severn Valley ware tradition implies an indigenous development dating to around the mid 1st century AD. A similar problem exists with the presence of Savernake ware which occurs on several of the sites and accounts for a significant percentage of the Bagendon assemblage. This was originally dated by Clifford (1961b) to AD 10–60. If Savernake ware is largely a post-conquest industry whose distribution is mainly due to the military supply system (Swan 1975, 46), it is difficult to understand how it appears to have achieved such a widespread distribution on sites of immediate post-conquest date throughout south and east Gloucestershire. Both the Severn Valley and Savernake industries may represent local native developments in the 1st century AD which continued to flourish into the Roman period.

The two Duntisbourne sites are of particular interest in view of their proximity to the Bagendon complex and the fact that both sites produced Savernake wares, handmade and wheelmade SVWEA

Table 7.24   Comparison of fabrics from Middle Duntisbourne, Duntisbourne Grove and Court Farm.

SITE	Middle Duntisbourne				Duntisbourne Grove				Court Farm			
Fabric	no	%	wt	%	no	%	wt	%	no	%	wt	%
MIA									109	24.4	578	22.8
H2	2	0.2	12	0.2	1	0.05	6	0.06	3	0.06	48	1.9
L00	4	0.5	51	0.7	32	1.7	184	1.8	1	0.2	2	0.08
L4					11	0.6	88	0.9	1	0.2	3	0.1
Native wares												
MALVL2	24	2.7	113	0.15	73	3.9	508	5				
MALVL1	126	14.2	428	5.7	563	29.8	1548	15.1	10	2.2	35	1.4
GROG	22	2.4	104	1.4	68	3.6	450	4.4	14	3	121	4.8
Imports												
ARRETINE	3	0.3	8	0.1								
SAMIAN					2	0.1	16	0.2	7	1.6	10	0.4
CGWSOX					16	0.8	63	0.6				
GABTR1A					1	0.05	2	0.02				
GABTR3	3	0.3	4	0.05								
GABTN	15	1.7	70	1	1	0.05	6	0.06				
NOGWH	21	2.4	163	2.2	31	1.6	130	1.3				
FWBUFF	6	0.7	11	0.15								
FWOX/WS	4	0.5	40	0.5					2	0.5	2	0.07
AMP	5	0.6	40	0.5	18	1	530	5.2	6	1.3	119	4.7
Local/Regional												
SVWEA1	67	7.6	534	7	305	16.1	1781	17.4				
SVWEA2	320	36	1321	17.5	281	14.9	1266	12.3				
SVWEA3	30	3.4	175	2.3	15	0.8	132	1.3	41	9.2	251	9.9
SAVGT	154	17.4	4080	54.2	195	10.3	2892	28.2	30	6.7	764	30
WMBBW	12	1.4	32	0.4	44	2.3	117	1.1	58	13	176	7
DORBB1					3	0.2	10	0.1	9	2	14	0.6
SWWSOX									1	0.2	10	0.4
LOCGOX	3	0.3	5	0.07	59	3.1	96	0.9	12	2.7	140	5.5
LOCGW8	26	2.9	269	3.6	14	0.7	58	0.6	79	17.7	111	4.4
LOCGW	32	3.6	55	0.7	74	3.9	247	2.4	47	10.5	133	5.2
CRUMBS	6	0.2	15	0.2	83	4.4	125	1.2	17	3.8	19	0.7
TOTAL	885	100	7530	100	1890	100	10255	100	447	100	2536	100

and imported finewares and amphora. The range of imports, comprising early sigillata, Gallo-Belgic wares and Spanish and Italian amphora, is directly comparable to material already recorded from Bagendon and Ditches (Trow 1988) and are so far unique to this locality. No other imports of this range and date have been recorded from elsewhere in Gloucestershire. Other sites with Gallo-Belgic imports are limited to Birdlip, Cowley with TN, probably post-conquest (Parry 1998, 76), to Frocester, with post-conquest TN and a single sherd of TR1A, and Cirencester, with post-conquest TN only. The existence of such early prestigious wares at satellite sites apparently beyond the Bagendon earthwork complex is unexpected, as such wares are traditionally seen as the preserves of the inhabitants of the large territorial 'oppida'. There is little evidence at comparable sites, such as Silchester, of further redistribution into the hinterlands. This could suggest a different social organisation in the West, perhaps more polyfocal with the existence of a number of wealthy elites

concentrated in one district. A further addition to the three foci already highlighted, namely Ditches, Middle Duntisbourne and Duntisbourne Grove, is the small number of less well-provenanced but contemporary wares from Duntisbourne Abbots reported on by Fell (1964), which included a native copy of an imported butt beaker.

A comparison of the fabric groups from Ditches, Middle Duntisbourne and Duntisbourne Grove (Table 7.25) using the categories defined by Trow (1988, 64) shows quite a good degree of consistency between Ditches and Duntisbourne Grove. Middle Duntisbourne by contrast shows a much higher proportion of early SVW by sherd count and more Savernake ware by weight. The percentage of imports by sherd count is closest between Ditches and Middle Duntisbourne with slightly less from Duntisbourne Grove, although with the much bigger assemblage from Ditches has a greater range of forms. Imports from Middle Duntisbourne and Duntisbourne Grove closely mirror those from both Bagendon and Ditches which range in date

Table 7.25   Comparison of fabric groups from Middle Duntisbourne, Duntisbourne Grove and Ditches.

FABRICS	Ditches				Middle Duntisbourne				Duntisbourne Grove			
	WT	%	NO	%	WT	%	NO	%	WT	%	NO	%
GROUP A Limestone-temp	12112	21.6	944	24.5	604	8	156	17.6	2334	22.8	680	36
GROUP B Grog-tempered	6525	11.6	501	13	638	8.5	89	10	2225	21.7	370	19.6
GROUP C Inclusion free	3925	7	400	10.4								
GROUP D Wt early SVW	11252	20	753	19.5	1496	19.9	350	39.6	1401	13.7	297	15.7
GROUP E Savernake	10493	18.7	323	8.4	4080	54.2	154	17.4	2892	28.2	195	10.3
GROUP F Imports, fw/amp	1847	3.3	292	7.6	605	8	83	9.4	805	7.8	83	4.4
OTHER	9973	17.8	645	16.6	107	1.4	53	6	598	5.8	265	14
TOTAL	56127	100	3858	100	7530	100	885	100	10255	100	1890	100

from the late Augustan to AD 40–60. The group from the latter site includes Arretine, South Gaulish samian, Gallo-Belgic wares (TR1A platter, TR1C platter Cam. 7 variant, TR2 cup Cam 56, TR3 girth beaker and butt beaker; TN Cam. platter forms 5, 7, 8 and 14), North Gaulish butt beaker and whiteware flagon and Spanish amphorae. Many of these occur in the backfill of the inner enclosure ditch, and are thought to have been deposited in the Claudian or Claudio-Neronian periods (Trow 1988, 73). This would exactly parallel the abandonment of the main ditches at both Middle Duntisbourne and Duntisbourne Grove.

Roman

The largest Roman assemblage, from Birdlip Quarry dating from the later 2nd–4th centuries, has been reported on separately. A smaller but significant group of later Roman wares from Weavers Bridge is of a similar date.

In addition to these two assemblages, a number of early and later Roman assemblages were present at other sites. Amongst the earlier material are single sherds of Savernake ware from St Augustine's Lane and St Augustine's Farm South, with four sherds from Daglingworth Quarry. Further possible early Roman material came from Duntisbourne Abbotts-Duntisbourne Leer, Trinity Farm and Lynches Trackway. The last-named produced some 140 sherds of 1st–2nd century date mixed with a few early Iron Age pieces. Approximately half the sherds came from a very fragmented, fine oxidised white-slipped flagon. Also present were sherds of DORBB1 including a flat-rimmed bowl of 2nd-century type, a carinated, cordoned bowl in a grey, sandy ware, SAVGT and SVWEA2. Finally a pre-Flavian SG samian cup, Drag 24/5, along with Savernake ware and MALVL2 was recovered from chainage 9652 on the Stratton to Nettleton improvement.

Later Roman sherds from Sly's Wall South comprised six sherds including OXFRS mortaria. The Cirencester-Burford Road produced 55 badly abraded sherds of 2nd–4th date range, Witpit Lane just two residual sherds. The assemblage from Latton 'Roman Pond' was very poorly preserved,

with discoloured, abraded sherds, mainly bodysherds. Several fabrics were present, including OXFWH mortaria, OXFRS, DORBB1, SAVGT, SVWOX, SWWSOX, Central Gaulish samian and various greywares indicating a date range from the later 2nd to 4th centuries. Further poorly preserved Roman sherds (c. 50 in total) were recovered from north of the Stratton to Nettleton improvement, including eight sherds from a very worn 2nd century samian dish (Drag 36). Other sherds, DORBB1, SVWOX, OXFRS and local greywares suggest a later Roman date. Another very fragmentary, poorly preserved assemblage of some 300 sherds with an average sherd weight of just 3 g came from Field's Farm. The majority of the sherds (67%) came from just three vessels: an everted rim black-burnished jar with an acute lattice in a sandy ware imitating DORBB1, a grey sandy, handled flagon and a SVWOX type jar all suggestive of a late 2nd–3rd century date.

EARLY/MIDDLE SAXON POTTERY
By Paul Blinkhorn

Duntisbourne Leer

The assemblage comprised a single sherd weighing 3 g from context 229. It is an organic tempered fabric, with moderate chaff voids and a single, rounded grain of quartz c. 0.5 mm (not illustrated).

Latton Watching Brief

The assemblage comprised three sherds, with a total weight of 14 g. Two, a rim sherd from a jar (Fig. 7.16.199) and a small body sherd, were from context 5900 (22), and the other, a rim sherd or foot-ring base fragment, from context 5900 (24) (Fig. 7.16.198). The rim sherd from 5900 (22) is in a fine, slightly micaceous fabric with sparse fine chaff voids and has a lightly burnished outer surface. It has a simple, slightly everted profile. The bodysherd contains a greater amount of chaff, and sparse angular limestone fragments c. 2 mm. The third sherd is in a similar fabric, although the limestone is considerably finer, less than c. 0.5 mm.

Catalogue of illustrated sherds

198   Rim sherd or foot-ring base fragment. Ctx 5900 (chainage 24).
199   Rim sherd, fine slightly micaceous fabric, sparse fine chaff voids, lightly burnished outer surface, simple slightly everted profile. Ctx 5900 (chainage 22).

Discussion

The four sherds are generally unremarkable, although their recovery is of interest, as such pottery is scarce in the region. The size, form and fabric of the sherds makes it impossible to date them closely, other than to place them in the early/middle Saxon period (c. AD 450–850).

198   199

0   100 mm

Figure 7.16   Saxon pottery from Duntisbourne Leer and Latton.

THE POST-ROMAN POTTERY
By Paul Blinkhorn and Nigel Jeffries

Street Farm

Introduction

The post-Roman pottery assemblage from Street Farm comprised 1216 sherds with a total weight of 22,784 g. Despite being small the assemblage is considered worthy of detailed analysis as there is a general paucity of published material of this period from the region, with the medieval and post-medieval assemblages from the East and North Gate sites in Gloucester (Vince 1983) providing one of the few comparanda.

Fabric descriptions and chronologies

The pottery occurrence per fabric type by number and weight of sherds is shown in Table 7.26. Fabric codes appear in brackets.

Oolitic limestone wares (F200/F355)

Oolitic-limestone gritted wares of the Cotswolds tradition. Some of the sherds are fragments of tripod pitchers (eg. Fig. 7.17.202) which can be stylistically paralleled with vessels from Gloucester and Selsey Common (McCarthy and Brooks 1988, fig. 219, nos 1491 and 1497). Such fabrics are present in the Gloucestershire type series (Vince 1983, 126, fabric TF44). One of the known production centres for the ware is the village of Minety, some 7.5 km to the

south-west of Latton, which produced pottery from the 12th to the late 15th centuries (Vince 1983; Mellor 1994). The unglazed jar from Latton (Fig. 7.17.200) has form parallels with vessels from Great Somerford and Old Sarum in Wiltshire (McCarthy and Brooks 1988, fig. 102, nos 404 and 406).

Brill/Boarstall ware (F352)

Sandy buff- to red-coloured ware produced at kilns in south-west Buckinghamshire (Mellor 1994). It was mainly produced from the 13th century until around the Dissolution, although some kilns continued into the 17th century (Mellor 1994, 111).

Tudor green ware (F403)

Fine, white fabric with bright green glazes. The likely source for these vessels is the Farnham area of Hampshire (Pearce 1992, 1). The tradition has been given a broad date range of c. AD 1380–1550 (Orton 1988, 298).

Cistercian ware (F404)

Smooth red fabric with a dark brown/black glaze. The main vessel forms are wheel-thrown, thin-bodied cups and posset pots. Numerous known production centres around England, with the greatest concentration in Yorkshire. The general date-range for the tradition is c. AD 1475–1550 (McCarthy and Brooks 1988, 402).

Red earthenwares (F427, 432, 439, 440 and 441)

Wares of this type form the bulk of the post-medieval assemblage (Table 7.26), as is the case with other contemporary sites in the region (eg. Mellor 1984, fiche II E9). All the fabrics at this site have varying quantities of red or black ironstone inclusions, up to 0.5 mm in a poorly sorted matrix (F432, F439, F440), although there is a sandier fabric which also has moderate white quartz sand, and calcareous inclusions (F441). It is highly likely that the Street Farm pots are the products of local, as yet undiscovered kilns, as wares such as these were produced at numerous sources throughout England and usually had a localised distribution (Jennings 1981, 157). The one exception to this is F427, which could be from a different source, possibly the Wiltshire/Oxfordshire border. The same fabric has been found at Eynsham Abbey, Oxfordshire (Blinkhorn and Jeffries forth-coming). The Street Farm assemblage entirely comprises sherds from medium- to large-bodied forms such as jugs and pancheon bowls. The date for these wares is variable, but usually spans the period c. AD 1500–1750 (Mayes 1968, 55; Orton and Pearce 1984, 36).

Frechen stoneware (F405)

Distinctive grey German stoneware with a speckled brown 'tiger' or 'orange-peel' salt glaze, generally imported into England from the second half of the 16th

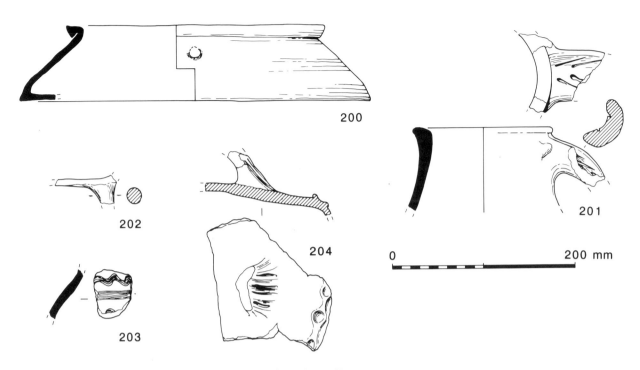

Figure 7.17   Medieval and post-medieval pottery from Street Farm.

Table 7.26   Street Farm, quantification of post-Roman pottery fabrics by number of sherds and weight (in grammes) per fabric.

Ware	Fabric code	No. of sherds	Weight
Oolitic wares	F202	134	2631
Brill/Boarstall	F352	2	12
Tudor Green	F403	2	68
Cistercian wares	F404	21	157
Red Earthenwares	F427, 432, 439, 440, 441	398	11938
Frechen Stoneware	F405	2	13
Tin-Glazed Earthenwares	F417	1	13
Staffs wares	F414, 417	20	293
Westerwald Stoneware	F413	4	45
Staffs Stoneware	F444	6	87
Staffs Salt-glazed Stoneware	F443	17	82
Nottingham Stoneware	F445	8	202
Jackfield Wares	F550	1	3
Early Porcelain	F428	12	30
Creamwares	F418	27	258
Pearlwares	F447	22	201
Transfer-printed Earthenwares	F448	9	45
Mocha/ Yellow wares	F442	103	1243
Basalt Wares	F449	2	41
Miscellaneous c. 19th/20thC wares	F437, 438	436	4800
Total		1216	22,784

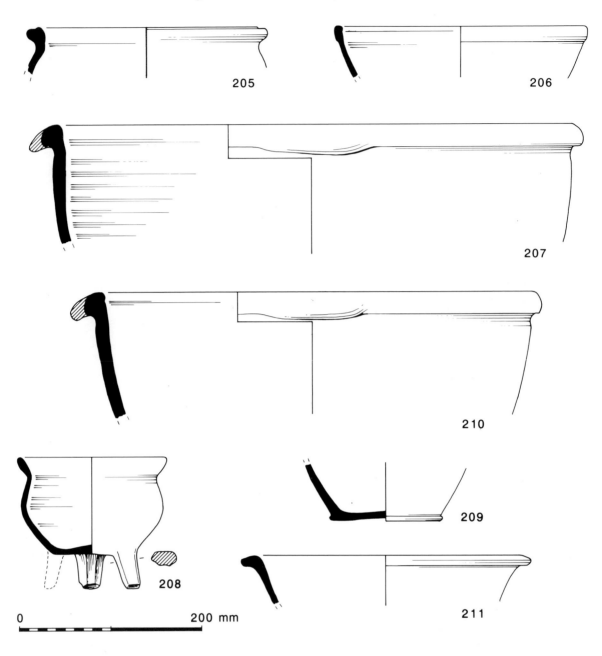

Figure 7.18   Medieval and post medieval pottery from Street Farm.

century. It occurs on most contemporary sites until the late 17th century (Jennings 1981, 117–8).

Tin-glazed earthenwares (F417)

Red-buff fabric with occasional 0.5 mm rounded black ironstone and sparse 0.2 mm sub-rounded red ironstone. Only one sherd, from a plate, occurred at Latton. It is decorated with an 'arc and chain' pattern, which is paralleled by two unstratified sherds from a waster dump at the Limekiln Potteries in Bristol (Jackson and Beckey 1991, figs 9 and 10, nos 82 and 95). Tin-glazed earthenwares were produced on a large scale in London, from *c.* 1613 onwards (Orton 1988, 298) and Bristol from *c.* 1630. The paucity of tin-glazed

earthenwares at this site is paralleled in the smaller assemblage from the nearby pipeline trench excavations at Street Farm.

Staffordshire type wares (F414 and F446)

This group includes both manganese (F414) and slip-decorated wares (F446). Both types have a date range of 1690 until 1760 (Barton 1961, 160–8). They have been discussed at length in many publications (eg. Celeria and Kelly 1973; Kelly and Greaves 1974). Wares of this type, despite being called Staffordshire-types, were also made in Bristol. The fabric of the Street Farm sherds suggest that they were all from a Bristol source (Barton 1961, 160–8).

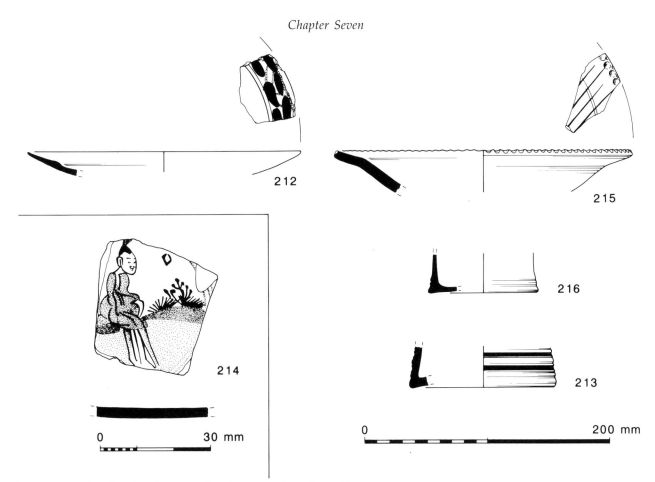

Figure 7.19   Medieval and post-medieval pottery from Street Farm.

Westerwald stoneware (F413)

German import. Uniform light grey stoneware fabric decorated with cobalt blue and/or manganese purple slip. The predominant forms are mugs, chamber pots and jugs, although the only form-diagnostic sherd from Street Farm site is a mug base (Fig. 7.19.213). The sherds in the assemblage date from the early 18th century, suggested by incised border lines and coloured motifs with combed stems and leaves (Jennings 1981, 123).

Staffordshire brown salt-glazed stoneware (F444)

Stoneware of this type was being made in Staffordshire from *c.* 1675 onwards (Jennings 1981, 219). It has a uniform light grey fabric with occasional black ironstone inclusions. The vessels were usually partially dipped in a white engobe and a ferruginous wash, and then salt-glazed. The rim forms from this assemblage all appear to be from tankards or mugs.

Staffordshire salt-glazed stoneware (F443)

White-bodied stoneware, produced in a large range of both ornamental and utilitarian forms. The sherds in this assemblage are the cheaper mug and bowl forms. The material was made in large quantities in Staffordshire from *c.* 1675 until *c.* 1780/1800 (Jennings 1981, 222).

Nottingham stoneware (F445)

Fine, lustrous brown glazed stoneware with a buff to grey coloured uniform fabric. A common feature of this ware is a thin white or grey margin between the fabric and the glaze. The majority of this assemblage comprises mugs, with the occasional base sherd of a bowl occurring. The date range for this pottery is *c.* 1700–1800 (Jennings 1981, 219).

Table 7.27   Witpit Lane, post-Roman pottery.

Context	Cotswolds-type Oolitic ware	Brill/ Boarstall	Red Earthenwares ware
5	24 (202)	1 (3)	1 (8)
7	2 (42)		
13			1 (7)
15			1 (8)
19			2 (31)
24	15 (171)		

Table 7.28   Burford Road, post-Roman pottery.

Context	Frechen Stonewares	Red Earthenwares	Metropolitan Slipware	Staffordshire Slip-trailed Ware	Misc 19/20thC wares
105		1 (5)			
206		2 (37)		1 (3)	8 (13)
209		1 (1)			1 (1)
310	1 (4)				
401		1 (1)			
406		2 (257)			
419		4 (51)			
523			2 (19)		
540		4 (39)			
661		4 (23)			

Table 7.29   Westfield Farm, post-Roman pottery.

Context	Medieval Shelly-Limestone Coarseware	Red Earthenwares	Misc. 19/20thC Wares
9		1 (280)	
10			1 (3)
21	1 (26)		
29		1 (5)	

Jackfield wares (F550)

Compact uniform dark brown/black fabric with a thick lustrous black glaze. Made in Staffordshire from *c.* 1750 (Jennings 1981, 230). Only one example was found in the Street Farm assemblage.

Basalt ware (F449)

Black stoneware used mainly for coffee- and tea-pots. It was produced in Staffordshire, from 1750 until the 19th century (Mellor 1984, fiche II, A3).

Porcelain (F428)

The earlier imported and English porcelain at Street Farm is classified separately from the miscellaneous *c.* 19th century types (F437), as London polychrome, European and 'Chinaman in the grass' porcelain from China (Fig. 7.19.214) can be stylistically dated. The non-English material probably came to the site from the port of Bristol, which imported such wares in massive quantities. Broadly speaking, this group has a date range of *c.* 1750+.

Creamwares (F418)

Cream-coloured buff earthenware made with the same calcined flint clay as Staffordshire white salt-glazed stonewares (Jennings 1981, 227). However, creamwares were fired at a different temperature and coated with a lead glaze, resulting in a rich cream colour. They were first produced in the 1760s (Mellor 1984, 217).

Pearlwares and transfer printed pearlwares (F447)

Pearlwares represent a progression from creamwares. The same clay was utilised, but the vessels were fired at a different temperature, resulting in an improved surface which was ideal for applied decoration. Much of this assemblage comprises blue-stained, painted shell-edged plates. These were an early 19th-century development (Mellor 1984, fiche II, D1).

Transfer-printed white earthenwares (F448)

This ware has an off-white to buff uniform fabric. The transfer-printing of earthenwares was a common form of decoration for tablewares from the early 19th century onwards. It is likely that the source for this pottery was Staffordshire.

Mocha/Yellow wares (F442)

By the 1830s, transfer-printed earthenwares had all been replaced by black, green, pink, grey and brown transfer prints. Both wares had the same hard, white, slightly sandy fabric and thick yellow glaze, although the Mocha wares, made in Staffordshire, were usually tea-pots, with a brown fern-like transfer decoration made from a mixture of tobacco and urine (Mellor 1984, fiche II, A3).

Miscellaneous c. 19th-century wares (F437, F438)

This broad group encompasses 19th-century Victorian 'Willow pattern' and a few Victorian stonewares (F438). However, the prominent type within this group

Table 7.30 Daglingworth Quarry, post-Roman pottery.

Context	Cotswolds-type Oolitic Ware	Red Earthenwares	Misc 19/ 20thC Wares
107	1 (12)	4 (395)	
116		1 (5)	1 (16)
120			10 (80)

is white-glazed earthenwares which were mass-produced in Staffordshire from the mid 19th century onwards (Mellor 1984, 209).

Discussion

The overwhelming majority of the medieval sherds are oolitic limestone-tempered wares of the Cotswolds tradition (McCarthy and Brooks 1988, fig. 219). The assemblage, despite being small in size, contains virtually the full range of domestic vessel types, include a curfew, or fire-cover, from context 559 (Fig. 7.17.204). The only other medieval wares present at the site are two sherds of Brill/Boarstall ware, which are worthy of note, as the products of this industry are rarely found to the west of Oxfordshire or Buckinghamshire (Mellor 1994, 117).

Table 7.31 Court Farm, post-Roman pottery.

Context	Red Earthenwares	Staffs Stoneware
16	1 (35)	
290	1 (49)	
345	1 (45)	
486	6 (101)	1 (16)

The late-medieval transitional and post-medieval wares are largely unremarkable. However, the presence of large quantities of such wares, along with fragments of medieval coarsewares, followed chronologically by Cistercian, red earthenware and Tudor Green vessels, suggests that the site was occupied continuously from the 12th/13th century until the post-medieval period.

The range of fabrics and forms on the site increased during the later post-medieval period. The social pastimes of the 18th and 19th centuries mainly centred around the consumption of ale and tea within the household and the Street Farm pottery assemblage reflects this general trend. A range of stone- and manganese-ware mugs and tankards were present, as were exotic, sometimes ornamental, tablewares such as pearlwares, porcelain and creamwares. The earthenwares, the pottery used for food preparation and storage, include a range of bowls (storage/mixing vessels), dishes, pancheons (Fig. 7.18.207) and a dripping dish. The exact start date of these wares is uncertain, although they were thought to be in general use in the region from *c.* 1500 onwards (see above). At this site, they occur in sealed contexts (such as 119 and 440) with medieval coarsewares, and also in other

contexts (eg. 173 and 262) containing Cistercian wares. Whilst these facts could be taken to imply that the earthenwares pre-date 1500, the small assemblage sizes and the real possibility of redeposition of pottery means that this cannot be suggested with confidence, as residuality may be a factor.

Table 7.32 Exhibition Barn, post-Roman pottery.

Context	Cotswolds-type Oolitic Ware	Red Earthenwares
2		1 (2)
8	1 (1)	
13	1 (5)	

There were no post-medieval North Devon gravel-tempered or Donyatt wares in the assemblage. These were produced in the same range of utilitarian forms as the red earthenwares, and, in the later 17th century, comprised some 17% of the non-local assemblage from Gloucester (Vince 1983, 139). An explanation for the absence of these wares at Street Farm may be that Gloucester received them directly from sources via the River Severn. However, the products of the 17th-century kilns at Ashton Keynes, only 4 km to the south-west of Latton, are also absent from the site. Such wares comprise between 10% and 50% percent of the pottery from 17th-century contexts in Gloucester (Vince 1983, 139). Their absence at Street Farm suggests that there was a hiatus in the occupation of the site at that time. The date ranges of the later wares, which include Mocha wares, Victorian 'Willow Pattern' and white glazed earthenwares suggest that occupation continued until the mid-19th century.

Catalogue of illustrated sherds (Figs 7.17–7.19)

200 CO1: F200, ctx 446. Grey fabric with brown surfaces, basepad scorched to a pale orange-brown. Single hole pierced, pre-firing, just below the rim.

201 CO2: F200, ctx 409. Grey fabric with brown outer surface.

202 CO3: F200, ctx 462. Grey fabric with buff-brown surfaces.

203 CO4: F200, ctx 458. Grey fabric with brown surfaces. Outer surface has a thin, dull, sage-green glaze.

204 CO5: F200, ctx 559. Uniform dark grey fabric. Inner surface is heavily smoked and has a patchy, thin sage-green glaze.

205 RE1: F401, ctx 589. Uniform dark reddish-brown fabric. Inner surface has a black glaze extending up to the lip of the rim.

206 RE2: F401, ctx 267. Uniform brick-red fabric. Inner surface has a brown manganese glaze up to the edge of the rim.

207 RE3: F439, ctx 305. Uniform brick-red fabric.

Inner surface has a patchy, light green glaze up to the edge of the rim.

208 RE4: F439, ctx 276. Uniform light brick-red fabric. Inner surface has a light brown glaze extending just over the lip of the rim.

209 RE5: F440, ctx 551. Uniform brick-red fabric. Inner surface has a dark brown manganese glaze.

210 RE6: F441, ctx 305. Uniform brick-red fabric. Inner surface has a brown manganese glaze up to the edge of the rim.

211 RE7: F441, ctx 196. Uniform, brick-red, sandy fabric. Rim and inner surface has a light green glaze up to the lip of the rim.

212 TG1: F417, ctx 276. Uniform buff fabric. Decorated with a hand-painted brown and blue 'chain and arc' pattern and a white glaze.

213 WEST1: F413, ctx 227. Uniform grey coloured fabric. External surface has cobalt blue bands beneath a grey salt-glaze.

214 PO1: F428, ctx 255. Hard paste fabric. Internally blue-enamelled Chinese Porcelain.

215 SW1: F444, ctx 198. Uniform buff fabric. Internally decorated with a combed brown slip beneath a lemon coloured glaze.

216 SW2: F444, ctx 786. Uniform buff fabric. Decorated internally and externally with a brown manganese glaze with a single cordon of rilling at the foot of the base.

Pottery from the other sites

Tables 7.27–7.32 list the number and weight of sherds per context by fabric type for the remainder of the sites. The fabrics are as described for the Street Farm assemblage except for two wares which were not present at that site, as follows:

Frechen stoneware (F405)

A uniform grey stoneware fabric with grey/brown salt-glaze. The main forms are mugs and tankards, although there are no form-diagnostic sherds in the assemblage. Produced in Frechen, Germany, and imported into England from *c.* 1550 onwards.

Metropolitan Slipware (F416)

Well-sorted matrix with occasional sub-rounded red ironstone/mica inclusions. The main forms are flat and hollow wares, although there are no form-diagnostic sherds in the assemblage. The ware is characterised by decorative trails of white pipe-clay over an iron-rich body clay, which varies in colour from a light brown through to a reddish-brown, with a brown or black glaze. Produced in Harlow, Essex, from *c.* 1615 onwards (Jennings 1981, 97).

The majority of sherds from context 24 at Witpit Lane were leached and abraded.

THE COINS
By John A. Davies

Introduction

A total of 291 coins from seven sites were examined. Each site-specific assemblage was analysed individually, and is summarised in Table 7.33. The entries are organised as follows: small find number, context number, identification, date range, obverse, reverse, diameter, mint.

Field's Farm

Two coins were recovered from Field's Farm. They are both Roman, dating from the mid- to late 4th century.

217 SF1, ctx 13, Constantine I, follis AD 330–1. Obv. CONSTANTINVS MAX AVG. Rev. GLORIA EXERCITVS, 2 standards

218 SF10, ctx 2, House of Theodosius, AE4, AD 388–402. Obv. Ill. Rev. [VICTORIA AVGGG]

Daglingworth Quarry

Two Roman coins of late 4th-century date were recovered.

219 SF1, Gratian, AE3, AD 367–75. Obv. Ill. Rev [GLORIA NOVI SAECVLI]

220 A gold solidus in good condition was recovered from the line of the new road by a labourer near Dowers Lane Underpass, Daglingworth, not associated with any archaeological site. It was presented by the Highways Agency to Cirencester City Council and is now in the Corinium Museum. The coin of Honorius is of the common VICTORI AAVGGG type, minted in Milan from AD 395–402 (as RIC X, 1206, Kent 1994)). The mintmark is M / D COMOB in which the lower M is close to an N, as often seen in this type. This type is a very rare find on settlement sites and it may therefore be a survivor from a hoard. This coin was examined by Paul Booth of the Oxford Archaeological Unit.

Burford Road

The Burford Road group numbers four coins. Two are very worn Roman examples which can only be broadly dated. The earlier example is a sestertius of the Antonine period of the middle 2nd century. The other is an irregular minim, which would have been struck between the late 3rd and mid-4th century.

There are two post-Roman coins, both farthings of Charles II (1660–85), from context 620.

221 SF 5, ctx 310, Antonine emperor Sestertius (incomplete) 138–80. Obv and Rev Ill.

222 SF 1, ctx 208, Illegible AE4 275–364 10 mm diam.

223–4 SF 8, ctx 620, Charles II Farthing 1660–85

Street Farm

225 SF10, ctx 281, a French 10 centimes piece of the Emperor Napoleon III (1852–70).

St Augustine's Lane

226   SF1, u/s, Constantine I, a follis, AD 307. Obv FL VAL CONSTANTINVS NOB C. Rev GENIO POP ROM. Trier RIC 6: 720b.

Weavers Bridge

The second largest coin group came from Weavers Bridge. The 51 coins are all Roman and all are base metal issues. A chronological summary employing Reece's Issue Periods (1972) is provided in Table 7.34. The assemblage is sufficiently large to allow meaningful comparison with other Romano-British sites. They comprise a tight chronological group which is restricted to the late Roman period. There are no issues of the Augustan System present. The normally ubiquitous antoniniani of the years from AD 260 to 275 are also completely absent. The earliest examples are two irregular antoniniani (barbarous radiates) of the late-3rd century, both of which are the later types of reduced size, or minims. Two other late antoniniani, of the British Empire, are also present.

Coin loss for the period AD 294–330 is always lighter than for the preceding and succeeding periods. A presence is attested during that time at Weavers Bridge by three issues. However, the major episode of coin deposition was between AD 330–48. The coins in question are the most commonly encountered mid-Constantinian folles, in particular the GLORIA EXERCITVS, 1 standard type. The mints of origin of these coins is summarised in Table 7.35, which shows Trier to have been the principal supplier during the years in question. The coin list subsequently drops away sharply. There are just two irregular 'falling horseman' minims. The assemblage ends prior to the Valentinianic period, whose coins tend to be relatively numerous on sites occupied after AD 364.

The very tight chronological grouping of the Weavers Bridge coins can be emphasised by separating them into the four main chronological phases (Table 7.36). Those from Phase D dominate the assemblage, accounting for 85.1% of the total.

Despite this predominance of coins belonging to the period AD 330–348, their condition and distribution suggests that they do not belong to a hoard. They are associated with a midden deposit (57) and appear to represent evidence for an episode of occupation at this site.

Table 7.33   Summary of the coin assemblages, all sites.

Site	Roman	Later	Total
Field's Farm	2		2
Daglingworth Quarry	2		2
Burford Road	2	2	4
Street Farm		1	1
St Augustine's Lane	1		1
Weavers Bridge	51		51
Birdlip Quarry	230		230
Total	288	3	291

227   SF 28, ctx 57, Barbarous radiate, Minim, 275–84, No legend, Pin figure, 13.

228   SF 52, ctx 57, Barbarous radiate, Minim, 275–84, Figure holding shield, 11.

229   SF 47, ctx 57, Carausius, Antoninianus, 287–93, Illegible, [PAX AVG], vertical sceptre, 20.

230   SF 24, ctx 57, Allectus, Antoninianus, 293–6, IMP C ALLECTVS PF AVG, PA[X A]VG.

231   SF 42, ctx 57, Illegible, Antoninianus, Illegible, Illegible.

232   SF 2, ctx 51, Maximian, Follis, 307, DN MAXIMIANO PFS AVG, ROMAE AETER, London, RIC6: 100.

233   SF 15, ctx 71, House of Constantine, Follis, 319–20, Illegible, [VICTORIAE LAETAE] PRINC PERP.

234   SF 43, ctx 51, Crispus, Follis, 322, [IVL] CRISPVS NOB CAES, BEATA TRANQVILLITAS, Trier, RIC 7: 347.

Table 7.34   Chronological summary of the coins from Weavers Bridge.

Period	Date	Number	%
11	(275–94)	4	8.5
12	(294–317)	1	2.1
13a	(317–30)	2	4.3
13b	(330–48)	38	80.9
14	(348–64)	2	4.3
Total		47	
Unphasable			
3rd– 4th C		4	
Total Roman		51	

235   SF 46, ctx 57, Constantius II, Follis, 330–1, FL IVL CONSTANTIVS NOB C, GLOR[IA EXE]RC[ITVS], 2 standards, Trier, RIC 7: 521.

236   SF 66, ctx 57, Constantine I, Follis, 332–3, VRBS ROMA, Wolf and twins, Trier, RIC 7: 542.

237   SF 8, ctx 51, Constantine I, Follis, 332–3, CONSTANTINOPOLIS, Victory on prow, Trier, RIC 7: 548.

238   SF 30, Constantine I, Follis, 333–4, VRBS ROMA, Wolf and twins, Trier, RIC 7: 553.

239   SF 57, ctx 57, Constantine I, Follis, 333–4, CONSTANTINOPOLIS, Victory on prow, Trier, RIC 7: 554.

240   SF 48, ctx 57, House of Constantine, Follis, 335–7, Illegible, GLOR[IA EXERC]ITVS, 1 standard, Trier, RIC 7: 586.

241   SF 29, ctx 57, House of Constantine, Follis, 330–1, Illegible, GLORIA EXERC[ITVS], 2 standards, Lyons, RIC 7: 236.

Table 7.35   Weavers Bridge, 4th-century mint distribution.

Period	12		13a		13b	
	No.	%	No.	%	No.	%
London	1	100.0				
Trier			1	100.0	13	76.5
Lyons					2	11.8
Arles					1	5.9
Aquileia					1	5.9
Total	1		1		17	
Irregular					3	

242   SF 40, ctx 51, Constantius II, Follis, 330–1, CONSTANTINVS IVN NOB C, GLORIA EXERCITVS, 2 standards, Lyons, RIC 7: 238.

243   SF 12, ctx 57, House of Constantine, Follis, 330–5, Illegible, [GLORIA EXERCITVS], 2 standards.

244   SF 51, ctx 57, House of Constantine, Follis, 330–5, Illegible, [GLORIA EXERCITVS], 2 standards.

245   SF 25, ctx 57, Constantine I, Follis, 3305, [VR]BS [R]O[MA], Wolf and twins.

246   SF 36, ctx 57, Constantine I, Follis, 330–5, [CONSTAN]TI[NOPOLIS], Victory on prow.

247   SF 38, ctx 51, Constantine I, Follis, 330–5, CONSTANTINOPOLIS, Victory on prow

248   SF 10, ctx 51, Helena, Follis, 337–40, FL IVL HE[LENAE AVG], P[AX] PV[BLICA], Trier, RIC 8: 47.

249   SF 55, ctx 57, House of Constantine, Follis, 337–40, —STANTI—, VIRTVS AVGG NN, Trier, RIC 8: 53

250   SF 37, ctx 57, Constantine I, Follis, 335–7, CONSTANTI—, GLORIA [EXERCITVS], 1 standard.

251   SF 9, ctx 51, House of Constantine, Follis, 335–40, Illegible, [GLORIA EXERCITVS], 1 standard.

252   SF 3, ctx 57, Constantius II, Follis, 337–40, FL IVL CONSTANTIVS AVG, GLOR[IA EXERCITVS], 1 standard.

253   SF 11, ctx 57, House of Constantine, Follis, 335–40, Illegible, GLORIA EXER]CITVS, 1 standard.

254   SF 49, ctx 57, House of Constantine, Follis, 335–40, Illegible, [GLORIA EXERCITVS], 1 standard.

255   SF 50, ctx 57, House of Constantine, Follis, 335–40, —PF—, [GLORIA] EXER[CITVS], 1 standard.

256   SF 53, ctx 57, House of Constantine, Follis, 335–40, Illegible, [GLORIA EXERCITVS], 1 standard.

257   SF 6, ctx 57, Helena, Follis, 337–40, Illegible, [PAX PV]BLICA.

258   SF 68, ctx 57, Theodora, Follis, 337–40, Illegible, PIETAS [ROMANA].

259   SF 45, ctx 57, Constantine I, Irregular follis, 341–6, CONSTANTINOPOLIS, Victory on prow, 11.

260   SF 5, ctx 57, House of Constantine, Irregular follis, 341–6, Illegible, [GLORIA EXERCITVS], 1 standard, 12.

261   SF 64, ctx 57, Constans, Irregular follis, 341–6, CONSTANS PF AVG, GLORIA EXERC[ITVS], 1 standard, Trier, 14.

262   SF 67, ctx 57, Constans, Follis, 347–8, CONSTANS PF AVG, VICTORIAE DD AVGG Q NN, Trier, RIC 8: 186.

263   SF 54, ctx 57, Constantius II, Follis, 347–8, [CONSTANTI]VS PF AVG, [VICTORIAE DD AVGG Q] NN, Trier, RIC 7: 193.

264   SF 41, ctx 57, House of Constantine, Follis, 347–8, CO—, [VICTORIAE DD AVGG Q NN], Trier, RIC 8: 193.

265   SF 7, ctx 57, Constans, Follis, 347–8, CONSTANS PF AVG, VICTORIAE DD AVGG Q NN, Trier, RIC 8: 195

266   SF 22, ctx 57, Constans, Follis, 347–8, CONSTANS PF AVG, [VICTORIAE DD AVGG Q NN], Trier, RIC 8: 196.

267   SF 17, ctx 57, House of Constantine, Follis, 347–8, [CONSTANTI]VS PF AVG, [VICTORIAE DD AVGG Q] NN, Arles, RIC 8: 95.

268   SF 35, ctx 57, House of Constantine, Follis, 347–8, Illegible, [VICTORIAE DD AV]GG Q [NN], Aquileia, RIC 8: 82/83.

269   SF 34, ctx 57, House of Constantine, Follis, 347–8, Illegible, [VICTORIAE DD AVGG Q NN].

270   SF 44, ctx 57, House of Constantine, Follis, 347–8, Illegible, VICTORIAE DD AVGG Q NN.

271   SF 27, ctx 57, Illegible, Follis, 330–48, Illegible, Illegible.

272   SF 13, ctx 51, House of Constantine, Irregular AE4, 354–64, No legend, FEL TEMP REPERATIO], falling horseman, 11.

273   SF 62, ctx 57, House of Constantine, Irregular AE4, 354–64, No legend, [FEL TEMP REPARATIO], falling horseman, 11.

274   SF 19, ctx 57, Illegible, AE4, 275–364, Illegible, Illegible, 9.

275   SF 60, ctx 57, Illegible, AE3, 260–402, Illegible, Illegible.

Table 7.36   Weavers Bridge, relative numbers of coins, separated into four phases.

	No.	%
Phase A (To AD 259)	-	
Phase B (259–96)	4	8.5
Phase C (296–330)	3	6.4
Phase D (330–402)	40	85.1

276–7   SF 31 and SF 33, ctx 57, bronze fragments. Possibly originally two 3rd–4th century coins. No diagnostic elements remain, to be certain..

Birdlip Quarry

This is the largest of the individual site groups, with 230 coins. All are Roman and they are essentially common issues. All but five are base metal. The silver types are four denarii and an antoninianus, all of the late 2nd-/early 3rd-century. The whole assemblage has a date-range from the mid 1st century to the end of the 4th century. A chronological summary is shown in Table 7.37. The 21 Issue Periods referred to are those established by Reece (1972). The percentages for each period are also shown, for comparative purposes.

The chronological range of the coins runs from a single 1st-century coin, a Vespasian issue of AD 71–9, through to the House of Theodosius, representing the final years of Roman Britain. There is a sizeable group of aes belonging to the 2nd century, especially to the reigns of Antoninus Pius and Marcus Aurelius. The degree of wear on these coins indicates a prolonged period of circulation. It is known from hoard evidence that such aes could have stayed in circulation for decades. It is likely that these particular coins belonged to an initial period of occupation at the site sometime between AD 160–180/90. The as of Vespasian would also have been deposited during that period of activity. The denominations of these coins of the Augustan System are summarised in Table 7.38.

Sestertii are the most prolific type prior to the end of the 2nd century, when denarii became more common. The denarii are the only silver coins to be recovered from the site. Two of these (cat. 292–3) are, however, base metal examples.

The assemblage exhibits steady coin loss through the 3rd century but the total escalates profoundly after AD 250. Coin numbers increase on all Romano-British sites after AD 259, which represents the widespread adoption of base metal antoniniani across the province. However, the proportion of finds from Birdlip which date from Reece's Periods 10 and 11 is within the high range for Britain. In particular, there are groups of antoniniani of the emperors Gallienus and Claudius II, which are accompanied by rarer issues of Valerian I and II, Postumus, Marius and Aurelian. Irregular antoniniani, or barbarous radiates, also comprise a sizeable component. There are 38 examples, of which half are minims (14 mm or less). This may be evidence for increased activity at the site from the final third of the 3rd century.

The assemblage continues steadily through the 4th century, with especially strong loss between AD 317–348. After this, deposition falls away sharply and remains much lighter through to the end of the century. Mintmarks are legible on most of the 4th-century coins and allow an analysis of the mints supplying coin to the site.

A small group of eight folles, dated to AD 320–5, were found within a metre of each other on the surface of Ermin Street. All but one are in clear, fully legible,

condition. Four were struck at London, two at Trier and one at Lyons. They appear to represent a purse group, which can be dated to shortly after AD 325 (Table 7.39).

The overall chronological distribution of the Birdlip coins can be analysed by dividing them into four phases (Table 7.40), as employed by Reece (1987). When shown in such a manner, some notable features become apparent. The early coinage (Phase A) comprises a significant presence but represents the lightest phase. Late 3rd-century coinage (Phase B) is remarkably high and dominates the assemblage. The coins from the early 4th century (Phase C) are also well-represented. This period is usually much lighter on all categories of Romano-British site. Later 4th-century coinage (Phase D) usually dominates site assemblages. Although well represented here, it is significantly lighter than Phase B and approximately equal to Phase C. A floruit at the site between the late 3rd and mid 4th century is apparent. This high ratio of Phase B: Phase D coins is a feature associated with urban sites in Britain (Reece 1987). Rural settlements tend to have a higher ratio of Phase D coins.

Table 7.37   Chronological summary of the coins from Birdlip Quarry.

Period	Date	Number	%
1	(To AD 41)	-	
2a	(41–54)	-	
2b	(54–69)	-	
3	(69–96)	1	0.5
4	(96–117)	-	
5	(117–38)	1	0.5
6	(138–61)	7	3.4
7a	(161–80)	2	1.0
7b	(180–93)	1	0.5
8	(193–222)	5	2.4
9a	(222–83)	2	1.0
9b	(238–59)	2	1.0
10	(259–75)	48	23.3
11	(275–94)	45	21.8
12	(294–317)	8	3.9
13a	(317–30)	36	17.5
13b	(330–48)	37	18.0
14	(348–64)	3	1.5
15a	(364–78)	7	3.4
15b	(378–88)	-	
16	(388–402)	1	0.5
Unphasable			
1st –2nd C		1	
3rd –4th C		23	
Total Roman		230	
Non-coin		1	
GRAND TOTAL		231	

Table 7.38 Birdlip Quarry, denominations of the Augustan System coins.

Issue Period	Denarius	Sestertius	Dupondius	As	Dupondius/As
3				1	
4					
5				1	
6		6			1
7a		2			
7b			1		
8	5				
9a	1			1	
Total	6	8	1	3	1

277 SF 431, ctx 34, Vespasian, As, 71–9, SC; eagle on globe.

278 SF 762, ctx 270, Hadrian, As, 117–38, Illegible, Illegible.

279 SF 1099, ctx 71, Illegible, As, 69–138, Illegible, Illegible

280 SF 1655, ctx 1500, Antoninus Pius, Sestertius, 138–61, —VS—, Ill. Salus stg. l. by altar.

281 SF 1565, ctx 1266, Antoninus Pius, Sestertius, 138–61, ANTONINVS AVG PI—, Ill; SC. Fem. fig. l., holding sceptre r.

282 SF 1728, ctx 1509, Antonine emperor, Sestertius, 138–61, Illegible, Illegible.

283 SF 1533, ctx 1210, Faustina I, Sestertius, 141–61, DIVA FAVSTINA, AVGVSTA; SC, Rome, RIC 3: 1127.

284 SF 763, ctx 270, Faustina I, Dupondius/as, 141–61, DIVA FAVSTINA, [AVGV]STA; SC, Rome, RIC 3: 1172.

285 SF 162, ctx 18, Faustina I, Sestertius, 138–61, Illegible, Illegible.

286 SF 3, ctx 7, Marcus Aurelius, Sestertius, 164–5, [M AVR]EL ANTONINVS AVG ARMENIACVS IMP,

TR POT [XIX] IMP II COS III; SC, Rome, RIC 3: 902.

287 SF 539, ctx 265, Marcus Aurelius, Sestertius, 173–4, M ANTONINVS AVG TR P XXVIII, Ill. Fig. seated l. (Jupiter or Roma).

288 SF 1528, ctx 1217, Faustina II, Sestertius, 145–6, FAVSTINAE AVG PII AVG FIL, P[VDI]CITIA; SC, Rome, RIC 3: 1381.

289 SF 148, ctx 18, Commodus, Dupondius, 180, —MODVS ANTONI—, LIB AVG TR P—, Rome, Robertson 2: 73.

290 SF 1572, ctx 1266, Septimius Severus, Denarius, 197–8, —AVG IMP X, Ill. Salus seated l.

291 SF 904, ctx 29, Septimius Severus, Denarius frag., 193–211, —VERVS—, —OR—; arm holding staff?

292 SF 1563, ctx 1268, Septimius Severus, Base Denarius, 193–211, Illegible, —IC—; Victoria stg. l.

293 SF 1569, ctx 1266, Julia Domna, Base Denarius, 193–6, Illegible, PI[ETAS A]VG.

294 SF 1710, ctx 1503, Elagabalus, Denarius, 218–22, [IMP] ANTONINVS PIVS AVG, SVMMVS SACERDOS AVG, Rome, RIC 4: 146.

295 SF 24, ,u/s, Severus Alexander, Denarius frag., 222–35, Illegible, [AEQVI]TAS AVG, , RIC 4: 127.

296 SF 1519, ctx 1198, Severus Alexander, As, 222–35, —SEV ALEXANDER AVG, LIBER[ALITAS —]; SC.

297 SF 430, ctx 128, Valerian I, Antoninianus, 253–9, IMP C P LIC VALERIANVS AVG, Illegible.

298 SF 1180, ctx 829, Valerian II, Silver antoninianus, 253–60, PCL VALERIANVS NOB CAES, PIETAS AVGG, Rome, RIC 5: 20.

299 SF 26, ctx 7, Gallienus, Antoninianus, 260–8, Illegible, [DIANAE CONS AVG] antelope walking l, RIC 5: 180.

300 SF 205, ctx 18, Gallienus, Antoninianus, 260–8, —LIENVS A—, MARTI PACIFERO, Rome, RIC 5: 236.

301 SF 83, ctx 7, Gallienus, Antoninianus, 260–8, G———VG, FORTVNA REDVX, Siscia, RIC 5: 572.

Table 7.39 Birdlip Quarry, 4th-century mint distribution.

Period	12		13a		13b		14		15a	
	No.	%	No.	%	No.	%	No.	%	No.	%
London	4	66.7	7	30.4						
Trier	2	33.3	11	50.0	17	73.9				
Lyons			3	13.6						
Arles					6	26.1			1	50.0
Heraclea			1	4.5						
Aquileia									1	50.0
Total	6		22		23		-		2	
Irregular					5		2			

Table 7.40 Birdlip Quarry, relative numbers of coins, separated into four phases.

	Total	%
Phase A (to AD 259)	21	10.2
Phase B (259–96)	93	45.1
Phase C (296–330)	44	21.4
Phase D (330–402)	48	23.3

302 SF 1582, ctx 1311, Gallienus, Antoninianus, 260–8, [GALLI]ENVS AVG, Ill. (Blurred striking). Fem. fig. stg. l..

303 SF 36, ctx 7, Gallienus, Antoninianus, 260–8, Illegible, Ill. Fortuna stg. L.

304 SF 564, ctx 128, Gallienus, Antoninianus, 260–8, Illegible, Ill., Fides stg. l..

305 SF 154, ctx 7, Claudius II, Antoninianus, 268–70, IM- — AVG, [PROVID] AVG, Rome, RIC 5: 87.

306 SF 1547, ctx 1244, Claudius II, Antoninianus, 268–70, IMP C CLAVDIVS AVG, FIDES EXERCI.

307 SF 31, ctx 7, Claudius II, Antoninianus, 268–70, Illegible, Ill. Genius stg. l.

308 SF 145, ctx 18, Claudius II, Antoninianus, 268–70, Illegible, Illegible.

309 SF 150, ctx 18, Claudius II, Antoninianus, 268–70, Illegible, Illegible.

310 SF 749, ctx 230, Claudius II, Antoninianus, 268–70, Illegible, Illegible.

311 SF 270, ctx 31, Claudius II, Antoninianus, 270, DIVO CLAVD[IO], [CO]NSEC[RATIO], altar, , RIC 5: 261.

312 SF 40, ctx 7, Claudius II, Antoninianus, 270, DIVO CL[AVDIO], [CONSECRATIO]; eagle, , RIC 5: 266.

313 SF 662, ctx 272, Postumus, Silver Antoninianus, 259–68, IMP C POSTVMVS PF AVG, [HE]RC PACIF[ERO], Principal mint, Elmer 299.

314 SF 1578, ctx 1313, Postumus, Antoninianus, 259–68, IMP C POST[VMVS PF AVG], MONE[TA A]VG, Principal mint, Elmer 336

315 SF 613, , ctx 268, Postumus, Antoninianus, 259–68, Illegible, [PAX AVG], Principal mint, Elmer 566.

316 SF 44, ctx 7, Postumus, Antoninianus, 259–68, IMP C POSTVMVS PF AVG, ORIENS AVG, Principal mint, Elmer 568.

317 SF 761, ctx 272, Postumus, Silver antoninianus, 259–68, IMP C POSTVMVS PF AVG, ORIENS AVG, Principal mint, Elmer 568.

318 SF 111, ctx 7, Marius, Antoninianus, 268, IMP C M [AVR MARIVS AVG], VICTORIA AVG, Cologne, RIC 5: 18

319 SF 160, ctx 34, Victorinus, Antoninianus, 268–70, Illegible, {PROVIDENTIA AVG], Trier, Elmer 743.

320 SF 15, ctx 2, Victorinus, Antoninianus, 268–70, Illegible, [VICTORIA] A[VG], Trier, Elmer 744.

321 SF 113, ctx 14, Victorinus, Antoninianus, 270–4, Illegible, [SALVS AVG].

322 SF 1661, ctx 1500, Tetricus I, Antoninianus, 270–4, Illegible, [PAX] A[VG], Cologne, Elmer 771.

323 SF 743, ctx 230, Tetricus II, Antoninianus, 270–4, —TET—, [PIET]AS AV[GG], Cologne, Elmer 773.

324 SF 29, ctx 7, Tetricus I, Antoninianus, 270–4, IMP TETRIC[VS PF AVG], [HILA]RITAS AVGG, Trier, Elmer 789.

325 SF 1698, ctx 1518, Tetricus I, Antoninianus, 270–4, Illegible, [SPES PVBLICA], Cologne.

326 SF 118, ctx 14, Tetricus I, Antoninianus, 270–4, Illegible, [SPES PVBLICA], Cologne.

327 SF 95, ctx 2, Tetricus I, Antoninianus, 270–4, Illegible, [SPES PVBLICA], Cologne.

328 SF 144, ctx 18, Tetricus I, Antoninianus, 270–4, Illegible, [SPES PVBLICA], Cologne.

329 SF 840, ctx 276, Tetricus I, Antoninianus, 270–4, Illegible, [SPES PVBLICA].

330 SF 279, ctx 2, Tetricus I, Antoninianus, 270–4, Illegible, LAETI[TIA —], Trier.

331 SF 245, ctx 31, Tetricus I, Antoninianus, 270–4, Illegible, [SPES —].

332 SF 1518, ctx 1198, Tetricus I, Antoninianus, 270–4, Illegible, LAE[TITIA—], Trier.

333 SF 343, ctx 34, Tetricus I, Antoninianus, 270–4, Illegible, Illegible.

334 SF 630, ctx 14, Tetricus I, Antoninianus, 270–4, Illegible, Illegible.

335 SF 115, ctx 14, Tetricus I, Antoninianus, 270–4, —VS C—, PI[ETAS] —, Cologne.

336 SF 7, ctx 7, Tetricus I, Antoninianus, 270–4, Illegible, [PIETAS —], Cologne.

337 SF 59, ctx 7, Tetricus II, Antoninianus, 270–4, Illegible, [SPES —].

338 SF 275, ctx 34, Tetricus II, Antoninianus, 270–4, Illegible, SPES —.

339 SF 458, ctx 34, Tetricus II, Antoninianus, 270–4, Illegible, [C]OME[S AVG].

340 SF 17, Tetricus II, Antoninianus, 270–4, Illegible, Illegible.

341 SF 835, ctx 230, Tetricus I/II, Antoninianus, 270–4, Illegible, Illegible, ewer.

342 SF 139, u/s, Gallic Empire, Antoninianus, 259–74, Illegible, Ill. Fem. fig. stg. l.

343 SF 143, ctx 18, Illegible, Antoninianus, 268–74, Illegible, Illegible.

344 SF 94, ctx 2, Aurelian, Antoninianus, 270–5, Illegible, CONCORDIA MILITVM.

345 SF 1529, ctx 1224, Illegible, Antoninianus, 260–74, Illegible, Illegible.

346 SF 452, ctx 182, Tetricus II, Irregular Antoninianus, 270–4, —ESP TETRICVS CA—(irregular lettering), PAX [AVG].

347 SF 1541, ctx 1225, Barbarous radiate, 270–84, Gallienus, Hilaritas.

348 SF 116, ctx 14, Barbarous radiate, 70–84, [CO]NSECR[ATIO], [CO]NSECR[ATIO].

349 SF 153, ctx 7, Barbarous radiate, 270–84, Claudius II, Altar.

350 SF 227, ctx 31, Barbarous radiate, 270–84, [DIVO CL]AVD[IO], Altar.

351 SF 1531, ctx 1224, Barbarous radiate, 270–84, Tetricus I, PAX AVG; vertical sceptre.

352 SF 105, ctx 7, Barbarous radiate, 270–84, Tetricus I, Pax Aug.

353 SF 75, ctx 7, Barbarous radiate, 270–84, No leg. Tetricus I, S—— AVG; Pax, vertical sceptre.

354 SF 210, ctx 1, Barbarous radiate, 270–84, Tetricus I, —CO—.

355 SF 760, ctx 14, Barbarous radiate, 270–84, Tetricus I, —VS—.

356 SF 1730, ctx 1509, Barbarous radiate, 270–84, , Female figure standing right.

357 SF 1690, ctx 1501, Barbarous radiate, 270–84, —TRICVS CA— (Tetricus II), No legend. Pin figure.

358 SF 1689, ctx 1508, Barbarous radiate, 270–84, Tetricus II, Female figure standing left.

359 SF 1552, ctx 1228, Barbarous radiate, 270–84, Tetricus II, Female figure with cornucopiae standing l.

360 SF 1554, ctx 1227, Barbarous radiate, 270–84, —TETRICV— (Tetricus II), Female figure.

361 SF 1525, ctx 1211, Barbarous radiate, 270–84.

362 SF 124, ctx 14, Barbarous radiate, 270–84, Pin figure.

363 SF 880, ctx 223, Barbarous radiate, 270–84.

364 SF 973, ctx 7, Barbarous radiate, 270–84, Pin figure.

365 SF 1113, ctx 704, Barbarous radiate, 270–84, Tetricus II.

366 SF 634, ctx 128, Barbarous radiate, 270–84.

367 SF 1526, ctx 1211, Barbarous radiate, Minim, 275–84, Pin figure.

368 SF 1527, ctx 1211, Barbarous radiate, Minim, 275–84, Altar derivative.

369 SF 375, ctx 34, Barbarous radiate, Minim, 275–84, Tetricus I, Pax.

370 SF 624, ctx 128, Barbarous radiate, Minim, 275–84, Tetricus I, Sacrificial implements.

371 SF 1540, ctx 1225, Barbarous radiate, Minim, 275–84, Tetricus II.

372 SF 27, ctx 7, Barbarous radiate, Minim, 275–84, Invictus to r.

373 SF 147, ctx 18, Barbarous radiate, Minim, 275–84.

374 SF 272, ctx 31, Barbarous radiate, Minim, 275–84.

375 SF 759, ctx 272, Barbarous radiate, Minim, 275–84, No legend, Border only.

376 SF 766, ctx 272, Barbarous radiate, Minim, 275–84, Tetricus II, Salus.

377 SF 815, ctx 272, Barbarous radiate, Minim, 275–84.

378 SF 831, ctx 278, Barbarous radiate, Minim, 275–84, No leg, No leg, ewer.

379 SF 850, ctx 251, Barbarous radiate, Minim, 275–84.

380 SF 893, ctx 454, Barbarous radiate, Minim, 275–84, No leg, No leg.

381 SF 927, ctx 431, Barbarous radiate, Minim, 275–84.

382 SF 1086, ctx 122, Barbarous radiate, Minim, 275–84.

383 SF 1538, ctx 1225, Barbarous radiate, Minim fragment, 275–84.

384 SF 1024, ctx 721, Barbarous radiate, Fragment, 270–84.

385 SF 469, ctx 34, Carausius, Antoninianus, 287–93, Illegible, MARS VLTOR, RIC 5: 89.

386 SF 86, ctx 7, Carausius, Antoninianus, 287–93, IMP CA[RAVSIV]S PF AVG, PAX AVG; vertical sceptre, London, RIC 5: 101.

387 SF 30, ctx 7, Carausius, Antoninianus, 287–93, —C CARAVSIVS PF AVG, PAX AVG; trans. sceptre, Illegible.

388 SF 60, ctx 7, Allectus, Antoninianus, 293–6, [IMP] C ALLECTVS PF AVG, LAETITIA AVG, London, RIC 5: 22.

389 SF 43, ctx 7, Allectus, Quinarius, 293–6, IMP C ALLECTVS PF AVG, VIRTVS AVG, London, RIC 5: 55.

390 SF 321, ctx 31, Allectus, Quinarius, 293–6, IMP C ALLECTVS PF AVG, VIRTVS AVG, 'C' mint, RIC 5: 128.

391 SF 468, ctx 14, Illegible, Antoninianus, 260–96, Illegible, Illegible.

392 SF 61, ctx 7, Licinius, Follis, 310–12, IMP LICINIVS PF AVG, GENIO POP ROM, London, RIC 6: 209c.

393 SF 103, ctx 7, Constantine I, Follis, 316,

CONSTANTINVS P AVG, SOLI INVICTO COMITI, London, RIC 7: 75.

394 SF 10, ctx 2, Constantine II, Follis, 317, FL CL CONSTANTINVS IVN NC, SOLI INVICTO COMITI, London, RIC 7: 117.

395 SF 626, ctx 72, Constantine I, Follis, 313–17, IMP CONSTANTINVS AVG, SOLI INVICTO COMITI, London.

396 SF 345, ctx 53, Constantine I, Follis, 320, CONSTANTINVS MAX AVG, VICTORIAE LAETAE PRINC PERP, London, RIC 7: 170.

397 SF 1686, ctx 2012, Crispus, Follis, 320–1, CRISPVS [NO]BIL C, VIR[TVS EXERCIT], London, RIC 7: 194.

398 SF 1685, ctx 2012, Crispus, Follis, 323–4, CRISPVS NOBIL C, BEAT TRANQLITAS, London, RIC 7: 274.

399 SF 1697, ctx 2012, Crispus, Follis, 323–4, CRISPVS NOBIL C, BEAT TRANQLITAS, London, RIC 7: 275.

400 SF 1696, ctx 2012, Constantine II, Follis, 323–4, [CONSTANT]INVS IVN NC, BEAT TRAN]QLITAS, London, RIC 7: 287.

401 SF 837, ctx 30, Constantine II, Follis, 323–4, CONSTANTINVS IVN NC, BEAT TRAN]QLITAS, London, RIC 7: 287.

402 1514, ctx 1179, Crispus, Follis, 324–5, FL IVL CRISPVS, PROVIDENTIAE CAESS, London, RIC 7: 295.

403 SF 21, ctx 2, Constantine I, Follis, 313–15, IMP CONSTANTINVS AVG, SOLI INVICTO COMITI, Trier, RIC 7: 40.

404 SF 14, ctx 2, Licinius, Follis, 313–15, IMP LICINIVS PF AVG, GENIO POP ROM, Trier, RIC 7: 57.

405 SF 1523, ctx 1211, Crispus, Follis, 320, CRISPVS NOB CAES, VIRTVS EXERCIT, Trier, RIC 7: 260.

406 SF 238, ctx 31, Constantine I, Follis, 321, CONSTANTINVS AVG, BEATA TRANQVILLITAS, VO/TIS/XX, Trier, RIC 7: 303.

407 SF 1719, ctx 1519, Constantine I, Follis, 322, CONSTA—, [BEATA TRA]NQVILLITAS, Trier, RIC 7: 341.

408 SF 48, ctx 7, Constantine I, Follis, 322, CONST-ANTINVS AVG, BEATA TRANQVILLITAS, VO/TIS/XX, Trier, RIC 7: 341.

409 SF 42, ctx 7, Crispus, Follis, 322, [IVL] CRISPVS NOB CAES, BEATA TRANQVILLITAS, Trier, RIC 7: 347.

410 SF 261, ctx 31, Crispus, Follis, 322–3, IVL CRISPVS NOB CAES, BEATA TRANQVILLITAS, Trier, RIC 7: 376.

411 SF 337, ctx 136, Constantine I, Follis, 323, CONSTANTINVS AVG, BEATA TRAN[QVILLITAS], VO/TIS/XX, Trier, RIC 7: 390.

412 SF 164, ctx 31, Crispus, Follis, 321–3, IVL CRISPVS NOB CAES, BEATA TRANQVILLITAS, VO/TIS/XX, Trier, RIC 7: 426.

413 SF 1684, ctx 2012, Constantine I, Follis, 323–4, CONST[AN]TIN[VS AVG], SARMAT[IA DEVICTA], Trier, RIC 7: 429.

414 SF 1687, ctx 2012, Fausta, Follis, 324-5, Illegible, SPE]S REIPVBLICAE, Trier, RIC 7: 460.

415 SF 330, ctx 31, Helena, Follis, 327–8, FL HELENA AVGVSTA, SECVRITAS REIPVBLICE, Trier, RIC 7: 508.

416 SF 1, ctx 7, Constantine I, Follis, 330–1, [VRBS ROMA], Wolf and twins, Trier, RIC 7: 522.

417 SF 1560, ctx 1313, Constantine I, Follis, 332–3, CONST[ANTINOPOLIS], Victory on prow, Trier, RIC 7: 543.

418 SF 141, ctx 72, Constantine I, Follis, 332–3, CONSTANTINOPOLIS, Victory on prow, Trier, RIC 7: 543.

419 SF 1208, ctx 760, Constantine I, Follis, 332–3, CONST[ANTINOPOLIS], Victory on prow, Trier, RIC 7: 543.

420 SF 872, ctx 246, Constantine II, Follis, 333–4, CONSTANTINVS IVN, GLORI]A EXERC[ITVS], 2 standards, Trier, RIC 7: 550.

421 SF 280, ctx 2, Theodora, Follis, 337–40, Illegible, P[IETAS] ROMANA, Trier, RIC 8: 65.

422 SF 1694, ctx 2012, House of Constantine, Follis, 321, Illegible, BEAT[A TRANQV]ILLITAS, Lyons, RIC 7: 125.

423 SF 237, ctx 31, Constantine I, Follis, 321, CONSTANTINVS AVG, BEATA TRANQVILLITAS,, Lyons, RIC 7: 129.

424 SF 464, ctx 128, Constantine I, Follis, 323–4, CONSTANTINVS AVG, SARMATIA DEVICTA, Lyons, RIC 7: 222.

425 SF 33, ctx 7, Constantine I, Follis (incomplete), 330, [CON]STANTIN[VS AVG], [GLORIA E] XERCITVS, 2 standards, Arles, RIC 7: 341.

426 SF 1521, ctx 1210, House of Constantine, Follis, 330–1, Illegible, [GLORIA EXERCITVS], 2 standards, Arles, RIC 7: 345.

427 SF 1576, ctx 1313, Constantine II, Follis, 333, CONSTANTINVS IVN NC, GLORIA EXERCITVS, 2 standards, Arles, RIC 7: 371.

428 SF 1561, ctx 1313, Constantine I, Follis, 333–4, CONSTANT[INVS] MAX AUG, GLORIA EXERCITVS, 2 standards, Arles, RIC 7: 375.

429 SF 200, ctx 53, Delmatius, Follis, 336, FL DELMATIVS [NOB C], GLORIA EXERC[ITVS], 1 standard, Arles, RIC 7: 399.

430 SF 4, ctx 7, Constantine I, Silvered Follis, 324–5, CONSTANTINVS AVG, PROVIDENTIAE AVGG,

Siscia, RIC 7: 183.

431 SF 267, ctx 31, Constantine II, Follis, 325–6, FL IVL CONSTANTIVS NOB C, PROVIDENTIAE CAESS, Heraclea, RIC 7: 78.

432 SF 660, u/s, House of Constantine, Follis, 310–13, Illegible, SOLI INVICTO COMITI.

433 SF 620, ctx 128, Licinius, Follis, 313–7, IMP LICIMIVS PF AVG, GENIO POP ROM.

434 SF 31, ctx 7, House of Constantine, Follis, 310–13, CON—, VICTORIAE LAETAE PRINC [PERP].

435 SF 240, ctx 31, Constantine I, Follis, 316–20, CONSTANTINVS AVG, VICTORIAE LAETAE PRINC PERP.

436 SF 1387, ctx 929, Constantine I, Follis, 316–20, CONSTANTINVS AVG, VICTORIAE LAETAE PRINC PERP.

437 SF 260, ctx 31, Licinius, Follis, 319–24, IMP LICINIVS AVG, VOT/XX.

438 SF 1695, ctx 2012, Crispus, Follis, 320–1, CRISPVS NOB CAES, VIR[TVS] EXERC[IT].

439 SF 1558, ctx 1224, Licinius, Follis, 320, LICINIVS IVN NOB C, [VIRTVS] EXERCIT.

440 SF 92, ctx 2, Crispus, Follis, 320-1, NOB CAES, VIRTVS EXERCIT.

441 SF 266, ctx 31, Crispus, Follis, 320–3, PVS NOB CAES, [BEATA TRANQVILLITAS].

442 SF 93, ctx 2, House of Constantine, Follis, 321–4, Illegible, [CAESARVM NOSTRORVM], VOT/X.

443 SF 635, ctx 128, House of Constantine, Follis, 321–4, Illegible, [CAESARVM NOSTRORVM], VOT/X.

444 SF 134, ctx 18, House of Constantine, Follis, 321–4, Illegible, [CAESARVM NOSTRORVM], VOT/X.

445 SF 395, ctx 34, Constantine I, Follis, 323–4, —TINVS AVG, DN CONSTANTINI MAX AVG; VOT/XX.

446 SF 96, ctx 2, Helena, Follis, 324–5, Illegible, [SECVRITAS REIPVBLICE].

447 SF 18, ctx 2, House of Constantine, Follis, 317–20, Illegible..Helemted bust r., Illegible.

448 SF 79, ctx 136, Constantine II, Follis, 330–5, FL IVL CO[NSTAN]TIVS NOB C, GLORIA EXERCITVS, 2 standards.

449 SF 9, ctx 7, House of Constantine, Follis, 330–5, CONSTANT—, [GLORI]A EXE[RCITVS], 2 standards.

450 SF 1517, ctx 1198, Constantine I, Follis, 330–5, [CONSTANTINOPOLIS], Victory on prow.

451 SF 1573, ctx 1313, Constans, Follis, 337–40, [FL IVL CONST]ANS AVG, GLORIA EXER[CITVS], 1 standard, Trier, RIC 8: 85.

452 SF 1592, ctx 1311, House of Constantine, Follis, 340, Illegible, [GLORIA EXERCITVS], 1 standard,

Arles, RIC 8: 56.

453 SF 325, ctx 31, Constantine I, Follis, 330–5, [VRBS ROMA], Wolf and twins.

454 SF 225, ctx 1, Constantine I, Follis, 330–5, [CONSTAN]TINOPOLIS, Victory on prow.

455 SF 1664, ctx 1500, House of Constantine, Follis (frag.), 335–40, Illegible, [GLORIA EXERCITVS], 1 standard.

456 SF 1556, ctx 1309, House of Constantine, Follis (frag.), 335–40, Illegible, [GLORIA EX]ERC[ITVS], 1 standard.

457 SF 1610, ctx 1311, House of Constantine, Follis, 335–40, Illegible, [GLORIA EXERCITVS], 1 standard.

458 SF 89, ctx 7, House of Constantine, Follis, 335–40, Illegible, [GLORIA EXERCITVS], 1 standard.

459 SF 70, ctx 7, House of Constantine, Follis, 335–40, Border missing, [GLORIA EXERCITVS], 1 standard.

460 SF 28, ctx 7, House of Constantine, Follis, 335–40, Illegible, [GLORIA EXERCITVS], 1 standard.

461 SF 25, ctx 7, Constantius II, Follis, 335–40, [FL IVL CONST]ANTIVS NOB [C], [GLORIA EXERCITVS], 1 standard.

462 SF 6, ctx 7, Constans, Follis, 337–40, —STANS AVG, [GLORIA] EXERCITVS, 1 standard.

463 SF 278, ctx 2, House of Constantine, Follis, 335–40, CONSTANTI—, GLORIA [EXERCITVS], 1 standard.

464 SF 1532, ctx 1224, Helena, Follis, 337–40, [FL IVL H]ELENAE AVG, [PAX PV]BLICA.

465 SF 1666, ctx 1500, House of Constantine, Irregular Follis, 341–6, Illegible, [GLORIA EXERCITVS], 2 standards.

466 SF 1575, ctx 1313, Constantine I, Irregular Follis, 341–6, VRBS ROMA, Wolf and twins.

467 SF 2, ctx 7, Constantine I, Irregular Follis 341–6, [CONSTANTINOPOLIS], Victory on prow.

468 SF 667, ctx 136, Constantine I, Irregular Follis, 341–6, CONSTANTINOPOLIS, Victory on prow.

469 SF 1244, ctx 760, Constantine I, Irregular Follis, 341–6, CONSTANTINOPOLIS, Victory on prow, As Lyons.

470 SF 22, ctx 7, House of Constantine, Follis, 347–8, Illegible, VICTORIAE DD AVGG Q NN], Trier, RIC 8: 207.

471 SF 1571, ctx 1313, House of Constantine, Follis, 347–8, Illegible, [VICTORIAE DD AVGG Q NN]].

472 SF 254, ctx 91, Constans, Follis, 347–8, CONSTANS PF AVG, [VICTORIAE DD AVGG Q NN].

473 SF 110, ctx 7, House of Constantine, Irregular AE4, 354–64, Illegible, [FEL TEMP REPARATIO]; falling horseman.

474   SF 448, ctx 128, House of Constantine, Irregular AE4, 354–64, Illegible, [FEL TEMP REPARATIO]; falling horseman.

475   SF 12, ctx 7, , Illegible minim, 340–64, Illegible, Illegible.

476   SF 370, ctx 34, Valens, AE3, 367–75, —S PF AVG, SECVRITAS REIPVBLICAE, Arles, RIC 9: 17b.

477   SF 130, ctx 7, Valentinian I, AE3, 364–7, DN VALENTINIANVS PF AVG, GLORIA R[OMAN-ORVM], Aquileia, RIC 9: 7a.

478   SF 32, ctx 7, House of Valentinian, AE3, 364–78, Illegible, [GLORIA ROMANORVM].

479   SF 91, ctx 7, Valens, AE3, 364-78, DN VALEN—, SECVRITAS REIP[VBLICAE].

480   SF 8, ctx 7, House of Valentinian, AE3, 364-78, Illegible, [SECVRITAS REIPVBLICAE].

481   SF 274, ctx 34, Valens, AE3, 364-78, DN VALEN—, SECVRITAS REIPVBLICAE.

482   SF 246, ctx 34, House of Valentinian, AE3, 364–78, Illegible, [SECVRITAS REIPVBLICAE].

483   SF 1048, ctx 736, House of Theodosius, AE4, 388–95, Illegible, SALVS REIPVBLICAE.

484   SF 1682, ctx 1534, Illegible, AE4, 320–78, Illegible, Illegible.

485   SF 11, ctx 7, Illegible, AE3, 320–78, Illegible, Illegible.

486   SF 165, ctx 40, Illegible, AE4, 341–402, Illegible, Illegible.

487   SF 166, ctx 1, Illegible, AE4, 275–364, Illegible, Illegible.

488   SF 170, ctx 31, Illegible, AE4, 275–364, Illegible, Illegible.

489   SF 1736, ctx 1624, Illegible, AE3, 260–378, Illegible, Illegible.
490   SF 1656, ctx 1500, Illegible, AE3, 260–378, Illegible, Illegible.

491   SF 1650, ctx 1500, Illegible, AE3, 260–378, Illegible, Illegible.

492   SF 88, ctx 7, Illegible, AE3, 260–378, Illegible, Illegible.

493   SF 132, ctx 18, Illegible, AE3, 260–378, Illegible, Illegible.

494   SF 1702, ctx 1501, Illegible, AE3/4, 260–402, Illegible, Illegible.

495   SF 1703, ctx 1501, Illegible, AE4 frag., 260–402, Illegible, Illegible.

496   SF 1678, ctx 2002, Illegible, AE3/4 frag., 260–402, Illegible, Illegible.

497   SF 1551, ctx 1244, Illegible, AE indet frags, 260–402, Illegible, Illegible.

498   SF 201, ctx 18, Illegible, AE3, 260–402, Illegible, Illegible.

499   SF 1190, ctx 815, Illegible, AE3, 260–402, Illegible, Illegible.

500   SF 1520, ctx 1210, Illegible, AE3, 270–402, Illegible, Illegible.

501   SF 336, ctx 38, Illegible, AE4, 270–402, Illegible, Illegible.

502   SF 128, ctx 7, Illegible, AE4, 275–402, Illegible, Illegible.

503   SF 133, ctx 18, Illegible, AE4, 275–402, Illegible, Illegible.

504   SF 290, ctx 90, Illegible, AE4, 275–402, Illegible, Illegible.

505   SF 1557, ctx 1235, Fragment, 3rd/4th century.

506   SF 129, ctx 7, Fragments, 3rd/4th century.

BROOCHES
By D. F. Mackreth

A total assemblage of 18 brooches was recovered from 4 sites: 6 from Duntisbourne Grove, 6 from Middle Duntisbourne, 5 from Birdlip Quarry and 1 from Court Farm. All were examined, and attributed, where possible, to one of the following typological categories: Colchesters, Colchester Derivatives, Late La Tène, Aucissa and Related, Trumpet and Penannular. All are copper alloy, unless otherwise stated.

Colchesters *(Fig. 7.20)*

507   Middle Duntisbourne, sf 29, ctx 288. The spring is covered with corrosion including a considerable quantity of iron possibly pointing to an ancient repair. The wings cannot be seen. The relatively short hook has a pointed end. The bow profile was forged and there are facets down each rear corner, the evidence for others down the front edges is equivocal. The bow is plain apart from three stamped circles arranged 2 and 1. The catch-plate was pierced, but it is impossible to tell whether it was fretted.

508   Middle Duntisbourne, sf 28, ctx 256. The wings are plain and the hook short. The plain bow had an octagonal section, its profile being forged. The catch-plate has largely gone but enough remains to show that it had been pierced with square-cornered openings.

509   Duntisbourne Grove, sf 136, ctx 135. In very poor condition, the type is assured, and the hook was short.

The only reliable guide to what is likely to have been common in most of southern England in the late pre-Roman Iron Age is the King Harry Lane cemetery (Stead and Rigby 1989) where brooches such as these Colchesters are common. Because the condition of the present examples is poor, detailed analysis of parallels

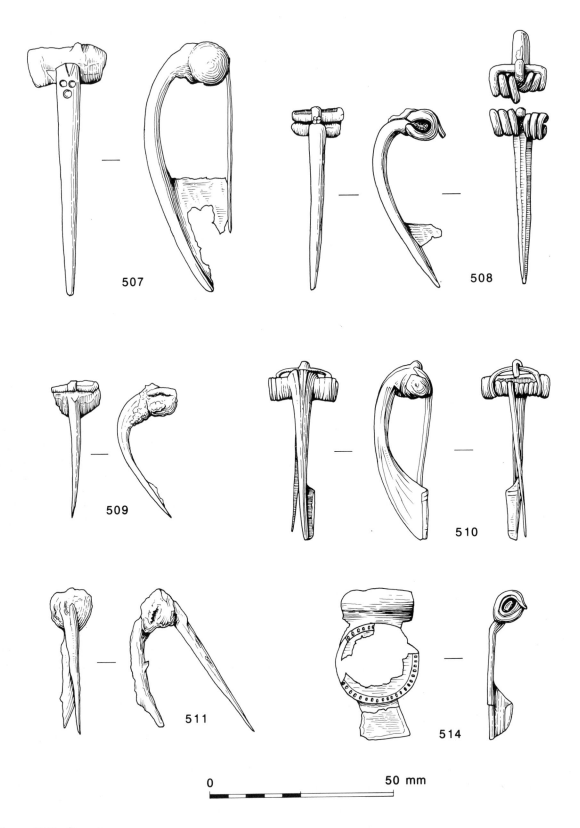

Figure 7.20 Brooches.

in the four phases is not really possible. However, all three here had their profiles forged, none is particularly small or has any feature pointing specifically to a late date in the development of the type. In this they match the bulk of those in the cemetery, excluding obviously early and late ones. The former are defined by their almost straight bows and the marked kick at the top of the profile, the latter are small and are cast with minimal finishing. The dating of the cemetery is therefore important.

The King Harry Lane report (ibid., 84) assigns the following dates to each phase: Phase 1 - AD 1–40, Phase 2 - AD 30–55, Phase 3 - AD 40–60, Phase 4 - AD 60+. The cemetery could have begun as early as *c.* 15 BC (ibid., 83), but a conservative view was taken and it was suggested that the cemetery lasted significantly beyond the Roman conquest. Therefore, all Phase 1, half of Phase 2 and practically nothing of Phase 3 would be pre-conquest, while Phase 4 can be ignored. However, there is a striking absence of well-known post-conquest types which flooded the market in the first 10–15 years after the arrival of the Roman army, there being only one Colchester Derivative (grave 316.4), and no standard Hod Hill. However, these types were being used in quantity a few hundred metres away, and there is also a commensurate lack of samian at a time when it was being imported in vast quantities (ibid., 113) and was abundant in the developing town. If, however, a possible start-date of 15 BC is used, and the phasing adjusted appropriately, then virtually all of the imbalance disappears. Consequently, the following dating is proposed: Phase 1 - 15 BC-AD 30; Phase 2 - AD 20–40; Phase 3 - AD 35–50; Phase 4 - AD 45+. What should be revealed, whatever the dating, is what was the common floruit of the main types in use at the time.

This argument covers brooches from a well-furnished cemetery, in which ordinary residuality, a common condition of standard occupation sites is not a factor, and it shows that the Colchester is frequently found on sites with Claudian deposits. Those brooches, which occur in contexts dating to the first 10–15 years after AD 43 are clearly devolving rapidly and it is very much a moot point as to whether they are actually only survivors in use. However, brooches such as nos 507–509 were made from about AD 10/20 and their manufacture had ceased by the conquest. The difficulty is establishing the point at which they become purely residual. The writer's opinion is that these three must have been residual by AD 60 and possibly not by AD 50 and, in default of better evidence, they should have passed out of use by AD 50/55.

Only brooch 507, with its stamped circles, has a distinctive feature. Brooches with such stamps are almost invariably larger than average, often have moulded wings and occasionally have grooves across the foot. The most extreme example comes from Cheriton, Kent, which has stamps down each side of the bow sweeping out along the top of the catch-plate (Tester and Bing 1949, 33, fig. 6, 3). The frequency

of stamps in the King Harry Lane cemetery is unequivocal: Phase 2, G53, G152, G399, G433; Phase 3, G23; unphased D170, G177. Both G399 and D170 have the almost straight bows which mark the earliest strand of British Colchesters. In other words, if the cemetery is treated as an ordinary site, such brooches were going out of use in Phase 3 and most should have ceased to be used by the conquest, which suits the general tenor of the main series as a whole.

Colchester Derivative *(Fig. 7.20)*

510 Duntisbourne Grove, sf 6, ctx 27. The spring is held by the Polden Hill method: an axis bar through the coils is lodged in pierced plates at the ends of the wings, the chord being secured by a rearward-facing hook. Each wing has a buried moulding at its end. The hook is part of a skeuomorph of the Colchester's hook, otherwise the bow is plain. The return of the solid catch-plate has a buried moulding across its top.

Most Polden Hills can be assigned to a major group without difficulty, and, had the present piece had a moulding rising from the wings on each side of the head, the same would be true here. However, despite this, the overall proportions, the minimal decoration on the wings, coupled with the skeuomorph of the hook, show that the brooch belongs to the second half of the 1st century. A determining feature in placing the brooch more exactly would have been the style of any piercing in the catch-plate, but the catch-plate here is too small to have been so treated. Bearing in mind that the chief variety of Polden Hill had developed by the end of the 1st century (Mackreth 1996, 301), and that brooch 510 betrays no sign of that development, it may date to before AD 75.

Late La Tène *(Fig. 7.20)*

511 Middle Duntisbourne, sf 7, ctx 45. Iron. The integral spring has four coils and an internal chord. The bow is a circular-sectioned rod, the lower bow with the catch-plate is missing.

512 Middle Duntisbourne, sf 21, ctx 41. Half the spring and internal chord from a brooch of Nauheim or Drahtfibel Derivative type. (not illustrated).

513 Birdlip Quarry, sf 363, ctx 34. As 6. (not illustrated).

Without the bows, very little can be said about brooches 512 and 513. Both are almost certainly 1st century AD, and may have lasted to near the end of the century. However, brooch 511 is recognisably related to the *Drahtfibel*. Without the framed catch-plate, one cannot be sure that this example is one, but its proportions would not be out of place (cf. Mackreth 1992, 123, fig. 113, 21). The type developed in as much as it sometimes has a fretted catch-plate, and examples occur in Phases 1 and 2 burials at King Harry Lane showing that this feature belongs to pre-conquest times (Stead and Rigby 1989, 342, fig. 141, 270.5; 310, fig. 113, 143.5). The dating available for examples with or without catch-plates, some of the latter possibly having been genuine Drahtfibeln, is as follows: Ower, Dorset, before AD 25 (Woodward 1987, 97, fig. 52, 217, 219); Kelvedon, Essex, 1st century BC-AD 43, and Tiberian- AD 40 (Rodwell 1988, 67, fig. 53, 3, 5); Werrington, Peterborough, 2nd/1st century BC - AD 50/60 (Mackreth 1988, 90, fig. 20,1); Station Road, Puckeridge, Herts, two examples, c. AD 25?-Claudius (Partridge 1979, 35, fig. 6.1–2); Gussage All Saints, mid 1st century, two examples (Wainwright 1979, 108, fig. 82, 3, 1056); Thetford, c. AD 45–61 (Mackreth 1992, 123, fig. 113, 24); Bagendon, AD 50–60 (Clifford 1961b, 167, fig. 29,4). Apart from excluding all brooches dating after AD 100, all those in iron with dates recorded by the writer are gathered here. The emphasis is on the first half of the 1st century or earlier. By AD 60 all were either residual or very long-lived survivors in use.

Rosette *(Fig. 7.20)*

514 Duntisbourne Grove, sf 8, ctx 43. The separate spring is housed in a case formed by folding two flaps round it at the top of the bow. This is a single plate shaped as a disc and fantail and was once covered by an applied repoussé plate, the remains of which preserve part of a beaded border on the disc.

This Rosette stands almost at the very end of a development which began in the middle of the 1st century BC, the last stage was to substitute a hinged pin for the sprung one. Beginning again with the King Harry Lane cemetery, two brooches of this variety occurred in Phase 2 (Stead and Rigby 1989, 290, fig. 99, 67.2,3) showing that, on the revised dating offered, it had arrived before the Roman conquest. Other dated examples are: Bagendon, AD 20/25–43/5 (Clifford 1961b, 175, fig. 32,2); Bancroft, pre-conquest-late 1st century (Mackreth 1994a, 291, fig. 132, 17); Colchester, AD 43/44–48, and AD 49–60 (Hawkes and Hull 1947, 83, pl. 94, 81, 83); Bagendon, AD 43/45–47/52 and AD 50/60 (Clifford 1961, 175, fig. 32, 3, 4); Colchester, AD 44–60 and AD 54–60 (Niblett 1985, 116, fig. 74, 22, 24); Baldock, AD 50–70 (Stead and Rigby 1986, 113, fig. 46, 100); Colchester, AD 60–80? (Crummy 1983, 8, fig. 3, 17). Again, any context later than AD 100 has been omitted. What is striking about these examples is that there is only one example dating after AD 60, and that should be residual, as the terminal date for pieces still in use should be hardly later than AD 50/55.

Langton Down *(Fig. 7.21)*

515 Duntisbourne Grove, ctx 5. The spring is housed like that in brooch 514. The condition is very poor and all that can be said is that the brooch was a reeded Langton Down, without any beading.

The King Harry Lane cemetery is again the chief source of information on the chronology of the Langton Down. The condition of this brooch is so poor that all that

need be noted is that it appears to have been reeded and to have had no beading. The latter means that the brooch probably belongs to the first half of the overall floruit. The type lasted a little longer than the Colchester and could still be seen in use in AD 55, but probably not by AD 60.

Aucissa and related types *(Fig. 7.21)*

516 Duntisbourne Grove, sf 3, ctx 6. Apparently a standard uninscribed Aucissa, the beading to be expected down the bow cannot be seen, but the surface is in poor condition.

517 Birdlip Quarry, sf 792, ctx 308. The same as the last, but in very poor condition.

518 Duntisbourne Grove, sf 15, ctx 64. The moulded head-plate had been reduced to a minimum, the bow is now an almost flat straight-sided strip with a flute down each side and a sunken moulding down the middle. The foot tapers in quickly from a slight triple cross-moulding.

These have rolled-over heads to house the axis bar of the hinged pin, and have separately made foot-knobs sweated on. The first two show no signs of having any early features such as rolled-under heads, extra ridges or punched dot decoration down the bow, or stamps or eyes on the head-plates. Both should be standard uninscribed Aucissas. The Aucissa lies at the very end of a development which started with the Alesia sometime in the middle of the 1st century BC (Duval 1974). The end of the Aucissa itself comes when it develops through examples like brooch 517 to the Hod Hill. As the Hod Hill in all its manifestations had fully developed by the time of the conquest, the parent had patently passed out of manufacture and so those found in Roman contexts in this country should be survivors in use. The Hod Hill, apart from one element, can be shown to be passing out of use in the period AD 60-70, therefore, the terminal date of the Aucissa should be considered to be at least 10–15 years earlier. The actual transition to the Hod Hill, represented by brooch 518, was very short and examples should perhaps have the same dating as the Aucissa proper.

Trumpet *(Fig. 7.21)*

519 Birdlip Quarry, sf 1200, ctx 837. The spring had been mounted in a pierced lug behind the head of the bow which is very narrow. On top is an unpierced tab. The trumpet head is minimal and most of it is straight-sided down to the knop. This has a triple cross-moulding in the middle separated from a single one top and bottom by a flute. The lower bow has a rounded front and a projecting foot.

A definite variety of the Trumpet found mainly in the south-west, hardly east of Wiltshire/Dorset and hardly north of the Avon in Warwickshire. There are obviously sub-groups, but these have yet to be fully

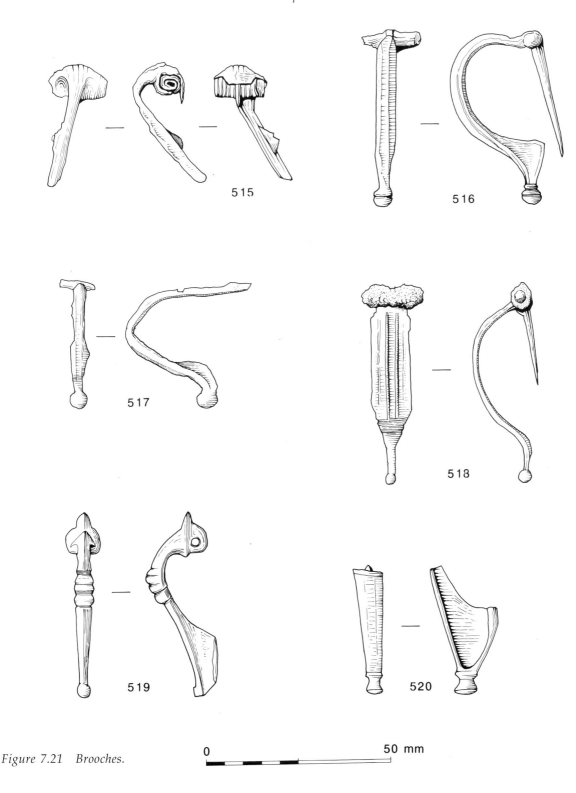

Figure 7.21   Brooches.

0   50 mm

distinguished. The chief features which define the general variety are the narrow head springing from a head-plate, generally slim lines, almost exclusive use of cross-mouldings for the knop and use of the single lug for holding the spring. Few are dated: Nettleton, AD 69–117 (Wedlake 1982, 127, fig. 53, 54); Caerleon, AD 80–100 (Brewer 1986b, 170, fig. 54, 3); Leicester, late 1st century (Clay and Pollard 1994, 145, fig. 74, 24); Alcester, Warks., Hadrianic-Antonine

(Mackreth 1994b, 167, fig. 79, 57). These few indicate that they date to the general floruit of the Trumpet type at large.

Unclassified *(Fig. 7.21)*

520   Birdlip Quarry, sf 98, ctx 2. Only the lower bow survives. It is broad at the fracture, flat in front, and tapers down to a foot which is suspended below the

catch-plate and is made up of two discs separated by a flute.

The writer has isolated three other catch-plates with the same style of foot-knob, but none has the upper bow, therefore the type is largely unidentified. All belong to the south-west and may be related to a widespread and poorly dated group which all have the same basic lower bow and prominent base moulding, but none close to the present example (cf. Hawkes 1947, 54, fig. 9, 12; Farwell and Molleson 1993, 87, fig. 67, 2), unless one from Bristol is acceptable (Hattatt 1985, 96, fig. 40, 408). Precise dating is rare, considering the numbers known: Dorchester, late 1st into the 2nd century (Green 1981, fig. 66); Camerton, AD 90–200 (Wedlake 1958, 225, fig. 52, 23); Chew, 2nd century (Rahtz and Greenfield 1977, fig. 114, 12).

Penannulars *(Fig. 7.22)*

All have circular-sectioned rings and straight pins, and all were forged.

521   Middle Duntisbourne, sf 12, ctx 39. Each terminal is turned back along the ring and has a groove across each end with a deep flute between.

522   Middle Duntisbourne, sf 36, ctx 288. Here the same style of terminal has five grooves across it.

In discussing the dating of these two brooches, only examples with the same characteristics have been chosen. These are, for brooch 521, the deep flute between a groove across each end, and for brooch 522, three or more equal value grooves. Brooch 521 before AD 60/65: Bagendon, AD 20/25–43/45 (Clifford 1961b, 184, fig. 36, 10); Hod Hill, before AD 50 (Brailsford 1962, 13, fig. 11, E17: Richmond 1968, 117–9); Longthorpe, Peterborough, *c.* AD 45–60/65 (Frere and St Joseph 1974, 46, fig. 24, 13); Waddon Hill, Stoke Abbot, *c.* AD 50–60 (Webster 1981b, 62, fig. 25, 11); Prestatyn, AD 70s–160 (Mackreth 1989, 98, fig. 40–27). Brooch 522, probably always before AD 60/65: Longthorpe, Peterborough, *c.* AD 45–60/65 (Frere and St Joseph 1974, 46, fig. 24, 14), and Claudian-Neronian (Dannell and Wild 1987, 87, fig. 21, 12); Tewkesbury, AD 140–160 (Hannan 1993, 68–70, fig. 19, 12).

523   Court Farm. Sf 2, ctx 132. Each terminal consists of two close-set discs which, although very worn, still preserve evidence of having been knurled. The wrap-round of the pin has two grooves round it, stopped at the top of the pin by two more.

The dating recorded by the writer is: Cirencester, AD 49–70/5 (Wacher and McWhirr 1982, 92, fig. 25, 17); Leicester, AD 90-100 (Kenyon 1948, 252, fig. 82, 10); Bancroft, late 1st-late 2nd century (Mackreth 1994a, 302, fig. 137, 54); Baldock, AD 120–150 (Stead and Rigby 1986, 122, fig. 49, 157); Ravenglass, AD 200–350/70 (Potter 1979, 69, fig. 26, 11). The range runs from the latter part of the 1st century to the 3rd century, it is possible that any after AD 200/225 should be regarded as having been residual in its context.

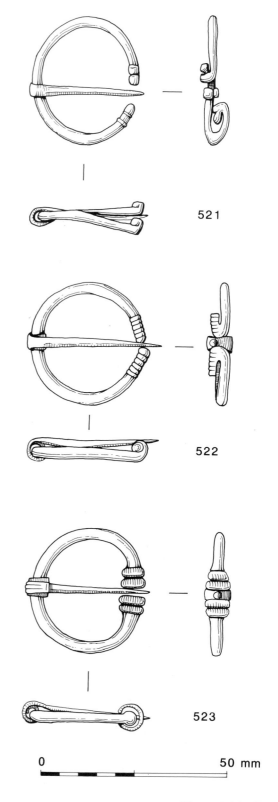

Figure 7.22   Brooches.

Fragment

524 Birdlip Quarry, sf 1581, ctx 1268. The pin and half of a bilateral spring, very probably from a Colchester Derivative. If so, it would date to before AD 150/175 by which date the bulk of British bow brooches had ceased to be made and used. (not illustrated).

COPPER ALLOY OBJECTS
By Ian R. Scott

Birdlip Quarry

Introduction

The assemblage of copper alloy objects is small, but contains a few interesting pieces. The total assemblage of copper alloy, excluding brooches and coins, comprises approximately 92 items. This is the number of copper alloy objects from all contexts and includes possible casting waste and scrap. Ident-ifiable objects comprise 62 pieces, the remainder is miscellaneous scrap, melted waste or unidentifiable fragments. There are a number of more recent pieces including a lower leg and foot from a hollow cast figure and a button. Thirty two objects have been included in the published catalogue.

The assemblage is small and as such provided only limited information regarding the occupation and use of the site. Personal ornaments (cat. 525–535) and military items (cat. 538–543) are well represented. Amongst the other finds a well preserved spoon is notable (cat. 536).

The military finds are interesting, because they repeat a pattern noted elsewhere in towns and on civilian sites in Roman Britain in the 2nd and 3rd centuries (Bishop 1991). A number of sites have produced small numbers of items of military equipment. On any one site, they would not be significant in themselves, but the recurring pattern of occurrence makes for greater interest. The range of items found comprises predominantly sword fittings (chapes and sword belt holders) and belt or baldric fittings (decorative plates and terminals). It is notable that there are pieces of military metalwork of 2nd-century and later date from Cirencester, which was abandoned as a military post before the end of the 1st century. Many of the civilian sites where military items occur are on major roads and it may be that the archaeological evidence points to the presence of small numbers of soldiers guarding way points. The pattern is too regular to be accounted for by casual loss alone, and is much more likely to represent some

Table 7.41   Copper alloy casting waste and possible scrap materials from Birdlip Quarry.

Context	Sf No.	Description
7	80	melted waste or scrap
7	80	melted waste or scrap
34	232	waste or scrap ? from casting
86	269	waste, ? casting
128	536	sheet, fragts
415	888	sheet fragts
519	921	sheet fragts, could be scrap
519	960	sheet fragts
893	1333	waste or scrap
1235	1543	plate fragts, irregular, possibly with cut edges
1244	1548	sheet, folded, ? scrap

Table 7.42   Miscellaneous fragments of strip, sheet, bar, wire and rings from Birdlip Quarry.

Context	Sf No.	Description
1210	1522	rod/bar fragment, square section
14	426	sheet fragment, slightly curved
31	257	sheet, thin
31	292	sheet, small fragment, could be piece of small collar
34	276	sheet, cast, fragment, poor surfaces
142	339	plate/sheet fragment, 1 straight edge
278	821	sheet fragment, bent
1210	1539	sheet, tinned surface, very thin
1501	1729	plate or sheet fragment, scored
7	72	strip, tapering
31	168	wire, twisted length
128	455	wire loop
1283	1586	Wire
u/s	152	wire, twisted
u/s	1237	? wire or very thin strip, curved
u/s	1327	wire or pin, tapered and bent
128	715	wire, twisted, within heavy encrustation, ? could be organic material

form of military presence. We know from surviving strength reports for Roman garrisons (Thomas and Davies 1977; Bowman and Thomas 1983, 154) that many soldiers were on detached duties away from their notional base. Sometimes they were on detachment as small garrisons at distant locations, sometimes they were acting as escorts.

In addition to the identifiable pieces, a quantity of casting waste and possible scrap metal was recovered (Table 7.41) as well as miscellaneous pieces of wire, sheet, strip, sheet, etc, which cannot be identified to function (Table 7.42).

Catalogue

Personal (Fig. 7.23)

525   Bracelet fragment. The object is formed from a tapering thin strip decorated with fish-scale like pattern. L 56 mm; sf 198, ctx 18.

526   Bracelet fragment, D-shaped cross-section with cast cable decoration on the external face, and plain squared terminals with slightly raised edge. L 56 mm; sf 1583, ctx 1297.

527   (not illustrated) Bracelet fragment, D-shaped cross-section, with cast cable pattern on outer face. L 13 mm; sf 1419, ctx 986.

528   (not illustrated) Possible bracelet fragment of lentoidal cross-section, rolled into a tight loop. L 19 mm; sf 1567, ctx 1266.

529   Finger ring with cast cable decoration on outer face. D 21 mm; sf 1313, ctx 880.

530 Finger ring, plain and heavy with small oval setting for a stone or a glass inset, which is missing. L 24 mm; sf 816, ctx 270.

531 (not illustrated) Finger ring, small fragment including plain oval setting and small section of plain band. L 11 mm; sf 149, ctx 18.

532 Chain links formed from lengths of wire looped at each end. L 92 mm; sf 455, ctx 128.

533 Hair pin, large circular slightly domed head with fine lines around the edge. L 82 mm; sf 73, ctx 7. Although not common, flat-headed Roman hairpins do occur and include pins decorated in similar fashion to this example (Cool 1990, 154-7, figs 3, 8 and 4, 1)

534 (not illustrated) Pin, much corroded with no details of any head or eye, bent. L 33 mm; sf 52, ctx 7.

535 (not illustrated) Pin or needle with traces of casting lines along the tapering stem. The end away from the point also tapers slightly and is incomplete or unfinished. L 88 mm; sf 1029, ctx 774.

Household (Fig. 7.23)

536 Spoon, well-preserved, with complete bowl and handle. The bowl narrows slightly towards the handle. The handle tapers to a point and is of circular cross-section. It is attached to the bowl by means of a cranked junction. There is no sign of tinning which might be expected. L 110 mm; sf 1660, ctx 1501. Typical later Roman spoon, comparable to examples from Colchester (Crummy 1983, 69, no. 2014) and Verulamium (Goodburn 1984, 41, no. 19).

537 Cast bell-shaped terminal on an iron stem of circular cross-section. D 17 mm; sf 1535, ctx 1210. Possibly a lock pin (Birley 1997, 30–34). This object type has also been discussed by Allason-Jones (1985) and she has adduced evidence for a number of related uses including as terminals for knife handles (ibid. pl. II) and decorative heads for rivets pivot bars on hinging sheaths for dolabra and axes (ibid. pl. III).

Military (Fig. 7.23)

538 Sword belt holder fragment, comprising the lower decorative portion of a belt fitting. The heart-shaped terminal is decorated with a fine incised cross. L 45 mm; sf 741, ctx 34. This is a 2nd-3rd-century type. (For the type see Oldenstein 1976, 95–101, Taff. 12–3).

539 Sword chape fragment. The object has been flattened. L 49 mm; sf 1566, ctx 1266. A 2nd- or 3rd-century type (see Oldenstein 1976, 110-14, Taf. 18).

540 Cast open-work plate fragment. The surface is tinned. L 33 mm; sf 1394, ctx 880. Possibly part of a belt plate or of a pendant heart-shaped belt terminal (eg. Oldenstein 1976, Taf 31).

541 Cast girdle plate tie-ring for segmented armour. There is no burring of the short stem which would indicate that the loop had not been used. L 26 mm;

sf 1536, ctx 1210. Fastening for lacing together the so-called lorica segmentata. This particular form of attachment dates to the late 1st and 2nd century and conforms to Webster's type 1 (Webster 1992, 116–8, nos 45–51).

542 Acorn terminal attached to a length of curved bar. L 25 mm; sf 1546, ctx 1236.

543 (not illustrated) Roundel fragment formed from thin sheet. L 25 mm; sf 512, ctx 128.

Fastenings (Fig. 7.23)

544 (not illustrated) Tack, slightly domed circular head. D 27 mm; sf 19, ctx 2.

545 (not illustrated) Tack, slightly domed circular head. D 20 mm; sf 526, ctx 14.

546 (not illustrated) Tack, with damaged flat head. D 16 mm; sf 969, ctx 270.

547 Domed stud, formed from beaten sheet copper alloy and packed at the back. D 26 mm; sf 574, ctx 140.

548 (not illustrated) Domed stud, formed from beaten sheet copper alloy with traces of packing material, probably lead, but no trace of attachment. D 17 mm; sf 746, ctx 253.

549 (not illustrated) Domed stud, formed from beaten sheet copper alloy with traces of whitish packing material probably lead. D 16 mm; sf 814, ctx 206.

550 (not illustrated) Domed stud, formed from beaten sheet copper alloy with traces of whitish packing material, probably lead; possible scar at the back in the centre. D 14 mm; sf 436, ctx 181.

551 (not illustrated) Large domed stud, with scar for attachment loop. D 44 mm; sf 1052, ctx 780. It is possible that this item is from a military baldric of 2nd-century date or later.

552 (not illustrated) Washer, circular formed from thin sheet. It has a central perforation and very slight traces of an edge or border. D 28 mm; sf 735, ctx 253.

553 (not illustrated) Washer, circular formed from thin sheet. Its central perforation is oval. D 29 mm; sf 5, ctx 7.

Miscellaneous

554 (not illustrated) Ring, of circular cross-section. D 42 mm; sf 1612, ctx 1262.

555 (not illustrated) Ring, incomplete, of circular cross-section. D 20 mm; sf 1564, ctx 1313.

Unidentified

556 (not illustrated) Small cast fragment, not identifiable. L 23 mm; sf 78, ctx 447.

Burford Road *(Fig. 7.24)*

557 Shield-shaped mount of copper alloy. The top of the shield is slightly convex and the sides gently curve

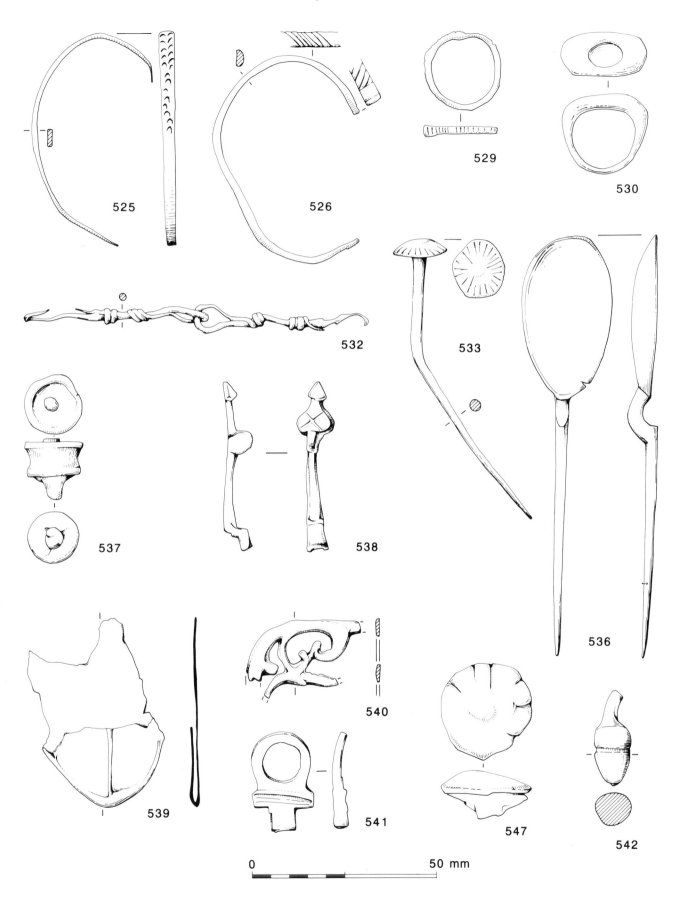

Figure 7.23   Copper alloy objects from Birdlip Quarry.

from the top to the point. The face of the shield is very slightly convex and decorated with what is probably a unicorn or possibly a dragon, although lacking wings. In heraldic terms the beast is passant. The dragon is inlaid with enamel, but the enamel is too decayed to be certain of its original colour. The mount was attached by means of a stout stem of circular section on the back of the shield. The stem has a hammered end and the remains of a thin washer are still attached. L 19 mm; sf 3, ctx 306.

Both pendants and studs, or mounts, decorated with heraldic motifs are well known. Many are shield-shaped and similar in appearance and size to this example (Griffiths 1986; Griffiths 1989; Goodall and Woodcock 1991). Pendants are more common than studs, but there are comparable examples of shield-shaped studs from London and elsewhere (Goodall and Woodcock 1991, fig. 13, nos 12, 14 and 20–26; Griffiths 1995, 69–71, fig. 53, esp. nos 77–78). They could be used as harness mounts, but other uses are attested, including to decorate dog collars, the straps of spurs and the varvels of hawks (Goodall and Woodcock 1991, 240). Griffiths (1986, figs 2a–2c) has classified the mounts and pendants according to form and the Burford Road mount with its shield with curving sides conforms to his Type 1a. The object can only be dated on typological grounds, but generally shield-shaped mounts and pendants are dated to the late 13th or 14th century after the emergence of a fully developed system of heraldry. The use of heraldry for decorative purposes on harness, dress and furnishings grew in popularity during the 13th century (Cherry 1991).

Street Farm

There are only 12 copper alloy objects, four of which are buttons of post-medieval or modern date (Table 7.43). In addition there is a pin with a round wound wire head, the cast handle from a key, and an embossed stud. These are all post-medieval in date. There is decorative plate, which may be the escutcheon for the handle of a drawer and which is probably 19th- or 20th-century in date. Finally, there is a tiny irregular quatrefoil plate from context 889.

IRON OBJECTS
By Ian R. Scott

Birdlip Quarry

Introduction and methodology

Recording at the analytical stage was intended to provide a basic record of the complete assemblage. The archive comprises pro forma record sheets on which the following data is entered: Context and small find number, x-ray plate number, object identification, written description often with a sketch, and measurement(s). Of the 425 objects comprising the assemblage, 217 were recorded in some detail on pro forma record sheets. For the remaining 208 objects a summary record sufficed.

Table 7.43   Street Farm, the copper alloy objects by context.

Ctxt	Sf no	Identification
metal detector	13	button, flat circular with loop
173		key handle, detached from shank
268		button, flat circular, tinned, with single attachment loop
305		strip with 2 holes
446		sheet with folded edges
458	9	pin with round head formed from wire, plated
611		button, large flat
730		button, flat circular, small
768	25	disc, ?coin
768	26	plate, decorative, possibly from furniture
784	24	stud, embossed sheet, incomplete, probably cu alloy
889	32	plate, quatrefoil, decorative, v small

The assemblage is medium-sized and contains a small number of interesting pieces. The total assemblage comprises between 950 and 1100 nails, *c.* 1200 hobnails and approximately 425 other items from all contexts. The latter include 217 objects which were recorded in detail. The published report contains details of 146 objects.

Boot cleats

A number of small boot cleats were recovered. All are of similar size varying between 15 mm to 20 mm long in the body and are summarised in Table 7.44.

Catalogue

Personal (Fig. 7.25)

558   D-shaped single loop buckle. The loop is of square cross-section. The pin is attached by a rolled over loop. L 29 mm; sf 1202, ctx 759.

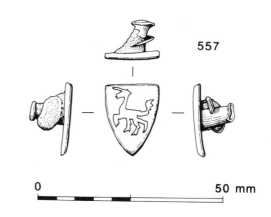

557

0   50 mm

Figure 7.24   Medieval harness mount from Burford Road.

559 (not illustrated) Pin from a brooch with a sprung pin. L 56 mm; sf 1400, ctx 880.

560 Folding knife with short blade with strongly curved back. The blade pivots on an iron pin which passes through the wooden handle and is secured by a sheet iron ferrule. Part of the wooden handle survives. L 65 mm; sf 1559, ctx 1225.

Writing (Fig. 7.25)

561 Stylus, fragment, with moulding at junction of scriber and stem. The eraser is missing. L 54 mm; sf 161, ctx 40.

Household (Fig. 7.25)

562 Knife with deep blade and curved edge. It has a thin solid handle. L 156 mm; sf 1737, ctx 1529.

563 (not illustrated) Socketed blade, possibly from knife. L 76 mm; sf 258, ctx 31.

564 (not illustrated) Spoon handle of subrectangular cross-section, with a small piece of the round bowl surviving. The handle is broken. L 78 mm; ctx 1290.

565 (not illustrated) Vessel fragment. From a shallow pan with sloping sides. Formed from sheet. L 110 mm; sf 1548, ctx 1225.

Buckets (Fig. 7.25)

566 (not illustrated) Bucket hoop, two fragments, from a wooden bucket. The diameter of the hoop is c. 330 mm. L 245 mm and 131 mm; sf 820, ctx 348.

567 (not illustrated) Bucket hoop, four fragments. The diameter of the hoop is c. 310- 320 mm. L 140 mm, 139 mm, 103 mm and 100 mm; sf 830, ctx 348.

568 Bucket handle fragment of rectangular section with U-section grip. L 200 mm; sf 707, ctx 246.

569 (not illustrated). Bucket handle mount with well-formed eye of round cross-section. The att-achment plate is incomplete and bent. L 45 mm; ctx 7, Sf 63.

570 Bucket handle mount, well-made, similar to 569, but with more of attachment plate extant. L 55 mm; sf 868, ctx 431.

Locks, keys and door furniture (Figs 7.25–6)

571 Bar spring padlock bolt with two loops, from a padlock with a straight hasp, which would have passed through the loops. It comprises two bars each of which originally terminated in a loop. L 172 mm; sf 46, ctx 7.

572 (not illustrated) Barb-spring padlock key, formed from tapering strip, with rolled-over loop at the narrower end with part of a suspension ring in situ. The bit at the wider end is broken. L 190 mm; sf 408, ctx 34.

573 (not illustrated) Barb-spring padlock key, similar to 572. L 190 mm; sf 1699, ctx 1543.

Table 7.44 Boot cleats by context from Birdlip Quarry.

Context	Sf No.	Description	No.	Size (mm)
2		boot cleat	1	L 26
29	940	boot cleat	1	L 28
90	248	boot cleat	1	L 26
128	663	boot cleat	1	L 25
128	706	? boot cleat	1	L 30
136	379	boot cleat	1	L 17
206	640	boot cleat	1	L 16
276	481	boot cleat	1	L 25
291	916	boot cleats, heavily encrusted	13	n/a
347	828	boot cleat	1	L 27
372	833	boot cleat	1	L 20
377	842	boot cleat		L 29
421	859	boot cleats	2	L 15 L 22
421	866	boot cleat	1	L 19
421	873	boot cleats	2	L 15 L 16
746	1026	boot cleat	1	L 20
778	1063	boot cleat	1	L 25
780	1057	boot cleat	1	L 22
1500	1651	boot cleat	1	L 39

574 Lever lock key, with square bit with horizontal slots. The handle is pierced for suspension and decorated. L 91 mm; sf 1549, ctx 1244.

575 Hinge strap from a loop hinge. Found with an incomplete second strap. L 243 mm; sf 13, ctx 7.

576 (not illustrated) Hinge plate, fragmentary from a loop hinge. L 86 mm; sf 513, ctx 14.

577 (not illustrated) Chain link, oval. L 48 mm; sf 674.

Horse gear and cart fittings (Fig. 7.27)

A number of horseshoes and fragments have been recovered although only a few can be dated on typological grounds. Fullering is a post-medieval feature which is found on only two shoes.

There continues to be debate in some quarters about whether or not there were Romano-British horseshoes. There are six shoes which have narrow webs with lobate expansions (cat. 579, SFs, 1680, 1738, 1722 and 1734 and the horseshoe from context 2013, Table 7.45) for which a Roman date has been claimed. John Clark in the recent Museum of London volume *The Medieval Horse and its Equipment* (Clark 1995, 95–6) is more sceptical. He is reluctant to accept a Romano-British date while adducing the evidence for a medieval date. The evidence from Birdlip would seem to support a sceptical view since the two horseshoes from putative Roman contexts (cat. 579 and 1734) were embedded in the heavily rutted 4th-century road surface. The other examples are from post-Roman contexts in the same area.

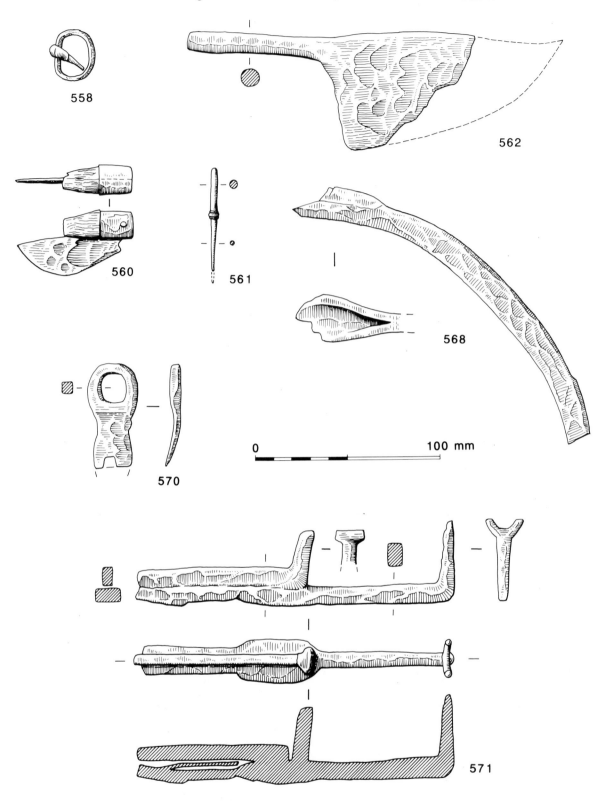

Figure 7.25   Ironwork from Birdlip Quarry.

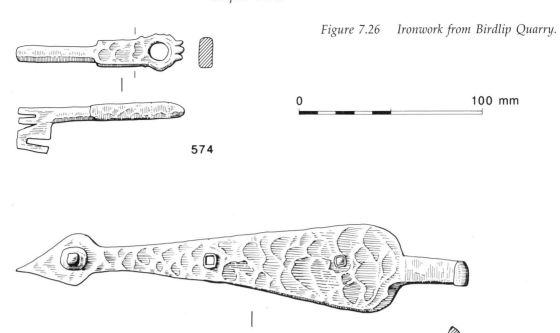

Figure 7.26   Ironwork from Birdlip Quarry.

574

575

578   Ctx 1533, horseshoe, complete, fullering, L 130 mm, post-medieval.

579   Ctx 1589, SF 1727, horseshoe complete, with 6 nail holes, narrow web with expansions, very large calkins and in situ fiddle key nail, L 116 mm, Romano-British or early medieval.

580   Ctx 2012, SF 1700, horseshoe, almost complete, no calkins rounded heel, 6 nail holes, thin web, L 100 mm.
581   Ctx 2017, SF 1701, horseshoe complete, with heavy web, large calkins and 6 nails, L 119 mm.

Hipposandals (Fig. 7.28)

Hipposandals are a distinctive feature of Romano-British finds assemblages and a number of examples have been found at Birdlip Quarry (Table 7.46). Most of these comprise side wings. The best piece is the complete section of a Type II sandal from context 33. The side wings were joined together and forged into a loop which fitted over the front of the hoof. Hipposandals were classified by Aubert in 1929 and his typology is summarised and expanded in Manning's British Museum catalogue (1985, 63–6).

582   SF 757, Hipposandal front loop, 1, L 135 mm, II, sf 757, ctx 272.

Bridle bits

583   (not illustrated) Jointed mouth bar from a bit, one end was formed by folding and forging the bar to make a loop, the other end by simple rolling-over. L 83 mm; ctx 10.

584   (not illustrated) Jointed mouth bar from a bit, similar to cat. 583, but smaller. L 59; sf 82, ctx 7.

Cart fittings

585   (not illustrated) Linch pin with spatulate head and rolled- over loop. L 158 mm; sf 262, ctx 90.
586   Linch pin with spatulate head and rolled- over loop. L 175 mm; sf 1670, ctx 1505.

587   (not illustrated) Linch pin. Spatulate head with rolled-over loop from a linch pin. L 48 mm; sf 962, ctx 276.

Tools

Leatherworking tools *(Fig. 7.28)*

588   Blade fragment with a sinuous back, much corroded. Possibly a leatherworking knife. L 84 mm; sf 341, ctx 34.

Carpenter's tools *(Fig. 7.28)*

589   Gouge blade, pointed at one end and broken at the other. The cross-section is a half circular. L 63 mm; sf 366, ctx 34.

Agricultural tools and equipment *(Fig. 7.28–9)*

590   Reaping hook, socketed. It has a small strongly curved blade. L 113 mm; sf 1448, ctx 993.

591   Spud. L 137 mm; sf 1040, ctx 745.

592   Ox-goad. D 14 mm; sf 480, ctx 34.

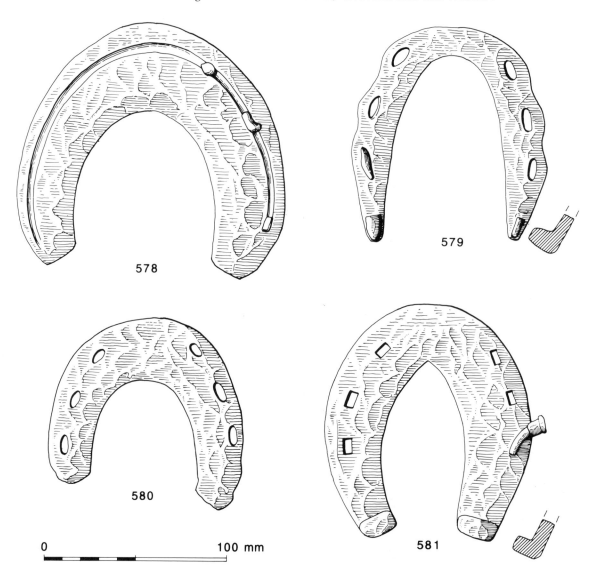

Figure 7.27   Horseshoes from Birdlip Quarry.

Table 7.45   Horseshoes by context from Birdlip Quarry.

Context	Sf No.	Description	Size (mm)	Object date
1307		horseshoe, complete, slight traces of fullering, no calkins	L108	post-med
1538		horseshoe, 3/4, toe portion	W103	
2002	1680	horseshoe fragment, heel from narrow branch with expansion	L 65	R-B or early-med
2012	1683	horseshoe, 1/2, no calkin, 3 possible nails, broad thin web	L 89	
2012	1683	horseshoe fragment, heel with calkin, no nail hole	L 65	
2012	1693	? horseshoe fragment, heel with no calkin, 1 possible nail	L 50	
2012	1704	horseshoe 1/2, thin web, no calkins, square heel	L 111	
2012	1738	horseshoe, 1/2, 3 nail holes, narrow web expansions and folded -over calkin	L 105	R-B or early-med
2012	1738	horseshoe 1/2, no calkin, 2 probable nail holes	L 112	
2013		horseshoe, 3/4, thin web with expansions		R-B or early-med
2029	1707	horseshoe, 3/4, heavy web, no calkins and square heel	L 116	
2029	1717	? horseshoe fragment, heel from narrow branch with ? expansion		
2029	1722	horseshoe fragment, heel with no calkin and 1 nail hole		R-B or early-med
2036	1711	horseshoe 3/4, thin web, no calkins and square heels	L 96	
2046	1739	horseshoe fragment, heel with no calkin, possible nail hole		
2048	1734	horseshoe, 4 extant nails, narrow web with expansions, no calkins		R-B or early-med
2048	1735	horseshoe fragment, heel with calkin		

394

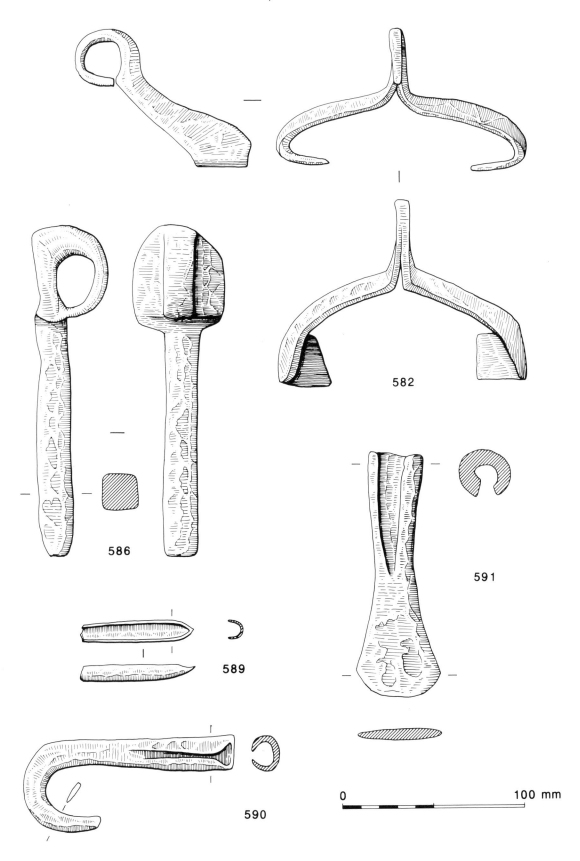

Figure 7.28   Ironwork from Birdlip Quarry.

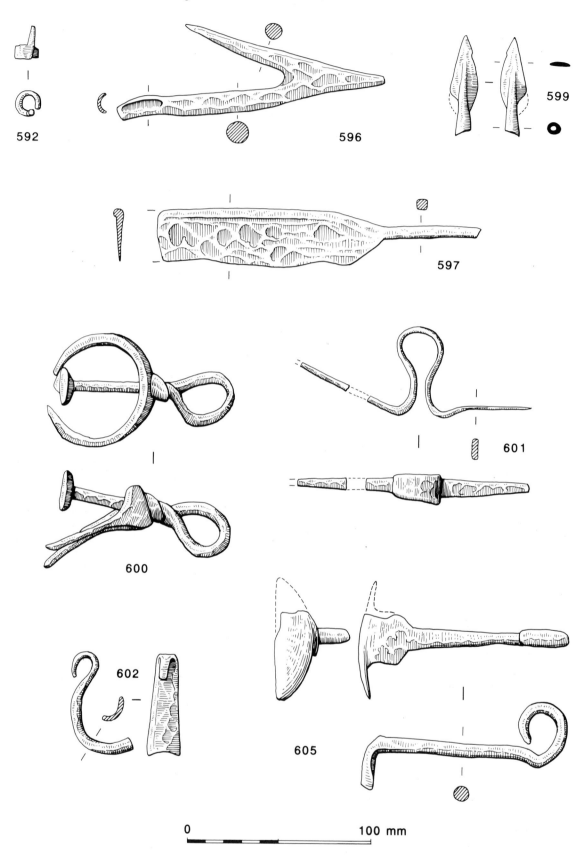

Figure 7.29   Ironwork from Birdlip Quarry.

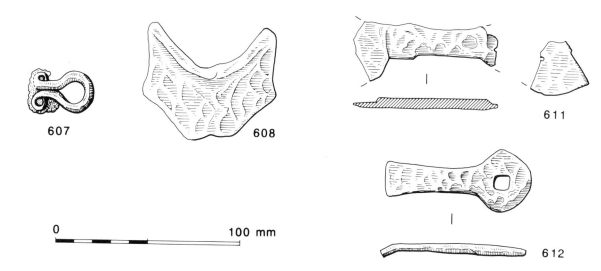

Figure 7.30 Ironwork from Birdlip Quarry.

593 (not illustrated) Ox-goad. D 19 mm; sf 114, ctx 745.

594 (not illustrated) Ox-goad. D 21 mm; sf 466, ctx 128.

595 (not illustrated) Ox-goad. D 21 mm; sf 805, ctx 270.

596 Barbed hook, with remains of a socket for attachment. L 146 mm; sf 231, ctx 84. Possibly a thatch hook.

597 Tanged blade with reinforced back, similar in section to a scythe blade but straight. L 176 mm; sf 65, ctx 7.

Weapons (Fig. 7.29)

598 Possible spearhead. A slim head with a much corroded slim ?leaf-shaped blade. The identification is not certain. L 133 mm; sf 1363, u/s.

599 Arrowhead, socketed, with leaf-shaped blade. L 51 mm; sf 1721, ctx 2029. Probably medieval.

Structural fixtures and fittings (Fig. 7.29)

600 Swivel comprising bar with looped eye and flattened head passing through a hole on an expansion in a ring. L 105 mm; sf 555, ctx 128.

Bindings

These comprise for the most part pieces of iron strip with nail holes and nails visible. In some instances they also have pierced expansions or terminals. Bindings can be parts of chests, applied to furniture or used structurally (Table 7.47).

Clamps, staples and other fastenings (Fig. 7.29)

These are defined as objects used for fastening together timberwork whether as parts of buildings, boxes and chests, or furniture. There are no clamps for use with stonework from Birdlip. Nails have not been listed simply because of their number. They were found in large numbers. The majority consisted of hand made wood nails. Smaller numbers of horseshoe nails and hobnails were also identified and are separately considered (Table 7.48).

601 Split spike loop, 1, L 123 mm, sf 1217, ctx 760.

Rings Table 7.49

A total of eight rings from a variety of contexts were recovered and these are summarised in table 7.49.

Table 7.46 Birdlip Quarry, hipposandals by context.

Context	Sf No.	Description	No.	Size (mm)	Type
7	77	hipposandal heel	1	L 79	I or II
14	123	hipposandal wing	1	L 84	I or III
33	214	hipposandal wing	1	L 95	I or III
272	757	hipposandal front loop	1	L 135	II
392	847	hipposandal wing point bent over	1	L 44	I or III
431	881	hipposandal wing	1	L 65	I or III
1266	1568	hipposandal wing	1	L 80	I or III
1287	1593	hipposandal wing	1	L 95	I or III

Table 7.47 Birdlip Quarry, bindings by context.

Context	Sf No.	Description	No.	Size (mm)
2	282	binding, fragment	1	n/a
4		binding, narrow rectangular strip with expansion at one end	1	L 64
7	37	binding, narrow strip	1	L 123
7	51	binding, with pierced expansion	1	L 104
7	106	binding, half round strip	1	L 126
7	112	binding, strip with eye at one end	1	L 89
15	47	? binding, curved strip	1	N/a
31	264	binding, terminal pierced by a nail hole	1	L 65
41	163	tapering bar, terminal expansion pierced	1	L 80
296	775	strip with large nail hole	1	L 82
383	670	binding, thin rectangular section, nail holes at each end	1	L 86
395	870	binding fragment, nail hole or notch	1	L 62
729	1272	strip, curved	1	L 62
849	1318	binding fragments, 1 with nail	3	L 70 L 55 N/a
1198		binding, 1 extant nail	1	L 37
1213		binding, thin cross-section, 1 extant nail hole	1	L 63
1318	1584	binding with 2 nail holes and small lug or tongue	1	N/a
1500	1653	? binding, strip, with 2 nail holes	1	L 55
1500	1658	? binding with circular expansion pierced with a nail hole	1	L 129
u/s	822	? binding, strip with pierced ? expansion	1	L 88

Table 7.48 Birdlip Quarry, clamps, staples, and other fastenings by context.

Context	Sf No.	Description	No	Size (mm)
7	56	U-shaped staple	1	L 44
14	677	clamp or large cleat	1	L 61
14	678	clamp or large cleat	1	L 70
33	215	rectangular washer	1	L 39
34	417	looped spike	1	L 65
53	220	split spike loop? formed from strip	1	L 40
72	606	split spike loop	1	L 80
86	252	dog fragment	1	L 82
108	299	L-shaped staple or nail	1	n/a
188	571	washer, square	1	L 32
206	910	U-shaped staple	1	n/a
840	1316	collar or ring formed from thin strip	1	D 19
1210	1534	clamp or collar of square section rod	1	L 44
1250	1550	clamp or dog	1	L 60
1500		clamp, formed of rectangular section strip	1	L 42
2004	1675	clamp or dog	1	L 127

Table 7.49 Birdlip Quarry, rings.

Context	Sf no	Description	No.	Size (mm)
2		ring, circular section	1	D 37
41	204	ring, or collar of sub-rectangular section	1	D 39
136	359	ring, circular-sectioned, large	1	D 62
392	843	ring, circular section	1	D 30
840	1390	ring, circular section	1	D 40
840	1396	ring of circular cross-section	1	D 50
848	1245	ring, fragmentary, circular section	1	D 70
1500	1659	ring, penannular rather than complete circle, sub-rectangular section	1	D 33

Miscellaneous objects of unidentified function (Figs 7.29–30)

602   Strongly curved object with rolled over loop or eye at one end. It is curved in cross-section. Uncertain function, possibly some form of handle. L 58 mm; sf 1505, ctx 34.

603   Ring attached by a rolled over loop to a sheet fragment. L 56 mm; sf 126, ctx 14. Possibly from a hipposandal of the rare Type 4 with rings attached to the side wings (Manning 1985, 65, fig. 16.4).

604   Handle or suspension loop. Slightly curved, it has a rolled loop or eye at one end and expands into a flange at the other. L 114 mm; sf 1270, ctx 729. Possibly the front loop from a hipposandal.

605   Handle or suspension loop. It has a rolled loop or eye at one end and expands into a flange at the other. The flange is sinuous in outline and joined to a larger object. L 115 mm; sf 1555, ctx 1227. Similar to 604.

606   Handle or suspension loop. It has a rolled loop or eye at one end and expands at the other. L 101 mm; sf 1731, ctx 1614. Possibly the front loop from a hipposandal.

607   Loop formed from rod or wire. L 37 mm; sf 171, ctx 19.

608   Plate fragment, very slightly curved, with a hole or cut-out with raised lip on one edge. Apparently regular outline. Function uncertain. L 72 mm; sf 357, ctx 34.

609   Plate fragment, very slightly curved, with a hole or cut-out on one edge. The hole has a raised lip. Function uncertain. L 59 mm; sf 1132, ctx 781.

610   Spiral ferrule or collar. D 18 mm; sf 1070, ctx 768.

611   Handle of sub-rectangular cross-section with the remains of circular flanges at each end. L 79 mm; sf 758, ctx 270.

612   Tapering strip or bar with expansion at one end, pierced by a square hole. L 80 mm; sf 163. ctx 41.

613   Hooked object formed from circular section rod with an eye at the other end. Function uncertain. L 117 mm; sf 467, ctx 276.

614   Peg or pin of rectangular cross-section with a eye or loop at one end. L 93 mm; sf 1537, ctx 1210.

615   Junction plate fragment, formed from sheet with rolled over loop at one end. L 19 mm; sf 545. ctx 1305.

Street Farm

Introduction

The ironwork comprises a small collection of exclusively post-medieval material. Much is undistinguished and most not worthy of further analysis or publication. There are 99 iron objects and 174 nails. The sample of nails is small and they have not been recorded in detail. The nails are tabulated by context and can be consulted in the archive.

Composition of the ironwork assemblage

The total number of objects of all types is 273. This comprises 174 nails and 99 other objects. The latter included 44 pieces, which can be described as miscellaneous pieces of rod, bar or sheet (Table 7.50). These cannot be identified to function.

Of the remaining 55 objects, 3 can be discounted because they are too small to identify and 3 are modern. The other 49 objects are made up as follows: 14 domestic objects, 15 pieces of structural metalwork, and 8 tools. In addition there are 3 pieces of chain, 2 items from footwear, a single horseshoe fragment and a sword chape. There are 5 items of uncertain identification.

The structural metalwork includes in addition to the usual collection of L-shaped and U-shaped, two H-hinges and two L-shaped drop hinge pintles. The tools include three balanced sickles of similar form but slightly different sizes. These are not closely datable. Other tools include part of a saw blade and as many as three chisels. The identification of two of these is not certain. The third is probably a smith's chisel or set. The assemblage is very small, but very much what might be expected from a small rural site of post-medieval date. A small number of pieces has been selected for illustration.

Date of the assemblage

Much of the metalwork is not closely datable. The nails cannot be closely dated, but all, with one modern exception from context 706, are hand-made. The domestic items include part of a kettle and keys and locks, which can be assigned a post-medieval date. The kettle is probably 18th- or 19th-century in date, possibly later. The locks and keys are of post-medieval form. None of the tools can be closely dated. Amongst the structural ironwork the H-hinges are almost certainly of 18th-century date. The two items of footwear - a patten (cat. 621) and a heel iron - can be dated. The patten is of 17th- or 18th-century date and the heel iron is probably of 19th- or 20th-century date. The date range of the metalwork seems to be 18th and 19th century rather than earlier, but with some possible 17th-century material.

Catalogue *(Figs 7.31–2)*

616   Smith's chisel of stout rectangular cross-section. L 127 mm; ctx 305.

617   Possible chisel, of rectangular section, with sub-rectangular head. L 85 mm; ctx 190.

618   Sickle, tanged, with triangular section blade. L 355 mm; ctx 611.

Not illustrated are two further sickles of similar form but larger size:
Sickle, similar to, but larger than, no. 618. L 411 mm; sf 6, ctx 319.

Sickle, similar to, but larger than, no. 618. L 444 mm; u/s

Table 7.50 Quantification of bar, block, plate, rod, sheet and wire by context from Street Farm.

Ctx	Description	No.
191	bar fragment, tapering	1
304	Bar/rod fragment	1
305	bar/rod cut at one end	1
328	Bar/ spike of rectangular section, tapering	1
438	bar/rod	1
605	bar fragment	1
611	bar/rod fragment	1
870	bar/rod	1
357	block, trapezoid section, dense	1
281	plate fragment, folded up at one end	1
717	plate fragment fused to stone	1
762	plate, pierced by 1 rectangular hole flanked by 2 smaller holes	1
889	plate fragment, curved	1
591	Rod	1
721	rod/nail fragment	1
199	sheet/plate fragment, small	1
304	sheet, thin folded	1
328	sheet, pierced by 1 nail hole and slightly curved	1
458	sheet/strip fragment, thin	1
589	sheet, curved	1
589	sheet, thin with lip	1
611	sheet, fragment, square	1
119	strip, thin slightly tapered and curved	1
197	strip, no extant nail holes	1
198	strip, no nail holes	1
262	strip, tapering, no nail holes	1
336	strip, irregular fragment, bent	1
357	strip/sheet fragments, 1 pierced by hole	1
389	strip, thin section, straight- sided, no nail holes	1
390	strip fragment, thin section, no nail holes	1
589	strip, no nail holes	1
589	strip, tapering	1
702	Strip	3
730	Strip	1
737	Strip	1
227	wire and other fragments	3
281	wire fragments	4

619   Sword chape, formed from thin sheet. L 91 mm; sf 31, ctx 878.

620   Clasp knife handle, with bone handle plates. No blade. L 106 mm; ctx 262.

621   Patten, comprising oval hoop with raised brackets at each end pierced for nails. L 175 mm, ctx 611.

622   Lever lock key, with broken bow. L 76 mm; sf 5, ctx 118.

623   Barb spring padlock bolt, with three springs. Two are formed by a single strip folded over the end of the bolt and secured by a pin or rivet. The bolt ends with a circular plate with raised edge. L 90 mm; ctx 262.

624   Bolt, with from a large stock lock. L 178 mm; ctx 305.

625   Latch, with small plate, formed from thick wire. L 114 mm; ctx 281.

626   H-hinge, broken with decorative terminals to one plate. L 165 mm; ctx 268.

627   H-hinge, half, with plain plate. L 152 mm; ctx 436.

628   Strap hinge with tapering strap pierced with 3 nail holes. L 90 mm; ctx 413.

629   L-shape staple for drop hinge. L 87 mm; ctx 470.

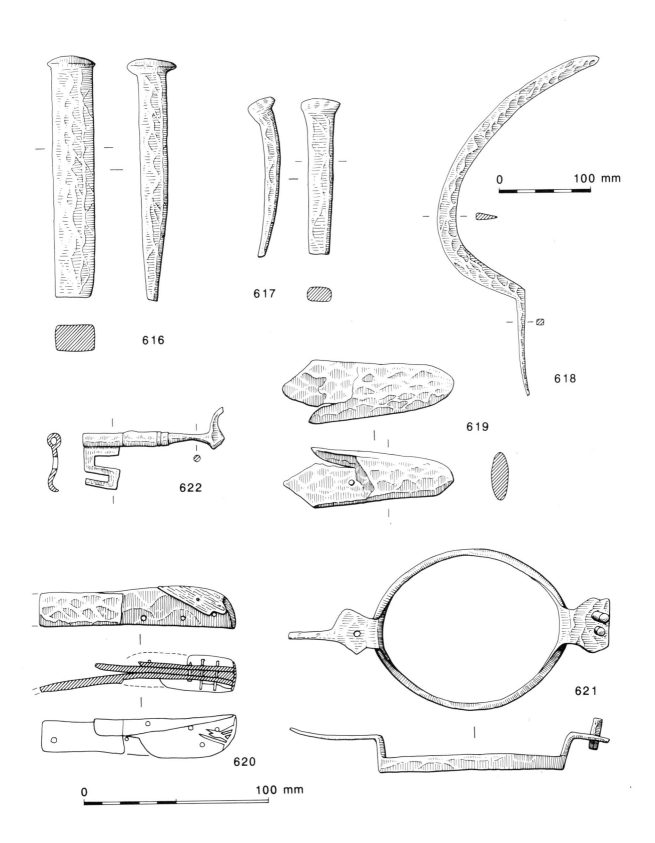

Figure 7.31   Ironwork from Street Farm.

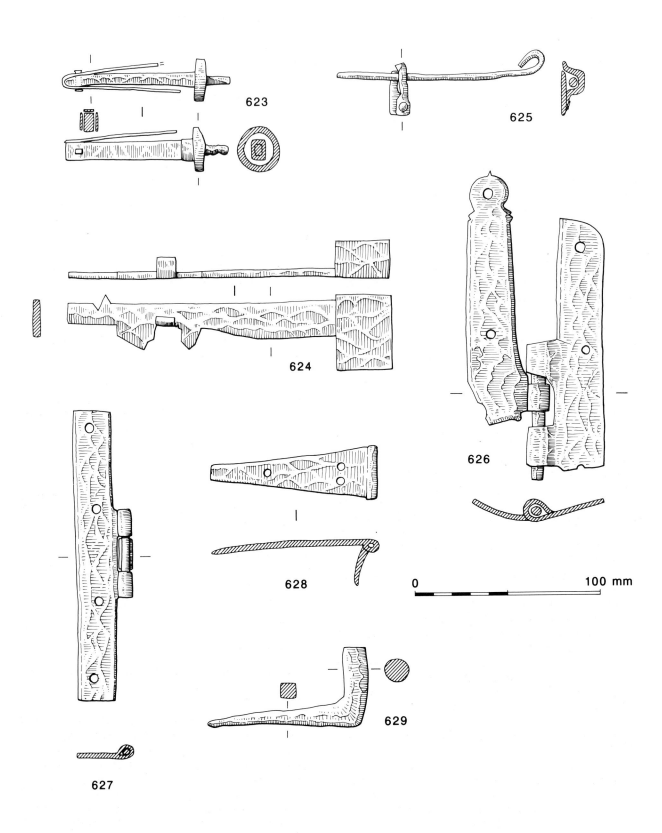

Figure 7.32   Ironwork from Street Farm.

Horse gear from other sites

The assemblage

Horse gear, including horseshoes and horseshoe nails, hipposandals and linchpins, were found in small numbers from a number of the sites along the line of the road (Table 7.51). The table exclude the items of horse gear from Birdlip Quarry which are reported on separately, and a single horseshoe fragment from Street Farm. Including watching briefs and 5 sections through Ermin Street, 17 sites have produced horsegear and/or horseshoe nails. Ten sites have produced horseshoe nails and 12 sites have produced horsegear other than horseshoe nails.

Horseshoes and hipposandals

The bulk of the finds comprise horseshoes. Most are characterised by broad heavy branches and rectangular countersunk nail holes and are probably of post-medieval date. A small number have fullering (eg. Table 7.51, nos 1, 4, 11–2, 20–23), which is a distinct post-medieval feature. A selection have been illustrated.

The most interesting finds are perhaps the hipposandals, three complete examples of which were recovered (cat. 630–1, Table 7.51, no. 29). The three complete examples are of two different forms. The side wings of cat. 630 originally met at the front and were formed into a rolled-over loop. The heel was hooked. This form was classified by Aubert as his form 2 (Manning 1972, 171). Cat 631 and 29 (Table 7.51) are two examples of Aubert's type 1 with side wings and a separate front loop. Again the heel is hooked.

The precise function of these items is a matter of debate. They were undoubtedly worn by horses, but under what circumstances is less clear. Given the lack of evidence for the shoeing of Roman horses (*pace* Manning 1976, 31), it has been suggested that the hipposandals were temporary shoes used when riding on metalled roads (Manning 1985, 63). There are two problems with this interpretation. First the number of hipposandals found is perhaps fewer than might be expected if they were regularly used. Secondly, and more pertinently, it would not have been possible to ride at any speed on a horse wearing hipposandals because the shoes would quickly work loose. A related problem was the probability that the shoes would chafe against the horse's legs. It is most probable that hipposandals were worn to protect damaged and injured hooves. Hipposandals which only cover half the hoof are known although they are rare. The existence of these half-shoes which would provide protection to only one side of the hoof is further evidence for the veterinary use of these pieces. A small selection of hipposandals have been illustrated and appear in the catalogue below.

Catalogue

Duntisbourne Grove (Fig 7.33)

630 Hipposandal, complete, Aubert Type 2 (Manning 1985, 63–6, fig. 16), sf 233, ctx 7.

Ermin Street (Figs 7.34–5)

631 Hipposandal, complete, Aubert type I, with wings, rear hook and front loop, 1, L 245 mm, sf 301, ctx 309.

632 Horseshoe, complete, quite broad heavy web; 7 rectangular nail holes arranged 3 and 4; no fullering or calkins; 3 in situ nails, L 115 mm; W 116 mm, sf 601, ctx 623.

633 Horseshoe, complete, quite broad heavy web; 7 rectangular nail holes arranged 3 and 4; no fullering or calkins, L 120 mm; W 120 mm, sf 602, ctx 624.

634 Horseshoe, complete, with broad heavy web; 8 rectangular nail holes arranged 4 and 4; no fullering or calkins, L 120 mm; W 120 mm, sf 603, ctx 624.

635 Horseshoe, complete, with broad heavy web; 8 rectangular nail holes arranged 4 and 4; no fullering or calkins, 1, L 115 mm; W 115 mm, sf 604.

Linch pins

The only cart or wagon fittings which could be identified were linch pins used to secure wheels on their axles. A single linch pin was recovered from Ermin Street section 6, but three further examples were found at Birdlip Quarry (cat nos 585–587). All four linch pins are of similar type with spatulate heads and rolled-over loops. This is one of the typical Romano-British linch pin forms (Manning 1972, 172–4).

Ermin Street (Fig. 7.35)

636 Linchpin, of Manning type 2b, with spatulate head and rolled over loop; rebate in stem, 1, L 170, sf 609, ctx 651.

LEAD OBJECTS
By Leigh Allen

A total of 36 lead objects were recovered: 24 from Birdlip Quarry, 7 from Street Farm, 4 from Weavers Bridge and 1 from Latton 'Roman Pond'.

Latton 'Roman Pond'

One miscellaneous fragment, recovered from context 228.

Weavers Bridge

The four fragments of lead consist of a fragment of casting waste from an unstratified context (cat. 640), a fragment of sheet from context 57 (cat. 638), a miscellaneous fragment from context 26 (cat. 641) and a pear-shaped spoon bowl without the handle from context 57 (cat. 639). Spoons with this shape of bowl appear to have been in production by the first half of the 2nd century (Crummy 1983, 69–70, fig. 73, nos 2012 and 2014).

Birdlip Quarry

The 24 objects comprise 3 weights (cat. 642–4), a trapezoidal fragment (cat. 645), a bung or plug

Table 7.51   Horseshoes and other horse gear (excluding horseshoe nails) by site and context.

Cat. No.	Context	Sf no	Identification	Nos	Size (mm)
Burford Road					
1	309		horseshoe, half, no calkin, 4 nail holes with fullering and 1 extant nail	1	
2	320		?horseshoe fragment	1	
3	323		horseshoe fragment, small, one part nail hole and rolled over calkin	1	
4	409		horseshoe fragment, 4 nail holes and fullering, no calkin	1	
5	573		horseshoe, half, wide side bar with 4 extant nail holes	1	
6	661	9	horseshoe, almost complete, 5 nail holes to each side	1	
Duntisbourne Leer					
7	214	4	?hipposandal fragments; curved plates	2	
Field's Farm					
8	50	9	horse or pony shoe, 1 extant calkin, 5 nail holes and 3 in situ nails	1	
11	310		horseshoe, half, no calkins but possible traces of fullering	1	L 119 mm
12	329		horseshoe, complete, with web of average width, and clear traces of fullering, no calkins; heavily worn at the toe; no nail holes visible to the naked eye.	1	L 108 mm; W 128 mm
Ermin Street					
18	720	701	horseshoe, half, no distinctive features	1	L 128 mm
19	769	703	horseshoe, half, possible fullering otherwise no distinctive features	1	L 136 mm
20	834	814	horseshoe, half, with 4 rectangular nail holes and fullering; no calkins	1	L 132 mm
21	836	810	horseshoe, complete, clear fullering, and right angle calkins; 8 nail holes	1	L 137mm; W 133 mm
22	836	811	horseshoe, complete, clear fullering, broad web, no calkins; 8 nail holes	1	L 135 mm; W 135 mm
23	839	813	horseshoe, complete, clear fullering, broad web, no calkins; 8 nail holes	1	L 118 mm; W 123 mm
Weavers Bridge					
24	13		horseshoe, 6 nail holes, some nails in situ	1	
25	13		horseshoe, 6 nail holes, some nails in situ	1	
26	2		horseshoe, 8 nail holes, fullering, no calkins	1	
27	4		horseshoe, small, 6 extant nail holes, no calkins	1	
28	4		horseshoe, small, fragment, 2 extant nail holes	1	
NOSNI					
29	Ch. 2500	2	hipposandal, complete, Aubert type I, with wings, rear hook and front loop	1	
Preston Enclosure					
30	160		horseshoe fragment, small	1	
31	surface cleaning		horseshoe fragment, no calkin, 3 extant nail holes	1	
Witpit Lane					
32	24		horseshoe fragment, no calkin, no fullering, 3 extant nail holes	1	

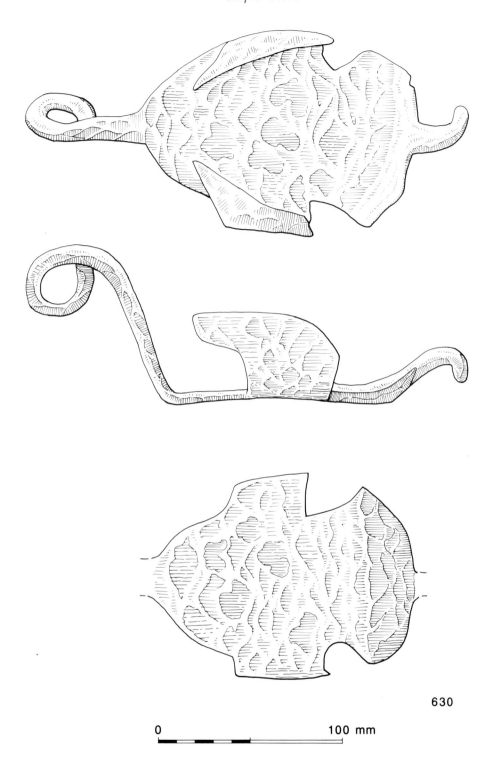

630

0   100 mm

Figures 7.33   Hipposandals from Duntisbourne Grove.

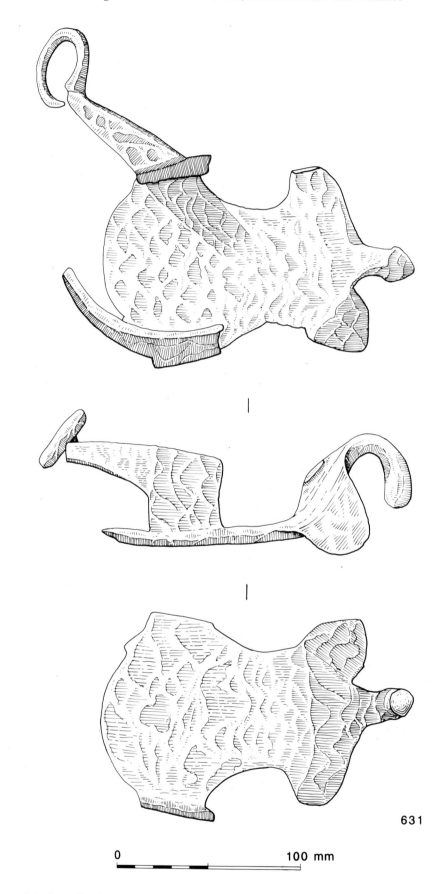

631

0   100 mm

Figure 7.34   Hipposandals from Ermin Street.

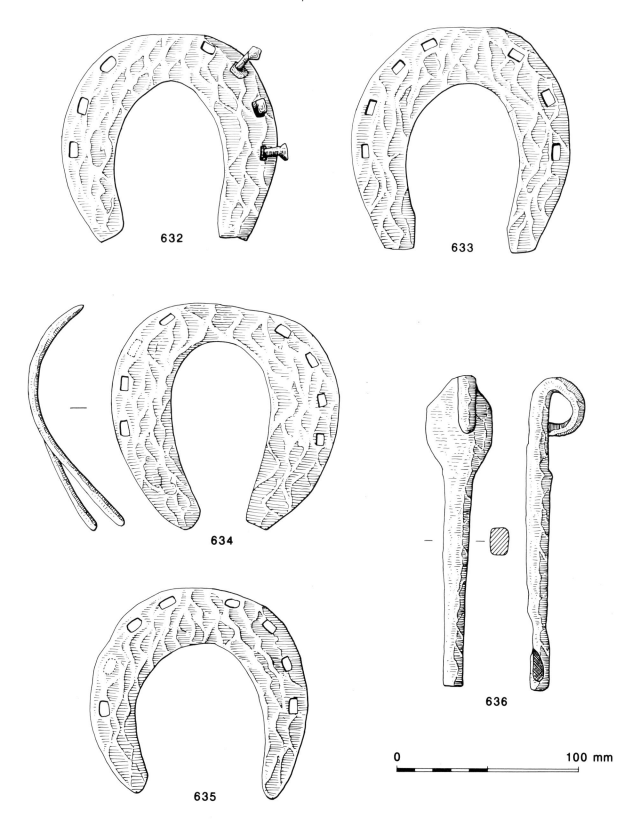

632

633

634

635

636

0   100 mm

Figure 7.35   Horseshoes and linch pin from Ermin Street.

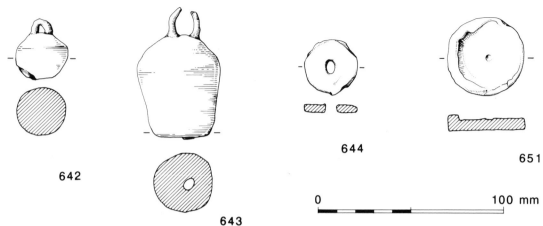

Figure 7.36 Lead objects.

(cat. 646), a sheet fragment (cat. 647), miscellaneous fragments and manufacturing waste. Two of the weights are hanging or steelyard weights (cat 642–643). The first of these, cat. 642, is a small globular weight with an iron loop attachment; a similar example was recovered from Bancroft, Buckinghamshire (Bird 1994b, 347, fig. 174, no. 308). The second (cat. 643), is a larger pear-shaped hanging type with an iron rod through the centre and a broken loop attachment. The other weight (cat. 646) is discoidal, with a central perforation (this object could feasibly have been used as a spindlewhorl) and similar examples have again been recovered from Bancroft (Bird 1994b, 347, fig. 174, no. 306). There is a large solid trapezoidal shaped fragment (cat. 645), a small mis-shapen plug or bung (cat. 646) with a domed head and a short shank, a fragment of irregularly shaped sheet (cat. 647) and five miscellaneous fragments.

The remaining objects are fragments of casting or cutting waste. The eight fragments of casting waste include small drips, droplets and spills produced during the working of lead, they also include a fragment of casting sprue (the metal that solidifies in the in-gate of a mould) which was recovered from occupation layer 227 (cat. 648). The four fragments of cutting waste were fragments of sheet, three with scored lines along one edge the fourth has a roughly scalloped edge.

Street Farm

The seven fragments consist of two window came fragments (identified by C Cropper), a weight, sheet fragments and cutting waste. One of the fragments of window came (cat. 649) is early post-medieval in date, and was extruded through a toothless mill, unlike the second fragment (cat. 650) which has widely spaced mill marks and probably dates to the 17th century or later. The weight is unstratified (cat. 651). It is circular, discoidal and has a raised lip around the circumference. There is a shallow indentation at the centre, and a similar example

is noted at Fishbourne, Sussex (Cunliffe 1971, 145, fig. 66, no. 10). The remaining objects consist of two fragments of fine lead sheet and two fragments of cutting waste, all of which are unstratified.

Catalogue of lead objects (Fig. 7.36)

Latton 'Roman Pond'

637   A miscellaneous fragment, ctx 228.

Weavers Bridge

638   Sheet, incomplete. Irregularly shaped fragment. L 27 mm, ctx 57.

639   Spoon, incomplete, lead. A pear-shaped spoon bowl, handle missing. L 37 mm. sf 32, ctx 57.

640   A fragment of casting waste, unstratified.

641   A miscellaneous fragment, ctx 26.

Birdlip Quarry

642   Weight, incomplete. Small globular hanging weight with an iron loop attachment. D 30 mm. sf 138, ctx 131.

643   Weight, incomplete. Large pear-shaped hanging weight with an iron rod through the centre and a broken loop attachment. L 68 mm. sf 55, ctx 31.

644   Weight, complete. Circular, discoidal weight with a central perforation. D 28 mm. sf 1662, ctx 1500.

645   Ingot fragment, incomplete. Solid trapezoidal fragment possibly from a lead pig or ingot. L 42 mm. sf 876, ctx 278.

646   Plug, incomplete. Small distorted dome headed plug with a short roughly circular sectioned shank. L:17 mm. sf 1663, ctx 1500.

647   Sheet fragment, incomplete. Fragment of lead sheet with one curved outside edge. L 52 mm. sf 125, ctx 14.

648 Casting sprue, incomplete. Fragment of cast lead from the in-gate of the mould. L 46 mm. sf 688, ctx 227. Casting waste was also recovered from contexts 2, 7, 31 and 72. Cutting waste was recovered from contexts 7, 41, 14 and 61. Miscellaneous fragments were recovered from contexts 2, 7, 10, 14 and 31.

Street Farm

649 Window came, incomplete. Short distorted fragment, extruded through a toothless comb. L 51 mm. ctx 749.

650 Window came, incomplete. Small distorted fragment bearing traces of widely spaced mill marks. L 34 mm, ctx 356.

651 Weight, complete. Circular discoidal weight with a raised lip around the circumference and a shallow indentation at the very centre. D: 40 mm, Sf 28, ctx 750.

Two fragments of cutting waste and two sheet fragments were recovered from unstratified contexts.

BONE OBJECTS
By Leigh Allen

There were eight objects of bone and one of horn. Six bone objects came from Birdlip Quarry, one from Ermin Farm and one from Weavers Bridge.

Birdlip Quarry

All six of the bone objects were pin fragments. Cat. 654 context 1236 is a highly polished headless pin, the top of the pin is flat and the shaft tapers smoothly from the head to the tip. It has been suggested that this type of pin belongs to the earlier part of the Roman period, losing popularity in the first half of the 3rd century (Crummy 1979, 157–158). Cat. 653 from context 798 and cat. 652 from context 278 are both examples of pins with hand cut globular heads with shanks that swell at the centre, they are both highly polished and have the tips of the points missing. This type of pin has a postulated date range of *c.* AD 200– late 4th/early 5th century (Crummy 1979, 158–161, fig. 1, no. 3). Similar examples have been recovered from sites A and B at Shakenoak, Oxfordshire (Brodribb et al. 1971, 110–11, fig. 37, no. 2), at Fishbourne, Sussex (Cunliffe 1971, 147–148, fig. 68, no. 23) and at Colchester (Crummy 1983, 21–22, fig.19). Cat. 655 from floor layer 729 is a roughly cut pin rectangular in section with a head delineated from the shank by slightly notched shoulders, there is some degree of polish over the whole length of the pin. Cat 656 and 657 are fragments of highly polished pin shafts.

Ermin Farm

A highly polished drilled boar's tooth of a type commonly referred to as amulets was recovered from context 3 (cat. 658). Their use can be traced back to the Roman period where they were favoured by Germanic mercenaries and were worn hung from necklaces or

mounted in metal sheaths (MacGregor 1985, 109). A similar example was recovered from Shakenoak, Oxfordshire in a late 3rd-4th context (Brodribb et al. 1971, 110–111, fig. 37, no. 2).

Weavers Bridge

Nine fragments from a decorated handle were recovered from context 57 (cat. 659), it is square in section with a circular longitudinal perforation for the insertion of a tang from a whittle tanged implement. The handle is decorated with irregularly spaced (sometimes overlapping) ring and dot motif. A similar object was recovered from Shakenoak, Oxfordshire and is late Roman or Saxon in date (Brodribb et al. 1971, 110–111, fig. 37, no. 3).

Ermin Street

A damaged and fragmentary object of horn was recovered from context 623 (cat. 660), it consisted of two fragments from a vessel. A circular disc of *c.* 51 mm would have formed the base of the vessel. It was found together with a curved fragment from the cylindrical body. The object is most probably a horn beaker, a conventional form of drinking vessels from the 17th century onwards (Hardwick 1981, 37–40). It is however worth noting that horn vessels were also used as medicine measures. During the Crimean war they were used in preference to glass vessels which often smashed whilst in transit. Traces of a green powdery substance were present at the base of the vessel (this substance has not been identified for this report).

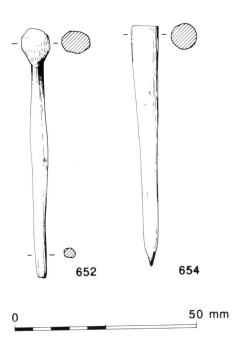

Figure 7.37 Bone objects.

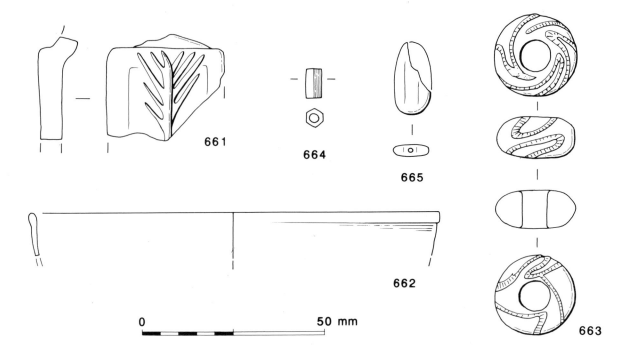

Figure 7.38   Roman glass from Birdlip Quarry.

Catalogue *(Fig. 7.37)*

Birdlip Quarry

652   Pin, incomplete, roughly worked with a hand-cut globular head, the shank has a slight swelling at the centre, the tip is missing, there are traces of polish on the head and shank. L 66 mm. sf 883, ctx 278.

653   Pin, incomplete, with a hand-cut globular head, the shank has a slight swelling at the centre, the tip is missing, highly polished. L 50 mm. sf 1087, ctx 798.

654   Pin, complete, headless pin, the top of the head is flat and the shaft tapers smoothly from the head to the tip. The whole pin is highly polished. L 64 mm. sf 1562, ctx 1236.

655   Pin, complete, roughly cut, rectangular in section and curved along its length, the head is delineated from the shank by slightly notched shoulders. L 91 mm. sf 1253, ctx 729.

656   Pin, incomplete, shank fragment, broken at both ends, circular section, tapers smoothly along its length and is highly polished. L 42 mm. sf 1291, ctx 848.

657   Pin, incomplete. Tip and a fragment of the shank of a pin. The fragment has a circular section, tapers smoothly along its length and is highly polished. L 30 mm. sf 1588, ctx 1412.

Ermin Farm

658   Boars tusk, incomplete, broken at upper edge, highly polished and perforated with a circular hole at the upper edge for suspension. L 86 mm. sf 1, ctx 3.

Weavers Bridge

659   Handle, incomplete, nine fragments from a decorated handle for a whittle tanged implement. The handle is square in section with a circular longitudinal perforation for the tang. The decoration consists of irregularly spaced (sometimes overlapping) ring and dot motif. L 103 mm. sf 4, ctx 57.

Cowley Underbridge Trench 6

660   Two fragments from a horn vessel. A circular disc *c.* 51 mm which forms the base of the vessel and a curved strip from the cylindrical body of the vessel. There are traces of a green powdery substance (unidentified) at the base of the vessel, sf 606, ctx 623.

ROMAN GLASS FROM BIRDLIP QUARRY *(Fig. 7.38)*
By Denise Allen

The excavations produced 34 fragments of Roman vessel glass and 3 beads. Most of the vessel glass fragments are very small and completely featureless, and therefore defy further identification. Twenty-two are blue-green in colour, and of these, 9 can be recognised as representing large, thick-walled vessels, almost certainly bottles of common 1st-2nd century types.

Vessels

Thirteen fragments are from colourless vessels, of which two are sufficiently diagnostic to identify their forms.

410

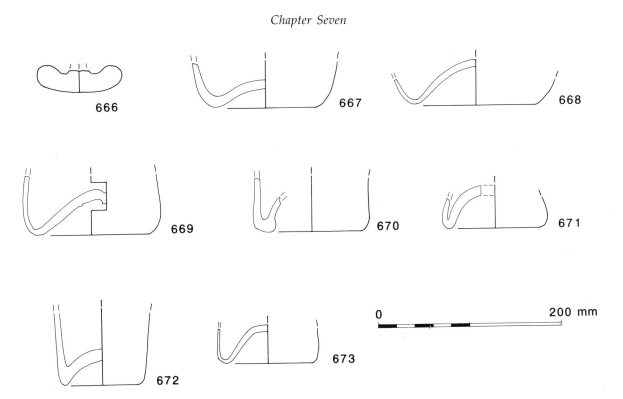

Figure 7.39   Post-medieval bottle glass.

661   Sf 319, ctx 125. Shoulder fragments of an unguent bottle of greenish-colourless glass. Blown in a square-section body mould; part of a moulded vertical palm leaf extant on one side, and apparently part of another just visible. Width of sides *c.* 32 mm.

This decorated shoulder fragment represents a rare form of unguent bottle, dating to the late 2nd or 3rd century. They often have moulded designs on their bases, with the figure of Mercury or some other deity, together with letters in each corner. The vessels are often called Mercury flasks for this reason. A rare variant has moulded designs on the sides. This almost always takes the form of a pattern resembling a palm branch, as here, or sometimes a thunderbolt. A complete example of the former was found in a 4th-century grave from Trier in Germany (Goethert-Polaschek 1977, 183, 1141, taf. 24.260b). The form has recently been discussed with reference to a similar fragment found during excavations at Colchester (Cool and Price 1995, 152–3, nos 1182–1183, fig. 9.6).

662   Sf 284, ctx 31. Rim fragment of a cup of colourless glass. Rim fire-rounded and thickened and turned slightly inward, diameter *c.* 110 mm. The form most likely to be represented here is a cylindrical cup with slightly inturned rim and two concentric base-rings. They were the most popular glass drinking vessel during the period *c.* AD 170–240. Thirty-nine examples were represented amongst finds from recent excavations at Colchester (Cool and Price 1995, 83–5, nos 476–533, fig. 5.12).

Beads

663   SF 1570, ctx 1281. Annular bead of pale green glass, with snaking twisted cable of blue and white. Diameter 20 mm, height 10 mm. Translucent greenish annular beads with two-colour twisted cables have been classified by Guido as Class 9A, and dated to the 1st century BC-1st century AD (1978, 77, plate II.14).

664   Ctx 16, Small hexagonal-sectioned green bead, length 8 mm, diam. 4 mm. This is a very common Roman type, which cannot be closely dated (Guido 1978, 96, fig. 37.9).

665   SF 1185, ctx 140. Fragment of an oval, flat-sectioned bead of blue-green glass, with single longitudinal perforation. Length *c.* 19 mm, width *c.* 6 mm. Another bead of common Roman type, in use throughout the period (Guido 1978, 99, fig. 37.17).

POST-MEDIEVAL GLASS
By Cecily Cropper

Summary *(Fig. 7.39)*

Fragments of post-medieval and modern glass were recovered from a selection of sites along the route. A small number of earlier fragments are from bottles dating to the 17th and early to mid-18th centuries (Exhibition Barn, Burford Road, Middle Duntisbourne). Later 18th-century bottle fragments were present at Court Farm and Latton 'Roman Pond'. Modern glass (19th and 20th century fragments) came from Trinity Farm, Lynches Trackway, Daglingworth Quarry, Lower Street Furlong and Itlay.

The sites of Cherry Tree Lane and Street Farm produced glass of significant example or quantity to warrant a more detailed description (see below).

Cherry Tree Lane

Three base fragments of onion bottles of a 17th-/18th-century date were recovered from contexts 6 and 8. Also, a fragment of a linen smoother, or slick-stone occurred in context 1 (cat. 666). Such objects, used for all manner of smoothing purposes, occur on glasshouse sites in the 16th century, a period in which the handle is characteristic (Charleston 1984, 37). They are also known from earlier occupation sites. A late Saxon/early medieval example occurred within an 11th-century context at Yarmouth, Norfolk (Rogerson 1976, fig. 51, no. 13). Diameters would appear to increase through time and the diameter of the smoother from this site fits into the larger range of 90 mm. Similar-sized examples with remains of handles from 15th-century contexts came from St Peter's Street, Northampton, (Hunter and Oakley 1979, 296–8, fig. 130, nos GL38–9). A miscellaneous piece of amber glass from context 20 may be a piece of 'melt' glass. Impurities are present on the surface and within bubbles in the glass itself. This, together with the linen smoother, may indicate the presence of a glass-house within the area.

666 Ctx 1. Linen smoother, perimeter fragment and remains of the stem-like handle. Weathered opaque with iridescence and some surface loss. Diam. *c.* 88 mm. ?16th century.

Street Farm

Glass was present in 50 contexts, the majority of which produced fragments of mixed dates from the late 17th to the 20th century. One solitary fragment of Roman glass came from context 273. Overall there is little of note, the assemblage being fragmentary and primarily of window and bottle glass. The bottle glass fits into existing typologies and a few diagnostic fragments are dateable.

Window glass

Very little post-medieval window glass was represented: only contexts 258, 737, 749 and 812 produced glass of a 17th-or 18th-century date. This was green-tinted, 1–1.5 mm thick and finely grozed where worked edges were still present. The rest of the window glass was of a 19th-or 20th-century date, represented in contexts 190, 225, 227, 235, 258, 304, 312, 313, 389, 420, 443,458, 545, 589, 591, 605, 611, 706, 784.

Vessel glass

Two diagnostic vessels were represented. The solid, drawn stem of an 18th-century wine glass came from context 268 and a 20th-century tumbler came from

context 227. Four undiagnostic sherds of mixed dates came from contexts 232, 267, 420 and 605.

Bottle glass

Bottle fragments came from virtually all contexts with glass. The catalogue below lists only those fragments that are illustrated, and in a chronological order. Only bases are illustrated as these fragments form the most comprehensive evidence for chronological development. Rim fragments were poorly represented. Two fragmentary rims, of an early 18th-century date came from context 611, and the four other examples are of 19th-century types.

667 Ctx 551. Onion bottle base; shallow, 'hummock-shaped kick, rounded heel. Globular body, light green. Late 17th-early 18th century. Rpd: 107 mm. (Dumbrell 1983, fig. b,.62, c. 1715; Hume 1961, "ideal squat form", no. 7, 102–3, fig. 3.99, *c.* 1685–1715.

668 Ctx 240. Onion bottle base; oblique angle of remaining lower body and the high kick suggest this is probably a late form of onion bottle. Light yellow-green. Rpd: 125 mm. Early 18th century. (Hume 1961, nos 10 and 11, 103, fig. 4.100, *c.* 1710–30.

669 Ctx 446. Mallett bottle base; relatively high, conical kick, rounded heel and slightly sagged base. Body rises steeply from a base that is wider than shoulder. Light olive-green. Rpd: 112 mm. Early 18th century. (Dumbrell 1983, figs a and b, 79, *c.* 1720–40; Hume 1961, no. 12, 103, fig. 4, 100, *c.* 1725–35).

670 Ctx 237. Cylindrical bottle base; sagged base, relatively high kick and acute heel. Light green. Rpd: ? Mid-18th century. (Dumbrell 1983, figs c and d (small bottle), 101, *c.* 1750–60; Hume 1961, nos 16 and 19 (taller version of no. 16), 104, fig. 4, 100).

671 Ctx 227. Cylindrical bottle base; relatively high, domed kick, acute heel, sagged base. Weathered opaque. Rpd: 80 mm. Mid-late 18th century. (Haslam 1984, type no. 11, fig. 41, 233, Hume 1961, type nos. 19 and 20, 104-5, fig. 5, 101, 1750–1770).

672 Ctx 443. Cylindrical bottle base; relatively shallow, domed kick, acute heel and slightly sagged base. Dark olive green. Late 18th century. (Haslam 1984, no. 13, fig. 41, 233, which he has classed under Hume's no. 21 type, an "...evolved cylindrical" form, 105, fig. 5, 101, *c.* 1770–1800).

673 Ctx 240. Cylindrical bottle base; relatively high, sub-conical kick, rounded heel, slightly sagged base. Late 18th to early 19th century. (Hume 1961, no. 22, 105, fig. 5, 101, *c.* 1790–1820; Dumbrell 1983, figs g–i,.101, *c.* 1790–1820, a "...transitional form just prior to the three part mould era...").

The above catalogue chronicles the basic development of the wine bottle from the early 'onion' bottles of the late 18th century to the later pre-mechanised early 19th-century cylindrical forms, although 19th-century mechanised examples are also represented (not

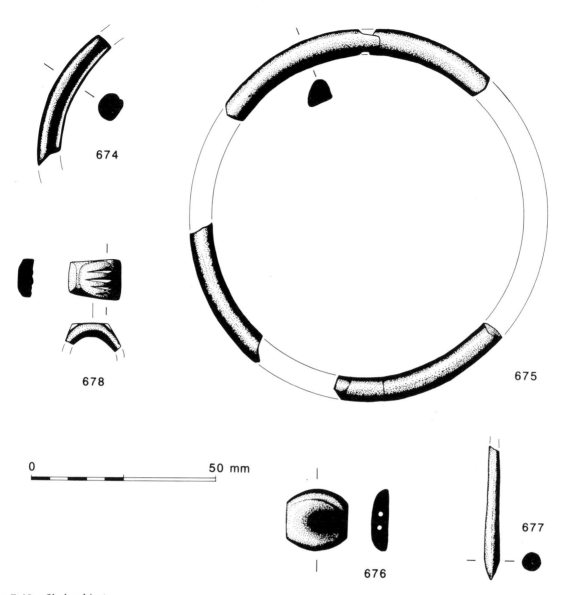

674

678

0   50 mm

676

675

677

Figure 7.40   Shale objects.

illustrated). This would indicate the long-lived nature of occupation at Street Farm. No medieval or early post-medieval glass was found.

SHALE OBJECTS *(Fig. 7.40)*
By Philippa Bradley

Shale bracelets are relatively common in Iron Age and Roman contexts (eg. Lawson 1976; Cunliffe 1984c, 396; Bird 1994a). Both bracelets are well finished and were probably lathe-turned. The Kimmeridge area of Dorset is the likely source for the shale (Calkin 1953). The example from Birdlip Quarry, with its internal groove, can be paralleled at Bancroft (Bird 1994, 368–9, fig. 191, no. 419). Although they are conventionally

described as bracelets they may also have been armlets or anklets (*cf.* Laws 1991, 234).

674 Birdlip Quarry, ctx 1 (topsoil). Fragment from a simple shale bracelet with a grooved line on the inside. Circular section, slightly flattened on one side. Original diameter *c.* 75 mm. Width 6 mm, height 7 mm. Condition good.

675 Preston Enclosure, ctx 132. Eleven fragments from a simple undecorated shale bracelet, very finely worked. Eight fragments conjoin, the remaining three probably belong to the same object. Probably circular section originally but now incomplete. Original diameter *c.* 85 mm. Width 6 mm (max.), height 8 mm (max. surviving). Condition fair but laminating.

Table 7.52   Summary of worked stone objects, all sites.

Site	Rotary Querns	Saddle Querns	Whetstones	? Slingstones	Other	Total
Hare Bushes North					1 pebble-hammer	1
Cherry Tree Lane Compound					1 point sharpener	1
Highgate House					1 spindle whorl	1
Birdlip Quarry	6	1	2	5	1 disc; 1 polisher	16
Middle Duntisbourne					1 quern fragment	1
Duntisbourne Grove		2 rubbers		1	2 quern fragments	5
Street Farm			2		1 millstone fragment	3
Ermin Farm				1		1
Preston Enclosure		2				2
Norcote Farm		1				1
Total	6	6	4	7	9	32

JET OBJECTS
By Martin Henig

Three jet objects were recovered from Birdlip Quarry comprising a spacer bead (cat. no. 676), a broken pin (cat. no. 677) and a broken finger-ring (cat. no. 678). The bead has been perforated twice and has been polished. A slightly larger example comes from a Period 2 grave at Butt Road, Colchester (c. AD 320–450; Crummy 1983, 34 fig. 36, 1447). The pin has a swollen waist and has a re-sharpened and polished point. Jet pins are relatively common and can be paralleled at a number of sites including Colchester (Crummy 1983, 27, fig. 24), Silchester (Lawson 1976, 257–8, fig. 7) and an almost identical example was found at Dalton Parlours (Clarke 1990, 122, fig. 90, 1). The finger-ring (349) is less easy to parallel but a plain rectangular bezel was found at Caerleon (Brewer 1986a, 144, fig. 145, 18) and a similar ring was found at Dalton Parlours (Clarke 1990, 122, fig. 90, 9).

676   Sf 273, ctx 31. Ovoid plano-convex spacer bead with two piercings. Length 17 mm, width 14 mm.

677   Sf 598, ctx 128. Shank of hairpin, expanding towards point, which appears to have been reshaped after breakage. The head is missing. Length 33 mm (max. surviving). Compare with Crummy 1983, 34, no. 1447; Allason-Jones 1996, 29, no. 50 (York).

678   Sf 829, ctx 349. Finger-ring, with externally faceted hoop and angled shoulders ornamented with four grooves. Less than half of the ring remains. The external diameter is no more than c. 16 mm, internal 12 mm. The width varies from 7–10 mm towards the bezel. Like much jet jewellery, it was probably designed to be worn by a woman, perhaps in this case a girl. The form of ring is related to the keeled ring (Johns 1996, 48–9), characteristic of the 3rd century, but rarely made from jet. There are, however, examples of jet rings of this type from York (Allason-Jones 1996, 36, no. 161) and the Rhineland, from Cologne and probably Wiesbaden (Hagen 1937, 106, no. A6 and 108, no. A16). Sf 829, ctx 349.

Allason-Jones emphasises the importance of the jet outcrops around Whitby, Yorkshire, and the importance of the York jet industry (1996, 11–14), but other materials were used (ibid. 6–7) and the relationship between the Rhineland jet industry and that in Britain and the sources of its raw material await further study. In this case, it is assumed that the three objects originated in Whitby.

THE WORKED STONE
By Fiona Roe

Introduction

The worked stone demonstrates how different varieties of hard stone were imported into Gloucestershire from the Neolithic until the medieval period or later. Ten of the excavated sites produced stone artefacts, amounting to 32 objects in total (Table 7.52). Twenty one pieces of local stone used in building were collected from Birdlip Quarry, six of which showed evidence of working. The objects include 1 piece of millstone, 15 quern fragments and 4 whetstones, all of which have proved to be of value for supplementing previously available information about the use of imported stone in central Gloucestershire and north Wiltshire, an area previously barely surveyed. Examination of further finds of worked stone in local museums has helped to fill out the picture. There have also been some unusual finds from the Neolithic period (Duntisbourne Grove), the Neolithic/Bronze Age (Norcote Farm) and the Roman period (Birdlip Quarry), all of which have wider implications.

Hare Bushes North

An early prehistoric pebble-hammer (Fig. 7.41.679, ctx 1010), made from a quartzite pebble was recovered, together with flint debitage, from a tree-throw hole. Pebble-hammers of this type are relatively common nationally (Roe 1979, 36), although only two others have previously been recorded from Gloucestershire (Davis *et al.* 1988, 152, no. 910, 153, no. 87).

They appear to have had a long period of use, mainly from the Mesolithic to the Bronze Age (Roe 1979, 36). This example has two worn facets at the end, possibly representing secondary use as a grinding stone after it had broken in half.

Duntisbourne Grove

Neolithic querns made from May Hill sandstone had not previously been recorded, either in Gloucestershire or elsewhere, so the two rubber fragments (Fig. 7.41.680–681) from the secondary fill of pit 94 are of some interest. The stone had been brought

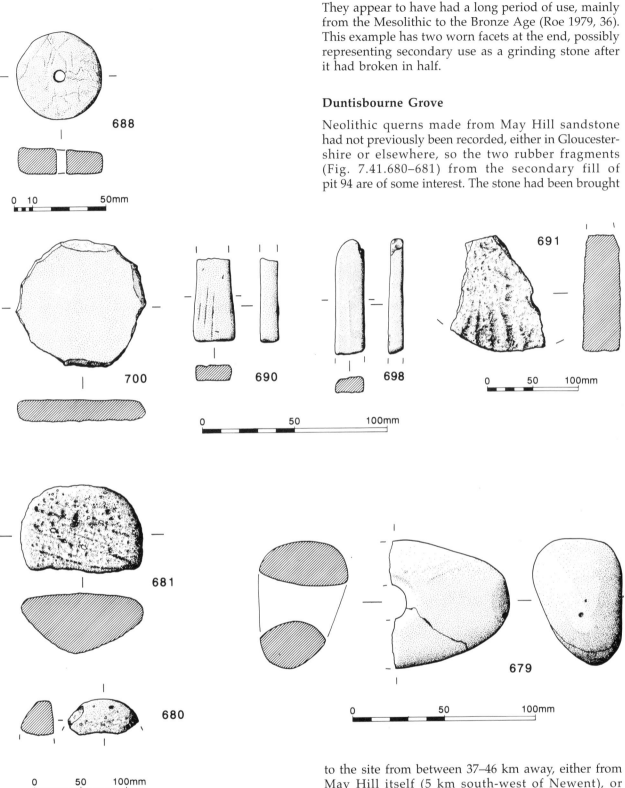

Figure 7.41   Stone objects.

to the site from between 37–46 km away, either from May Hill itself (5 km south-west of Newent), or from the Malverns. Pit 94 also contained flints, including leaf arrowhead tips and a chisel arrowhead, and it was one of a group of earlier prehistoric features in the south-west corner of the site.

Two further sites with worked May Hill sandstone from Neolithic contexts are now known from the area. Both are chambered Cotswold-Severn long barrows near Northleach, Glos. The Hazleton long cairn was constructed over a spread of domestic rubbish which included securely stratified quern and rubber fragments made from May Hill sandstone (Saville 1990, 176, 231, fig. 176). At The Burn Ground, Hampnett, half of a small saddle quern was found built into the cairn material (Grimes 1960, 75, fig. 32), and this too was made from May Hill sandstone (Gloucester Museum).

A small chip (cat. 682) of Forest of Dean Upper Old Red Sandstone came from the upper fill (ctx 168) of pit 142, a feature which also contained worked flints (cat. 34). The fragment originates from *c.* 41–48 km away. The pit again belonged to the group of early features in the south-west corner of the site. This variety of quernstone had not previously been recorded from an early prehistoric context, but there is also a further find from Norcote Farm, described below. The same pit at Duntisbourne Rouse also produced a small quartzite pebble from the upper fill, and this, like similar finds from Birdlip Quarry described below, could have been used as a slingstone.

Another quern fragment, of Upper Old Red Sandstone, came from context 53, the fill of ditch 44 (cat. 683) and could be Roman or earlier.

Middle Duntisbourne

A quern fragment of Upper Old Red Sandstone (cat. 684) was found in gully 194, beside trackway 137. The long period of use for this type of sandstone means that it could date to any time from the late Iron Age to the medieval period.

Norcote Farm

At Norcote Farm, a probable saddle quern fragment made from quartz conglomerate (cat. 685) was recovered from an evaluation area which had produced a lithics scatter although the quern fragment was unstratified. It had been brought some 45–50 km to the site.

Preston Enclosure

A worn fragment of saddle quern (cat. 687), made from May Hill sandstone, came from the fill of middle Iron Age enclosure ditch 59. May Hill sandstone saddle querns are common on early and middle Iron Age sites in the region. A second piece of saddle quern (cat. 686), of Upper Old Red Sandstone, came from a rubbish deposit in a tree-throw hole. This material occurs less frequently on earlier Iron Age sites, but there was a small proportion of Upper Old Red Sandstone at Salmonsbury, including a complete large saddle quern (Dunning 1976).

Ermin Farm

Small quartzite pebbles, collected locally, could have been used as slingstones, and an Iron Age example came from context 83.

Highgate House

The main fill of the Iron Age enclosure ditch produced a complete spindlewhorl (ctx 210, cat. 688, Fig. 7.41). It is made from a fine-grained Jurassic limestone which is likely to have been obtained locally (Richardson 1972). A somewhat similar spindlewhorl of late Iron Age/early Roman date came from Ditches hillfort at North Cerney (Trow 1988, 55, fig. 28, no. 6).

Cherry Tree Lane

Point sharpeners are ubiquitous, and the example from Cherry Tree Lane could be of any date from prehistoric onwards. It is weathered, including the single groove, and made from Pennant sandstone, brought to the site from the Bristol Coalfield some 48 km away. This was a versatile material, and was used during the Roman period for whetstones (cf. Hunter 1985, 71, fig. 8.2) and roofing tiles (cf. Timby 1998a).

Birdlip Quarry

The largest collection of stone artefacts comes from the Roman site at Birdlip Quarry and comprises seven quern fragments, two whetstones and seven other pieces. It is the only site from which building stone was recovered. Not all of the objects are typical of other Roman sites in Gloucestershire, while others appear to belong to earlier occupation in the area.

Standard materials

There are four rotary quern fragments made from Upper Old Red Sandstone quartz conglomerate, obtained from the Forest of Dean or the Wye Valley. This variety of stone was widely used for querns, and finds are known from a further 27 Roman sites in Gloucestershire alone. At Birdlip Quarry, one quern (cat. 697, ctx 368) came from a context dating to before AD 250, while three others (cat. 693 and 696, ctx 31, ctx 190) are from contexts dating to after AD 350.

Niedermendig lava was less widely used in the area, and only seven previous finds from Roman sites in Gloucestershire have been recorded to date. The single rotary quern fragment from Birdlip Quarry (cat. 699, ctx 1198) was unstratified, but it has a raised rim on the upper circumference, which suggests an early date. Similar querns were found at Usk (Welfare 1995). There is one Kentish Rag whetstone, which is of the typical cigar shape (cat. 690, Fig. 7.41). It was also unstratified, but similar whetstones are known from 13 Roman sites in Gloucestershire. Two other objects which are fairly common on Roman sites in the area are a polisher of quartzite (cat. 694, ctx 34) and a disc made from Jurassic limestone (Fig. 7.41.700, ctx 1325). Quartzite pebbles could have been picked up locally, and similar polishers are known from Bishop's Cleeve (Roe 1998, 130) and Kingscote (Gutierrez and Roe 1998, 176). Stone discs, possibly used for gaming, have been recorded from various local sites, including Kingscote (Gutierrez and Roe 1998, 176) and Frocester (Price forthcoming). These objects were often made from broken roofing tiles of various materials, and tiles at Birdlip were made from local Jurassic limestone.

Non-standard materials

Two objects, a quern and a whetstone, stand out as different from the general range of Roman finds in this area. The rotary quern (Fig. 7.41.691) is made from igneous rock which could not have been obtained locally. A thin-section (R 290) has shown that the rock is an altered gabbro, the main components of which are lathes of altered plagioclase (probably andesine) set in plates of altered pyroxene which are now nearly all altered to chlorite. Gabbro is found most abundantly in areas such as northern England, north Wales and Scotland (Sutherland 1982) but is uncommon further south. The Birdlip gabbro is not comparable to either the hornblende gabbro from the Mount Sorrel complex in Leicestershire (Le Bas 1968, 48) or the Coverack gabbro from the Lizard in Cornwall. Evidence from fieldwork has confirmed that a match can be made with the Squilver gabbro (formerly referred to as the Pitcholds intrusion) which occurs in the Shelve area just north of Bishops Castle in south Shropshire (Blythe 1943), 105 km from Birdlip Quarry.

Another mineral resource found in the Shelve area is lead, and this is known to have been used by the Romans (Haverfield 1908, 263). Thus, the quern might have been brought to Birdlip together with supplies of lead. Shelve is only 27 km from Wroxeter, and from there, the easiest route would have been by boat down the Severn to Gloucester, and then down the Ermin Way to Birdlip. This would perhaps have involved a less arduous journey than if lead had been obtained from the Mendips.

A whetstone (cat. 698, Fig. 7.41) is made from a fine-grained, very slightly micaceous, black sedimentary rock, clearly foreign to Gloucestershire. This could have come from Ordovician rocks in Wales, perhaps even from the Hope shale, which occurs in the same locality as the Squilver gabbro (Blythe 1943, 169). A somewhat similar whetstone came from the Bishop's Cleeve Roman site (Roe 1998, 128).

Objects that may relate to earlier occupation

A fragment of a May Hill sandstone saddle quern (cat. 695) from colluvium or hillwash seems likely to belong to earlier occupation in the area, and is perhaps related to the scatter of prehistoric pits. The five small quartzite pebbles, which were probably utilised as slingstones, are also of likely prehistoric date.

Street Farm

This site serves to demonstrate the long timespan during which Upper Old Red Sandstone. was utilised. Quartz conglomerate was used for a millstone, a fragment of which came from a medieval/post-medieval context (329). Another medieval example came from Tewkesbury Abbey Meadow (Hoyle 1993, 231). Coal Measures Sandstone was widely used for whetstones from at least the Roman period (Moore 1978), and there are examples of Roman date from Gloucestershire (Gutierrez and Roe 1998) while a medieval example is known from Holm Hill, Tewkesbury (Hannan 1997, 131). A medieval/post-medieval example was recovered from Street Farm (cat. 703) and a whetstone made from Norwegian Eidsborg schist cam from the same context. This Norwegian Rag is common on medieval sites in England, and there are further examples from post-medieval and later contexts at Southgate Street, Gloucester (Roe in prep.).

Discussion

The materials

Jurassic limestones are unsuitable for use as grinding materials, and it was always necessary to import hard, quartzose sandstones for querns, millstones and whetstones into this area of Gloucestershire. Only two objects from the excavations are made from local limestone, a late Iron Age spindlewhorl from Highgate House, Cowley (Fig. 7.41.688), and a Roman gaming disc, made from a piece of broken roofing tile or flat stone from Birdlip Quarry (Fig. 7.41.700).

The other type of stone which occurred naturally in the area was quartzite or quartzitic sandstone, in the form of pebbles in scattered Pleistocene Drift (Richardson 1933). It is possible that small quartz pebbles were used as slingstones; and the seven examples range from Neolithic to Iron Age or Roman in date. Quartzite pebbles were also used as polishers during the Roman period (Birdlip Quarry, cat. 694) and as early prehistoric pebble-hammers (Hare Bushes North, cat. 679). There are limitations to the ways in which a smooth, hard material such as quartzite can be utilised, and it is unsuitable for whetting, so the number of quartzite artefacts other than slingstones is small.

Most of the worked stone consists of varieties of stone that were brought to Gloucestershire from some distance. There are nine different kinds of imported stone, seven of which came from England and Wales, while the other two, Niedermendig lava and Norwegian Rag, came from overseas. These imported materials were used for 21 objects, consisting of 15 querns, 1 millstone, 4 whetstones and a point sharpener.

Upper Old Red Sandstone was the most frequently used quern material. Duntisbourne Grove is the first site at which Upper Old Red Sandstone has been recorded from early prehistoric contexts, and so it is now possible to show that this use of quartz conglomerate and pebbly sandstone for grinding extended over nearly six millennia, from the Neolithic period until the early 20th century. During the early and middle Iron Age it was apparently less popular than May Hill sandstone, but it was utilised for rotary querns in some quantity during the Roman period, as demonstrated by finds from Birdlip Quarry and numerous other sites in Gloucestershire. It appears to have been used continuously until about 1914 (Tucker 1971, 238). Millstones, as from Street Farm (cat. 701), were an important later product.

The excavation at Duntisbourne Grove has also shown that May Hill sandstone was first brought into the Cirencester area in the Neolithic period, and was used for saddle querns until rotary querns became current in the region. At that point, Upper Old Red Sandstone seems to have become the preferred grinding material, both in Gloucestershire and the surrounding areas. During the Roman period May Hill sandstone seems temporarily to have been ignored, but it was used again for querns, although perhaps sporadically, during the Anglo-Saxon and medieval periods.

The Roman period saw some innovations in quern materials, with new types of stone being traded into the area, although always in smaller quantities than Old Red Sandstone. Querns of Niedermendig lava were brought to many sites in Britain from the Roman period onwards. Millstone Grit was also widely traded, and is now known from ten Roman sites in Gloucestershire, although there have been no finds from these excavations. The rotary of Squilver gabbro, however, stands out as being the only known quern made from this type of stone, either in Gloucestershire or elsewhere, although further research may well produce more examples.

The four whetstones are all from Roman or later contexts, and all were brought into Gloucestershire over considerable distances. The whetstone of black shale from Birdlip Quarry (cat. 698) is unusual, but the find may be accounted for because of the gabbro quern, as both types of stone, and indeed lead ore, occur in the same area of Shropshire near the Welsh borderland. It may have been convenient to transport these commodities together within the same trading network. At Maiden Castle, the Iron Age whetstones were probably being brought to the site through a distribution network of metalworking ores (Laws et al. 1991, 232). By contrast, Kentish Rag (cat. 690, Birdlip Quarry) was generally used for whetstones throughout the Roman period, but the trade seems to have died out afterwards. This seems to be the only variety of stone among those considered here that was very widely utilised, but for a relatively short period only. Whetstones of Coal Measures sandstone had a much longer period of use, from at least Roman times until the 19th century (Moore 1978), and there is a probable connection with the distribution of Millstone Grit. It is therefore no surprise to find a Coal Measures sandstone whetstone from a medieval/post-medieval context at Street Farm (cat. 702). The same context produced another long lived whetstone material, Norwegian Rag or Eidsborg schist which was a Saxon innovation but had a long history of subsequent use (Crosby and Mitchell 1987). Pennant sandstone also had a long useful life, and fits into the general picture of conservative use of specific types of stone.

Chronological overview

The worked stone is a good representative collection for Gloucestershire, covering a lengthy timespan from Neolithic to medieval/post-medieval times, with gaps only in the early Iron Age and Saxon periods. The early prehistoric period shows the beginning of a long tradition in the use of both Upper Old Red Sandstone and May Hill sandstone, with subsidiary use of quartzite pebbles. The excavations at Duntisbourne Grove and Norcote Farm have provided the first evidence in the area for Neolithic trade in quern materials. This was probably a different distribution network for that of Neolithic stone axes, since the querns were a good deal heavier, and were transported over shorter distances, perhaps only up to 37–50 km.

The same two quern materials were still in use during the later prehistoric period. These excavations have shown that, far from being an Iron Age innovation, the use of Old Red Sandstone and May Hill sandstone was already well-established by that time. By the earlier part of the Iron Age, however, May Hill sandstone seems to have been the preferred material for saddle querns. At Salmonsbury hillfort, for example, there was a considerably higher proportion of May Hill Sandstone saddle querns (Cheltenham Museum). The use of locally collected quartzite pebbles also lasted until at least the Roman period.

From medieval times onwards, traditional lithic materials still continued to be used. The Old Red Sandstone and Coal Measures sandstone from Street Farm were far from being innovations, while Eidsborg schist had first been brought in from Norway in the 9th century. Millstone Grit and Niedermendig lava were also still being used, although they are not represented among the finds of later date from these excavations. All these traditional materials did not go out of use until the 20th century.

Catalogue *(Fig. 7.41)*

Hare Bushes North

679 Two fragments of pebble-hammer, burnt, hour-glass perforation, made from unevenly shaped pebble, two worn facets at end; B 82 mm, max D 50 mm, quartzite, fill of tree-throw hole 1011, Neolithic? Sf 1, ctx 1010.

Duntisbourne Grove

680 Small fragment from rubber for saddle quern, hog backed, slightly convex grinding surface, worn, B now 75 mm, max D now 33.5, May Hill sandstone, fill of prehistoric pit 94, middle Neolithic. Sf 257, ctx 111.

681 Fragment of rubber for saddle quern, hog backed, slightly convex grinding surface, worn, B 126.5 mm,

max D 61 mm, May Hill sandstone, fill of prehistoric pit 94, middle Neolithic. Sf 258, ctx 111.

682 Small chip with no clear evidence of working, but a quern material, Upper Old Red Sandstone, fill of pit 142, Neolithic. Sf 210, ctx 168

683 Quern fragment, Upper Old Red Sandstone, quartz conglomerate, upper fill of quarry ditch 44, Roman? Sf 10, ctx 53.

Middle Duntisbourne

684 Quern fragment with one worked surface, Upper Old Red Sandstone fill of gully 194, beside trackway 137, medieval? Ctx 138.

Norcote Farm

685 Part of quern, probable saddle type, Upper Old Red Sandstone quartz conglomerate, in area of Neolithic/Bronze Age occupation. Sf 3, ctx 146.

Preston Enclosure

686 Fragment saddle quern with concave grinding surface; Upper Old Red Sandstone, fill of tree-throw hole 14, middle Iron Age. Sf 8, ctx 8.

687 Small fragment saddle quern, worn thin, concave grinding surface, May Hill sandstone, fill of enclosure ditch 59, middle Iron Age. Ctx 64/65.

Highgate House

688 Spindlewhorl, disc type with straight bored hole, diam 45 mm, th 13.5 mm, diam of hole 6.5 mm, Jurassic limestone, fine-grained micaceous, main backfill of enclosure ditch 212, late Iron Age. Sf 1, ctx 210.

Cherry Tree Lane

689 Small slab used as point sharpener, roughly weathered, one fairly coarse groove, L 93 mm, B 61 mm, D 23.5 mm, Pennant sandstone within colluvium, undated. Ctx 6.

Birdlip Quarry

690 Fragment small, slender whetstone, rectangular cross section, worn sides, L 43 mm, B max 22mm D max 10 mm, Kentish Rag. Sf 1490, ctx u/s.

691 Fragment of rotary quern, disc type, traces of grooved grinding surface, thin section, R290, Th 47 mm, roughly trimmed edge, igneous, fairly coarse-grained gabbro from Squilver Hill, Shropshire, upper part of midden, Period 2B, phase 6. Sf 263, ctx 31, Area B.

692 Fragment rotary quern, upper stone with part of central hole, worn shiny around outer edge, Upper Old Red Sandstone, quartz conglomerate, upper part of midden, Period 2B, phase 6, AD 350+. Sf 287, ctx 31, Area B.

693 Fragment rotary quern, lower stone, good grooving of grinding surface; Upper Old Red Sandstone quartz conglomerate, upper part of midden, Period 2B, phase 6. Sf 296, ctx 31, Area B.

694 Pebble with slight traces of use as polisher on three sides; quartzitic sandstone, floor/rubble layer possibly associated with late building, Period 2B, phase 6. Sf 1200, ctx 34, Area A.

695 Quern fragment, probably from saddle quern, May Hill sandstone, colluvium over wall 35, residual from Iron Age? Period 2B, phase 6. Sf 281, ctx 90, Area A.

696 Fragment rotary quern with part of central hole, neatly trimmed circumference and trace of small hopper, Upper Old Red Sandstone quartz conglomerate, within corn dryer 42, probably backfill, Period 2A, phase 2. Sf 496, ctx 190, Area B/D.

697 Fragment rotary quern, upper stone, top surface pecked into shape, possibly a small hopper, Upper Old Red Sandstone quartz conglomerate, rubble backfill of well 277. Sf 836, ctx 368.

698 Small whetstone with wear on two edges, split off larger slab; L 60 mm, B 16 mm, D 9 mm, black, fine-grained shale, probably Ordovician from Shropshire, material from around hearth 756, includes early and late material. Sf 1283, ctx 875, area A.

699 Fragment rotary quern, upper stone, possible traces of raised rim around circumference on upper side, Niedermendig lava, unstratified. Sf 1542, ctx 1198, area 2.

700 Disc, unevenly worked edge; diam 67 mm, Th 11 mm, Jurassic limestone fine-grained, soil accumulation over stone surface. Sf 1604, ctx 1325, Area 2A.

Street Farm

701 Fragment from large millstone with part of central hole and keyhole shaped socket for rhynd fittings; Upper Old Red Sandstone, quartz conglomerate, posthole associated with surface 382, medieval/post-medieval. Sf 17, ctx 329.

702 Whetstone, rectangular slab type with two grooves from use as sharpening stone, grey sandstone probably Coal Measures sandstone, charcoal layer associated with oven 516, medieval/post-medieval. Sf 18, ctx 500.

703 Whetstone, long and slender, weathered; Eidsborg schist, charcoal layer associated with oven 516, medieval/post-medieval. Sf 19, ctx 500.

Building stone from Birdlip Quarry

Three different varieties of Jurassic limestone were used for the building stone, and the probability is that they were all collected locally. A light coloured oolitic limestone was used for the three earliest pieces only, a broken block of dressed building stone from part of an oven (cat. 713, structure 646, ctx 199), and two large post-pads (cat. 716–717, ctx 297, 298) consisting of rectangular blocks of limestone with square-socketed holes. They date to before AD 250. Such limestone can be found in the Inferior Oolite of Leckhampton Hill, but also occurs in the Lower Freestone at Cowley itself (Richardson 1972, 79, 85). It can be worked as a freestone, which facilitates any shaping that might be needed.

The later building stone, dated to after AD 250–300, is all, with one exception, made from fine-grained Jurassic limestone. A coarse-grained, shelly and oolitic limestone, perhaps from Cowley Wood or nearby (Richardson 1972, 112), was used for a suggested entrance marker or threshold stone (cat. 721, ctx 841) found in the drystone wall of structure 1452 but this was probably not its original purpose. The finer-grained limestone, which again could have come from Cowley, or else from only a few km away, was used for 17 pieces. There are three blocks of building stone (cat. 706, 719, 724, contexts 34, 730, 1323), one of which (cat. 719) has a groove of unknown purpose crudely pecked round three sides. Another large piece is a post-pad (cat. 715, ctx 353), which has a square socket in a partly shaped rectangular block, the bottom half of which was left rough. It had been re-used as post-packing. No definite pieces of roofing tile survived, although of the remaining 13 small fragments of fine-grained limestone, the three thinnest (cat. 704, 714, 722, contexts 7, 223, 848) may be pieces of roofing tile. Another ten somewhat thicker, but still small fragments have been interpreted, on the basis of worn surfaces, as paving slabs.

Catalogue

704 Fragment roofing tile or more probably paving stone, Jurassic limestone, fine-grained, occupation layer general cleaning, Period 2B, phase 6. Ctx 7, Area A.

705 Fragment possible paving stone, burnt, Jurassic limestone, fine-grained, modern drain. Ctx 12, Area A.

706 Block of burnt stone, probably building stone, Jurassic limestone, fine-grained, floor/rubble layer possibly associated with building, Period 2B, phase 6. Ctx 34, Area A.

707 Fragment possible paving stone, burnt, Jurassic limestone fine-grained, medieval lynchet. Ctx 38

708 Weathered slab, possible paving stone, burnt, Jurassic limestone fine-grained, fill of pit 39. Ctx 40, Area B/D.

709 Fragment possible paving stone, burnt, Jurassic limestone fine-grained, occupation layer, Period 2B, phase 3. Ctx 72, Area E.

710 Fragment possible paving stone, burnt, Jurassic limestone, fine-grained, modern topsoil. Ctx 95.

711 Fragment possible paving stone, Jurassic limestone, fine-grained, upper part of midden, Period 2B, phase 6. Sf 668, ctx 128, Area B.

712 Fragment possible paving stone, weathered, slightly burnt, Jurassic limestone, fine-grained, upper part of midden, Period 2B, phase 6. Sf 676, ctx 128, Area B.

713 Part of rectangular block of dressed building stone, burnt, Jurassic limestone, oolitic, light coloured, part of oven, structure 646, Period 1, phase 1. Ctx 199, Area C.

714 Fragment roofing tile or paving stone, Jurassic limestone fine-grained, rough stone surface or path, Period 2A, phase 5. Ctx 223, Area B.

715 Large post pad with square socket, top part of pad partly shaped into a rectangular block, bottom half left rough, Jurassic limestone fine-grained, reused as post packing Period 2A, phase 2. Sf 353, ctx 276, Area D.

716 Large post pad; nearly square block with a square socket, Jurassic limestone, oolitic, light coloured, probable post setting, paired with 298, Period 1, phase 1. Sf 722, ctx 297, Area C.

717 Large post pad, rectangular block with square socket, Jurassic limestone, oolitic, light coloured, paired with 297, Period 1, phase 1. Sf 774, ctx 298, Area C.

718 Fragment possible paving stone, burnt Jurassic limestone, fine-grained, occupation layer next to wall 775, Period 2A, phase 5. Ctx 705, Area A.

719 Approximately rectangular grooved block with crudely pecked out groove running round three sides, Jurassic limestone, fine-grained, drystone wall of structure 1452, Period 2A, phase 4. Sf 1335, ctx 730, Area A.

720 Fragment with worn surface, possible paving stone, Jurassic limestone fine-grained, occupation layer, Period 2A, phase 3–5. Ctx 825, Area A.

721 Very large elongated block, about the size for a threshold stone, one side weathered, especially in centre where it may first have been worn down, other side is crudely grooved, Jurassic limestone, coarse, shelly and oolitic, drystone wall of structure 1452, Period 2A, phase 4. Sf 1502, ctx 841, Area A.

722 Fragment from burnt slab, possible tile or paving stone, Jurassic limestone, fine-grained, mixed accumulation including material from oven/hearth 1035, Period 2A, phase 4. Ctx 848, Area A.

723 Fragment from slab, possible paving stone, Jurassic limestone, fine-grained, debris from hearth 1035, Period 2A, phase 3. Ctx 914, Area A.

724 Block of possible building stone, Jurassic limestone, fine-grained, stone surface over roadside ditch, Period 2A, phase 2. Sf 1603, ctx 1323, Area 2A.

Burnt Stone

Burnt Jurassic limestone, changed in colour to either pink or grey, was recovered from 11 of the sites. The largest amount came from Birdlip Quarry (11 fragments) and the impression gained was of burnt building stone, probably including paving stones. This material could be the result of an unintentional fire. Five sites produced negligible amounts of burnt stone: Burford Road (6 fragments), Preston Enclosure (2), Street Farm (2), Weavers Bridge (2) and Hare Bushes North (1). At five other sites, all of which had some prehistoric occupation, burnt stone was present in noteworthy amounts. At Trinity Farm, pits of late Neolithic/Beaker date contained pottery, flint and burnt stone amounting to 47 fragments, although there was no worked stone. Other sites where prehistoric activity correlates with finds of burnt stone are Middle Duntisbourne (47 fragments), Duntisbourne Grove (32 fragments), Highgate House (19 fragments) and Court Farm (13 fragments). More work is needed on the possible uses for this burnt stone, which is of frequent occurrence on prehistoric sites in the region.

THE FIRED CLAY
By Alistair Barclay

Introduction

The overall assemblage is relatively small and consists of 249 fragments weighing a total of 1.081 kg from 14 of the excavated sites. The fired clay was recovered from a variety of feature types including pits, ditches, a midden and hillwash deposits. The total assemblage includes only a few object fragments (loomweights (19, 125 g) and briquetage containers (2, 31 g)), while most of the fired clay consists of amorphous fragments. The assemblage includes some evidence for textile production in the form of loomweight fragments from Court Farm and Weavers Bridge, a few fragments of Droitwich briquetage from Highgate House that indicate inter-regional exchange and an important group of fired clay from a Neolithic pit at Duntisbourne Grove. There was no evidence for structural clay (with timber impressions) or for metalworking debris (eg. moulds or crucibles).

Methodology

The material was quantified by number of fragments and weight. The fired clay occurs in a range of fabrics. It was examined for evidence of wattle or other impressions, possible objects and structural pieces.

Fabrics

Nat:	No added temper or inclusions.
Sand:	Sandy clay matrix with no other inclusions.
Coarse sand:	Coarse quartz sand.
Shell:	Coarse shell platelets.
Sandy:	(Briquetage) coarse quartz sand with occasional voids from burnt out organics and rare quartzite grit.

Quantification

Table 7.53 gives a breakdown of the quantity (number of fragments, weight) of material from each site and context. In, general, the overall quantity of fired clay was low with relatively few sites producing more than 10 fragments.

Loomweights

The only identifiable objects relating to textile production were the possible loomweight fragments from Court Farm and Weavers Bridge. These were identified by their flat edges and in two cases by perforations. It is assumed that they derive from triangular loomweights. Neither of these fragments were very large with the heaviest piece weighing only 37 g. Triangular loomweights can be of either Iron Age or early Roman date. At Court Farm four fragments from contexts 286 and 317 were found with either Iron Age or Roman pottery, while a further two fragments from context 402 were possibly residual. At Weavers Bridge the 13 identifiable fragments were found with later Roman pottery in context 57. If this date is accepted at face value then it could be suggested that either the fragments are redeposited residual material or that they actually belong to objects other than loomweights.

Briquetage salt containers

Two fragments of possible briquetage salt containers from contexts 111 and 228 were recovered from late Iron Age features at Highgate House (identified by E Morris). Both fragments are small with the larger weighing only 25 g. They are manufactured from sandy fabrics, although one (context 111) also has larger quartzite grits and burnt out organics, that would approximate to so-called Droitwich briquetage from the West Midlands (cf. Hurst and Rees 1992, 200–1). If the identification of these pieces as Droitwich briquetage is correct, then this indicates that the site was involved in specialised exchange on an inter-regional basis as outlined by Morris for the Iron Age (1994a, 384–6).

Amorphous fired clay

The majority of the fired clay consists of oxidised amorphous fragments. This material no doubt derives from ovens and hearths used for domestic and industrial activities. Most but not all of this material is fired a reddish-brown colour. In addition, a significant quantity (11, 230 g) of unburnt clay was recovered from the lower fill of well 277 (context 368) at Birdlip Quarry. Of interest is the quantity of fired clay from the Neolithic pit (fill 168) at Duntisbourne

Table 7.53   Fired clay, all sites.

Context	No.	Weight (g)	Fabric	Comment
Highgate House				
111	1	25	? Briquetage	Droitwich briquetage
128	1	15	Shelly	One oxidised surface
228	1	6	? Briquetage	Droitwich briquetage
Middle Duntisbourne				
216	1	2	Shelly	Amorphous
256	1	4	Nat.	Amorphous
330	13	5	Sandy	Amorphous
Duntisbourne Grove				
108	1	2	Sandy	Amorphous
113 <13>	4	6	Nat.	Amorphous
168 <15>	29	110	Nat.	Amorphous
168 <10>	86	278	Nat.	Amorphous
168 Sf 199	31	76	Nat.	Amorphous
228	2	3	Coarse sand	Amorphous
Trinity Farm				
57	10	64	Nat.	Amorphous
Burford Road				
309	1	1	Nat.	Amorphous
Cherry Tree Lane				
6	8	15	Sandy	Amorphous
Witpit Lane				
7	1	1	Nat.	Amorphous
Preston Enclosure				
87	2	12	Nat.	Finger moulded amorphous lump
285	1	5	Clay pellets	Amorphous
St Augustine's Farm South				
3127	1	<1	Nat.	Amorphous
Lower Street Furlong				
31	2	27	Calc. gravel	Amorphous
Court Farm				
286	1	37	Nat.	Flat side. Probable loomweight fragment
317	3	13	Nat.	As above.
402	2	48	Nat.	Two fragments with broken perforations. Probable loomweight fragments.
Weavers Bridge				
57	12	23	Nat.	Loomweight fragment ?
57	1	4	Calc. gravel	Loomweight fragment ?
NOSNI96				
CH6300(2)	13	14	Organic	Amorphous
Birdlip Quarry				
81	1	10	Shelly	Amorphous
368 <48>	11	230	Nat.	Amorphous unburnt clay
619	3	1	Nat.	Amorphous
1225	1	20		Amorphous
1313	4	14	Nat.	Amorphous
Total	249	1081		

Table 7.54   Ceramic building material, all sites.

Site Code	Total weight (g)	Roman tile weight (g)	Medieval and later tile weight (g)	Misc tile weight (g)
Cirencester Watching Brief	125	75	-	50
Weavers Bridge	1635	950	675	10
Court Farm	575	525	-	50
Preston Enclosure	375	-	375	-
Westfield Farm	325	-	325	-
Middle Duntisbourne	10	-	-	10
Lynches Trackway	45	-	-	45
Burford Road	1795	1375	50	370
Exhibition Barn	250	250	-	-
Norcote Farm	395	-	300	95
Street Farm	8300	150	5575	2575
Cherry Tree Lane	585	300	-	285
NOSNI	275	50	225	-
Birdlip Quarry	12490	11350	-	1140
TOTAL	27180	15025	7525	4630
Percentage of total	100%	55%	28%	17%

Table 7.55   Summary of Roman tile types, all sites.

Site Code	Total weight of Roman tile (g)	Tegulae A		Imbrices B		Tubuli C		Plain tiles D		Bricks	
		No.	(g)	No.	(g)	No.	(g)	No.	(g)	No.	(g)
Cirencester Watching Brief	75					1	75				
Weavers Bridge	950	2	300					3	650		
Court Farm	525	1	350					2	175		
Burford Road	1375	1	200			1	50	4	1125		
Exhibition Barn	250	1	250								
Street Farm	150					2	150				
Cherry Tree Lane	300	1	75			2	225				
NOSNI	50							1	50		
Birdlip Quarry	11350	19	5950	4	475	7	250	33	4525	1	150
Total	15025	25	7125	4	475	13	750	43	6525	1	150
%	100%		47%		3%		6%		43%		1 %

Table 7.56   Summary of Roman fabric types, all sites.

	Fabric 1	Fabric 2	Fabric 3	Fabric 4	Fabric 5	Fabric 6	Fabric 7
Weight (g)	8125	700	2200	300	275	200	322
%	54	4.7	14.7	2	1.8	1.3	21.5

Grove. Fired clay is a rare find from Neolithic contexts and when it does occur it tends to be in rather small quantities. The relatively high quantity of, albeit amorphous fired clay, from a Neolithic pit in association with pottery, worked flint and charred plant remains is of some importance as a probable indicator of domestic activity. Small quantities of fired clay were found in a pit deposit associated with later Neolithic Peterborough Ware at Cam, Glos. (Smith 1968, 24–5) and from Stanton Harcourt, Oxon (Hamlin 1963).

CERAMIC BUILDING MATERIAL
By Leigh Allen

Introduction

A total assemblage of ceramic building material weighing 27, 180 kg was recovered from 15 of the excavated sites (Table 7.54).

Methodology

The whole assemblage was initially scanned and divided into either Roman or medieval material. The medieval material was weighed but no further analysis of type or fabric was undertaken. The Roman tile fragments were weighed, measured (where a complete dimension existed) and assigned to one of the following tile type categories: tegula (A), imbrex (B), tubulus (C), plain tile (D) or brick (E). Fragments without distinguishing characteristics or measurable thicknesses were assigned to the miscellaneous category. The fragments within the five recognisable tile type categories were examined macroscopically with a x20 hand lens and seven distinct fabric types were identified.

Summary

The results of the analysis are tabulated below (Table 7.54), giving the total weight in grammes of the Roman, medieval and miscellaneous fragments recovered from each of the individual sites.

Roman tile

The tile types are summarised in table 7.55. Tegulae were identified by the existence of a flange, a groove at the base of the flange or traces of an incised semi-circular design or signature at one end of the tegula. There were 25 fragments of tegulae in the assemblage weighing 7125 g (47% of the total Roman material).

Imbrices are the curved tiles which cover the tegulae flanges on a roof, they taper along their length. There were only four fragments from imbrices identified in the assemblage weighing 475 g (3% of the total).

Tubuli were identified by the presence of a key for plaster or remains of the perforation in the side through which the air would have passed. There were 13 fragments weighing 750 g (6% of the total Roman material).

The plain tile category includes fragments of tile with thicknesses that range from 17–39 mm (fragments with a thickness greater than 40 mm have been classified as bricks (see below). These fragments could originate from tile types A–C although they have none of the distinguishing features mentioned above. Alternatively they may be from any one of the great variety of floor tiles or pilae. There were 43 fragments of plain tile weighing 6525 g (43% of the total).

There was one fragment of brick recovered weighing 150 g (1% of the total Roman material). It may have originated from a floor or bonding tiles such as a Lydion, pedalis or sesquipedalis.

Tile Fabrics (Table 7.56)

Seven distinct fabric types were identified. Fabric 1 was predominant comprising 8125 g of tile (54% of the total assemblage). This fabric has a soft, soapy matrix, reddish-pink in colour with a variable degree of streaks and swirls of badly mixed lighter coloured clay. The inclusions comprise abundant very fine quartz, abundant fragments of grog and frequent fine mica particles. Tile fragments of this fabric have been recovered from other excavations in Gloucestershire notably at Fairford, Claydon Pike (Palmer *et al.* in preparation) and Somerford Keynes. Its source is probably the nearby tile kilns of Minety in Gloucestershire.

Medieval tile

The total assemblage includes 7525 g of medieval tile, no further analysis of tile type or fabric has been carried out.

Conclusions

The total quantity of tile recovered was very small and the fragments were very abraded. There were only 15, 025 g of tile identifiable as Roman, nearly 50% of which came from fragments classified as plain tiles which could originate from a wide variety of floor tile types. The other large group consists of roof tiles, predominantly tegulae with very few examples of imbrices.

WATERLOGGED WOOD
By N Mitchell

Introduction

An assemblage comprising the remains of 14 water-logged wooden posts and/or stakes, largely of oak, were recovered from Lynches Trackway, Latton 'Roman Pond' and Weavers Bridge.

Lynches Trackway

A single well-preserved oak stake was recovered. It had been cut to a point on three faces by a broad flat axe leaving one third of the point untooled. Measuring 950 mm long and 85 mm in diameter it is roundwood with heartwood, sapwood and bark intact.

Table 7.57   Slag identification, all sites.

Site	Context	Sf no.	Identification	Mass	Comment
Birdlip Quarry	33	156	HB or Slag Cake	1480.0	130*120*50mm
	781	1146	SSL/CIN	6.5	
Duntisbourne Grove	26		CIN?	4.0	
Burford Road	206		Clinker	17.0	
Cherry Tree Lane	6		HB	133.5	55*50*25mm
Preston Enclosure	202		SSL?	35.0	
St Augustine's Lane	143		Clinker?	14.0	
Westfield Farm	12		SSL	130.0	
Street Farm	17		SSL/CIN	3.0	
	119		Clinker	29.0	
	199		Clinker?	110.0	
	304		Coal/Shale?	293.0	
	719		Clay Lining	82.0	
	870		Slag/Clinker?	200.0	
	888		SSL	85.0	
	889		Clinker	3.5	
Court Farm	286	4	SSL	67.0	
	33		CIN	19.0	
	43		SSL	48.5	
Weavers Bridge	57		Limestone?	23.0	Ca DETECTED
NOSNI 96	9	2590	Clinker	744.0	
Trinity Farm	9	1	Limestone?	41.0	Ca DETECTED
Ermin Farm	5	8	Crucible		Cu, Sn minor Pb

Latton 'Roman Pond'

One willow or poplar stake, sf 99, and the remnants of five oak posts were recovered. The willow/poplar stake is the only well preserved wood from the site and was recovered from ditch fill 316. It is the tip of a small roundwood stake measuring 106 x 36 mm and has been cut to a point with four long axe marks. Its function is unknown.

The remnants of three oak posts, sfs 114–116 were retrieved from an alignment of ten postholes orientated north-south (postholes 288, 300 and 315). They appear to have been roundwood but only the tough heartwood survives and there is no evidence for tooling or even shaping to a point. Although they only survive to between 150 and 210 mm in length they are estimated to have been at least 180 mm in diameter. A fourth posthole, fill 319, similarly produced a badly decayed remnant of an oak post, sf 132 with no evidence of tooling. Two other oak stakes, approximately 300 x 45 mm have been radially split but are too poorly preserved to show tool-marks.

Weavers Bridge

The five stakes, (sfs 105, 106, 107, 108 and 139) are of oak heartwood and are well preserved only at their points with sapwood surviving in patches. They are all characterised by their long, slender points resulting from very regular axing. They have numerous axe marks creating seven or eight faces of tooling on the point of each stake. Only 108 differs in having four major faces of tooling with the edges finely chamfered to create four smaller faces. Their slightly flattened tips show that the stakes were, at least in part, driven into the ground.

SLAG AND RESIDUE
By G. McDonnell

Introduction

The material classed as slags and other residues recovered from the excavations are described and listed in Table 7.57. Sieved residues from soil samples were examined using magnetic susceptibility to assess the presence of (iron) metalworking debris. These results are given in Table 7.58.

Slag classification

The slags were visually examined and the classification is solely based on morphology. In general slags and residues are divided into two broad groups; diagnostic and non-diagnostic slags. The diagnostic slags, can be attributed to a particular industrial process. These comprise the ironworking slags, ie. smelting or smithing slags, and the non-ferrous residues, eg. crucibles. The non-diagnostic residues cannot be directly ascribed to a process, but may be identified with a process by association with diagnostic residues, eg. clay furnace lining with smelting slag.

Table 7.58   Magnetic Susceptibility Results (Units x 10⁻⁸ m³/kg).

Context	S.S. No	Mass (g)	Mag Sus	Corrected
198	15	148	123	42
204	26	92	107	58
266	93	42	150	179
267	98	68	268	197
532	58	169	125	37
532	59	97	165	85
532	60	76	120	79
885	125	61	37	30
1127	131	74	98	66
Standard	HS	18	1200	3333

Ferrous diagnostic slags and residues

Hearth bottom (HB) - a plano-convex accumulation of fayalitic slag formed in the smithing hearth. The dimensions (major diameter*minor diameter*depth in mm) are given in the Comment column (Table 7.57).

Smithing slag (SSL) - randomly shaped pieces of fayalitic slag generated by the smithing process.

Hammer scale (HS) - it occurs in two forms, flake and spheroidal. The former is believed to derive from scaling (oxidation) of the surface of the iron being worked, and would be removed from the metal during hammering and deliberately knocked from the surface prior to insertion in the fire. Spheroidal scale is formed during fire welding. Slag is trapped between the two pieces of iron being welded and is ejected during hammering of the weld which form droplets that freeze in flight.

Cinder (CIN) - high silica smithing debris, often formed at the reaction zone between the smithing slag and the hearth lining.

Non-ferrous diagnostic residues

Crucible - fragments or complete ceramic vessels used to melt non-ferrous metals.

Non-diagnostic slags and residues

Cinder (Cin) - a high silica slag that can be formed by high temperature reaction between silica and ferruginous material. It can be ascribed to either the non-diagnostic slags or the diagnostic slags depending on its iron content and morphology.

Furnace/hearth lining (FL or HL) - the clay lining of an industrial hearth, furnace or kiln which has been subjected to high temperature oxidising conditions. It is characterised by a vitrified surface inner face. In some cases the tuyere mouth may be preserved. Furnace Lining is considered non-diagnostic, since it cannot be ascribed to a process on grounds other than archaeological association, i.e. there is as yet no diagnostic feature which will distinguish vitrified lining from a smithing hearth from that from an iron smelting furnace.

Clinker - clinker or ash probably derived from steam boilers.

Other Material (Other) - which normally comprises fragments of fuel etc., and in this instance includes coal/shale

Discussion of slag types

The identification of the slags is given in Table 7.57. The majority of fragments were either smithing slags (SSL or SSL/CIN) or of modern derivation, probably clinkers from fireboxes (notably Street Farm). The quantity of smithing debris recovered was small and it can all be considered as 'background' noise. The modern material probably derives from steam powered engines. The clay lining (Street Farm, context 719) and the slag/clinker lining (Street Farm, context 870) probably could have derived from some (modern) industrial process. The following discussion relates to individual pieces that require specific attention.

Birdlip Quarry

This large pieces of slag (1480 g) from context 33 is either a large hearth bottom derived from smithing or a slag cake formed by tapping the slag from a smelting furnace into a small pit in front of the furnace. The slag lacks the vesicular appearance of hearth bottoms, and has clearly been fully liquated.

Soil samples from an oven (context 199) were sieved and the residues sent for examination to assess the presence of metalworking residues. The samples were weighed and their magnetic susceptibility measured. It would be expected that if the oven/hearth had been used for ironworking then hammerscale, other micro-slags and metal fragments would be present in the samples. These residues have very high magnetic susceptibility and their presence could be readily detected without recourse to microscopic study. The results are given in Table 7.58. They have been corrected to a standard mass of 50 g, and the values obtained from a sample of hammerscale are also provided. These results demonstrate that there is no enhanced magnetic susceptibility due to ironworking, but that there may be some enhancement due to burning.

Weavers Bridge

This piece from context 57 is not a slag, but probably altered limestone or other sedimentary rock. XRF analysis detected calcium as the major element.

Ermin Farm

Fragments of crucible were recovered from enclosure ditch 49 (segment 6, fill 5). XRF analysis detected copper, tin and a low level of lead, indicating the melting and casting of tin bronze.

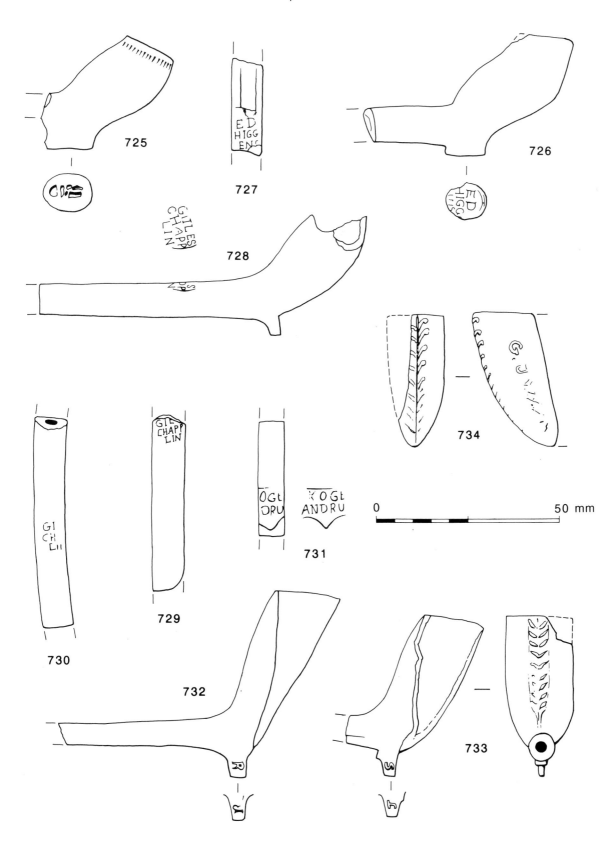

Figure 7.42   Clay pipes.

Table 7.59   Stem-bore diameters.

Context	Wide	Medium	Narrow	Date	Bowl dates
749 (3)	18	0	0	-1680	1670–1700
258 (1)	0	7	8	1720+	*c.* 1725–50
611	2	3	6	1725+	18th–19th
227 (3)	0	0	14	1720+	*c.* 1830–65

Conclusions

Identification of the slags has shown no evidence for metalworking in the areas excavated. The presence of ironworking debris at Birdlip Quarry, Cherry Tree Lane Compound, Preston Enclosure, Westfield Farm, Street Farm and Court Farm should be noted for future excavations in adjacent areas. It should be noted that all the evidence points to the slags deriving from smithing, but with such small samples it is not possible to be completely certain that some of the slags may be smelting slags. In particular the large piece from Birdlip Quarry could be a smelting slag, but if there was further evidence for smelting 10–100s kg of slag would be expected.

CLAY PIPES
By W R G Moore

Street Farm

An assemblage of 149 fragments of clay tobacco-pipes was recovered. This report provides an illustrated study of the makers' marks and the bowl forms (Fig. 7.42). The bowls have been classified and dated by reference to the Gloucester typology (Peacey 1979, 45-9) and that published for southern England (Oswald 1975, 54–5).

The assemblage forms a small group of marked pipes that can be compared with other similar finds from the Wiltshire/Gloucestershire border, such as those from the nearby village of Brinkworth (Oak-Rhind 1980).

Makers' marks

725   Gauntlet incuse on the base of a bowl similar in form to Gloucester type 2b (1630–60). The well-known gauntlet mark is thought to have been used by the Gauntlet family working in Amesbury during the 17th century. However, it was widely copied both in the south-west and elsewhere (Atkinson 1970, 212–13). In Wiltshire and Somerset the incuse gauntlet mark has been dated to the period *c.* 1640–60 (Oswald 1975, 63). Ctx 812.

726–7   ED/HIGG/ENS One unstratified example occurs as an incuse mark on the base of a bowl similar to Gloucester type 7 (1690–1710). A second example

from context 232 occurs as an incuse mark on a thick stem. Edward Higgens was working at Salisbury 1698–1710 and perhaps also worked at Cirencester (Atkinson 1980, 69). Many examples of his pipes have been found both in Wiltshire and Gloucestershire (Peacey 1979, 63; Atkinson 1980, 69). In the latter county, pipes by this maker are much more numerous than those of any other maker (Peacey, ibid).

728–730   GILES/CHAPP/LIN Three examples occur as incuse marks on thick stems. The first and clearest example, from context 749, retains the lower part of a bowl with a small, well-defined spur, comparable with Southern England type 11 (*c.*1690–1700). The other examples are from contexts 285 and 773. Giles Chaplin (ob. 1714) was a potter and pipemaker living at nearby Ashton Keynes (Atkinson 1980, 73; Oak-Rhind 1980, 356). Examples of his pipes are known from Wiltshire and Gloucestershire (Peacey 1979, 63; Atkinson 1980, 73; Oak-Rhind 1980).

731   ROGE/ANDRU Occurs as an incuse mark across a stem from context 258. Roger Andrews was apprenticed at Marlborough in 1718. His pipes can therefore be dated *c.* 1725–50 (Oak-Rhind 1980, 354). Further examples of his marked stems have been noted from Brinkworth, Brimscombe and Marlborough (Peacey 1979, 63; Oak-Rhind 1980, 354).

732   I/R Small serif initials in relief on the sides of a slightly pointed spur. The letter 'I' appears to have been recut over a letter 'R'. From context 227. The incomplete bowl is large, plain and upright in form and can be dated *c.* 1830–60. Possibly associated with the Ring family of Bristol (Price and Jackson 1984).

733   J/S Small serif initials in relief on the sides of a pointed spur. From context 269. The bowl is decorated along the back seam (and probably the front one as well though it is largely missing) with simple oak-leaf decoration. The bowl shape resembles Gloucester type 16 (1830–70). Such J/S marks have been found in quantity all over Wiltshire (Atkinson 1970, 215). The most likely maker is John Skeanes who was working in Salisbury 1858–75 (Oswald 1975, 198).

734   G.J(AME?)... Serif letters in relief with only the first letter clear, reading down the side of an incomplete bowl from context 119. The bowl was decorated along the front seam with a simple leaf design and dates from *c.* 1820–60. Makers' marks of this sort are rare particularly in the 19th century (Oswald 1975, 70). No parallel has been found for this particular mark, though the maker was possibly George James, working in Bristol 1817–48 (Oswald 1975,154).

Unmarked bowls

735–6 Two bowls, one of them complete, from context 749 are similar to Gloucester type 4 (1670–1700).

737   A bowl with most of the upper part missing, from context 358, has a small well defined forward spur, similar to cat. 729. The bowl shape is southern England type II (*c.* 1690–1714).

Decorated bowls

Four 19th-century decorated bowls without maker's marks were recovered. Two of these, a fluted bowl from context 227 and a bowl showing footballers from context 936, are post-1850.

738 A 19th-century bowl, from context 227, has a distinctive feature that suggests it was made in Bristol - a large splayed foot with a tail joined to the stem. The bowl itself has simple oak-leaf decoration along both front and back seams. Similar examples have been found in Bristol in deposits dated 1850–65 (Price and Jackson 1984, 284, fig. 6, 13 and 14).

There is a fragment from another similar pipe with a tailed foot from context 267.

Plain stem fragments *(Table 7.59)*

Williams (1997) has pointed out that the small numbers of stem fragments available are not sufficient for stem bore dating by statistical methods to be carried out. Nevertheless, the four largest groups of stem fragments, each with 11–18 stems, were examined to gain some general impression of date. The results, it must be admitted, are not very informative and add little to the dating gained from the bowls. The bore diameters referred to are wide (7/64″ or greater), medium (6/64″) or narrow (5/64″ or less). The general tendency is for stem bores to decrease: widen in the mid 17th century, then become medium, and by the mid 18th century, narrow (Walker 1967; Oswald 1975, 92–5).

Two marked clay pipe fragments from Cirencester

Context 1 produced 10 stem fragments among which were two pieces bearing maker's marks.

739 ...ODEN/ELY The incomplete mark is incuse, with serif letters impressed along a thin stem. Maker's mark type (4) of Noah Roden (II), Working 1824–55 at Broseley, Shropshire (Atkinson 1975, 77).

740 W SO.../BRO... The incomplete and worn mark shows small serif letters in relief along a thin stem. William Southern was in business at Broseley using such marks from 1829 to 1850 (Atkinson 1975, 83).

It is interesting to note that very few Broseley pipes dating from the period *c.*1720–1850 have been recorded in Gloucestershire (Peacey 1979, 68).

Chapter 8: Environmental Evidence

ANIMAL BONE

Middle Duntisbourne and Duntisbourne Grove
By Adrienne Powell

Introduction

Almost all of the excavated animal bone from Duntisbourne Grove and Middle Duntisbourne) came from the enclosure ditches (98% and 99% respectively). This simplifies comparisons between the two sites as the complicating factors of intra-site variation in disposal and survival can be discounted. For the same reason, however, comparisons with other sites are rendered difficult: at sites where a variety of features have produced animal bone, comparison of the feature types can show the impact of these factors on species representation, whereas it is impossible to judge the extent of their biasing effect in the Duntisbourne assemblages. Most aspects of the two assemblages are discussed separately by site. Others, however, such as the size of the livestock, are considered together to facilitate comparison with other sites in the area.

Methodology

Bone has been identified to species where possible, and sheep and goat bones have been distinguished using the criteria of Boessneck (1969) and Payne (1985). The sheep- and cattle-sized categories include vertebrae, which could not be identified to species, and ribs. Bone in these categories has not been included in the percentage of identifiable bone, although this figure does include fragments which were only identifiable as bird.

The assemblage was recorded using the zonal system described by Serjeantson (1996). This produced a basic fragment count, or number of identifiable specimens (NISP). Since differential fragmentation and survival may affect the relative proportions of species and anatomical elements present in an assemblage, the minimum number of elements (MNE) was used in addition to the NISP. This was based on the sum of the most frequent zone for each element and was calculated for the three main domestic animals only. Minimum numbers of individuals (MNI) were derived from the most common element in the MNE counts for these species, taking size into account.

The incidence of burning and butchery was quantified, with the latter categorised as either chop marks or knife cuts. The incidence of carnivore and rodent gnawing was also recorded. Root etching was ubiquitous in both assemblages. Since this will have affected the observed incidence of butchery and gnawing as well as indicating the degree of post-depositional alteration, the amount of root etching was assessed for each context as a whole as: light, where etch lines are present on few or none of

the bones; moderate, a greater incidence and more of a fragment's surface area affected; or heavy, where the majority of fragments and most or all of the surface area are affected.

Ageing was based on tooth wear and epiphyseal fusion, although the latter is generally less reliable. Timing of epiphyseal closure is based on Sisson and Grossman (Getty 1975). Tooth wear was recorded after Grant (1982), and attribution to wear stages and respective ages was based on Payne (1973) for sheep and goats, Halstead (1985) for cattle and O'Connor (1988) for pigs. Age was also estimated for horse from measurements of the crown heights of cheek teeth, following Levine (1982).

The material was sexed where possible: horses, cattle; sheep and goats using pelves (Getty 1975, Grigson 1982), and pigs using the morphology of the upper and lower canine teeth (Schmid 1972).

Measurements taken are based on von den Driesch (1976) and Payne and Bull (1988). Data accumulated and validated in the Animal Bone Metrical Archive Project (Centre for Human Ecology 1995) for contemporary sites in southern England were used for comparison.

Duntisbourne Grove

The species composition is summarised in Table 8.1 for both hand-retrieved and sieved bone. There is a total of 4518 fragments in the hand-retrieved assemblage, of which only 571 (13%) are identifiable to species. Only mammal bones are represented and these consist primarily of cattle, sheep/goat and pig (95%), with a small amount of horse and a few wild mammal bones. Sheep bones are present, but no goat bone has been identified; therefore all sheep/goat remains are subsequently referred to as sheep. The sieved bone does not add to the species list.

Table 8.1 Summary fragments count, Duntisbourne Grove.

Taxon	Hand	Sieved	Total No.	%
Horse	26		26	4
Cattle	339	5	344	59
Sheep/goat	71	2	73	13
Sheep	8		8	1
Pig	124	1	125	22
Roe deer	2		2	0.3
Fox	1		1	0.2
Cattle-sized	54	5	59	
Sheep-sized	10	2	12	
Unidentified	3883	132	4015	
Total	4518	147	4665	
% Identified	13		12	

Most of the bone (84% of hand-retrieved fragments) came from the southern linear ditch, 9; and half of the remainder came from ditch 8.

Table 8.2 summarises some taphonomic characteristics of the assemblage; unidentified bone is excluded. The severity of root etching is immediately apparent. This, and the high proportion of isolated teeth, indicate substantial post-depositional alteration of the bone. As a consequence of the high degree of root etching there is little evidence of either gnawing or butchery and the types of butchery marks present also show the effect of etching. Chop marks are more frequent than knife cuts, in contrast to the usual pattern at Iron Age or rural Romano-British sites such as Birdlip Bypass and Birdlip Quarry (Dobney and Jaques 1990; Ayres and Clark nd.), but the fine, shallow nature of knife marks makes them more vulnerable to obliteration by root erosion. No rodent gnawing was observed but, as with knife marks, this would be more easily obscured or destroyed by root etching than would canid gnawing. Burnt bone is also infrequent.

The fragmentation in the identifiable material is a further indication of the poor preservation: less than one third of the fragments were more than 50% complete (five or more zones present). Although this is a greater proportion than at Middle Duntisbourne (less than one quarter) where the bone is in better condition (see below), in view of the degree of root etching and frequency of loose teeth at Duntisbourne Grove this is likely to be due to reduced identifiability of small fragments.

Relative abundance of the main domestic mammals

The relative abundance of the three main domestic animals is compared in Figure 8.1 using the different methods of quantification (NISP, MNE, MNI). Whichever method is used, cattle remains are the most frequent, with pig the next most frequent and sheep bones a relatively minor component. This pattern is an unusual one for contemporary sites in the Cotswolds and it is probable that differential preservation has, to some extent, biased the assemblage.

Analyses of Iron Age assemblages have often shown (Maltby 1981; Maltby 1985; Wilson 1996) that

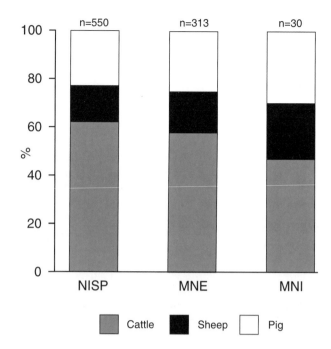

Figure 8.1   Representation of the main domestic species at Duntisbourne Grove.

cattle remains are more common, compared with sheep and pig, in ditches, particularly external ones, than in other features and in some cases this can be clearly linked to the adverse preservational environment of an open ditch biasing the assemblage in favour of the more robust bones of cattle. For example, at Rooksdown (Powell and Clark 1996) the proportion of loose teeth in the ditches (19–27%) was comparable with Duntisbourne Grove, and far higher than in pits; likewise, the relative frequency of cattle bones was greater in the ditches.

Hence the source contexts of the assemblage and the high representation of loose teeth at Duntisbourne Grove suggest potential survival bias in favour of cattle. The representation of body parts in the three main species corroborates this.

The minor contribution of sheep is unusual for this period and this region, where sheep husbandry is an important part of the economy at most sites of middle

Table 8.2   Taphonomy of the animal bone assemblage from Duntisbourne Grove.

Type	Degree			Total	
				No.	%
Root etching (by context)	Light	Moderate	Heavy		
	11	25	64	44	
Burned	Charred	Calcined			
	33	67		6	1
Gnawed	Surface	Heavy			
	92	8		36	6
Loose teeth	-	-	-	144	25
Butchered	Chopped	Cut	Sawn		
	63	13	25	16	2

Iron Age date (Cunliffe 1991). That this is not simply poor survival of the smaller domesticates is suggested by the contrasting high representation of pig which distinguishes this site from others in the region. Differential disposal of pigs and sheep might have had some role in this pattern: for example, at Birdlip Quarry (Ayres and Clark nd.) pig bones comprised a greater proportion of the domestic mammal material from ditch contexts (19% in Period 1 and 31% in Period 2) than in the assemblage as a whole (8% in both periods). However, at Duntisbourne Grove the suite of terrestrial molluscan species present indicates a locally wooded environment (see Robinson, chapter 8) which would indeed have been more supportive of non-intensive pig husbandry than sheep herding.

Body part representation and butchery

The distribution of cattle, sheep and pig skeletal elements in the assemblage is shown in Table 8.3. The various skeletal elements of cattle and sheep have a similar pattern of occurrence: predominantly limb bones, followed by girdle bones then other elements. The main differences between these two species are the smaller numbers of sheep carpals, tarsals and phalanges, and the greater number of cattle mandibles. The former is a common observation and is a retrieval bias, while the latter may reflect differential disposal or preservation. Pig skeletal elements are more evenly represented.

This pattern is also demonstrated in Figure 8.2, which shows (for each species) the actual number of body parts present as a percentage of the figure expected if whole carcasses were deposited, derived from the MNI. Only elements occurring in all three species are included: hence horn cores, fibulae, lateral phalanges and metapodials, and carpals and tarsals (with the exception of the astragalus and calcaneus) are excluded. In addition, the elements have been grouped into anatomical regions: *head* comprises skull and mandibles; *axial* is atlas, axis, scapula and pelvis; *limb* is the major limb bones; and *extremities* includes astragalus, calcaneus, metapodials (the MNE is halved for pig) and medial phalanges. Table 8.3 suggests that all parts of an animal's carcass eventually found their way into the ditches, and, with the possible exception of cattle mandibles, it seems that in general there was no appreciable systematic bias between species in the disposal of any skeletal parts. Hence the results in Figure 8.2 are due to differential survival and retrieval.

The figure shows that cattle body parts, particularly mandibles and with the exception of axial elements, have survived better than those of sheep and pig, whereas sheep are poorly represented by all except limb bones. The even representation of pig skeletal elements, observed in Table 8.3, is apparent here in the consistent degree of survival of head, axial and limb elements. The better representation of head parts in comparison with sheep and cattle is due to their more solid and robust structure.

Table 8.3 *Minimum number of elements of the main domestic mammals at Duntisbourne Grove.*

Element	Cattle	Sheep	Pig	Total
		Species		
Horn core	7	-	-	7
Cranium	3	1	4	8
Mandible	17	3	5	25
Atlas	2	1	-	3
Axis	1	-	-	1
Scapula	9	4	8	21
Humerus	19	7	7	33
Radius	9	6	8	23
Ulna	5	1	2	8
Pelvis	10	4	14	28
Femur	7	1	3	11
Tibia	28	9	12	49
Astragalus	11	1	1	13
Calcaneus	14	1	2	17
Tarsals	5			5
Carpals	3			3
Metacarpal	12	3	4	19
Metatarsal	4	6	2	12
Lateral metapodial	-	-	4	4
Phalanx I	11	1	1	13
Phalanx II	6	1	1	8
Phalanx III	2			2
Total	185	50	78	313
% main domestics	59	16	25	
MNI	15	6	9	30
% MNI	50	20	30	

There are several sets of articulating bone in the assemblage although erosion of the bone surface often made it difficult to be certain that two bones did articulate. Those groups present are all cattle: a left distal humerus with proximal radius and ulna; a left and a right radius/ulna pair; one left metacarpal with articulating first phalanges; two left metatarsals with articulating first phalanges; a right distal tibia with astragalus and calcaneus; and a left metatarsal with navicular-cuboid, lateral cuneiform, one first and one second phalanx. The phalanges of this last group are fused while the metatarsal is distally unfused; this indicates that the animal was between two and a half and three years old. This group is also the only one which shows any evidence of butchery: the first phalanx exhibited a chop mark at the proximal end which may be the result of skinning. All of these articulating groups came from ditch group 9.

The distribution by species of the sparse butchery evidence is given in Table 8.4: most of the observed butchery marks occur on cattle bones, unsurprisingly since they are the most frequently occurring in the assemblage but this also represents the highest frequency within a species, 4% in contrast to the 1% of both sheep and pig material. The sawn elements are all horn cores with saw marks at the base where the horn sheath was removed. The remainder of the butchery marks on cattle bones indicate division of

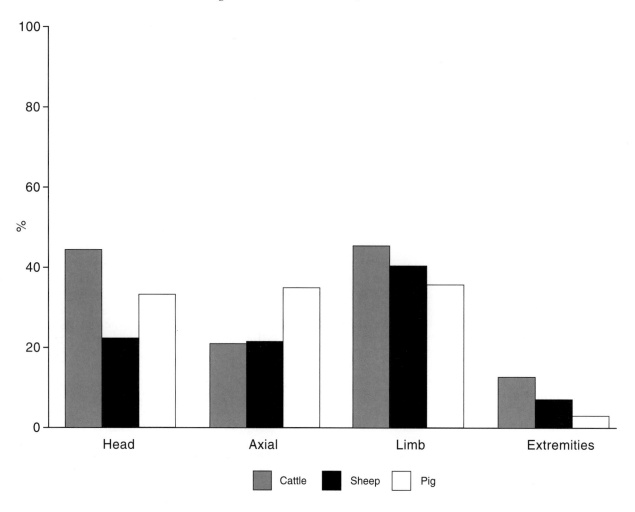

Figure 8.2   Body part representation at Duntisbourne Grove.

the carcass, primarily at the major limb bone joints. However, there are also two pelves where the ilium bears chop marks on the ventral or medial surfaces; these suggest subdivision of the trunk into smaller units once the limbs had been removed.

The single sheep bone bearing evidence of butchery is a radius with a mid-shaft knife cut, probably from filleting. The single butchered pig bone is a humerus with a chop mark, probably from disarticulation, on the distal shaft.

Table 8.4   Distribution of butchery marks by species at Duntisbourne Grove.

Species	Chopped	Cut	Sawn	Total No.	%
Cattle	8	1	4	13	4
Sheep		1		1	1
Pig	1			1	1
Cattle-sized	1			1	2
Total	10	2	4	16	2

Age and sex of the main domestic mammals

The principal caveat in the interpretation of epiphyseal fusion data is that the unfused, porous bones of immature animals are more vulnerable to taphonomic destruction than those of adults and hence the age profile derived from this information may be biased in favour of mature animals. This can be particularly misleading in the case of pigs where most individuals will be slaughtered while immature. This biasing factor is particularly relevant to consideration of this assemblage in view of the evidence for post-depositional alteration.

The fusion data for cattle (Table 8.5) suggest that no animals were slaughtered until they reached two years of age; approximately one third of the bones came from animals which died in their third year and the remainder from animals which survived into full adulthood. This pattern is partially borne out by the dental data (Table 8.6), particularly if the 18-30 month old specimens died at the older end of that age range. Although one third of the specimens came from fully mature adults, including elderly animals, the toothwear data do show a higher proportion of young adults (at least three years old) dying than does the

Table 8.5   Cattle epiphyseal fusion, Duntisbourne Grove.

Age at Fusion	Element	Fused	Unfused	Total
7–10 months	Scapula	8		8
7–10 months	Pelvis	12		12
12–15 months	Radius, p	8		8
15–18 months	Phalanx II	6		6
15–20 months	Humerus, d	20		20
20–24 months	Phalanx I	10		10
24–30 months	Tibia, d	13	7	20
24–30 months	Metapodial, d	5	2	7
36 months	Clacaneus	7	3	10
36–42 months	Femur, p	3	1	4
42–48 months	Radius, d	1		1
42–48 months	Femur, d	1	2	3
42–48 months	Tibia, p	3		3
Total		97	15	112

Table 8.7   Sheep epiphyseal fusion, Duntisbourne Grove.

Age at fusion	Element	Fused	Unfused	Total
3–4 months	Humerus, d	5		5
3–4 months	Radius, p	4		4
5 months	Scapula	2		2
5 months	Pelvis	3		3
5–7 months	Phalanx II		1	1
15–20 months	Tibia, d	1		1
20–24 months	Metapodial, d	1		1
36 months	Calcaneus	1		1
36–42 months	Femur, p		1	1
42 months	Radius, d		1	1
Total		17	3	20

bone fusion information. The absence of younger juveniles could be a consequence of poor survival, as mentioned above; however, the lack of even loose deciduous teeth implies the absence is likely to be genuine, since the durability of teeth means they are often the last elements to be lost in a poorly preserved assemblage.

The age profile suggests that dairying was not a major part of the site economy: two thirds of the animals died in an age range suitable for optimising carcass weight against continued feed costs. The remaining animals were probably draught beasts and/or breeding cows, although the two are not mutually exclusive. All four of the sexable cattle pelves are female.

As a consequence of the small size of the sheep assemblage, there is little ageing information for this species. Although most of the bones are fused (Table 8.7) there is no evidence for fully adult animals, whereas the few juvenile bones present include one from an individual which died in its first year. The absence of skeletally mature animals is borne out by the dental evidence (Table 8.6): the oldest mandible is from an animal between three and four years old, while the remaining six are spread between one and three years of age.

Thus, as with most of the aged cattle material, the sheep ageing data show only animals culled at

optimum meat yielding ages. There is no evidence to suggest that milk or wool were major products of the sheep husbandry: although the absence of lambs younger than one year could be a preservation bias, this would not have affected the contribution of old animals. Two of the three sexable pelves are male.

The fusion evidence for pigs (Table 8.8) suggests that while no animals died in their first year of life, over half died in their second year, but in the absence of ageable late-fusing elements, the proportion which survived beyond full skeletal maturity is unknown. Most of the ageable mandibles are sub-adult. According to Habermehl's (1975) timings for late-maturing pigs, these jaws would have come from animals in their second year and so the predominance of mandibles at this wear stage agrees with the epiphyseal fusion evidence.

Hence the age profile of the Duntisbourne Grove pigs points to non-intensive pig husbandry. There are seven male canines and two female.

Other mammals

Horse is the best represented of the remaining species and most of this material comes from ditch 8. This feature is therefore responsible for the predominance of pelvic fragments and loose teeth in the horse assemblage but also produced three skull fragments and an atlas. Other contexts produced a scapula, radius and more loose teeth. The MNI, derived from the pelvis, is three.

Table 8.6   Cattle, sheep and pig toothwear, Duntisbourne Grove.

Cattle	0–1 months	1–8 months	8–18 months	18–30 months	30–36 months	Young adult	Adult	Old adult	Senile	Total
				2	4	6	4	1	1	18

Sheep	0–2 months	2–6 months	6–12 months	1–2 years	2–3 years	3–4 years	4–6 years	6–8 years	8–10 years	Total
				3	3	1				7

Pig	Neo-natal	Juvenile	Immature	Sub-adult	Adult	Elderly				Total
				4	1					5

Table 8.8   Pig epiphyseal fusion, Duntisbourne Grove.

Age at fusion	Element	Fused	Unfused	Total
12 months	Scapula	5		5
12 months	Humerus, d	7		7
12 months	Radius, p	8		8
12 months	Pelvis	15		15
12 months	Phalanx II	1		1
24 months	Tibia, d	2	2	4
24 months	Metapodial, d	1	1	2
24 months	Phalanx I		1	1
24–30 months	Calcaneus	1	1	2
Total		40	5	45

Where the state of fusion can be determined, none of the bones are unfused and the fused distal radius indicates the presence of an animal older than three and a half years. Further ageing data for the horse assemblage is given by the loose cheek teeth in Table 8.9. All have produced estimates of similar age range: adult but not old animals which, unless broken down through overwork or poor condition, would still have been of working age. Three of the pelvic fragments retain the pubis, allowing the sex to be determined: all are male. None of the horse material shows butchery marks.

Table 8.9   Horse cheek teeth crown heights, Duntisbourne Grove.

Context	Element	Side	Estimated age range	Comment
25	P_2	Right	8–9 years	
28	P_3 / P_4	Left	7–8.75 years	
28	M_1 / M_2	Left	6.5 –9 years	
162	P^2	Right	9–10 years	*
162	P^3	Right	8–9 years	*
162	$P^3 – M^2$	Left	7–9.75 years	
228	M^3	Left	7–8 years	

* same tooth row

Wild mammals are represented by fox (*Vulpes vulpes*) and roe deer (*Capreolus capreolus*). Fox is unspecialised and versatile in its habitat requirements (Harris and Lloyd 1991) and so the single bone occurring in this assemblage may either be from a scavenger around the site or an animal hunted further afield for its fur. In contrast, roe deer prefer the availability of some woodland as cover (Staines and Ratcliffe 1991). Hence the elements present (scapula and radius, from different ditches) suggest the proximity to the site of a stand of woodland since whole carcasses were brought back to the site, whereas if the animals had been hunted further away the carcasses might have been butchered at the kill site and only the meat and skin with attached extremities brought back.

Middle Duntisbourne

This assemblage is slightly larger than that from Duntisbourne Grove, comprising 5035 fragments in the hand retrieved assemblage (Table 8.10). Most of the bone in the this assemblage (90% of the hand retrieved material) came from the southern ditch of the enclosure (context 4). The amount of identifiable bone, although low at 856 fragments (17%), is greater than at Duntisbourne Grove. The three main domestic mammals comprise an even greater proportion of the assemblage at Middle Duntisbourne (99% of the identifiable bone) and birds, absent at Duntisbourne Grove, occur in small numbers here.

The degree of root etching on bone from Middle Duntisbourne (Table 8.11) is much less severe than at Duntisbourne Grove. The lower frequency of isolated teeth is probably a reflection of this, although it might be due to differential disposal of heads (that is, more were originally deposited in the Duntisbourne Grove ditches). The rate of survival of heads is similar between the two sites (38% at Middle Duntisbourne and 37% at Duntisbourne Grove, for cattle, sheep and pig together) and the relative frequencies of skulls and mandibles in the two assemblages are also the same. Since the minimum number of skulls is based on diagnostic zones (eg. zygomatic or occipital condyle), a set of badly preserved, highly fragmented skulls can yield the same result as a group of intact skulls. However, because of the fragmentation, an assemblage containing the former would have a higher proportion of isolated maxillary teeth than an assemblage containing the latter; the less an assemblage has been affected by fragmentation, the greater the bias should be towards loose mandibular teeth, since cattle and sheep incisors, which are only present in the mandibles, readily fall out of their alveoli. Hence, at Duntisbourne Grove maxillary teeth comprise 63% of the total number of loose teeth, whereas at Middle Duntisbourne they are only 48% of the total.

Although fewer contexts at Middle Duntisbourne contain bone which has been heavily affected by root etching, less than one third of the contexts contain

Table 8.10 Summary fragments count, Middle Duntisbourne.

Species	Hand	Sieved	Total	
			No.	%
Horse		1	1	0.1
Cattle	267	11	278	31.0
Sheep/goat	203	5	208	24.0
Sheep	51		51	6.0
Pig	324	12	336	38.0
Hare	3		3	0.3
Bird	8		8	1.0
Cattle-sized	135	12	147	
Sheep-sized	122	9	131	
Unidentified	3922	194	4116	
Total	5035	244	5279	
% Identified	17		17	

Table 8.11   Taphonomy, Middle Duntisbourne.

Type	Degree			Total	
				No.	%
Root etching (by context)	Light 27	Moderate 36	Heavy 38	45	
Burned	Charred 65	Calcined 35	20	2	
Gnawed	Surface 82	Heavy 18	78	7	
Loose teeth	-	-	-	81	9
Butchered	Chopped 69	Cut 24	Both 7	29	2

bone which has only been marginally affected. Consequently, the observed incidence of gnawing and butchery marks is similar to that at Duntisbourne Grove, although slightly more of the butchery marks at Middle Duntisbourne are knife cuts.

Relative abundance of the main domestic mammals

The contributions of cattle, sheep and pig to the assemblage are shown in Figure 8.3, comparing NISP, MNE and MNI. The results are similar whichever method of quantification is used. Cattle remains, around one third of the three main species in this assemblage, are far less frequent than at Duntisbourne Grove (50-63%). This difference is consistent, in view of the argued survival bias in favour of cattle bones, with the lower degree of post-depositional alteration at Middle Duntisbourne.

Sheep are far better represented than at Duntisbourne Grove, and is the most frequently occurring

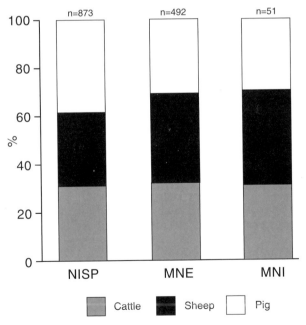

Figure 8.3   Representation of the main domestic species at Middle Duntisbourne.

species in the MNE and MNI figures. This is a more typical pattern for contemporary Cotswold sites, although the occurrence is still relatively low, and the contribution of pig in comparison to sheep is consequently less at Middle Duntisbourne. However, pig is more frequent overall than at Duntisbourne Grove, although this is not as marked as in sheep and is only apparent in the NISP and MNE figures. As at Duntisbourne Grove, the high proportion of pig in the assemblage is consistent with molluscan evidence suggesting the local environment included woodland.

Body part representation and butchery

The presence of the various skeletal elements is shown in Table 8.12 and Figure 8.4, the latter following the same method as in Figure 8.2. The very high representation of pig heads, in comparison with both other pig body parts and the heads of the other two species, is plain and reflects the frequency of both crania and mandibles. A similar, although not so marked, contrast with cattle and sheep skulls was observed in the Duntisbourne Grove assemblage. The sturdy construction which is responsible for this

Table 8.12   Minimum number of elements of the main domestic mammals, Middle Duntisbourne.

Element	Species			Total
	Cattle	Sheep	Pig	
Horn core	-	-	-	0
Cranium	2	3	12	17
Mandible	7	10	24	41
Atlas	1	1	-	2
Axis	-	1	-	1
Scapula	12	23	29	64
Humerus	13	14	7	34
Radius	9	22	2	33
Ulna	3	10	5	18
Pelvis	25	26	17	68
Sacrum	1	0	0	1
Femur	11	10	11	32
Tibia	20	35	11	66
Fibula	-	-	-	0
Patella	1	-	1	2
Astragalus	12	4	2	18
Calcaneus	24	5	5	34
Tarsals	3	1	1	5
Carpals	1	-	1	2
Metacarpal	5	2	2	9
Metatarsal	6	8	5	19
Lateral metapodial	-	-	-	0
1st Phalanx	3	5	2	10
2nd Phalanx	1	-	1	2
3rd Phalanx	1	-	1	2
Lateral phalanx	-	-	-	0
Total	161	180	139	480
% main domestics	34	38	29	
MNI	16	20	15	51
% MNI	31	39	29	

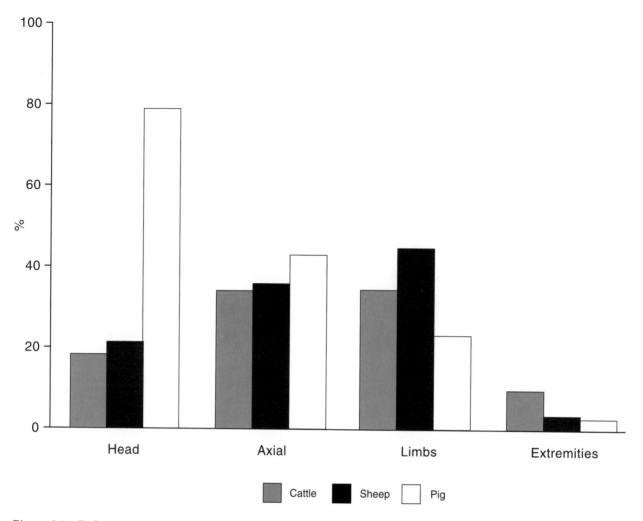

Figure 8.4   Body part representation at Middle Duntisbourne.

pattern is also the major cause of the discrepancy between the NISP and MNE relative proportions of pig versus sheep (Figure 8.3); there are far more identifiable fragments surviving from pig skulls and contributing to the minimum value than there are for sheep: seven and two, respectively, per 'skull'.

Figure 8.4 also shows that, in contrast to Duntisbourne Grove, sheep remains have survived better than those of cattle in all groups except extremities, although the difference is notable only in the limb group. This is probably a reflection of the better preservation of the bone from Middle Duntisbourne, as is the higher representation of axial elements for all three species. It is, however, possible that the relatively low occurrence of pig limb bones, in comparison with cattle and sheep and the frequency of pig heads and axial bones, is due to a disposal bias.

There are only two sets of articulating bones in this assemblage: a cattle right proximal radius and ulna, and a sheep left proximal radius and ulna. Neither pair showed any evidence of butchery.

There is little difference between the species in incidence of butchery marks (Table 8.13), but they are slightly more common on the cattle material. The majority of these may be interpreted as division of the carcass: primarily removal and jointing of the limbs (at the elbow or hip, for example), but also removal of the mandible from the cranium (chop mark at the hinge), separation of the body into sides (chop marks through the proximal end of a rib and the transverse processes of thoracic and lumbar vertebrae) and smaller units (a lumbar vertebra chopped transversely through the caudal end). Filleting is manifested in a single scapula with cuts concentrated around the origin of the spine.

The evidence for sheep butchery, like cattle butchery, consists entirely of disarticulation marks: separation of the forelimb from the trunk by cutting between the ribs and scapula; the hindlimb from the trunk at the hip; jointing of the limbs at the elbow and hock; and, as with cattle, division of the trunk into sides and smaller units. The evidence on pig bones is more limited than for either cattle or sheep, but shows disarticulation of the mandible and limbs. In contrast to the pattern on sheep, a scapula with a chop mark on the rim of the glenoid suggests that pig forelimbs were separated from the trunk at that point, rather than as a unit with the scapula.

Table 8.13   Distribution of butchery marks by species, Middle Duntisbourne.

Species	Chopped	Cut	Both	Total No.	Total %
Cattle	6	3		9	3
Sheep	2	3	1	6	2
Pig	4	1		5	1
Cattle-sized	3	0	1	4	3
Sheep-sized	5			5	4
Total	20	7	2	29	2

Ageing and sexing of the main domestic mammals

It was suggested for the Duntisbourne Grove assemblage that the scarcity of juvenile material might be related to the poor preservation, similarly, the greater proportion of juvenile and immature remains at Middle Duntisbourne may be a consequence of the comparatively better preservation.

The cattle epiphyseal fusion data (Table 8.14) show a moderate proportion of first year mortalities, with unfused pelvic fragments comprising 17% of ageable elements. Three of these are probably from the same animal, a neonate. There is no evidence in the bones for further mortality in the second year, but there is a great increase in the third year: 50% of bones from individuals between two and three years of age are unfused. Thereafter, animals apparently survived through to skeletal maturity. These fully adult animals are, however, under-represented in the toothwear data (Table 8.15), as are the neonates. Otherwise, the two sets of data broadly agree. The much smaller sample of ageable mandibles and teeth in this assemblage may explain the absence of the age groups which are rare at Duntisbourne Grove (old adult and senile), however, the most frequent age group in that assemblage (young adult) is completely absent at Middle Duntisbourne.

Table 8.14   Cattle epiphyseal fusion, Middle Duntisbourne

Age at Fusion	Element	Fused	Unfused	Total
7–10 months	Scapula	10		10
7–10 months	Pelvis	29	8	37
12–15 months	Radius, P	10		10
15–18 months	2nd Phalanx	1		1
15–20 months	Humerus, D	8	1	9
20–24 months	1st Phalanx	3		3
24–30 months	Tibia, D	11	5	16
24–30months	Metapodial, D	3	1	4
36 months	Calcaneus	5	13	18
36–42 months	Femur, P	3	2	5
42–48 months	Radius, D		2	2
42–48 months	Femur, D	2	1	3
42–48 months	Tibia, P	3	1	4
Total		88	34	122

Taking into account the possible effect of the better preservation at Middle Duntisbourne, the age profile suggests an approach to cattle husbandry similar to Duntisbourne Grove. The first year kill-off is not great enough to indicate more than a small-scale role for dairying and, although culled from a narrower age range than at Duntisbourne Grove, prime meat carcasses are predominant. Only one of the 11 sexable pelves is male.

As a consequence of the much greater presence of sheep in this assemblage, there is also much more fusion data (Table 8.16) than at Duntisbourne Grove and comparison of the two samples is affected. A few animals died in their first year (3% of bones in this age range), but the greatest mortality occurred in the second year animals, with another peak in the three to three and a half year range. Only a little less than one third of these late-fusing bones come from animals which survived into full adulthood. As with cattle, the sheep toothwear data do not show these older animals, and they also suggest a much greater mortality of animals in their first year than does the fusion evidence, including a possible neonate. The dental age profile resembles Duntisbourne Grove except for the larger number of first year deaths: since three of these four specimens came from animals which died between 6 and 12 months of age, it is likely they represent individuals too weak to survive their first winter who died or were culled for meat. The sexed elements are predominantly female: 14 pelves and an atlas, compared with only 4 male pelves.

The fusion evidence for the Middle Duntisbourne pigs (Table 8.17) shows the same high second year mortality as Duntisbourne Grove, with a second peak between two and two and a half years and no animals surviving beyond three and a half years. The dental data agree with these major kill-off peaks: although a few animals died towards the end of their first year, 59% of the mandibles came from sub-adults, probably animals between one and two years old and the remaining mandibles (25%) are adult with the lower third molar in early wear, corresponding to the two to two and a half year fusion peak. Most of the sexable canines, 13 out of 17, are male. While more males would be expected in the sub-adult group and more females in the adults, the sample of both aged and sexed mandibles is too small to offer convincing support: one adult and two sub-adult mandibles and one female sub-adult.

Other mammals

Few bones from species other than the three main domesticates are present at Middle Duntisbourne. The single horse bone is the cranial portion of an axis which exhibits no signs of butchery or gnawing. The three hare bones are a fragment of tibia and two left pelves, the latter being comparable in size with brown hare (*Lepus europaeus*) rather than the smaller mountain hare (*L. timidus*). There has been some debate over whether brown hare was present in Britain before the Roman period (Coy 1984; Tapper 1991),

Table 8.15   Cattle, sheep and pig toothwear, Middle Duntisbourne.

Cattle	0–1 months	1–8 months	8–18 months	18–30 months	30–36 months	Young adult	Adult	Old adult	Senile	Total
			1	2	3		2			8

Sheep	0–2 months	2–6 months	6–12 months	1–2 years	2–3 years	3–4 years	4–6 years	6–8 years	8–10 years	Total
	1		3	2	3	1				10

Pig	Neo-natal	Juvenile	Immature	Sub-adult	Adult	Elderly				Total
	-	1	3	12	5	-				21

Table 8.16   Sheep epiphyseal fusion, Middle Duntisbourne.

Age at fusion	Element	Fused	Unfused	Total
3–4 months	Humerus, D	12	0	12
3–4 months	Radius, P	16	0	16
5 months	Scapula	15	0	15
5 months	Pelvis	30	1	31
7–10 months	1st Phalanx	3	1	4
15–20 months	Tibia, D	10	3	13
20–24 months	Metapodial, D	0	4	4
36 months	Calcaneus	3	2	5
36–42 months	Femur, P	1	1	2
42 months	Radius, D	1	3	4
42 months	Ulna, P	1	6	7
42 months	Femur, D	2	1	3
42 months	Tibia, P	1	2	3
Total		95	24	119

although Coy made definite identifications of it in both late phases at Danebury (1984), and it has also been identified at several other Iron Age sites, for example, Owslebury (Maltby 1987) and Groundwell Farm (Coy 1982). The reason for its presence is not straightforward. According to Caesar (Edwards 1952) the Britons had a taboo against eating hare; furthermore, hare would have been a part of the local wild fauna, as it is abundant in arable areas with associated woods or hedgerows for shelter (Tapper 1991), and thus the bones could be non-anthropogenic. None of the hare bones show evidence of butchery or gnawing damage.

Birds

Of the eight bird bones, six (all limb bones save one scapula) belong to the domestic fowl (*Gallus gallus*). Three of these, from the same context, are comparable in size with bantams. Bantam-size bones also occurred in the late period at Danebury, in addition to a larger type of fowl (Serjeantson 1991a). All of the ageable bones are adult and there are two sexable tarsometatarsi: one male (spurred) and one female (unspurred). There is no evidence of butchery, which is consistent with Caesar's claim (Edwards 1952) that the Britons kept fowl but did not eat them. Domestic

fowl bones are present in small numbers at the contemporary Cotswold sites of Bagendon (Jackson 1961; Rielly 1990), Ditches (Rielly 1988) and Birdlip Bypass Period 2 (Dobney and Jaques 1990). The two other bird bones are a distal radius from a duck, probably mallard (*cf. Anas platyrhynchos*) and an ulna from a redwing (*Turdus iliacus*).

Size of livestock at Duntisbourne Grove and Middle Duntisbourne

The full suite of measurements taken on the Duntisbourne Grove and Middle Duntisbourne bones appears in appendices 2–3, with only the more frequent ones discussed here. Few bones are complete enough for greatest length measurements to be possible so only a few withers heights, using the factors in Driesch and Boessneck (1974) could be calculated (Table 8.18).

The four cattle withers heights, although within the range for cattle from contemporary southern British sites, suggest the Duntisbourne cattle were of average or below average size. Figure 8.5 compares distal tibia breadth in the Duntisbourne cattle to other 1st century AD and later Roman assemblages in the Cotswolds. These figures show, in agreement with the withers heights, that the Duntisbourne cattle tend to

Table 8.17   Pig epiphyseal fusion, Middle Duntisbourne.

Age at fusion	Element	Fused	Unfused	Total
12 months	Scapula	25	0	25
12 months	Humerus, D	5	0	5
12 months	Radius, P	1	0	1
12 months	Pelvis	18	0	18
12 months	2nd Phalanx	1	0	1
24 months	Tibia, D	5	3	8
24 months	Metapodial, D	0	6	6
24 months	1st Phalanx	2	1	3
24–30 months	Calcaneus	1	5	6
36–42 months	Ulna, P	0	1	1
36–42months	Femur, P	0	1	1
42 months	Radius D	0	1	1
Total		58	18	76

440

Table 8.18   Withers heights in metres, Middle Duntisbourne and Duntisbourne Grove.

Species	Site	Radius	Metacarpal	Metatarsal	Calcaneus
Cattle	Duntisbourne Grove	1.03	1.13	1.04	
	Middle Duntisbourne			1.13	
	ABMAP: mean, range	1.14, 1.02–1.26	1.10, 0.98–1.19	1.13, 1.03–1.28	
Sheep	Duntisbourne Grove				0.55
	Middle Duntisbourne				0.58, 0.53
	ABMAP: mean range				0.54, 0.50–0.59

be smaller than their local contemporaries. There is also no visible improvement in cattle size until the later assemblages of the 3rd–4th centuries. This size increase is clear in Figure 8.6, which plots tibia distal depth against distal breadth for the Duntisbournes and the 2nd–4th century Birdlip Quarry material. These form two largely separate groups with only a few overlapping values. The narrow range and the lack of smaller animals in the Iron Age assemblage from Birdlip (Figure 8.5) may be a reflection of the small

sample size; comparison of humerus trochlea breadth (Figure 8.7) shows a similar size range present at the Duntisbournes and Iron Age Birdlip, with the Birdlip Quarry assemblage containing larger animals than the Iron Age sites.

The three sheep withers heights fit into the average and above part of the range, derived from calcaneus only, for contemporary southern British sites. The comparison of distal tibia breadth in sheep from the Duntisbournes and other Cotswold assemblages

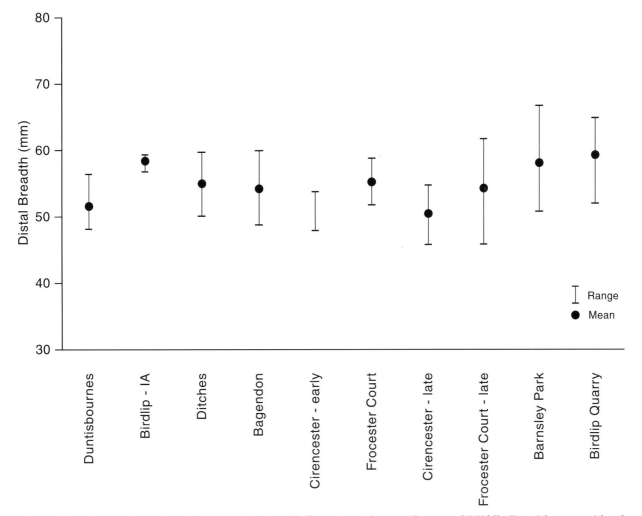

Figure 8.5   Comparison of cattle distal tibia breadth from Duntisbourne Grove and Middle Duntisbourne with other Cotswolds sites.

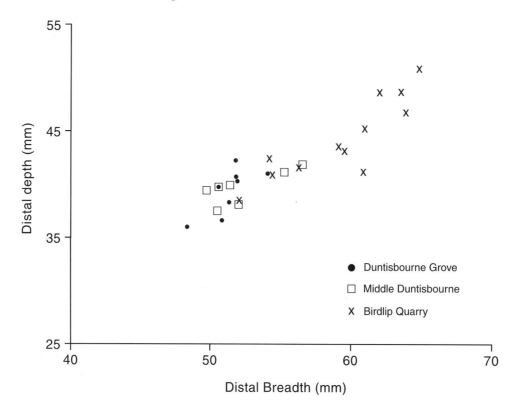

Figure 8.6   Comparison of tibial distal breadth against tibial distal depth in cattle.

(Figure 8.8) shows a similar size range in most of the 1st century assemblages and less variation than in the same measurement for cattle. The Ditches sheep, however, are slightly larger than their contemporaries. Otherwise, as argued by Rielly (1988), there is no apparent increase in the size of sheep until the later

Roman period in the Cotswolds. Figure 8.9 shows that, while most of the Birdlip Quarry measurements are larger than those from the Duntisbournes, all of the distal tibias from Middle Duntisbourne lie within the lower half of the range from Birdlip. If the smaller specimen from Duntisbourne Grove is excluded, the minimum value for the distal breadth (Figure 8.8) is 21.5, comparable with the lower limit at Ditches. Other measurements do not show such a degree of differentiation: the scattergram of distal humerus measurements (Figure 8.10) shows far more congruence between the size ranges at the Duntisbournes and Birdlip Quarry.

No withers heights could be calculated for pigs since the high kill-off of immature animals means there are no complete long bones. The length of the lower third molar (Figure 8.11) suggests there was no change in the size of pigs between the late Iron Age and the late Romano-British period. The range present in the Duntisbourne assemblages is similar to that in the Ditches material, although the latter has a slightly lower mean size as does the later Birdlip Quarry sample. In contrast, the teeth from the Iron Age features at Birdlip Bypass are relatively small, as can also be seen in Figure 8.12. The outlying Iron Age third molar from Birdlip, with a large anterior breadth, is probably from a wild boar (Payne and Bull 1988). Comparison of the Duntisbournes and Birdlip Quarry in Figure 8.13, plotting distal humerus, shows larger animals at the latter in contrast to the third molar data. However, the sample of measurable pig bones is too small at Birdlip Quarry (below) to draw a firm conclusion from this.

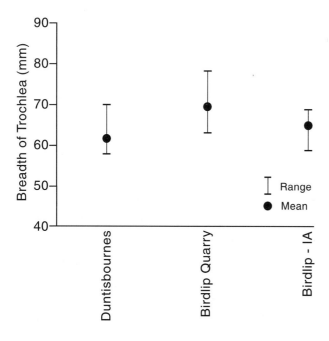

Figure 8.7   Cattle distal humerus. Comparison of humerus trochlea breadth in cattle.

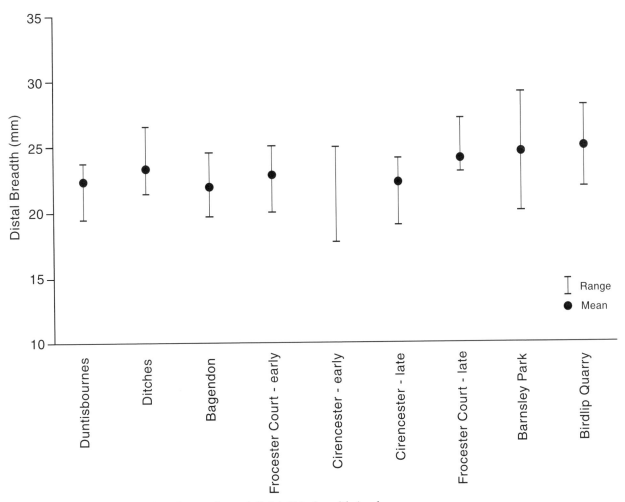

Figure 8.8   Sheep distal tibia. Comparison of distal tibia breadth in sheep.

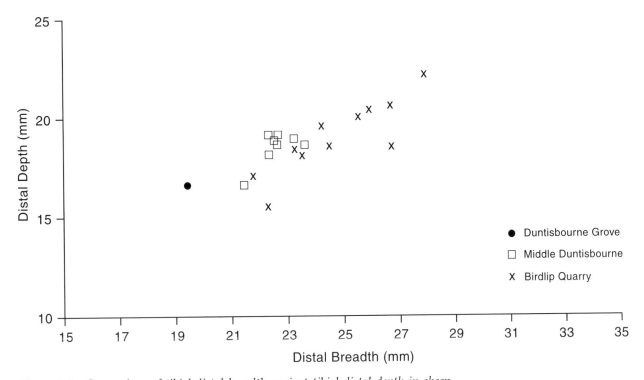

Figure 8.9   Comparison of tibial distal breadth against tibial distal depth in sheep.

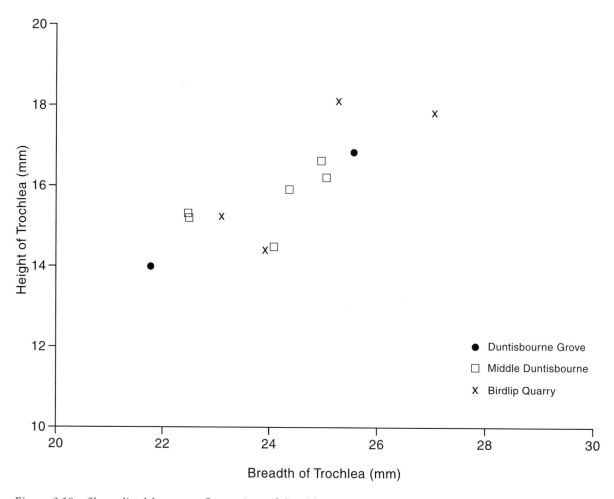

Figure 8.10   Sheep distal humerus. Comparison of distal humerus measurements in sheep.

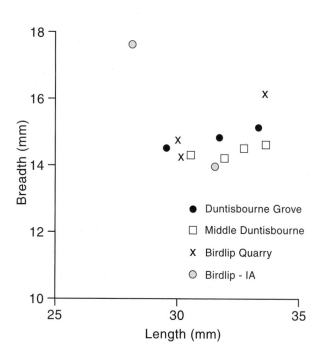

Figure 8.11   Pig third molar length.

Pathology

The incidence of pathology in these two assemblages is surprising low, but in view of the post-deposition modification by root etching and solution it would be expected that much fine pathology would be lost. In particular, surface indications of infection and small areas of proliferative bone indicating early stages of pathological conditions would be unlikely to survive. However, arthropathies in the domestic mammals are robust manifestations which should be visible even with this degree of post-burial damage and the low frequency is concommitant with the age profile for cattle.

There is just one pathological specimen from Duntisbourne Grove, a distal fragment of a cattle tibia (context 15) with small osteophytes at the sites of tendon insertion laterally and medially. This is almost certainly an age-related manifestation with slow, progressive ossification of the tendon extremities during maturity.

At Middle Duntisbourne, the majority of lesions are in cattle. A cattle metatarsal from context 45 shows some articular extension of the medial condyle, but without associated arthropathies, and this is probably a reflection of maturity. An interesting specimen from context 330, another distal tibia, has incomplete sub-

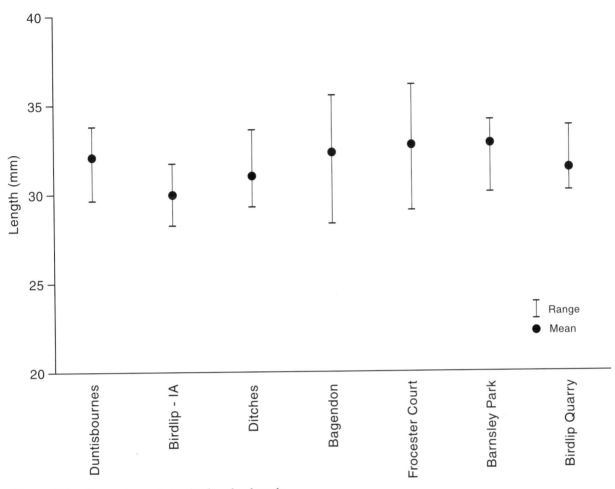

Figure 8.12   Comparison of pig third molar lengths.

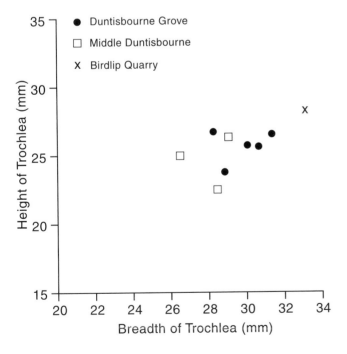

Figure 8.13   Comparison of distal humerus measurements in pig.

chondral bone anteriorly and laterally, and this has resulted in the development of an isolated facet. This is certainly a sub-clinical condition and probably congenital in origin rather than being the result of injury or stress.

There are two instances of infection in the Middle Duntisbourne cattle. A calcaneus has a smooth bony extrusion medially, which is probably the result of a healed or healing infection (context 85), and a mandible (context 45) shows resorption of the bone below the second molar lingually.

A pig mandible (context 57) also has evidence of infection with the loss of the first molar and resorption of the bone around the alveolus. The two other pathological pig specimens both result from trauma; a bony flange on the spine of a scapula from context 218 is probably the result of injury, and a juvenile lateral metapodial has a healing fracture of the distal end (context 69).

A single pathological sheep specimen from context 69, a juvenile mandible, shows possible infection of the mandibular symphysis.

Oral pathology

This category of pathology is often the most common in archaeological material, partly because of the

Plate 8.1   Lateral view of hypoplastic pig third molar.

resistance to destruction of mandibles and teeth, and these two assemblages are no exception. Specimens showing evidence of infection have already been described; the two other, more frequently represented, categories dealt with here are congenital and developmental.

Congenital conditions are present in all three of the main species. In the Duntisbourne Grove assemblage there is a cattle right mandible which retained a third molar with a reduced distal cusp and a left mandible with no second premolar: these two traits are often recorded in archaeological cattle and seem to be particularly common in Iron Age and Romano-British assemblages. Congenitally absent teeth also occur in the Middle Duntisbourne material, but here it is the pigs which are affected: three mandibles lack the first premolar, a frequent occurrence in domestic pigs (Miles and Grigson 1990). This assemblage also contained a cattle left mandible with an accessory nutrient foramen below the second premolar lingually and a sheep right mandible with accessory foramen on the buccal surface below the third premolar. All of these conditions, save the absent first premolar in pigs, were also present in the assemblage from the nearby Ditches hillfort (Rielly 1988).

Developmental anomalies, in the form of hypoplasia and tooth rotation, only occur in the pig material in these two assemblages. Hypoplasia occurs in two specimens from Middle Duntisbourne: a mandible from context 217 with the third molar in early wear (Grant 1982 stage c) shows a deep (7.5 mm) band of small pits on all three cusp units of this tooth (Plate 8.1), the first unit is the most severely affected, with the concentration of pits leading to some areas of dentine exposure; the lower third of the crown is unaffected as is the adjacent second molar. The second specimen is a maxilla from context 45, with the third molar again the affected tooth. In this example, although only the first and second cusp units are affected, the damage is much more severe than in the mandible: only the lower half (7.3 mm) of the crown has enamel present, the upper half has dentine fully exposed (Plates 8.2–3). The tooth was erupting but had not yet come into wear. In both these cases a genetic cause can be excluded

since only part of the crown surface area is affected (Hillson 1986).

Hypoplasia can have local causes, for instance injury or abscess (Miles and Grigson 1990), however, in these two examples malnutrition or systemic infection during crown formation are probably more likely and the extent of the effect suggests the cause was prolonged over several months (Miles and Grigson 1990). There may be a correlation with weaning and associated stress. Weaning age is two months in a husbandry system where young pigs are economically important and there are two farrowings a year (Lauwerier 1983). In a less intensive system, such as suggested by the age profiles for the Duntisbourne assemblages, the animals might be older when weaned, closer to the three to four months of wild boar (Macdonald and Barrett 1993). Crown formation of the third molar starts in modern pigs at this age, with the third molar starting slightly later (McCance *et al.* 1961). These timings may have been later in the archaeological animals, as eruption is in wild and unimproved types (Bull and Payne 1982) and the delaying effect of undernutrition on third molar crown formation (McCance *et al.* 1961) is also a complicating factor, but the hypoplastic third molars at Middle Duntisbourne might have resulted if animals were

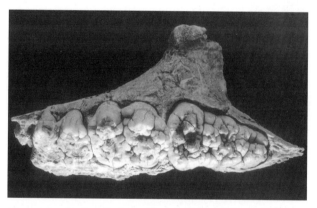

Plate 8.2   Occlusal view of hypoplastic pig maxillary third molar.

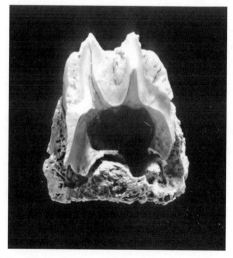

Plate 8.3   Cross section of hypoplastic tooth in plate 8.2.

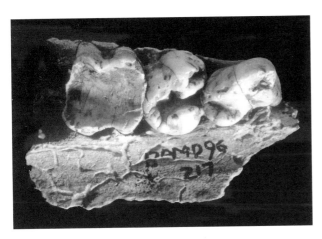

Plate 8.4 Occlusal view of pig maxilla (Middle Duntisbourne, context 217) showing rotated third and fourth molars.

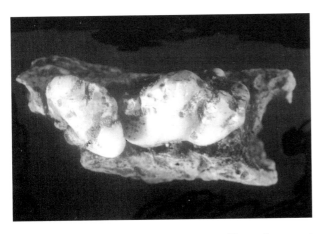

Plate 8.5 Occlusal view of pig maxillary fragment (Middle Duntisbourne, context 84) showing rotated first premolar.

weaned in a bad year with a poor crop of pannage to feed them over the autumn and winter.

Rotation of the teeth arises from overcrowding of the tooth row (Miles and Grigson 1990). One of the possible causes of overcrowding is undernutrition, which prevents the jaws from reaching their proper length and affects the maxilla to a greater extent than the mandible (McCance *et al.* 1961). This would explain why all the examples of rotated teeth in the Duntisbourne assemblages are in the maxilla. The teeth most affected are the latest erupting ones (Miles and Grigson 1990), which in a pig cheek tooth row means the second to fourth premolars and the third molar (Bull and Payne 1982).

The incidence is similar in both assemblages: there are three examples of rotated teeth at Middle Duntisbourne (MNE maxilla = 20) and one at Duntisbourne Grove (MNE = 7). The affected teeth are the first, third and fourth premolars and, in one case, both third and fourth premolars (Plate 8.4). The degree of rotation varies from slight to *c.* 45° and, with the exception of the first premolar (Plate 8.5), is in an

anti-clockwise direction. The affected first and third premolars also show crowding and overlapping with adjacent teeth. The maxilla containing the hypoplastic third molar described above also has evidence of overcrowding: the fourth premolar is not rotated and none of the teeth anterior to it are present, but the position of the partially erupted third molar seems to indicate a degree of impaction.

A further effect of undernutrition is relatively short third molars (McCance *et al.* 1961). If undernutrition was the cause of overcrowding in these examples still it was not severe enough to result in third molars differing in length from those at other sites in the region (see above, Figure 8.12).

Discussion

How far are the relative proportions of species, assessed from the recovered remains, an accurate representation of the original species composition? This is the important question to bear in mind when considering the relationship between Duntisbourne Grove and Middle Duntisbourne and between these and other sites in the area. It has often been noted (eg. King 1978; Reilly 1988) that cattle tend to be over-represented by NISP counts. Hence use of MNI figures in inter-site comparisons will reduce the general bias in favour of cattle caused by factors such as better survival and subsequent identifiability of bones from this species and greater retrieval (compared with sheep and pig) of their smaller skeletal elements.

Further problems lie in the potential for intra-site variation in the distribution of species. Spatial patterning of species has been investigated at several Iron Age sites in central southern Britain, for example Winnall Down (Maltby 1985), Owslebury (Maltby 1987) and Mingies Ditch (Wilson 1985; 1996). Maltby (1981; 1985) and has shown that there is a tendency for cattle and horse to occur more frequently in ditches and quarries than in pits, and that bone tends to be more degraded in ditches than in pits. Wilson (1996) has argued that '...it is not the exact species composition which is important in determining bone distributions at sites but the size of bones or the size of species individuals.' Furthermore, the bones of younger animals and small-to medium-sized species suffered demonstrably more damage at Mingies Ditch than the bones of older animals or larger species (Wilson 1985; 1996). Both disposal practices and differential survival are implicated in spatial variation of species proportions.

No similar studies for sites in the Cotswolds have been published, although in some cases, such as at Duntisbourne Grove and Middle Duntisbourne, the absence of more than one feature type prevents such analysis. However, this does mean that when comparing assemblages the relative proportions of sheep and cattle cannot be taken at face value as reasonably accurate reflections of species present originally, or easily be used to discuss site status, function or economy.

The representation of cattle, sheep and pig are shown in Figure 8.14 for late Iron Age and Romano-British assemblages from the area. The biasing effect of poor preservation will have inflated the contribution of cattle in the assemblage from Duntisbourne Grove. Of the three other Iron Age sites close to the Duntisbournes, Bagendon (Rielly 1990) has a low percentage of cattle and high sheep with the bone retrieved entirely from pits, while the assemblage from Ditches (Rielly 1988), with a higher percentage of cattle, was retrieved entirely from ditches. Unpublished data from Ditches (Rielly pers. comm.) indicates a reduced contribution by cattle in the non-ditch features. The Iron Age assemblage from Birdlip Bypass (Dobney and Jaques 1990) came from both pits and ditches and has cattle slightly more frequent than sheep, but the high degree of gnawing observed suggests considerable post-discard alteration could be biasing the assemblage towards cattle. Hence at all of these site, except Bagendon, the frequency of sheep in the husbandry could be underestimated. However, the relative sizes of the species means that cattle probably still made the greater contribution to the diet.

The relative proportions of sheep and pig are likely to be affected less by spatial variation than the relationship between cattle and these smaller domesticates. However, prolific breeding by pigs allows a far higher kill-off of juvenile animals than in cattle or sheep while still maintaining a viable population. Since the bones of these juveniles are more

susceptible to destruction it follows that the proportion of pigs in a site economy will almost always be underestimated, especially where preservation is poorer. This may be offset to some degree by the relatively robust cranial bones.

Pigs seem to be relatively common at both Middle Duntisbourne and, particularly, Duntisbourne Grove. The relationship between pig and sheep in assemblages from these and other late Iron Age and Romano-British assemblages from the area is shown in Figure 8.15. This confirms that pigs are more frequent at the Duntisbournes; even at Middle Duntisbourne they are still more common (although only little more than at Iron Age Birdlip) than at any other site, including 1st-century Cirencester (Thawley 1982). This high representation of pigs is consistent with the molluscan evidence (see Robinson, this chapter) at both sites for local woodland which would have provided food in autumn. The pathology on the pig teeth from these sites does suggest, however, that this food source was not always sufficient to prevent some members of the herd from suffering nutritional stress. Pig would have been a more important part of the meat diet at both sites than sheep.

Of the minor species in these two assemblages, the very small number of horse bones is comparable with The Ditches (Rielly 1988) and Bagendon (Rielly 1990) but contrasts with their representation at Iron Age Birdlip (Dobney and Jaques 1990). The low numbers of wild animals indicates hunted food was not an important contribution to the diet at either site, in spite of the presence of woodland which would have offered shelter to deer.

The age profiles of the three main domestic mammals show broad similarities between the Duntisbourne sites and the assemblages from Ditches and Bagendon. The cattle show some variation in the numbers of older immatures versus younger adults killed, with the former more numerous at Middle Duntisbourne and Bagendon and the latter more numerous at Duntisbourne Grove and Ditches. However, variation in preservation may account for some of this and all are alike in having minimal numbers of very young or very old animals. This pattern contrasts the typical Romano-British pattern, as seen at Birdlip Quarry, suggesting that the cattle in these sites were reared as all-purpose animals.

The sheep age profile is likewise similar at all these site: very few young and older animals and more animals dying before maturity than in cattle. Only a few clips could have been produced before these sheep were slaughtered, whereas the use of cattle as draught beasts, particularly in the absence of horses, would have been vital in an arable economy.

The age range of the pigs reflects a non-intensive husbandry with few younger juveniles culled in their first year. Although it must be remembered that this age group may be under-represented, if more animals were allowed to over-winter, the consequent extra pressure on food sources could explain the pathology observed in the pig teeth at Duntisbourne Grove and Middle Duntisbourne.

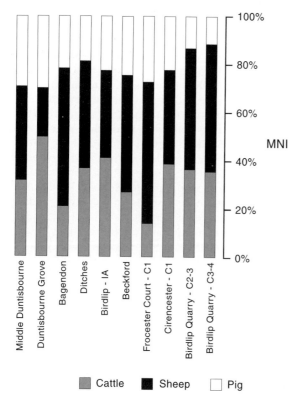

Figure 8.14   Representation of the main domestic animals at 1st-century and later sites in the Cotswolds.

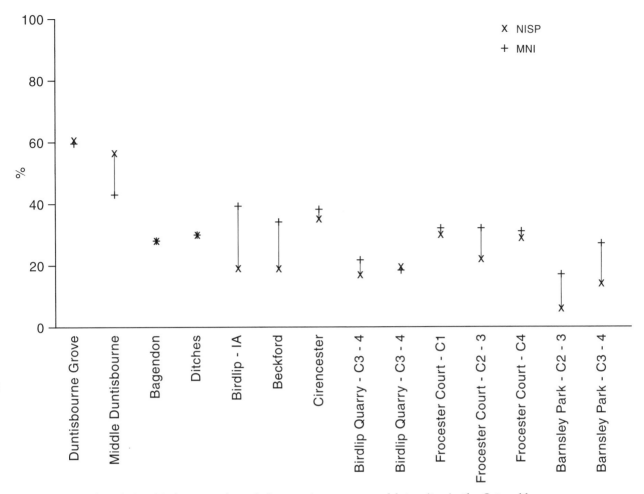

Figure 8.15   The relationship between pig and sheep at 1st-century and later sites in the Cotswolds.

Hence, although the relative frequencies of the domestic mammals differ, both Middle Duntisbourne and Duntisbourne Grove show in their treatment of these species an unspecialised, mixed husbandry which appears to be characteristic of contemporary sites in this part of the Cotswolds.

Birdlip Quarry
By Kathy Ayres and Kate M. Clark

The assemblage. For methodology see middle Duntisbourne and Duntisbourne Grove above.

Bone was recovered through hand excavation and sieving of bulk samples, and the hand retrieved assemblage totalled 11,355 fragments. This total is smaller than that estimated during the assessment due to the reconstruction of bones which had been fragmented post-excavation.

Period 1 produced a total of 2415 fragments of animal bone, of which 905 (45%) could be identified to species, while the assemblage from period 2 was much larger, comprising a total of 8948 fragments, 3737 (46%) of which could be identified to species. The NISP and MNI values are given in Table 8.19.

Table 8.19   Numbers of identified species (NISP) and minimum number of individuals (MNI) at Birdlip Quarry.

	Period 1			Period 2		
	NISP	%	MNI	NISP	%	MNI
Cattle	401	44	13	1788	46	35
Sheep/goat	272	30	18	1093	28	52
Sheep	-	-	-	6	<1	-
Goat	1	<1	-	1	<1	-
Pig	57	6	5	265	7	12
Horse	143	16	4	499	13	8
Dog	22	2	5	53	1	7
Cat	-	-	-	7	<1	-
Red deer	-	-	-	9	<1	-
Roe deer	-	-	-	4	<1	-
Hare	-	-	-	3	<1	-
Fox	1	<1	-	2	<1	-
Bird	8	<1	-	4	<1	-
Water vole	-	-	-	3	<1	-
Cattle size	159	-	-	307	-	-
Sheep size	24	-	-	41	-	-
Unident.	1327	-	-	4863	-	-
Total	2415	-	-	8948	-	-

Species representation

Domestic mammal remains (Table 8.19) dominated the assemblages in both periods 1 and 2, the most frequent of these being cattle, sheep/goat, horse and pig. The relative proportions of these were similar between the periods, but varied within each according to the method of quantification used. Cattle were the most abundant species according to the NISP, with sheep/goat second and horse being more frequent than pig. When MNI counts are considered, sheep/goat are the most numerous.

Dogs were well represented. Measured elements are detailed in Tables 8.20.8.22, and although no complete limb bones were available from which to estimate shoulder height, the measurements do give some indication of the characteristics of the individuals represented.

The remains from the earlier period, representing at least five dogs, are those of two types, and, described in terms of modern animals, were medium-sized terriers and labradors. However, the pair of mandibles from context 597 suggest that the "labrador" type had a rather heavier jaw than would be expected in the modern breed, and similarly in context 1584 the "terrier" sized mandibles are also notably robust. This latter pair of mandibles exhibited an area of periostitis around the mental foramen of the right jaw, with the infection extending from the tooth socket to the ventral surface of the mandible.

At least a further seven dogs are represented in the later period, including a partial skeleton from the well (context 847), which comprised the skull, mandibles, higher vertebrae and ribs. This dog has the broad facial aspect of modern Staffordshire terrier crosses, although the atlas and axis suggest that the animal would have been rather taller (Clark 1996).

Context 2018 from a pit produced the remains of at least two young puppies, probably less than four weeks of age, but the remainder of the dogs are either adult or sub-adult. There was very little wear noted on any of the teeth, including those from the earlier period, but tooth wear in dogs is notoriously unreliable as an age indicator due to the diversity of dog eating habits and a propensity to chew.

Period 2 also produced seven cat bones. Morphology and size of the bones suggested domestic rather than wild cat, and the function of the animals was probably that of vermin control.

Several species of wild mammal occurred in low numbers and, with the exception of a single fox bone from period 1, they were only recorded from period 2. Small quantities of domestic and wild bird were recorded from both periods.

Anatomical distribution of domestic mammal bone

All parts of the cattle skeleton were recorded in both assemblages, with a predominance of higher meat yielding bones and mandibles (Tables 8.23–24). Metapodials were also present in high frequencies and, although recorded in lesser quantities, the presence of smaller bones such as tarsals and phalanges indicates the presence of whole carcasses on site. The assemblage from period 2 included an

Table 8.20   Dog measurements: appendicular, Birdlip Quarry.

Element	Period	Context	R/L	Measurement	(mm)
Axis	C2/C3	307		Length including dens	45.7
				Dorsal length	49.6
				Breadth at cranial facies	30.9
	C3/C4	847*		Length including dens	44.9
				Dorsal length	41.4
				Breadth at cranial facies	26.2
Atlas	C3/C4	847*		Cranial breadth	27.8
				Caudal breadth	27.2
				Height	25.6
Scapula	C3/C4	84	L	Breadth of glenoid	26.2
Humerus	C2/C3	372	R	Distal breadth	28.2
				Min. shaft diameter	11.5
	C3/C4	84	L	Distal breadth	38.3
				Min. shaft diameter	14.8
	C3/C4	83	R	Distal breadth	37.3
				Distal depth	31.6
				Min. shaft diameter	15.0
Radius	C3/C4	84	L	Proximal breadth	22.2
Femur	100-200 AD	1057	L	Distal breadth	26.1
				Min. shaft diameter	10.5
Tibia	C3/C4	800	L	Proximal breadth	32.3
				Min. shaft diameter	12.2

* partial skeleton

Table 8.21   Dog measurements: mandibular (all tooth measurements taken at alveolus), Birdlip Quarry.

Measurement C4	Period	100–300 AD	C2/C3	C2/C3	C3/
	Context	1584	323	597	847*
	R/L	R	L	R	L
Length M3–P1		69.1		80.3	68.9
Length M3–P2		62.4			64.7
Length of molar row		32.1		39.5	32.4
Length P1–P4		38.1		42.9	36.9
Length P2–P4		32.3		36.3	32.5
Length carnassial alveolus		18.9		23.0	21.0
Thickness of jaw below M1		10.1	12.3	11.9	10.7
Height of vertical ramus					48.5
Height of mandible behind M1		20.0	22.4	26.5	22.8
Height of mandible between P2 and P3		16.4		21.3	20.3

Table 8.22   Cranial measurements from partial dog skeleton in context 847, Birdlip Quarry.

Measurement	(mm)
Otion to otion	48.5
Breadth occipital condyles	35.8
Breadth foramen magnum	19.0
Euryon to euryon	56.6
Breadth at post-orbital constriction	37.2
Breadth at ectorbitales	45.9
Breadth at entorbitales	31.9
Height of occipital triangle	50.1
Length of carnassial	16.6

Table 8.23   Minimum number of elements (MNE), Birdlip Quarry, Period 1.

	Cattle	Sheep/goat	Pig	Horse
Horn core	0	0	0	0
Mandible	13	18	3	1
Atlas	5	1	0	1
Axis	3	0	0	3
Scapula	7	3	2	3
Humerus	11	6	5	1
Radius	8	10	1	2
Ulna	2	1	1	1
Metacarpal	7	6	0	3
Pelvis	4	4	1	3
Sacrum	1	0	0	1
Femur	5	7	4	2
Tibia	8	12	4	1
Astragalus	3	1	0	3
Calcaneum	4	1	0	3
Nav-Cuboid	2	0	0	0
Metatarsal	7	9		4
1st Phalanx	11	4	1	8
Total	101	83	22	40

Table 8.24   Minimum number of elements (MNE), Birdlip Quarry, Period 2.

	Cattle	Sheep/goat	Pig	Horse
Horn core	2	1	0	0
Mandible	28	35	12	7
Atlas	11	1	1	2
Axis	6	1	0	3
Scapula	35	4	5	7
Humerus	24	20	7	6
Radius	24	34	2	8
Ulna	21	2	2	3
Metacarpal	25	18	1	5
Pelvis	15	5	1	7
Sacrum	2	0	0	2
Femur	17	22	8	6
Tibia	24	52	11	3
Astragalus	18	2	2	3
Calcaneum	18	1	2	4
Nav-Cuboid	4	0	0	0
Metatarsal	21	38	3	5
1st Phalanx	62	4	1	17
Total	357	240	58	88

articulated cattle tibia, calcaneum and navicular cuboid, recovered from well 891.

The relative abundance of anatomical elements of sheep was again similar in both periods with high frequency of mandibles, radii, tibiae and metatarsals (Tables 8.23–24). Other prime meat-bearing bones were recorded in quantities, particularly in the larger assemblage from the later period. Few parts of the head (apart from mandibles) or the feet were present but it is possible that the fragmented nature of the crania and the small size of the foot bones causing a retrieval bias leading to under-representation when compared to the more robust skeletal elements. In general, it would appear most likely that the sheep assemblage derives from the processing of whole carcasses, rather than from joints brought to the site.

The most frequent body parts of pig in both assemblages were main limb bones such as humerus, femur and tibia (Tables 8.23–24). Scapula and pelvis were also present, but there were few smaller bones such as phalanges. There were higher frequencies of mandibles and teeth in period 2. The analysis of element representation for pig is always compromised, however, by the immaturity of the slaughtered animals. Pigs offer no secondary products beyond manure, and there is therefore no incentive to maintain them beyond optimum meat contribution weight which is before skeletal maturity. Because of their fecundity, breeding stock can be kept low. Therefore, there will normally be an excess of juveniles over adults both in the herd and in the processed bone but unfortunately juvenile bone survives poorly in the soil. The numerical results that can be obtained from a pig assemblage, therefore, are likely to be significantly biased towards adult animals, whose actual presence would most likely have been a significant minority.

Many of the parts of the horse skeleton were present in the assemblages (Tables 8.23–24). In period 1 an articulated radius and ulna occurred in a ditch context, and in the later period, groups of bones included an articulated ulna and radius from a well context, and an astragalus and calcaneum in a layer.

Ageing and sexing of the main domestic mammals

In period 1, all of the earlier-fusing elements of cattle (up to approximately 2 years) were fused, except for one bone (Table 8.25). Thereafter, mortality increased, but there was also evidence for some cattle having reached 3–4 years or more. The dental data was dominated by evidence for mature cattle. Of the 17 mandibles available for ageing, 12 were aged as adult or older and 4 as senile. The only evidence for cattle under the age of 1 year in this period was a mandible aged to less than 8 months. The larger set of fusion data in period 2 emphasised the advanced age of the cattle with a lack of evidence for animals dying under the age of 1 year, and few animals dying under 3 years (Table 8.26). Again, there was evidence for most

Table 8.25 Cattle fusion data, Period 1, Birdlip Quarry.

Age at Fusion	Element	Fused	Unfused	Total
7–10 months	Scapula D	8	0	8
12–15 months	Radius P	6	1	7
15–20 months	Humerus D	10	0	10
20–24 months	1st Phalanx	11	0	11
24–30 months	Tibia D	6	1	7
24–30 months	Metacarpal D	4	2	6
24–30 months	Metatarsal D	4	0	4
36 months	Calcaneum	1	2	3
36 months	Femur P	3	1	4
42 months	Femur D	4	0	4
42–48 months	Humerus P	2	4	6
42–48 months	Radius D	2	1	3
42–48 months	Tibia P	1	1	2
Total		62	13	75

Table 8.26 Cattle fusion data, Period 2, Birdlip Quarry.

Age at Fusion	Element	Fused	Unfused	Total
7–10 months	Scapula, D	44	0	44
12–15 months	Radius, P	45	1	46
15–20 months	Humerus, D	27	2	29
20–24 months	1st Phalanx	58	0	58
24–30 months	Tibia, D	23	1	24
24–30 months	Metacarpal, D	18	1	19
24–30 months	Metatarsal, D	19	2	21
36 months	Calcaneum	3	7	10
36 months	Femur, P	10	4	14
42 months	Femur, D	16	5	21
42 months	Ulna, P	0	3	3
42–48 months	Humerus, P	9	5	14
42–48 months	Radius, D	9	3	12
42–48 months	Tibia, P	7	5	12
Total		288	39	327

Table 8.27 Sheep/goat fusion data, Period 1, Birdlip Quarry.

Age at fusion	Element	Fused	Unfused	Total
3–4 months	Humerus, D	4	4	7
3–4 months	Radius, P	3	1	4
3–4 months	Humerus, P	0	1	1
5 months	Scapula	1	1	2
20–24 months	Metacarpal, D	3	0	3
20–24 months	Metatarsal, D	3	1	4
36 months	Calcaneum	1	0	1
36 months	Femur, P	2	0	2
42 months	Radius, D	1	1	2
42 months	Tibia, P	1	0	1
Total		19	9	27

animals surviving beyond 3 years and a lower, but still high, proportion of those surviving over the age of 4. The dominance of mature cattle was further supported by the dental data with 31 of the 41 mandibles and loose teeth available being aged as fully adult or older. Of these, 14 were from senile animals. A small quantity of evidence for animals which had not reached 1 year, and also for older juveniles, was recorded.

The fusion data for sheep/goat in period 1 (Table 8.27) indicated the presence of very young animals, with an unfused metatarsal indicating a foetal lamb. Bones that fuse between 1–3 years and or later were represented. In contrast to the fusion data, there was no dental evidence for individuals aged under 1 year, and most animals were killed between 1 and 4 years, with the majority aged 3–4 years at slaughter (Fig. 8.16). Two mandibles were aged at 8–10 years, indicating some very old animals on site. The data from period 2 shows little evidence in either the fusion (Table 8.28) or dental data for very young lambs, with the majority of mandibles aged to over 1 year and evidence in the fusion data for high mortality in the 3rd and 4th years. The available

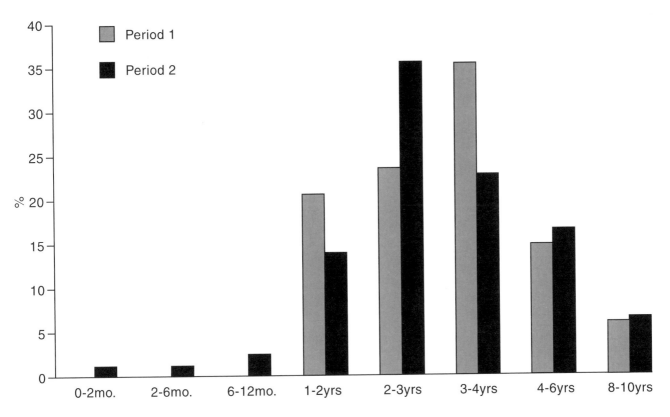

Figure 8.16   Sheep/goat dental data. Period 1: n=34; Period 2: n=90.

Table 8.28   Sheep/goat fusion data, Period 2, Birdlip Quarry.

Age at fusion	Element	Fused	Unfused	Total
3–4 months	Humerus, D	7	0	7
3–4 months	Radius, P	8	2	10
3–4 months	Humerus, P	3	2	5
5 months	Scapula	3	0	3
15–20 months	Tibia, D	14	3	17
20–24 months	Metacarpal, D	7	4	11
20–24 months	Metatarsal, D	4	3	7
36 months	Femur, P	1	4	5
42 months	Radius, D	1	4	5
42 months	Tibia, P	2	2	4
42 months	Ulna, P	2	0	2
42 months	Femur, D	1	3	4
Total		53	27	80

Table 8.30   Pig fusion data, Period 2, Birdlip Quarry.

Age at fusion	Element	Fused	Unfused	Total
12 months	Humerus, D	0	3	3
12 months	Radius, P	1	0	1
12 months	Scapula	1	1	2
24 months	Metacarpal, D	0	1	1
24 months	Metatarsal, D	0	3	3
24 months	Tibia, D	2		2
24–30 months	Calcaneum	0	2	2
36–42 months	Ulna, P	0	1	1
36–42 months	Femur, P	0	2	2
36–42 months	Femur, D	0	2	2
36–42 months	Tibia, P	1		1
Total		5	15	20

Table 8.29   Pig fusion data, Period 1, Birdlip Quarry.

Age at fusion	Element	Fused	Unfused	Total
12 months	Radius, P	1	0	1
24 months	Tibia, D	1	0	1
36–42 months	Ulna, P	0	1	1
36–42 months	Femur, P	0	1	1
Total		2	2	4

mandibles corroborate this high kill-off in the 2–4 year age range and the pattern is similar to period 1, although the highest peak was a year earlier. Five mandibles were aged as senile.

Fusion data for pig from period 1 consist of evidence for animals killed in the 2–3 year age group (Table 8.29). Two mandibles were available for ageing and indicated one immature and one sub-adult animal. In period 2 (Table 8.30), there was a higher proportion of immature bones in the pig assemblage than was recorded for cattle and sheep, with evidence for animals under the age of 1 year and little evidence of animals surviving past 2 years. The majority of

Table 8.31   Horse fusion data, Period 1, Birdlip Quarry.

Age at fusion	Element	Fused	Unfused	Total
9–12 months	Scapula, D	6	0	6
10–12 months	2nd Phalanx	2	0	2
12–15 months	1st Phalanx	7	0	7
15 months	Metapodial, D	10	0	10
15–18 months	Humerus, D	1	0	1
15–18 months	Radius, P	2	0	2
24 months	Tibia, D	2	0	2
36 months	Calcaneum	1	1	2
36–42 months	Femur, P	1	1	2
42 months	Humerus, P	1	0	1
42 months	Radius, D	2	0	2
42 months	Ulna, P	1	0	1
42 months	Femur, D	2	0	2
42 months	Tibia, P	1	0	1
Total		39	2	41

Table 8.32   Horse fusion data, Period 2, Birdlip Quarry.

Age at fusion	Element	Fused	Unfused	Total
9–12 months	Scapula, D	11	0	11
10–12 months	2nd Phalanx	6	0	6
12–15 months	1st Phalanx	14	0	14
15 months	Metapodial, D	14	0	14
15–18 months	Humerus, d	10	0	10
15–18 months	Radius, P	14	0	14
24 months	Tibia, D	1	0	1
36 months	Calcaneum	4	1	5
36–42 months	Femur, P	5	2	7
42 months	Humerus, P	4	0	4
42 months	Radius, D	17	0	17
42 months	Ulna, P	0	3	3
42 months	Femur, D	6	0	6
42 months	Tibia, P	4	0	4
Total		110	6	116

mandibles were aged as sub-adult (11 out of 20), few very young or very old animals represented.

Pig canine teeth and dental alveoli were sexed and of the four recorded from period 1, two could be identified as male and two as female. Out of the upper and lower canines recorded in period 2, 14 could be sexed as female and 10 as male.

The majority of horse bones from both periods 1 and 2 were fused (Tables 8.31–2) and indicated adult animals, as did the loose teeth available for ageing. In the later period most were clustered around the ages of 7–10 years but some were aged up to 20 years.

A dog humerus with a fused distal end from period 1 indicated an animal over the age of 6–8 months, and in period 2 a pit produced the remains of at least two young puppies probably less than four weeks of age, with the remainder of the dogs either aged as adult or sub-adult. There was very little wear noted on any of the teeth.

All the cat bones recorded from period 2 were fully fused indicating adult cats rather than kittens.

Metrical data

The measurements from Birdlip were studied to investigate the possibility of any changes in size between the early and late Roman period although no significant differences could be observed. Measurements for the main domestic species are shown in Appendix 8.4, with the Animal Bone Metrical Archive Project data (Centre for Human Ecology 1996) from contemporary sites for comparison. The majority of measurements taken from Birdlip in the early Roman period are compatible with those listed in ABMAP although anomalies include a low value for distal breadth of cattle tibia and a high value for greatest length of sheep metacarpal. The latter measurement was also seen to be high at Portway (Noddle 1984). In both periods height of the cattle humerus trochlea was smaller than those from ABMAP. In period 2 the greatest length of cattle tibia was small, although it had high measurements of distal breadth as seen at Frocester Court (Noddle 1979) and Barnsley Park (Noddle 1985). Both the distal depth and breadth at Birdlip were larger than those in ABMAP.

Withers heights were calculated for cattle, sheep and horse from greatest lengths of long bones using formulae of Matolcsi, Teichert and Kiesewalter respectively (von den Driesch and Boessneck 1974). Only two withers heights could be calculated for cattle from the earlier period: 1.12 m and 1.19 m. The larger database of measurements in the later period provided more heights which ranged from 0.95 m to 1.2 m.

Only one withers height was available in either of the periods for sheep, period 1 gave a value of 0.56 m and period 2 of 0.67 m.

Withers heights for horse could be calculated for both periods, and are shown in Figure 8.17, again with the inclusion of comparable ABMAP data for period 2 (there is no useable comparative sample for period 1). The later Birdlip horses are noticeably at the lower end of the ABMAP range.

The shape of cattle metapodials is sexually dimorphic, with bulls having more robust bones than cows (Higham 1969); proximal breadth and depth were plotted to establish whether sexes could be determined in the assemblage. No clustering could be observed in the plotted metatarsals, but the metacarpals show two 'groups' of measurements (Fig. 8.18), of which the larger bones could be bulls and the smaller, cows. Alternatively, as the metacarpal is an early fusing bone, the figure may illustrate different age groups, such as young but skeletally immature animals, and older animals, thereby supporting the ageing data. Although these are not the best measurements for differentiating sexes, there were too few of the more suitable ones.

Wild mammals

The only evidence of wild species in period 1 was fox (*Vulpes vulpes*), represented by a scapula recovered from a well context. In period 2, both red deer

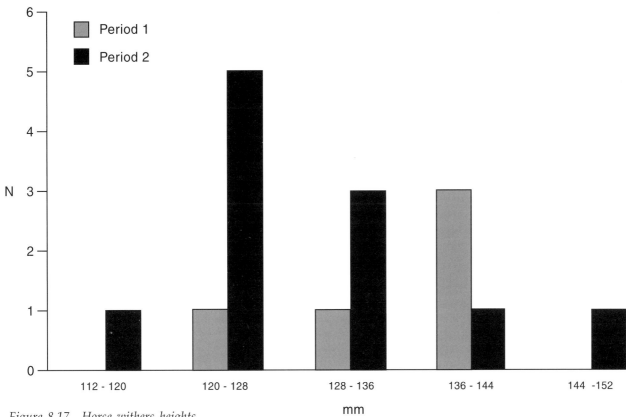

Figure 8.17   Horse withers heights.

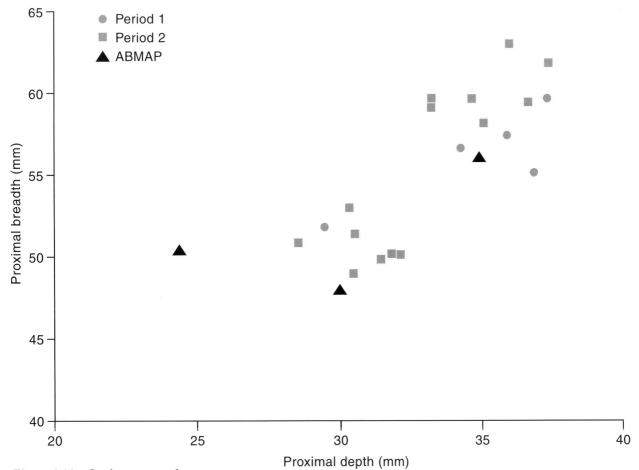

Figure 8.18   Cattle metacarpals.

(*Cervus elaphus*) and roe deer (*Capreolus capreolus*) were identified, with the former being the more numerous. Four of the nine red deer fragments recorded were antler, but femur and tibia were also present. A fused tibia and the ageable teeth indicated adult animals. Four fragments of roe deer were identified; humerus, ulna, metatarsal and a patella, which also indicated adults. Hare (*Lepus europaeus*) and fox were found in low frequencies, with three fragments of hare and two of fox identified, consisting of long bones and metatarsals. Three bones, two upper incisors and a femur, were identified as water vole (*Arvicola terrestris*).

Birds

Eight bird bone fragments were identified from period 1, six from domestic fowl, a thrush (*Turdus sp.*) humerus, and a woodcock (*Scolopax rusticola*) tibia. Medullary bone was identified in three specimens of the domestic fowl. This is a deposit of bone formed within bones of female birds and is required for the production of eggshell. The bone is deposited some weeks before the eggs are laid. While the eggshells are being formed the medullary bone is depleted and after the last egg is laid the normal internal structure is regained (Driver 1982). It is most easily recognised in long bones due to deposition in the relatively large marrow cavity and was identified in two femora and a tibia of domestic fowl in the Birdlip assemblage. Four bird bones were identified in the assemblage from period 2, three belonged to domestic fowl and one was mallard (*Anas platyrhynchos*).

Butchery

The majority of bones with identified butchery marks were recorded from contexts in the main occupation areas. Butchery data can be seen in Tables 8.33–34.

Butchery marks were identified on 19% of cattle bone fragments in both periods. Both heavy and light marks were recorded, indicating methods using both heavy chopping instruments and knives. In the earlier period they were most numerous on mandibles and scapula, although the main long bones were frequently marked and evidence was recorded on the extremities. In the later period marks were observed on all elements, including skull and phalanges. The marks are consistent with primary butchery techniques, of the initial dressing of the carcasses, disarticulation of joints (such as the shoulder and pelvis) and also the defleshing of bones. Those on the mandible could possibly indicate its detachment from the rest of the skull and removal of the tongue. The marks on the various skull fragments could be indicative of the disarticulation of the skull from the mandibles and neck, and the removal of the horn and core. Marks on the phalanges suggest skinning.

The majority of marks on sheep/goat bones were made by knives, although some chop marks were identified. In period 1, chop marks occurred on a metacarpal and a scapula indicating the disarticulation of the ankle and shoulder joint

Table 8.33   Butchery data, Period 1, Birdlip Quarry.

	Chop	Knife	Chop and Knife	Total
Cattle	17	45	14	76
Sheep/goat	1	11	2	14
Pig	2	3	1	6
Horse	1	6	0	7
Cattle size	3	4	1	8
Sheep size	0	1	0	1
Unidentified	4	32	1	37
Total	28	102	19	149

Table 8.34   Butchery data, Period 2, Birdlip Quarry.

	Chop	Knife	Chop and Knife	Sawn	Total
Cattle	102	199	32	0	333
Sheep/goat	8	67	1	0	76
Pig	5	17	0	0	22
Horse	1	9	0	0	10
Dog	1	1	0	0	2
Red deer	2	2	0	0	4
Cat	0	1	0	0	1
Cattle size	4	4	0	0	8
Sheep size	0	2	0	0	2
Unidentified	7	98	6	1	112
Total	130	400	39	1	570

respectively and filleting marks were observed on scapula and main limb bones. In period 2, the marks were most frequent on the radius and tibia, but were also present on other meat bones as well as astragalus and metapodials. They are mainly indicative of filleting.

Both chop and knife marks were observed on pig bones, but knife marks were again more frequent in both periods. In period 1 these suggest the detachment of the mandible and disarticulation of the shoulder joint, and the filleting of meat from long bones and scapula, and in the later period they occurred mainly on the limb bones, scapula and pelvis.

Butchery marks were also identified on horse bones in both assemblages. A chop mark on an ulna and six examples of knife marks on limb bones and metapodials were present in the 2nd to 3rd century assemblage. Ten marks were recorded on horse bones in period 2 and included one chop mark on a radius and nine knife marks on meat bones, metatarsals and phalanges. Ribs and vertebrae of main domesticates showed evidence of butchery.

In the later period four marks were recorded on red deer bones. Two marks were observed on dog bones, a knife mark on an ulna and a chop mark on a fibula, and one knife mark was recorded on the tibia of a cat which might again have been the result of skinning.

The burning and smashing of cattle and horse long bones may be indicative of the extraction of marrow. This occurred on six cattle metatarsals and metacarpals, and two horse metatarsals.

Gnawing

Gnaw marks, predominantly inflicted by dogs, were observed on 4% of the bones from period 1 and 5% of those from period 2 and were recovered from all context types, with a higher percentage in wells, which may result from the better preservation of bone in these contexts. In period 1 a higher proportion was retrieved from Area A. The majority of gnaw marks were recorded on bones of the four main domestic species (Table 8.35–36). Both heavy and surface gnawing was observed on the bones. Surface gnawing on sheep/goat bones was most frequent, although one instance of rodent gnawing was noted on a sheep/goat bone from the earlier period. Heavier gnawing was more prevalent on the bones of cattle and had often resulted in the destruction of the epiphysis. Two examples of puncture marks were recorded on a cattle-sized rib fragment in period 1 and a fox bone in period 2. A single dog bone from period 2 showed superficial gnawing. There were two instances of feline gnawing on a sheep pelvis and a domestic fowl femur.

Burning

Burnt bones accounted for only 1% of the total assemblage from periods 1 and 2 (Table 8.37). In period 1 evidence for burning was present on bones of sheep, horse and unidentified fragments and in the

later period on cattle, cattle-sized, sheep/goat and unidentified fragments. In period 1 the majority of the burnt fragments of bone were recovered from ditches and hearths in Area A; in period 2, most were from the corn dryer fill and occupation layer by fragment count, but from pits by percentage.

Pathology

The most notable characteristic of the pathological assemblage is the incidence of established and advanced arthropathy. Table 8.38 summarises the distribution of the lesions, all but one of them in the lower limbs, with hindlimbs most commonly affected. The degree of joint damage is remarkable. Those lesions designated as degenerative all comprise substantial reactive bone around the joint margin (periarticular exostoses) together with expansion of the articular area and eburnation and grooving of the subchondral bone (Plate 8.6). Cases described as septic have suffered complete destruction of all or part of the joint surface and this is associated with

Table 8.37 Burning data, Birdlip Quarry.

Period	Burned	Calcined	Charred	Partly	Total	%
1	26	1	0	5	32	1
2	51	15	1	10	77	1
Total	77	16	1	15	109	

Table 8.35 Gnawing data, Period 1, Birdlip Quarry.

	Heavy	Surface	Digested	Punctured	Rodent	Total
Cattle	14	8	0	0	0	22
Sheep/goat	7	26	0	1	1	35
Pig	4	5	0	0	0	9
Horse	4	1	0	0	0	5
Dog	0	1	0	1	0	2
Cattle-sized	0	0	0	1	0	1
Unidentified	5	4	1	0	0	10
Total	34	45	1	3	1	84

Table 8.36 Gnawing data, Period 2, Birdlip Quarry.

	Heavy	Surface	Digested	Punctured	Rodent	Total
Cattle	86	52	0	0	0	138
Sheep/goat	46	134	0	0	0	180
Pig	13	19	0	0	0	32
Horse	7	7	0	0	1	15
Dog	0	1	0	0	0	1
Cattle-sized	0	3	0	0	0	3
Unidentified	10	81	3	1	1	96
Total	162	297	3	1	2	465

Table 8.38   Arthropathic conditions, Birdlip Quarry.

Period	Species	Context	Element	Epiphysis	Status
1	Cattle	852	Metatarsal	D	Articular extension
	Horse	953	Metatarsal	P	Septic
			3rd tarsal	P D	Septic
			Central tarsal	D	Septic
2	Cattle	18	1st Phalanx	D	Degenerative
		84	Metatarsal	P	Degenerative
		206	Metatarsal	P	Degenerative
		815	Metatarsal	P	Septic
		848	Femur	P	Eburnation
		861 / 880	1st Phalanx	P	Degenerative
		1501	Metacarpal	D	Degenerative
			1st Phalanx	P	Degenerative
			Centroquartal	D	Degenerative
	Horse	984	Metatarsal	P	Degenerative
		1228	Astagalus		septic

proliferative infected bony growth. In the case of the 2nd-/3rd-century horse hindlimb from context 953, there has been total collapse and integration of the remains of the third tarsal into the proximal metatarsal, with the degeneration and infection extending into the central tarsal above (Plate 8.7).

A significant observation in this assemblage is the lack of early arthropathic manifestations, and there are two broad explanations that can be forwarded in a collection of this size based on the cattle data. The animals may have been slaughtered at an advanced age, or perhaps in a slaughter pattern which includes only juveniles/young adults and elderly cattle. Alternatively, the progression of the disease has been accelerated by repeated stresses such as those imposed by draught or traction or work over hard surfaces. The latter explanation is often more attractive

because of its narrative potential, but analysts are becoming more aware of the complexities of arthropathic change in animals and the external conditions which stimulate it. In the case of the Birdlip cattle assemblage, the ageing data suggest that the pattern of joint abnormality is consistent with the presence of elderly animals.

This absence of such asymptomatic joint remodelling as discrete articular extension is unusual, even in small assemblages. Morphological adjustments to joint surfaces, usually sub-clinical, and age-related manifestations reflecting some degree of maturity within the group are common. In the case of the animals from Birdlip this category of naturally occurring remodelling is missing, but advanced joint degradation is well represented. Here, the second hypothesis, that of repeated unnatural stress, has to

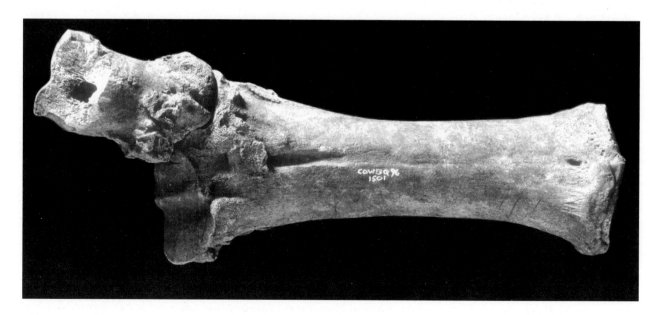

Plate 8.6   Cattle lower forelimb showing degenerative osteoarthropathy.

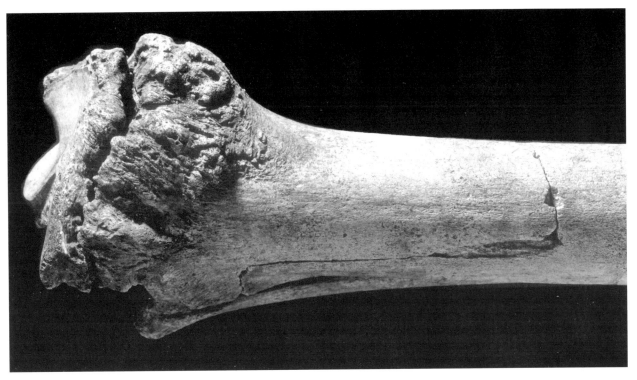

Plate 8.7   Horse metatarsal and third tarsal showing advanced arthropathy.

be considered seriously and is supported by the eburnated femoral head specimen from context 848. This is unfused, and therefore represents an animal less than about three years of age. This is a very young age indeed for cattle to suffer normal degenerative arthropathy, and it may be far more likely that the animal was subjected to repeated stresses in the hindquarter.

The effects of working over hard surfaces are seen in a case of splints in a horse metatarsal from the 3rd/4th century group (context 84). Splints are bony enlargements which are a result of localised periostitis and occur most commonly in modern horses under the age of six years who are doing strenuous work on hard or uneven surfaces, or who strike the lower limb with the inside of the opposing hoof. In the Birdlip specimen the lesions are on the lateral side so the latter aetiology does not apply. It is more likely that excessive concussion before the animal reached adulthood caused inflammation of the interosseous ligament binding the cannon bone to the smaller metatarsals, and the inflammation spread to the covering periosteum. New bone growth is subsequently stimulated by the irritation and strain.

The remainder of the infectious lesions visible in the assemblage are discrete and unrelated. In the 3rd-/4th-century cattle, a mandible has an infection of a tooth socket with resorption and recession of the bone around the alveolus, and a 2nd-/3rd-century second phalanx has an infection at the site of the medial ligament insertion. A pig calcaneum has a severe infection of the distal end which has resulted in the complete destruction of the articulation; this is undoubtedly due in the first instance to a penetrating wound.

There is only one instance of sheep periodontal disease, with a left mandible exhibiting an abscess from the 3rd-/4th-century context 846. This lack of oral disease in sheep from this period is as notable as the high incidence of advanced arthropathy in the cattle, and adds considerably to the very individual character of this bone assemblage. The only other lesion in sheep remains is a partially healed fracture of a distal tibia, with well developed callus and evidence of infection. A single instance of trauma in cattle is an ossified haematoma on the caudal border of a scapula, probably the result of a strong blow.

Congenital abnormalities are all from the 2nd-/3rd-century material. A horse jaw exhibits an extra mental foramen, and a pair of cattle maxillary third molars have very abnormal wear, due almost certainly to the absence of the third cusp in the opposing mandibular molars. A cattle mandible from context 1505 does indeed show a very reduced third cusp on the third molar with abnormal wear. This mandible has also suffered the loss of the first molar, with the alveolus filling but with infection, recession and resorption of the jawbone. A pair of dog mandibles from period 1 exhibited an area of periostitis around the mental foramen of the right jaw, with the infection extending from the tooth socket to the ventral surface of the mandible.

Worked bone

Only one worked fragment of bone was recorded in the 2nd–3rd century assemblage. This was an unidentified fragment and may have been a waste piece. A fragment of red deer antler in period 2 had been worked and there were four knife marks identified on antler. An unidentified fragment of bone had also been worked.

Sieved bone

Animal bone was also recorded from 5 sieved samples in period 1, and 11 in period 2 (Table 8.39). Cattle remains were the most frequently identified in period 1, although period 2 showed a higher proportion of sheep. However, the number of bones recorded from each sample was not large. In period 1 the fill of the possible votive pot (sample 123) contained frog *(Rana temporaria)*, toad *(Bufo sp.)*, indeterminate amphibian and shrew *(Sorex sp.)* bones which were probably not deposited ritually. Ageing data indicated the presence of mature cattle and horse and juvenile pig. Period 2 contained a higher proportion of sheep bone, and fragments of cattle, pig, horse and dog and cat were also identified.

Spatial analysis

Although bones were recovered from nearly all parts of the site, in both periods 1 and 2 the majority were excavated from the main occupation areas, A-E. In period 2, bone was also excavated from part of Roman Ermin Street. In both assemblages, the largest proportion came from area A alone (52% of period 1, and 38% of period 2). Within these areas, bone was recovered from a number of different contexts which have been grouped into types. In both periods bone was recorded from ditches, layers, pits, wells and structural remains, and in period 1, a single hand-retrieved bone was excavated from a possible votive deposit. Although similar proportions were excavated from the various areas in each period, the distribution of bones by context type differed between the two. In period 1, the majority of bones were recovered from ditches and layers, with similar proportions from each; whereas in the later period, a larger proportion was excavated from layers (62%) and fewer from ditches.

Cattle bone predominated in most areas in both periods although there were exceptions. In period 1, Area 1 had a much higher proportion of horse, although the number of bones excavated from this area was small (66). Similarly in Area 2a, identified as a dump, the assemblage consisted solely of cattle and cattle-

sized bone fragments, but the total number of bones was only 23. Cattle and horse fragments were the most frequent in the culvert trench and well 277. Dog was present only in the assemblages from the main occupation areas. Cattle bone was the most frequent in all context groups, although the structural remains had almost equal proportions of sheep/goat. Apart from the sieved bone described above, the votive deposit consisted of only one fragment of hand-retrieved bone and this could not be identified to either species or element level. In period 2, the predominance of cattle remains in most areas was again noted, an exception being area D where sheep were most frequent. Dog was present over a larger area in this period. In both periods the percentage of horse relative to other species was higher outside the main occupation areas. In contrast to period 1, the majority of bones were excavated from layers and again cattle bone was the most frequent in all but the structural deposits.

Most parts of the skeleton were present in the main areas of occupation in period 1, although a predominance of cattle skull fragments and teeth was noted in Area 2A. There was little difference in the distribution of anatomical elements in the context groups. The data from period 2, however, could indicate differential deposition. Main areas of occupation such as A, B and D had higher proportions of limb bones, and fewer fragments of the head and feet, whereas in those areas on the edges of the site, the reverse is true. In Area E and the nearby well (context 891), feet were represented in much higher proportions, and in the section of Ermin Street which had been excavated, there was an abundance of parts of the skull. This could indicate food debris deposited in the main areas of occupation and primary butchery waste outside of these. This was most notable with cattle bone and can be seen in Figure 8.19.

Discussion

The relative abundance of the main domestic species and the age profiles are similar between the two periods and allow them to be discussed together. Cattle were the most frequent species by fragment count although the higher MNI of sheep/goat suggests the important contribution of both these species to the husbandry of the site.

Table 8.39 Number of identified specimens from samples, Birdlip Quarry.

	Cattle	Sheep/goat	Pig	Horse	Dog	Cat	Cattle	Sheep size	Frog size	Toad	Amphibian	Shrew	Uniden.	Total
Period 1														
> 10mm	25	4	3	31			2	1					4	70
Pot fill			0					8	2		1	2	1	14
Period 2														
> 10 mm	5	13	2	2	3			1					11	37
10–4 mm		1			2	3		1					1	8

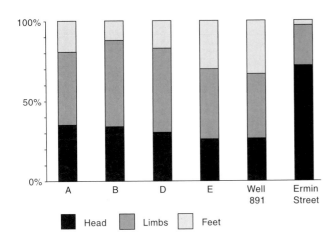

Figure 8.19   Representation of cattle body parts by area.

King, in his survey of British sites (1978), identified cattle husbandry as dominant in the Roman period and concluded that the more 'Romanised' settlements (eg. villas and towns) had fewer sheep than native sites, which continued the Iron Age pattern (King 1991), this trend spreading and becoming more marked in the later Roman period. However, this pattern is based largely on fragments counts which, as argued in the analysis of the Duntisbourne assemblages, will over-represent the contribution of cattle to an assemblage. Hence, although NISP proportions show that by the 4th century this more 'Romanised' pattern of high proportions of cattle occurred at both urban and rural sites near to Birdlip, examination of the MNI proportions (Fig. 8.20) shows that, as at Birdlip, sheep equalled or outnumbered cattle in numbers of animals present.

The predominance of aged cattle was particularly evident in the later period with senile animals the most numerous. This indicates that a role for cattle at Birdlip was as working draught animals. This is also suggested by the advanced arthropathy of the species which indicated stresses through work.

The identification of all parts of the body suggests whole carcasses were present on site. The presence of immature animals does suggest that some animals were slaughtered locally at an age which optimised meat return for food costs. The almost complete absence of very young animals is notable but may well be explained by poor preservation of the bones of younger animals. Maltby (1981) recognises this emphasis of mature cattle in the Roman period but such a high proportion of senile animals at Birdlip is unusual in that this pattern has more frequently been seen on military and urban sites rather than rural, which have evidence for cattle of all ages in their assemblages. However, predominance of mature cattle was also seen at the nearby rural sites of Haymes and Portway and high proportions of mature cattle were also recorded from Frocester Court Villa (Noddle 1979) and Barnsley Park (Noddle 1985).

The keeping of a sheep population for meat in both periods was implied by the peaks in age profile at approximately 2–4 years. Older animals which would have been kept for their wool and milk were also represented, although the absence of loomweights and rarity of spindle whorls in the small finds assemblage suggests that most wool may have left the site as raw fleeces. There was little evidence for very young animals indicating little consumption of young on site or, as with cattle, this could be due to preservational bias. Both Grant (1989) and Maltby (1981) note the increasing importance of meat in the Roman period although they observe that wool production would also have continued. High proportions of immature and mature sheep were recorded at Barnsley Park, Portway and Frocester Court (Noddle 1979; 1984; 1985).

High percentages of immature pigs were also noted at sites in the vicinity. This is a typical pattern for pigs because of their high fertility rate and lack of secondary products, which means there is less reason to keep most of them to maturity. This also means that the role of pig in the site economy is almost certainly understated because of the lesser likelihood of juvenile bones surviving.

In both periods the butchery evidence indicated the dismembering of the carcass and subsequent filleting of the meat from the bones of the main food animals. Grant (1989) observed the change in butchery techniques from the Iron Age to the Roman period, with the use of heavier chopping tools becoming more frequent than the cutting of ligaments by knife, although the latter method continued to be used.

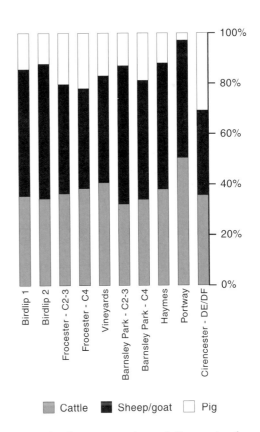

Figure 8.20   Representation of the main domestic mammals at Birdlip and contemporary Cotswolds sites.

In Birdlip, there was a predominance of knife marks on both cattle and sheep bones and Maltby (1989) observed that although chop marks predominated on urban sites where carcasses were more heavily butchered, knife marks were still more frequent on rural sites even in the later Romano-British period. This may be because there is unlikely to have been a specialist butchery practice on rural sites, as there were in towns, and traditional practices were still in use.

Horse is often recorded on Roman sites but is rarely very common and the high proportion of horse bones recorded at Birdlip is unusual. Although butchery marks have been observed on some horse bones at Birdlip, they could have been the result of skinning of the carcasses rather than the removal of meat for human consumption (Grant 1989). In both periods the horses were aged as adult and they would have been used as working animals. According to Hyland (1990) horse power could have been utilised for all farm duties other than 'heavy ploughing'. The pathological evidence has indicated the work related conditions in the Birdlip bones. Particularly high frequencies of horse were also noted at Heneage, Haymes and Portway, although the species was present in most of the sites mentioned above.

The frequency of wild species at Birdlip was not high and it is unlikely that they contributed much to the diet. Deer could be a source of food, or raw material in the form of antler for working and the evidence suggests it was used for both purposes at Birdlip. Femur and tibia were both recorded indicating hunted carcasses brought back to site, and an antler with cut marks was also recorded which may have been used for working. Wild species were found only at the larger sites such as the villa at Barnsley Park (Noddle 1979) where red, roe and fallow deer (*Dama dama*) were all present but again would not have contributed to the diet to any great extent. The settlement and shrine at Portway has an absence of wild species and Vineyards Farm only had small frequencies but included dog, cat, deer, fowl, goose and other bird (Noddle 1984).

Excavations of Iron Age and very early Roman date had taken place previously at Birdlip, the site being situated *c.* 1.5 km further north. Cattle was also identified as the most frequent species by fragment count in this assemblage (Dobney and Jacques 1990), although the wet-sieve data shows a predominance of sheep. The age profiles were similar to that of the later assemblages described in this report with a predominance of mature cattle and immature and mature sheep. Wild species were also rare. The measurements were compared between the different assemblages, and although no change had been found between the two later Roman periods as noted above, the maximum of many of the measurement ranges in these were higher than those in the Iron Age assemblage (Table 8.40). Jewell (1962) identified the presence of small cattle in the Roman period but also greater variation in size than in the Iron Age with the appearance of larger stock. Possible reasons for this include the importation of stock and the improvements in size of native stock. There may also have been regional variations in size.

The animal bone assemblage from Birdlip did not reflect a wealthy site. Cattle and sheep were mainly kept until old which indicates they were utilised fully until too old for working or were barren, with fewer animals kept mainly for their meat. The high incidence of severe pathologies also indicates some cattle and horse being overworked which suggests limited replacement. The assemblage from Birdlip does fit in with those from nearby rural and urban sites and appears to be typical of the Cotswolds region. At present it is not certain how the Roman site relates to the earlier Iron Age site situated nearby, but the assemblages from both periods were very similar and imply a continuation of husbandry practices.

Other sites
By Adrienne Powell

Summary

Apart from the sites discussed above, none of the other animal bone assemblages from the road scheme were considered worthy of any analysis beyond the assessment stage.

Table 8.40   Comparison of measurements from Iron Age (Dobney and Jacques 1990) and Roman periods, Birdlip Quarry.

Species	Element	Measurement	Iron Age	Period 1	Period 2
Cattle	Radius	BFp	60.55 –63.75	-	61.30 –81.80
	Humerus	Bd	67.60 –79.65	70.00	66.00 –85.00
		BT	59.00 –68.85	65.90	50.60 –78.30
	Tibia	Bd	57.05 –59.60	40.30	52.20 –65.10
	Metacarpal	GL	170.80 –176.20	-	171.00 –82.00
		Bp	43.25 –54.50	51.80 –62.90	49.00 –61.80
	Metatarsal	GL	196.10	212.00 –225.00	184.00 –23.00
		Bp	39.75 –44.00	39.60 –51.50	41.20 –53.00
Horse	Humerus	Bd	74.95 –75.25	71.00	68.00 –78.00
	Radius	BFp	66.10	72.00 –73.70	54.30 –80.10

The assemblages were examined in their entirety, with the exception, due to time constraints, of Street Farm and Weavers Bridge. The total identifiable fraction was estimated for the latter two sites in the same way as for the larger assemblages (Table 8.41).

The condition of the bone affects its identifiability and the amount of other information which can be recovered, and hence an assemblage's suitability for further analysis. Therefore, the condition of the examined bone was rated on a scale of 1 to 5 for each group of fragments (context or bag). Condition 1 describes bone in excellent or very good preservation, with little post-depositional damage; condition 2 describes bone which may be identifiable to species but which may not retain fully such other data as butchery or gnawing; condition 3 describes bone identifiable to species and element but with little other information preserved; condition 4 indicates few bones identifiable beyond element; and condition 5 describes greatly altered material, only identifiable as 'bone' (Table 8.42). The proportions of the main domestic animals in the identified fraction of the assemblage has also been calculated (Tables 8.43), although as with condition, sites with assemblages containing less than 100 fragments are excluded.

Highgate House

The bone from this site comes from features ranging from prehistoric to Romano-British in date, but most is from the middle-late Iron Age contexts. The level of identification overall is low (17%) and the condition of the bone is moderate to poor. The bones of cattle are the most frequent in all the dated groups and include an articulating adult radius and ulna pair. Sheep/goat and horse bones are also frequent, the former including neonatal material. Pig is present in low numbers. A skull and partial skeleton of a water vole (*Arvicola terrestris*) occurs in a sample from the undated context 139. Butchery marks, gnawing and burning are present.

Five Mile House

Two bones in poor condition were retrieved from this site, the single identifiable bone is sheep/goat.

Duntisbourne Leer

A single unidentifiable fragment of bone was recovered.

Field's Farm

There is only one identifiable bone in this assemblage, a pelvis from an adult horse, the remainder consist mainly of eroded fragments, including some splinters of sheep-sized long bone.

Daglingworth Quarry

The large identifiable portion of this assemblage consists of a partial toad skeleton.

Ermin Street sections

Much of the bone in this assemblage is in good condition, and a high proportion is identifiable to species (70%). Almost half of these are sheep/goat, both adult and juveniles represented, with the remainder largely cattle and pig, equally divided, and one specimen of horse. Gnawmarks are present.

Lynches Trackway

The condition of the bone from this site is variable: the early Iron Age/Romano-British and some of the undated material is in good condition, and most of the early Romano-British bone is moderately well preserved. However, the remainder of the bone, including the largest group from the site, the Iron Age/Romano-British material, is in poor condition, resulting in a relatively low degree of identifiability overall (17%). Cattle bones are the most frequent in all the dated groups, while the proportion of sheep/goat appears to increase through time. Horse bones are present in the early Romano-British material. The skull of a small vole in the undated group may represent a burrowing intrusion. The assemblage is not large enough or closely enough dated to yield much information on husbandry practice.

Burford Road

Most of the bone in this assemblage is from medieval to post-medieval and post-medieval/modern contexts. The later material is mostly in moderate condition, while the remainder is largely in poor condition. The single identifiable Romano-British bone is cattle, while sheep/goat and pig are present in the medieval to post-medieval material, and horse, cattle and sheep/goat bones are present in the post-medieval/modern.

Cherry Tree Lane

The bone in this assemblage is in poor condition, consisting mainly of eroded unidentifiable fragments. The identifiable bone consists of fragments of cattle humerus, pelvis and femur.

Norcote Farm

The bone is poorly preserved and largely unidentifiable, the identifiable bone consists of a horse pelvis from the undated material, and 2 fragments of cattle tibia from the 1st century AD.

Witpit Lane

Although most of the bone from this site is in poor condition, some is moderately well preserved. Nevertheless, the identifiable fraction is small: a cattle humerus and a loose lower third molar from an adult sheep in the post-medieval contexts, and a horse second phalanx from the late 12th–14th century.

Table 8.41 Bone from the remaining smaller assemblages.

Site		?BA	Prehistoric	IA/ prehistoric	EIA/RB	M-LIA	LIA	IA	IA/RB	ERB	LRB
Highgate House	Total		13	168		176	254	48			
	Ident.		1	22		25	40	13			
Five Mile House	Total										
	Ident.										
Duntisbourne Leer	Total									1	
	Ident.									0	
Field's Farm	Total									6	
	Ident.									0	
Daglingworth Quarry	Total										
	Ident.										
Ermin St Sections	Total										
	Ident.										
Lynches Trackway	Total				22				218	99	
	Ident.				14				19	24	
Burford Road	Total									1	
	Ident.									1	
Cherry Tree Lane	Total		4					2			
	Ident.		0					0			
Norcote Farm	Total									8	
	Ident.									2	
Witpit Lane	Total										
	Ident.										
Preston Enclosure	Total					685					
	Ident.					157					
St Augustine's Lane	Total	6	48								
	Ident.	6	0								
St Augustine's Farm South	Total		99								
	Ident.		3								
Ermin Farm	Total					32		47			
	Ident.					7		16			
Cirencester Road	Total										
	Ident.										
Lower Street Furlong	Total		7								
	Ident.		0								
Westfield Farm	Total										
	Ident.										
Latton Roman Pond	Total									41	32
	Ident.									4	8
Court Farm	Total	1	1					90	31	255	
	Ident.	0	0					4	5	66	
nosniwb	Total										
	Ident.										
cirenwb	Total										
	Ident.										
latwb	Total										
	Ident.										
swglwb	Total										
	Ident.										
Total	Total	7	172	168	22	893	254	187	249	411	32
	Ident.	6	4	22	14	189	40	33	24	97	8

RB	?RB/ later	RB/ medieval	RB/ post-medieval	Medieval	Medieval/ post-medieval	Prehistoric/ post-medieval	Post-medieval/ modern	Undated	Total
8								85	752
1								25	127
							2		2
							1		1
									1
									0
54									60
1									1
							27		27
							25		25
								44	44
								31	31
							1	30	370
							0	6	63
1					20		14	7	43
0					4		9	2	16
					24	2		19	51
					4	0		0	4
								57	65
								1	3
			10				19		29
			1				2		3
									685
									157
							2	17	73
							2	3	11
									99
									3
								45	124
								16	39
								1	1
								0	0
									7
									0
19							1	32	52
0							0	0	0
36	185	6	26					413	739
9	0	3	8					39	71
7				2			22	69	478
5				2			1	3	86
								42	42
								17	17
								1	1
								1	1
								14	14
								8	8
								1	1
								0	0
125	185	6	26	12	44	2	88	877	3760
16	0	3	8	3	8	0	40	152	667

Table 8.42   Condition of the animal bone in the smaller assemblages.

Site	Date	Condition				
		1	2	3	4	5
Highgate House	? Prehistoric					100
	Iron Age/prehistoric			9	21	70
	Middle-late Iron Age			22	65	13
	Late Iron Age		4	25	71	
	Iron Age			8	92	
	Romano-British				75	25
	Undated		1	48		51
	Sub-total		1	22	51	26
Lynches Trackway	Early Iron Age/Romano-British		100			
	Iron Age/Romano-British					100
	Early Romano-British			79	21	
	Post-medieval					100
	Undated		13	10		77
	Sub-total		7	22		65
Preston Enclosure	Middle-late Iron Age			41	37	22
Ermin Farm	Middle-late Iron Age		41	38		22
	Iron Age		2	79	11	9
	Undated			53	47	
	Sub-total		11	59	21	9
Latton Roman Pond	Early Romano-British		3	6	84	6
	Late Romano-British		22	3		75
	Romano-British		2	41	17	39
	? Romano-British/later					100
	Romano-British/medieval		83	17		
	Romano-British/post-medieval.		8	69		23
	Undated		1	61	17	20
	Sub-total		3	40	14	43
Street Farm	Medieval		10	48	35	6
	Medieval/post-medieval		17	75	8	
	Post-medieval/modern Modern		46	13	38	2
	Undated	3	20	25	30	21
	Sub-total	2	24	28	32	14
Court Farm	?Bronze Age			100		
	Prehistoric					100
	Iron Age	1	1	17	66	16
	Iron Age/Romano-British				65	35
	Early Romano-British		18	33	10	38
	Romano-British			86		14
	Medieval		100			
	Post-medieval				100	
	Undated			17		83
	Sub-total		10	24	27	38
Weavers Bridge	Late Romano-British			97	3	
	Undated		2	3	94	
	Sub-total			79	20	

Table 8.43   Main domestic mammals in the smaller assemblages.

Site	Date	% of identified fragments				No.
		Horse	Cattle	Sheep	Pig	
Highgate House	? Prehistoric		100			1
	Iron Age/prehistoric	27	68		5	22
	Middle-late Iron Age		60	40		25
	Late Iron Age	13	68	15	5	40
	Iron Age	19	63	19		16
	Romano-British		100			1
	Undated	23	5	5	5	22
Lynches Trackway	Early Iron Age/Romano-British		93	7		14
	Iron Age/Romano-British		63	37		19
	Early Romano-British	21	58	21		24
	Undated	17	17			6
Preston Enclosure	Middle-late Iron Age	13	39	41	5	157
Ermin Farm	Middle-late Iron Age		29	71		7
	Iron Age	6	6	75	13	16
	Undated			100		16
Latton Roman Pond	Early Romano-British	100				4
	Late Romano-British		100			8
	Romano-British	89	11			9
	Romano-British/medieval	67	33			3
	Romano-British/post-medieval	50	38	13		8
	Undated	51	49	3		39
Street Farm	Medieval	15	23	38	23	13
	Medieval/post-medieval	33		67		6
	Post-medieval/modern	14	41	27	9	22
	Undated	20	20	18	7	55
Court Farm	Iron Age	25	75			4
	Iron Age/Romano-British		20	80		5
	Early Romano-British	17	36	30	2	66
	Romano-British			100		5
	Medieval			100		2
	Post-medieval	100				1
	Undated		33		67	3
Weavers Bridge	Late Romano-British	6	61	30	3	64
	Undated	71		24		17

Preston Enclosure

Most of the bone in this assemblage is in moderate to poor condition and the proportion of identifiable bone is 23%. The bones of cattle and sheep/goat, in similar proportions, comprise the bulk of the identifiable material, while horse, followed by pig, is less frequent. The only bones of other species present are two of dog. Measurable bones are present, as is evidence of gnawing.

St Augustine's Lane

The condition of the bone in this assemblage is variable. Those from the Bronze Age and post-medieval contexts are in moderately good condition, the former comprises six loose adult horse teeth, and the latter an adult sheep/goat mandible and a cattle tibia which has been sawn through. The remaining bone, from prehistoric and undated contexts, is in poor condition, the identifiable material being cattle.

St Augustine's Farm South

The condition of the bone in this assemblage is poor, largely due to the high frequency of eroded or calcined material. The identifiable bones are two fragments of a horse radius and one cattle bone, large mammal limb bone fragments are frequent in the remainder.

Ermin Farm

The bone from this site, particularly that from the Iron Age contexts, is mostly in moderate to good condition. Sheep/goat bones predominate in the identified material and include ageable jaws and bones. Cattle is the only other species present in the middle to late Iron Age contexts, however horse and pig (the latter more frequent than cattle and including a male canine) are also present in the Iron Age contexts. Burnt and gnawed bone occurs. Although there is a relatively high proportion of identifiable bone present (31%), much of the bone is from undated contexts, and the quantity of identifiable bone is small.

Cirencester Road

A single unidentifiable fragment of bone is present.

Lower Street Furlong

Several fragments of eroded large mammal long bone, unidentifiable to species.

Westfield Farm

The bones from this site are in poor condition, the high fragment count in the Romano-British and undated material being due to the presence in each case of one highly fragmented long bone from a large mammal.

Latton 'Roman Pond'

This group of bones is one of the largest of the smaller assemblages, but has a low proportion of identified material, due to the high degree of fragmentation and the poor condition of much of the bone, although a substantial proportion is in moderate condition. Horse and cattle bones dominate the assemblage, sheep/goat is only represented by two bones. The fragmentary head, vertebrae and ribs of an adult male horse occur in the undated, possibly Roman ditch upcast (context 395), and it is possible that the limb bones from other contexts come from the same animal, which may have been a disturbed burial.

Street Farm

This site produced bone from features ranging in date from the medieval to post-medieval/modern, of which *c.* 50% were examined. There is a high level of identification and the condition of the bone is moderate to good overall, although it is poorer in the earlier groups. Sheep/goat bones are the most frequent of the domestic species in the medieval and medieval to post-medieval groups and, although the bones of cattle become more frequent in the post-medieval/modern group, sheep/goat bones are still numerous and include a pathological specimen of a radius. Horse and pig bones are also present. Other species represented are cat (several bones from an undated context) and unidentified bird (two bones) in the post-medieval/modern group. Butchery marks are present. The estimated number of identified bones from each period was not large enough to justify more detailed work.

Court Farm

The bone from this site comes from features ranging from Iron Age to post-medieval/modern, however most of the material is Iron Age and Romano-British, and most of the identifiable bone comes from Romano-British contexts. The higher level of identifiability in this group is related to the condition of the bone: moderate to good, whereas the bone from the other groups is more poorly preserved. Sheep/goat bones are the most frequent overall and include, in the early Romano-British group, a pair of right and left goat frontals and horn cores, the only positively identified goat in the entire assemblage. Also in this group, cattle bones are slightly more common than sheep/goat, horse bones are relatively frequent, pig is present and gnawed and burnt bone occurs. Measurable bones are present.

Weavers Bridge

The proportion of this assemblage which was examined (69%) has a low content of identified bone, although the condition of the assemblage is moderate as a whole. Cattle bones are the most frequent, but sheep/goat are also frequent. Horse and pig are present in lower numbers in the dated contexts, the former including loose juvenile cheek teeth. One bird bone is present.

Watching brief: NOSNI section

A high proportion of the few bones present are identifiable, but although some of the material is in moderately good condition (2), much of it is poorly preserved. Most of the identifiable fragments are cattle, with sheep/goat also common, one bone each of horse and pig occurs.

Watching brief: Cirencester section

The single bone recovered is of pig.

Watching brief: Latton section

The few bones in this assemblage are in poor condition (4), the identifiable material consists mainly of cattle, with one sheep/goat bone.

Watching brief (SWGLWB)

One bone unidentifiable to species.

Conclusion

The opportunity for comparing animal husbandry at different periods and in different environments, provided by this project's transect across the Cotswolds, cannot unfortunately be realised, since the quantity of identifiable bone from the smaller assemblages is too little to make meaningful comparisons. However, it may be said that in all the assemblages containing more than 100 fragments, whether Iron Age or Romano-British, cattle is the species most frequently represented, except at Preston Enclosure, Ermin Farm, and the medieval and medieval/post-medieval groups from Street Farm, where sheep/goat bones are more frequent.

HUMAN SKELETAL MATERIAL
By Angela Boyle

Trinity Farm

A small quantity of burnt bone was recovered from the fill (9) of a Beaker pit. Only 2 g of cremated bone was present and nothing was identifiable.

St Augustine's Lane

A pit (3109) was found within a ring ditch, though it was not centrally located. It was interpreted as a possible secondary cremation burial and was found to contain a small quantity of unidentifiable burnt bone. This was present in the 4–0.5 mm residue.

Lynches Trackway

A single skeleton (103) was found in a tightly crouched position on its left side within a small oval grave cut (101) and oriented north-west-south-east. The grave was located on the scarp of a hill (Chapter 3, Fig. 3.33). Approximately half of the grave had been removed by the machine cut for a footpath. The skeleton was virtually complete and preservation was excellent. The assessment of age was based on stage of epiphyseal fusion (Gentry Steele and Bramblett 1988) and degree of dental attrition (Brothwell 1981, 72) and was estimated as 17–25 years. Skull and pelvic morphology indicated that the skeleton was male (Workshop 1980). Stature was estimated at 1.67 m using the formula of Trotter and Gleser (reproduced in Brothwell 1981, 101). Details of the dentition appear in Table 8.44

The burial was unaccompanied, and, although the crouched position is suggestive of a prehistoric date it is not necessarily indicative of one. However, two samples of human bone produced radiocarbon dates of 355–289 cal BC and 235–33 cal BC (2 sigma R24151/22) which places the burial in the middle Iron Age.

Table 8.44 Lynches Trackway Skeleton 103, dentition.

-	-	-	-	-	-	-	-	-	-	-	-	-	6	7	-
8	7	6	5	4	3	2	1	1	2	3	4	5	6	7	8

- indicates tooth and socket absent

Cirencester, Watching Brief

A single cremation burial (2) was recovered during the watching brief north-west of Whitelands Wood. It was badly damaged and there were only three sherds of Roman pottery associated. In addition five iron nails were also present. It is therefore possible that the burial had originally been placed within a wooden box of the type defined by Philpott (1991, 12–21). The results of the analysis of the cremated bone appear in the table below.

Birdlip Quarry

A small quantity of cremated bone (988) was recovered from within a pottery vessel (978). The vessel had been placed near the entrance of a building and may have been a foundation deposit. The fill associated with a second vessel was also sampled but found to contain no cremated bone. Both vessels were Roman in date. Only a very small quantity of cremated bone was present in the 4–0.5 mm residue and nothing was identifiable.

Weavers Bridge

A broken and incomplete skull (sf 1) was recovered from an undated layer of silty clay (4). It was assessed as a male individual of 33–45 years on the basis of skull morphology (Workshop 1980) and dental attrition (Brothwell 1981, 72). The date of the skull is uncertain.

CHARRED AND WATERLOGGED PLANT REMAINS
By Ruth Pelling

Introduction

Excavation of sites along the route of Roman Ermin Street included a sampling program for the recovery of charred and waterlogged plant remains. The volume of deposit sampled varied depending on the period and nature of the site excavated, and ranged from 2 to 104 litres. Samples were processed at the Oxford Archaeological Unit. Charred remains were processed by bulk water separation and flots retained on a 500 µm mesh. Dried flots were submitted for assessment. Waterlogged deposits were usually subsampled and 1 kg processed by a simple wash over technique. The flots were collected onto 250 µm sieves and kept wet. One sample from below Ermin Street was recognised as waterlogged at the processing stage only. A total of 17 litres was processed by bulk flotation and the flot was kept wet.

Methods

All flots were first assessed by scanning under a binocular microscope at x10 magnification. The abundance of charred remains and the character of the species present was noted. Samples were selected for analysis on the basis of this assessment.

Selected flots were sorted at x10 to x20 magnification. Identifications of seeds and chaff were made based on morphological characteristics and by reference to the modern comparative collection held at the Oxford University Museum. Nomenclature and taxonomic order follows Clapham *et al.* (1989).

Charcoal was identified from several of the sites. Fragments were picked out from the 2 mm mesh. For small flots all fragments were extracted and examined. For larger flots, notably from Birdlip Quarry, the first 10 or 20 fragments randomly selected were examined and the remaining fragments examined in transverse section to ensure no additional species were present. Each fragment was fractured and examined in transverse section at magnification of x20 and x40, and in tangential and radial longitudinal sections at x100 and x200 magnification. Identifications were made by reference to the key for European Hardwoods in Schweingruber (1978) and by comparison with modern reference material.

The results are shown in Tables 8.45–8.59. In the case of cereals the plant part identified is given (grain, rachis etc.). In all other identifications the plant part is the seed, nutlet etc. unless otherwise stated. Quantification of cereal grains was based on embryo ends. The quantification of *Corylus avellana* (hazel) nut shell fragments was based on the number of fragments held within the 2 mm mesh. Smaller fragments could not be identified with certainty and were in some cases too numerous to be manageable. Using the number of fragments is a somewhat arbitrary method of quantification given the potential for variation of fragment size. It is the method most commonly used, however, and does provide an indication of general relative abundance.

Sites included in the assessment but for which no further identifications were made are included in the discussion but not in the tables.

The Neolithic period *(Tables 8.45–8.47)*

Birdlip Quarry

Eleven possible prehistoric samples were taken from nine pits. Two samples which contained useful quantities of charred material were analysed in detail (Tables 8.45 and 8.47, samples 5 and 88). Three further samples (from contexts 202, 356 and 361) contained single grains of *Triticum* sp. (wheat), indeterminate

cereal grain and a fragment of *Corylus avellana* (hazel) nut shell.

Sample 5 is the only sample which was taken from a context (pit 88) containing dateable material. Flint flakes of possible early Neolithic date were recovered from this shallow, oval pit. Sample 88 was taken from a nearby pit (pit 620). Small numbers of poorly preserved grain were recovered from both samples. Grains of *Triticum* sp. (wheat) were most commonly identified, one of which was from a hulled variety. Several other *Triticum* sp. grains were more hulled than naked in appearance with a flat ventral surface and slight longitudinal ridges suggesting the grains had been charred while held inside a tightly fitting glume. Distortion was such, however, that it was not possible to definitely assign grain as hulled or naked. *Hordeum* sp. (barley) forms a secondary group of cereal grains. Fragments of *Corylus avellana* (hazel) nut shell were by far the most common component of the samples. A total of 321 fragments were identified in sample 5 and 51 fragments from sample 88.

Duntisbourne Grove

Twelve samples from prehistoric contexts contained charred material, of which five were analysed in detail. All twelve samples were taken from pits containing Neolithic flintwork and other general debris thought to be related to domestic activity. Five samples were selected for detailed analysis, three from pit 94, and two from pit 142. The results are displayed in Table 8.45. All five samples contained large amounts of *Corylus avellana* (hazel) nut shell fragments. Occasional cereal grains were also identified. Occasional grains of *Triticum* sp. (wheat) were identified in sample 10 (pit 142) one of which could be identified as being of a hulled variety. The presence of *T. spelta* is suggested by a single glume base in sample 14. A second glume base could not be identified. *T. spelta* is not known prior to the Bronze Age. It is likely, therefore, that sample 14, taken from the uppermost fill of pit 142 (context 143) contains some later contamination.

Table 8.45 Neolithic charred plant remains.

Site	Birdlip Quarry		Duntisbourne Grove				
Sample	5	88	8	12	13	10	14
Context	89	619	113	111	113	168	143
Type	Pit 88	Pit 620	Pit 94	Pit 94	Pit 94	Pit 142	Pit 142
Volume (litres)	44	14	10	30	52	28	14
Triticum sp. hulled grain	-	1	-	-	-	1	-
Triticum sp. grain	11	1	-	-	-	2	-
Hordeum sp. grain	2	1	-	-	2	1	-
Cerealia indet grain	18	5	2	-	2	6	2
Tritcum cf. *Spelta* glume base	-	-	-	-	-	-	1
T. spelta/dicoccum glume base	-	-	-	-	-	-	1
Corylus avellana nut shell frags.	321	51	189	128	307	332	68
Chenopodiaceae seeds	-	1	-	-	-	-	-
Gramineae, small seeded	1	-	-	-	-	-	-

Table 8.46   Late Neolithic/Bronze Age charred remains.

Site	Trinity Farm			Duntisbourne Leer
Sample	1	2	3	1
Context	9	11	2	3
Date	LN/EBA	LN/EBA	LN/EBA	LN/BA ?
Type	PIT 10	PIT 8	PIT 12	PIT 4
Volume (litres)	104	20	28	12
Hordeum sp. grain	2	-	-	-
Cerealia indet grain	4	-	-	-
T. spelta/dioccum glume base	2	-	-	-
Corylus avellana nut shell frags.	143	29	66	743
Chenopodiaceae seeds	1	-	-	-

Table 8.47   Early prehistoric charcoal.

Site		Birdlip Quarry		Trinity Farm	Duntisbourne Grove	
Sample		5	88	1	8	13
Context		89	619	9	113	113
Pomoideae	Apple, hawthorn etc.	11	7	9	9	14
cf. Pomoideae		-	-	1	-	-
cf. Prunus sp.	Sloe, plum, bullace etc.	6	-	-	3	-
Corylus sp.	Hazel	3	3	8	8	5
Quercus sp.	Oak	-	-	2	-	-
Indet		-	-	-	-	1
Abundance of charcoal		++	+	+	+	+

+ = identifiable fragments present; ++ = common

Free-threshing wheat was not positively identified. Grains of *Hordeum* sp. (barley) were identified in sample 10 from pit 142 and sample 13 from pit 94.

Three samples contain identifiable charcoal, two of which (8 and 13) were examined in detail. Both samples contain Pomoideae charcoal (apple, pear, hawthorn etc.) and *Corylus* sp. (hazel) while sample 8 also contained some possible *Prunus* sp. (sloe, plum, bullace, etc.). A *Crataegus* sp. (hawthorn) stone was provisionally identified in sample 15 (pit 142) during the assessment. This suggests that the Pomoideae charcoal may be of hawthorn.

The late Neolithic/early Bronze Age period

Trinity Farm

Single samples were taken from each of the three pits (8, 10 and 12) located in the north-east corner of the excavation area which contained Beaker pottery. All three samples produced fragments of *Corylus avellana* (hazel) nut shell. In addition, sample 1 (pit 10) produced a spikelet fork of *Triticum* sp. (wheat) and two grains of *Hordeum* sp. (barley). The *Triticum* glume bases were too poorly preserved to enable identification to species. A single seed of indeterminate Chenopodiaceae, identified from sample 1, was the only weed seed recovered (Table 8.46).

No obvious differences in assemblage were noticed between pits, other than a slightly greater quantity of material in pit 10 (sample 1) which is likely to be related to a greater volume of material sampled.

The Bronze Age period

St Augustine's Farm South

A total of 39 samples were taken from ditch segments and from the two pits. Scanning of the samples indicated the presence of very infrequent cereal in two samples (sample 1, context 2010 and sample 22, context 3184), consisting of two indeterminate grain and one barley rachis. Two samples (13, context 3022 and 17, context 3113) also contained occasional fragments of *Quercus* sp. (oak) charcoal.

St Augustine's Lane

Seven samples were assessed for charred plant remains. The scanning results indicate a general background of very poorly preserved cereal grains, only two of which, a *Triticum* grain and a *Hordeum* grain, were identifiable.

Miscellaneous earlier prehistoric features

Duntisbourne Leer

Three samples were taken from pit features. One sample taken from the fill of pit 4 (sample 1) produced

Table 8.48 The later prehistoric charred plant remains.

		Highgate House	Ermin Farm	Ermin Farm
	Sample	11	1	7
	Date	M-L IA	MIA	MIA
	Type	Ditch	Ditch	Ditch
	Volume (litres)	18	17	32
Triticum spelta	spelt wheat grain	-	-	2
Triticum sp. hulled	wheat grain, hulled	4	3	6
Triticum sp.	wheat grain	1	-	2
Hordeum sp.	barley grain, hulled	1	-	4
Hordeum sp.	barley grain	3	1	1
Cerealia indet	grain	5	2	7
Triticum spelta	spelt wheat glume base	-	3	8
Triticum spelta	small glume base	-	1	-
Triticum cf. *spelta* glume	glume base	-	2	2
Triticum spelta/dicoccum	spelt/emmer wheat glume base	-	10	50
Triticum spelta/dicoccum	spelt/emmer rachis internode	-	2	-
Cerealia indet	detached embryo	-	-	1
Corylus avellana	hazel nut shell fragments	-	-	1
Silene sp.		-	-	1
Montia fontana	Blinks	-	-	1
Chenopodium album L.	Fat hen	-	-	1
Chenopodium sp.		-	1	-
Atriplex sp.	Orache	-	1	-
Chenopodiaceae		-	-	3
Vicia/Lathyrus sp.	Vetch, Tare/Vetchling	-	-	1
Leguminosae small seeded		-	1	4
Labiate		-	-	3
Polygonaceae		-	-	1
Solonaceae		-	-	1
Galium aperine L.	Goosegrass, Cleavers	-	2	1
cf. Compositae gall		-	-	3
Eleocharis palustris	Common spikerush	-	-	1
Cyperaceae		-	-	10
Bromus subsect *Eubromus*	Brome grass	1	1	20
Bromus sterillis	Barren brome	-	-	7
Gramineae	Grass, large seeded	1	2	23
Gramineae	Grass, small seeded	-	10	26
Weed indet		-	4	10
Total cereal grain		14	6	21
Total cereal chaff		-	18	61
Total weeds		2	22	117
Total items		16	46	200

a large quantity of *Corylus avellana* (hazel) nut shell, 743 fragments in a total of 12 litres of deposit. No cereal remains were present. The dating is unclear for this pit, but it is thought to be Neolithic or early Bronze Age (Table 8.46).

The earlier prehistoric economy

The charred plant remains, when taken together, provide a broad picture of the economy of the region from the early Neolithic into the Bronze Age. The evidence from Birdlip Quarry is very useful as it may be the earliest example of charred plant remains from the region to date.

The remains are likely to represent the waste from food preparation or the accidental burning of crops during processing activities involving heat. General low density cereal cultivation is suggested from the early Neolithic until at least the early Bronze Age. Both wheat and barley were being cultivated. A glumed wheat which is likely to be emmer (*Triticum dicoccum*) was cultivated although identification was not possible. The cultivation of both emmer and bread-type wheat, hulled and naked six-row barley is known from the evidence of other Neolithic and early Bronze Age sites (Helbaek 1952; Moffet *et al.* 1989; Greig 1991). There appears to be no increase in the extent of cereal cultivation in the region into the Bronze Age. Indeed, the evidence is less extensive in the early Bronze Age than for the Neolithic.

Wild food resources are likely to have formed a major component of the diet alongside cereals. Hazel nut shell forms a major component of the assemblages throughout the early prehistoric period. Assessment of the relative importance of hazelnut and cereals is difficult given that hazel nuts were quantified by shell fragments and cereals by whole grain. It is also likely that other wild resources were utilised which have not left any evidence in the archaeological record. Fruits have been recorded from Neolithic and Bronze Age sites, notably crab apple, raspberry, blackberry, sloe and hawthorn (Moffet *et al.* 1989). Again, it is difficult to assess the relative importance of such finds given the differential chances of preservation. Cereal grain may come into contact with fire in the course of processing and hazelnut shell may be thrown onto fires once the kernel had been removed. While crab-apples may be heated in order to dry them, fruits would not generally come into contact with fire other than during cooking, and are therefore likely to be under-represented in the archaeological record. So, while no fruit remains were recovered from the prehistoric sites, the association of large numbers of hazelnut shell with cereal remains and fruits on other sites of the same period would suggest a similar utilisation of such wild resources. The charcoal suggests that suitable woodland or scrub habitats within which such fruits could be found, were available.

The later prehistoric period

The middle Iron Age (Table 8.48)

Preston Enclosure

Thirty samples were taken from the enclosure ditch and internal features. Nine samples were assessed of which eight contained low densities of charred remains. Occasional cereal remains were present, although preservation was such that grain and glume bases could only be identified as far as hulled *Triticum* sp. (emmer/spelt wheat). Occasional grains of *Hordeum* sp. (barley) were present and very infrequent weed seeds including a small legume and a Cyperaceae. Fragments of *Quercus* sp. (oak) charcoal were provisionally identified from one pit (context 8).

Ermin Farm

Seven samples were assessed. Two samples taken from ditch sections (contexts 17 and 32) were analysed in detail. *Triticum spelta* (spelt wheat) is represented by both grain and glume bases. More poorly preserved glume bases could not be identified to species so are recorded as *T. spelta/dicoccum* (spelt/emmer). *Hordeum* sp. (barley) was also recorded, including grains which display clear signs of being hulled. The wheat grains outnumber barley grains.

A single fragment of *Corylus avellana* (hazel) nut shell may suggest the collection of wild nuts.

Weed seeds were present in both samples. Grasses form the major component of the weed flora in both assemblages, including *Bromus* subsect *Eubromus* (brome grass) and *Bromus sterillis* (barren brome) as well as large seeded unidentifiable grasses. Small seeded grasses were also common. It is not unusual to find large numbers of grass seeds in prehistoric charred assemblages and it has been suggested that large proportions of grasses are associated with shallow cultivation (Jones 1984b). They could also grow as arable weeds invading from the field margins. Seeds of *Bromus* spp. can be frequent in Iron Age grain assemblages and occasionally dominate which has led to suggestions of deliberate harvesting (eg. Hubbard 1975; Jones 1978). Large grasses may have entered the assemblage as a contaminate of grain, but small seeded grasses must have come in through another route.

Eleocharis palustris (common spike rush) requires at least seasonal flooding, while many of the Cyperaceae are characteristic of damp ground. *Eleocharis palustris* is today not regarded as an arable weed but is more characteristic of damp grassland. It is a species commonly associated with charred cereal assemblages from the Iron Age period which has led to a generally widely held view of cultivation of agriculturally marginal land reaching onto the floodplains in regions like the Upper Thames Valley. These species may indicate the similar cultivation of marginal land which was either seasonally flooded itself or close enough for rhizomous species to invade. Given the number of grass seeds it is also possible that the seeds have entered the assemblage with cut grass. *Galium aperine* which was present in both samples, is an autumn germinating species and commonly associated with autumn sown crops. The remaining weed species are generally common species of arable or disturbed ground, or were too poorly preserved to enable identification to species.

The samples are dominated by weed seeds and glume bases, that is, the by-products of cereal processing. Chaff and weeds together form 87% of the assemblages of sample 1 and 89% of sample 7. Some cereal processing was clearly taking place on the site, albeit possibly on a small scale. It is not clear whether cereals were being produced at the site. It is difficult to assess the relative importance of cereal production on the strength of two samples. It does appear, however, given the general paucity of remains and the scarcity of cereal grains, that cereal production was not on a large scale. Furthermore, cereal grain is less likely to be burnt the further from the site of production it moves and the greater the perceived value becomes. It is likely, therefore, that cereal grains were an important commodity and that whole spikelets were being brought into the site and small quantities were processed when and as they were needed.

Highgate House

A total of 28 samples were taken from enclosure ditch sections, pits and occupation layers. Several samples from upper pit fills contained modern cereal debris interpreted as the remains of stubble burning. Of the remaining samples, small quantities of charred cereal remains were noted in sixteen samples during the assessment. The charred remains include very occasional grains of *Triticum* sp. (wheat) including occasional grains identifiable as *T. spelta* (spelt wheat) or hulled *Triticum* sp. (spelt/emmer wheat), occasional grains of *Hordeum* sp. (barley) and occasional indeterminate grains. A single *Arrhenatherum* tuber (pit 122) and a hazelnut shell fragment (context 139) were also noted. The largest of the samples (11/12) taken from an enclosure ditch terminus (feature 131) was fully sorted and analysed.

Sample 11/12 contained a total of 14 cereal grains. No *Triticum* grains could be convincingly assigned as *T. spelta*, although 4 grains were identifiable as hulled wheat. Hulled grains of *Hordeum* sp. (barley) were identified. Two weed seeds were present, a single *Bromus* subsect *Eubromus* and a large grass.

On the evidence of the charred remains agricultural activity appears to have been minimal. Preservation was poor thus it is likely that the absence of cereal chaff is a reflection of preservation. The cereals identified are in keeping with evidence for the Iron Age elsewhere in southern Britain. It is not possible to comment on cereal processing activities given the absence of chaff and weed seeds.

Middle Duntisbourne

Eight samples were submitted for assessment. The samples were taken from enclsoure ditch fills (contexts 4, 121, 120 and 310). Four samples contained occasional grains of hulled wheat, slightly more frequent *Hordeum* sp. (barley) and very occasional weed seeds. Fragments of Pomoideae (apple, hawthorn etc.) and *Quercus* sp. (oak) charcoal were noted. The samples were not sorted and analysed fully. The remaining samples contained very occasional indeterminate cereal grains. The samples suggest some settlement activity but do not indicate any arable cultivation or cereal processing on any notable scale. It is possible that more intensive settlement activity is located nearby.

Duntisbourne Grove

Seven samples were taken from ditch fills (contexts 9 and 114) and five contained small quantities of charred material which were noted in the assessment. Cereal remains include *Triticum* sp. (wheat) grain some of which may be free-threshing bread-type wheat,

and *Hordeum* sp. (barley grain). Nut shell fragments of *Corylus avellana* (hazel) were fairly numerous. It is probable that the remains represent residual redeposited material given the occurrence of early prehistoric activity. Charcoal noted during the assessment included much *Corylus/Alnus* and Pomoideae sp. (apple, hawthorn etc.) charcoal, again very similar to the early prehistoric charcoal assemblage

Miscellaneous later prehistoric features

Cherry Tree Lane (Table 8.49)

A total of thirteen samples were assessed for their charred plant content from Cherry Tree Lane. Samples were taken from two possible hearths (4 and 15) and from pits 12, 13, 35 and 47 and from ditch 40. Samples from the hearth features were very rich in charcoal. Two samples from each hearth were selected for identification of the charcoal, which was demonstrated to consist almost entirely of Pomoideous wood (apple, hawthorn etc.). Very occasional fragments of *Prunus* sp. (sloe, bullace etc.) charcoal were present. It is likely that the Pomoideae charcoal is derived from construction material of the features. Provisional identifications suggest that the charcoal in the remaining hearth samples is also of Pomoideae wood. Two samples from pits 12 and 13 (samples 10 and 9) contained one or two grains of *Triticum spelta*, *Hordeum* sp. and indeterminate cereals. The samples were not examined in detail. The remaining samples were devoid of any charred remains.

Cereal cultivation and the economy of the later prehistoric period

The analysis of the charred plant remains from the later prehistoric sites provides some information regarding the economic activities of the settlements. The cereal remains that have been identified fit the evidence from elsewhere that the principle cereal crop cultivated in southern Britain at the time was spelt wheat (Helbaek 1952, Greig 1991). Hulled barley was cultivated as a secondary crop. There is no evidence for the cultivation of emmer wheat on any of the sites. It is likely, therefore that emmer had been totally replaced by spelt wheat by this time.

In contrast to sites within the Upper Thames Valley area of Oxfordshire and the Wessex chalklands, cereal cultivation appears to have been on a small scale. While further detailed sampling is needed to provide a more conclusive picture it does appear on present evidence that the major agricultural developments and expansion witnessed elsewhere in southern Britain did not occur in the region until the Roman period. The concentration of cereal remains is very low and the weed flora is a fairly limited one in comparison to sites such as Ashville (Jones 1978) and Barton Court Farm (Jones 1986). There is an absence of the large numbers of weed species usually associated with increased intensification of arable agriculture such as

Table 8.49   The charcoal from Iron Age features at Cherry Tree Lane.

		Sample 3	1	11	12
		Context 5	5	9	9
Pomoideae	apple, hawthorn etc.	19	17	17	20
Prunus sp.	cherry, blackthorn	1	3	3	-
Abundance of charcoal		++++	++++	++++	++++

+ = identifiable fragments present; ++ = common; +++ = frequent; ++++ = abundant

large numbers of leguminous weeds and species of marginal land. The assemblages are perhaps more in line with those from floodplain sites such as Mingies Ditch in the Windrush Valley (Jones and Robinson 1993), where there appears to have been a much greater reliance on the pastoral element of the economy.

There is some evidence to suggest that cereal cultivation was supplemented by the collection of wild food plants. Nut shell fragments of *Corylus avellana*, an *Arrhenatherum* tuber and even wild grasses such as *Bromus* subsect *Eubromus* and *B. sterillis*, could have been harvested.

ERMIN STREET

Four samples, all from buried soils beneath Ermin Street were processed for the retrieval of charred plant remains (Trench 9, context 925; Trench 10, context 1059 (2 samples), Trench 8, context 877). A further sample, 602 (Trench 6, context 673), taken from deposits immediately below the construction layer of Ermin Street (Fig. 5.3) was found to contain waterlogged plant material. This was examined for evidence of the local environment of the road immediately prior to its construction. A total of 17 litres was processed by bulk water flotation and the flot collected onto a 250 µm mesh and kept wet.

The samples taken for charred plant remains produced one *Triticum spelta/dicoccum* (spelt/emmer wheat) glume base and occasional charcoal flecks only. No further comment is made on these samples.

The detailed results of analysis of sample 602 are displayed in Table 8.50. Species of damp ground, meadows or marsh predominate, generally suggestive of a damp grassland or meadow flora. The major damp grassland species present is *Ranunculus repens* (creeping buttercup), while the *Carex* species (sedges) are also included in this group, although not all species are characteristic of damp ground. Other damp grass species include, *Potentilla anserina*, *Veronica* subgen *Beccabunga* (water-speedwell), *Juncus articulatus* gp. (rush) and *J. bufonius* gp. (toad rush). Drier grassland and pasture species form a more minor group. These include *Ranunculus parviflorus* (small-flowered buttercup), *Viola* subgen *Melanium* (pansy), *Stellaria media* (lesser stichwort), *Aphanes arvensis* (parsley-piert) and *Carduus* sp. (thistle).

Arable or ruderal species are well represented in the sample. These include notably *Arenaria* sp. (sandwort), *Atriplex* sp. (orache), *Urtica dioica* (stinging nettle). Other species include *Stellaria media* (chickweed), *Chenopodium album* (fat hen), *Polygonum aviculare* (knotgrass), *Hyoscyamus niger* (henbane) and *Valerianella dentata* (narrow-fruited cornsalad). Generally, these species are of a more ruderal than arable nature.

In conclusion, the flora represented by the sample indicates an open grassland vegetation with a wetter marshy area over which the road has passed. Some ruderal elements are also present.

WEAVERS BRIDGE

Four samples were assessed for their potential for charred plant remains, two of which, sample 6 from a buried soil horizon and sample 8 from a drainage channel of unknown date, contained useful quantities of material.

Two samples, samples 6 and 7, contained useful quantities of waterlogged plant remains. Sub-samples of 1 kg were processed by hand using a simple wash-over technique for the retrieval of waterlogged remains. The samples were taken from the fills of two man-made channels, features 127 and 20. Subsamples of 1 kg were examined.

Charred plant remains *(Table 8.51)*

The charred assemblages are dominated by cereal remains. The identifiable cereal grains are dominated by free-threshing *Triticum* sp. (bread-type/rivet wheat). Short, plump grains were most frequently identified and recorded as 'compact'. Occasional longer narrow grains were also recognised and recorded as 'elongated', while intermediate grains were classified separately. Given the inherent difficulties in the identification of free-threshing wheat grains to ploidy level, no attempt was made to identify grains to species. Well preserved free-threshing wheat rachis was present, however, in both samples. Rachis of tetraploid wheat was quite common in sample 6, while a single rachis node each of tetraploid and hexaploid wheats were present in sample 8. Further, more poorly preserved, rachis fragments could not be identified to ploidy level.

It is now generally thought that the tetraploid wheat identified from many sites in England, from the early medieval period onwards, is *Triticum turgidum* (rivet wheat). Documentary evidence is available for its cultivation from the early post-medieval period

Table 8.50   The waterlogged plant remains from Ermin Street.

		Sample	602
		Context	673
		Volume	17
Ranunculus acris subsp. *acris*	Meadow Buttercup		3
Ranunculus cf. *acris*	cf. Meadow Buttercup		2
Ranunculus repens	Creeping Buttercup		35
Ranunculus cf. *reprens*	cf. Creeping Buttercup		37
Ranunculus acris/repens/bulbosus	Buttercup		56
Ranunculus parviflorus	Small-flowered Buttercup		5
Papaver cf. *dubium*	Long-headed Poppy		4
Papaver agremone	Long Prickly-head Poppy		5
Fumaria sp.	Fumitory		1
Viola subgen *Melanium*	Pansy		23
Labiate			1
Cerastium spp.	Mouse-ear Chickweed		37
Stellaria media agg.	Chickweed		7
Stellaria graminea	Lesser Stitchwort		1
Caryophyllaceae			4
Arenaria sp.	Sandwort		16
Montia fontana subsp. *chondrosperma*	Blinks		4
Chenopodium album	Fat Hen		1
Atriplex spp.	Orache		19
Chenopodiacae			3
Potentilla anserina	Silverweed		1
Potentilla reptans	Creeping Cinquefoil		3
Aphanes arvensis	Parsley-piert		67
Aethusa cynapium	Fool's Parsley		4
Polygonum aviculare	Knotgrass		2
Polygonum sp.	Knotgrass/Persicaria		5
Rumex cf. subgen *acetosa*	Sorrel		1
Rumex spp.	Docks		8
Polygonaceae			1
Urtica dioica	Common Nettle		25
Urtica urens	Small Nettle		3
Corylus avellana	Hazel nut, shell fragment		1
Hyoscyamus nigra	Henbane		2
Veronica subgen *Beccabunga*	Water-speedwell		2
Galeopsis sp.	Hemp-nettle		1
Sambucus nigra	Elder		1
Valerianella cf. *carinata*	Keel-fruited Cornsalad		1
Valerianella dentata	*Narrow-fruited Cornsalad*		8
Carduus sp.	Thistle		3
Sonchus asper	Spiny Milk- or Sow-Thistle		1
Juncus articulatus gp.			2
Carex spp.	Sedges, 3 sided		112
Carex spp.	Sedges, 2 faced		1
Gramineae	Grass, small seeded		1
Indet			4
<0.5 mm, 1/10			
Arenaria sp.	Sandwort		3
Juncus bufonius *gp.*	*Toad Rush*		3
Juncus articulatus gp.			1
Juncus sp.			1

Table 8.51   Charred plant remains, Weavers Bridge.

		Sample	6	8
		Context	28	92
		Type	Ditch	Soil
		Volume	14	20
CEREAL GRAIN				
Triticum sp.	Free-threshing wheat, compact grain		4	15
Triticum sp.	Free-threshing wheat, intermediate grain		-	6
Triticum sp.	Free-threshing wheat, elongated grain		1	6
Triticum sp.	Wheat grain		1	14
Hordeum sp.	Barley grain		-	1
Hordeum sp.	Hulled grain		-	3
Avena sp.	Oats grain		2	1
CEREAL CHAFF				
Cerealia indet			4	29
Triticum sp.	Free-threshing hexaploid wheat, rachis node		-	1
Triticum sp.	Free-threshing tetraploid rachis node		17	1
Triticum sp.	Free-threshing wheat, rachis node		6	9
Triticum sp.	Free-threshing wheat, basal rachis node		2	1
Hordeum sp.	Barley, rachis node		1	-
Avena sp.	Oats, awn fragment		-	1
Cereal sized	Indet. culm node		1	-
OTHER EDIBLE PLANTS				
Corylus avellana	Hazel nut shell frags.		-	1
Vicia/Lathyrus/Pisum sp.	Cultivated vetch/ beans/ pea etc.		-	8
WEEDS				
Agrostemma githago sp.	Corn cockle		-	1
Stellaria media agg.	Chickweed		-	1
Chenopodiaceae			1	-
Vicia/Lathyrus sp.	Vetch/tare		-	2
Leguminosae small seeded			-	1
Galium sp.	Goosegrass		-	1
Anthemis cotula L.	Stinking mayweed		-	1
Bromus subsect *Eubromus*	Grass, large seeded		1	2
Gramineae			1	1
Weed indet			2	2

(Moffett 1991), while *Triticum durum* (macaroni wheat) the other tetraploid free-threshing wheat is poorly suited to the British climate (Percival 1921). The hexaploid wheat would be a variety of bread wheat. Hexaploid wheat rachis tends to be less well preserved than tetraploid wheat and as such may be under-represented.

It is likely that the two types of wheat chaff had different uses, and therefore experience differential preservation. Bread-type wheats are more likely to be awnless, so are generally more palatable to animals and as such more likely to be used as animal feed. Rivet wheat, however, tends to produce a good quality straw and is therefore more likely to be used as thatch. In addition, there was some evidence from West Cotton, Northamptonshire, to suggest that they were sometimes grown together as a maslin (Campbell forthcoming b). Bread-type wheats produce a far superior flour for bread baking, while rivet wheat flour is more suited for biscuits, but the two flours can be mixed together for a useful multi-purpose flour (Percival 1934).

Hordeum sp. (barley) and *Avena* sp. (oats) were very occasionally identified in both samples. Both species are frequently identified as secondary crops from medieval contexts. Large legumes were also recorded from sample 8 although they were poorly preserved with no testa or hilum left to enable identification.

The weed flora was very limited in both samples. The species present are all common in medieval cereal assemblages and were frequent weeds of cornfields.

Waterlogged plant remains *(Table 8.52)*

Sample 6 produced frequent aquatic species, notably seeds of *Oenanthe aquatica* agg. (water dropwart) and *Schoenoplectus lacustris* (bulrush), which are characteristic of slow-flowing or stagnant water. Other species characteristic of slow-flowing or shallow water were present including *Apium nodiflorum* (fool's watercress), *Sagittaria sagittifolia* (arrow head) and *Sparganum* sp. (bur-reed). *Nuphar lutea* (yellow water-lilly) and *Zannicella palustris* (horned pondweed) will also grow in slow-flowing or still water in ditches

Table 8.52   Waterlogged plant remains, Weavers Bridge.

| Species | Sample | 6 | 7 |
	Context	128	22
Ranunculus cf. Acris L.	Meadow Buttercup	2	-
Ranunculus cf. Repens L.	Creeping Buttercup	5	9
*Ranunculus cf. Bulbosus.*L.	Bulbosus Buttercup	-	1
Ranunculus susect *Ranunculus*	Buttercup	8	-
Ranunculus sugen *Batrachium*	Crowfoot	88	13
Nuphar lutea (L.) Sm.	Yellow water lily	2	-
Lychnis flos-cuculi L.	Raggen Robin	1	-
Cerastium sp.	Mouse-ear chickweed	-	6
Myosoton aquaticum (L.) Moench.	Water Chickweed	32	42
Stellaria media agg.	Chickweed	4	5
Caryophyllaceae		3	1
Chenopodium sp.	Goosefoot	3	-
Atriplex patula/hortensis	Orache	18	11
Atriplex sp.	Orache	-	9
Chenopodiaceae		4	2
Rubus fruticosus agg.	Bramble, Blackberry etc.	-	1
Rubus sp.		-	1
Potentilla anserina L.	Silverweed	3	2
Rosaceae type thorn		-	1
Oenanthe aquatica agg.	Water-Dropwort	322	1
Apium nodiflorum (L.) Lag.	Fool's Watercress	23	1
Torilis japonica (Houtt) D.C	Upright Hedge-Parsley	1	-
Umbelliferae		3	-
Polygonum aviculare agg.	Knotgrass	4	2
P.lapathifloium L.	Pale Persicaria	69	19
P.persicaria L.	Red Shank, Persicaria	-	8
P.convolvulus (L.) A.Love	Black bindweed	2	4
Polygonum sp.		11	17
Rumex hydrolapathum Hudson	Water Dock	1	-
R. maritimus L.	Golden Dock	11	14
Rumex sp.		10	13
Polygonacae		3	1
Urtica dioica L.	Common Stinging Nettle	10	13
U. urens L.	Small Nettle	2	-
Menyanthes trifoliata L.	Bogbean	1	-
Solanum sp.	Nightshade	2	1
Mentha sp.	Mint	43	-
Galeopsis sp.	Hemp-Nettle	-	1
Lycopus europaeus L.	Gipsywort	15	-
Plantago *major* L.	Plantain	3	6
Sambucus nigra L.	Elder	-	1
Arctium cf. *Lappa* L.	Great Burdock	-	1
Carduus/Cirsium sp.	Thistle	2	3
Leontodon sp.	Hawkbit	-	1
Picris echioides L.	Bristly Ox-tongue	-	2
Sonchus asper (L.) Hill	Spiny Milk-Thistle	3	4
Taraxacum sp.	Dandelion	-	1
Compositae		1	6
Alisma plantago-aquatica L.	Water Plantain	61	12
Sagittaria sagittiflia L.	Arrow-head	4	5
Potamogeton sp.	Pondweed	4	4
Zannichellia palustris L.	Horned Pondweed	38	-
Juncus effusus agg.	Rushes	8	-
J. bufonis agg.	Rushes	2	-
J. articulatus agg.	Rushes	9	-
Juncus sp.	Rushes	3	-
Sparganium sp.	Bur-Reed	8	-
Scheonoplectus lacustris (L.) Palla	Bulrush	38	-
Eleocharis palustis (l.) (Roemer & Schultes)	Common Spike-Rush	12	2
Carex sp.	Sedges	22	8
Cyperaceae		5	2
Indet		12	11

or ponds, as well as in faster flowing rivers. *Nuphar lutea* requires a pH of 6.0 or greater. Several other species will grow on the muddy sub-strata on the edge of slow-flowing rivers or ditches, including *Alisma plantago-aquatica* (water plantain), *Menyanthes trifoliata* (bog bean) and *Rumex maritimus* (golden dock). *Myosoton aquaticum* (water chickweed) and *Lycopus europaeus* (gipsy wort) generally grow on the banks of rivers or ditches. Overall, the aquatic and semi-aquatic species of sample 6 are suggestive of a slow-flowing shallow ditch with tall dense vegetation.

The terrestrial or semi-terrestrial plants represented include species which could have been growing in wetter parts of grassland or meadows close to the ditch, including *Eleocharis palustris* (common spike rush) which requires at least seasonal flooding, the *Juncus* species (rushes) and *Lychnis flos-cuculi* (ragged robin). *Ranunculus* cf. *acris*, *R.* cf. *repens* and *Potentilla anserina* (silverweed) are also common in damp meadows and grassland. The remaining terrestrial species, such as *Uritica dioica* (stinging nettle) are suggestive of drier disturbed habitats including settlement sites.

The aquatic component is much less significant in sample 7, with only a single seed each of *Oenanthe aquatica* agg, and *Apium nodiflorum*, while seeds of *Potamogeton* (pond weed) are rare. Species characteristic of the muddy sub-strata on the edge of ponds and ditches have generally increased including *Myosoton aquaticum* and *Rumex maritimus*, while *Ranunculus* subsect. *Batrachium* and *Alisma plantago-aquatica* are fewer. A less watery, muddy ditch is suggested by the flora.

Terrestrial species are more common in sample 7. Marshy or damp ground species are present, but much less common than in sample 6, with some *Ranunculus* cf. *repens* and *Potentilla anserine* and occasional *Eleocharis palustris* and *Carex* spp. (sedges). Other grassland and/or meadow species include *Leontodon* sp. (hawkbit) and *Ranunculus bulbosus* (bulbous buttercup). Species of disturbed or cultivated ground are generally fairly common such as *Atriplex* sp. (orache), *Polygonum* spp., *Urtica dioica*, *Solanum* sp., *Sambucus nigra* and *Taraxaccum* sp. (dandelion) all of which could have been growing within the settlement.

Discussion

The dating evidence is unclear, however, the charred remains are typical of assemblages of medieval date, while tetraploid wheats are not found prior to the 11/12th centuries. Indeed sample 6 also contained a mollusc, a species of Helicinae, generally thought to be a medieval introduction.

The waterlogged assemblages provide some information regarding the ditches from which they were taken. Sample 6 suggests that ditch feature 127 contained shallow slow-flowing water. Sample 7 suggests that ditch 20 possibly contained very little water. Both samples contained terrestrial species characteristic of disturbed habitats such as would be expected within a settlement.

THE ROMAN PERIOD AT BIRDLIP QUARRY

A total of 93 samples of Roman date were scanned in order to assess the quality and quantity of charred remains. Charred remains were noted in 64 samples. A total of 18 samples contained sufficient quantities (greater than 20 items) to merit detailed analysis.

Samples representing both the Period 1 and Period 2 occupation of the site were selected for analysis. The features represented include a corn dryer, a pit containing possible corn dryer or similar waste, ovens, a hearth, a ditch section and a well. Samples sizes range from 2–40 litres. Nine samples were selected for the analysis of wood charcoal. Larger flots were split and a fraction ranging from 1/16 to ˇ was sorted.

Cereal remains

Cereal remains were dominated by hulled wheat. *Triticum spelta* (spelt wheat) was identified by both grain and glume bases. No evidence of *Triticum dicoccum* (emmer) was identified. Poorly preserved indeterminate hulled *Triticum* sp. grains and glumes are also likely to be of *T. spelta*. *T. spelta* is the principle cereal crop of southern Britain in the Romano-British period (Greig 1991). Two rachis nodes of free-threshing *Triticum* sp. (bread-type/rivet wheat) were recorded, but no grain (Tables 8.53–8.55).

Several of the *Triticum spelta* grains were noticeably short and plump, yet still displayed distinct signs of being charred while tightly held within glumes. Grains were recorded as short, elongated or intermediate. Long grains tended to outnumber short grains, although intermediate grains form the greatest category.

The glume bases identified from the richer corn dryer and pit samples were quite variable in size and shape. Several glume bases showed morphological characteristics of *Triticum spelta*, but were very small and narrow. These glumes were perhaps from spikelets with single rather than double or triple grains. A further group of glume bases were large with no prominent dorsal keel, but the angle at the ventral keel was too sharp to allow identification as *T. spelta*. Some well preserved spikelet forks retained fragments of rachis internode. Given the absence of any definite *T. dicoccum* it is thought that the glume bases are all likely to be of *T. spelta* and that the variation is that which would occur naturally within a population.

Loose fragments of rachis internode were identified as hexaploid wheat (spelt/bread-type wheat) on the basis of the strong lines on the dorsal surface. Where there was no glume base attached they could not be identified as *T. spelta*.

Hordeum sp. (barley) grains occur in similar numbers of *Triticum* sp. in the Period one samples with the exception of pit 180, but only forms 3.5% of the total grain in Period two. In six-row *Hordeum vulgare* each rachis node generally produces three fertile florets, the outer two of which are generally asymmetrical, resulting in a ratio of two 'twisted' asymmetrical lateral grains to one 'straight' or symmetrical grain. The identification of occasional asymmetrical lateral grains therefore attests to the presence of six-row barley. The identification of two-row barley is more difficult and it can only be stated that it may have been present. *Avena* sp. (oats) is a possible third minor cereal crop represented by nine grains. A single floret base of a wild *Avena* species does, however, raise the possibility that the *Avena* grains are also of wild varieties.

Ecological implications of weeds

The seeds of weed species form a very minor component of the majority of assemblages with the exception of one oven sample (24, context 204) in which they form the major component of the assemblage (Table 8.53). Weeds seeds in Period one samples are dominated by grasses, notably in sample 24. Grass seeds commonly occur in high numbers in prehistoric and Romano-British assemblages and then decrease, as do perennial weed species generally, with the increasing practice of deep ploughing in the early medieval period (Jones 1984b). The assemblage in sample 24 also includes species which are commonly associated with grassland such as *Linum catharticum* (fairly flax), *Prunella vulgaris* (self heal) and small seeded legumes (medicks, clovers etc.). Some species of *Carex* (sedges) are characteristic of damp grassland while *Odontites verna* (red barstia) and *Plantago media/lanceolata* (plantain) can also occur as grassland species. The assemblage is therefore more characteristic of a grassland than arable flora but may have resulted from the collection of rough herbage growing at the edge or on the headlands of arable fields for use as hay or fuel.

Some evidence of the soil types cultivated during the Period one occupation is available. *Linum catharticum* has a strong dependence upon fresh soils and open conditions including grassland, heaths and moors (Godwin 1975) and is especially common and characteristic of calcareous grassland, although is not confined to basic soils (Clapham *et al.* 1989). It will also grow as a heathland plant. *Odontites verna* is characteristic of heavy clay soils. *Prunella vulgaris*, and *Plantago media/lanceolata* are characteristic of neutral or basic soils.

The samples from pit 180, probably also Period one, again contain a large number of grass seeds (Table 8.54). Some of the larger grass seeds such as the *Bromus* subsect *Eubromus* (brome grass) may have entered the assemblage as contaminates of grain, further suggested by the presence of two germinated grains. The greatest number of grasses are, however, small seeded which suggests they have not entered the assemblage as contaminates, but are likely to have derived from fuel. Again there is some evidence regarding the types of soil cultivated. *Anthemis arevensis* (corn chamomile) is a calcicolous arable weed, while species of heavy calcareous clay soils are again present, including *Odontites verna* and *Anthemis cotula* (stinking mayweed), a species which became widespread during the Roman period. Other species are common weeds of arable or ruderal habitats, such as

Stellaria media (chickweed), *Chenopodium album* (fat hen) and *Rumex* sp. (docks) and are ubiquitous in charred cereal assemblages.

Seeds of grasses are common in the Period two samples but are less dominant than in earlier samples (Table 8.55). Large seeded grasses including *Bromus* subsect *Eubromus* are more frequent suggesting they have entered the assemblage as contaminates of the grain. Species characteristic of heavy calcareous clay soils (*Anthemis cotula* and *Odontites verna*) are quite frequent. Occasional species commonly associated with damp grassland are present such as *Carex* sp. (sedges), *Eleocharis palustris* (common spikerush) and *Ranunculus acris/repens/bulbosus* (buttercup). *Eleocharis palustris* requires at least seasonal flooding, suggesting some cultivation of rather marginal land.

Generally, the weed flora is characteristic of the calcareous soils of the region. There is some cultivation of heavier clay soils, locally present within soils overlying limestone, and of marginal wetter ground, for example at the bottom of river valleys. All the weed species represented could have been growing locally. The collection of rough grass herbage, possibly for hay or fuel, is also suggested.

Sample composition *(Fig. 8.21–8.22)*

Period one

Overall, the Period One samples contain 52.9% chaff, while four of the seven samples each contain more than 50% chaff. Grain forms 18.3% of the samples overall and weeds 32.4% (Table 8.53). Generally, the samples are characteristic of cereal processing waste derived from the later stages of processing. The variation between samples is discussed by feature type. *Triticum* and *Hordeum* sp. grains occur in similar numbers while *Avena* sp. forms a very minor component.

Ovens

Four samples from ovens contained charred plant remains, three of which contained sufficient quantities for analysis (samples 14, 22 and 24). The fourth sample (50) contained a single indeterminate grain and a glume base. Two samples were derived from oven 213 (sample 22 and 24), and one (14) from oven 199. Samples 14 and 22 have similar compositions. In both cases cereal grain forms the minor component, less than 20%. Cereal chaff dominates, mostly glume bases. Weed seeds are a fairly minor component and are dominated by both small and large seeded grasses. Mixed charcoal assemblages were present in each sample, including the charcoal of *Prunus* sp. (sloe, bullace, plum etc.), *Quercus* sp. (oak), *Fraxinus* sp. (ash) and Pomoideae (apple, hawthorn etc.). The ovens are thought to be for industrial rather than domestic use, thus the assemblages are likely to represent the remains of mixed fuel, including cereal processing waste which may have been used as kindling.

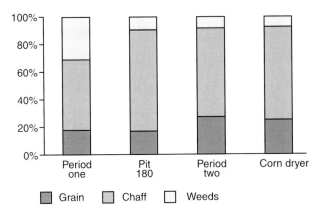

Figure 8.21 Birdlip Quarry, composition of samples by period.

Sample 24, taken from oven 213 is very different in that over 90% of the assemblage consists of weed seeds (Table 8.53). Grasses predominate, of which there are several identifiable as *Poa annua* type. *Plantago media/ lanceolata* and *Odontites verna*. are also significant species. The weed seeds are generally small in size. Cereal grain slightly outnumbers chaff which consists of glume bases only, although given the differential survival rates of grain and chaff (Boardman and Jones 1990) it is possible that the chaff is under-represented. It is unlikely that the large number of grassland weeds have derived from cereal processed. As discussed above it is more likely that the assemblage derives from the remains of hay or roughage which has been used as fuel or kindling.

Well (feature 288)

A sample of charred material was taken from one of the wells. The sample is dominated by chaff (95% of the sample), notably glume bases. Cereal grain and weeds form a very minor component. The sample is again likely to represent glume bases and other by-products of cereal processing which have been used as fuel. The absence of weed seeds would suggest that a late stage of processing spikelets is represented and that weed seeds had been sieved off at an earlier stage. The remaining well samples contain occasional glume bases and occasional grain including *Hordeum* sp. (barley).

Other features

A further 18 samples from ditch fills, hearths, a gully and a mortar deposit contain scatters of charred remains. Generally, these consist of one or two indeterminate grains. Three samples did contain sufficient material for full analysis. The samples were from a hearth, a ditch section and a gully. All three samples contain low densities of chaff, grain and weed seeds in varying proportions. Grain of both *Triticum* sp. and *Hordeum* sp. are present. Occasional chaff fragments include *T. spelta* glume bases. The weeds are all common species of cultivated or disturbed ground. Such assemblages are interpreted as rep-

resenting general background scatters of remains. A mixed charcoal assemblage, including *Prunus* sp. (sloe, plum etc.) *Fraxinus* (ash) and Pomoideae (hawthorn, apple, pear etc.) from the hearth is presumably derived from fuel (Table 8.56). There was no evidence for the use of chaff as fuel, although this could be a result of preservation.

Pit 180 (Table 8.54)

Three samples were taken from pit 180, possibly a Period one feature, from three successive fills (contexts 181, 207, 208). The density of remains is exceptionally high, ranging from 213.6 to 4992 items per litre. Glume bases always outnumber grain, although the ratio of grains to glumes varies considerably from 2:47 in the lower sample (28, context 208) to 1:1.4 in the upper sample (17, context 181). Given the differential survival rate of grains and chaff (Boardman and Jones 1990) the ratio of glumes to grain may have been higher still. It is certainly unlikely that grain is under-represented. Sprouted coleoptiles are present in all three samples in varying numbers. They form a minor component of sample 17 (1 per litre of deposit), but are present in large numbers in sample 28 (418.7 per litre). Germinated grain is present in each sample with approximately 24% of wheat grains in sample 28 showing clear signs of germination. Germinated grains are less frequent in the other samples but are present. Rachis fragments of wheat, including many of hexaploid wheat and some identifiable as *Triticum spelta*, were quite common in sample 28. Awn fragments are very frequent in the two lower samples (21 and 28), both as charred remains and silica skeletons. Weeds form minor components of the lower samples but are slightly more conspicuous in sample 17 (20% of the sample).

The greater number of glumes than grains in all three samples is indicative of processing waste, possibly re-used as fuel, rather than an accidentally burnt product. The much greater number of grains in sample 17 than the earlier samples suggests some accidental burning of product or spoilt crop which

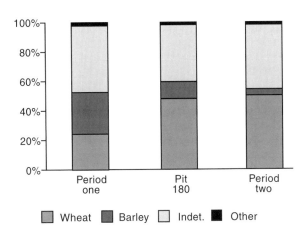

Figure 8.22 Birdlip Quarry, composition of grain by period.

Table 8.53   Charred seeds and chaff From Period 1, Birdlip Quarry.

	Sample	14	22	24	46	48	121	125
	Context	198	209	204	347	368	918	1061
	Period	1	1	1	1	1	1	1
	Fraction (%)	100	100	100	100	100	100	100
	Volume (litres)	37	10	28	32	20	16	
	Feature type	oven	oven	oven	ditch	well	hearth	gully
GRAIN								
Triticum spelta (Spelt Wheat) short, sprouted		-	-	-	-	-	-	-
Triticum spelta short		1	-	-	1	-	-	-
Triticum spelta long, sprouted		-	-	-	-	-	-	-
Triticum spelta long		-	-	-	-	-	-	-
Triticum spelta intermediate, sprouted		-	-	-	-	-	-	-
Triticum spelta intermediate		1	2	-	2	2	-	-
Triticum spelta immature grain		-	-	-	-	-	-	-
Triticum sp. hulled (hulled Wheat), sprouted		-	-	-	-	-	-	-
Triticum. sp. hulled		2	2	3	3	-	-	2
Triticum sp.(Wheat)		2	2	-	-	2	4	1
Hordeum vulgare (six-row Barley) hulled, lateral grain		-	-	-	-	-	2	2
Hordeum sp. (Barley) hulled sprouted		-	-	-	-	-	-	-
Hordeum sp. hulled		-	1	-	1	-	2	10
Hordeum sp.		-	5	1	-	1	6	4
Avena sp. (Oats)		-	1	-	-	-	-	1
cf. *Secale cereale* (Rye) sprouted		-	-	-	-	-	-	-
Triticum/Secale (Wheat/Rye)		-	-	-	-	-	-	-
Cerealia indet		10	17	3	9	3	6	11
CHAFF								
Triticum spelta glume base		23	55	2	2	35	-	1
Triticum spelta small glume base		-	-	-	-	3	-	-
Triticum cf. *spelta* glume base		3	2	-	1	7	-	1
Triticum sp. glume base		32	79	2	19	59	-	2
Triticum spelta rachis internode		-	-	-	-	3	-	-
Triticum cf. *spelta* rachis internode		-	-	-	-	-	-	-
Triticum sp. hexaploid rachis internode		-	4	-	1	16	-	-
Triticum sp. hulled wheat rachis internode		-	-	-	-	-	-	-
Triticum sp. hexaploid free-threshing rachis node		-	-	-	-	1	-	-
Triticum sp. free-threshing rachis node		-	-	-	-	-	-	-
Triticum sp. rachis internode		3	3	-	1	9	-	-
Triticum sp. awn fragments (silica & charred)		-	-	-	-	-	-	-
Hordeum sp. rachis internode		-	-	-	-	-	-	-
Avena sp. awn fragment		-	-	-	-	-	-	-
Cerealia indet rachis internode		-	-	-	-	-	-	-
Cerealia indet basal rachis node		-	-	-	-	-	-	-
Cerealia indet sprouted coleoptile		-	-	-	-	-	-	-
Cerealia indet detached embryo		-	-	-	-	-	-	-
Cereal size culm node		-	-	-	-	-	-	-
Corylus avellana (Hazel) nut shell frags		-	-	-	1	-	-	-
WEEDS								
Ranunculus acris/repens/bulbosus (Buttercup)		-	-	-	-	-	-	-
Silene sp. (Campion)		-	-	-	-	-	-	-
Stellaria media agg. (Chickweed)		-	-	-	-	-	-	-
Chenopodium album (Fat Hen)		-	-	-	-	-	-	1
Chenopodium sp. (Fat Hen, Goosegrass)		-	-	-	-	-	-	-
Atriplex sp. (Orache)		-	-	-	-	-	-	-
Linum catharticum (Fairy Flax)		-	-	4	-	-	-	-
Vicia/Lathyrus sp. (Vetch/Tare)		-	1	-	-	-	-	-
Leguminosae small seeded		-	2	8	-	-	-	3
Crataegus sp. (Hawthorn) stone		-	-	-	-	-	-	-

Table 8.53 continued.

	Sample	14	22	24	46	48	121	125
	Context	198	209	204	347	368	918	1061
	Period	1	1	1	1	1	1	1
	Fraction (%)	100	100	100	100	100	100	100
	Volume (litres)	37	10	28	32	20	16	
	Feature type	oven	oven	oven	ditch	well	hearth	gully
Umbelliferae		-	-	-	-	-	-	-
Polygonum persicaria (Knotgrass)		-	-	-	-	-	-	-
Fallopia convolvulus (Black Bindweed)		-	-	-	-	-	-	-
Rumex sp. (Docks)		4	2	-	-	1	-	2
Rumex sp. tubercles		-	-	2	-	-	-	-
Polygonaceae		-	1	-	-	-	-	2
Odontites verna (Red Barstia)		-	2	16	-	-	-	1
Prunella vulgaris (Selfheal)		-	-	2	-	-	-	-
Labiate		-	-	-	-	-	-	-
Plantago media/lanceolata (Plantain)		-	-	25	-	-	1	2
Anthemis cotula (Stinking Mayweed)		-	-	-	-	-	-	-
Anthemis arvensis (Corn Chamomile)		-	-	-	-	-	-	-
cf. *Tripleurospermum inodorum* (Scentless Mayweed)		-	3	-	-	-	-	-
Lapsana communis (Nipplewort)		-	-	-	-	-	-	-
Compositae		-	5	5	-	-	-	-
Eleocharis palustris (Common Spike Rush)		-	-	-	-	-	1	-
Carex sp. (Sedges)		-	-	5	-	-	-	2
Cyperaceae		-	-	1	-	-	-	-
Bromus subsect *Eubromus* (Brome Grass)		2	-	-	-	-	1	-
Bromus subsect *Eubromus* sprouted		-	2	-	-	-	-	-
Bromus sterilis (Barren Brome)		-	1	-	-	-	-	-
Poa annua type (Annual Meadow-grass)		-	-	23	-	-	-	9
Avena sp. (wild Oat) floret base		-	-	-	-	-	-	-
Avena sp. (Oat) awn fragment		-	-	-	-	-	-	-
Gramineae large seeded (Grass)		5	9	2	-	-	1	-
Gramineae small seeded		2	7	9	4	-	1	3
Gramineae tuber		-	-	-	-	-	-	-
Prunus/Craetagus type thorn		-	-	-	-	-	-	-
Indet bud		-	-	-	-	-	-	-
Weed indet		4	2	27	-	2	6	1
	Total Grain	16	30	7	16	8	20	31
	Total Chaff	61	143	4	24	133	0	4
	Total Weeds	17	37	129	9	3	22	26
	Total	94	210	129	45	144	31	35

Table 8.54   *Charred seeds and chaff from pit 180, Birdlip Quarry.*

	Sample	17	21	28
	Context	181	207	208
	Period	1	1	1
	Fraction	100%	100%	1/16
	Volume	10	2	6
	Type	Pit	Pit	Pit
GRAIN				
Triticum spelta (Spelt Wheat) short, sprouted		1	-	-
Triticum spelta short		10	6	-
Triticum spelta long, sprouted		-	-	-
Triticum spelta long		-	-	-
Triticum spelta intermediate, sprouted		4	3	5
Triticum spelta intermediate		71	15	19
Triticum spelta immature grain		6	-	-
Triticum sp. hulled (hulled Wheat), sprouted		7	18	4
Triticum sp. Hulled		117	42	5
Triticum sp. (Wheat)		106	51	4
Hordeum vulgare (six-row Barley) hulled lateral grain		1	-	-
Hordeum sp. (Barley) hulled sprouted		-	-	-
Hordeum sp. hulled		45	2	-
Hordeum sp.		72	-	1
Avena sp. (Oats)		2	1	-
cf. *Secale cereale* (Rye) sprouted		-	-	-
Triticum/Secale sp. (Wheat/Rye)		1	1	-
Cerealia indet		275	120	20
CHAFF				
Triticum spelta glume base		421	375	105
Triticum spelta small glume base		32	56	130
Triticum cf. *spelta* glume base		23	108	65
Triticum sp. glume base		455	968	1064
Triticum spelta rachis internode		1	9	2
Triticum cf. *spelta* rachis internode		-	-	6
Triticum sp. hexaploid rachis internode		16	5	127
Triticum sp. hulled, rachis internode		2	-	7
Triticum sp. hexaploid free-threshing rachis		-	-	-
Triticum sp. free-threshing rachis node		-	1	-
Triticum sp. rachis internode		24	2	17
Triticum sp. awn fragments (silica & charred)		-	+++	+++
Hordeum sp. rachis internode		1	-	3
Avena sp. awn fragment		1	46	27
Cerealia indet rachis internode		1	-	11
Cerealia indet basal rachis node		-	-	2
Cerealia indet sprouted coleoptile		10	69	157
Cerealia indet detached embryo		7	9	-
Cereal size culm node		-	-	1
Corylus avellana (hazel) nut shell fragment		-	-	-
WEEDS				
Ranunculus acris/repens/bulbosus (Buttercup)		-	-	-
Silene sp. (Campion)		-	-	-
Stellaria media agg. (Chickweed)		2	1	-
Chenopodium album (Fat Hen)		-	-	-
Chenopodium sp. (Fat Hen, Goosegrass)		-	-	1
Atriplex sp. (Orache)		2	-	-
Linum catharticum (Fairy Flax)		-	-	-
Vicia/Lathyrus sp. (Vetch/Tare)		-	-	-
Leguminosae small seeded		1	2	3
Crataegus sp. (Hawthorn) stone		-	-	-

Table 8.54 continued.

	Sample	17	21	28
	Context	181	207	208
	Period	1	1	1
	Fraction	100%	100%	1/16
	Volume	10	2	6
	Type	Pit	Pit	Pit
Umbelliferae		-	-	-
Polygonum persicaria (Knotgrass)		-	-	-
Fallopoia convolvulus (Black Bindweed)		-	-	1
Rumex sp. (Docks)		14	4	4
Rumex sp. Tubercles		-	-	-
Polygonaceae		-	-	-
Odontites verna (Red Barstia)		4	4	-
Prunella vulgaris (Selfheal)		-	-	-
Labiate		-	-	-
Plantago media/lanceolata (Plantain)		-	-	1
Anthemis cotula (Stinking Mayweed)		-	-	1
Anthemis arvensis (Corn Chamomile)		2	-	-
cf. *Tripleurospermum inodorum* (Scentless Mayweed)		4	12	3
Lapsana communis (Nipplewort)		1	-	-
Compositae		-	-	1
Eleocharis palustris (Common Spike Rush)		-	-	-
Carex sp. (Sedges)		-	-	1
Cyperaceae		-	-	1
Bromus subsect *Eubromus* (Brome Grass)		17	11	3
Bromus subsect *Eubromus* sprouted		-	-	2
Bromus sterilis (Barren Brome)		1	1	-
Poa annua type (Annual Meadow-grass)		-	-	-
Avena sp. (wild Oat) floret base		-	-	-
Avena sp. (Oat) awn fragment		-	1	-
Gramineae large seeded (Grass)		19	12	36
Gramineae small seeded		213	119	20
Gramineae tuber		1	-	-
Prunus/Crataegus type thorn		-	-	-
Indet bud		-	-	1
Weed indet		44	22	12
	Total Grain	718	259	58
	Total Chaff	994	1648	1724
	Total Weeds	325	189	91
	Total	2037	2096	1873

Table 8.55   Charred seeds and chaff from Period 2, Birdlip Quarry.

	Sample	1	3	4	23	31	32	138	2
	Context	33	43	81	190	222	221	1265	41
	Period	2	2	2	2	2	2	2	2
	Fraction	100%	100%	100%	1/4	1/16	100%	100%	100%
	Volume	23	28	28	19	30	28	32	40
	Type	CD	CD	CD	CD	CD	CD	pit	pit
GRAIN									
Triticum spelta (Spelt Wheat) short, sprouted		-	-	-	-	-	17	-	-
Triticum spelta short		-	-	-	2	9	-	1	2
Triticum spelta long, sprouted		-	1	-	-	-	10	-	-
Triticum spelta long		-	2	-	-	13	46	-	-
Triticum spelta intermediate, sprouted		-	-	-	1	-	-	-	-
Triticum spelta intermediate		-	-	1	2	7	-	5	2
Triticum spelta immature grain		-	-	-	-	-	-	-	-
Triticum sp. hulled (hulled Wheat) sprouted		-	-	-	-	-	-	-	-
Triticum sp. Hulled		2	3	7	11	18	67	16	10
Triticum sp. (Wheat)		2	3	-	7	64	88	19	6
Hordeum vulgare (six-row Barley) hulled lateral grain		-	-	-	-	-	-	-	-
Hordeum sp. (Barley) hulled sprouted		-	-	-	-	-	2	-	-
Hordeum sp. hulled		-	-	-	-	-	6	-	-
Hordeum sp.		-	-	3	1	2	14	1	2
Avena sp. (Oats)		-	-	1	-	-	2	1	-
cf. *Secale cereale* (Rye) sprouted		-	-	-	-	1	-	-	-
Triticum/Secale sp. (Wheat/Rye)		-	-	-	-	-	-	-	-
Cerealia indet		9	7	27	25	79	191	36	17
CHAFF									
Triticum spelta glume base		5	1	33	88	198	176	1	13
Triticum spelta small glume base		-	-	-	26	27	38	-	1
Triticum cf. *spelta* glume base		-	-	2	-	18	3	-	2
Triticum sp. glume base		16	32	43	89	622	443	2	37
Triticum spelta rachis internode		-	-	-	-	2	-	-	-
Triticum cf. *spelta* rachis internode		-	-	-	-	-	-	-	-
Triticum sp. hexaploid rachis internode		-	2	1	7	17	10	-	-
Triticum sp. hulled, rachis internode		-	-	-	-	-	-	-	-
Triticum sp. hexaploid free-threshing rachis node		-	-	-	-	-	-	-	-
Triticum sp. free-threshing rachis node		-	-	-	-	-	-	-	-
Triticum sp. rachis internode		-	-	3	3	17	3	-	-
Triticum sp. awn fragments (silica & charred)		-	-	-	-	-	-	-	-
Hordeum sp. rachis internode		-	-	-	-	-	-	-	-
Avena sp. awn fragment		-	-	-	-	2	5	-	-
Cerealia indet rachis internode		-	-	-	-	-	-	-	-
Cerealia indet basal rachis node		-	-	-	-	-	-	-	-
Cerealia indet sprouted coleoptile		-	2	1	8	22	8	-	-
Cerealia indet detached embryo		2	-	-	-	5	12	-	-
Cereal size culm node		-	-	-	-	-	-	-	-
Corylus avellana (Hazel) nut shell fragments		-	-	-	-	-	-	-	-
WEEDS									
Ranunculus acris/repens/bulbosus (Buttercup)		-	-	-	-	-	-	2	-
Silene sp. (Campion)		-	-	-	-	-	-	-	1
Stellaria media agg. (Chickweed)		-	-	1	-	-	-	-	-
Chenopodium album, (Fat Hen)		-	-	-	-	-	-	-	-
Chenopodium sp. (Fat Hen/Goosefoot)		2	-	-	1	1	1	-	-
Atriplex sp. (Orache)		-	-	-	-	-	2	-	-
Linum catharticum (Fairy Flax)		-	-	-	-	-	-	-	-
Vicia/Lathyrus sp. (Vetch/Tare)		-	-	-	1	-	1	-	-
Leguminosae, small seeded		1	-	2	1	-	-	11	-
Crataegus sp. (Hawthorn) stone		-	-	-	-	-	-	2	

Table 8.55 continued.

	Sample	1	3	4	23	31	32	138	2
	Context	33	43	81	190	222	221	1265	41
	Phase	2	2	2	2	2	2	2	2
	Fraction	100%	100%	100%	1/4	1/16	100%	100%	100%
	Volume	23	28	28	19	30	28	32	40
	Type	CD	CD	CD	CD	CD	CD	pit	pit
Umbelliferae		-	-	-	-	1	-	-	-
Polygonum persicaria (Knotgrass)		-	-	-	2	-	-	-	-
Fallopia convolvulus (Black Bindweed)		-	-	-	-	4	-	-	-
Rumex sp. (Docks)		1	-	1	4	1	3	2	-
Rumex sp. Tubercles		-	-	-	-	-	-	-	-
Polygonaceae		-	1	-	-	1	-	-	-
Odontites verna (Red Barstia)		1	-	2	10	-	1	4	2
Prunella vulgaris (Selfheal)		-	-	-	-	-	-	-	-
Labiate		-	-	-	-	1	-	-	-
Plantago media/lanceolata (Plantain)		-	-	-	-	-	-	1	-
Anthemis cotula (Stinking Mayweed)		1	1	-	-	1	-	-	-
Anthemis arvensis (Corn Chamomile)		-	-	-	-	1	-	-	-
cf.*Tripleurospermum inodorum* (Scentless Mayweed)		-	-	-	-	1	-	-	-
Lapsana communis (Nipplewort)		-	-	-	-	-	-	-	-
Compositae		1	-	-	-	-	6	-	-
Eleocharis palustris (Common Spike-rush)		-	-	-	-	-	-	1	-
Carex sp. (Sedges)		-	-	-	-	-	-	1	-
Cyperaceae		-	-	2	-	-	-	-	-
Bromus subsect *Eubromus* (Brome Grass)		1	-	3	3	11	52	-	-
Bromus subsect *Eubromus* sprouted		-	-	-	-	-	-	-	-
Bromus sterilis (Barren Brome)		-	-	-	-	-	3	-	-
Poa annua type (Annual Meadow-grass)		-	-	-	-	-	-	1	-
Avena sp. (wild Oat) floret base		-	-	-	-	-	-	-	-
Avena sp. (oat) awn fragment		-	-	-	-	-	-	-	-
Gramineae large seeded (Grass)		-	2	3	4	7	1	3	5
Gramineae small seeded		7	8	4	4	2	9	1	6
Gramineae tuber		-	-	1	-	-	-	-	-
Prunus/Craetagus type thorn		-	-	-	3	-	-	-	-
Indet bud		-	-	-	2	-	-	-	1
Weed indet		-	2	9	2	4	4	2	1
	Total Grain	13	16	39	49	193	443	79	39
	Total Chaff	23	37	83	221	930	698	3	53
	Total Weeds	15	14	28	37	36	83	31	16
	Total	51	67	150	307	1159	1224	113	108

C.D. = corn dryer

Table 8.56   *Charcoal identifications from Birdlip Quarry.*

	Sample	4	23	32	17	125	22	121	14	138
	Context	81	190	221	181	885	209	918	198	1265
	Feature	42	42	42	180	1030	213	-	199	1263
Prunus sp.	Plum, sloe, bullace etc.	4	2	3	1	-	4	2	-	5
cf. *Prunus* sp.		-	-	-	-	-	2	-	-	-
Pomoideae	Apple, pear, hawthorn etc.	2	10	3	1	15	11	6	2	4
cf. *Pomoideae*		-	-	-	1	-	-	-	-	-
Fraxinus sp.	Ash	2	2	-	16	5	1	-	8	1
cf. *Fraxinus* sp.		-	-	2	-	-	-	1	-	-
cf. *Rhannus* sp.	Buckthorn	4	5	-	-	-	-	1	-	-
Quercus sp.	Oak	6	1	-	1	-	2	-	-	-
Indet		2	-	2	-	-	-	-	-	-

Table 8.57   *Composition of the assemblages from the corn dryer, Birdlip Quarry.*

Sample	Type	% germinated grain		No. items	Items per 1	Glum:grain	Sprout:grain	% Weeds	Silica	Charcoal
		Total	Wheat							
4	Bowl	-	-	150	5.3	2.1	1:39	18.7	-	++
23	Bowl	2	4.3	302	15.9	4.1:1	1:6.1	10.6	-	+++
31	Flue	-	-	1167	38.9	4.5:1	1:7.1	3.1	-	+
32	Flue	6.1	11.8	1224	43.7	1.5:1	1:22.2	6.8	-	+
17	Pit	1.7	3.7	2136	213.6	1.3:1	1:42	19.9	-	+
21	Pit	7.8	15.6	2105	1052.5	5.6:1	1:3.4	8.9	++	-
28	Pit	19	24.3	1872	312.0	23.5:1	2.7:1	4.8	++	+

has been subsequently used as fuel. Samples 17 and 21 are of similar composition to the corn dryer deposits, ie. they are likely to have derived from the processing of a cereal crop for consumption/storage.

Sample 28 contains a much greater number of sprouted coleoptiles than any other sample (418.7 per litre, 8.4% of total assemblage). A minimum of 24% of the wheat grains show signs of germination. This figure may be much higher, but many grains are poorly preserved. The numbers of sprouted coleoptiles and germinated grains would seem too high to have occurred naturally in an average harvest. The deposit appears to be most characteristic of malting waste, the detached glumes and sprouts resulting from the rubbing of malted grain. The process of malting is discussed in relation to corn dryers below. If not malting waste, this figure would suggest the burning of a spoilt crop, perhaps as the result of a wet harvest. The large number of rachis internodes and awn fragments suggests that whole ears were processed rather than individual spikelets. A similar deposit recently recovered from a pit at Stratford Road, Alcester (Mudd and Booth forthcoming) has been interpreted as malting waste (the 'cumins') on the basis of the large number of sprouted coleoptiles and glume bases and that the majority of grains showed clear signs of germination (only one grain could definitely be identified as not germinated) (Pelling forthcoming a). Several corn dryers have been interpreted as producing evidence for malting (Van der Veen 1989) including an example at Bancroft Villa, Milton Keynes (Pearson and Robinson 1994) and Catsgore (Hillman 1982). The

known examples of possible malting waste from both corn dryers and pits are all of spelt wheat, while the brewing of wheat beer by the Romans is documented by Pliny (Book XVIII).

The assemblages of the pit fills are similar in nature to those of the lower fills of the corn dryer in that they are very rich in the by-products of an intensive processing activity. It seems likely that if not directly related then the pit contains refuse from a similar structure.

Period two

The Period two samples are dominated by the corn dryer (Table 8.57). The greatest component overall is chaff, forming 64.2% of the total assemblage, the majority of which is glume bases. Weeds form only 8.2% over all. The assemblages are characteristic of the very final stages of processing of a tough glumed wheat. The straw and weeds must have been removed at an earlier stage. Wheat forms 51% of the overall grain component, while indeterminate grain forms 44%. Barley and oats are a very minor component.

The corn dryer (feature 42)

Samples were analysed from both the flue and the bowl/stoke hole of the corn dryer and from the post-abandonment fill. Three samples are assumed to be related to the primary function of the feature, two from the flue (samples 31/34, context 222 and 32/33, context 221) and one from the bowl (sample 23, context

488

190). A summary of the composition of samples is shown in Table 8.57. Glume bases and grains of *Triticum spelta* (spelt wheat) dominate the cereal assemblage, while occasional grains of *Hordeum* sp. (barley) and *Avena* sp. (oats) are present as minor components.

Samples 31/34, 32/33 and 23 are characterised by very large quantities of glume bases, very occasional weeds and few grains, although grain is slightly more numerous in sample 32 (context 221) from the upper flue. The density of remains is high, exceptionally so in the lower flue fill, sample 31 (617.6 items per litre). Small numbers of germinated cereal grains were identified from samples 23 (context 190) and 32 (context 221). Very occasional detached coleoptiles (sprouted embryos) were present in each sample.

Samples 1 (context 33), 3 (context 43) and 4 (context 81) were taken from the post-abandonment fills of the corn dryer. The density of remains is much lower than those in the primary fills (2.2 to 5.4 items per litre). The compositions are much more mixed. Chaff still forms the greatest category of remains, but only makes up about half of the assemblage. Grain and weeds occur in similar quantities. Germinated grain and detached coleoptiles are very infrequent. Preservation of cereal grains was poor. The majority were 'clinkered' in appearance, suggesting high degrees of heat. These samples are likely to represent mixed cereal processing waste and accidentally charred grain. Occasional germinated grain may be expected in an average cereal crop.

The botanical evidence of so-called 'corn dryers' has been addressed in detail by Van der Veen (1989). From the analysis of the botanical assemblages from corn dryers from 21 sites she concludes that they should be regarded as multi-functional structures. The botanical evidence was interpreted as indicating that both the roasting of deliberately germinated grain for the production of malt and the preparation of grain for food production (ie. parching prior to de-husking, milling etc.) and storage (ie. drying) are associated with T-shaped corn dryers. Experiments conducted by Reynolds and Langley (1979), however, suggest that the structures were not actually very suitable for drying grain. Storage of clean grain is unlikely outside Roman military granaries, while hulled spikelets could be dried sufficiently on a barn floor or even in the field. Drying of grain prior to storage is therefore unlikely. Spelt appears to be the only cereal used in the malting process, while both spelt and barley have been recorded from corn dryers in association with evidence for processing prior to storage or consumption.

The roasting of deliberately germinated grain for the production of malt would result in a large number of detached coleoptiles. If roasting took place while grains were still in their glumes, rubbing of the grains would remove glumes and coleoptiles simultaneously. It would also be expected that the greater number of grains would show signs of germination. Van der Veen provides an arbitrary figure of 75% for a minimum number of germinated grains (1989). The waste

product of such a process would include glume bases, sprouted coleoptiles and occasional grain, some of which may have germinated. Accidental burning would result in glumes and grain in similar numbers with the majority of grain (say >75%) showing signs of germination.

Processing for consumption/preparation of food covers a range of possible stages/categories including the drying of damp or immature spikelets for the recovery of spoilt harvests or for greencorn, and the parching of spikelets for the removal of glume bases. Accidental burning would result in approximately equal proportions of grain and glume bases with occasional sprouted coleoptiles. General waste which may be burnt as fuel would consist of glume bases, occasional sprouted coleoptiles and occasional grains, a small proportion of which could show signs of germination.

The issue is somewhat compounded by the use of chaff as fuel. Straw and glume bases, mixed with wood and/or peat where available, appear to have been the favoured fuel for all forms of grain parching, especially malting (Hillman 1982). Straw and glume bases would have been readily available if cereal processing was taking place and would have had less effect on the taste of malt than other forms of fuel. Any chaff generated by the activities at the corn dryer is likely to have been thrown straight back in to be used as fuel for the next episode of use. The denser chaff fragments and occasional cereal grains and weed seeds could therefore be expected in the ashes of the bowl/stoke pit, while the deposits in the flue might contain a greater percentage of accidental loss during processing. Some mixing could occur, especially where fuel is blown up into the bowl or material which has built up in the bowl raked down into the fuel.

The high numbers of glume bases must indicate the use of the waste products of cereal processing reused as fuel. The higher proportion of glumes in the bowl/stoke-hole than the upper flue deposits is presumably related to the greater proportion of fuel in that deposit. A mix of wood charcoals including Pomoideae (hawthorn, apple etc.), *Quercus* (oak) and *Fraxinus* (ash) suggests that some wood was also used as fuel. The higher percentage of grain in the upper flue deposits (sample 32) is likely to be due to accidental loss through the processing floor. The number of germinated grains and of sprouted coleoptiles are within a range which would be feasible for occasional spoilt grains within a harvest. The glume-rich deposit in the lowest of the flue samples (context 222) is likely to represent a general build up of small chaff which has trickled down into the base of the flue over successive episodes of use. No germinated grain was present and the number of sprouted coleoptiles is low. The deposits all suggest the activities taking place within the corn dryer involved the processing of grain for consumption, rather than for malting. It must be considered, however, that only the later episodes of use are likely to be represented in the deposits with evidence regarding earlier stages probably having been removed. Therefore, while there is no confirmation of malting as a function of the structure, there is also no evidence to indicate that it did not take place at some point.

In summary, the assemblages within the corn dryer indicate that the charred remains are, at the very least, the product of an episode of waste disposal, probably taking the form of burning cereal processing by-products as fuel. The more likely interpretation of the material is that it represents successive episodes of waste disposal, that waste having been directly derived from episodes of use of the corn dryer in which roasting spikelets or ears of spelt wheat took place for the purpose of processing prior to consumption.

The emergence of corn dryers in the 3rd century AD has been linked to the increase in large-scale cereal processing. Van der Veen (1989) suggests large-scale processing and then storage of clean grain. While clean grain was certainly stored in Roman military granaries, where it was then available for transport when needed, it is unlikely that grain would normally be stored clean in a Romano-British rural settlement. The glumes of hulled wheat provide protection against damage from infection as well as from insect attack. It is more likely that the emergence of corn dryers is related to increased social organisation and that they eventually became commonplace within non-military settlements of any size for use in malting for brewing purposes and for preparation of grain for consumption.

The later, post-abandonment deposits within the corn dryer (samples 1, 3 and 4) are clearly very different in nature to those associated with the original function of the structure. They are more likely to represent general background scatters of the waste products of cereal processing episodes.

Other pits

A further eleven samples from Period 2 pits contained charred plant remains. The majority of these contained occasional indeterminate grains and glume bases. Two samples (138 and 2) (Table 8.55) contained slightly more charred remains and so were analysed in full. Charred remains occur in low concentrations (3.5 and 2.7 items per litre). The cereal remains were dominated by indeterminate and hulled wheat grain and glumes. Weeds and chaff were more numerous than grain in sample 2 suggestive of processing debris. In general, the pit samples contain the low density background scatters of charred seeds and chaff which tend to be common on Romano-British rural sites. The density of remains is much lower than in pit 180.

General discussion

The cereal-based economy at Birdlip Quarry was dominated by spelt wheat, with some barley consumption and possibly oat. The processing of cereals was clearly taking place within the settlement. A background scatter of processing waste including occasional grains, glume bases and weed seeds were recovered from the majority of features sampled. This waste is unlikely to have been redeposited deliberately but rather is likely to have derived from scatters of waste which were generally present. Some more intensive processing is indicated by the remains recovered from the corn dryer and pit 180. The corn dryer provides evidence for the use of such features in the dehusking of glume wheats prior to consumption or storage. There is evidence that the processing waste was used as fuel. It is also possible that at least some of the remains in pit 180 have derived from the by-products of malting spelt wheat for brewing purposes. The weed flora provides some evidence for the cultivation of heavy clay and calcareous soils which could be found locally and possibly some evidence of the cultivation of seasonally marshy ground as might be found in the river valleys. The arable weeds actually form a minor component of the samples. The greater weed element of the assemblages is derived from a grassland flora, suggestive of open, calcareous grassland. The bulk of the arable weed seeds are therefore absent and are likely to have been removed at an earlier stage than is represented, possibly before the cereals even entered the assemblages. At least some of the grassland flora may have entered the site in the form of locally gathered turves or roughage, possibly used as hay or fuel.

Comparable published assemblages from within the Gloucestershire region are rare, although charred assemblages have been recovered from a middle Iron Age to early Roman site on the Birdlip Bypass (Straker 1998). Comparable material has been recovered from Roman sites within the Upper Thames Valley (Robinson and Wilson 1987) and from elsewhere in southern Britain such as Bancroft Villa (Pearson and Robinson 1994). An overview of Romano-British material in southern Britain is provided by Greig (1991). The cereal assemblage from Birdlip Quarry fits the pattern for Romano-British sites in southern Britain in which spelt wheat is the principle cereal, although smaller quantities of free-threshing wheat and of emmer wheat which was not present at Birdlip Quarry, are often recorded, as is hulled barley. The assemblages are similar to those at Bancroft Villa in that the later stages of processing (principally de-husking) are represented while the earlier stages in which the straw and the bulk of the weed seeds are removed. Bancroft Villa, however, is a high-status site in which grain was clearly stored for some period of time, as attested by grain-storage pests. The assemblages were interpreted as being derived from grain that was produced on smaller and lower status sites from which the grain was mostly exported and then stored in spikelet form at the villas. At Birdlip Quarry the dominance of assemblages representing the final stages of processing (malting and de-husking) is a result of the corn dryer and large pit assemblages. These structures suggest some degree of social organisation and centralisation of certain cereal processing activities, probably commonplace on rural Romano-British settlements of this size by the later Roman period.

THE MEDIEVAL PERIOD AT STREET FARM

Eight samples were taken from within the kitchen building dating from the 13th to the early 16th century. Samples were taken from successive floor deposits and from an oven. Original sample sizes ranged from 1 to 12 litres. Five samples, all of which were clearly rich in charred remains were selected for detailed analysis. The oven sample was included in the analysis. Two samples were selected for the identification of charcoal (Tables 8.58–8.59).

Crop species

Cereal crops are represented by grain with occasional chaff fragments (Table 8.58). Free-threshing *Triticum* sp. (bread-type/rivet wheat) is the predominant cereal crop in all samples apart from that taken from the oven (sample 7). This sample, in which wheat and barley occur in similar numbers, contains a much lower number of cereal grains, and as such the ratio of cereal types cannot be taken as statistically representative. Overall, short, plump free-threshing *Triticum* grains, recorded as 'compact', were most numerous. A few longer narrow grains recorded as 'elongated' were also identified. Intermediate grains are classified separately. Occasional rachis nodes identifiable to ploidy level were also present. Given the inherent difficulties in distinguishing between ploidy level on the basis of grain, no attempt was made to identify free-threshing wheat grain to species. The rachis nodes, however, demonstrate the presence of both tetraploid and hexaploid wheat. The tetraploid wheat is likely to be of *Triticum turgidum* (rivet wheat), which appears to have been cultivated from the early medieval period (Moffett 1991), rather than *T. durum* (durum wheat) which is poorly suited to the British climate (Percival 1921). The hexaploid wheat would be a variety of bread wheat.

Hexaploid wheat, *Triticum aestivum* type (bread-type wheat), is less frequently identified by the rachis in the samples, although it is unclear how representative this is as the hexaploid rachis tended to be more abraded, thus suggesting that some of the more poorly preserved *Triticum* rachis which was not assigned to ploidy level could also be hexaploid. It is also likely that the two types of chaff may have had different uses and as a result experience different chances of preservation by charring. Hexaploid free-threshing wheat is more likely to be awnless and to be used fodder as it is more palatable to the animals, and so is less likely to be charred, while tetraploid wheat tends to give a good quality straw and is more likely to be used for thatch. The likelihood of preservation is also dependent on context. It is therefore very difficult to assess the relative importance of hexaploid and tetraploid wheats. There was some evidence from West Cotton to suggest that the two wheats were sometimes grown together as a maslin (Campbell forthcoming b). Bread-type wheat has far superior qualities for bread baking, while rivet wheat provides a good flour for biscuits, but the two wheats

can also be used together as a useful multi-purpose flour (Percival 1934). When both species are grown, either together as a maslin, or separately, they provide added insurance against crop loss as the two crops have different tolerance to infections or frost, thus where one is damaged the other may survive.

Hordeum sp. (barley) and *Avena* sp. (oats) are present in all samples. All seeds identified as *Avena* were recorded as grain. Although this means that any wild oats will be recorded as cultivated, given the absence of floret bases this provides the only reasonable impression of the relative importance of oats in the samples. Oats and barley occur in very similar numbers overall, although the ratios vary from sample to sample. The numbers of barley and oats are similar in sample 1 and 3. In samples 4 and 7, barley is approximately three times as frequent as oats, while oats forms only a minor component of sample 8. The two species were commonly grown together as a mixed crop or drage (Slicker van Bath 1963). They have uses together as a pottage (Bennett 1960) and also for brewing, evidence of which was recovered from West Cotton (Campbell forthcoming b). Each crop can equally be grown and used on its own, for example as pot barley and rolled oats, as well as for flour and individually for brewing. Markham provides documentary evidence for the use of oats on their own for brewing (Markham 1681).

Leguminous crops are represented by *Vicia sativa* subsp. *sativa* (cultivated field vetch) and *Vicia faba* (field bean). The majority of legumes were poorly preserved and lacked their testa and hilum. This group was simply recorded as cultivated *Vicia/Lathyrus/Pisum* sp. which is distinguished from seeds of weed/wild varieties of *Vicia/Lathyrsus* sp. on the basis of size. Pulses are generally poorly represented in archaeological contexts. They are not usually exposed to fire during processing, and if used as fodder the whole plant is fed to the animal therefore leaving little waste to be burnt as fuel. The threshing waste is, however, recommended as a substitute for cereal chaff as a fuel for drying malt by Markham (1681). Evidence for the use of legume chaff as fuel is provided by seeds occurring in ovens in association with large quantities of legume pod fragments at West Cotton (Campbell unpublished). If the structure is domestic in nature then the beans may have been charred during cooking accidents. *Vicia sativa* spp *sativa* is likely to have been grown as animal fodder, thus it may have entered the deposits as fuel, although it could also provide a human famine food. Documentary evidence attests to its cultivation from the early 13th century AD, while examples from West Cotton were recovered from the first half of the 12th century, thought to be the earliest record in Britain (Campbell 1994).

Seeds of *Brassica/Sinapis* spp. were present in three of the samples taken from floor deposits (samples 1, 3 and 4). Seeds of any of the *Brassica/Sinapis* species could have been used as condiments. They also have uses in brewing, both as a flavouring, and as an addition to ale as a means to reduce fermentation (Man and Weir 1984, 14). Large numbers of brassica seeds

Table 8.58   Charred plant remains from Street Farm.

	1	3	4	7	8
Context	500	517	503	602	613
Vol (litres)	2	4	12	1	1
Fraction	100%	100%	100%	100%	50%
Feature type	Layer	Layer	Layer	Oven	Layer
Triticum sp. free-threshing, compact grain	29	113	46	6	102
Triticum sp. free-threshing, intermediate grain	16	30	11	-	19
Triticum sp. free-threshing, elongated grain	-	-	-	5	14
Triticum sp. wheat grain	27	64	36	6	62
Hordeum vulgare lateral grain	2	-	-	-	-
Hordeum sp. hulled	13	36	28	9	18
Hordeum sp. hulled, germinated	-	1	-	-	-
Hordeum sp.	8	-	19	7	15
Avena sp. Oat grain	20	30	15	6	5
Cerealia indet grain	58	132	89	17	87
Triticum sp. hexaploid rachis	-	2	1	-	4
Triticum sp.tetraploid rachis	1	2	4	-	7
Triticum sp. naked rachis	3	3	-	-	32
Hordeum/Secale rachis internode	1	-	9	-	8
Cerealia indet rachis internode	-	2	-	-	
Cerealia indet embryo	-	3	-	-	2
Cerealia indet sprouted embryo	-	1	-	-	
Cereal size culm node	-	-	-	-	2
Vicia sativa subsp. *sativa*	1	2	6	1	
cf. *Vicia faba*	-	2	4	-	17
Vicia/Lathyrus/Pisum sp.	19	17	46	10	-
Papaver sp.	-	-	1	-	-
Brassica cf. *Nigra*	-	1	-	-	-
Brassica/Sinapis sp.	1	5	3	-	-
Stellaria media agg.	-	-	1	-	-
Montia fontana subsp. *fontana*	-	1	-	-	-
Caryophyllaceae	1	-	-	-	-
Chenopodium album	-	2	1	1	-
Chenopodium sp.	-	-	1	-	-
Atriplex sp.	-	4	7	2	-
Chenopodiaceae	-	-	13	-	3
Vicia/Lathyrus sp.	4	-	3	-	6
Medicago lupinula	-	1	6	1	11
Leguminosae small seeded	20	-	65	6	39
Rosaceae type thorn	-	-	-	-	1
Polygonum persicaria	-	-	1	-	1
Polygonum convulvulus	-	-	2	-	-
Polygonum sp.	-	-	4	-	-
Rumex sp.	2	3	21	4	6
Polygonaceae	-	2	3	-	-
Polygonaceae/Cyperacacea	-	-	3	-	-
cf. *Anagalis* sp.	3	1	6	-	-
Lithospermun arvensis	-	-	-	-	4
Odontites verna/Euphrasia sp.	-	1	13	1	1
Plantago major	-	2	6	-	-
Galium apernine	-	-	1	-	2
Sambucus nigra	-	-	2	-	-
Anthemis cotula	3	11	61	1	5
Chrysanthemum segetum	-	-	1	1	-
Compositae	-	12	7	-	1
Eleocharis palustris	-	1	8	-	2
Carex sp.	-	-	7	-	-
Cyperacacea	2	-	5	1	-
Phalaris sp.	1	-	-	-	-

Table 8.58 continued.

	1	3	4	7	8
Context	500	517	503	602	613
Vol (litres)	2	4	12	1	1
Fraction	100%	100%	100%	100%	50%
Feature type	Layer	Layer	Layer	Oven	Layer
Granineae large seeded	9	10	19	3	12
Granineae small seeded	1	15	10	-	1
Weed indet	2	13	45	3	14
Total grain	173	406	244	56	322
Total chaff	5	14	44	0	61
Total legumes	20	21	56	11	19
Total weeds	49	85	326	24	109
Total	247	526	670	91	511

were recovered from the floors of malt-houses at West Cotton (Campbell unpublished). The seeds also often occur in faecal deposits of medieval date, further indicating their use as a spice (Greig 1991). While they do occur as ruderal weeds, they certainly were being cultivated by the medieval period, both for their seeds and their leaves. Either origin is possible for the examples in these deposits.

The weed assemblage

The weed seeds form approximately 20% of the assemblages in four of the five samples. The species represented are generally common weeds of arable or disturbed ground. Sample 12 conversely produced a greater number of weed seeds than cereal grains, with weed seeds forming some 48.7% of the assemblage.

Leguminous weeds form the major group of weeds in all samples. *Medicago lupulina* L. (black medick) was identified where sufficient seed coat remained, while *Vicia/Lathyrus* sp. (vetches) were distinguished from cultivated legumes on the basis of size. The category of small seeded Leguminoseae includes seeds of shape similar to the *Medicago lupulina* but which lacked any seed coat, as well as other small legumes not identifiable as *Vicia/Lathyrus*. Leguminous weeds generally increase in frequency during the late Saxon and early medieval period, for example at the Raunds sites in Northamptonshire (Campbell forthcoming). This may reflect decreasing soil fertility resulting from the agricultural expansion from the 13th century, or the deliberate cultivation or encouragement of natural swards of grass and legumes for animal fodder. Leguminous weeds also tend to occur in large numbers in association with large numbers of cultivated legumes, for example in medieval deposits at Eynsham Abbey, Oxfordshire (Pelling forthcoming b). Climbing leguminous weeds could be growing up with cultivated varieties of the same species, for example, wild and cultivated varieties of *Vicia sativa*. It is possible, therefore, that the leguminous weeds are simply a common weed of cultivated legumes and that increases in number reflect increases in the cultivation of legumes.

Species normally associated with wet ground or damp grass land are present in each sample, most notably sample 4. *Montia fontana* and *Eleocharis palustris* both require at least seasonal flooding. They are known in association with cereal assemblages from the Iron Age onwards, leading to their interpretation as arable weeds, even though they are not regarded as weeds today. Their presence as an arable weed is usually taken to suggest the cultivation of marginal land, possibly that the arable fields go down onto the flood plain of the river Churn. Several of the species of *Carex* are also commonly associated with wet or damp ground. Some evidence is provided regarding the type of soils utilised. The presence of fairly frequent seeds of *Anthemis cotula* and *Odontites verna* suggest the cultivation of rather heavy calcareous claylands, while the seeds of *Papaver* sp. suggest some well drained, lighter calcareous soils may have been cultivated. Some indication is also provided of the cultivation of lighter acid sandy soils by the presence of *Chrysanthemum segetum*.

The remaining weed species include common ruderals such as members of the Chenopodiaceae and Polygonaceae families. Such weeds could have been growing in the settlement area itself or as arable weeds, and are ubiquitous among charred cereal assemblages. Some poorly preserved grasses were present. Cereal grains may be included in the group, while other grasses may have been growing on the headlands of arable fields.

The charcoal

Charcoal of *Ulmus* sp. (elm) and *Quercus* sp. (oak) were present in each of the two samples selected for charcoal analysis (Table 8.59). Two fragments of Pomoideae charcoal (apple, pear, hawthorn etc.) were also identified in sample 4. *Quercus* charcoal is commonly found in archaeological contexts and is a naturally favoured wood for construction purposes. One fragment of *Quercus* charcoal was attached to an iron nail. It has been noticed that *Ulmus* increases in proportion to other wood charcoal during the medieval period (Mark Robinson pers. comm.). Rackham (1986) refers to the deliberate collection of *Ulmus* timbers from hedgerows during the medieval period, if not for construction purposes then at least for repair work. The wood is likely to have been reused as fuel in the oven or hearth within the building.

Acknowledgements

I would like to thank Gill Campbell for giving me permission to quote unpublished work and to Gill Campbell and Mark Robinson for their assistance with identifications and comments on the text.

Table 8.59   Charcoal from Street Farm.

	Sample	4	5
	Context	503	552
Quercus	Oak	4	38
Ulmus sp.	Elm	15	4
Pomoideae	Apple, pear, hawthorn etc.	2	-

LAND AND FRESHWATER MOLLUSCA
By Mark Robinson

Introduction

The route of the A417/419 runs entirely over calcareous substrata from the Oolitic Limestone of the Cotswold Hills between Birdlip and Cirencester, the cornbrash on the edge of the Thames Valley below Cirencester to the Pleistocene terrace gravels of the Thames system around Cricklade. Such conditions might seem ideal for the palaeoecological investigation of mollusca from archaeological sediments and buried soils. However, the Jurassic limestones of the Cotswolds and the Pleistocene gravels derived from them are hard. Deeper soil profiles over them tend to be circumneutral rather than calcareous unless they have been disturbed, so are not always conducive to the survival of shells. The brashy nature of the limestone, other than where it is in the form of Pleistocene gravel, can present problems of interpretation for land molluscs because some species which are usually characteristic of woodland can also find favourable conditions in the interstices to the fills of archaeological features (Evans and Jones 1973, 125).

During the excavations, snail shells were observed in the sediments at many of the sites and extensive sampling was undertaken. A total of 90 samples, from 17 excavations, was assessed for the range of molluscs present in them and their archaeological implications. All the samples yielded at least some snails, although in many cases the concentrations were very low or the results were of limited archaeological significance. On the basis of the assessment, eight sites were selected for detailed analysis: Highgate House, Field Farm, Middle Duntisbourne, Duntisbourne Grove, Trinity Farm, Latton 'Roman Pond', Street Farm and Weavers Bridge. Subsequently, further sections were cut through Ermin Street and a buried soil suitable for detailed analysis was found at Dartley Bottom.

Methods and results

Sub-samples weighing 1 kg were weighed out for each sample, broken up in water and any shells which floated were poured off onto a 0.5 mm mesh and dried. The residue was then sieved over a 0.5 mm mesh and dried. Both the flots and residues were sorted under a binocular microscope and any shells picked out. The shells were examined at up to x50 magnification and identified with reference to the collections of the Oxford University Museum of Natural History. The results are listed in a table for each site (Tables 8.60–8.65, 8.67–8.69), which lists the minimum number of individuals recorded for each sample. *Cecilioides acicula* has been excluded from the totals because it is a deeply burrowing species. It proved necessary to analyse some of the charred plant remains flots from Dartley Bottom and Duntisbourne Grove for molluscs. In the case of Duntisbourne Grove sample 6 there were sufficient shells that the equivalent of a 1 kg sample could be counted. Shells were sparse in the other samples so only the presence of species was recorded. Nomenclature for land snails follows Waldén (1976).

The lower samples from Latton 'Roman Pond' were waterlogged and some contained macroscopic plant remains. Sub-samples, weighing 1 kg, from these contexts were washed over onto a 0.25 mm mesh, sorted under a binocular microscope and the seeds from them identified at up to x50 magnifications using reference material. The results are given in Table 8.66, the nomenclature following Clapham *et al.* (1989).

Highgate House

The results from a sequence of samples from colluvial sediments in Trench 3 through what is now a small dry valley (section 18) are given in Table 8.60. Molluscs were virtually absent from the lowest colluvial sediments excavated (samples 36, 34, 33) apart from a very few shell fragments of terrestrial species. The occurrence of a few shells of *Lymnaea truncatula* and *Anisus leucostoma*, which are stagnant water to amphibious species, in sample 32 (context 306) suggests that there was formerly water seepage in the valley. The deposit was of Bronze Age, or perhaps earlier, date. Molluscs were absent from the overlying colluvial sediments.

Table 8.60   Molluscs, Highgate House.

Column/Section	18			
Sample	36	34	33	32
Context	312	308	307	306
Depth (m.)				0.4 - 0.5
Lymnaea truncatula (Müll.)	-	-	-	1
Anisus leucostoma (Mill.)	-	-	-	5
Cochlicopa sp.	-	-	1	-
Trichia hispida gp.	1	1	-	-

Field's Farm

A column of samples was investigated through the ditch fill of a square barrow of probable early Roman date (section 6) and the molluscs listed in Table 8.61. The ditch was cut into limestone. The lowest sample, from context 52, had a strong rock-rubble element to the fauna, represented by *Discus rotundatus* and *Oxychilus cellarius*. This was a result of the high limestone content of the primary fill, which had fallen in from the monument. Rupestral conditions also seem to have favoured *Punctatum pygmaeum*. The lower deposits of the ditch (context 52, 51 and 50) also contained high concentrations of dry-ground open-country molluscs, especially *Vallonia excentrica* but also *Pupilla muscorum*, *V. costata* and *Helicella itala*. Another open-country species from the ditch, *Vertigo pygmaea*, is not restricted to dry habitats. These species would have been reflecting the more general conditions on the site. Above context 52, the stone content of the ditch fill declined and the rock-rubble species almost disappeared. Numbers of all shells apart from *Cecilioides acicula*, a burrowing species, were very much reduced in the uppermost sample, from context 20.

Table 8.61   Molluscs, Field's Farm.

Column/section	6			
Sample	18	18	18	18
Context	52	51	50	20
Depth (m.)				
Pomatias elegans (Müll.)	-	2	1	-
Carychium cf. *tridentatum* (Risso)	-	2	1	-
Cochlicopa sp.	-	4	1	-
Vertigo pygmaea (drap.)	4	5	5	-
Pupilla muscorum (L.)	9	2	1	1
Vallonia costata (Müll.)	5	6	1	-
V. excentrica Sterki	11	18	2	1
Vallonia sp.	7	24	6	2
Punctum pygmaeum (Drap.)	10	7	1	-
Discus rotundatus (Müll.)	10	-	-	-
Vitrina pellucida (Müll.)	2	-	-	-
Vitrea cf. *contracta* (West.)	2	1	1	-
Aegopinella pura (Ald.)	-	1	-	-
A. nitidula (Drap.)	2	2	1	-
Oxychilus cellarius (Müll.)	11	-	-	-
Limax or *Deroceras* sp.	7	8	9	2
Cecilioides acicula (Müll.)	4	3	9	7
Helicella itala (L.)	3	2	1	1
Trichia hispida gp.	13	56	10	1
Cepaea nemoralis (L.)	-	1	-	-
Cepaea sp.	-	1	-	-
Total (excluding *Cecilioides acicula*)	96	142	41	8

Ermin Street, Trench 8, Dartley Bottom

A low concentration of shells was found to have survived in the soil sealed beneath Ermin Street and above the limestone bedrock in Trench 8. Although there were insufficient shells for detailed analysis in a sample column through the buried soil (context 877), an adequate assemblage was recovered from a bulk sample (sample 800). The results are given in Table 8.62. The fauna was characteristic of woodland, obligate open-country species being absent. Shells of *Carychium* cf. *tridentatum* were the most numerous but a full range of woodland species was present including *Ena obscura*, *Discus rotundatus*, *Oxychilus cellarius* and *Cochlodina laminata*. Relatively undisturbed, long-established woodland was suggested by the occurrence of *Acicula fusca*.

Table 8.62   Molluscs, Ermin Street, Trench 8, Dartley Bottom.

Column / Section	8
Sample	800
Context	877
Acicula fusca (Mont.)	+
Carychium cf. *tridentatum* (Risso)	++
Cochlicopa sp.	+
Vertigo sp.	+
Acanthinula aculeata (Müll.)	+
Ena obscura (Müll.)	+
Discus rotundatus (Müll.)	+
Vitrea sp.	++
Nesovitrea hammonis (Ström)	+
Aegopinella pura (Ald.)	+
A. nitidula (Drap.)	+
Oxychilus cellarius (Müll.)	+
Cochlodina laminata (Mont.)	+
Trichia hispida gp.	+

Middle Duntisbourne

A rich molluscan sequence was obtained from a closely-sampled column through a late Iron Age enclosure ditch (ditch 4, Fig. 3.39, section 29). The shells were somewhat eroded but still fully identifiable and the results are given in Table 8.63. They showed that several changes in environment occurred during the life of the ditch.

The primary fill of the ditch (context 58, samples 70–68) was clay loam almost devoid of shells. Above this was clay loam with much limestone rubble (context 57, samples 67–61). It contained a high concentration of shells, almost all of which are woodland species. One of the more numerous molluscs, *Discus rotundatus*, can also occur in rock-rubble faunas, living in the interstices between the stones, as can two other species from these samples, *Vitrea* cf. *contracta* and *Oxychilus cellarius*. However, a balanced woodland fauna was present, including many individuals of *Carychium* cf. *tridentatum*, which does not occur in rubble habitats. Most of the woodland species, such as *Aegopinella pura*, *A. nitidula*, *Cochlodina laminata* and *Trichia striolata* are still widespread in woodland on calcareous substrates in England. There were also several individuals of *Acicula fusca* and *Ena montana*, two species of limited distribution which tend to characterise old woodland (Kerney and Cameron 1979, 54–100). Around 2.5% of

Table 8.63   Molluscs, Middle Duntisbourne.

Column/Section	29															
Sample	70	69	68	67	66	65	64	63	62	61	60	59	58	57	56	55
Context	58	58	58	57	57	57	57	57	57	57	56	56	56	153	153	153
Depth (m.)	1.35-1.40	1.30-1.35	1.25-1.30	1.20-1.25	1.15-1.20	1.10-1.15	1.05-1.10	1.00-1.05	0.95-1.00	0.90-0.95	0.85-0.90	0.80-0.85	0.75-0.80	0.70-0.75	0.65-0.70	0.60-0.65
Acicula fusca (Mont.)	-	-	-	1	-	-	-	-	1	2	-	-	-	-	-	-
Carychium cf. *tridentatum* (Risso)	-	-	-	10	3	10	5	17	38	71	5	10	5	1	6	-
Cochlicopa sp.	-	-	-	1	2	-	-	3	5	4	-	-	-	-	-	-
Vertigo pygmaea (Drap.)	-	-	-	-	-	-	-	-	-	-	-	-	-	-	-	1
Pupilla muscorum (L.)	-	-	-	-	-	-	-	-	-	-	-	-	-	-	-	-
Vallonia costata (Müll.)	-	-	-	-	-	1	-	1	-	1	1	1	-	-	1	-
V. excentrica Sterki	-	-	-	-	-	-	-	1	1	-	-	-	-	-	-	-
Vallonia sp.	-	-	-	3	1	2	-	1	1	-	3	-	-	1	-	-
Ena montana (Drap.)	-	-	-	-	1	-	-	-	-	-	-	-	-	-	-	-
E. obscura (Müll.)	-	-	-	-	1	-	-	-	-	-	-	-	-	-	-	-
Punctum pygmaeum (Drap.)	-	-	-	1	-	-	1	1	-	2	-	-	-	-	1	-
Discus rotundatus (Müll.)	-	1	1	14	13	12	9	7	15	21	2	2	1	-	3	-
Vitrina pellucida (Müll.)	-	-	-	-	-	-	-	-	-	-	-	-	-	1	-	-
Vitrea cf. *contracta* (West.)	-	-	-	2	1	-	-	2	4	6	2	-	-	-	-	-
Nesovitrea hammonis (Ström)	-	-	-	-	-	-	-	-	-	-	-	-	-	-	-	-
Aegopinella pura (Ald.)	-	-	-	1	3	-	-	3	2	4	-	1	2	-	1	-
A. nitidula (Drap.)	-	-	-	2	4	1	-	5	8	8	-	-	-	-	2	-
Oxychilus cellarius (Müll.)	-	-	-	3	6	1	1	3	1	1	-	1	-	-	1	-
Limax or *Deroceras* sp.	-	-	-	3	1	7	-	1	1	1	1	2	-	1	-	-
Cecilioides acicula (Müll.)	-	-	-	1	1	-	-	5	5	1	-	1	-	-	-	-
Cochlodina laminata (Mont.)	-	-	-	-	-	1	1	-	3	1	-	-	-	-	-	-
Clausilia bidentata (Ström)	-	-	-	-	1	-	2	-	1	1	-	-	-	-	-	-
Helicella itala (L.)	-	-	-	-	-	-	-	-	-	-	-	-	-	-	-	-
Trichia striolata (Pfeiff.)	-	-	-	3	14	11	14	5	12	14	-	-	-	-	-	-
T. hispida gp.	-	1	-	3	3	1	4	4	7	2	2	1	-	1	1	-
Arianta arbustorum (L.)	-	-	-	-	1	2	-	-	-	-	-	-	-	-	-	-
Helicigona lapicida (L.)	-	-	-	-	-	-	-	-	-	-	-	-	-	-	-	-
Cepaea sp.	-	-	-	-	-	-	-	1	-	1	-	-	-	-	-	-
Arianta or *Cepaea* sp.	-	-	-	-	1	1	-	-	1	2	-	-	1	-	1	1
Helicellidae indet.	1	-	-	-	-	-	-	-	-	-	-	-	-	-	-	-
Total excluding *Cecilioides acicula*	1	2	1	47	55	51	37	55	101	142	16	18	9	5	17	2

the shells were from open country species of the genus *Vallonia*. *V. excentrica* was present in addition to *V. costata*, which does also occur in low numbers in woodland (Evans 1972, 156–7).

There was a decrease in the concentration of shells in the clay loam of the next layer in the ditch (context 56, samples 60–58). *Trichia striolata* disappeared and the old woodland species were absent. However, *Carychium* cf. *tridentatum* was the most numerous mollusc and the proportion of open country species remained low. Similar conditions seem to have prevailed in the lower part of the layer of stony clay loam above (context 153, samples 57–56). Only two shells were found in the top sample from this layer (sample 55).

Shell numbers increased in the clay loam of context 54 (samples 54–51) and remained high in the lower two-thirds of context 55 (samples 50–46), the next layers up the sequence. The most numerous shells were from

the genus *Vallonia*, which comprises open country species. *Vallonia costata* was the best represented amongst those which could be attributed to species. There was a significant presence of *Carychium* cf. *tridentatum*, which also occurs on long grass but otherwise there were few shells of woodland species. The calcite internal plates of the slugs *Limax* or *Deroceras* were well-represented.

Shell numbers declined somewhat in sample 45, increasing again in the top two samples from the ditch (context 55, samples 44–43). *Carychium* cf. *tridentatum* was absent. Shells from the genus *Vallonia* predominated, with both *V. costata* and *V. excentrica* present. There was a slight presence of two other open country species, *Pupilla muscorum* and *Helicella itala*.

The primary fill of the ditch presumably accumulated rapidly after it had been dug. The fauna of context 57 (samples 67–61) suggested conditions of old woodland. It is possible that the enclosure had

54	53	52	51	50	49	48	47	46	45	44	43
54	54	54	55	55	55	55	55	55	55	55	55
0.55-	0.50-	0.45-	0.40-	0.35-	0.30-	0.25-	0.20-	0.15-	0.10-	0.05-	0-
0.60	0.55	0.50	0.45	0.40	0.35	0.30	0.30	0.20	0.15	0.10	0.05
-	-	-	-	-	-	-	-	-	-	-	-
3	9	2	3	7	22	7	1	-	-	-	-
-	1	-	-	2	1	-	2	-	-	-	-
1	4	1	1	-	-	1	-	-	2	-	1
-	-	-	-	-	2	-	-	-	-	1	1
1	2	2	1	3	5	2	1	-	2	3	3
1	-	-	-	-	4	3	2	2	4	4	4
1	9	5	2	3	19	6	1	5	5	13	15
-	-	-	-	-	-	-	-	-	-	-	-
1	1	-	2	5	3	-	-	-	-	-	-
3	6	-	1	1	-	1	-	-	-	-	2
-	-	-	-	-	-	-	-	-	-	-	-
-	-	-	1	3	1	1	-	-	-	1	1
-	-	-	-	1	-	-	-	-	-	-	-
-	1	-	1	-	3	-	-	-	-	1	-
2	2	1	-	-	5	1	1	1	-	-	-
-	-	-	-	-	-	-	-	-	-	-	-
8	8	14	19	17	12	8	18	10	1	1	3
-	2	-	-	-	-	1	-	-	-	1	-
-	-	-	-	-	1	-	-	-	-	-	-
1	1	1	1	-	-	-	-	-	-	1	1
-	1	-	-	-	1	2	-	1	-	1	2
3	1	-	-	-	-	-	-	-	-	-	-
6	12	10	4	8	9	5	7	7	5	2	3
-	-	-	-	-	-	-	1	-	-	-	-
-	-	1	-	-	-	-	-	-	-	-	-
1	-	-	1	-	-	-	-	-	-	-	-
2	1	1	-	-	2	1	1	-	-	-	-
-	-	-	-	-	-	-	-	-	-	-	-
34	59	38	36	47	93	38	36	26	19	28	36

been constructed in an area of woodland and regeneration was allowed to occur over the ditch. The few shells of *Vallonia* sp. could have been the result of the interior being kept open. The faunal changes with the deposition of contexts 56 and 153 (samples 60–56) probably reflected changing environmental conditions although the site seems to have remained wooded.

The virtual absence of shells from the top of context 153 (sample 55) was probably the result of the site being cleared. Throughout the period of deposition of context 54 and the lower two-thirds of context 55 (samples 54–46) the surrounds of the ditch were open. It is possible that there was some scrub on the site in a hedge alongside the ditch but tall herbaceous vegetation in the ditch would be sufficient explanation for the occurrence of the shade-loving species. The top three samples from context 55 (samples 45–43) showed fully open conditions without any tall vegetation in the ditch.

Duntisbourne Grove

Two samples were analysed from the bottom of two sections through a large rock-cut ditch of late Iron Age date (ditch 114, Fig. 3.43, sections 30 and 29). A short column of samples was also investigated from a small Iron Age ditch 9 (section 15). The results are given in Table 8.64. Samples 6 and 9 from ditch 114 contained rich woodland faunas, with numerous shells of *Carychium* cf. *tridentatum. Discus rotundatus, Vitrea* cf. *contracta* and *Oxychilus cellarius* were also well represented. While the last three species can live in rock rubble habitats, *C. tridentatum* does not. There were smaller numbers of other shade-loving species which do not occur in rock-rubble faunas including *Ena obscura, Clausilia bidentata* and *Trichia striolata*. There was only a slight presence of molluscs of open habitats in the form of one shell of *Vertigo pygmaea* and several shells of *Vallonia costata. V. pygmaea* does not occur in woodland but *V. costata* has been recorded in low numbers in woodland (Evans 1972, 156-7). These samples were from low in the fill of the ditch, so it seems unlikely that they post-dated the abandonment of the enclosure made by the ditch, unless it had a very short life. it seems more likely that either the enclosure was indeed set in woodland or that hedges along either side of the ditch had merged.

Molluscs were sparse from section 15 (samples 5, 4, 2) from ditch 9. The assemblages included *Pupilla muscorum, Vallonia excentrica* and *Helicella itala*. They indicated very different conditions from those suggested by the assemblages from the large Iron Age ditch, woodland species being entirely absent.

Trinity Farm

Molluscs were recovered from one of a group of late Neolithic to Beaker shallow rock-cut pits (section 11, context 11). They included both open-country species (*Pupilla muscorum* and *Vallonia excentrica*) and shade-loving species (*Discus rotundatus* and *Oxychilus cellarius*) (Table 8.65). While *D. rotundatus* and *O. cellarius* could represent a rock-rubble element to the fauna, the assemblage was small and conditions need by no means have been fully open.

Latton 'Roman Pond' macroscopic plant remains and Mollusca *(Fig. 4.30)*

Field observations by OAU suggested that the hollow which had been interpreted as a Roman pond was, on the basis of topography, a palaeochannel in the lower gravel terrace rather than a dug feature. This was confirmed by excavating a trench across it. The feature

Table 8.64   Molluscs, Duntisbourne Grove.

Column/Section	30	29	15		
Sample	9	6	5	4	2
Context	134	87	74	64	47
Depth (m.)					
Carychium cf. *tridentatum* (Risso)	27	47	-	-	-
Cochlicopa sp.	4	4	-	-	-
Vertigo pygmaea (Drap.)	-	1	-	-	-
Pupilla muscorum (L.)	-	-	+	-	+
Vallonia costata (Müll.)	2	6	-	-	-
V. excentrica Sterki	-	-	+	-	+
Vallonia sp.	1	1	+	-	+
Ena obscura (Müll.)	1	-	-	-	-
Punctum pygmaeum (Drap.)	1	1	-	-	-
Discus rotundatus (Müll.)	18	12	-	-	-
Vitrina pellucida (Müll.)	2	1	-	-	-
Vitrea cf. *contracta* (West.)	8	12	-	-	-
Nesovitrea hammonis (Ström)	1	1	-	-	+
Aegopinella pura (Ald.)	3	6	-	-	-
A. nitidula (Drap.)	1	2	-	-	-
Oxychilus cellarius (Müll.)	8	15	-	-	-
Limax or *Deroceras* sp.	1	-	-	-	-
Cecilioides acicula (Müll.)	4	3	+	-	+
Cochlodina laminata (Mont.)	1	-	-	-	-
Clausilia bidentata (Ström)	1	1	-	-	-
Helicella itala (L.)	-	-	+	-	-
Helicellinae indet.	-	-	-	-	+
Trichia striolata (Pfeiff.)	5	6	-	-	-
T. hispida gp.	4	10	+	+	+
Arianta arbustorum (L.)	1	1	-	-	-
Cepaea nemoralis (L.)	-	3	-	-	-
Total excluding *Cecilioides acicula*	90	130			

+ present

was shown to be shallow, with gently sloping sides and to overlie leached Pleistocene terrace gravels. The gravel bed of the channel showed involutions characteristic of tree-throw holes, which contained woody organic sediments and redeposited gravel. Some of these features cut yellowish-brown clay which overlay the gravel. The tree-throw holes were covered by a dark grey-brown humic alluvial clay (context 506), which graded upwards into peaty clay (context 505). The peaty clay was cut by some ditches and a grey gravelly clay loam ploughsoil extended a short distance from the north-west edge of the channel, partly covering the ditches. The ploughsoil and peat were overlain by mottled grey brown alluvial clay loam (contexts 504, 503, 502). A ploughsoil, which supported the modern turf, had been created from the top part of the alluvium in recent years (context 501).

A column of samples was taken through these sediments (section 501). Shells and organic remains other than roots were absent from the lowest two samples (context 507, 0.50–0.55 m, context 506, 0.47–0.50 m). The next three samples (context 506, 0.43–0.47 m, context 505, 0.40–0.43 m, 0.35–0.40 m) contained badly preserved waterlogged seeds

(Table 8.66). Some *Alnus/Corylus* (alder/hazel) charcoal, a waterlogged *Crataegus/Prunus* (hawthorn/sloe) thorn and two waterlogged prickles of *Rubus* sp. were also present in the sample from context 506, 0.43–0.47 m. The sample from context 505, 0.40–0.43 m also contained two carbonised nut shell fragments of *Corylus avellana* (hazel). The remains from context 506, 0.43–0.47 m suggested dry fen scrub or carr grew in the palaeo-channel. Seeds of fully aquatic plants were absent, but there were many seeds of *Eupatorium cannabinum* (hemp agrimony), a plant of damp shaded habitats including fen woods. A scrub element was suggested by the remains of *Rubus fruticosus* agg. (blackberry), *Crataegus* or *Prunus* sp. (hawthorn or sloe) and *Sambucus nigra* (elder). While it is possible that remains of more substantial trees had not been preserved, remains would have been expected to survive from *Alnus glutinosa* (alder), the tree most likely to have been growing on the channel bed prior to clearance. The other seeds were mostly from species which will grow in damp scrub such as *Ranunculus* cf. *repens* (buttercup), *Viola* S. *Viola* sp. (violet) and *Ajuga reptans* (bugle) although they are by no means restricted to this habitat. Preservation was very poor in the two samples above, but seeds of *E. cannabinum* were absent and there was a decline in the number of remains from shrubs, perhaps suggesting conditions becoming more open. The burnt fragments of hazelnut shell were perhaps from nearby prehistoric activity.

Remains were entirely absent from context 504, 0.30–0.35 m but mollusc shells were recovered from context 503, 0.27–0.30 m, context 502, 0.20–0.27 m and context 501, 0– 0.20 m (Table 8.67). The occurrence of the flowing water mollusc *Valvata piscinalis* confirmed the riverine origin of the alluvial sediments. There was also a stagnant water to amphibious component of the fauna comprising *Lymnaea truncatula* and *Anisus leucostoma* which probably flourished in pools left by receding floodwaters. The majority of shells, however, were from species favoured by damp grassland including *Carychium* sp., *Vallonia pulchella* and *Trichia hispida* gp. These three faunal elements are particularly characteristic of grassland on the

Table 8.65   Molluscs, Trinity Farm.

	Column/Section	11
	Sample	2
	Context	11
	Depth (m.)	
Vertigo pygmaea (Drap.)		1
Pupilla muscorum (L.)		2
V. excentrica Sterki		1
Vallonia sp.		2
Discus rotundatus (Müll.)		5
Oxychilus cellarius (Müll.)		2
Cecilioides acicula (Müll.)		631
Cepaea sp.		1
Total excluding *Cecilioides acicula*		14

Table 8.66   Waterlogged seeds, Latton 'Roman Pond'.

Column / Section		501		
Sample				
Context		506	505	505
Depth (m)		0.43–0.47	0.40–0.43	0.35–0.40
Ranunculus cf. *acris* L.	Meadow buttercup	-	-	1
R. cf. *repens* L.	Creeping buttercup	2	-	-
Viola S. *Viola* sp.	Violet	1	1	-
Atriplex sp.	Orache	2	1	-
Rubus cf. *fruticosus* agg.	Blackberry	12	3	-
Chaerophyllum temulentum L.	Rough chervil	1	-	-
Mentha cf. *aquatica* L.	Water mint	-	2	3
Ajuga reptans L.	Bugle	2	5	8
Sambucus nigra L.	Elder	8	1	1
Eupatorium cannabinum L.	Hemp agrimony	34	-	-
Juncus sp.	Rush	1	-	-
Carex sp.	Sedge	1	2	5
Total		64	15	18

floodplain of the Upper Thames that is managed as hay meadow (Robinson 1988). The few shells of *Vallonia excentrica* in the uppermost sample were perhaps a reflection of recent drainage and cultivation. However, the numerous shells of *Carychium* sp. in this sample showed that cultivation had not been occurring for long.

Table 8.67   Molluscs, Latton 'Roman Pond'.

Column/Section	501		
Sample			
Context	503	502	501
Depth (m.)	0.27–0.30	0.20–0.27	0–0.20
Valvata piscinalis (Müll.)	-	-	1
Carychium sp.	1	31	28
Lymnaea truncatula (Müll.)	-	8	6
L. peregra (Müll.)	-	-	1
Anisus leucostoma (Mill.)	-	2	5
Bathyomphalus contortus (L.)	1	-	-
Succinea or *Oxyloma* sp.	1	1	-
Cochlicopa sp.	-	5	9
Vertigo pygmaea (Drap.)	-	-	2
Vertigo sp.	-	2	-
Pupilla muscorum (L.)	-	-	1
Vallonia pulchella (Müll.)	1	10	6
V. excentrica Sterki	-	-	4
Vallonia sp.	5	31	34
Acanthinula aculeata (Müll.)	-	1	-
Punctum pygmaeum (Drap.)	-	1	1
Vitrea sp.	-	-	1
Nesovitrea hammonis (Ström)	-	1	-
Aegopinella pura (Ald.)	-	1	-
Zonitoides nitidus (Müll.)	-	1	-
Limax or *Deroceras* sp.	-	12	10
Cecilioides acicula (Müll.)	-	-	1
Helicellinae indet.	-	-	1
Trichia hispida gp.	3	38	28
Total excluding *Cecilioides acicula*	12	145	138

Table 8.68   Molluscs, Street Farm.

Column/Section	28
Sample	2
Context	365
Depth (m.)	
Vertigo pygmaea (Drap.)	1
V. excentrica Sterki	6
Vallonia sp.	13
Vitrina pellucida (Müll.)	1
Cecilioides acicula (Müll.)	3
Helicella itala (L.)	1
Trichia hispida gp.	1
Arianta or *Cepaea* sp.	1
Total excluding *Cecilioides acicula*	24

The "pond" probably had its origin as a minor channel re-working the top of the gravels in the Late Devensian. It could have been dry throughout most of the Holocene and trees grew on its bed. However, a rise in the water table resulted in the preservation of organic material in tree-throw holes and the soil becoming humic. Following clearance, fen peat which supported scrub began to develop in the palaeochannel. By analogy with events further downstream in the Upper Thames Valley, the rising water table was perhaps occurring in the 1st millennium BC as a response to tree clearance in the Cotswolds (Robinson 1992a). A radiocarbon date of 2943±63BP (R24151/19) was obtained on waterlogged seeds from the bottom of the organic sequence (context 506, 0.43–0.47). Some cultivation, perhaps of Iron Age or Roman date occurred alongside the palaeochannel. Subsequently, alluvial clay partly filled the palaeochannel. Again by analogy with the evidence from further downstream, there were major episodes of overbank alluviation in the Roman and late Saxon to medieval periods as a result of erosion in the Cotswolds caused by extensive cultivation on the slopes (Robinson 1992a). The evidence of the molluscs from the alluvium for hay meadow also fits into the general pattern of the region. Hay meadow became extensive on the floodplain of the Upper Thames in the medieval period.

Street Farm

A sample was examined from a buried soil overlying the terrace gravels in the south-east corner of the site (Fig. 6.2) and perhaps sealed by Ermin Street (section 28, context 365). The snails from it (Table 8.68) gave evidence of open conditions, with *Vallonia excentrica* predominating. The assemblage was too small to determine whether the soil supported grassland or arable vegetation.

Weavers Bridge

A column of alluvial clay sediment was examined from the floodplain of the river Churn near the Roman midden. The lowest part of the sequence (context 92) was dark grey silty clay which overlay the Pleistocene gravels and contained some charred plant remains, including cereals. Above was grey silty clay (context 91). The molluscs are listed in Table 8.69. The majority of the shells from the alluvium were of aquatic or amphibious species, *Lymnaea truncatula* being particularly abundant. Shells of snails of vegetated permanently marshy habitats and of fully terrestrial habitats were almost absent. *L. truncatula* is an amphibious species characteristic of wet mud as well as small bodies of stagnant water. It probably flourished along with *Anisus leucostoma* in the pools left by retreating floodwaters in the spring. When the floodplain dried out in the spring, they would have retreated into cracks. Such a fauna occurs on low-lying flood pastures in the Upper Thames Valley (Robinson 1988). The shells of some of the other aquatic species, for example *Planorbis planorbis* and *Gyraulus albus* had probably been deposited from the river by floodwater.

Table 8.69 Molluscs, Weavers Bridge.

Column / Section	23		
Sample	2	3	5
Context	92	91	91
Depth (m.)			
Carychium cf. *minimum* (Müll.)	-	-	1
Lymnaea truncatula (Müll.)	9	47	39
L. peregra (Müll.)	3	4	1
Planorbis planorbis (L.)	2	5	1
Anisus leucostoma (Mill.)	2	4	7
Bathyomphalus contortus (L.)	1	-	-
Gyraulus albus (Müll.)	-	1	-
Succinea or *Oxyloma* sp.	-	1	-
Vallonia pulchella (Müll.)	-	-	1
Candidula or *Cernuella* sp.	1	-	-
Trichia hispida gp.	1	2	1
Pisidium sp.	1	-	-
Total	20	64	51

The occurrence of a shell of *Candidula* or *Cernuella* sp. in sample 2 suggested that context 92 post-dated the Roman midden because they are regarded as medieval introductions to Britain. This was confirmed by the Saxon/medieval character of the charred plant remains from the deposit (see Pelling, above).

THE CHURN VALLEY PROFILE AND SEDIMENTARY SEQUENCE
By Rob Scaife

Introduction

A 12 m long trench (BAULT96 Trench 2) was excavated through alluvial sediments to investigate well-preserved organic deposits which had been identified in the original auger sampling transect (Cores 11 and 14) (Fig. 8.23). The trench was positioned well-preserved organic deposits which had been identified in the original auger sampling transect (Cores 11 and 14) (Fig. 8.23). The trench was positioned within a shallow depression marking the infilled course of a stream channel. This appears to have been the main channel of the river Churn before the river was canalised on the western side to lengthen the mill leat or pound, effectively cutting off this meander. The parish boundary between Baunton and Bagendon follows the meander rather than the more recent channel to the west.

Trench 2

The trench was excavated primarily for the investigation of environmental remains. Samples were taken for pollen, macroscopic plant and insect remains, mollusca and charred plant remains. Samples for radiocarbon dating were also obtained. Artefacts were absent except for a sharpened oak post (sample 24) from the lowest deposit in the channel (see Mitchell, Chapter 7). This sediment, about 0.3 m thick, was a slightly gleyed fine sandy silt with frequent waterlogged organic inclusions. This was overlain by a discontinuous deposit of grey and brown gleyed silt, which, at the eastern end of the trench, was separated from the upper layers by a thin band of sand. The middle third of the channel was a grey sandy silt up to 0.3 m thick. The upper deposits were an orange-brown silt and clay with fine gravel inclusions, overlain by a similar but more clayey sediment under the modern topsoil. It is not clear that any of these deposits can be interpreted as upcast from the mill pound, as identified in Evaluation Trench 549.

The macroscopic plant and insect remains from this section were poorly preserved and unremarkable (see Pelling, this chapter), reflecting mostly fen and aquatic species. However, pollen preservation was good, providing evidence of vegetation from both the local and wider catchments. Two pollen columns were taken (samples 13 and 14). That from the eastern end of the trench (sample 14) was found to have a more complete profile and was analysed in detail (see Scaife, this chapter).

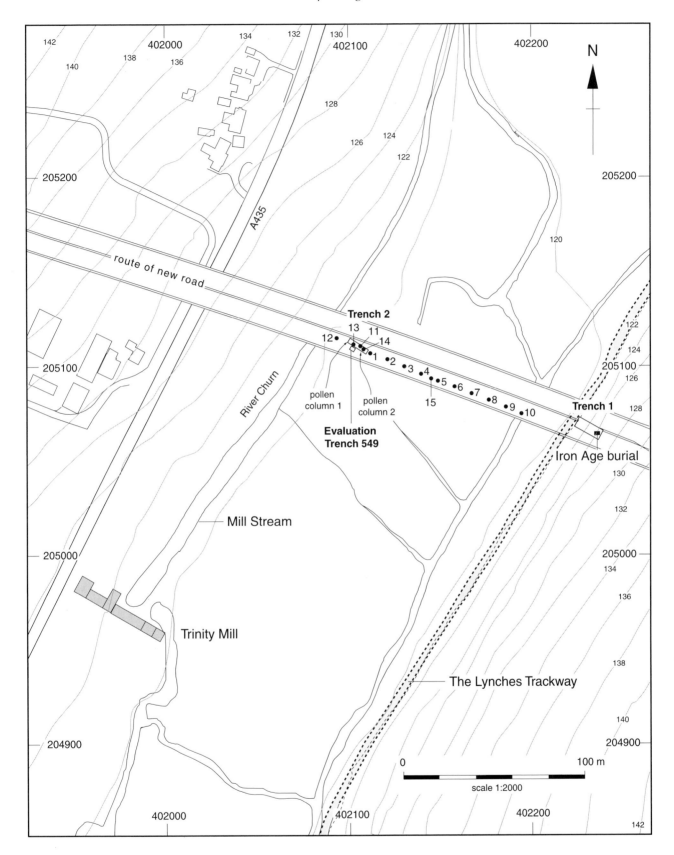

Figure 8.23   Churn Valley, plan of borehole locations and Mill stream.

The Churn Valley alluvial sediments

A cross-valley stratigraphical transect was carried out to assess the overall depth and character of the alluvial fills of the Churn Valley along the road corridor (Fig. 8.24). From this survey, a suitable point was chosen for pollen coring (Russian/Jowsey). Only the lower half of the sediment profile was sampled since the upper, alluvial stratigraphy was very gleyed and oxidised. A 1.25 m sequence was recovered and comprised inorganic, grey, alluvial clays with silt. Due to the local alkalinity of the bedrock and the highly inorganic character of the material examined, little pollen was expected. This was found to be the case with poor preservation. Preliminary pollen counts were obtained only with great difficulty. The data should, therefore, be treated carefully. The very substantial numbers of pre-Quaternary palynomorphs also attest to this and reflect the derived (allochthonous) origins of the sediment and possibly much of the pollen.

Pollen spectra obtained from the basal levels of the alluvial fill of the valley contained a greater number of trees with *Quercus* (oak) and *Corylus avellana* type (hazel/sweet gale) with some *Tilia* (lime) and *Fraxinus* (ash). Herbs are more important in the upper levels and are dominated by Lactucae (dandelion types) and Poaceae (grasses). The former were in general poorly preserved and are strong evidence of differential preservation (through oxidation and gleying) and the resulting skewed pollen spectra. This is also evidenced by the substantial numbers of fern spores and pre-Quaternary palynomorphs already noted.

Because of the poor pollen preservation and absence of dating (due to absence of suitable organic material), no detailed interpretations can be made. However, the presence of hazel, oak, ash and lime pollen provides evidence of woodland on the drier valley side areas above the floodplain. Lime in the lowest level is interesting and may be attributed to lime woodland which has also been evidenced at Latton 'Roman Pond'. Radiocarbon dating of the latter to the late Bronze Age may indicate that the lowest levels here are also of late Bronze Age date although the 'lime decline' occurred at different times in different regions. Subsequently, oak and hazel woodland was predominant. Indications of a reduction in woodland in upper levels is associated with increased herbs including cereal pollen. This may be evidence for woodland clearance and agriculture such as has also been discussed for Latton 'Roman Pond'. However, as noted, there is strong evidence for differential pollen destruction and information here must be regarded with care.

Cyperaceae (sedges) reflect the character of the 'on-site' vegetation which appears to have been sedge/grass fen marginal to the river. This would have been subject to overbank deposition of sediments. Little more can be deduced from this site as pollen preservation and absolute numbers of grains were very poor.

POLLEN ANALYSIS OF THE CHURN VALLEY RIVER CHANNEL
By Rob Scaife

Introduction

The primary sediment sequences of the river Churn valley and the secondary fills of the river channel were initially assessed for pollen and spore content (CAT 1991; Scaife 1997). Whilst some pollen was present in the primary valley fills (see above), preservation and absolute pollen frequencies were not sufficient to warrant full pollen analysis. Pollen was, however, identifiable and countable in the fill of the channel. Given the limestone geology of the region, that is, on Jurassic Oolite on both sides of the valley and Forest marbles on the tops of the hill, it is somewhat surprising that such pollen is present.

At the evaluation stage a small hand-dug trial pit recovered some organic deposits which when assessed were found to have good pollen preservation (CAT 1991a, 48–49). Although it was speculated that the pollen sequence may have a Saxon component, and this has been repeated in publication (Gerrard 1994a; 97), no dating evidence was obtained. Radiocarbon dates from the current project produced two late medieval dates of 1421–1471 cal AD (R24151/20, 2 sigma) and 1431–1482 cal AD (R24151/211; 2 sigma).

Stratigraphy

Two monolith samples were taken from the excavated section (Fig. 8.25). Of these, monolith B appeared to have the most complete and undisturbed profile. Consequently, it was this profile which was pollen analysed. The stratigraphy was described in the laboratory at the same time as sampling for pollen was carried out. The stratigraphy comprises:

Depth cm: 0–4 Orange/brown clay and silt (10YR 6/8) to 7.YR 5/8).
6–8 Large stone
8–22 Grey sandy silt (2.5Y 4/2) with freshwater molluscs. Sand band from 19-20 cm.
22–46 Grey (2.5Y 4/2) gleyed brown (5Y 5/8). Evidence of fine roots now eroded.
46–72 Grey, fine sandy silt (5YR 4/1). Less gleying than above. Freshwater molluscs to base.
72–73 Sand and silt with occasional pebbles to 3 cm.
73 Base of profile.

Pollen methodology

Samples for pollen analysis were obtained directly from the open sections using monolith trays. These monoliths were sub-sampled for pollen analysis in the laboratory of the Department of Geography,

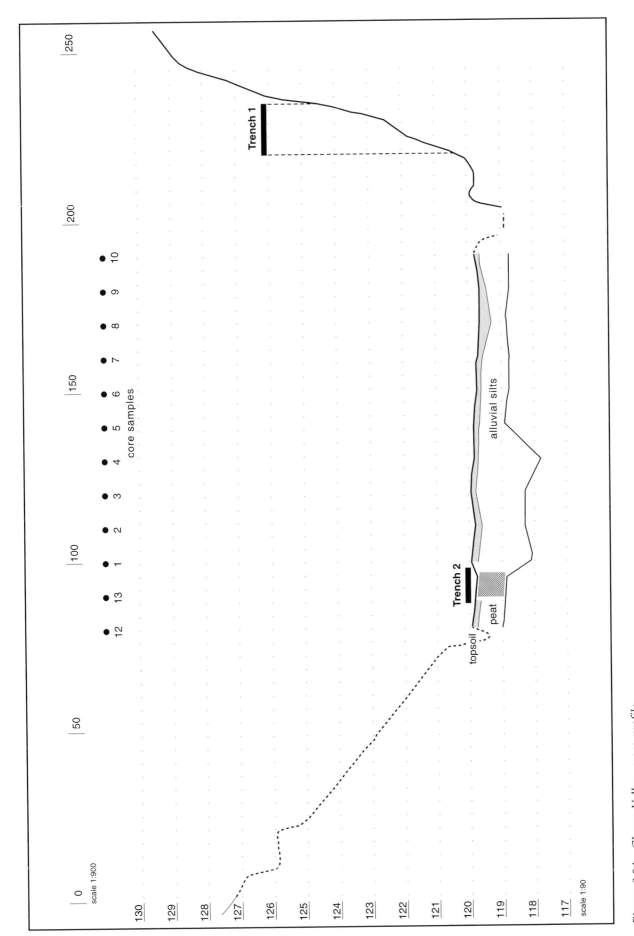

Figure 8.24 Churn Valley, cross profile.

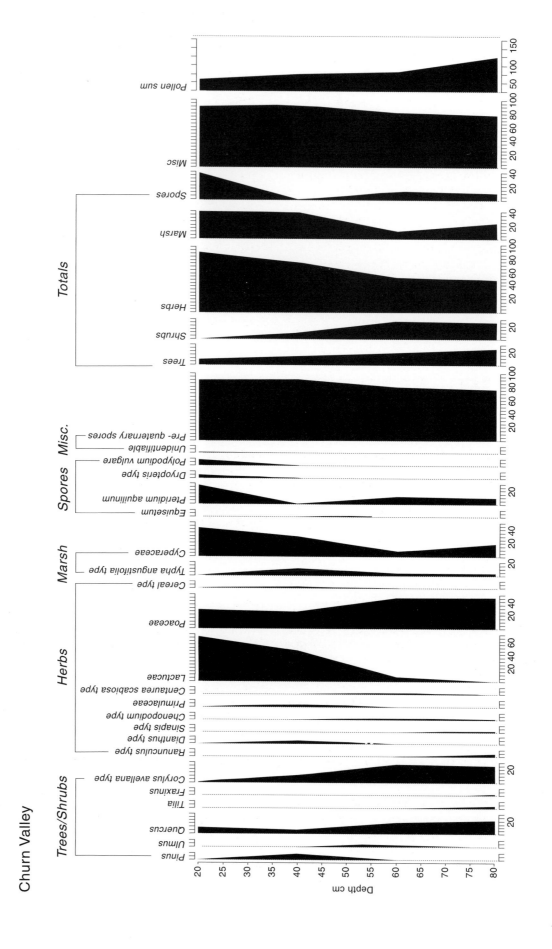

Figure 8.25 Churn Valley, pollen diagram.

University of Southampton. Samples of 2–3 ml were taken at 40 mm intervals. Standard procedures were used for the extraction of the sub-fossil pollen and spores (Moore and Webb 1978; Moore *et al.* 1991). These are described in more detail in appendix 8.4. Pollen counts of *c.* 400 grains of dry land taxa and extant mire/aquatic and spores were counted. These data are presented in standard pollen diagram form (Fig. 8.25) with the pollen sum comprising dry-land pollen as a percentage of its sum and mire taxa and spores as percentages of these groups plus the total of dry-land taxa for each level. Absolute pollen frequencies were calculated using the addition of a known number of exotic spores (*Lycopodium*) to a known volumes of sample. Pollen taxonomy generally follows that of Moore and Webb (1978) modified according to Bennett *et al.* (1994) in accord with Stace (1991). The pollen diagram was plotted using *Tilia* and *Tilia* Graph. These procedures were carried out in the Department of Geography, University of Southampton.

Pollen data

A diverse pollen flora was found comprising a total of 109 taxa recorded in the 18 levels examined which contained pollen. Absolute pollen frequencies average *c.* 50,000 grains/ml with higher values between 56–60 cm (to 168,000 grains/ml.). It should, however, be noted that pollen becomes less well preserved towards the top of the profile with relative expansion of taxa, especially Lactucae, with robust exines. This is indicative of differential preservation in favour of these taxa and thus some possible skewing of the data. This is undoubtedly due to the alkalinity of the site and gleying which has taken place in the upper sedimentary units.

Overall, the pollen spectra are dominated by a diverse range of herbs/assemblages with few trees and shrubs. There are indications of a number of different plant communities including strong evidence of arable/cereal cultivation and possibly pastoral land use. Other cultivated crops recorded include *Cannabis sativa* and interestingly, *Vitis*. These are discussed further below. The range of herbs present can be attributed to these communities plus the autochthonous aquatic/marsh components.

Two local pollen assemblage zones (l.p.a.z.) have been delimited on the inherent changes in the pollen spectra which appear to correspond with stratigraphical changes in the sediment fills of the channel. These zones are characterised from the base of the profile as follows:

l.p.a.z. CHURN:1 (72–42 cm) Delimited by greater herb diversity than zone 2 above with higher percentage values of *Plantago lanceolata* (to 11%), *Plantago major* type (4%), *Ranunculus* type (5%), *Rumex* spp., *Sanguisorba minor* and *Cannabis sativa* type. Cereal pollen becomes progressively more important towards the top of the zone (to 40%). *Vitis vinifera* is

present (72 cm and 56 cm). Tree and shrub pollen although subordinate to herbs have higher values in this zone. *Quercus* (11%) and *Fraxinus* (5%) are most important with sporadic records of *Betula, Ulmus, Tilia, Taxus, Fagus* and *Juglans*. Shrubs comprise *Corylus avellana* (5%), *Salix, Euonymus, Cornus* and *Viburnum*. Marsh and aquatic taxa are dominated by Cyperaceae (to 10%) with *Typha angustifolia/ Sparganium* and *Potamogeton. Nymphaea, Callitriche, Lemna, Iris* and possibly *Isoetes* are also present.

l.p.a.z. CHURN: 2 (42–4 cm) The change to this zone corresponds with stratigraphical change to more heterogeneous sediments and poorer pollen preservation. There are reductions in *Plantago lanceolata* (to <5%), *Fraxinus, Ranunculus* type, *Plantago lanceolata, Sanguisorba minor*. Cereal pollen is important at the base of the zone but declines upwards. There are expansions of Cyperaceae, *Pteridium aquilinum* and particularly derived pre- Quaternary palynomorphs (Jurassic). There remains a relatively diverse herbaceous component. Tree and shrub pollen is diminished (<10%) with declining *Fraxinus. Quercus* remains the most important/consistent taxon.

Discussion and inferred vegetation

This study of the channel was undertaken to date the feature and to characterise the local environment and particularly the local land use. Preservation of pollen in limestone terrains is unusual and this provides the first detailed pollen analysis for this region.

The depositional environment

Since the site is a river channel, marginal aquatic and aquatic taxa might be expected in the pollen spectra. This is the case although such types are frequently under-represented in pollen assemblages due to production of small quantities of pollen and the fact that liberated pollen is readily dispersed in flowing water. This is of course less so in still-water lake habitats. Here, a range of marsh, aquatic and marginal aquatic attest to slow flowing water. *Nymphaea, Myriophyllum verticillatum, Callitriche, Lemna* and *Potamogeton* are the typical aquatic plants. Marginal reeds comprised *Iris, Alisma Plantago-aquatica, Typha angustifolia* and/or *Sparganium, Littorella* and Cyperaceae. Although the latter are important in the assemblages, they may also be referable to the wetter areas of the water meadow. This similarly applies to a number of taxa which may also have been growing in the floodplain water meadow including *Caltha* type, *Succisa, Filipendula ulmaria*, and Apiaceae type 3 (such as *Oenanthe*). In l.p.a.z. CHURN:2, there is a very marked increase in the numbers of reworked pre-Quaternary (Jurassic) palynomorphs. These may indicate some form of land use change which was responsible for bedrock erosion and inclusion of these geological microfossils.

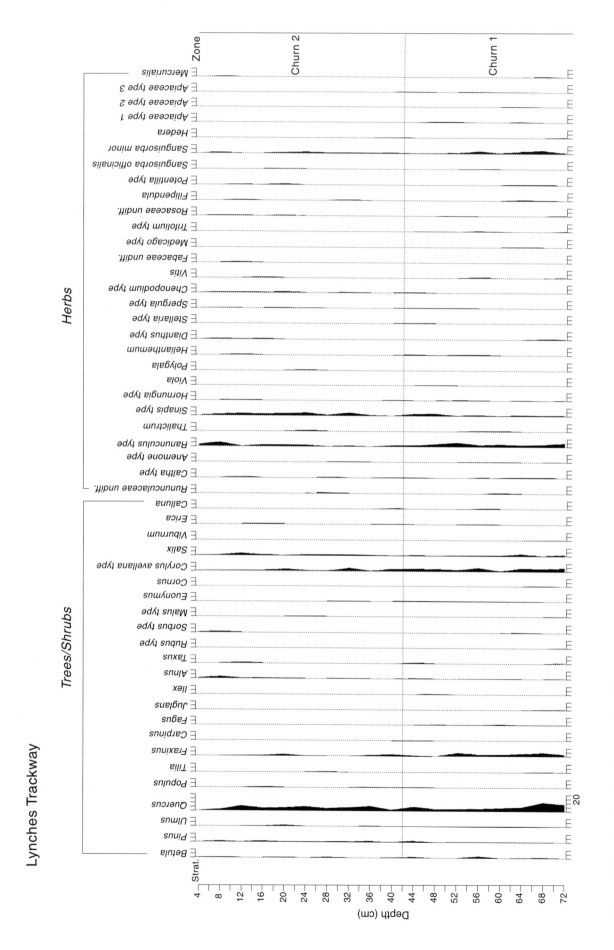

Figure 8.26a Lynches Trackway, pollen diagram.

Lynches Trackway

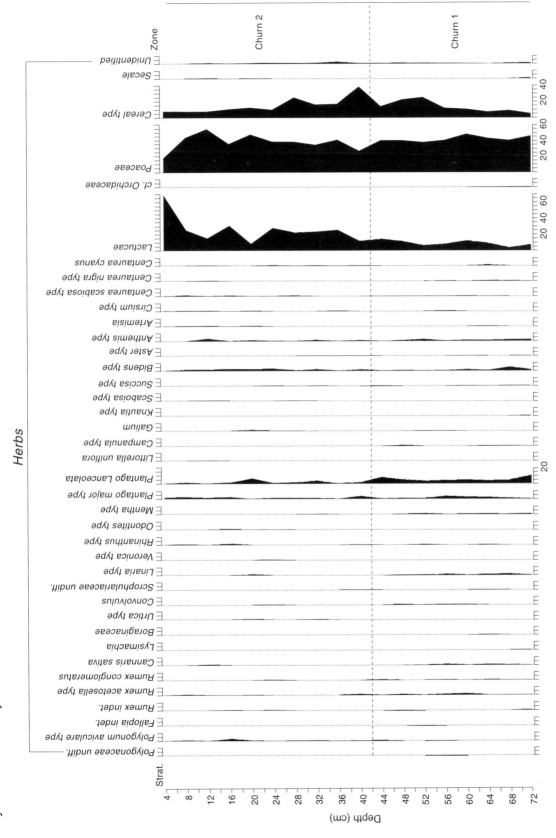

Figure 8.26b Lynches Trackway, pollen diagram.

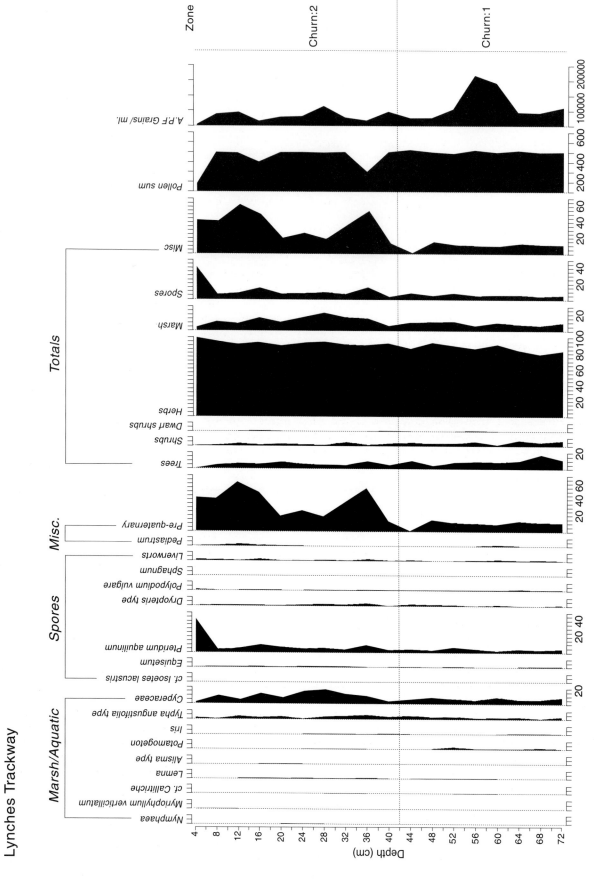

Lynches Trackway

Figure 8.26c Lynches Trackway, pollen diagram.

The agricultural environment

There is strong evidence both for cultivation of crops and for pastoral grassland. The latter is most likely to derive from the extensive water meadows growing on the floodplain of the Churn valley and is evidenced by the higher percentages of Poaceae and associated taxa associated with tall grassland/meadow. Typical pastoral indicators are *Plantago lanceolata, Ranunculus* type, *Thalictrum, Rumex acetosella* type, *R. obtusifolius/ conglomeratus* type, *Sanguisorba officinalis,* Asteraceae types (including *Centaurea scabiosa* type, *C. nigra* type, Lactucae) and possibly Orchidaceae. Many other taxa may also be referable to this habitat but whose pollen does not allow differentiation to a lower taxonomic level; for example *Rhinanthus* type. *Mentha* type, *Campanula* type and *Lysimachia.* In addition to the tall grassland of the floodplain/water meadow, there is also evidence for short turf grassland. Whilst Poaceae in part are attributable, the presence of *Helianthemum* and *Sanguisorba minor* and *Polygala* are significant. These taxa are substantially under-represented in pollen spectra due to their low growing form and entomophily. They are, however, diagnostic calcicolous plants typical of short turf, species rich calcareous grassland growing today on chalk and limestone. It is not possible to state where this habitat was but it may be postulated that the upper, grazed slopes of the valley side interfluves are the most likely source. Taphonomy of the pollen should also be considered in that it is also not possible to define to what extent pollen has been fluvially transported down the river/catchment rather than deposited via normal airborne means.

The cultivated crops

Cultivated plants are more easily delimited in pollen assemblages than pastoral elements. Here there is a clear importance of cereal cultivation along with *Cannabis sativa* (hemp) and *Vitis* (viticulture).

Arable cultivation

Cereals are largely dominated by *Triticum* (wheat) and *Hordeum* type (barley) with some *Secale* (rye). These are also associated with weeds of disturbed and cultivated ground (segetals) including *Centaurea cyanus* (blue cornflower), *Polygonum aviculare, Fallopia convolvulus, Spergula/Spergularia,* Chenopodiaceae, Brassicaceae (*Sinapis* type), *Artemisia.* Wheat, barley and especially rye, are crops typical of medieval cultivation. The latter has generally been regarded as a Roman introduction, although, there is an increasing number of records from the late prehistoric, Bronze Age and Iron Age periods (Chambers 1989). However, its importance in later periods, especially the medieval is unquestioned. It is frequently associated with *Cannabis sativa* and *Linum* (Godwin 1975, 414) and this appears to be the case here although absolute pollen numbers of *Secale* are small. Since *Secale* is anemophilous and produces substantial quantities

of pollen it seems that rye was not of especial local significance. *Triticum* and/or *Hordeum* (wheat/barley), however, are the principal crops present and, given the high percentages values of associated weeds, were likely to have been cultivated in close proximity on the adjacent valley side. It must also be considered that with the proximity of the mill, local crop processing may also have been responsible for liberating pollen trapped in the husks of cereals (Robinson and Hubbard 1977; Scaife 1986; 1995).

Cereal pollen is more abundant in the middle of the profile (60–30 cm) and occurs after a reduction of *Plantago lanceolata* (ribwort plantain) and *Ranunculus* type (buttercups). This might be tentatively attributed to a change from pastoral to arable land-use in field(s) adjacent to the pollen sample site.

Viticulture

The presence of *Vitis vinifera* (grape) is somewhat unusual and important. Whilst there are frequent seed records of grape especially from the Roman and later periods these are largely attributed to imports. Jones and Legge (1987) provide the earliest radiocarbon record with a Neolithic seed from Hambledon Hill. Records of pollen are, however, more likely to be attributable to local viticulture. Godwin (1975) records a single Holocene pollen record obtained by K. Barker from medieval deposits adjacent to Lanercost Priory dated to 1150–1350 AD. Chambers (personal communication and in press) has found pollen at Mingies Ditch, Oxfordshire in an Iron Age ditch context. Possible Romano-British bedding trenches in Northamptonshire (Brown and Meadows pers. comm.) have been attributed to vine cultivation and are associated with pollen (Brown pers. comm.). Saxon vine pollen has also been found at Market Lavington, Wiltshire (Allen pers. comm.). Thus, there is an increasing number of records of vine cultivation in England during the later prehistoric and historic periods. The pollen record (3 grains) obtained from the Churn valley river implies local viticulture.

Hemp cultivation

Cannabis sativa L. is present especially in l.p.a.z. CHURN:1 and a single record in CHURN:2. This is typical of medieval pollen records implying the importance of *Cannabis* as a crop for production of hemp used for rope and coarse textiles. This is particularly useful as a dating/marker in pollen spectra in the north-west of England (e.g. Dumayne-Peaty and Barber 1998) and is also frequently associated with cultivation of rye and flax (Godwin 1967; 1975). This was undoubtedly a locally grown crop in the Churn valley.

The woodland/arboreal flora

The small percentage values/small absolute pollen frequencies suggest that the landscape was largely open with pastoral and arable agriculture predominant.

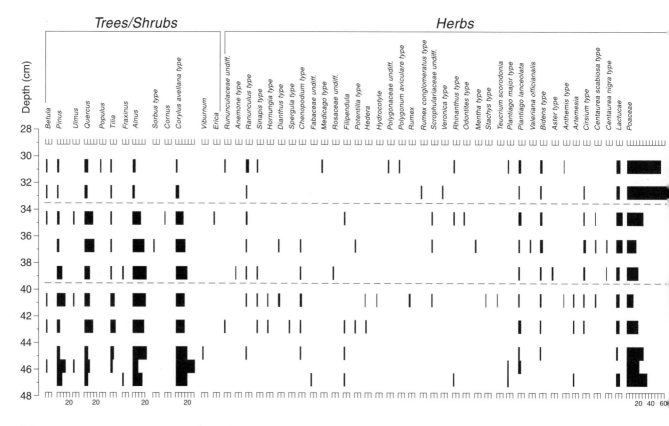

Figure 8.27   Latton 'Roman Pond', pollen diagram.

Sporadic occurrences of *Betula* (birch), *Pinus* (pine), *Alnus* (alder), *Juglans* (walnut), *Populus* (poplar) and *Carpinus* (hornbeam) are attributed to long distant transport from extra-regional sources. *Juglans* is regarded as a Roman introduction adding further evidence of a historic date for the sequence. *Quercus* (oak) and *Corylus avellana* (hazel) possibly represent areas of coppice managed woodland. *Fraxinus* (ash) is under-represented in pollen spectra (Andersen 1970; 1973) and as such the records in zone 1 imply that it was relatively more important locally. Other poorly represented taxa include *Fagus* (beech) *Salix* and *Ilex* (holly) and it is possible that these were also growing locally although fluvial transport from up- stream must also be considered. *Salix* was most likely growing along the margins of the river channel as it does today.

Conclusion

Pollen analysis carried out on the sediment fills of the river has provided information on the medieval palaeovegation, palaeoeconomy and environment of the Churn valley. The data obtained are some of the very few obtained from limestone areas of Britain. Such areas do not usually offer potential for pollen preserving environments. Preservation has occurred here because the river channel has remained con- tinuously waterlogged. Furthermore, there are few pollen analytical studies of recent/historic sediments. The study illustrates an open agricultural environment with possibly pastoral use of water meadows but with cereal cultivation (wheat/barley and rye) and hemp

(*Cannabis* for its bast fibres) and importantly local viticulture. Where trees are present, these are oak and hazel, possibly managed woodland with local ash.

POLLEN FROM LATTON 'ROMAN POND'
By Rob Scaife

Introduction

Pollen analysis has been carried out on the organic, peat and silty peats which have accumulated in a shallow depressions in the basal Devensian gravels (Fig. 8.27). Preliminary analysis (Scaife 1997) showed that there was sufficient pollen to enable detailed pollen counts to be made. Subsequently, additional monoliths and samples for radiocarbon dating were obtained. Dating has shown that the peats accumulated during the late Bronze Age. Pollen analysis has been undertaken on one of the profiles in conjunction with plant macro and insect analysis by Dr Mark Robinson providing information on the local vegetation and environment.

Methodology

See Churn Valley, above.

Stratigraphy

The peat and sediment stratigraphy as recorded in the monolith is described as follows and is related to the contexts recorded in the field although depths are slightly discordant.

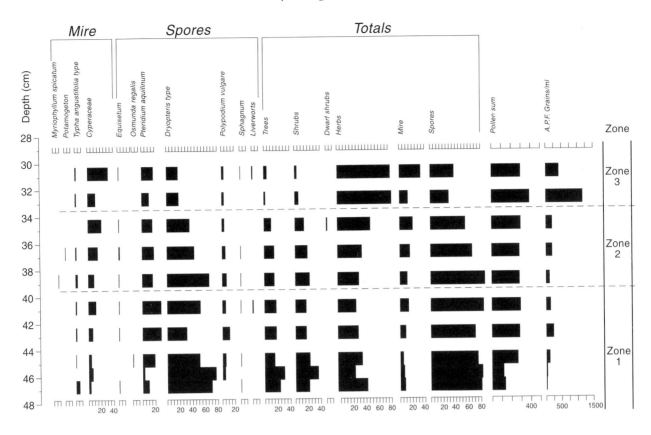

Depth cm

0–27	Topsoil. Brown (contexts 510-511). Upper plough soil and modern turf with underlying clay/silt 'B' horizon
27–31	Pale brown chalky marl (context 512). Slightly more organic than overlying soil.
31–45	Black, highly humified, detrital peat with silt (context 513).
45–47	Transition (context 514).
47–50	Buff silt/marl. Lower alluvium? (context 515).
50–64	Coarse grit/marl with limestone fragments. Basement/natural or Devensian colluvium?

Palynology *(Fig. 8.27)*

Three pollen zones have been recognised. The lower, zone 1 (48-39 cm) has been defined by the generally higher percentages of tree pollen in particular, *Tilia* (lime) and *Pinus* (pine). *Quercus* (oak), *Alnus* (alder) and *Corylus avellana* type (hazel and sweet gale) are the other principal trees and shrubs. Herbs are relatively important (48% of total pollen) with Poaceae (grasses) dominant (to 38%). *Plantago lanceolata* (ribwort plantain), Lactucae (dandelion types) and range of sporadically occurring herbs are also present. These also include large poaceae (cereal type). There are high values of monolete (*Dryopteris* type) fern spores and *Pteridium aquilinum* (bracken). Between 38–40 cm, (zone: 1/2 boundary), *Tilia* declines to much

lower percentage values and *Pinus* from just above. *Quercus*, *Alnus* and *Corylus avellana* type remain important. Herbs remain broadly similar in importance with some indications ofexpansion towards the top of the zone. From 33–34 cm. (zone 3) there is a marked reduction in percentages of tree pollen to <5%. Conversely, Poaceae (grasses) expand sharply to 75%. There is also a slight increase in Large Poaceae (cereal type).

Throughout the profile, marsh and aquatic taxa comprise predominantly Cyperaceae (sedges) which become more important in the upper, zone 3 (to 35% tdlp+mire). *Typha angustifolia* type (bur reed and reed mace) are consistent Throughout. *Osmunda regalis* (royal fern) is present at 44-45cm (zone 1). There are few true aquatic taxa with only single occurrences of *Myriophyllum* and *Potamogeton* type. *Alnus* (zone 1 and 2) is also attributable to wetland fen-carr or fringing aquatic.

Inferred vegetation and suggested dating

Both the preliminary assessment study of an adjacent monolith and this analysis have provided evidence of woodland in local pollen assemblage zone 1. this consisted of oak, lime and hazel on drier soils with some evidence of lime on wetter areas (carr woodland probably at some distance) or from more localised growth marginal to the river. Pine also present in zone 1 may be attributed to long distance transport but, percentages to 18% are enigmatic and may represent some local or near regional growth.

The lowest levels of the sequence (Zone 1) represent the period of dominant lime woodland evidenced from southern and eastern Britain during the middle and early part of the later Holocene (Moore 1977; Scaife 1980; Grieg 1982) and which sibsequently remained well into the late prehistoric period in many areas. It should be noted that *Tilia* is under-represented in pollen spectra due to its insect (rather than wind) pollination (Andersen 1970; 1973). Production of small numbers of pollen grains during the height of summer when leaves are present on trees also negates widespread dispersal of its pollen. Its marked decline in many pollen profiles was in the past attributed to climatic change (Godwin 1940; 1956) but is now widely attributed to forest clearance and agriculture (Turner 1962). A model of paludification has also been presented by Waller (1994). Whilst the lime decline has now been demonstrated as asynchronous (Baker *et al.* 1979) with dates spanning the late Neolithic (Scaife 1980) to the Saxon period (Baker *et al.* 1979) the majority of dates appear to be from the late Bronze Age. This is the case here where lime declines at 40–39 cm. Radiocarbon measurements of this organic sequence produced a date of 2943±63 BP (1258–1020 BC) (NZA-8579, R24151/9). This, therefore, places the vegetation sequence within the late Bronze Age, suggested in earlier assessments on the basis of the vegetation and especially the presence of the 'lime decline' (zones 2/3 boundary). Removal of lime at this time may form part of the changing land use patterns of this period due to increasing land pressure with need for more agricultural land (Ellison and Harris 1972).

In pollen zone 2, although lime is greatly diminished, considering its under-representation in pollen spectra (Andersen 1970; 1973), oak, hazel and alder remain important woodland elements. This suggests that areas of dominant lime were cleared whilst other areas of deciduous woodland remained. From 34–33 cm, (zone 3), there is further evidence of an increase in local woodland clearance and expansion of herb communities which similarly appear to be pasture with expansion of grasses and other herbs and also of cereal cultivation which may perhaps be attributed to more intensive Iron Age agriculture.

Conclusions

Radiocarbon dating has placed the age of this organic accumulation in the late Bronze Age thus providing the necessary dating framework within which to place the environmental data obtained. The habitats suggested by the pollen show an initial woodland of oak, lime and hazel in the vicinity. Subsequently, there are two phases of woodland decline, most likely through human clearance for agriculture. In the first, lime becomes less important (in zone 2) and subsequently all other remaining tree types, that is, oak, hazel and alder (pollen zone 3). Quantities of pine noted largely in zone 1 are enigmatic and may represent some local growth. If so, this is rather an unusual occurrence. Concurrent with the reduction of woodland is the expansion of herbs indicative of arable and pastoral agriculture.

MARINE SHELL
By G Campbell

Summary of Results

Approximately 270 identifiable and 120 fragmentary marine shells were recovered from eight sites. All of the shell was from oyster, and all of the identifiable shells were the Roman or edible oyster *Ostrea edulis* L. The upper and lower valves were counted within each context, and the number of fragments were counted for the smaller groups and estimated for the larger groups.

Refitting was not attempted, but the assemblage comprised a minimum of 140 individual oysters. Upper and lower valves occurred in relatively similar amounts regardless of site or deposit. Shells appear to be confined to deposits resulting from intense human activity (middens, pit fills and floor surfaces principally) during the Roman era. The great majority of the deposits comprised only one or two shells, with two exceptions:

1   Birdlip Quarry. A small group of 33 shells in the sequence of occupation layers 1318, 1322, 1324 and stone surfaces 1323, 1319.

2   Weavers Bridge. The largest single group at any of the sites includes the largest single group in one deposit, a midden (context 57) containing 154 shells.

Discussion

The number of individuals from the midden deposit at Weavers Bridge is still probably too small for any conclusions regarding Roman oyster bed management to be statistically valid, despite this being the largest single group in the assemblage. Of greater importance is the association of oyster shell with other materials in the same contexts. The dates of these contexts can identify whether the consumption of oysters was restricted to a specific period of time, or was occurring throughout the Roman period. It is clear from the similar number of upper and lower valves recovered that oysters were not served 'on the half-shell' principally.

Note on the hand-recovered terrestrial shell

Terrestrial snails were recovered from one or two deposits at seven sites. Since these were recovered only in small numbers, it is unlikely that any were collected as food. This view is reinforced by the small size of the shells; the larger shells are more likely to be the Common Garden Snail, (*Helix aspersa*) rather than that mammoth of British land snails, the Roman or Apple Snail (*H. pomatia*). The groups are biased heavily towards the larger snails, and therefore of no value in reconstructing deposit formation or ecology.

Chapter 9:   Discussion

THE EARLY PREHISTORIC PERIOD
By Alistair Barclay and Alan Lupton

Palaeolithic and Mesolithic

During the course of the road scheme excavations, the only evidence for Palaeolithic activity recovered was a handaxe of uncertain providence. Mesolithic activity was restricted to stray finds of lithic material from a small number of sites. The near absence of Mesolithic material fits the present pattern of settlement activity as recorded within this area (Darvill 1987, 25 and 28; Holgate 1988, map 9). Since the evidence for early Mesolithic activity is very rare the microlith from Cherry Tree Lane is an important addition. In contrast the numerous later Mesolithic sites identified by Holgate are distributed on the higher ground of the Cotswolds and the Corallian Ridge to the south (1988, map 9). Later Mesolithic sites near the road corridor and within the Churn valley include Bagendon, South-moor Grove, Birdlip and Coates (Holgate 1988, table 1). In addition, a number of important mesolithic scatters have been preserved on relic ground surfaces beneath both Neolithic and Bronze Age barrows in the Cotswolds (Lambrick 1988; Saville 1990; Marshall 1997).

The earlier Neolithic

The evidence for the earlier Neolithic recovered from the excavations is slight and can generally be interpreted as belonging to small-scale domestic activity. However, the corridor of the road scheme passes through an area of important monuments and the evidence it has produced greatly adds to the understanding of how the surrounding landscape was inhabited and utilised during this period.

Earlier Neolithic activity is represented by a group of pits containing pottery and flint at Duntisbourne Grove and collections of lithic material in tree-throw holes, later features, or in the ploughsoil. This range of evidence is typical for the Upper Thames region and for southern England in general (Holgate 1988). The evidence for settlement in this period is scarce all over the country and earlier Neolithic occupation sites in particular are notoriously ephemeral (Hodder 1990, 244). Our present under-standing of early Neolithic settlement is that it is not permanent, and the general picture we have is one of small-scale mobile communities that left little or no trace in the archaeological record (see Thomas 1991). A number of houses or structures have been identified in the Cotswolds, preserved beneath barrows. These tend to be associated with surface scatters of cultural material, some of which is concentrated in midden-like deposits, along with hearths and occasional pits. Only at Sale's Lot is it possible to recognise a definite rectilinear house, while at Hazleton North

and somewhat further to the east at Ascott-under-Wychwood the structures were perhaps more flimsy and maybe little more than screens or windbreaks (Saville 1990; unpublished info.).

Our knowledge of the period is very much biased towards the well-known monuments, which around the route include long cairns and causewayed enclosures (Holgate 1988, fig. 6.2). For the area around the Churn Valley Holgate has collated all of the settlement evidence and has identified a small number of probable and possible domestic sites recorded as lithic scatters (1988). These sites are generally located on higher land and on the edge of the Cotswolds and a number cluster in the Bagendon area close to the causewayed enclosure at Southmore Grove, Rendcomb (Trow 1985). A slight concentration of sites in the area of the Churn valley (Holgate 1988, map 14) coincides with the occurrence of early Neolithic monuments, but it also reflects an area of concentrated fieldwork. Holgate has suggested that the majority of earlier Neolithic activity appears to have concentrated on the central uplands of the Cotswolds, with some evidence for expansion over the Cotswolds and into the lower lying areas of the Severn and Upper Thames valleys as the period progressed.

Two causewayed enclosures are known from cropmarks near the route, one at Down Ampney near Latton and the other at Southmore Grove just north of Bagendon (Trow 1985; Darvill 1987). Fieldwalking over the enclosure at Southmore Grove produced a concentration of Mesolithic as well as early-mid Neolithic flints (Saville 1985, 19). Near to the enclosure at Down Ampney is the cropmark of a possible oval barrow (Leech 1977, map 3). Just north of Bagendon and beyond the area of the road scheme are the excavated enclosures known as Crickley Hill (Dixon 1979, 147) and Peak Camp (Darvill 1982), both of which it is suggested took on a more domestic role during a late stage of their history.

Pottery is particularly rare in non-funerary contexts, so the finds at Duntisbourne Grove are of considerable significance. Comparative material is limited with most material coming from the excavations of monuments in the Cotswolds. Traces of early Neolithic occupation prior to the construction of the tombs were sealed beneath the long barrows of Hazleton North (Saville 1990, 240) and Sale's Lot (O' Neil 1966), and consisted of postholes and stakeholes, pottery, flint, hearth areas, saddle querns and rubbers, animal bone and hazelnut shells. On the lowlands in the Severn Valley and just north of the road scheme, a pit containing flint and approximately one third of an early Neolithic pottery bowl was found in Berkeley Street, Gloucester (Hurst 1972, 38). However, in the Upper Thames such pit deposits are extremely rare (Holgate 1988, maps 16–7). This might be because the practice of pit digging in this region became more common towards the end of the

4th millennium cal BC. Other settlement areas may be represented by flint scatters located during field surveys of the north Cotswolds (Marshall 1985; Holgate 1988). Mention has already been made of domestic sites preserved under long cairns, but other features have also been found beneath round barrows. At Guiting Power recent investigations identified a scatter of early Neolithic flintwork along with charcoal from which a radiocarbon determination of 3786–3644 cal BC (4929±78BP) has been obtained (Marshall 1997, 286).

The environment at this time is likely to have consisted of small cleared areas within woodland, which would have been used for habitation or small-scale cultivation. There is some evidence for the cultivation of cereals, for example at Hazleton North (Saville 1990, 240), alongside the exploitation of wild foods. As such, the plant remains found in the pits at Duntisbourne Grove would confirm this pattern of reliance on a mixture of wild and domesticated resources.

The later Neolithic

Changes in artefacts, settlement patterns and monument types are evident from the middle through to the later Neolithic. Most apparent is the abandonment of long cairns and causewayed enclosures before the end of the 4th millennium cal BC. There is evidence that certain of the long cairns were deliberately blocked and some of this activity is associated with the deposition of Peterborough Ware (Darvill 1987, 66–7). There is evidence for considerable social change, instability and even conflict. At Crickley Hill on the Cotswold escarpment, the defended middle Neolithic hilltop settlement was violently destroyed (Dixon 1979, 147), while arrowheads were also a prominent feature of the flint assemblage at the nearby site of Peak Camp (Darvill 1981; 1982).

Perhaps as a result of this activity, the later Neolithic is less visible in the landscape than the preceding phase and evidence for settlement of this date is scarce in the region.

In contrast to the early Neolithic very few monuments appear to have been built in the later 4th millennium BC. In the Cotswold uplands a possible long mound was built across the enclosure at Crickley Hill, while at Signet Hill, Burford, a possible bank barrow was laid out across the enclosure (Darvill 1987, 77; Barclay and Hey in press). Another possible monument of this date could be the Soldier's Grave, Frocester (Darvill 1987, 74). On the gravel terraces the cursuses at Lechlade and Buscot are likely to belong to the middle Neolithic. These new monument types are likely to have been constructed at a time when Peterborough Ware was in use. This type of pottery is rare in the area and most of the findspots are located on higher ground and from the blocking of long cairns or from pit deposits. Some pottery of this date was found in a pit at Duntisbourne Grove (see Chapter 2). Elsewhere Peterborough Ware associated deposits have come from pits at Salmonsbury Camp and

Bourton-on-the-Water, and from just beyond the Cotswolds at Cam near Dursley in the Severn Valley (Darvill 1987, 68–9). To the south of the region at Home Farm, Blunsdon a single pit containing Peterborough Ware and flint was found (Phillips 1971). From the gravels the only recorded finds are the few possible sherds from the top of the cursus ditch (Barclay in prep. b), while Peterborough Ware associated pit deposits are far more common in the east part of the Upper Thames Valley (Thomas 1991, fig. 7.4).

In contrast, Grooved Ware, which is thought to overlap with the final use of Peterborough Ware, is almost absent from the Cotswold uplands, but is generally more common on the gravel terraces around Lechlade (Thomas 1991, fig 7.4; Barclay in prep. b). Again it must be emphasised that although the density of findspots is far less than that of the Oxford region, this difference is partly a factor of the scale of fieldwork that is associated with mineral extraction and development. To the south of the road scheme an isolated Grooved Ware pit was found at Tower Hill, Ashbury just on the edge of the Downs (Barclay in prep. c), while Grooved Ware associated deposits are very common in the adjacent areas of the eastern part of the Upper Thames Valley and from the Avebury area (Thomas 1991, fig 7.8).

By the late Neolithic the Cotswold uplands may have been largely abandoned, with the river valleys, notably the Upper Thames and the Severn, becoming the focus for both domestic and ritual activity. Two cursus monuments, located at Buscot and Lechlade in the Upper Thames Valley, may have developed into monument complexes during this phase and suggest a concentration of ritual activity in this area (Barclay *et al.* forthcoming). During this time there is evidence for increasing levels of long-distance exchange and contacts with other parts of the country; the concentration of sites in river valleys may, therefore, be no coincidence, as communities on the Cotswolds became more outward-looking. Pits containing Grooved Ware and other artefacts have been found around the Lechlade cursus and from the upper fill of its ditch (Barclay *et al.* in prep.), The Loders, Lechlade (Darvill *et al.* 1986), Roughground Farm, Lechlade (Darvill 1993, 9–15) and possibly Saintbridge, Gloucester (Garrod and Heighway 1984, 22–5).

Late Neolithic monuments are again rare, although two possible massive henges are known from Westwell near Burford and from Condicote near Stow, both of which are within 25 km of the road scheme (Atkinson 1951, 101; Saville 1983b). A number of smaller henges and hengiform ring ditches are known from the Lechlade area, one of which occurs just outside the cursus. Two radiocarbon dates obtained from charcoal recovered from the middle fill of the inner henge ditch at Condicote indicate a probable mid-late 3rd millennium date (2500-1750 cal BC 3670±100bp 95.4%; 2500–1900 cal BC 3720±80bp 95.4%). Some 53 sherds of probable Beaker pottery representing at least three vessels was recovered from the same level (Saville 1983b, 35, fig. 7), although both this material and the radiocarbon dates are likely to belong to secondary activity and not to the construction of the monument. These sites are likely to have been constructed either during the currency of Grooved Ware or during a phase when both Grooved Ware and Beaker pottery were being used during the later 3rd millennium BC.

An isolated Neolithic pit containing flint and antler fragments was found north of Court Farm, Latton, in the lower lying Churn/Upper Thames Valley (SMR No. SU09NE100). Other sites have produced additional late Neolithic artefacts, but these have not been associated with domestic structural evidence. There appears to have been some later Neolithic activity at Duntisbourne Grove, which is situated in the Churn Valley, as pit 94 contained Peterborough Ware and some later Neolithic flintwork, as well as earlier Neolithic material. This is of interest as it indicates some continuity of use of certain occupation areas, rather than the complete dislocation between the earlier and later Neolithic, which is often assumed. As discussed above, the pits may represent some form of structured, ritual activity as well as forming part of a possible settlement. It may be that certain sites retained their significance into the later Neolithic, perhaps referring to ancestors or traditional practices as a source of influence (eg. Bradley 1984, 78–79). The deposit of flintwork and a pebble hammer in a tree-throw hole at Hare Bushes North may also represent domestic activity or a similar structured deposit.

The discovery of the flint and worked stone artefacts in the Duntisbourne Grove pits also attests to contact between the Neolithic inhabitants of the road scheme area and surrounding regions. Flint does not naturally occur in the area, the nearest sources being the Marlborough Downs *c.* 25 km to the south-west, and in the river gravels of the Middle Thames valley. The sandstone saddle quern rubbers were probably derived from the May Hill area *c.* 40 km to the north-west, and saddle quern fragments of the same material have also been found in the spread of domestic rubbish over which the Hazleton North long cairn was constructed (Saville 1990). The presence of a piece of worked chert from Norcote Farm could also indicate exchange from the Thames Valley or as far afield as Portland in Dorset. Three pieces of worked chert were also recovered from the pre-long barrow occupation level at Hazleton North (Saville 1990, 154). Links with the Dorset coast may already be evident, as the raw material (if not the finished objects) for shale beads from the Notgrove and Eyford Hill long barrows and a shale pendant from Peak Camp would probably have been obtained from Kimmeridge (Darvill 1987, 64).

The Beaker period

The Beaker period spans the final part of the Neolithic and the start of the early Bronze Age (2500–1700 cal BC), and so the pattern of settlement is much like that for the later Neolithic described above. Beaker associated activity is perhaps more widespread than that associated with either Peterborough Ware or Grooved Ware. Darvill suggests that this represents a phase of expansion and re-colonisation with settlement occurring in both upland and lowland areas (Darvill 1987, 92). The road scheme investigations have significantly added to the number of sites, although the actual quantity of related material and the scale of activity appears to be small.

Beaker burials are also found in both upland and lowland areas, and may be found as flat burials, in cists, or insertions into earlier long mounds (as at Sale's Lot), or under round barrows. Round barrows and flat graves of Beaker date are also uncommon and there are only a few with dating evidence, for example those from Shorncote, Somerford Keynes (Barclay *et al.* 1995); Ivy Lodge Farm, Kings Stanley (Clifford 1950); Lechlade (Thomas and Holbrook 1998) and Lechmore, Horsley and Frampton on Severn (O'Neil and Grinsell 1960). However, just south of the road scheme is the major barrow cemetery at Lambourn, which contained a number of important Beaker burials (Case 1956–7; Richards 1986-90), while somewhat further south is the Avebury monument complex which has a wealth of Beaker associated material (Thomas 1991, 174–5).

There is a marked contrast between the high concentration of Beaker associated grave deposits found in the Oxford region of the Upper Thames with the low number found in the area of the road scheme. Although this is partly a result of less fieldwork, it none the less seems to support the view that this area of the Upper Thames was more of a backwater and somewhat marginal to the social developments occurring in Wessex and the Oxford region of the Upper Thames Valley, where more ostentatious burials and monuments were in evidence (see Thomas 1991). Bradley (1984, 90) has noted that burials are often less elaborate and the range of contemporary artefacts is more limited in these marginal areas. This is also evident in the type, quality and quantity of Beakers found in the region. However, there is another point worth making. The type of elaborate grave goods found in this area (flint dagger, bronze bracelet and probable copper earring) are different from those found in the Oxford region (Barclay 1999, 324). This regionalisation of certain grave goods could also suggest that the area had different social and economic links to those of the Oxford region.

What are traditionally termed Early style Beakers (see Case 1977) are very rare in Gloucestershire, either in burial or domestic contexts, and are mostly confined to Wessex and the south-east of England. In contrast, what are termed Middle and Late style Beakers are better represented. Research by the British Museum, however, indicates that the accepted Beaker typology and chronology is in doubt and in need of revision (Kinnes *et al.* 1991). There is some evidence to suggest that certain Middle style Beakers are amongst the earliest forms and this may be true for the Upper Thames region. The radiocarbon determinations of 2476–2142 cal BC (95% 3876±57bp NZA-8673) and 2462–2047 cal BC (95% 3836±58bp NZA-8674) obtained for the Beaker pits at Trinity Farm would certainly support this view. A somewhat similar date of 2500–1850 cal BC (95% 3710±100bp HAR-5499) was obtained from animal bone for a Beaker pit at Roughground Farm, Lechlade (Darvill 1993, 21).

Of the small number of burials recorded from this area three have radiocarbon dates. Two burials from Lechlade have dates of 2030–1740 cal BC (95% 3530±50bp BM-2980) and 1920–1760 cal BC (95% 3460±50bp BM-2981), respectively (Thomas and Holbrook 1998, 282) and the third is from Shorncote and has a date of 1980-1670 cal BC (95% 3480±60bp BM-2892) (Barclay *et al.* 1995). All three are late within the Beaker sequence and fall within the start of the 2nd millennium cal BC and within the early Bronze Age.

The evidence for Beaker associated activity in this area has been discussed by Darvill (1987), and includes a trough-shaped feature containing flintwork and Beaker sherds from Burnwood, east of Gloucester (Clifford 1964) and pits with Beaker sherds, flint and animal bone from Roughground Farm, Lechlade (Allen *et al.* 1993), pits containing Beaker sherds from The Warren, Toddington and a shallow ditch containing sherds near Oxpens Farm, Yanworth (Smith and Cox 1985). The assemblage from Trinity Farm is, therefore, of considerable significance as it contains finely made early style Beaker sherds, possibly the first Wessex/Middle Rhine sherds in a non-funerary context in this region.

As most of the Beaker 'settlement' sites that have been identified in the region are small, consisting of scattered pits and ditches, they contain little or no evidence for the subsistence activities that were being practised (Darvill 1987, 81–4). Roughground Farm, Lechlade provided evidence for the presence of domestic cattle and pigs, and although no cereal remains were recovered fragments of worked stone might have been used for crop processing. The absence of cereal remains might suggest an emphasis on a pastoral economy, if only locally, although it is unclear whether the feature was ever sampled for carbonised remains (Tim Allen pers. comm.). The samples from Trinity Farm present different evidence, indicating the presence of cereals (wheat and barley), but also the continued exploitation of wild resources (hazelnuts). This also suggests that economic strategies may have varied widely from settlement to settlement. As discussed above in the site description, however, it is possible that the contents of these pits may be some sort of special, structured deposit, so it is difficult to judge how representative they are of everyday activity or of the local or regional economy.

The early Bronze Age

There is very little evidence for post-Beaker early Bronze Age settlements (Darvill 1987, 111); flint scatters and stray sherds of pottery would appear to be the only indicators of their location. Nevertheless, the presence of numerous round barrows and stray finds suggest there was no lack of activity in this period. In this area the barrows are often found in pairs or groups of three such as those found at Shorncote approximately 5 km to the south (Barclay *et al.* 1995)

and occasionally are seen clustered together in small cemeteries. Within this region, barrow cemeteries are found particularly in the Cotswolds uplands, although they are much more common in parts of Wessex (eg. around Avebury) and in the Oxford Region of the Upper Thames Valley (Case 1963; Drinkwater and Saville 1984; Lambrick 1988). Near the road corridor the largest cemeteries occur at Hull Plantations, Longborough and Cow Common, Swell, with nine and ten barrows respectively (Darvill 1987, 99). Both these cemeteries are located within 3 km of the henge monument at Condicote (Saville 1979a, 119, fig. 1), while other relatively large cemeteries occur within the cursus monument complexes at Lechlade and Buscot (Barclay *et al.* forthcoming.).

Contiguous ring ditches, such as those seen at St Augustine's Farm South, are relatively uncommon, though comparable examples have been found at Dorchester-on-Thames (Whittle *et al.* 1992, 193–4, fig. 30) and Gravelly Guy, near Stanton Harcourt (Barclay *et al.* 1996, fig. 3). Inhumation under a burial mound was largely replaced by cremation as the dominant funerary rite as the period progressed.

In addition to the ring ditches excavated at St Augustine's Farm South, a number were noted on aerial photographs close to the route. Some of these were single, isolated examples; near Highgate House (NGR index no. SO 9512/3), east of Ermin Farm (SU 0699/1), west of Latton (SU 0895/35) and Court Farm (SU 0995/56). Others appeared to be located in pairs; Eysey, Latton (SU 1194/8), south of Driffield (SU 0798/1), St Augustine's Farm, Preston (SP 0500/9) and north of High Tun Farm, Duntisbourne Grove (SO 9906/4). No clearly contiguous ring ditches like those excavated were noted on the aerial photographs, though a crop mark south of Village Farm, Preston appears to represent a ring ditch with a smaller, sub-circular feature attached to it (SP 0400/4). In terms of location, the ring ditches excavated at St Augustine's Farm South add to the distinctive concentration of barrows along the lower part of the Churn Valley (cf. Darvill 1987, 95).

Although a wide variety of grave goods may be found with burials of this date, the particularly rich graves of the early Bronze Age 'Wessex Culture' (Piggott 1938), which are accompanied by bronze weaponry and other artefacts, are uncommon in the region. The most well-known example of this type is from Snowshill on the north Cotswolds, a burial under a large barrow which was accompanied by several pieces of bronzework and a polished stone battle axe (Greenwell 1890; Kinnes and Longworth 1985). However, like the example from the southern ring ditch at St Augustine's Farm South, many of the ring ditches that have been excavated in the region were found to contain a central cremation set in a simple pit, with few or no grave goods. It seems possible then, that although the central cremation deposit had been affected by ploughing, there may never have been any accompanying grave goods. The early Bronze Age urn sherd found in the ditch fill of the northern ring ditch is also of interest, as burials accompanied by Collared or Biconical Urns are not particularly common in Gloucestershire (Darvill 1987), although more recently Collared Urns have been found from funerary deposits at Guiting Power and Rollright both in the central Cotswolds (Lambrick 1988; Marshall 1997, 286). The sherd was, however, recovered from an upper fill of the ditch and given that the covering mound no longer survived could have derived from a destroyed secondary burial deposit.

The later Bronze Age

The excavations produced very little evidence for activity of this date. Apart from a small quantity of pottery no features or sites were identified. A number of linear ditches of uncertain prehistoric date were found at Norcote Farm and St Augustine's Farm South. No dating evidence was recovered, but as there was no apparent relationship to the Iron Age ditches found at St Augustine's Farm South and St Augustine's Lane, it is safer to assume that they are not necessarily of the same date, although a later Bronze Age date cannot be discounted.

The division of land using linear ditches and pit alignments is first apparent in the later Bronze Age, although there is little evidence for this in the area of the Upper Thames around the road scheme. At this time the evidence for conspicuous burial and the use of other ritual monuments disappears. The density of barrows and ring ditches dating to the earlier Bronze Age period recorded from this area contrasts with the low number of later Bronze Age settlements. Relatively little metalwork has been recorded in this area, although a hoard comprising two side-looped spearheads came from Down Ampney and a number of objects have been found as stray finds along the Churn Valley (Darvill 1987, 114–9).

Settlements are generally rare in this region. Later Bronze Age activity is recorded around Lechlade and a possible field system is known from Buscot Wick (Yates 1997). The most substantial settlement has, however, been found at Shorncote Quarry near Somerford Keynes. Excavation has revealed an enclosed cemetery of middle Bronze Age date and a major open settlement of mid to late Bronze Age date (Hearne and Heaton 1994; Barclay *et al.* 1995). The settlement is characterised by small post-built round houses, structures such as granaries, large pits some of which are waterholes and fencelines and is spread over an area of several hectares (Hearne and Heaton 1994; Carrie Hearne pers. comm.). It may not all be of one phase but rather represents the result of settlement shift.

In this region there is so far little evidence for the reorganisation of land into recognisable field systems. However, the discovery of the extensive late Bronze Age settlement at Shorncote Quarry indicates that permanently settled farmsteads or hamlets were indeed a feature of the later Bronze Age landscape in this region. Comparable permanently occupied settlements, such as the series of enclosures and possible roundhouse discovered at Corporation Farm

near Abingdon (Barrett and Bradley 1980, 251 and 258), have been discovered in adjacent areas (Yates 1997). However, the pattern of pit clusters, devoid of any traces of more permanent occupation or arable agriculture, revealed at Roughground Farm, near Lechlade (Allen *et al.* 1993, 27–35), albeit of middle Bronze Age date, suggests that other forms of settlement pattern and land-use also existed in the area.

THE LATER PREHISTORIC PERIOD *(Fig. 9.1)*
By Andrew Mudd

Early Iron Age

Little early Iron Age material was recovered from the excavations on this project and our understanding of this period remains poor. Sites yielding early Iron Age pottery include Lynches Trackway, Cherry Tree Lane and (probably) St Augustine's Lane (Chapter 3), all on the lower slopes of the Cotswolds. Some early elements were present among the predominantly middle Iron Age assemblages from Preston Enclosure and Court Farm, although there was no definable earlier activity associated with these sherds. The quantity of Iron Age pottery from colluvial and Roman deposits at Lynches Trackway strongly suggests that a site lies somewhere in the vicinity. It may lie completely outside the road corridor, but alternatively, the lack of any associated features from the road corridor here may be related to the relative 'invisibility' of this site, particularly under watching brief conditions. At Cherry Tree Lane, a pit contained material characteristic of later prehistoric 'burnt mound' deposits. It may have been part of a more extensive site of this type (whatever sort of activity it might represent) although it was not particularly close to an identifiable water supply which is sometimes seen as a feature of such sites. The probable early Iron Age pottery from the segmented ditches at St Augustine's Farm suggests some concern with boundary demarcation in this period, although the radiocarbon dates from St Augustine's Farm South were later and the complex as a whole is discussed with the middle Iron Age sites.

This sparse evidence for early Iron Age occupation conforms to the regional picture in the Cotswolds where known early Iron Age sites are mainly hillforts. These appear to fall into two groups (Darvill 1987, 126): the massive hilltop enclosures of Nottingham Hill (Gotherington) and Norbury Camp (Northleach with Eastington), and a large number of smaller, highly defended settlements such as Crickley Hill, Leckhampton Hill, and Chastleton. While this may be an oversimplification, it is probable that settlement had a strongly defensive element, with a greater intensity of occupation on the higher ground, and that non-hillfort settlement was genuinely sparse. The morphologically late hillforts, eg. Painswick Beacon, are far smaller than eg. Norbury, while such as Crickley Hill are distinctive scarp edge promontory

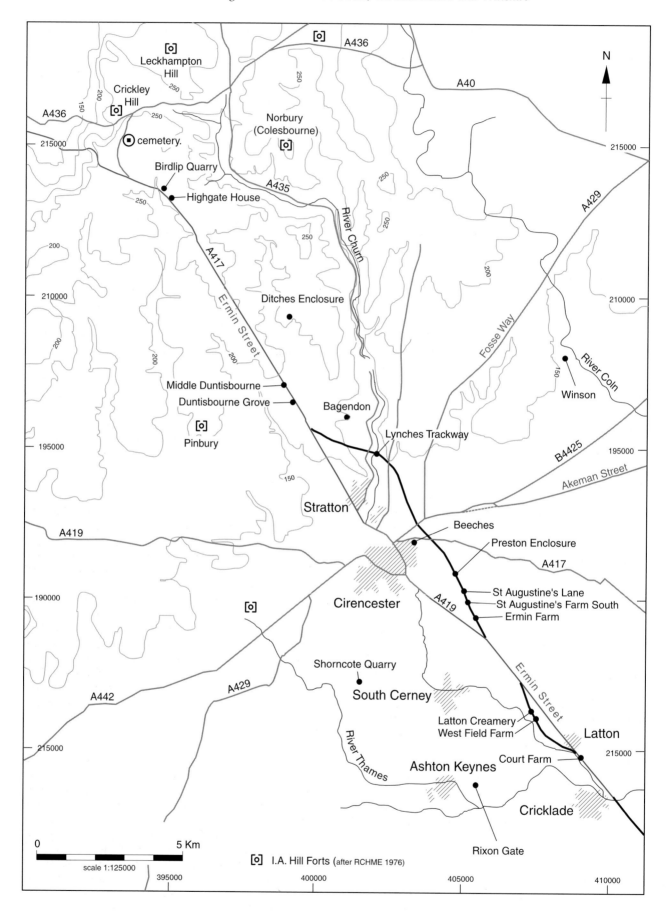

Figure 9.1   Distribution of later prehistoric sites.

sites. It seems that these sites existed in a politically unsettled climate, and, if the key site of Crickley Hill can be taken as representative of the smaller hillforts rather than a special case (something which only excavations on similar sites will be able to confirm), were periodically subject to destruction. It is tempting to see the final destruction of the Crickley Hill hillfort around 400 BC (Darvill 1987, 133–4) as reflecting a decisive change in settlement pattern which saw fewer but larger hillforts (such as Uley Bury and Salmonsbury), a greater density of non-hillfort settlement, and a regional shift towards the lower slopes and river valleys.

The early Iron Age in the Upper Thames region is characterised by sparse occupation, or at least occupation which is not easily detectable, and sites which are not tightly defined. Darvill (1987, 132–3) noted only two sites in Gloucestershire, the Loders and Roughground Farm, Lechlade. The former consisted of just a few pits while the latter had a wider scatter of pits and postholes with extensive linear boundary ditches (Allen *et al.* 1993, 36–47). Evidence of large-scale land division, probably a continuation of the same ditches, also comes from Butler's Field, Lechlade (Jennings 1998, 31–34). It has been suggested that this land division was part of a series of extensive terrritorial markers on the Upper Thames gravels which may have been related to the control of grazing rights (Darvill 1987 133). Possibly similar indications of land boundaries were found further up river in an evaluation near Lady Lamb Farm, Marston Meysey (WANHM 1995, 150). More settlement sites are known in the Oxford region where there is an indication of the intensification of arable farming particularly on the higher gravel terraces (Lambrick 1992, 90). Closer to Cirencester, evidence for early Iron Age occupation has proved elusive. At Latton Lands, west of the Creamery, two ditches forming part of an enclosure of late Bronze Age/early Iron Age date were evaluated (CAT 1995b). It is probable that these belonged to a settlement of some kind which at present lacks clear definition. The extensive (9 ha) settlement at Shorncote Quarry, Somerford Keynes, while dating to the 9th/8th centuries BC rather than any later, has been seen as evidence for non-intensive, shifting occupation at this time (Hearne and Heaton 1994, 17; Rawes and Wills 1996). Recent excavations adjacent to this site have corroborated this interpretation, indicating a pastoral emphasis to the occupation (Brossler *et al.* forthcoming). A continuation of this type of land use into the middle Iron Age can now be suggested for Shorncote, although a definition of the early Iron Age phases has proved difficult both in relation to the settlement structure and the associated pottery, and continuity of land use has yet to be demonstrated.

Middle Iron Age

The current project identified middle Iron Age settlement at Highgate House, Preston Enclosure and Ermin Farm, and evidence of probable settlement near Court Farm, Latton. In addition, radiocarbon dating

suggests that the segmented boundary ditches at St Augustine's Farm South/St Augustine's Lane are likely to have been of this date. The ditches at Norcote Farm and Lower Street Furlong, probably representing boundaries at some distance from settlement, are less securely dated, although a middle Iron Age origin appears most likely given the dating from the similar features at St Augustine's Farm South. This proliferation of activity lies in sharp contrast to the situation in the early Iron Age and is made more striking by the fact that, before excavation began, Highgate House was the only site of this date known from within the development corridor. Little new information came from the Upper Thames Valley. This is one of the most intensively studied archaeological landscapes in Britain (Fulford and Nichols 1992; Lambrick 1992), but it should be noted that most of the evidence for middle Iron Age settlement comes from below Fairford/Lechlade with the area south of Cirencester remaining comparatively unknown (Darvill and Gerrard 1994, 49).

Comparatively few settlement sites of middle Iron Age date in the Cotswold region have been examined by excavation and then only on a small scale (Darvill 1987, 140–2; Lambrick 1988, 125–127; Parry 1998). The evidence for the Gloucestershire Cotswolds has recently been reviewed by Parry (op. cit.), drawing largely from the Upper Windrush Valley and other Cotswold sites north of Cirencester. Darvill (1987, 140) identifed more than 30 middle Iron Age sites in Gloucestershire as a whole although many more may be indicated by cropmarks. The road scheme excavations do indicate that any reasonably large-scale investigation in the Cotswolds is likely to discover hitherto unknown sites. This has already been intimated by the unexpected discovery of a settlement at Winson within the corridor of the Esso Oil Pipeline (Smith 1986). Systematic fieldwork has led Marshall to estimate a spacing of Iron Age settlements every 1–2 km around Guiting (Marshall 1991, 22), although these may not be expected to be strictly contemporary. At the same time, the examination of the three middle Iron Age sites on the current project (Highgate House, Preston Enclosure, Ermin Farm), each of different form but almost identical date, underlines the hazard of attempting to date sites purely on the basis of cropmark morphology, let alone engage in any deeper economic or social analysis on that basis.

Settlement

Highgate House, Preston Enclosure and Ermin Farm have provided important new evidence for settlement in the region during the middle Iron Age. In the Cirencester area the only other securely dated settlement is at The Beeches, Nursery Field (Darvill and Holbrook 1994, 49) although here excavations have been limited. On the gravels a settlement within a rectangular enclosure is known at Westfield Farm, Latton within the scheduled area (Wilts. SMR SU09NE201), and further south-west settlements have been investigated at Shorncote Quarry

(Brossler *et al.* forthcoming) and Spratsgate Lane, Somerford Keynes (Darvill and Holbrook 1994, 49; Rawes and Wills 1997). In the Cotswolds the site at Birdlip Bypass has been partly examined (Parry 1998), but there is virtually nothing else assuredly of this date within a kilometre or so of Ermin Street (information from Glos. SMR). This paucity of information in the vicinity of the current project undoubtedly reflects a lack of archaeological investigation rather than the true picture of settlement at this time.

There is insufficient information from the region to attempt a synthesis of settlement or economic patterns. Iron Age sites in the Cotswolds which have undergone any sort of investigation by excavation tend to indicate far more complexity to their spatial organisation and development than is suggested by cropmark evidence (Lambrick 1988, 125–9; Parry 1998). The economic orientation of sites on the current project remains unclear given the limited areas excavated and the small quantity of material recovered. The lack of features for grain storage at the Preston sites may be significant and contrasts with some of the evidence from the Cotswolds such as that from Birdlip Bypass (Parry 1998), Guiting Manor Farm (Saville 1979b) and The Park, Guiting Power (Marshall 1990) where storage pits are common. This may suggest that grain production was more significant at these sites, although the suggestion must remain tentative. Further lines of evidence are required in order to attempt to establish the relative importance of one or other aspect of the economy of these sites, including the complete site layout and chronological range as well as more artefactual and palaeoenvironmental material. Probable grain storage pits were present at Highgate House but the numbers were small and do not, on present evidence, suggest a dominant arable component to the economy. As a point of contrast, at The Park, Guiting Power the size of some storage pits, with a capacity well in excess of what it is estimated that the relatively small farmstead could have produced, has led to the suggestion that the site had some kind of central storage and redistributive function (Marshall 1991, 22–23).

Preston Enclosure and Ermin Farm had simple layouts comprising one main phase. A consideration of the silting sequences in the enclosure ditches, as well as the pottery, suggests that occupation may have been relatively short-lived. The evidence from Highgate House is more difficult to interpret but may suggest a longer period of occupation. However, the radiocarbon dates from all these sites are very similar and indicate that they were occupied in the 4th-3rd centuries BC, with a slightly later end-date possible for Highgate House on the stratigraphic evidence. The radiocarbon dates are similar to those from Birdlip Bypass (Parry 1998, table 5) and compatible with those presented from The Park (Marshall 1991, table 3). At face value the dating fits in with the regional settlement pattern, identified principally from sites in the Upper Thames Valley, where middle Iron Age settlements do not continue into the late Iron Age

and Roman periods (Fulford and Nichols 1992, 27; Lambrick 1992b, fig. 27). This also appears to hold true for sites in the Cotswolds (Parry 1998, 55–56) although the evidence is still comparatively slight.

The shift in settlement, which appears to have taken place in the 2nd–1st centuries BC at the sites on the current project, leads to an archaeological enigma since no sites securely of this date were located and it is therefore unclear where the earlier settlements shifted to. The terminal occupation at Highgate House remains ill-defined and does not contribute to a resolution of the problem. The fragmentary remains at Court Farm, Latton, may be relevant, but the date and character of the Iron Age occupation here is too uncertain to be meaningfully discussed. The apparent gap between the middle Iron Age and 1st-century AD deposits at Birdlip Bypass has been examined (Parry 1998, 55) and, on the evidence of the admittedly limited excavations, seems to be genuine. At Guiting Power there seems to have been a local shift from a small settlement at The Park to a larger trapezoidal enclosure at The Bowsings in the later or late-middle Iron Age (Marshall 1991). The ditch here has been interpreted as defensive and the settlement seen as a local stronghold. If this is correct and the pattern applicable more widely, it is possible that there was a change to fewer but larger and more defendable sites in the later Iron Age. This is not a pattern which has been recognised generally (cf. Darvill 1987, 159), but with the notable exception of Claydon Pike in the Thames Valley, so few sites of this period have been defined it is certain that any new excavations will add substantially to, and perhaps radically alter, our understanding of the period.

Land boundaries

The segmented ditch complex at St Augustine's Farm South/St Augustine's Lane appears to be broadly middle Iron Age with possible earlier origins. This is unexpectedly late for this type of land division which is frequently found to date to the late Bronze Age or early Iron Age. The complex has been compared to the late Bronze Age/early Iron Age boundary ditches at Butler's Field, Lechlade (Jennings 1998), although in some respects there are notable contrasts. The Lechlade ditches comprised a sequence of recut ditches and regular pit alignments, the major element of which can be traced, fairly directly, for over 1 km. They may have demarcated a parcel of land of up to 250 ha within the confluence of the rivers Thames and Leach (ibid., 33). The boundary may have been the axis of an extensive field system, or a land division relating to the control of grazing. It can be seen as an expression of unitary authority, or at least an action sanctioned by a large, united social group. It is also significant that the boundary cut an earlier Bronze Age ring ditch, indicating a lack of interest in maintaining the monument. The ditches at St Augustine's Farm/ St Augustine's Lane may be interpreted differently. Although the full extent of this system remains unknown, its meandering and intermittent course suggests a more piecemeal scale of activity. Its respect for the earlier ring ditches is evidence that land use in the intervening period had not obliterated the burial monument, and the ditches may be seen as evidence of either a continuity of earlier land demarcation, or a reaffirmation of traditional boundaries with respect to the monument. A curious and possibly similar act of reaffirmation may be interpreted from the site at Birdlip Bypass, where a middle Iron Age rectangular enclosure was established concentrically around a Bronze Age ring ditch (Parry 1998).

The irregular, and intermittent character of the boundary ditches at St Augustine's Farm has similarities with those recently excavated at Shorncote Quarry (Brossler *et al.* forthcoming). These were not closely dated but appear to be largely middle Iron Age. They were characterised by lines of pits and irregular short lengths of ditch joined to form meandering boundaries and partial enclosures. The excavated part of the complex covered about 3 ha. Settlement appeared to be sparse but the ditches were associated with occasional isolated or small groups of buildings. The complex appears to represent incoherent and unplanned boundary definition undertaken on a small scale.

The recognition of this type of irregular field pattern may have important implications for an understanding of Iron Age settlement and land use in the region. On the gravels south of Cirencester an irregular pattern of ditches can be seen from cropmarks in the Latton area, at Westfield Farm (Scheduled Ancient Monument 899) and west of Street Farm (Scheduled Ancient Monument 899). These were largely unexamined in the current project and remain to be analysed in detail. Most have not been included in the Royal Commission's cropmark survey of the area, although some of those at Westfield Farm have and exhibit a similar alignment to the known Iron Age enclosure in this field (Wilts. SMR SU09NE201). Here the boundaries are not dated by archaeological investigation but they are clearly distinct from the rectilinear ditches of the Roman settlement and a later prehistoric date seems highly likely. East of Latton 'Roman Pond' a number of ditches were examined during the watching brief. Prehistoric pottery has been recovered from a ditch in this field (Wilts. SMR SU09NE525) (CAT 1997). However, the current project recovered only Roman sherds from some of the ditches and it remains unclear whether distinct prehistoric and Roman systems existed here or can be recognised from the cropmarks. One of the dominant east-west cropmarks has been identified as a palaeochannel. Others also appear to be natural drainage features, although it is possible that they were redug as ditches. The irregular linear features at Court Farm (Plate 4.3) appear more likely to be natural gullies or ice-wedge casts.

The present lines of evidence discussed suggest that the land around Cirencester, both on the gravels and on the Cotswold margins, may not have been intensively settled until the middle Iron Age, with a concomitant need for boundary definition coming

rather later to this area than further down river. The nature of the boundaries requires much more investigation, particularly in the Latton area, but it can be suggested that colonisation (which probably took the form of the intensification of existing practices rather than the exploitation of new ground) generally took place on a smaller scale than it did further down the Thames Valley at Lechlade where there is evidence for land division on a much larger scale in the early Iron Age, and tightly defined areas of settlement and land use by the middle Iron Age at Claydon Pike (Hingley and Miles 1984, fig. 4.4).

The pollen sequence from Latton 'Roman Pond' provides some corroboration of relatively late woodland clearance in this region. Although the sequence cannot be dated precisely, it suggests that the later Holocene dominant lime woodland (Pollen Zone 1) persisted beyond the later Bronze Age (2943+/-63 BP; 1258–1020 cal BC) and that clearance which is represented by the 'lime decline' therefore probably took place in the early Iron Age. A second decline in tree pollen occurred later on, probably in the middle Iron Age although an even later date cannot be ruled out (Pollen Zones 2/3). This led to the establishment of a predominantly agricultural landscape of pasture and arable. The relatively late clearance of woodland in the region with the establishment of a predominantly pastoral land use in the Iron Age is a model which has already been arrived at independently from the study of hydrological changes on the Thames floodplain further down river (Robinson and Lambrick 1984; Lambrick and Robinson 1988; Robinson 1992b). Overbank alluviation here has been seen to relate to a later phase of arable expansion which took place from the middle to late Iron Age onward and was probably related to the cultivation of winter-sown cereals in the valley catchment. The current project offers general confirmation of this model, but the development of settlement and land use in the region is still imperfectly understood. It is possible, for instance, that in the Iron Age the Upper Thames Valley in the Cirencester region had more in common with the Cotswold uplands than with the valley further down river.

Late Iron Age

Late Iron Age sites were investigated at Duntisbourne Grove and Middle Duntisbourne. Each comprised a large enclosure or partial enclosure lacking any evidence of internal features or a focus of occupation. The character of these sites is therefore uncertain, but the nature and quantity of finds from the ditches would suggest that they can be regarded as settlements and probably of high status. Both sites were occupied at the same time and their use was restricted to a few decades around the middle of the 1st century AD. An earlier phase of site layout was detected at Middle Duntisbourne, but this remains undated and it is unclear whether or not the 1st-century AD occupation represents a continuation, an expansion, or a re-founding. There is certainly nothing to indicate occupation in the 2nd–1st centuries BC at either of the sites and with the possible exception of Highgate House, this period appears to remain genuinely unrepresented on the current project.

The dating of the Duntisbourne sites is particularly interesting in view of their relationship to the 'Bagendon complex' whose status as a Dobunnic political centre is unchallenged, but whose precise nature and date remain controversial (Darvill 1987, 164–7; Trow 1988; 1990). Excavations at Ditches hillfort have revived the debate as to whether the occupation at both this site and Bagendon itself were pre- or post-conquest (Rigby 1988; Trow 1988, 73–76). Only tiny proportions of these sites have been excavated and the dating will certainly be subjected to further revision in the future. The same applies to the Duntisbourne sites. Furthermore, the nature of archaeological evidence means that it is not usually amenable to such precise discrimination, and the material from the Duntisbourne sites suffers many of the limitations which apply to the dating of Bagendon and Ditches. However, the singular characteristic of the Duntisbourne sites is that they were crossed by Roman Ermin Street which, at face value, was later than those occupations. The sequence of ditch deposits at both these sites has been presented in some detail (Chapter 3) to elucidate the development of each site and to try to establish whether the assemblages of material can be shown to be contemporary with the use of the ditches (and therefore pre-dating the road), rather than being incorporated at a later date. The balance of evidence suggests that accumulations of primary deposits almost certainly relate directly to the occupations on those sites, rather than being later backfills. It is reasonable to assume that similar deposits are sealed by the road, although of course, this relationship could not be investigated. The molluscan evidence from Middle Duntisbourne is particularly important since there is a strong indication that woodland was regenerating over the ditches while they were silting up, indicating a long-term natural process of infilling (see Robinson, Chapter 8). Furthermore, the distribution and size of pottery sherds suggests that the occupation was continuing while the ditches were silting up and woodland overtaking them, contradicting any suggestion that this associated material could have been re-deposited through later activity. The clearance of the woodland took place near the top of the fill sequence, and probably related to Roman road construction, as supported by the woodland mollusca from beneath Ermin Street at Dartley Bottom. An extrapolation of the Middle Duntisbourne sequence to the ditches at Duntisbourne Grove is not unreasonable, although the stratigraphy here is more ambiguous and the molluscan evidence less complete. The pattern of infilling at Duntisbourne Grove also appears to have been different and the site may have been abandoned earlier while the ditches were still largely open. Later, the sides of the partly infilled ditches were quarried. To judge by the pottery from the backfilled quarry this activity dated to after the conquest, and on

circumstantial grounds may be linked to the construction of the Roman road. The conclusion from the foregoing is that Iron Age deposits with significant assemblages of 1st-century pottery predate the construction of Roman Ermin Street, and by implication the conquest itself. The pottery assemblages include imported Gallo-Belgic wares, whiteware butt beakers, Savernake Ware and early Severn Valley wares along with Malvernian limestone-tempered jars and bowls of the Iron Age tradition.

As yet the regional late Iron Age/early Roman settlement pattern remains undefined, with sites such as Bagendon, Ditches hillfort and now the Duntisbournes yielding little more than site-specific interpretations and further questions. The topic has wide implications for the nature of the native Dobunnic polity and its interaction with the Roman invaders in the Cirencester area (Trow 1990; Darvill and Holbrook 1994, 49–56). It is worth noting, however, that the short-lived occupations at the Duntisbourne sites are untypical of the pattern established from excavations in the Thames valley and elsewhere, where sites which commence in the late Iron Age normally show evidence of continuity on the same site until well into the Roman period (Fulford and Nicholls 1992, 27). This may well relate to considerations of status, with exclusively farming settlements receiving a stimulus to production, but the fortunes of politically significant sites more dependent upon relations with the new centres of power. The decline of Bagendon, for instance, was probably related to the development of the civilian settlement at Cirencester by the 60s AD, while the early Roman villa at Ditches developed from a centre of the native tribal autocracy (Trow 1990, 113). It has been suggested that the Duntisbourne sites were part of the 'Bagendon complex' and their woodland/woodland margin location may have been important in their economic orientation, which would have been relatively specialised within the local settlement system. Their rather specialised nature and connection with the centre of a potentially volatile political system may explain why the settlements failed to survive into the Roman period, although it should be emphasised that there is no indication that they were physically destroyed by the Romans and may, indeed, have been abandoned before the conquest. The impression that the enclosures were deliberately slighted by the construction of Ermin Street needs to be resisted since it is clear that the Roman road was constructed with the single-minded objective of linking the forts at Cirencester and Gloucester (Chapter 5). It does not betray any deviation from this course, certainly not in the vicinity of the Duntisbourne enclosures, and the fact that it crossed them can only be a coincidence.

The distribution of other late Iron Age sites in the region is difficult to ascertain. A large number of cropmark enclosures are known although none are assuredly of this period. Two possibilities lie within about a kilometre of Ermin Street. One is part of a rectangular enclosure visible south of Blacklains

Farm, Brimpsfield. This lies near a linear ditch running for about 350 m between Gowanlea and Sidelands (Glos. SMR 7214) which is similarly undated. The other is a very clear subrectangular enclosure covering about 2 ha at The Ash, Watercombe Farm, Elkstone (Glos. SMR 4701; RCHME 1976, 54) which has superficial similarities to Duntisbourne Grove. However, the form of Ditches hillfort should warn against attempting to date sites from cropmark evidence alone since this site is similar to middle Iron Age hillforts (RCHME 1976, fig. opp. xxvi) and may in fact be middle Iron Age in origin (Darvill 1987, 163). South of Cirencester, Iron Age occupation is known from both Westfield Farm and Court Farm, Latton near to the Scheduled Roman settlements. At present it is unclear whether final Iron Age settlement is represented and therefore whether continuity into the Roman period is likely. Certainly the trackway at Court Farm appears to be early Roman (Chapter 4) and would suggest that a settlement pre-dating Ermin Street already existed at Field Barn (Wilts. SMR SU09NE303), becoming connected to the Roman road at the earliest opportunity. At Westfield Farm, the hexagonal ditched enclosure which later formed the focus of the Roman farmstead, appears Iron Age and, if continuity of occupation could be demonstrated, a similar trajectory of development can be envisaged. Further south at Rixon Gate, Ashton Keynes, there appears to be a continuity from the late Iron Age into the Roman period (Newman 1994, 83–4). This rather superficial interpretation of the evidence from sites south of Cirencester would suggest a marked contrast to the fortune of the Duntisbourne sites. However, the current project has indicated the need for detailed research on Iron Age settlement and landuse in the Cirencester area and a more precise chronological definition. The difficulty of establishing the presence of occupation in the 2nd and 1st centuries BC in the region has been mentioned and distinction between continuity and the re-occupation of sites needs careful consideration in any future research in this area. The label 'Iron Age' on the basis of (often limited) pottery, is clearly inadequate. Judicious radiocarbon dating has been shown to be an effective supporting technique, and mollusc evidence occasionally invaluable for site-specific and wider interpretations.

THE ROMAN PERIOD *(Fig. 9.2)*
By Andrew Mudd

A number of sites of the Roman period were examined on the project. These included, at Field's Farm, an early roadside funerary monument, together with adjacent trackway ditches on both sides of Ermin Street; and a later Roman roadside settlement at Birdlip Quarry. Other sites yielded more peripheral features, such as quarry pits and boundary ditches at Court Farm and Westfield Farm, Latton; and field boundaries at Latton 'Roman Pond' and land to the east, as well as at Exhibition Barn, Baunton. A late Roman midden, almost certainly related to a nearby settlement, was examined at Weavers Bridge. In addition to these sites, Ermin Street was investigated with seven cross-sections north of Cirencester and several other partial excavations. The Fosse Way/Akeman Street (Burford Road) was sectioned with less useful results. The Lynches Trackway and a probable ditched trackway at Norcote Farm, Preston, were unexpected Roman discoveries.

With minor exceptions the current project has not added to the number of known sites in the region. This, in itself, is of some interest in the vicinity of a major Roman town (and dyke system of arguably comparable importance) and contradicts the expectations expressed in the initial desk-based assessment of the Cirencester-Stratton section of the route, which effectively predicted the discovery of hitherto unknown sites in the hinterland of Roman Cirencester (CAT 1990a, 36). However, the subsequent trial trench evaluation here also revealed little of note (CAT 1991a, 136), and the excavations have largely confirmed this picture. South of Cirencester the route bypassed several known sites, but with the possible exception of Weavers Bridge (where finds were made in the evaluation but the site was not identified as a possible settlement), there were no totally new discoveries. The same is true of the northern section of the route where the site at Birdlip Quarry, identified at the Stage 2 survey, was the only other settlement investigated. It is worth noting, therefore, that the number of sites examined by excavation was unaffected by any redesign or realignment of the route undertaken as impact mitigation after Stage 2 (the mitigation measures on Scheduled Ancient Monument 899 at Latton being to reduce the impact on known sites rather than a response to new information), and to that extent the results reflect the real distribution of Roman sites within this transect of landscape.

The pattern of Roman settlement around Cirencester has been discussed briefly by Holbrook (1994, 85–86), who has overturned earlier suggestions, derived almost exclusively from the distribution of villas, of a lack of settlement close to the Roman town. The results of the present project do not directly contradict his assertion, for, despite the observations presented above, it is clear from cropmarks and surface finds that occupation of the Roman period is both dense and widespread in this area. A large number of sites are known to lie close to the course of the new route corridor and it may be regarded as fortuitous that more Roman sites were not encountered within it. The lack of substantial new sites within the road transect may, however, suggest that the known distribution of Roman sites is not radically different from the true pattern in this area. This is in direct contrast to conclusions (above) on the distribution of later prehistoric sites.

The sites examined on the current project provide little basis for an overall assessment of the development of settlement and landscape in the Roman period. However there are a few interpretations whose implications are worth pursuing in this discussion.

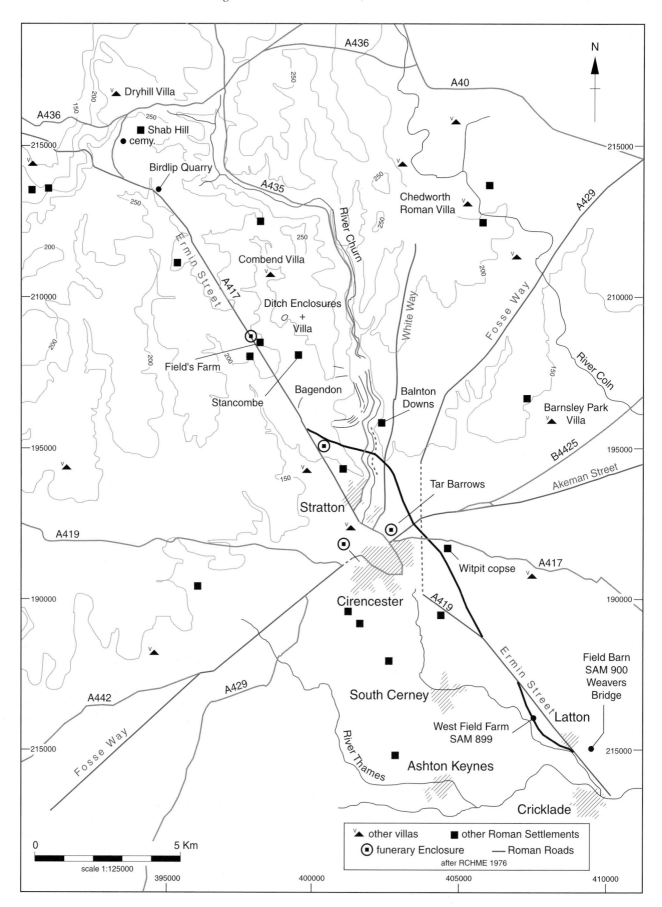

Figure 9.2 Distribution of Roman sites.

Ermin Street

The earliest activity identified in the Roman period was probably the construction of Ermin Street. While there is little direct evidence of the date of its initial construction from anywhere along its length and no further information on the matter from the current project, the position of the Leaholme fort (occupied *c.* AD 50–70) on the same alignment as the road, has been used to suggest that the road was constructed very shortly after the conquest of the region (Darvill and Holbrook 1994, 52). This view is not contradicted by any evidence from the current project. None of the sections through the road offered a straightforward interpretation and dating evidence was limited. Notwithstanding this, the stratigraphic sequences from the deeper trenches (particularly Trenches 6 and 8) indicate that the road was regularly repaired, at least throughout the 1st and 2nd centuries, and possibly into the 3rd century. It remains uncertain whether these were local repairs undertaken in response to particular difficulties in negotiating the major dry valleys which the road crossed, or whether they reflect something more systematic. In either case it appears that the route between Cirencester and Gloucester was sufficiently important to warrant maintenance throughout, at least, the early Roman period. At Birdlip Quarry there was clear evidence for a widening of Ermin Street in the early 4th century. In contrast to the earlier constructions this was a very rudimentary surfacing which appears to owe nothing to military engineering practice. The surfacing appears to have been too extensive to have exclusively served the settlement at Birdlip Quarry (although this must remain a possibility) and may rather imply a more extensive redesign of the road. There was no direct support for this interpretation from elsewhere, except perhaps at Field's Farm where part of a late surface adjacent to Ermin Street was exposed. An undated cobbled surface was also found at Daglingworth in a similar position. The later surfaces in the sections through Ermin Street were either truncated, or proved impossible to date with any confidence. Despite these various uncertainties, a widespread remodelling of Ermin Street in the early 4th century should be considered as a serious proposition and one which would carry implications for changes in the region at this time, adding to a picture of widespread development which has emerged from a number of villa excavations.

A discussion of the political/administrative context for the maintenance of this section of Ermin Street lies outside the scope of this report. However, it can be noted that while a number of sites elsewhere in Britain show roads remodelled throughout the Roman period, these are normally considered in terms of the local development of a settlement, rather than as a strategic undertaking demanded or sanctioned at a higher level of authority. On the current project, where a major Roman road was examined independent of nearby settlement, there are indications that a regional explanation may be appropriate, although the spatial and chronological patterns of the road system and its development require much more research.

Settlement and land-use

At Field's Farm, the square funerary enclosure was undoubtedly an early monument. There are grounds for considering it to be the earliest of the group of features on this site, almost certainly pre-dating the trackway and roadside ditches, and possibly pre-dating the roadside quarry pits (although these need not have been related to the first construction of Ermin Street). A 1st-century date for the funerary monument receives some support from the limited pottery present in the ditch silts and, in view of the stratigraphic interpretation, appears highly likely. The discussion of this monument has emphasised its probable role as an overt symbol of Roman affinity positioned for maximum public visibility. That it was associated with the settlement at Field's Farm is plausible in view of the interpretation of the site sequence which indicates that the roadside and trackway ditches were positioned in relation to the funerary monument, rather than vice versa, thereby forming the link between the monument and the settlement. The site can therefore be seen as an early statement of Roman allegiance by inhabitants of the settlement. Whether this represents Romanization is a question which can only be addressed by an examination of the settlement itself. Possible similar monuments in the region have been discussed (Chapter 4). Neither the cropmark south of Daglingworth Quarry (Glos. SMR 4783) nor the Tar Barrows appear to be very close to contemporary settlement although both may have been sited adjacent to roads.

At Court Farm the trackway which served the Roman settlement at Field Barn was also shown to be early, although precise dating was not possible. The trackway ditches were respected by the dense quarry pitting which ran in a corridor on this side of Ermin Street and which the pottery evidence suggests to have been largely of 1st-century date. This line of evidence has been used to suggest that a settlement at Field Barn existed in the pre-Conquest period and became linked to Ermin Street early on (see late Iron Age discussion, above). Rather like Field's Farm this may be seen as an example of a landowner taking advantage of Ermin Street at an early opportunity, although again this idea requires further substantiation.

Features within the Scheduled Ancient Monument 899, roughly between Westfield Farm and Street Farm, comprised mainly field boundaries peripheral to the known Roman settlement. This cropmark complex, which shows superimposed Iron Age and Roman features, has been identified as a key site for the understanding of Iron Age settlement and land use in the Cirencester area (see middle Iron Age discussion, above), and may be equally important in understanding the Roman transition. The mitigation strategy within the Scheduled area was designed to minimise disturbance to archaeological deposits, and it is not surprising that few conclusions can be reached regarding the Roman occupation here. The chief value of the excavations at Latton 'Roman Pond' lay in the pre-Roman environmental sequence from the peat deposits. The Roman ditches examined were less informative, although the tentative identification of the ditch in the centre of the 'pond' with an extensive rectilinear system of land division suggests further complexities to the site which require investigation. At Westfield Farm a Roman ditch could be seen to correspond to a major land boundary which was respected by a zone of quarrying alongside the present Cerney Wick Road. This is not a known Roman road and an interpretation of this evidence remains problematic. The field boundaries east of Latton 'Roman Pond' received some attention during the watching brief. A Roman date is likely for some of them although their correlation with the cropmarks is not straightforward. There is at present insufficient evidence for interpreting the pattern of activity in this field, and the discovery of a small quantity of early to middle Saxon pottery on the eastern side of the field suggests that the cropmarks and the limited interventions by excavation are an insufficient basis for understanding activity in this area. Early Saxon pottery has already come from a pit in this field (Wilts. SMR SU09NE400).

Another Roman field boundary was investigated at Exhibition Barn. This lay among a series of intercutting boundary ditches which appear to show a continuous development from Roman times through to the modern era. The suggestion of a continuity of administrative frameworks and boundaries from the late Roman through to the medieval period has been an abiding theme in studies of the region (Gerrard 1994a, 95–7) although this can rarely be demonstrated with physical evidence. Exhibition Barn was the only site where there was reasonable evidence for the continuous evolution of a field boundary across this period, but the alignment of the primary Roman ditch was different from the later ditches and any suggestion of administrative significance can probably be ruled out.

Settlement pattern

There are a large number of Roman settlements known from the region, both in the Cotswolds and in the Thames Valley. Very few have been excavated in the Cotswolds and there is an assumption that many are villas without good evidence (Jan Wills pers. comm.). The contrasting distributions of settlement types – with the abundance of villas in the Cotswolds and apparently lower status sites more common in the Thames Valley – has been remarked upon on a number of occasions and explanations have taken account of various possible social, historical and environmental factors (Miles and Hingley 1984; Hingley 1984; Miles 1988). On a more specific level, the Roman occupation in the eastern Cotswolds, and its links with the more intensively studied Upper Thames Valley

region around Oxford, has recently been reviewed (Booth 1998). This review need not be repeated here but it is worth re-iterating the point that the view of a villa-dominated Cotswolds is largely based on superficial evidence and there has been very little opportunity to understand the rural settlement pattern as a whole (ibid., 13). In the western Cotswolds there has been a recent synthesis of the Roman 'small towns' of Gloucestershire (Bourton-on-the-Water, Wycomb, Coln St Aldwyns and Dorn) and their role in the regional pattern of settlement and communications (Timby 1998a). Timby largely concerns her discussion with the origin and functions of the 'small towns', although, following from a discussion of the villa at Kingscote, there is also some consideration of rural settlement distributions and hierarchies. Both these themes are of some relevance to the nature and function of the Roman roadside settlements at Weavers Bridge and Birdlip Quarry examined on the current project, and are explored here.

The spacing of the 'small towns' along the Fosse Way and Akeman Street (at every 20–35 km – about a day's journey) suggests that they had a function in relation to the *cursus publicus* and, although definitive evidence is lacking, would probably have been provided with posting stations. There are also some intermediate settlements (including perhaps Bourton) which may or may not have had this role (Timby 1998a, 430–1). Along Ermin Street, the spacing between Gloucester, Cirencester and Wanborough is approximately regular and about the same distance. It is possible that intermediate posting stations were not required on this route, although Timby (among other authors) suggests Birdlip would have been a logical place to site one in response to the difficulty of ascending the scarp. In terms of the buildings excavated, the settlement at Birdlip Quarry lacks an indication of any kind of official involvement and a far more likely location for a *mansio* is at Birdlip itself, where a 'villa type' building was discovered near the present Royal George Hotel (RCHME 1976, 40). However, it should be noted that relay stations (*mutationes*) and the lower classes of resthouse, the *praetoria* and *tabernae*, have not been defined archaeologically and may correspond to the more informal kind of waystation suggested for Birdlip Quarry. Indeed, it has been suggested that a change of animals may have been provided at minor intermediate points between *mansiones* (Black 1995, 89). There is certainly evidence from Birdlip Quarry that cattle, and the unusually high number of horses, were overworked and there is the suggestion of an occasional official presence from the small collection of military metalwork. Taken together, these strands of evidence may point to the settlement's role in providing transport for the *cursus publicus*. South of Cirencester, Smith has cited Latton as a 'roadside settlement' (1987, 247, fig. 1) although the site at Latton Lands (Wilts. SMR SU09NE316) can be discounted as a settlement on the evidence of an evaluation by Wessex Archaeology in 1996, while both known settlements (Westfield Farm and Field Barn) are at a distance from Ermin Street. The value of this classification must therefore be doubted. Timby mentions Cricklade as a settlement with a possible official role although this site is also a slight distance from Ermin Street and is at present too ill-defined to be meaningfully discussed. The midden investigated on the current project at Weavers Bridge lay close to the assumed crossing point of the Thames and within about 10 m of Ermin Street, but, while the character of any associated settlement remains unknown, a function in relation to the road is improbable on current evidence. Of more interest is a Roman settlement, about 400 m further south-east, known from surface finds and the record of a Roman building (Wilts. SMR SU19SW309 and 310). This lies on the line of Ermin Street between Weavers Bridge and Calcutt and must be a candidate for a posting-station of some kind. It lies in a similar relation to Cirencester as Birdlip does, about half way to the next town.

Timby has also discussed settlement patterns in relation to rural estates and the possibility of defining two- or three-tier settlement hierarchies of 'estate centres', more modest villas and non-villa establishments within individual large estates. The question of tenurial arrangements is, however, difficult to recognise from the archaeological record and has largely been left unresolved for Birdlip Quarry (Chapter 4). It is therefore unknown whether this settlement was dependent upon a nearby villa (or indeed a non-villa centre) or operated independently. There are no known villas particularly close to Birdlip Quarry whose elevated position appears to have been typically avoided by villas. The nearest villa (or estate centre?) to Birdlip Quarry may have been Great Witcombe, lying at the foot of the scarp, about 5 km to the west in a direct line. The villa at Combend (RCHME 1976, 35) lies equidistant to the south-east. The status and date of the much closer sites at Birdlip/Birdlip Bypass are still unclear. It is worth noting, therefore, that Birdlip Quarry does not easily fit within either of the models of tenurial organisation proposed by Applebaum (cited in Hingley 1989, 100-110). The site certainly does not appear to come into the category of an estate workers' settlement adjacent to a villa. It is more likely to fall into Applebaum's second category, that of a 'peripheral holding', although its distance from the most likely estate centres means that it may have been the most peripheral of dependent settlements. In view of this it is possible that it was tenurially independent. Esmonde Cleary has discussed the possible existence of a class of *coloni* who, despite being legally free men, may have owed rents and labour service to an estate owner (1989, 114).

The problem of defining settlement relationships and hierarchies is bound in with the debate (discussed by Timby, op. cit., 432–3) as to whether villas were in essence economic units functioning within the wider rural economy, or whether they were primarily elite residences, and whether they need have been situated within (or anywhere near) their putative estates. The debate cannot be pursued with much profit in this report. However, it is interesting to note from Timby's statistics on the number of settlements within a 12 km orbit of Cirencester (coincidentally, covering the length of this road project almost exactly), the ratio of villas (11) to non-villa settlements/probable settlements (52) is the same or slightly lower than that around Bourton (6 villas to 24 non-villas – ibid., table 20). This tends to suggest that the oft-remarked high density of villas near Cirencester is matched by a high density of non-villa settlements, showing, even at this crude level of analysis, that the region was settled by a wide social range and with the possible further implication that one required the other. This may be taken to support the idea of a pattern of villa distribution based in the rural economy, rather than one which reflected the favoured retreats of the urban elite. However, the proposal essentially suffers, like other analyses of settlement patterns, from a suspect database and, despite the valuable inventory of sites compiled by the Royal Commission (RCHME 1976), much more work is required to identify the distribution, nature and development of settlements in the region before the social and economic landscape can be examined with any confidence.

Birdlip Quarry

The excavations at Birdlip Quarry have contributed modestly to an understanding of settlement form and development in the Cotswolds. The importance of this settlement lies in the recognition of a farming community of strongly native character which persisted and developed from the later 2nd century through to the later 4th century. While the continuity of native forms of settlement is well documented from other parts of Roman Britain, and were undoubtedly the vast majority in the northern and western regions (Hingley 1989, 31), the Cotswolds are commonly regarded as an area where Roman influence was strong and where pre-Roman traditions might not have been expected to last long. The settlement was certainly not located in a peripheral or 'backward' region beyond Roman influence and its existence cannot be explained in such terms. On the contrary, its founding beside one of the most highly visible monuments of the Roman conquest, namely the Roman military road between the *civitas* capital at Cirencester and the *colonia* at Gloucester, and well within a day's travel of either city, indicates that the symbols of Roman power and civilisation would have been pervasive. The indifference to this influence is striking and seems only explicable if it is assumed that the inhabitants were wedded to a social and economic way of life which was deep-rooted and at the same time highly viable.

In the analysis and discussion of the Birdlip Quarry settlement (Chapter 4) certain aspects of the Iron Age tradition have been explored. This discussion has been aided by some of the unusually well-preserved evidence of structural detail, development and finds distribution from the site. It has been suggested that there were fundamental structuring principles to

Iron Age settlement which were adhered to, at least during Period 1 (up to the mid 3rd century). The circular stake-walled structures of the later 2nd to early 3rd centuries are not only of native form, but archaeologically indistinguishable from houses built 500 years or more earlier, except perhaps in their larger size. It is suggested that the circular form was integral to the social life of the inhabitants, although this need not imply (and would seem inherently unlikely) that all aspects of social life remained unchanged over this period. The orientation of the doorway to the south-east is also an Iron Age tradition, one which is held to have been related to the position of sunrise, perhaps particularly at the winter solstice. That this orientation was important is emphasised by the fact that it resulted in the roundhouse facing away from Ermin Street. The tradition appears to have been further emphasised by the fact that the first roundhouse (structure 1463) was replaced in exactly the same position by the second roundhouse (structure 1464). This may have been because the house had become dilapidated, but the fact that the earlier drainage gully was deliberately filled in and then redug suggests that the process was a formal refounding, perhaps related to the death of the house owner or some other event which needed commemoration. The distribution of finds in relation to the roundhouse indicates that midden material was deposited at the front of the building and on the left hand side (looking towards the building). There is some indication that this was a standard practice in the Iron Age, although this subject requires more research. There has also been some discussion of the distribution of finds within the roundhouses and the later structures in this area as well as over the site in general. Although no clear patterns were identified it is felt that the presentation of this data is useful for exploring some ideas about the way material culture was used.

The change of site organisation in the mid to later 3rd century (Period 2A) corresponds to a clear change in vernacular architecture. A stone-founded circular or polygonal building (structure 1452) replaced the stake-walled roundhouses. This was of a very similar size to the earlier buildings and in an almost identical position. It is unclear whether this reflected any changes in the nature or social organisation of the settlement. There are a number of late 3rd-century stone-founded circular buildings known from southern Britain and possible parallels have been sought. However, on present evidence they do not appear to represent a distinct vernacular type and may have incorporated a variety of structural techniques and have had a variety of uses. The changes in the early to mid 4th century were the most radical in the settlement's history and may reflect a fundamental break with the pre-Roman past. The buildings are difficult to interpret but it appears that large circular structures (and therefore the earlier forms of social organisation) were abandoned in favour of rectangular buildings. There also appears to have been a change in the pattern of rubbish disposal with material now deposited both next to the structures and in a more distant midden. The reasons for the abandonment of the settlement in the later 4th century are also obscure, although it is possible that this was part of a regional reorganisation of the settlement pattern which resulted in fewer but larger settlements.

Although the position of the Birdlip Quarry settlement in the regional pattern is not known it was probably not a particularly rare type. A comparison with the settlement at Barnsley Park suggests that Birdlip Quarry may have been similar, or have had similar elements, up until the mid 4th century (Fig. 4.110). At Barnsley Park the villa then developed, while Birdlip Quarry was abandoned. Up until that point there are observable similarities between the excavated (ie. southern) part of Birdlip Quarry and the southern compound at Barnsley Park, both in the type of buildings present and their sequence and date of construction. It is possible that this represents the development of a particular kind of farming group in the region. The evidence from Birdlip Quarry would suggest that within the mixed farming settlement this group had a particular role which was concerned with tending cattle and horses. Their position beside Ermin Street suggests that the provision of transport may have been an aspect of this specialism. Although there is nothing from the archaeological evidence to suggest a formal role as a posting-station, there is a suggestion that it may have served as a relay-station (*mutatio*) as well as a waystation for low-ranking or unofficial travellers.

THE POST-ROMAN PERIOD *by Andrew Mudd*

There was very little evidence of post-Roman occupation from the excavations on the project. The only buildings excavated were the medieval kitchen block and overlying agricultural buildings at Street Farm, Latton. On a number of sites the turnpike and other roads and trackways were examined. Most of the other sites revealed disparate evidence of post-Roman activity, consisting of miscellaneous finds, quarries, ditches and features relating to agricultural land use.

Settlement

The lack of evidence for post-Roman occupation may be considered unsurprising since the new road avoided existing settlements many of which are likely to have been the focus of occupation from at least the later Saxon period. There is evidence of this from a number of the nearby churches which have been shown to have pre-Conquest origins. These include Duntisbourne Abbotts, Duntisbourne Rouse, Daglingworth and Preston (Heighway 1984, 230; Gerrard 1994a, 95). The dearth of evidence of rural occupation in the 5th–7th centuries (and the ambiguity of much of the urban evidence) is a regional phenomenon (Heighway op. cit., 227). It is possible that these sites also lie under later settlements, but such continuity is not documented nationally and appears to be unlikely in the Cirencester region.

The shortage of evidence at this time is probably attributable to the poverty of material culture and the deficiency of archaeological features, perhaps combined with a decreased population after the Roman period.

In view of the regional background, the presence of early Saxon pottery north-west of the present village of Latton attains a significance well beyond the meagre quantity of material recovered. Early Saxon pottery has already come from a pit in this field (Wilts. SMR SU09NE400), and the current evidence re-inforces a suggestion of a settlement here. No features of this date were recognised in the watching brief and there is no clear indication of settlement from the cropmarks, although, since features from this period can be notoriously difficult to recognise unless large areas are stripped archaeologically, this absence is not altogether surprising. The location of this site between the Roman settlement and the medieval village at Latton may suggest a gradual shift of settlement focus.

The excavations at Street Farm demonstrated the presence of occupation on the western side of Ermin Street, away from the centre of the village, from the 13th or 14th century. Although only a kitchen block was defined, this would almost certainly have been associated with a dwelling lying closer to the road. It must be considered a possibility that this was one of a row of houses here whose croft boundaries endured until the modern period, although this has not been shown to be the case since the surviving property boundaries examined proved to be post-medieval or not closely datable. The presence of a focus of medieval settlement away from the village core would have implications for the nature of village development. It remains unclear whether this offshoot might have had functions relating to the road, as well as, presumably, an agricultural basis.

The status of the 12th–14th century finds from south of Witpit Lane is unclear. It may be the site of a ploughed-out medieval settlement, although more field work would be required to substantiate this. Deserted settlements of various types and dates are suggested to be quite common in Gloucestershire (Aston and Viner 1984, 282), and in particular there is the expectation that farms deserted at the time of enclosure ought to be identifiable (Gerrard and Viner 1994, 135). There appears to have been little recent work on medieval and later settlement dynamics, although it is interesting to note that at Frocester it was suggested that a number of small settlements existed until the 12th century, after which there appears to have been a nucleation in the present village (Aston and Viner 1984, fig. 10). The present project contributes little to the theme of deserted settlements although some speculation about the demise of the post-medieval buildings at Street Farm after Inclosure has been offered.

Cultivation

The evidence for ridge and furrow cultivation was almost continuous through the parishes of Preston and Latton, and less common, or entirely absent, elsewhere. This confirms, but does not substantially add to, the picture of ridge and furrow distribution in the vicinity of Cirencester (Gerrard 1994b, fig. 41), which has been shown to lie predominantly on the eastern and southern sides of the town (the parishes of Preston and Siddington). The shortage of evidence for cultivation in the northern section of the project, which closely followed Ermin Street, is to be expected. However, its absence in the parishes of Baunton and Bagendon in the Cirencester and Stratton Bypass section is noteworthy and, particularly when considered in the light of the lynchets found at Birdlip Quarry, Cowley, this contrast does not seem explicable in terms of geology. It may well rather reflect a difference in the history of land use between these areas. As noted by Gerrard (1994b, 118) very little excavation has been carried out on medieval agricultural remains around Cirencester, however, there is good documentary evidence for a number of parishes such as Cowley, (eg. VCH). This discussion therefore comprises little more than a few comments and observations, although the evidence, as far as it goes, does support the general trends.

In the main, medieval ridge and furrow comprised long narrow strips with a reversed S-shaped plan, whereas the post-medieval furrows tended to be straighter and more widely spaced. Both types of ridge and furrow were found on the current project. In the Latton area, most of the ridge and furrow recorded and visible as cropmarks was broad and widely spaced (about 15-16 m apart), and respected the post-Inclosure field boundaries. At Westfield Farm, two distinct patterns of ridge and furrow existed. The earlier phase of ploughing comprised narrow furrows, spaced at about 7-m intervals, which ran parallel to a Roman field boundary. These were replaced by post-medieval 'broad rig' furrows which ran in a different direction. The earlier furrows were uncommonly narrow and in that respect were similar to examples at Gwithian in Cornwall which were dated to the 9th or 10th century (Taylor 1975). There is, however, absolutely no evidence for such an early chronology for any of the furrows examined during the course of these excavations, and it is furthermore unclear to what extent the narrowness of furrows can be attributed to an accident of survival rather than a direct outcome of early agricultural practice. Regardless of absolute date, the fact that the early furrows at Westfield Farm respected the alignment of the Roman field boundary can be taken as evidence that the Roman features were still visible during the medieval period and were incorporated into the new landscape.

In the parish of Preston, two patterns of ridge and furrow were evident at St Augustine's Farm South, Site Na. In this case both patterns were quite narrowly spaced. The broader north-east – south-west furrows, which were also found at Site O, correspond to the direction of the pre-Inclosure strip fields mapped in 1770. The narrower furrows at Site Na, running east-west, are presumably earlier although this cannot be demonstrated. If this assumption is correct it implies a change in cultivation practice which was earlier than, and unrelated to, Inclosure. Just south of St Augustine's Lane the single furrow in Site Nb running east-west corresponds to the alignment of the strip fields here in 1770. The field north of St Augustine's Lane with the narrow east-west furrows had been enclosed by 1770 and there is no record of the strip field system. This absence applies to much of the land between St Augustine's Lane and Witpit Lane, which had been enclosed by 1687 (the first cartographic record of the parish). It is therefore unclear whether the extensive ridge and furrow here is derived from the pre-Inclosure layout or not. The irregularly-spaced, post-medieval ridge and furrow at Preston Enclosure may pre- or post-date the Inclosure of these fields, or it may represent traces of two systems on the same alignment. There is a suggestion that the 'narrow rig' at the Witpit Lane site was medieval rather than later, but the pottery evidence, abundant though it is, is not conclusive since it may all have been residual. At Norcote Farm the broad but narrowly-spaced furrows contained post-medieval finds. From this latter site it appears that, while closely-spaced furrows can often be shown, or reasonably assumed to be medieval rather than later, this is not an invariable rule.

The cultivation lynchets at Birdlip Quarry, Cowley, were unique on this project. They suggest quite intensive arable cultivation here in the medieval period, which was presumably undertaken from the shrunken village at Stockwell, the nearest contemporaneous settlement in the parish, which lay a little over 1 km to the north-west (Glos. SMR 5758). This settlement is documented from the 13th century and was evidently depopulated during the late 18th century following the enclosure of the open field. It is not known when the lynchets themselves fell out of use. The field was known simply as South Field by the time of the 1847 tithe survey, suggesting that the lynchets may not have been visible by then. Cultivation terraces have also been recorded just south of Stockwell (Glos. SMR 6710) and ridge and furrow a little further south still (Glos. SMR 14858). Arable cultivation here appears to have been quite extensive in the medieval period, contrary to any implication from the place-name that the settlement may have had a pastoral specialism.

Boundaries

Post-Roman boundary ditches and walls were recorded at a number of sites. In general these scattered features contributed little to an understanding of the pattern and development of physical land units. Some aspects of the apparent continuity of boundary ditches from the Roman period has been mentioned in Chapters 4 and 6. In some cases, such as Latton 'Roman Pond', the continuity of boundary definition can be related to physical factors – in this case the division between well-drained terrace soils and the wetter peat – which remained a governing factor in land use. The persistence of boundaries alongside

Ermin Street can be attributed to the continued presence and use of the road, although it is possible that the quite precise coincidence of Roman and post-Roman ditches at Birdlip Quarry might reflect active maintenance of the boundary rather than merely the existence of the road as a topographic determiner. At Exhibition Barn, Baunton (Chapter 4) it has been suggested that an addition to a Roman boundary system was made during the initial post-Roman re-organisation of the landscape. This would seem to point to the evolution of boundary ditches from the Roman to medieval and, in this instance, the modern period, although this site stands as a somewhat isolated example and the wider implications for landscape development are unclear.

The proposition that Roman boundaries and administrative units in this region continued into the medieval period was raised many years ago (Finberg 1955) and has been revisited periodically since then (Reece and Catling 1975; Slater 1976; Reece 1984). One aspect of this topic is the suggestion that parish boundaries may represent the fossilization of Anglo-Saxon and perhaps earlier estates (Gerrard 1994a, 95). However, archaeological evidence has been able to contribute relatively little to this line of enquiry. At the evaluation stage of the current project the parish boundaries between Daglingworth-Baunton, Daglingworth-Bagendon, Baunton-Cirencester and Preston-Driffield were singled out as being of particular research interest (CAT 1991a, 135–6), although such boundaries need not have been defined by man-made, nor any kind of archaeologically recognisable feature. The Preston-Driffield (formerly Harnhill) boundary at Harnhill Road was targeted with two evaluation trenches to either side of it (CAT 1991a, 106–112), but failed to find any boundary-related features. The only parish boundaries specifically targeted at Stage 3 was the junction of Daglingworth, Baunton and Bagendon at Warren Gorse House Area 2. Extant drystone walls were recorded, as well as the probable foundation of an earlier wall, but although these were undated they seem unlikely to be very ancient, and there were no underlying boundary features.

Water management

Relict river channels and later drainage ditches were revealed at Weavers Bridge. The complex of inter-cutting features gave some indication of the dynamic nature of the Churn river system between the Roman and early modern period, although no firm conclusions could be drawn concerning the overall pattern or chronology of its development.

Of some interest were the results of investigations of the Churn Valley sediments north of Trinity Mill, Baunton (Chapter 8). Here a pollen sequence from waterlogged sediments in the former river channel yielded evidence of viticulture in the valley. Two radiocarbon dates, from levels in the profile similar to those yielding the pollen, produced dates within the 15th century (Appendix 1, samples 21 and 22). There appears to be no reason to doubt these dates except that they are rather later than most dated evidence for viticulture in this country (see Scaife, Chapter 8). It is conventionally thought that climatic deterioration from the end of the 13th century was responsible for the abandonment of vine cultivation (Platt 1978, 94-95), and there appears to be little documentary evidence for its continuation after this (Dyer 1989, 62). However, the current evidence would suggest that it did continue albeit, perhaps, on a small scale. It can be noted that the south-east-facing slope of the Churn valley here may have been an exceptionally favourable site for grape cultivation. Much of the parish of Baunton was an estate of Cirencester Abbey before the Dissolution (L Viner, pers. comm.) which offers a possible tenurial context for this practice.

The radiocarbon dates also appear to have implications for the date at which the river channel was put out of use. Survey by RCHME (McOmish and Lewis 1991) has indicated that the channel formed an integral part of the operation of the water-meadows in this part of the Churn Valley, providing a source for feeder channels which supplied drains running

south and east. The water-meadows were used as specialised pasturage for sheep and are thought to have been constructed between *c.* 1600 and *c.* 1750. However, this dating is only an approximation, based on examples drawn from Wessex, and the Churn Valley water-meadows themselves do not appear to be closely documented. It is possible that the operation of the water-meadows, which essentially involved channelling water from the northern and western sides of the floodplain into the carriers and drains on the southern and eastern side, while at the same time still needing to maintain the flow to the stream for Trinity Mill, was instrumental in the demise of the original channel. The current dating suggests that the channel suffered a loss of flow and was becoming choked in the 15th century, although it presumably still functioned for several centuries after that. This somewhat indirect reasoning may suggest that the water-meadows were actually a 15th-century rather than later construction, although clearly there may have been other reasons for the silting up of the river channel, including perhaps the enlargement of the mill stream.

Appendices

APPENDIX 1

Radiocarbon Age Determinations
By Andrew Mudd

Introduction

A total of 22 radiocarbon dating determinations were made (Samples R24151/1–22). Four were conventional radiometric dates (Samples 2, 3, 4 and 7) provided by The University of Waikato, New Zealand. Twelve (Samples 8, and 11 to 21) were single AMS dates and six were 'enhanced precision' AMS dates using the weighted mean of three replica dates from a sample (Samples 1, 5, 6, 9, 10 and 22). The AMS dating was undertaken by Rafter Radiocarbon Laboratory, New Zealand. Calibrations are obtained from Bard *et al.* 1993, Kramer and Becker 1993, Linick *et al.* 1993, Pearson and Stuiver 1993, and Stuiver and Pearson 1993.

Highgate House (Samples 1–4)

All four dates appear reasonable and are internally consistent. Sample 1 was an articulated horse talus and calcaneum from the primary fill of the ditch terminal. The replicated AMS determination gave a very precise date of 2310±33 BP calibrated to 402–360 BC and 281–256 BC at the 95% confidence level, and to 396–374 BC at the 68% confidence level.

Sample 2 was an articulated cattle radius and ulna, Sample 3 a cattle jaw with teeth, and Sample 4 a horse tibia. These three samples were from the secondary rubble infill of the main ditch and the conventional determinations yielded virtually identical dates calibrated to the late 4th to mid 1st century BC. The dates are imprecise but their consistency is mutually supporting. Together with Sample 1 they suggest an occupation in the 3rd to 4th centuries BC, rather than later.

Preston Enclosure (Samples 5–8)

Sample 6, a cattle radius, gave an erroneous date due to a low collagen yield and can be discounted. The other dates appear to be acceptable. Sample 5, a cattle ulna from the primary fill of the enclosure ditch, gave a replicated AMS determination of 2258±43 BP, calibrated to 396–188 BC at the 95% confidence level. Sample 7, horse teeth and jaw fragments from higher up in the same ditch, gave a less precise conventional date of 2200±50 BP, calibrated to 385–99 BC (95% confidence). Sample 8, which was a charred grain of barley from the fabric of shell-tempered pot (Fabric H5), gave an AMS date of 2309±57 BP (471-466 BC and 416–199 BC at the 95% confidence level). These three dates are mutually consistent.

Ermin Farm (Samples 9–10)

Both samples were submitted for replicated AMS dates. Sample 9 was a cattle horn core from the lower fill of ditch 63 and yielded a date of 2178±34 BP, calibrating to 363–111 BC (95% confidence level). Sample 10, rib fragments from the upper fill of ditch 68, yielded a slightly earlier date of 2306±36 BP, calibrating to 403–357 BC and 287–250 BC (95% confidence level) and 395–371 BC (68% confidence level). Sample 10 must be considered to be from a less secure context than Sample 9. It may have been redeposited from earlier in the occupation, accounting for the earlier date, although there is nothing to suggest that it could have predated the enclosure ditches.

St Augustine's Farm South (Samples 11–14)

There were very few suitable items for dating from this site. Sample 11 came from the segmented ditch 2005, and Samples 13 and 14 from nearby and probably associated pits. All three samples were fragments of animal bone from near the base of the respective features and were submitted for AMS dating. Sample 11 was dated to 2294±59 BP, calibrating to 409–193 BC; Sample 13 was dated to 2237±68 BP, calibrating to 403-96 BC; and Sample 14 was dated to 2234±56 BP, calibrating to 396–125 BC, all at the 95% confidence level. These dates are all very close and there seems little doubt that the associated features are of middle Iron Age date, rather than any earlier.

Sample 12 was a collection of small broken fragments of bone, probably originally one piece, and came from the lowest fill of the northern ring ditch. An AMS determination yield a date of 3482±60 BP, calibrating to 1940–1644 BC. This date is much as expected and there is no reason to doubt it.

Duntisbourne Grove (Samples 15-16)

Both samples were charred hazelnuts from Neolithic pits and submitted for AMS dating. Sample 15 (pit 94) was associated with animal bone, worked flints and Peterborough Ware and yielded a date of 4761±57 BP, calibrating to 3654–3370 BC (95% confidence level). Sample 16 (Pit 142) was associated with flintwork and burnt clay and yielded a date of 4717±60 BP, calibrating to 3641–3354 BC (95% confidence level). These dates are very close.

Trinity Farm (Samples 17–18)

Both samples were charred hazelnuts from pits associated with Beaker pottery and were submitted for AMS dating. Sample 17 was dated to 3876±57 BP, calibrating to 2476–2142 BC. Sample 18 gave a virtually identical date of 3836±58 BP, calibrating to 2462–2130 BC and 2076–2047 BC.

Latton 'Roman Pond' (Sample 19)

This sample comprised a collection of charred seeds and thorns extracted from the macroscopic environmental sample at the base of the peat sequence (Context 506). It yielded an AMS date of 2943±63 BP, calibrating to 1376–929 BC at the 95% confidence level. This provides an approximate date for a rise in the water table and the onset of peat growth in this valley.

Churn Valley stream deposits (Samples 20–21)

Both samples were of waterlogged organic remains taken from the pollen column within the stream channel and were submitted for AMS dating. Sample 20, was a small collection of twigs from near the base of the waterlogged sequence (68 cm). It yielded a date of 462±57 BP, calibrating to AD 1401–1517 and AD 1587–1623 (95% confidence level). Sample 21 was a slightly larger sample of pollen processing residue from higher up in the sequence (40–60 cm). It yielded a date of 441±57 BP, calibrating to AD 1406–1527 and AD 1555–1633 (95% confidence level). It dates are virtually

identical. At the 68% confidence level a date in the 15th century is preferred for both these samples (AD 1421–1471 and AD 1431–1482 respectively).

Lynches Trackway burial (Sample 22)

This sample was a long bone from the isolated human inhumation. A replicated AMS determination yielded a date of 2130±47 BP. This calibrates to 355–289 BC and 235–33 BC at the 95% confidence level. While the dating is imprecise, the burial appears to be securely Iron Age. A date in the later 1st or 2nd century BC (195–60 BC) is indicated at the 68% confidence level.

Conclusions

With the exception of Sample 6, the dates appear to be valid. Some of the middle Iron Age dates have a broad calibrated date range and are not particularly useful individually, although in their consistency they do support the general trends. The replicated AMS dates have been shown to be particularly useful since, in the absence of closely datable pottery, their precision appears to enable discrimination between the earlier and later parts of the middle Iron Age. The middle Iron Age sites at Highgate House, Preston Enclosure and Ermin Farm therefore appear to date to the 3rd and 4th centuries BC, rather than later. The unexpected middle Iron Age dates from St Augustine's Farm would seem to indicate broadly contemporary activity here.

Table A1 Radiocarbon age determinations.

Laboratory Number	Context Number	Radiocarbon Age (BP)	d¹³C (⁰/₀₀)	Material	Context Type	Calibrated date range (95% confidence)
Highgate House						
R24151/1 NZA 8670	130	2305±57	-22.2	Horse talus and calcaneum	Primary fill of main ditch	
		2284±57	-22.2			
		2342±59	-22.2			402-360 cal BC*
		2310±33*				281-256 cal BC*
R24151/2	210	2200±70	-25.5+/-0.2	Cattle radius and ulna	Secondary rubble infill over primary ditch fill 208	395-44 cal BC
R24151/3	210	2190±60	-26.4+/-0.2	Cattle teeth and mandible	As above	389-49 cal BC
R24151/4	228	2200±60	-27.9+/-0.2	Horse tibia	Secondary rubble infill of possible recut	391-57 cal BC
Preston Enclosure						
R24151/5 NZA 8573	135	2301±57	-21.9	Cattle ?ulna	Primary fill of enclosure ditch	
		2172±57	-21.7			
		2302±57	-21.7			
		2258±43*				396-188 cal BC*
R24151/6 NZA 8576	45	1709±61	-23.7	Cattle ?radius	Primary fill of enclosure ditch	
		1810±59	-22.7			
		1752±57	-23.6			
		1758±34*				216-394 cal BC*
R24151/7	4	2200±50	-24.7+/-0.2	Horse teeth and mandible	Middle/upper fill of enclosure ditch	400-364 cal BC / 274-264 cal BC

Table A1Radiocarbon age determinations, continued.

Laboratory Number	Context Number	Radiocarbon Age (BP)	d¹³C ($^0/_{00}$)	Material	Context Type	Calibrated date range (95% confidence)
R24151/8 NZA 8670	279	2309±57	-22.5	Single charred grain	Only fill of pit 280	471-466 cal BC
						416-199 cal BC
Ermin Farm						
R214151/9 NZA 8579	57	2152±58	-21.3	Cattle horn core	Lower fill of ditch 63	363-111 cal BC*
		2188±65	-21.2			
		2195±57	-21.2			
		2178±34*				
R24151/10 NZA 8616	71	2334±54	-21.7	Animal rib bone	Upper fill of ditch 68	
		2263±60	-21.6			
		2328±56	-21.6			403-357 cal BC*
		2306±36*				287-250 cal BC*
St Augustine's Farm South						
R24151/11 NZA 8766	2024	2294±59	-21.3	Animal bone	Lowest fill of ditch 2005 (cut 2008)	409-193 cal BC
R24151/12 NZA 8614	3094	3482±60	-20.8	Animal bone	Lowest fill of northern ring ditch (cut 3097)	1940-1644 cal BC
R24151/13 NZA 8615	3010	2237±68	-21.8	Animal bone	Primary fill of pit 3011	403-96 cal BC
R24151/14 NZA 8619	3080	2234±56	-22	?Cattle long bone	Fill near base of pit 3083	396-125 cal BC
Duntisbourne Grove						
R24151/15 NZA 8671	113	4761±57	-23.8	Charred hazelnut	Primary fill of pit 94	3654-3370 cal BC
R24151/16 NZA 8672	168	4717±60	-24.3	Charred hazelnut	Secondary fill of pit 142	3641-3354 cal BC
Trinity Farm						
R24151/17 NZA 8673	7	3876±57	-23.8	Charred hazelnut	Single fill of pit 8	2476-2142 cal BC
R24151/18 NZA 8674	9	3836±58	-24.1	Charred hazelnut	Single fill of pit 10	2462-2130 cal BC
						2076-2047 cal BC
Latton 'Roman Pond'						
R24151/19 NZA 9119	506	2943±63	-25.9	Charred plant material		1376-929 cal BC
Lynches Trackway						
R24151/20 NZA 9082	68 cm	462±57	-27.4	Waterlogged plant material (twigs)	Base of profile	Cal AD 1401-1517
						Cal AD 1587-1623
R24151/21 NZA 9083	40-60 cm	441±57	-29	Waterlogged plant material (twigs)		Cal AD 1406-1527
						Cal AD 1555-1633
R24151/22 NZA 8620	103	2217±56	-19.7	Human femur	Crouched inhumation 103	
		2069±65	-20			
		2088±57	-19.9			355-289 cal BC*
		2130±47*				235-33 cal BC*

* weighted mean calculation

APPENDIX 2

Table A2   Animal bone measurements from Middle Duntisbourne.

Cattle	Scapula	GLP	BG	LG	SLC		
		56.2	41.0	47.3	44.8		
		61.0		49.8	46.1		
		56.4		47.0	39.8		
		60.7			45.4		
	Humerus	Bd	BT	HT			
		71.4	59.4	36.3			
		74.2	64.4	38.4			
		74.9	61.7	36.4			
		78.2		39.3			
			61.1	36.9			
	Radius	BFp					
		61.4					
		63.6					
	Tibia	Bd	Dd				
		49.8	39.4				
		52.1	38.1				
		51.5	39.9				
		55.4	41.1				
		56.7	41.8				
		50.7	39.7				
		50.6	37.5				
		53.8					
		53.2					
	Calcaneus	GL					
		115.7					
		124.8					
	Metacarpal	Bp	Dp				
		48.5	29.9				
	Metatarsal	GL	Bp	Dp	SD	Bd	Dd
		206.8	41.9	40.0	23.5	53.9	28.7
						51.2	
Sheep	Scapula	GLP	BG	LG	SLC		
		28.5	18.2	22.4	16.6		
		30.9	20.4	24.4			
		27.3		20.2	16.1		
		29.7		24.0	17.4		
		27.4		22.3	15.5		
	Humerus	Bd	BT	HT			
		23.5	22.5	15.2			
		27.3	25.1	16.2			
		27.8	24.4	15.9			
		28.2	24.1	14.5			
		29.0	25.0	16.6			
			22.5	15.3			
			16.4				

APPENDIX 2 continued

Table A2   Animal bone measurements from Middle Duntisbourne.

	Radius	BFp					
		25.1					
		26.8					
		23.6					
		25.5					
		24.6					
	Tibia	Bd	Dd				
		22.4	19.1				
		23.3	18.9				
		22.7	19.1				
		22.6	18.8				
		22.6	18.8				
		22.7	18.6				
		22.4	18.1				
		23.7	18.6				
		21.5	16.6				
	Calcaneus	GL					
		50.5					
		46.4					
Pig	M₃	Length	Breadth				
		30.6	14.3				
		32.8	14.5				
		32.0	14.2				
		33.7	14.6				
	Scapula	GLP	BG	LG	SLC		
		34.2	23.9	28.0	22.5		
		30.9	21.4	28.0	19.9		
		33.2	22.7	26.1	23.3		
		30.5	21.0	26.0	20.2		
		31.0	22.9	27.0	19.9		
		31.5	23.3	27.4			
		32.7		27.5	21.7		
		30.5					
		30.1					
					21.8		
	Humerus	Bd	BT	HT	HTC		
		34.2	28.6	22.4	14.9		
			29.2	26.2	17.8		
			26.6	24.9			
	Tibia	Bd	Dd				
		27.0	25.0				
		25.8	22.5				
		25.0	23.5				
		26.6	23.5				
Domestic fowl	Scapula	Dic		Radius	Bd		
		10.6			6.2		
	Ulna	Bp		Femur	Bp		Dp
		7.8			12.4		10.5
	Tarsometatarsus	Bd					
		12.1					

APPENDIX 3

Table A3   Animal bone measurements from Duntisbourne Grove

Cattle	Scapula	GLP	BG	LG	SLC		
		56.2	41.0	47.3	44.8		
		61.0		49.8	46.1		
		56.4		47.0	39.8		
		60.7			45.4		
Humerus	Bd	BT	HT				
		71.4	59.4	36.3			
		74.2	64.4	38.4			
		74.9	61.7	36.4			
		78.2		39.3			
			61.1	36.9			
	Radius	BFp					
		61.4					
		63.6					
	Tibia	Bd	Dd				
		49.8	39.4				
		52.1	38.1				
		51.5	39.9				
		55.4	41.1				
		56.7	41.8				
		50.7	39.7				
		50.6	37.5				
		53.8					
		53.2					
	Calcaneus	GL					
		115.7					
		124.8 '					
	Metacarpal	Bp	Dp				
		48.5	29.9				
	Metatarsal	GL	Bp	Dp	SD	Bd	Dd
		206.8	41.9	40.0	23.5	53.9	28.7
						51.2	
Sheep	Scapula	GLP	BG	LG	SLC		
		28.5	18.2	22.4	16.6		
		30.9	20.4	24.4			
		27.3		20.2	16.1		
		29.7		24.0	17.4		
		27.4		22.3	15.5		
	Humerus	Bd	BT	HT			
		23.5	22.5	15.2			
		27.3	25.1	16.2			
		27.8	24.4	15.9			
		28.2	24.1	14.5			
		29.0	25.0	16.6			
			22.5	15.3			
			16.4				
	Radius	BFp					
		25.1					
		26.8					
		23.6					
		25.5					
		24.6					

APPENDIX 3 continued

Table A3   Animal bone measurements from Duntisbourne Grove

	Tibia	Bd	Dd				
		22.4	19.1				
		23.3	18.9				
		22.7	19.1				
		22.6	18.8				
		22.6	18.8				
		22.7	18.6				
		22.4	18.1				
		23.7	18.6				
		21.5	16.6				
	Calcaneus	GL					
		50.5					
		46.4					
Pig	M₃	Length	Breadth				
		30.6	14.3				
		32.8	14.5				
		32.0	14.2				
		33.7	14.6				
	Scapula	GLP	BG	LG	SLC		
		34.2	23.9	28.0	22.5		
		30.9	21.4	28.0	19.9		
		33.2	22.7	26.1	23.3		
		30.5	21.0	26.0	20.2		
		31.0	22.9	27.0	19.9		
		31.5	23.3	27.4			
		32.7		27.5	21.7		
		30.5					
		30.1					
					21.8		
	Humerus	Bd	BT	HT	HTC		
		34.2	28.6	22.4	14.9		
			29.2	26.2	17.8		
			26.6	24.9			
	Tibia	Bd	Dd				
		27.0	25.0				
		25.8	22.5				
		25.0	23.5				
		26.6	23.5				
Domestic fowl	Scapula	Dic		Radius	Bd		
		10.6			6.2		
	Ulna	Bp		Femur	Bp	Dp	
		7.8			12.4	10.5	
	Tarsometatarsus	Bd					
		12.1					

APPENDIX 4

Pollen procedure and methodology

Standard pollen procedures have been used for the extraction of the preserved pollen and spores. These procedures are detailed in Moore and Webb (1978) and Moore *et al.* (1991). This was carried out in the Department of Geography, University of Southampton.

· Samples of 2–3 ml size.
· HCL 10% to decalcify.
· Deflocculation with 10% NaOh.
· Sieving at 150u for removal of the coarse fraction.
· Sieving at 10u (residue kept) for removal of clay.
· Hydrofluoric acid (boiling) digestion of silica.
· -Erdtman's acetolysis.
· Washing/centrifuging.
· Staining with aqueous safranin and mounting in glycerol jelly.

Pollen was examined, identified and counted using an Olympus biological research microscope fitted with Leitz optics at magnifications of x400 and x1000 with normal transmitted and phase contrast lighting. An extensive pollen reference/comparative collection is available for identification of difficult/critical taxa (*Palaeopol*). Plant taxonomy follows that of Stace (1991). A pollen sum of generally 400 grains per level excluding marsh/aquatic types and spores was used where possible. Absolute pollen frequencies were calculated using Stockmarr *Lycopodium* tablets (Stockmarr 1971). Pollen taxonomy generally follows that of Moore and Webb (1978) and Moore *et al.* (1991) modified according to Bennett *et al.* (1994) in accord with Flora Europaea/Stace (1991). The data have been presented in standard pollen diagram form (Figs 8.25–7) with the pollen of dry-land taxa calculated as a percentage of their sum. Marsh types (incl. *Alnus*) and spores are as a percentage of the dry land sum+the sub-group. The pollen diagrams were plotted using *Tilia* and *Tilia* Graph. These procedures were carried in the Department of Geography, University of Southampton.

APPENDIX 5

Table A5   Summary of ceramic building material.

Site code	Context	Description	Type	Fabric	Weight	Date
Cirencester Watching Brief	1		Misc	-	50	-
	1		C	1	75	RB
Weavers Bridge	51	layer	D	3	550	RB
	57	Midden deposit	A	1	150	RB
	57		A	1	150	RB
	57		D	?	500	-
	57		D	?	175	-
	62	Fill of gully	D	1	50	RB
	80	Fill of circular feature	D	1	50	RB
	134	Large ditch	Misc	-	10	-
Court Farm	38	Fill of pit	D	1	100	RB
	223	Fill of recut ditch	D	1	75	RB
	314	Fill of quarry pit	A	1	350	RB
	482	Ditch fill	Misc	-	50	-
Preston Enclosure	93	Segment through gully	D	-	25	Med
	160	Fill of furrow	D	-	50	Med
	u/s	Furrow	D	-	300	Med
Westfield Farm	10	Fill of boundary ditch	Field drain	-	325	Modern
Middle Duntisbourne	12	Finds reference	Misc	-	5	-
	54	Fill of Roman ditch	Misc	-	5	-
Lynches Trackway	5	Cobbled surface	Misc	-	35	-
	6	Layer of silty clay	Misc	-	5	-
	12	Silty deposit	Misc	-	5	-
Burford Road	306	Pebbled surface	Misc	-	25	-
	318	Quarry pit fill	Misc	-	5	-
	320	Silt over surface	Misc	-	50	-
	323	Silty build up on surface	C	3	50	RB
	323		Misc	-	175	-

APPENDIX 5 continued

Table A5   Summary of ceramic building material.

Site code	Context	Description	Type	Fabric	Weight	Date
Burford Road	323		Misc	-	50	-
	325	Silty material on top of 323	Misc	-	35	-
	407	Compact surface	D/E	4	300	RB
	409	Silty build up on top of road surface	Misc	-		5 -
	419	Quarry fill	Misc	-	10	-
	523	Road make up	D/E	1	450	RB
	523		D	1	100	RB
	523		Misc	-	10	-
	523		D	-	50	Med
	525	Road make up	A	2	200	RB
	525		Misc	-	5	-
	661	Road make up	D/E	5	275	RB
Exhibition Barn	19	Fill of ditch	A	1	250	RB
Norcote Farm	9	Subsoil T.P 4	Misc	-	5	-
	18	Topsoil T.P 10	Misc	-	10	-
	20	Topsoil T.P 11	Misc	-	10	-
	37	Topsoil T.P 20	Misc	-	5	-
	44	Topsoil T.P 24	Misc	-	5	-
	47	Topsoil T.P 26	Misc	-	10	-
	50	Topsoil T.P 28	Misc	-	5	-
	60	Topsoil T.P 33	Misc	-	5	-
	62	Topsoil T.P 34	Misc	-	5	-
	101	Finds ref.	Misc	-	25	-
	102	Finds ref.	D	-	200	Med
	181	Ditch	Misc	-	10	-
	189	Plough soil	D	-	100	Med
Street Farm	1	Topsoil	D	-	25	Med
	191	Subsoil	Misc	-	50	Med
	196	Layer	Misc	-	100	Med
	197	Deposit overlying pit	D	-	200	Med
	198	Pit fill	D	-	50	Med
	199	Pit fill	Misc	-	50	Med
	225	Deposit above quarry pits	Misc	-	100	Med
	232	Secondary fill of pit	D/E	-	750	Med
	232		Misc	-	400	Med
	262	Surface within building	D	-	450	Med
	275	Primary fill of pit	Misc	-	125	Med
	291	Layer of dumping	D	-	75	Med
	304	Top fill of well	Misc	-	400	Med
	305	Fill of well	D/E	-	700	Med
	313	Spread of domestic rubbish	D	-	25	Med
	420	Fill of 19th century pit	Misc	-	50	Med
	551	Surface over oven	D	-	150	Med
	591	Fill of stone lined pit	Field drain	-	100	Modern
	605	Buried soil	D	-	100	Med
	611	Finds ref.	Field drain	-	1200	Med
	750		Misc	-	200	Med
	702		Misc	-	125	Med
	737		Misc	-	100	Med
	721		Field drain	-	150	Modern
	710		Misc	-	250	Med
	761		E	-	175	Med
	708		Misc	-	25	Med
	773		Misc	-	25	Med
	730		Misc	-	50	Med

APPENDIX 5 continued.

Summary of ceramic building material.

Site code	Context	Description	Type	Fabric	Weight	Date
Street Farm	780		Misc	-	50	Med
	762		Misc	-	25	Med
	706		Misc	-	50	Med
	734		Misc	-	100	Med
	758		D/E	-	450	Med
	952		D	-	275	Med
	873		Misc	-	300	Med
	713		C	1	75	RB
	887		C	1	75	RB
	762		E	-	625	Med
Cherry Tree Lane	2	Colluvial hill wash	Misc	-	25	-
	6		D	1	75	RB
	6		D	2	150	RB
	6		A	1	75	RB
	6		Misc	-	225	RB
	20	Modern topsoil	Misc	-	25	-
	27	Layer sealing burnt mound	Misc	-	10	-
NOSNI	1	Topsoil	D	-	50	Med
	4	Quarry	E	-	100	Med
	5		D	-	75	Med
	8	Occupation layer	D	1	50	RB
Birdlip Quarry	7	Occupation Layer	C	1	25	RB
	8	Modern land drain	Misc	-	25	-
	10	Fill of drain	Misc	-	25	-
	19	Occupation layer	D	1	100	RB
	31		E	2	150	RB
	34	Stone layer	D	1	150	RB
	34		D	1	50	RB
	34		Misc	-	50	-
	34		A	6	100	RB
	64	Fill of gully	Misc	-	25	-
	72	Occupation material	Misc	-	25	-
	79		A	1	150	RB
	83	Secondary fill of ditch	A	1	1000	RB
	83		D	3	325	RB
	86	Rubble layer	D	3	450	RB
	86		Misc	-	200	-
	86		D	1	50	RB
	90	Colluvium	A	6	100	RB
	90		D	1	50	RB
	90		Misc	-	25	-
	128	Cobbling	D	1	300	RB
	128		Misc	-	50	-
	128		D	1	50	RB
	128		C	1	50	RB
	128		C	1	25	RB
	131	Furrow fill	C	1	25	RB
	150	Lynchet fill	Misc	-	75	-
	157	Ditch fill	A	1	1350	RB
	206	Stoney occupation layer	A	1	600	RB
	223	Stoney layer	A	1	150	RB
	223		D	2	200	RB
	223		D	1	300	RB
	234	Ditch fill	A	3	200	RB
	250	Possible colluvium	D	1	25	RB

APPENDIX 5 continued.

Summary of ceramic building material.

Site code	Context	Description	Type	Fabric	Weight	Date
Birdlip Quarry	278	Trample layer	Misc	-	50	-
	656	Furrow fill	D	3	100	RB
	705	Occupation layer	C	3	50	RB
	729	Stone floor	D	1	200	RB
	729		D	7	100	RB
	729		D	1	250	RB
	729		A	7	150	RB
	729		A	7	75	RB
	729		D	7	50	RB
	738	Ditch fill	C	3	50	RB
	774	Rubble wall	D	7	75	RB
	807	Dumping layer	B	1	150	RB
	807		D	1	75	RB
	807		Misc	-	30	-
	815	Rubble layer	D	1	50	RB
	815		B	7	75	RB
	815		A	1	175	RB
	819	Ditch fill	B	7	100	RB
	846	Well fill	D	3	50	RB
	851	Ditch fill	Misc	-	10	-
	860	Well fill	Misc	-	100	-
	863	Post-hole fill	Misc	-	50	-
	903	Roman soil	Misc	-	100	-
	938	Occupation layer	A	7	250	RB
	953	Ditch fill	B	1	150	RB
	1005	Pitched stone	A	7	100	RB
	1009	Occupation layer	Misc	-	25	-
	1013	Make-up for floor	C	3	25	RB
	1060	Deposit of burnt material	D	7	50	RB
	1060		A	7	75	RB
	1064	Rubble	A	7	350	RB
	1064		A	7	500	RB
	1064		A	7	200	RB
	1064		D	7	600	RB
	1128	Stoney layer	Misc	-	50	-
	1139	Stone surface	Misc	-	25	-
	1140	Colluvium	D	3	50	RB
	1140		D	3	100	RB
	1140		D	3	50	RB
	1140		Misc	-	25	-
	1210	Post-occupation material	D	1	50	RB
	1210		Misc	-	75	-
	1224	Pitched stone	D	7	75	RB
	1225	Occupation layer	Misc	-	50	-
	1225		A	7	350	RB
	1236	Occupation deposit	D	1	275	RB
	1317	Cobbled surface	D	1	25	RB
	1500		A	1	75	RB
	1500		Misc	-	50	-
	1500		D	3	100	RB
	1500		D	3	50	RB
	1500		Misc	3	100	RB

A=Tegula,   B=Imbrex,   C=Tubulus,   D=Plain Tile,   E=Brick.

Bibliography

Gloucestershire County Record Office Sources

1773 Andrews and Drury WRO 12

Bagendon
1792 Enclosure Map and Award D475 P33
1838 Tithe Map and Award TI/14
1955 Excavation at Church D3459 box 126/1
1968 Air Photograph (aerofilms) GPS 33/1

Baunton
1768 Enclosure Map and Award D674b P1O
1849 Tithe Map and Award TI/19
1849 Tithe Map (copy) D674b P11
1858 Abbey Estate D674b P5

Brimpsfield
1838 Tithe Map and Award P58 SD2/1
1842 Enclosure Map and Award D1 388 Q/RI 29

Cirencester
1771 Draft Enclosure D674b P14
1795 Town Map PC 235
1838 Tithe Map D674b E40
1838 Tithe Map (copy) TI/55
1840 Lands adjoining the Churn D674b P20

Cowley
1847 Tithe Map and Award P102 SD2/1 E11

Daglingworth
1781 Enclosure Award D22
1838 Tithe Map and Award MF 1127 IR 30/13/63-145

Duntisbourne Abbots
1780 Enclosure Award Q/RI 56
1780 Enclosure Award P122a/SD 1

Duntisbourne Rouse
1837 Enclosure Map and Award Q/RI 62

Driffield
1801 Enclosure Award Q/RI 86

Elkstone
1824 Bryants Map Glos 180
1835 Enclosure Map and Award Q/RI 62
1841 Tithe Map TI/76

Gloucestershire Turnpike Roads 1976

North Cerney
1837 Tithe Map TI/45
1855 Enclosure Map and Award Q/RI 35

Preston
1687 Abbey Estate D674b P1
1770 Pre-Enclosure Parish D674b P2
1770 Draft Enclosure D674b P31

C18 Draft Enclosure D674b P29
1772 Enclosure Award D674b E91
1840 Abbey Estate D674b P4
1842 Parish and Village D674b P4
1858 Abbey Estate D674b P5
1884 Abbey Estate D674b P8

Stratton
1770 Pre-Enclosure Parish D674b 37-40
1772 Enclosure Map D674b E91
C18 Accounts for making mounds in Stratton field D674b E42
1858 Abbey Estate D674b P5

Syde
1838 Tithe Map TI/176

Winstone
1782 Enclosure Map and Award Q/RI 160
1842 Tithe Map and Award TI/199

Other
1327 Lay Subsidy Roll ROL G4
1744 Lands of Thomas Master (parishes of Stratton, Preston, Baunton, Cirencester) D674b P44
1850 Cotswold Estate (parishes of North Cerney, Winstone, Duntisbourne Abbots) D2525

Wiltshire County Record Office Sources

Latton
1805 Latton Enclosure Award EA/198

Published and unpublished sources (the latter appear in plain text)

Albert, W, 1972 *The turnpike road system in England 1663–1840*, Cambridge University Press
Allason-Jones, L, 1985 Bell-shaped studs?, in Bishop, M C, 95–108
Allason-Jones, L, 1996 *Roman jet in the Yorkshire museum*, The Yorkshire Museum, York
Allen, J R L and Fulford, M G, 1996 The distribution of south-east Dorset black burnished category 1 pottery in south-west Britain, *Britannia* **27**, 223–81
Allen, T G, 1990 *An Iron Age and Romano-British enclosed settlement at Watkins Farm, Northmoor, Oxon*, Thames Valley Landscapes: the Windrush Valley **1**, Oxford Archaeological Unit and Oxford University Committee for Archaeology, Oxford
Allen, T G, 1993 Abingdon Vineyard 1992: Areas 2 and 3, the Early Defences, *South Midlands Archaeology* **23**, 64–6
Allen, T G, 1994 A medieval grange of Abingdon Abbey at Dean Court Farm, Cumnor, Oxon., *Oxoniensia* **59**, 219–447

Allen, T G, Darvill, T C, Green, L S and Jones, M U, 1993 *Excavations at Roughground Farm, Lechlade, Gloucestershire: a prehistoric and Roman landscape,* Thames Valley Landscapes: the Cotswold Water Park, Volume **1**, OAU and Oxford University Committee for Archaeology, Oxford

Allen, T G, Miles, D and Palmer S, 1984 Iron Age buildings in the Upper Thames region, in Cunliffe, B W and Miles, D, 89–101

Allen, T G and Robinson, M A, 1993 *The prehistoric landscape and Iron Age enclosed settlement at Mingies Ditch, Hardwick-with-Yelford, Oxon.,* Thames Valley Landscapes: the Windrush Valley, Volume **2**, OAU and Oxford University Committee for Archaeology, Oxford

Andersen, S Th, 1970 The relative pollen productivity and pollen representation of north European trees, and correction factors for tree pollen spectra, *Danm Geol Unders* Series I, **I96**, 99

Andersen, S Th, 1973 The differential pollen productivity of trees and its significance for the interpretation of a pollen diagram from a forested region, in Birks, H J B and West, R G, 109–115

Anderson, A S, 1978 Wiltshire fine wares, in Arthur, P and Marsh, G, 373–92

Anderson, A S, 1979 *The Roman pottery industry of north Wiltshire,* Swindon Archaeol Soc Rep **2**, Swindon

Annable, F K, 1962 A Romano-British pottery in Savernake Forest, kilns 1-2, *Wilts Archaeol Nat Hist Mag* **58**, 142–55

Arms, J H D' and Kopff, E C 1980 *The Seabourne Commerce of Ancient Rome: Studies in Archaeology and History,* Mem Amer Academy in Rome, **36**,

Arthur, P and Marsh, G, 1973 *Early fine wares in Roman Britain,* BAR Brit Ser **57**, Oxford

Aston, M, and Viner, L, 1984 The study of deserted villages in Gloucestershire, in Saville, A, 1984c, 276–293

Atkinson, D R, 1970 Clay pipes found in Shaftesbury, *Proc Dorset Nat Hist and Archaeol Soc* **91**, 206–15

Atkinson, D R, 1975 *Tobacco pipes of Broseley, Shropshire,* privately published

Atkinson, D R, 1980 More Wiltshire clay tobacco pipe varieties, *Wilts Archaeol Nat Hist Mag* **72/73**, 63–74

Atkinson, R J C, 1951 A henge monument at Westwell near Burford, Oxon., *Oxoniensia* **14**, 84–7

Audouy, M forthcoming *North Raunds, Northamptonshire: Excavations 1977-1987,* English Heritage Monograph

Ayres, K E and Clark, K M, (nd.) The animal bones from Birdlip Quarry, Cowley, AML Report

Baker, C A, Moxey, P A and Oxford, M, 1979 Woodland continuity and change in Epping Forest, *Field Studies* **4**, 645–669

Balkwill, C J, 1978 The Bronze Age features, in Parrington, M, 25–30

Balaam, N D, Levitan, B and Straker, V 1987 *Studies in palaeoeconomy and environment in south-west England,* BAR Brit Ser **181**, Oxford

Bard, E, Arnold, M, Fairbanks, R G and Hamelin, B, 1993 ^{230}Th and ^{14}C ages obtained by mass spectrometry on corals, *Radiocarbon* **35**(1), 191–199

Barclay, A J, 1999 The discussion, in Barclay, A and Halpin, C, 309–325

Barclay, A J, in prep. a The prehistoric pottery, in Hey, G and Bell, C

Barclay, A J, in prep. b The prehistoric pottery in Barclay, A Miles, D, Moore, J, Vatcher, F and Vatcher, L

Barclay, A J, in prep. c Neolithic pottery in Cromarty, A, Campbell, G and Miles, D

Barclay, A J, Bradley, R, Hey, G and Lambrick, G, 1996 The earlier prehistory of the Oxford region in light of recent research, *Oxoniensia* **61**, 1–20

Barclay, A J and Glass, H with Parry, C, 1995 Excavations of Neolithic and Bronze Age ring ditches, Shorncote Quarry, Somerford Keynes, Gloucestershire, *Trans Bristol Gloucestershire Archaeol Soc* **113**, 21–60

Barclay, A J and Halpin, C, 1999 *Excavations at Barrow Hills, Radley, Oxfordshire. Volume I: The Neolithic and Bronze Age Monument Complex,* Oxford Archaeological Unit, Thames Valley Landscapes Monograph Volume **11**, Oxford

Barclay, A J and Harding, J 1999 *Pathways and Ceremonies: the cursus monuments of Britain and Ireland,* Neolithic Studies Group Seminar Papers **3**, Oxbow Monograph, Oxford

Barclay, A, J and Hey, G, 1999 Cattle, cursus monuments and the river: the development of ritual and domestic landscapes in the Upper Thames Valley, in Barclay, A and Harding, J, 67–76

Barclay, A, J, Miles, D, Moore, J, Vatcher F and Vatcher L, forthcoming The Lechlade Cursus excavations, 1961 and 1985 in, *Cursus monuments in the Upper Thames Valley: excavations at the Drayton and Lechlade cursuses* (A Barclay, G Lambrick, J Moore and M Robinson), Thames Valley Landscapes Monograph, Oxford

Barker, G and Gamble, C, 1985 *Beyond domestication in prehistoric Europe,* Academic Press

Barnwell, P S and Giles, C, 1997 *English farmsteads,* 1750–1914, RCHME, Swindon

Barrett, J and Bradley, R, 1980 The later Bronze Age in the Thames Valley, in Barrett, J and Bradley, R, 47–70

Barton, K J, 1961 Some evidence for two types of pottery manufactured in Bristol in the early 18th century, *Trans Bristol and Gloucestershire Arch Soc* **80**, 160–8

Barton, N, 1997 *Stone Age Britain,* Batsford, London

Barton, R N E, 1992 *Hengistbury Head Dorset. Volume 2: the late Upper Palaeolithic and early Mesolithic sites,* Oxford University Committee for Archaeology Monograph No. **34**, Oxford

Bateman, C, 1997 Land at Sherbourne House, Lechlade, Glos, unpub Cotswold Archaeol Trust Rep 97491

Bell, M and Limbrey, S, 1982 *Archaeological aspects of woodland ecology,* Assoc Environ Arch Symposia Volume 2, BAR Internat Ser **146**, Oxford

Bennett, K D, Whittington, G and Edwards, K J, 1994 Recent plant nomenclatural changes and pollen morphology in the British Isles, *Quaternary Newsletter* **73**, 1–6

Benson, D and Miles, D, 1974 *The Upper Thames Valley: an archaeological survey of the river gravels.* OAU Survey **2**, Oxford

Bird, S, 1994a Jewellery and ornament, in Williams, R J and Zeepvat, R J

Bird, S, 1994b The lead objects, in Williams, R J and Zeepvat, R J, 347–349

Birks, H J B and West, R G, 1973 *Quaternary plant ecology*, Blackwell, Oxford

Birley, A, 1997 *Vindolanda Research Reports, new series. Volume IV: The small finds. Fascicule II: Security: the keys and locks*, Greenhead, Hexham

Bishop, A, 1991 Soldiers and military equipment in the towns of Roman Britain, in Maxfield, A and Dobson, M J, 21–27

Bishop, M C, 1985 *The production and distribution of Roman military equipment, Proceedings of the Second Roman Military Equipment Research Seminar*, BAR Internat Ser **275**, Oxford

Black, E W, 1995 *Cursus Publicus: the infrastructure of government in Roman Britain*, BAR Brit Ser **241**, Tempvs Reparatvm, Oxford

Blagg, T F C and Millett, M, 1990 *The Early Roman Empire in the West*, Oxbow Monograph, Oxford

Blinkhorn, P and Jeffries, N, forthcoming Late medieval and post-medieval wares, in Keevill, G, Hardy, A and Dodd, A

Blockley, K, 1985 *Marshfield Piece excavations 1982–3: an Iron Age and Romano-British settlement in the south Cotswolds*, BAR Brit Ser **141**, Oxford

Blockley, K, 1989 *Prestatyn 1984–5. An Iron Age farmstead and Romano-British industrial settlement in North Wales*, BAR Brit Ser **210**, Oxford

Blythe, F G H, 1943 Intrusive rocks of the Shelve area, South Shropshire, *J Geol Soc* **99**, 169–204

Boardman, S and Jones, G, 1990 Experiments on the effects of charring on cereal plant components, *J of Archaeol Sci* **17**, 1–11

Boessneck, J A, 1969 Osteological differences between sheep (*Ovis aries* Linné) and goat (*Capra hircus* Linné), in Brothwell, D R and Higgs, E S, 331–358

Booth, P M, 1997 *Asthall, Oxfordshire: excavations in a Roman 'Small Town'*, Thames Valley Landscapes Monograph. No. **9**, Oxford Archaeological Unit, Oxford

Booth, P M, 1998 The regional archaeological setting of the Roman roadside settlement at Wilcote - a summary, in Hands, A R, 9–20

Booth, P M and Green, S, 1989 The nature and distribution of certain pink grog tempered vessels, *J Roman Pottery Stud* **2**, 77–84

Bowan, H C and Wood, D, 1968 The experimental storage of corn underground and its implications for Iron Age settlement, *University of London Institute of Archaeology Bulletin* **7**, 1–14

Bowden, M and McOmish, D, 1987 The required barrier, *Scottish Archaeological Review* **4**, 98–107

Bowman, A K and Thomas, J D, 1983 *Vindolanda: the Latin writing-tablets*, Britannia Monograph **4**, London

Boyle, A, Jennings, D, Miles, D and Palmer, S, 1998 *The Anglo-Saxon cemetery at Butler's Field, Lechlade, Gloucestershire. Volume 1: prehistoric and Roman activity and grave catalogue*, Thames Valley Landscapes Monograph Volume **10**, Oxford

Boyle, A and Chambers, R A, in prep. The Romano-British cemetery at Barrow Hills, Radley, in McAdam, E and Chambers, R A

Bradley, R, 1984 *The social foundations of prehistoric Britain*, Longman, London and New York

Bradley, R, 1985 The Bronze Age in the Oxford area - its local and regional significance, in Briggs, G, Cook, J and Rowley, T, 38–48

Brailsford, J W, 1962 *Hod Hill, volume one, Antiquities from Hod Hill in the Durden Collection*, London

Branigan, K and Fowler, P J, 1976, *The Roman West Country: classical culture and Celtic society*, David and Charles, Newton Abbot

Branigan, K and Miles, D 1988 *The economies of Romano-British Villas*, Sheffield

Brewer, R J, 1986a Other finger-rings and settings, in Zienkiewicz, J D, 144–5

Brewer, R J, 1986b The Roman brooches, in Zienkiewicz, J D, 168–172

Briggs, G, Cook, J and Rowley, T, 1985 *The archaeology of the Oxford region*, Oxford University Department of External Studies, Oxford

Brodribb, A C and Walker, D R, 1971 *Excavation at Shakenoak Farm, near Wilcote Oxfordshire, Volume II. Sites B and H*, privately published, Oxford

Brossler, A, Gocher, M and Laws, G, forthcoming Excavations of a late prehistoric landscape in the Upper Thames Valley at Shorncote Quarry, *Trans Bristol Gloucestershire Archaeol Soc*

Brothwell, D R, 1981 *Digging up bones*, British Museum (Natural History), Oxford University Press, 3rd edition

Brothwell, D R and Higgs, E S, 1969 *Science in archaeology*, Thames and Hudson, London

Brown, A E 1995 *Roman Small Towns in eastern England and beyond*, Oxbow Monograph **52**, Oxford

Brown, A E and Woodfield, C with Mynard, D C, 1983 Excavations at Towcester, Northamptonshire: the Alchester road suburb, *Northamptonshire Archaeol* **18**, 43–140

Buckman, J, 1863 Roman remains found at Latton, Wilts, *Wilts Archaeol and Nat Hist Magazine* **9**, 232–7

Bull, G and Payne, S, 1982 Tooth eruption and epiphyseal fusion in pigs and wild boar, in Wilson, B, Grigson, C and Payne, S, 55–71

Burgess, C B, 1974 The Bronze Age, in Renfrew, A C, 165-232, 291–329

Burrow, E J, Paine, A E W, Knowles, W H and Gray, J W, 1925 Excavations on Leckhampton Hill, Cheltenham, during the summer of 1925, *Trans Bristol Gloucestershire Archaeol Soc* **47**, 81–112

Calkin, J B, 1953 Kimmeridge coal-money: the Romano-British shale armlet industry, *Proc Dorset Nat Hist Archaeol Soc* **75**, 45–71

Campbell, G, 1994 The preliminary archaeobotanical results from Anglo-Saxon West Cotton and Raunds, in Rackham, J, 65–82

Campbell, G, forthcoming Plant and invertebrate remains from Saxon and medieval sites in North Raunds, in Audouy, M

Campbell, G, unpublished The charred plant remains from West Cotton

Case, H J, 1956-7 The Lambourn Seven barrows, *Berkshire Archaeol J* **55**, 15–31

Case, H J, 1963 Notes on the finds and ring ditches in the Oxford region. *Oxoniensia* **28**, 19–52

Case, H J, 1977 The Beaker culture in Britain and Ireland, in Mercer, R, 71–101

Case, H J and Whittle, A W R, 1982 Settlement patterns in the Oxford region; Excavations at the Abingdon causewayed enclosure and other sites, CBA Res Rep **44**, London

CAT 1990a A419/417 Cirencester and Stratton Bypass, Gloucestershire: Stage 1 archaeological assessment, unpublished

CAT 1990b A419 Latton Bypass: Stage 1 archaeological assessment, unpublished

CAT 1991a A419/417 Cirencester and Stratton Bypass, Gloucestershire: Stage 2 archaeological evaluation, unpublished

CAT 1991b A419 Latton Bypass: archaeological survey report, unpublished

CAT 1993 Preliminary statement on the results of an archaeological evaluation at Peewitt's Hill Farm, Cirencester, unpublished

CAT 1994a A419 Latton Bypass: southern extension: archaeological evaluation, unpublished

CAT 1994b A419/417. Cirencester and Stratton Bypass, Glos. Brief and specification for archaeological action, unpublished

CAT 1994c A419 Latton Bypass. Wiltshire Archaeological Rescue Works. Project Design, unpublished

CAT 1995a Mains relocation for A419(T) Latton Bypass, Wiltshire: archaeological assessment and walkover survey. CAT Report 95303, unpublished

CAT 1995b Latton Lands, Wiltshire: archaeological evaluation. CAT Report 95264, unpublished

Celeria, F S C and Kelly, J H, 1973 *A post-medieval pottery site with a kiln base found off Albion Square, Hanley, Stoke-on-Trent, Staffordshire*, Stoke-on-Trent Mus Archaeol Soc Report **4**, Stoke-on-Trent

Centre for Human Ecology, 1995 Animal bone metrical archive project (ABMAP). Draft report on the project phase for English Heritage, Centre for Human Ecology, Dept of Archaeol, University of Southampton

Centre for Human Ecology, 1996 Animal bone metrical archive project (ABMAP). Centre for Human Ecology, Dept of Archaeol, University of Southampton

Chamber, F. 1989 The evidence for early rye cultivation in north-west Europe, in Milles, A, Williams, D and Gardner, N, 165–175

Chambers, R, 1981 Dorchester by-pass, *CBA Group 9 Newsletter* **12**, 163–7

Chambers, R A, 1987 The late- and sub-Roman

Cemetery at Queenford Farm, Dorchester-on-Thames, Oxon., *Oxoniensia* **52**, 35–69

Champion, T C and Collis, J R, 1996 *The Iron Age in Britain and Ireland: recent trends*, J.R. Collis Publications, Department of Archaeology and Prehistory, University of Sheffield

Charleston, R J, 1984 *English Glass and the glass used in England c. 400–1940*, George Allen and Unwin, London

Cherry, J, 1991 Heraldry as decoration in the 13th century, in Ormrod, W, 123–34

Childe, V G, 1940 *Prehistoric communities of the British Isles*, Chambers, London

Clapham, A R, Tutin, T G, Moore, D M, 1989 *Flora of the British Isles*, 1st paperback edition(with corrections), Cambridge

Clark J, 1995 *The medieval horse and its equipment c. 1150 – c. 1450*, Medieval finds from excavations in London **5**, Museum of London

Clark, J G D, 1934 Derivative forms of the petit tranchet in Britain, *Archaeol J* **91**, 32–58

Clark, K M, 1996 Neolithic dogs: a reappraisal based on evidence from the remains of a large canid in a ritual feature, *Internat J of Osteoarchaeology* **6/2**, 211–9

Clarke, D L, 1970 *Beaker pottery of Great Britain and Ireland*, Gulbenkian Arch Series, Cambridge University Press

Clarke, D L, 1972 *Models in archaeology*, Methuen

Clarke, J C, 1990 Miscellaneous stone and ceramic artefacts (excluding structural stonework), in Wrathmell, S and Nicholson,, A, 120–126

Clay, P and Pollard R, 1994 *Iron Age and Roman occupation in the West Bridge Area, Leicester, excavations 1962–1971*, Leicester Museum Arts and Records Service, Leicester

Cleal, R M J, 1992 The Neolithic and Beaker pottery, in Gingell, C,

Cleal, R M J, 1999 Prehistoric pottery, in Barclay, A and Halpin, C, 195–210

Clifford, E M, 1937a A palaeolith found near Gloucester, *Antiq J* **16**, 91

Clifford, E M, 1937b The Beaker Folk in the Cotswolds. *Archaeologica* **86**, 119–62

Clifford, E M, 1950 The Ivy Lodge round barrow, *Trans Bristol Gloucestershire Archaeol Soc* **69**, 59–77

Clifford, E M, 1961 *Bagendon: A Belgic Oppidum. A record of the excavations of 1954-56*, Heffer, Cambridge

Clifford, E M, 1964 Two finds of Beaker pottery from Gloucestershire, *Trans Bristol Gloucestershire Archaeol Soc* **83**, 34–39

Clifford, E M, 1965 Early Iron Age pottery from Rodborough Common and Duntisbourne Abbots, *Trans Bristol Gloucestershire Archaeol Soc* **83**, 145–6

Clifford, E M, Garrod, D A E and Gracie, H S, 1954 Flint implements from Gloucestershire, *Antiq J* **34**, 178–87

Clough, T H McK and Cummins, W A, 1979 *Stone axe studies: archaeological, experimental and ethnographic.*

CBA Res Rep **23**, London

Clough, T H McK and Cummins, W A, 1988 *Stone axe studies 2*, CBA Res Rep **67**, London

Clutterbuck, J C, 1865 Prize essay on water supply, *Journal of the Royal Agricultural Society*, 2nd series, Vol. **1**, 271–287

Cohen, A and Serjeantson, D, 1986 *A manual for the identification of bird bones from archaeological sites*, London, Alan Cohen

Coleman, R J, 1996 Burgage plots of medieval Perth; the evidence from the excavations at Canal Street, *Proc Soc Antiq Scot* **126**, 689–732

Collingwood, R G and Richmond, I, 1969 *The archaeology of Roman Britain*, London

Colls, D, Etienne, R, Lequément, B and Mayet, F, 1977 L'épave Port-Vendres II et le commerce de la Bétique à l'époque de Claude, *Archaeonautica* **1**, 7–143

Cool, H E M, 1990 Roman metal hairpins from southern Britain, *Arch J* **147**, 148–82

Cool, H E M and Price, J, 1995 *Roman vessel glass from excavations in Colchester, 1971–85*, Colchester Archaeol Rep **8**, Colchester

Cooper, N, 1998 The supply of Roman pottery to Roman Cirencester, in Holbrook, N, 32450

Courtney, T and Hall, M, 1984 Excavations at the Perrotts Brook dyke, Bagendon 1983, *Trans Bristol and Gloucestershire Archaeol Soc* **102**

Coy, J P, 1982 The animal bones, in Gingell, C, 69–73

Coy, J P, 1984 The small mammals and amphibia, in Cunliffe, B W, 1984a, 526–27

Cracknell, S and Mahany, C, 1994 *Roman Alcester: southern extramural area, 1964–1966 excavations, part 2, finds and discussion*, Roman Alcester Ser **1**, CBA Res Rep **96**, London

Cromarty, A M, Campbell, G and Miles, D in prep. *Excavations at Tower Hill, Ashbury: a late Bronze Age hoard and its context*, Oxford Archaeological Unit, Thames Valley Landscapes Monograph

Crosby, D D B and Mitchell, J G, 1987 A survey of British metamorphic hone stones of the 9th–15th centuries AD in the light of potassium-argon and natural remanent magnetization studies, *J Archaeol Sci* **14**, 483–506

Crummy, N, 1979 Chronology of Romano-British pins, *Britannia* **10**, 157–163

Crummy, N, 1983 *The Roman small finds from excavations in Colchester, 1971–9*, Colchester Archaeol Rep **2**, Colchester

Cunliffe, B W, 1971 *Excavation at Fishbourne. Volume II The Finds*, Report of the Res Com, Soc of Antiq **27**, London

Cunliffe, B W, 1983 *Danebury: anatomy of an Iron Age hill-fort*, London, Batsford

Cunliffe, B W, 1984a *Danebury: an Iron Age hill-fort in Hampshire*. 2 vols CBA Res Rep Nos **51–52**, London

Cunliffe, B W, 1984b Iron Age Wessex: continuity and change, in Cunliffe, B W and Miles, D, 3–23

Cunliffe, B, W, 1984c Objects of Kimmeridge shale, in Cunliffe, B W, 396

Cunliffe, B W, 1986 Iron Age, in Darvill, T C, 30–33

Cunliffe, B W, 1991 *Iron Age Communities in Britain*, 3rd edition, London, Routledge

Cunliffe, B W, 1995 *Danebury: an Iron Age Hillfort in Hampshire. Volume 6: A hillfort community in perspective*, CBA Res Rep **102**, London

Cunliffe, B W and Miles, D, 1984 *Aspects of the Iron Age in Southern Britain*, Oxford University Committee for Archaeology Monograph **2**, Oxford

Cunliffe, B W and Poole, C, 1991 *Danebury: an Iron Age hillfort in Hampshire. Volume 4: The excavations 1979–88: the site*, CBA Res Rep **73**, London

Cunliffe, B W and Rowley, T, 1976 *Oppida, the beginnings of uurbanisation in barbarian Europe*, BAR Supplementary Series **2**, Oxford

Dannell, G B and Wild, J P, 1987 *Longthorpe II, The military works-depot: an episode in landscape history*, Britannia Monograph Series **8**, London

Darvill, T C, 1981 Excavations at the Peak Camp, Cowley, Gloucestershire - An interim note, *Glevensis* **15**, 52–6

Darvill, T C, 1982 Excavations at the Peak Camp, Cowley, Gloucestershire - Second interim note, *Glevensis* **16**, 20–5

Darvill, T C, 1984a Neolithic Gloucestershire, in Saville, A, 78–112

Darvill, T C, 1984b Birdlip Bypass project - first report: archaeological assessment and field survey, Western Archaeological Trust, unpublished report

Darvill, T C, 1986 *The archaeology of the uplands: a rapid assessment of archaeological knowledge and practice*, London. 30–3

Darvill, T C, 1987 *Prehistoric Gloucestershire*, County Library Services, Alan Sutton Publishing Ltd

Darvill, T C, 1993 Beaker period occupation, in Allen, T G, Darvill, T C, Green, L S and Jones, M U, 9–25

Darvill, T C and Gerrard C, 1994 *Cirencester: Town and Landscape. An urban archaeological assessment*, Cotswold Archaeological Trust Ltd, Cirencester

Darvill, T C, Hingley, R, Jones, M and Timby, J, 1986 A Neolithic and Iron Age site at The Loders, Lechlade, Gloucestershire, *Trans Bristol Gloucestershire Archaeol Soc* **104**, 27–48

Darvill, T C and Holbrook, N 1994 The Cirencester area in the prehistoric and early Roman periods, in Darvill, T C and Gerrard, N, 47–56

Davey, P 1980 *The Archaeology of the Clay Tobacco Pipe III*, BAR Brit. Ser **78**, Oxford

Davis, R V, Howard, H and Smith, I F, 1988 The petrological identification of stone implements from south-west England, in McKClough, T H and Cummins, W A, 141–162

Déchelette, J, 1904 *Les vases céramiques ornés de la Gaule romaine (Narbonnaise, Aquitaine et Lyonnaise)*, Paris

De Roche, C D, 1978 The Iron Age pottery, in Parrington, M, 40–74

Dewey, H and Bromehead, C E N, 1915 *The geology of the country around Windsor and Chertsey*, Mem Geol Survey, HMSO, London

Dickinson, B, 1986 Potters' stamps and signatures on samian, in Miller, L, Schofield, J and Rhodes, M, 186–198

Digby, H S N, 1977 Archaeological survey of the Latton to Blunsdon Thames Water pipeline, TAU

Digby, H S N, 1987 Archaeological survey of the Thames Water pipeline from Latton to Blunsdon, TAU Typescript Report

Digby, H S N, 1988 Archaeological Evaluation on the line of the proposed Latton Bypass, TAU Typescript Report

Dilke, O A W, 1971 *The Roman land surveyors: an introduction into agrimensores*, David and Charles, Newton Abbot

Dixon, K R and Southern, P, 1992 *The Roman cavalry from the 1st-3rd century AD*, Batsford, London

Dixon, P, W 1971 *Crickley Hill, Glos.*, Third interim report, Cheltenham, privately published

Dixon, P W, 1972 Crickley Hill 1969–71, *Antiquity* **46**, 49–52

Dixon, P W, 1973a Crickley Hill, Fifth Report, privately printed, Cheltenham

Dixon, P W, 1973b Longhouse and roundhouse at Crickley Hill, *Antiquity* **47**, 56–9

Dixon, P W, 1976 Crickley Hill 19697–2, in Harding, D W, 161–75, 424–9, 507–8

Dixon, P W, 1979 A Neolithic and Iron Age site on a hilltop in southern England, *Scientific American* **241.5**, 142–50

Dixon, P W, 1994 *Crickley Hill: the hillfort defences, University of Nottingham*, Department of Archaeology and Crickley Hill Trust

Dobney, K and Jaques, D, 1990 Animal bones from the excavations at Birdlip, Glos. AML Rep **36/90**

Dobney, K and Jaques, D 1998 The animal bone, in Parry, C, 80–84

Drinkwater, J and Saville, A, 1984 The Bronze Age round barrows of Gloucestershire: a brief review, in Saville, A, 1984b,128–39

Driver, J C, 1982 Medullary bone as an indicator of sex in bird remains from archaeological sites, in Wilson, B, Grigson, C and Payne, S, 251–4

Drury, P J, 1982a An interpretation of the structures, in. Great Oakley and other Iron Age sites in the Corby area, (D A Jackson) *Northamptonshire Archaeol* **17**, 3–23

Drury, P J, 1982b *Structural reconstruction: approaches to the interpretation of the excavated remains of buildings*, BAR Brit Ser **110**, Oxford

Dumayne-Peaty, L and Barber, K, 1998 Late Holocene vegetational history, human impact and pollen representivity variations in northern Cumbria, England, *Journal of Quaternary Science* **13**, 147–164

Dumbrell, R, 1983 *Understanding antique wine bottles*, Antique Collector's Club

Dunning, G C, 1932 Bronze Age settlements and a Saxon hut near Bourton-on-the-Water, Gloucestershire, *Antiquaries Journal* **12**, 279–93

Dunning, G C, 1976 Salmonsbury, Bourton-on-the-Water, Gloucestershire, in Harding, D W, 75-118, 373–401, 488–94

Duval, A, 1974 Un type particulier de fibule gallo-romaine précoce: la fibule "d'Alésia", *Antiquités Nationale* **6**, 67–76

Dyer, C, 1989 *Standards of living in the later middle ages*, Cambridge University Press, Cambridge

Edwards, H J (Trans.), 1952 *Caesar: The Gallic War*, London: Loeb Classical Library

Ellison, A, 1984 Bronze Age Gloucestershire: artefacts and distribution, in Saville, A 1984b, 113–127

Ellison, A and Drewett, P, 1970 Pits and postholes in the British early Iron Age: some alternative explanations, *Proc Prehist Soc* **37**, 183–94

Ellison, A and Harris, J, 1972 Settlement and land use in the prehistory and early history of southern England: a study based on locational models, in Clarke, D L, 911–962

Elsdon, S, 1994 The Iron Age pottery, in Dixon, P W, 203–41

English Heritage, 1991a *Management of archaeological projects*, 2nd edition, English Heritage, London

English Heritage, 1991b *Exploring our past: strategies for the archaeology of England*, English Heritage, London

Esmonde Cleary, A S, 1989 *The ending of Roman Britain*, Batsford, London

Evans, J G, 1972 *Land snails in archaeology*, London: Seminar Press

Evans, J G and Jones, H, 1973 Subfossil and modern landsnail faunas from rock-rubble habitats, *J Conchology* **28**, 103–129

Farwell, D E and Molleson T I, 1993 *Poundbury, Volume 2: the cemeteries*, Dorset Natural History and Archaeological Society, Monograph Series Number **11**, Dorchester

Fasham, P J 1985 *The prehistoric settlement at Winnall Down, Winchester*, Hampshire Field Club Monograph **2**, Hampshire

Fell, C I, 1961a Shenbarrow Hill Camp, Stanton, Gloucestershire, *Trans Bristol Gloucestershire Archaeol Soc* **80**, 16–41

Fell, C I, 1961b The coarse pottery of Bagendon, in Clifford, E M, 212-67

Fell, C I, 1964 The pottery, in Early Iron Age pottery from Rodborough Common and Duntisbourne Abbots (E M Clifford), *Trans Bristol Gloucestershire Archaeol Soc* **83**, 145–6

Fieller, N R J, Gilbertson, D D and Ralph, N G A, 1985 *Palaeobiological Investigations: Research Design, Methods and Data Analysis*, BAR Internat Ser **266**, Oxford

Finberg, H P R, 1955 *Roman and Saxon Withington: a study in continuity.* Leicester University College Dept. of English Local History, Occas Paper No **8**

Fitzpatrick A P, 1994 Outside in: the structure of an early Iron Age House at Dunston Park, Thatcham, Berkshire in Fitzpatrick, A P and Morris, E L, 68–72

Fitzpatrick A P, 1997 Everyday life in Iron Age Wessex, in Gwilt, A and Haselgrove, C, 73–86

Fitzpatrick, A P and Morris, E L, 1994 *The Iron Age in Wessex: recent work*, Association Française D'Etude de L'Age du Fer, Wessex Archaeology

Foster, J, 1986 *The Lexden Tumulus*, BAR Brit Ser **156**, Oxford

Foster, P, 1994 Interim report on the excavations

undertaken at Huntsman's Quarry, Naunton, Gloucestershire in 1994, Typescript report deposited with Gloucestershire SMR

Fox, C F, 1933 The distribution of man in East Anglia, c. 2300 BC–50 AD. A contribution to the prehistory of the region, *Proc Prehist Soc of East Anglia* **7.2**, 149–64

Fowler, P J, (ed) 1972 *Archaeology and the landscape. Essays for L V Grinsell*, Baker, London

Frere, S S, 1972 *Verulamium Excavations, volume 1*, Soc Antiq Res Rep No. **28**, London

Frere, S S, 1974 *Britannia - A History of Roman Britain*, 2nd edition, Sphere Books, London

Frere, S S and St Joseph, J K, 1974 The Roman fortress at Longthorpe, *Britannia* **5**, 1–129

Frere, S S, 1984 *Verulamium Excavations Volume 3*, Oxford University Committee for Archaeology Monograph No **1**, Oxford

Friendship-Taylor, R M and Friendship-Taylor, R E 1997 *From roundhouse to villa: the proceedings of a conference in 1993 to celebrate the Upper Nene Archaeological Society's 30th anniversary*, Nene Archaeological Society

Fulford, M, 1975 *New Forest Roman Pottery*, BAR Brit Ser **17**, Oxford

Fulford, M and Nichols, E, 1992 *Developing landscapes of lowland Britain. The archaeology of the British gravels, a review*, Soc Antiq Occas. Paper **14**, London

Gardiner, C I, 1932 Recent discoveries in the Stroud Valley, *Proc Cots Nat Hist Field Club* **24** (3), 163–80

Garrod, A P, and Heighway, C, 1984 *Garrod's Gloucester: Archaeological Observations 1974-81*, Western Archaeological Trust Excavation Monograph **6**, Bristol

Gates, T, 1975 *The Middle Thames Valley: an archaeological survey of the river gravels*, Berks Archaeol Committee Publication **1**, Reading

GCC 1990 A417 North of Stratton to Birdlip Improvement: archaeological survey Stage 2, Gloucestershire County Council, unpublished

GCC 1994 A417. North of Stratton to Nettleton improvement. Archaeological Survey. Stage 3 Project Design

GeoQuest Associates 1995 Geophysical surveys prior to the mains relocation for the A419(T) Latton Bypass, Wiltshire, Unpublished report for Thames Western Archaeological Trust Utilities and Mike Lang Hall

Gentry Steele, D and Bramblett, C A, 1988 *The anatomy and biology of the human skeleton*, A&M University Press, Texas

Gerrard, C, 1994a Cyrncaestre: A royal/ecclesiastical centre in the early medieval period, in Darvill, T and Gerrard, C, 87–97

Gerrard, C, 1994b Cirencestre: a medium-sized market town in the medieval period, in Darvill, T and Gerrard, C, 98–118

Gerrard, C and Viner, L, 1994 Cirencester: A medium-sized market town in the post-medieval period, in Darvill, T and Gerrard, C, 119–137

Getty, R, 1975 Sisson and Grossman's *The anatomy of the domestic animals*, Philadelphia: W B Saunders Co

Gibson, A and Kinnes, I, 1997 On the urns of a dilemma: radiocarbon and the Peterborough problem, *Oxford J of Archaeol* **16**, 65–72

Gillam, J P, 1970 *Types of Roman coarse pottery vessels in northern Britain*, 3rd edition, Oriel Press, Newcastle-upon-Tyne

Gillam, J P, 1976 Coarse fumed ware in North Britain and beyond, *Glasgow Archaeol J* **4**, 57-80

Gilmore, F, 1972 Animal remains, in Excavations at Beckford (A Oswald), *Trans Worcestershire Archaeol Soc Third Series* **3**, 18–28

Gingell, C, 1981 Excavation of an Iron Age enclosure at Groundwell Farm, Blunsdon St Andrew, 1976-7, *Wilts Archaeol Nat Hist Mag.* **76**, 33–75

Gingell, C, 1992 *The Marlborough Downs: A later Bronze Age landscape and its origins*, Wiltshire Archaeological and Natural History Society Monograph **1**, Devizes

Godwin, H, 1940 Pollen analysis and forest history of England and Wales, *New Phytologist* **39**, 370–400

Godwin, H, 1956 *The history of British flora: a factual basis for phytogeography*, Cambridge University Press, Cambridge

Godwin, H, 1967 The ancient cultivation of hemp, *Antiquity* **41**, 42–50

Godwin, H, 1975 *The history of the British Flora*, 2nd edition, Cambridge University Press, Cambridge

Goethert-Polaschek, K, 1997 *Katalog der romischen Glaser des Rheinischen Landesmuseums Trier* (Mainz am Rhein)

Goodall, J and Woodcock, T, 1991, Exhibits at Ballots: 3. Armorial and other pendants, studs and ornaments, *Antiquaries Journal* **71**, 239–47

Goodburn, R, 1978 Winterton: some villa problems, in Todd, M, 93–102

Goodburn, R, 1984 The non-ferrous metal objects, in Frere, S S, 19–67

Gracie, H S, 1962 Bagendon, the Iron Age Camp, *Trans Bristol Gloucestershire Archaeol Soc* **80**, 179

Grant, A, 1982 The use of tooth wear as a guide to the age of domestic ungulates, in Wilson, B, Grigson, C and Payne, S, 91–108

Grant, A, 1984 Animal husbandry in Wessex and the Thames Valley, in Cunliffe, B W and Miles, D, 102–119

Grant, A, 1989 Animals in Roman Britain, in Todd, M, 135–46

Green, C S 1981 Brooches

Green, C S, 1987 *Excavations at Poundbury, Volume I: the settlements*, Dorset Nat Hist and Archaeol Soc Monograph Series No. **7**, Dorchester

Green, L S, and Booth, P, 1993 The Roman pottery, in Allen, T and Robinson, M, 113–41

Greenwell, W, 1890 Recent researches in barrows in Yorkshire, Wiltshire, Berkshire, etc., *Archaeologia* **52**, 1–72

Gregory, T, 1992 *Excavations in Thetford, 1980–1982, Fison Way*, EAA Rep **53**, Gressenhall

Greig, J R A, 1982 Past and present lime woods of Europe, in Bell, M and Limbrey, S, 23–55

Greig, J R A, 1991 The British Isles, in Van Zeist, Wasylikowa and Behre (eds) *Progress in Old*

World Palaeobotany, Rotterdam; Balkema

Griffiths, N, 1986 *Horse harness pendants*, Finds Research Group 700–1700, Datasheet 5, Coventry

Griffiths, N, 1989 *Shield-shaped mounts*, Finds Research Group 700–1700, Datasheet 12, Oxford

Griffiths, N, 1995 Harness pendants and associated fittings, in Clark 1995, 61–71

Grigson, C, 1982 Sex and age determination of some bones and teeth of domestic cattle: a review of the literature, in Wilson, B, Grigson, C and Payne, S, 1982, 7–23

Grimes, W F, 1960 Excavations on defence sites 1939–1945: I, mainly Neolithic to Bronze Age. HMSO, London

Grimes, W, F and Close-Brooks, J, 1993 Caesar's Camp, Heathrow, Middlesex, *Proc Prehist Soc* **59**, 303–360

Grinsell, L V, 1957 Archaeological Gazetteer. *VCH* Wiltshire i, pt. 1

Grinsell, L V, 1966 A Palaeolithic implement from Poole Keynes, *Trans Bristol Gloucestershire Archaeol Soc* **85**, 207–8

Guido, M, 1978 The glass beads of the prehistoric and Roman periods in Britain and Ireland, *Soc of Antiq Res Rep* **35**, Thames and Hudson, London

Gutierrez, A, 1998 Ceramic rings, in Timby 1998a

Gutierrez, A and Roe, F, 1998 Stone objects, in Timby 1998a, 176–9

Gwilt, A and Haselgrove, C 1997 *Reconstructing Iron Age societies*, Oxbow Monograph **71**, Oxford

Habermehl, K H, 1975 *Die Alterbestimmung bei Haus- und Labortieren*. Berlin: Paul Verlag Parey

Hagen, W, 1937 Kaiserzeitliche Gagatarbeiten us dem rheinishen Germanien, *Bonner Jahrbücher* **142**, 77–144

Hajnalova, E 1991 *Palaeoethnobotany and archaeology*, IWGP 8th Symposium, Acto Interdisciplinaria Archaeologica Tomus **7**, Nitra

Hall, M and Gingell, C, 1974 Nottingham Hill, Gloucestershire, 1972, *Antiq* **48**, 306–9

Halstead, P, 1985 A study of mandibular teeth from Romano-British contexts at Maxey, in Pryor, F, 219–224

Hamlin, A, 1963 Excavations of ring ditches and other sites at Stanton Harcourt, *Oxoniensia* **28**, 1–52

Handford, M and Viner. D, 1984 *The Thames and Severn Canals towpath guide*

Hands, A R, 1993 *The Romano-British Roadside Settlement at Wilcote, Oxfordshire I. Excavations 1990–92*, BAR Brit Ser **232**, Oxford

Hands, A R, 1998 *A Romano-British roadside settlement at Wilcote, Oxfordshire. II. Excavations 1993–96*, BAR Brit Ser **265**, Oxford

Hannan, A, 1993 Excavations at Tewkesbury, 1972–74, *Trans Bristol and Gloucestershire Archaeol Soc* **111**, 21–75

Hannan, A, 1997 Tewkesbury and the Earls of Gloucester: excavations at Holm Hill, 1974–5, *Trans Bristol Gloucestershire Archaeol Soc* **115**, 79–231

Harden, D B, and Treweeks, R C, 1945 Excavations at Stanton Harcourt, Oxon., 1940 *Oxoniensia* **10**, 16–41

Harding, D W, 1971 *The Iron Age in the Upper Thames basin*, Clarendon Press Oxford

Harding, D W, 1976 *Hillforts: later prehistoric earthworks in Britain and Ireland*, Academic Press, London

Hardwick, P 1981 *Discovering horn*, Guildford, Lutterworth Press

Harris, S, and Lloyd, H G, 1991 Fox *The Handbook of British Mammals*, 3rd edition (eds in G B Corbet and S Harris), Oxford: Blackwell Science, 351–67

Haslam, J, 1984 The glass in Hassall, T G, Halpin, C E and Mellor, M, 232–249

Hassall, T G, Halpin, C E and Mellor, M 1984 Excavations in St Ebbes, Oxford, 1967–1976, Part II, Post-medieval domestic tenements and the post-dissolution site of the Greyfriars, *Oxoniensia* **49**,

Hattatt, R, 1985 *Iron Age and Roman brooches, a second selection of brooches from the author's collection*, Oxbow Books, Oxford

Haverfield, F, 1908 Romano-British Shropshire, in *VCH Shropshire vol I*, (ed W Page), London, 205–278

Hawkes, C F C, 1947 Britons, Romans and Saxons round Salisbury and in Chase, *Arch J* **104**, 27–81

Hawkes, C F C and Hull, M R, 1947 *Camulodunum, First Report on the excavations at Colchester, 1930–1939*, Rep of the Res Comm of the Antiq Soc of London, **14**, Oxford

Hearne, C M and Heaton, M J, 1994 Excavations at a late Bronze Age settlement in the Upper Thames Valley at Shorncote Quarry near Cirencester, 1992, *Trans Bristol and Gloucestershire Archaeol Soc* **112**, 17–57

Heighway, C M, 1983 *The East and North Gates of Gloucester and associated sites: excavations 1974 – 81*, Western Archaeological Trust. Excavation Monograph. No. **4**, Bristol

Heighway, C, 1984 Anglo-Saxon Gloucestershire, in Saville, A, 1984b, 225–247

Helbaek, H, 1952 Early crops in southern England. *Proc Prehist Soc* **18**, 194–233

Hey, G, Bayliss, A and Boyle, A 1999 Iron Age burials at Yarnton, Oxfordshire, *Antiquity* (September 1999)

Hey, G and Bell, C, in prep. *The Yarnton-Cassington Project, Neolithic and Bronze Age settlement and landscape*, Thames Valley Landscapes Monograph

Hick, S P, 1972 The impact of Man on the East Moor of Derbyshire from Mesolithic times, *Arch Journal* **129**, 1–21

Higham, C F W, 1969 The metrical attributes of two samples of bovine limb bones, *J of Zoology* **157**, 63–74

Hill, J D, 1996 Hillforts and the Iron Age of Wessex, in Champion, T C and Collis, J R, 95–116

Hillman, G, 1982 Evidence for spelting malt, in Leech, R, 137–41

Hillson, S, 1986 *Teeth*, Cambridge Manuals in Archaeology, Cambridge University Press

Hingley, R, 1982 Tomlin's Gate, Kiddington, *CBA Group 9 Newsletter* **12**, 154–5

Hingley, R, 1984a Towards social analysis in archaeology: Celtic society in the Iron Age of the

Upper Thames Valley, in Cunliffe, B W and Miles, D, 72–88

Hingley, R, 1984b Domestic organisation and gender relations in Samson, R, 125–148

Hingley, R, 1986 The Iron Age pottery, in Darvill, T, Hingley, R, Jones, M and Timby, J, 27–48

Hingley, R, 1989 *Rural Settlement in Roman Britain*, Seaby, London

Hingley, R, 1993 Early Iron Age pottery, in Allen, T G, Darvill, T C, Green, L S and Jones, M U, 40–4

Hingley, R and Miles, D, 1984 Aspects of the Iron Age in the Upper Thames Valley, in Cunliffe, B W and Miles, D, 52–71

Hinton, D A and Rahtz, P, 1966 Upton

Hodder, I, 1990 *The domestication of Europe: structure and contingency in Neolithic society*, Basil Blackwell, Oxford

Hodder, M A and Barfield, L H, 1990 *Burnt mounds and hot stone technologies: papers from the second international burnt mound conference. Sandwell, 12th-14th October 1990.* Sandwell Metropolitan Borough Council

Holbrook, N 1994 Corinium Dobunnorum: Roman Civitas Capital and Roman Provincial Capital, in Darvill, T and Gerrard, C, 57–86

Holbrook, N 1998 *The Roman town defences, public buildings and shops*, Cotswold Archaeological Trust, Cirencester

Holbrook, N, and Bidwell, P T, 1991 *Roman Finds from Exeter*, Exeter Archaeol Rep 4, Exeter

Holgate, R, 1988 *Neolithic Settlement of the Thames Basin.* BAR Brit Ser 194, Oxford

Household, H, 1983 *The history of the Thames and Severn canal* (new enlarged edition), Alan Sutton, Gloucester

Howe, M D, Perrin, J R and Mackreth, D F, 1980 *Roman pottery from the Nene Valley: A Guide*, Peterborough City Mus Occ Paper 2, Peterborough

Hoyle, J, 1993 Archaeological Review No. 17, in Rawes, *Trans Bristol Glos Archaeol Soc* 11, 231

Hubbard, R N K B, 1975 Assessing the botanical component of human palaeo-economies, *Bulletin of the Institute of Archaeology*, London 12, 197–205

Hume, N, 1961 The glass wine bottle in colonial Virginia, *J Glass Studies* 3

Hunter, A G, 1985 Building excavations in Southgate Street and Quay Street, Gloucester 1960, *Trans Bristol Glos Archaeol Soc* 103, 55–72

Hunter, J and Oakley, G E, 1979 The glass, in Williams, J H, 296–303

Hunter, R and Mynard, D, 1977 Excavations at Thorplands, near Northampton, 1970 and 1974, *Northampton Archaeology* 12, 97–154

Hurst, D and Rees, H, 1992 Pottery fabrics; a multi-period series for the County of Hereford and Worcester, in, Woodiwiss, S, 200–9

Hurst, H, 1972 Excavations at Gloucester, 1968–1971: First interim report, Antiq J 52, 24–69

Hyland, A, 1990 *Equus: The horse in the Roman World*, London: B.T. Batsford

Ireland, C, 1983 The pottery, in Heighway, C M, 96–124

Jackman, W T, 1962 *The development of transportation in modern England*, 2nd edition, Frank Cass, London

Jackson, D, 1983 The excavation of an Iron Age site at Brigstock, Northants, 1979–81, *Northamptonshire Archaeology* 18, 7–32

Jackson, J W, 1961 The animal bones, in Clifford, E M, 268–71

Jackson, R P and Beckey, I, 1991 Tin-glazed earthenware kiln waste from the Limekiln Lane potteries, Bristol, *Post-Medieval Archaeol* 25, 89–112

Jackson, R P J and Potter, T W, 1996 *Excavations at Stonea, Cambridgeshire, 1980-85*, British Museum, London

Jarrett, M G and Wrathmell, S, 1981 *Whitton: An Iron Age and Roman Farmstead in South Glamorgan.* University of Wales Press

Jennings, D, 1998 Prehistoric and Roman activity, in Boyle, A, Jennings, D, Miles, D and Palmer, S, 9–34

Jennings, S, 1981 *Eighteen centuries of pottery from Norwich*, EAA Rep 13, Norwich, the Norwich Survey

Jessup, R F, 1959 Barrows and walled cemeteries in Roman Britain, *Journal of the British Archaeological Association* 22, 1–32

Jewell, P A, 1962 Changes in size and type of cattle from prehistoric to medieval times in Britain. *Zeitschrift fur Tierzuchtung und Zuchtungsbiologie* 77/2, 157–67

Johns, C, 1996 *The jewellery of Roman Britain. Celtic and classical traditions*, UCL Press, London

Johnson, C, 1991 A419 Latton Bypass, Archaeological Report. Additional Report, Southern Extension. CAT Typescript 9165

Jones, G and Legge, A J, 1987 The grape (*Vitis vinifera* L.) in the Neolithic of Britain. *Antiquity* 61, 452–455

Jones, M, 1988 *Archaeology and the flora of the British Isles*, Oxford University Committee for Archaeology Monograph No 14, Oxford

Jones, M and Dimbleby, G, 1981 *The environment of man: the Iron Age to the Anglo-Saxon period*, BAR Brit Ser 87, Oxford

Jones, M K, 1978 The plant remains in Parrington, M,

Jones, M K, 1986 The carbonised plant remains, in Miles, D fiche 9, A1–9, B5

Jones, M K, and Robinson, M, 1983 The carbonised plant remains, in Allen, T G and Robinson, M, 120–123

Jones, M U, 1984a Regional patterns in crop production, in Cunliffe, B W and Miles, D, 120–125

Jones, M U, 1984b The ecological and cultural implications of carbonised seed assemblages from selected archaeobotanical contexts in southern Britain, PhD thesis, Oxford

Jones, M U, 1985 Archaeobotany beyond subsistence reconstruction, in Barker, G and Gamble, C, 107–128

Jones, R F J, 1991 *Britain in the Roman period: recent trends*, Sheffield, J R Collis Publications

Jope, E M, 1953–60 Medieval pot kilns at Brill, Buckinghamshire, *Records of Buckinghamshire*,

Vol **16**, 39–42

Keeley, H C M 1987 *Environmental archaeology: a regional review 2*, HBMC Occasional Paper **1**, London

Keevill, G D and Booth, P, 1997 Settlement, sequence and structure: Romano-British stone-built roundhouses at Redlands Farm, Stanwick (Northants) and Alchester (Oxon), in Friendship-Taylor, R M and Friendship-Taylor, D E,

Keevill, G, Hardy, A and Dodd, A, forthcoming *Excavations at Eynsham Abbey 1989–1992*, Oxford Archaeological Unit, Thames Valley Landscapes Monograph

Kelly, J H and Greaves, S J, 1974 *The excavation of a kiln base in Old Hall Street, Hanley, Stoke-on-Trent, Staffordshire. SJ 885475*, Stoke-on-Trent Mus Archaeol Soc Rep **6**, Stoke-on-Trent

Kent, J P C, 1994 *The Roman imperial coinage. Volume X. The divided Empire and the Fall of the western parts*, London, Spink

Kenyon, K M, 1948 *Excavations at the Jewry Wall site, Leicester*, Rep of the Res Comm of the Soc of Antiq of London, **15**, Oxford

Kerney, M P and Cameron, R A D, 1979 *A field guide to the land snails of Britain and north-west Europe*, London: Collins

King, A, 1978 A comparative survey of bone assemblages from Roman sites in Britain. *Bull of the Inst of Archaeol* **15**, 207–32

King, A, 1991 Food production and consumption - meat, in Jones, R F J,

King, A and Henig, M, 1981 *The Roman West in the Third Century*, BAR Internat Ser **109**, Oxford

King, A, and Soffe, G, 1994 The Iron Age and Roman temple on Hayling Island, in Fitzpatrick and Morris, 114–116

King, R, 1998 Excavations at Gassons Road 1993, in Boyle, A, Jennings, D, Miles, D and Palmer, S, 269–281

King, R, Barber, A and Timby, J, 1996 Burials at West Lane, Kemble, *Trans. Bristol Gloucestershire Arch Soc* **114**, 15–54

Kinnes, I, 1979 *Round barrows and ring ditches in the British Neolithic*, British Museum Occas Paper No **7**, British Museum, London

Kinnes, I, 1992 *Non-megalithic long barrows and allied structures in the British Neolithic*, British Museum Occasional Paper **52**, London

Kinnes, I A and Longworth, I H, 1985 *Catalogue of the excavated prehistoric and Romano-British material in the Greenwell collection*, London, British Museum Publications

Kinnes, I A, Gibson, A Ambers, J, Bowman, S, Leese, M and Boast, R, 1991 Radiocarbon dating and British Beakers: the British Museum Programme, *Scottish Archaeol Review* **8**, 35–68

Knight, D, 1984 *The Iron Age in the Upper Nene and Great Ouse Basin*, BAR Brit Ser **130**, Oxford

Kromer, B and Becker, B, 1993 *Radiocarbon* **35**(1), 125

Lambrick, G H, 1979 Berinsfield Mount Farm, *CBA Group 9 Newsletter* **9**, 113–5

Lambrick, G H, 1985 Stanton Harcourt, Gravelly Guy, *CBA Group 9 Newsletter* **16**

Lambrick, G H, 1988 *The Rollright Stones, megaliths, monuments and settlement in the prehistoric landscape*, English Heritage Archaeological Report **6**, London

Lambrick, G H, 1992a Alluvial archaeology of the Holocene in the Upper Thames Basin 1971–1991: a review, in Needham, S andMacklin, M G, 209–228

Lambrick, G H, 1992b The development of late prehistoric and Roman farming on the Thames gravels, in Fulford, M and Nichols, E, 78–105

Lambrick, G H and Robinson, M, 1979 *Iron Age and Roman Riverside Settlements at Farmoor, Oxfordshire* CBA Res Rep **32**, London

Lambrick, G H with Robinson, M, 1984 Holocene alluviation and hydrology in the Upper Thames basin, *Nature* **308** (No 5962), 809–14

Lambrick, G H and Robinson, M, 1988 The development of floodplain grassland in the Upper Thames Valley, in Jones, M, 55–75

Laubenheimer, F, 1985 *La Production des amphores en Gaule Narbonnaise sous le Haut-Empire*, Paris

Lauwerier, R C G M, 1983 Pigs, piglets and determining the season of slaughtering, *J Archaeol Science* **10**, 483–8

Laws, K, 1991 The shale, in Sharples, N M, 233–4

Laws, K, Roe, F, Peacock, D P S and Edmonds, M, 1991 The foreign stone in Sharples, N M, 229–233

Lawson, A J, 1976 Shale and jet objects from Silchester, *Archaeologia* **105**, 241–275

Leach, P, 1993 The pottery, in Woodward, A and Leach, P, 219–49

Le Bas, M J, 1968 Caledonian igneous rocks, in Sylvester-Bradley, P C and Ford, T D, 41–58

Leech, R H, 1977 *Upper Thames Valley in Gloucestershire and Wiltshire: An Archaeological Survey of the River Gravels*, Committee for Rescue Archaeology in Avon, Gloucestershire and Somerset, Survey No. 4, Bristol

Leech, R H, 1981 *Historic towns in Gloucestershire,.* Committee for Rescue Archaeology in Avon, Gloucestershire and Somerset, Bristol

Leech, R H, 1982 *Excavations at Catsgore 1970–1973: A Romano-British village*, Western Archaeological Trust Excavation Monograph **2**, Bristol

Lees, J, 1977 Romano-British pottery and flints at Winstone, *Glevensis* **11**, 30

Lees, J, 1979 Romano-British pottery and flints at Winstone, *Trans Bristol Gloucestershire Archaeol Soc* **96**, 90

Levine, M A, 1982 The use of crown height measurements and tooth eruption sequences to age horse teeth, in Wilson, B, Grigson, C and Payne, S, 223–50

Levitan, B, 1993 Vertebrate remains in Woodward, A and Leach, P, 257–301

Ling, R, 1992 A collapsed building façade at Carsington, Derbyshire, *Britannia* **23**, 233–236

Ling, R and Courtney, T, 1981 Excavations at Carsington, 1979–80, *Derbyshire Arch Journal* **110**, 58–87

Linick, T W, Long, A, Damon, P E and Ferguson, C W, 1993 *Radiocarbon* **35(1)**, 943

Liou, B, 1982 Informations archeologiques. Direction des recherches sous-marines, *Gallia* **40**, 437–54

Longworth, I H, 1984 *Collared Urns of the Bronze Age in Britain and Ireland*, Cambridge University Press

Luke, M and Dawson, M, 1997 The Biddenham Loop, Bedford, *South Midlands Archaeology* **27**, 2–5

Lupton, A and Williams, R J, 1997 Swindon to Gloucester A417/419 DBFO Roadscheme - Post-excavation Assessment and Publication Proposal. Vols. 1–2. Unpublished OAU document

Lyne, M A B and Jefferies, R S, 1979 *The Alice Holt/ Farnham Roman pottery industry*, CBA Res Rep **30**, London

Lynne, C, 1979 Deer Park Farms, *Current Archaeol* **113**, 193–198

Macdonald, D W and Barrett, P, 1993 *Mammals of Britain and Europe*,. Collins Field Guide

MacGregor, A, 1985 *Bone, antler, ivory and Horn. The technology of skeletal materials since the Roman times*, Croom Helm, London

Mackreth, D F, 1982 The brooches, in Wacher, J S and McWhirr, A, 88–92

Mackreth, D F, 1988 Excavation of an Iron Age and Roman Enclosure at Werrington, Cambridgeshire, *Britannia* **19**, 59–151

Mackreth, D F, 1989 Brooches, in Blockley, K, 87–99

Mackreth, D F, 1992 Brooches of copper alloy and iron, in Gregory, T, 120–128

Mackreth, D F, 1994a The brooches, in Williams, R J and Zeepvat, R, 285–303

Mackreth, D F, 1994b Copper alloy and iron brooches, in Cracknell, S and Mahany, C, 162–177

Mackreth, D F, 1996 Brooches, in Jackson, R and Potter, T, 296–327

Macready, S and Thompson, F H (eds) 1984 *Cross-channel trade between Gaul and Britain in the pre-Roman Iron Age*, Society of Antiquaries Occasional Paper (New Series) **4**, London

McAdam, E and Chambers R A, in prep. Excavations at Barrow Hills, Radley, Oxfordshire, 1983–85. Volume 2: The Romano-British Cemetery and Anglo-Saxon Settlement, Thames Valley Landscapes Monograph, Oxford

McCance, R A, Ford, E H R and Brown, W A B, 1961 Severe undernutrition in growing and adult animals. 7: Development of the skull, jaws and teeth in pigs, *Brit J of Nutrition* **15**, 213–24

McCarthy, M R and Brooks, C M, 1988 *Medieval pottery in Britain AD 900–1600*, Leicester University Press

McOmish, D and Lewis, C, 1991 Trinity Mill earthwork survey, RCHME Unpub MS

McWhirr, A D, 1976 *Archaeology and History of Cirencester*, BAR Brit Ser 30, Oxford

McWhirr, A D, 1981 *Roman Gloucestershire*. Alan Sutton Publishing Ltd, Gloucestershire

McWhirr, A D 1982 *Roman crafts and industries*, Princes Risborough, Shire Publication

McWhirr, A D, 1984 The cities and large rural settlements of Roman Gloucestershire, in Saville, A 1984c, 212–224

McWhirr, A D, 1986a *Houses in Roman Cirencester*. Cirencester Excavations III, Cirencester Excavation Committee

McWhirr, A D, 1986b *Roman Gloucestershire*. County Library Series, Alan Sutton Publishing Ltd

McWhirr, A D, Viner, L and Wells, C, 1982 *Romano-British Cemeteries at Cirencester*. Cirencester Excavations II, Cirencester Excavation Committee

Maltby, J M, 1981 Iron Age, Romano-British and Anglo-Saxon animal husbandry: a review of the faunal evidence in Jones, M and Dimbleby, G, 155–204

Maltby, J M, 1985 The animal bones, in Fasham, P J, 97–112

Maltby, J M, 1987 The animal bones from the excavations at Owslebury, Hants. An Iron Age and early Romano-British settlement. AML Rep **6/87**

Maltby, M, 1985 Patterns in faunal assemblage variability, in Barker, G and Gamble, C, 33–74

Maltby, M, 1989 Urban-rural variations in the butchering of cattle in Romano-British Hampshire, in Serjeantson, D and Waldron, T, 75–91

Man, R and Weir, R, 1984 *The Complete Mustard*, London

Manning, W H, 1972 The iron objects, in Frere, S S, 163–95

Manning, W H, 1976 *Catalogue of Romano-British ironwork in the Museum of Antiquities, Newcastle upon Tyne*, Newcastle upon Tyne

Manning, W H, 1985 *Catalogue of the Romano-British iron tools, fittings and weapons in the British Museum*, London

Manning, W H, Price, J and Webster, J, 1995 *Report on the excavations at Usk: the Roman small finds*. University of Wales, Cardiff

Margary, I D, 1973 *Roman Roads in Britain*, 3rd edition. London

Markham, G, 1681 *A Way to Get Wealth*

Marshall, A, 1978 Material from Iron Age sites in the Northern Cotswolds, *Trans Bristol Gloucestershire Archaeol Soc* **96**, 17–26

Marshall, A, 1985 Neolithic and earlier Bronze Age settlement in the Northern Cotswolds: A preliminary outline based on the distribution of surface scatters and funerary areas, *Trans Bristol Gloucestershire Archaeol Soc* **103**, 23–54

Marshall, A, 1989 The hillfort at Burhill, Buckland, Gloucestershire: evidence for occupation during the earliest phases of the Iron Age, *Trans Bristol Gloucestershire Archaeol Soc* **107**, 197–202

Marshall, A, 1990 Cotswold Archaeological Research Group: Research Report **5**

Marshall, A, 1991 Cotswold Archaeological Research Group: Research Report **6**

Marshall, A, 1994. The Bowsings, in Archaeological review 18 (ed. B Rawes), 1993, *Trans Bristol Gloucestershire Archaeol Soc* **112**, 204

Marshall, A, 1995 The Park, in B Rawes (ed) Archaeological review 19, 1994, Trans Bristol Gloucestershire Archaeol Soc 113, 197

Marshall, A, 1997 Guiting Power. In Archaeological review 21 (ed J Rawes and J Wills), 1996, *Trans Bristol Gloucestershire Archaeol Soc* 115, 285–8

Martin, E A, 1915 *Dewponds*

Mayes, P, 1968 A 17th century kiln at Potterspury, Northamptonshire, *Post-Medieval Archaeol* 2, 55–83

Maxfield, A and Dobson, M J 1991 V *Roman Frontier Studies 1989. Proc of the XVth International Congress of Roman Frontier Studies*, Exeter,

Meddens, B, 1993 Land mollusca, in Woodward, A and Leach, P, 253–255

Megaw, J V S and Simpson, D D A, 1979 *Introduction to British prehistory*, Leicester University Press

Mellars, P, 1974 The Palaeolithic and Mesolithic, in Renfrew, C,

Mellor, M, 1984 A summary of the key assemblages. A study of pottery, clay pipes, glass and other finds from fourteen pits, dating from the 19th century, in Hassall, T G, Halpin, C E and Mellor, M, 181–219

Mellor, M, 1994 A synthesis of middle and late Saxon, medieval and early post-medieval pottery in the Oxford Region, *Oxoniensia* 59, 17–218

Mercer, R 1977 *Beakers in Britain and Europe*, BAR Internat Ser 26, Oxford

Miles, A E W and Grigson, C, 1990 *Colyer's variations and diseases of the teeth of animals*, Cambridge University Press

Miles, D, 1984 Settlement in the Gloucestershire Thames Valley, in Saville A, 1984c, 191–211

Miles, D 1986 *Archaeology at Barton Court Farm, Abingdon, Oxon*, CBA Res Rep 50, Oxford Archaeology Unit Report 3. London and Oxford

Miles, D, 1988 Villas and variety: aspects of economy and society in the Upper Thames landscape, in Branigan, K and Miles, D, 60–72

Miles, D and Palmer, S, 1982 *Figures in a landscape: Archaeological investigations at Claydon Pike, Fairford/Lechlade, Gloucestershire - Interim report 1979–81*. Oxford, Oxford Archaeological Unit

Miles, D and Palmer, S, 1983 Claydon Pike, *Current Archaeol* 8, 88–91

Miller, L, Schofield, J and Rhodes, M, 1986 *The Roman quay at St Magnus House*, London Special Paper No. 8, London and Middlesex Archaeol Soc

Milles, A, Williams, D and Gardner, N 1989 *Beginnings of agriculture*, BAR Internat Ser 96, Oxford

Millett, M, 1990 *The Romanization of Britain. An essay in archaeological interpretation*, Cambridge

Moffett, L, 1991 The archaeobotanical evidence for free-threshing tetraploid wheat in Britain, in Hajnalova, E, 233–43

Moffett, L, Robinson, M A and Straker, V, 1989 Cereals, fruit and nuts: charred plant remains from Neolithic sites in England and Wales and the Neolithic economy, in Milles, A, Williams, D and Gardner, N, 243–61

Moore, D T, 1978 The petrography and archaeology of English honestones, *J Archaeol Sci* 5, 61–73

Moore, J (ed.), 1982 *Domesday Book 15: Gloucestershire*, Phillimore

Moore, P D, 1977 Ancient distribution of lime trees in Britain. *Nature* 268, 13–14

Moore, P D and Webb, J A 1978 *An illustrated guide to pollen analysis*, London: Hodder and Stoughton

Moore, P D, Webb, J A and Collinson, M E, 1991 *Pollen analysis*, Second edition. Oxford: Blackwell Scientific

Morris, P, 1979 *Agricultural buildings in Roman Britain*, BAR Brit Ser 70, Oxford

Morris, E L, 1982 Petrological report: Droitwich briquetage containers; seriation analysis by fabric type of the Iron Age pottery, in Saville, A, 14–19

Morris, E L, 1994a Production and distribution of pottery and salt in Iron Age Britain: a review, *Proc Prehist Soc* 60, 371–94

Morris, E L, 1994b Pottery, in Hearne and Heaton, 34–43

Morris, E L, 1996 Artefact production and exchange in the British Iron Age, in Champion, T C and Collis, J R, 41–66

Morris, E L, forthcoming The briquetage from Huntsman Quarry, Naunton, Glos

Mudd, A and Booth, P, forthcoming, Site of the former Hockley chemical works, Stratford Road, Alcester: Excavation 1994, *Trans. Birmingham and Warickshire Archaeol Soc*

Murphy, P and French, C, 1988 *The exploitation of wetlands*, BAR Brit Ser 186, Oxford

Mynard, D C and Zeepvat, R J, 1992 *Excavations at Great Linford, 1974–80. The Buckinghamshire Archaeol Soc Monograph Ser. No. 3*

Neal, D S, 1989 The Stanwick villa, Northants. An interim report on the excavations of 1984–88, *Britannia* 20, 149–168

Neal, D S, Wardle, A and Hunn, J, 1990 *Excavation of the Iron Age, Roman and medieval settlement at Gorhambury, St Albans*, English Heritage Archaeol Rep No 14, London

Needham, S and Macklin, M G, 1991 *Alluvial archaeology in Britain*, Oxbow Monograph 27, Oxford

Needham, S and Spence, A, 1996 *Refuse and disposal at Area 16 East Runnymede. Runnymede Bridge Research Excavations, Volume 2*, London: Brit Mus Press

Newman, C, 1994 An Iron Age settlement at Ashton Keynes, Wiltshire in Fitzpatrick and Morris, 81–85

Niblett, R, 1985 *Sheepen: an early Roman industrial site at Camulodunum*, CBA Res Rep 57, London

Noddle, B, 1979 The animal bones in Frocester Court Roman villa. second report 1968-77: The courtyard (H S Gracie and E G Price), *Trans Bristol Gloucester Archaeol Soc* 97, 51–60

Noddle, B, 1984 Animal bones, in The Romano-British Site on the Portway, near Gloucester (B Rawes) *Trans Bristol Gloucestershire Archaeol Soc* 102. 68–70

Noddle, B, 1985 The animal bones, in The excavation of a Romano-British rural establishment at Barnsley Park, Gloucestershire, 1961–1979: Part III (G Webster, P Fowler, B Noddle and L Smith)

Trans Bristol Gloucester Archaeol Soc **103**, 82–97

Noddle, B, 1986, The animal bones, in The Romano-British settlement at Haymes, Cleeve Hill, near Cheltenham (B Rawes) *Trans Bristol Gloucestershire Archaeol Soc* **104**, 61–93

Noddle, B, 1987 Mammalian remains from the Cotswold region: a survey of the literature from Palaeolithic to Roman times, and a more detailed account of the larger domestic mammals from some recent Romano-British excavations, in Balaam, N D, Levitan, B and Straker, V, 31–50

Noddle, B, 1991 Animal bones, in A prehistoric and Romano-British settlement at Vineyards Farm, Charlton Kings, Gloucestershire, (B Rawes) *Trans Bristol Gloucestershire Archaeol Soc* **109**, 25–89

Oak-Rhind, H, 1980 Distribution of clay tobacco pipes round their place of manufacture, in Davey, P, 349–61

OAU, 1996 Swindon to Gloucester A419/417 DBFO Scheme - Archaeological Project Design: General Strategy and Methodology. Unpublished OAU document

O'Connor, T P, 1988 *Bones from the General Accident Site, Tanner Row*, The Archaeology of York **15/2**,.CBA, London

Okun, Marcia L, 1989 An example of the process of acculturation in the early Roman frontier, *Oxford J of Archaeol*. **8(1)**, 41–54

Oldenstein, J, 1976 Zur Ausrustung romischer Auxiliareinheiten, *Bericht der Romisch-Germanischen Kommission* **57**, 1976, 49–284

O'Neill, H E, 1965 A Palaeolithic flint implement from Bourton on-the-Water. *Proceedings of the Cotswold Naturalists Field Club* **34.4**, 225–7

O'Neill, H E, 1966 Sale's Lot long barrow, Withington, Gloucestershire, 1962-1965, *Trans Bristol Gloucestershire Archaeol Soc* **85**, 5–35

O'Neill, H E and Grinsell, L V, 1960 Gloucestershire barrows, *Trans Bristol Gloucestershire Archaeol Soc* **79.1**, 5–149

Orton, C, 1988 *Excavations in Southwark, 1973–76, Lambeth 1973–79*

Orton, C and Pearce, J, 1984 The pottery in The excavations at Aldgate (A Thompson, F Grew and J Schofield) *Post-Medieval Archaeol* **18**, 34–66

Ormrod, W, 1991 *England in the Thirteenth Century*, Stamford

Oswald, A, 1975 *Clay Pipes for the Archaeologist*, BAR Brit Ser **14**, Oxford

Oswald, A, 1997 A Doorway on the Past: practical and mystic concerns in the orientation of roundhouse doorways, in. Gwilt, A and Haselgrove, C, 87–95

Oswald, F, 1936-7 *Index of figure-types on terra sigillata ("samian ware")*, Liverpool

Parker-Pearson, M, 1996 Food, fertility and front doors in the first millennium BC, in Champion, T C and Collis, J R, 117–132

Parrington, M, 1978 *The excavation of an Iron Age settlement, Bronze Age ring ditches and Roman features at Ashville Trading Estate, Abingdon (Oxfordshire) 1974–76*, Oxford Archaeological Unit Rep **1**, CBA Res Rep **28**, London, 25–30

Parry, C, 1998 Excavations near Birdlip, Cowley, Gloucestershire, 1987-8. *Trans Bristol Gloucestershire Archaeol Soc* **116**, 25–92

Partridge, C, 1979 Excavations at Puckeridge and Braughing, 1975–79, *Hertfordshire Archaeol* **7**, 28–132

Partridge C, 1981 *Skeleton Green. A late Iron Age and Romano-British site*. Britannia Monograph Series No. **2**

Payne, S, 1973 Kill-off patterns in sheep and goats: the mandibles from Asvan Kale. *Anatolian Studies* **23**, 281–303

Payne, S, 1985 Morphological distinctions between the mandibular teeth of young sheep, *Ovis*, and goats, *Capra. J of Archaeol Sci* **1**. 139–47

Payne, S and Bull, G, 1988 Components of variation in measurements of pig bones and teeth, and the use of measurements to distinguish wild from domestic pig remains. *Archaeozoologia* **2**, 27–66

Peacey, A, 1979 *Clay tobacco pipes in Gloucestershire*, Committee For Rescue Archaeology in Avon, Gloucestershire And Somerset Occ Pap **4**

Peacock, D P S, 1968 A petrological study of certain Iron Age pottery from western England, *Proc Prehist Soc* **34**, 414–27

Peacock, D P S, 1977 *Pottery and early commerce: characterisation and trade in Roman and later ceramics*, Academic Press

Peacock, D P S and Williams, D F, 1986 *Amphorae and the Roman Economy. An Introductory Guide*, London

Pearce, J, 1992 *Border Wares*, Post-medieval pottery in London **1**

Pearson, E and Robinson, M, 1994 Environmental evidence from the villa, in Williams, R J and Zeepvat, R, 565–84

Pearson, G W and Stuiver, M, 1993 *Radiocarbon* **35(1)**, 25

Pelling, R, forthcoming a, The charred plant remains, in Mudd, A and Booth, P

Pelling, R, forthcoming b The plant remains at Eynsham Abbey, Oxfordshire, in Keevill, G, Hardy, A and Dodd, A

Percival, J, 1921 *The wheat plant a monograph*, New York

Percival, J, 1934 *Wheat in Great Britain*, London: Duckworth

Phillips, B, 1971 Blunsdon St. Andrew, Home Farm. *Archaeological Review* **6**, 17

Philpott, R, 1991 *Burial practices in Roman Britain. A survey of grave treatment and furnishing A.D. 43–410*. BAR Brit Ser **219**, Oxford

Piggott, S, 1938 *The early Bronze Age in Wessex*, Proc Prehist Soc **4**, 52–106

Piggott, S, 1962 *The West Kennet long barrow, excavations 1955-56*, Ministry of Works Archaeol Rep **4**, London, HMSO

Platt, C, 1978 *Medieval England: a social history and archaeology from the Conquest to AD 1600*. Routledge & Kegan Paul, London

Pliny, *Natural History*, book XVIII, trans. H Rackham, 1968, London

Plouviez, J, 1995 A hole in the distribution map: the characteristics of small towns in Suffolk in Brown, A E, 69–80

Potter, T W, 1979 *Romans in north-west England, excavations at the Roman forts of Ravenglass, Westercrook and Bowness-on-Solway*, Cumberland and Westmorland Antiq and Archaeol Soc, Res Ser, **1**, Kendal

Powell, A and Clark, K, 1996 Animal bone from Rooksdown, AML Report, unpublished

Price, E G, 1983 Frocester, *Current Archaeol* **88**, 139–45

Price, E, forthcoming Excavations at Frocester Court, Gloucestershire

Price, R and Jackson, R, 1984 The Ring Family of Bristol, Clay tobacco pipe manufacturers, *Post-Medieval Archaeol* **18**, 263–300

Pryor, F, 1983 Gone but still respected: some evidence for Iron Age house platforms in lowland England, *Oxford J Archaeol.* **2** (2), 189–198

Pryor, F, French, C, Crowther, D, Gurney, D, Simpson, G and Taylor, M 1985 *Archaeology and environment in the Lower Welland Valley Vol 1*, EAA 27, Fenland Project Committee, Cambridge

Pugsley, A J, 1939 *Dewponds in fable and fact*

Purnell, F and Webb, E W, 1950 An Iron Age A site near Cheltenham, *Trans Bristol Gloucestershire Archaeol Soc* **69**, 197–9

Purnell, F and Webb, E W, 1976 An Iron Age A site near Cheltenham. *Trans Bristol Gloucestershire Archaeol Soc* **69**, 197–199

Rackham, J 1994 *Environment and economy in Anglo-Saxon England*, CBA Res Rep **89**, York

Rackham, O, 1986, *The history of the countryside*, Dent, London

Rahtz, P A and Greenfield, E, 1977 *Excavations at Chew Valley Lake*, DOE Archaeol Rep, **8**, London

Rawes, B, 1981 The Romano-British site at Brockworth, Glos, *Britannia* **12**, 45–77

Rawes, B, 1982 Gloucester Severn Valley ware, *Trans Bristol Gloucestershire Archaeol Soc* **100**, 33–46

Rawes, J and Wills, J, 1996 Archaeological Review No. 20 1995, *Trans Bristol Gloucestershire Archaeol Soc* **114**, 163–185

Rawes, J and Wills, J, 1997 Archaeological Review No. 21, *Trans Bristol Gloucestershire Archaeol. Soc.* **115**, 277–95

RCHME 1976 *Ancient and Historical Monuments in the County of Gloucester, 1: Iron Age and Romano-British Monuments in the Gloucestershire Cotswolds*, London

Reece, R, 1972 A short survey of the Roman coins found on fourteen sites in Britain, *Britannia* **3**, 269–276

Reece, R, 1981 Bagendon, in Archaeological Review No. 5, 1980 (ed. B Rawes), *Trans Bristol Gloucestershire Archaeol Soc* **99**, 173

Reece, R, 1984 The Cotswolds: an essay on some aspects and problems of Roman rural settlement, in Saville, A 1984c, 181–190

Reece, R, 1987 *Coinage in Roman Britain*, London

Reece, R, 1990 *Excavations, survey and records around Cirencester*. Cotswold Studies **2**, Great Yarmouth

Reece, R and Catling, C, 1975 *Cirencester: the development and buildings of a Cotswold town*. BAR Brit Ser **12**, Oxford

Renfrew, C, 1976 *British prehistory: a new outline*, Duckworth and Co. Ltd, London

Reynolds, P J, 1974 Experimental Iron Age storage pits: An interim report. *Proc Prehist Soc* **40**, 118–131

Reynolds, P J, 1979 *An Iron Age farm. The Butser experiment*

Reynolds, P, 1982 Substructure to superstructure, in Drury, P J, 173–198

Reynolds, P J, and Langley, J K, 1979 Romano-British corn-dryer: an experiment *Archaeol Journal* **136**, 27–42

Richards, J, 1986-90 Death and the past environment. The results of work on barrows on the Berkshire Downs, Berkshire *Archaeol J* **73**, 1–42

Richardson, B, 1986 Pottery, in Miller, L, Schofield, J and Rhodes, M, 96–138

Richardson, L, 1933 *Geology of the Country around Cirencester*, Memoir of the Geological Survey of Great Britain, Sheet 235. HMSO London

Richardson, L, 1972 (revised R D Beckinsale) *A handbook to the geology of Cheltenham and neighbourhood*, Geol Soc

Richmond, I A, 1959 The Roman Villa at Chedworth, *Trans Bristol Gloucestershire Archaeol Soc* **88**, 5–23

Richmond, I, 1968 *Hod Hill, volume two, Excavations carried out between 1951 and 1958 for the Trustees of the British Museum*, London

Rielly, K, 1988 The animal bones, in Excavations at Ditches hillfort, North Cerney, Gloucestershire, 1982-3 (S D Trow), *Trans Bristol Gloucestershire Archaeol Soc* **106**, 19–85

Rielly, K, 1990 The animal bones in 1990, Excavations, survey and records around Cirencester (R Reece), *Cotswold Studies* **2**, 28–38

Rielly, K and Trow, S D, 1988 The Ditches animal bone assemblage in its regional context in The animal bones in Excavations at Ditches hillfort, North Cerney, Gloucestershire, 1982–3 (S D Trow), *Trans Bristol Gloucestershire Archaeol Soc* **106**, 19–85

Rigby, V, 1982 The pottery, in Wacher, J and McWhirr, A, 118–98

Rigby, V, 1988 Gallo-Belgic wares, in Trow, S, 19–85

Rigby, V and Freestone, I, 1983 The flagons, in A mirror burial at Dorton, Buckinghamshire (M Farley), *Proc Prehist Soc* **49**, 291–3

Riley, D N, 1944 Archaeology from the air in the Upper Thames Valley, *Oxoniensia* **8-9**, 64–101

Roberts, J P, 1989 The Iron Age and early Roman site at Bagendon, Gloucestershire County Council, unpublished report

Robinson, M A, 1983 Landscape and environment in central southern Britain in the Iron Age, in Cunliffe, B W and Miles, D, 1–11

Robinson, M A, 1988 Molluscan evidence for pasture and meadowland on the floodplain of the Upper Thames basin, in Murphy, P and French, C, 101–112

Robinson, M A, 1992a Environment, archaeology and alluvium on the river gravels of the South Midlands, in Needham, S P and Macklin, M G, 197–208

Robinson, M A, 1992b Environmental archaeology of the river gravels: past achievements and future directions, in Fulford, M and Nichols, E, 47–62

Robinson, M and Hubbard, R N L B, 1977 The transport of pollen in bracts of hulled cereals, *J Archaeol Science* **4**,197–199

Robinson, M and Lambrick, G H, 1984 Holocene alluviation and hydrology in the Upper Thames basin, *Nature* **308**, 809–14

Robinson, M A and Wilson, R, 1987 A survey of environmental archaeology in the South Midlands, in Keeley, H C M, 16–100

Rodwell, K A, *1988 The prehistoric and Roman settlement at Kelvedon, Essex*, CBA Res Rep, **63**, Chelmsford Archaeol Trust, Rep **6**, London

Rodwell, W, 1976 Coinage, Oppida and the rise of Belgic power in south-eastern Britain, in Cunliffe, B W and Rowley, T,

Roe, D A, 1981 *The lower and middle Palaeolithic periods in Britain*. London

Roe, F, 1979 Typology of stone implements with shaftholes, in Clough, T H McK and Cummins, W A, 23–48

Roe, F, 1998 Worked stone, in Home Farm, Bishop's Cleeve: excavation of a Romano-British occupation site 1993–4, *Trans Bristol Glos Archaeol Soc* **116**, 117-139 (A J Barber and G T Walker), 128–30

Roe, F, forthcoming The worked stone, in Cotswold Archaeological Trust

Roe, F 1998 Worked stone, in Parry, C, 63–64

Roe, F, in prep. Whetstones from Southgate Street, Gloucester

Rogers, G B, 1974 *Poteries sigillées de la gaule centrale, Supplément à Gallia* **28**, Paris

Rogerson A, 1976 Excavations on Fuller's Hill, Great Yarmouth, *East Anglian Archaeol* **2**, 131–245

Ruben, I and Ford, S, 1992 Archaeological Excavations at Wallingford Road, Didcot, South Oxon., *Oxoniensia* **57**, 1–28

Rudder, S, 1779 *A New History of Gloucestershire 1779*

Rudder, S, 1804 *A history of Cirencester*

Russell, R, 1971 *Lost canals of England and Wales*, Devon

Russett, V, 1989a The Conversion to Dual Carriageway of the A 4167 Birdlip to Stratton Trunk Route. Gloucestershire County Council

Russett, V, 1989b The Stratton and Cirencester Bypass. Gloucestershire County Council

Samson, R, 1984 *The social archaeology of houses*, Edinburgh University Press

Sandford, K S, 1965 Notes on the gravels of the upper Thames floodplain between Lechlade and Dorchester, *Proc Geol Soc* **76**.1, 61–76

Saville, A, 1979a *Recent work at Cow Common Bronze Age cemetery, Gloucestershire*, Committee For Rescue Archaeology In Avon, Gloucesterhsire And Somerset Occas. Paper No. **6**

Saville, A, 1979b *Excavations at Guiting Power, Iron Age Site, Gloucestershire 1974*, Committee For Rescue Archaeology In Avon, Gloucestershire And Somerset Occas. Paper No. **7**

Saville, A, 1980 *Archaeological Sites in the Avon and Gloucestershire Cotswolds,*. Committee for Rescue Archaeology in Avon, Gloucestershire and Somerset

Saville, A, 1983a *Uley Bury and Norbury Hillforts: rescue excavations at two Gloucestershire Iron Age sites*, Western Archaeological Trust Excavation Monograph No. **5**, Bristol

Saville, A, 1983b Excavations at Condicote Henge monument, Gloucestershire, *Trans Bristol Gloucestershire Archaeol Soc* **101**, 21–48

Saville, A, 1984a Palaeolithic and Mesolithic evidence from Gloucestershire, in Saville, A, 1984c, 60–79

Saville, A, 1984b The Iron Age in Gloucestershire: a review of the evidence, in Saville, A, 113–127

Saville, A, (ed.) 1984c *Archaeology in Gloucestershire*. Cheltenham Art Gall and Mus and the Bristol and Gloucestershire Archaeol Soc, Cheltenham

Saville, A, 1985 The flint, in Trow, S O

Saville, A, 1990 *Hazleton North, Gloucestershire, 1979–82: The excavation of a Neolithic long cairn of the Cotswold-Severn group*. English Heritage Archaeological Report **13**

Saville, A and Ellison, A, 1983 Excavations at Uley Bury hillfort, Gloucestershire 1976, in Saville, A, 1983a, 1–24

Scaife, R G, 1980 Late-Devensian and Flandrian palaeoecological studies in the Isle of Wight. Ph D thesis. University of London, King's College

Scaife, R G, 1986 Pollen in human palaeofaeces: and a preliminary investigation of the stomach and gut contents of Lindow Man, in Stead, I M, Bourke, J B and Brothwell, D R, 126–135

Scaife, R G, 1995 Pollen analysis of the Lindow III food residues, in Turner, R C and Scaife, R G, 83–85

Scaife, R G, 1997 Pollen assessment, in Lupton, A and Williams, R J

Schmid, E, 1972 *Atlas of animal bones*. Elsevier, Amsterdam

Schweingruber, F H, 1978 *Microscopic wood anatomy*. Teufen: F Fluck-Wirth.

Sealey, P R, 1985 *Amphorae from the 1970 Excavations at Colchester-Sheepen*, BAR Brit Ser **142**, Oxford

Sellwood, L, 1984 Tribal boundaries viewed from the perspective of numismatic evidence, in Cunliffe, B W and Miles, D, 191–204

Serjeantson, D, 1991a The bird bones, in Cunliffe, B W and Poole, C, 479–81

Serjeantson, D, 1991b Rid Grasse of Bones: a taphonomic study of the bones from midden deposits at the Neolithic and Bronze Age site of Runneymede, Surrey. *International J of Osteoarchaeol* **1**, 73–89

Serjeantson, D, 1996 The animal bones, in Needham, S and Spence, A, 194–222

Serjeantson, D and Waldron, T 1989 *Diet and Crafts in*

Towns: The evidence of animal remains from the Roman to the Post-Medieval periods, BAR Brit Ser **199**, Oxford

Sharples, N M, 1991 *Maiden Castle: Excavations and field survey 1985–6*. English Heritage Archaeol Rep **19**, London

Sheldon, H, 1981 London and south-east Britain, in King, A and Henig, M, 363–381

Shepherd, W, 1972 *Flint. Its origin, properties and uses*, London, Faber and Faber

Slade, H P, 1877 *A short practical treatise on dewponds*

Slater, T R, 1976 The town and its region in the Anglo-Saxon and medieval periods, in McWhirr, A D, 81–108

Slicker van Bath, B H, 1963 *The agrarian history of western Europe 500–1859*, London

Smith, I F, 1968 Report on late Neolithic pits at Cam, Gloucestershire, *Trans Bristol Gloucestershire Archaeol Soc* **87**, 14–28

Smith, I F, 1972 Ring ditches in eastern and central Gloucestershire, in Fowler, P J, 157–67

Smith, I F, 1976 The Neolithic, in Renfrew, 100–136

Smith, I F and Darvill, T, C, 1990 The prehistoric pottery, in Saville, A, 141–152

Smith J T, 1985 Barnsley Park Villa; its interpretation and implications, *Oxford J Archaeol.* 4 No. **3**, 341–352

Smith J T, 1992 The buildings: a commentary, in Mynard, D C and Zeepvat, R J, 121–130

Smith, R and Cox, P, 1985 *The past in the pipeline: Archaeology of the Esso Midline*. Salisbury

Smith, R F, 1987 *Roadside settlements in lowland Roman Britain*, BAR Brit Ser **157**, Oxford

Smith, R J C, 1986 Winson. In Archaeological Review 10, 1985 (ed. B Rawes), *Trans Bristol Gloucestershire Archaeol Soc* **104**, 246

Sørenson, M-L S and Thomas, R (eds) 1989 *The Bronxe Age-Iron Age transition in Europe*, BAR Internat Ser **483**. Oxford

Spencer, B, 1983 Limestone-tempered pottery from South Wales in the late Iron Age and early Roman periods, *Bull Celtic Stud* **30** (1982-3), 405–19

Stace, C, 1991 *New flora of the British Isles*. Cambridge: Cambridge University Press

Staines, B W and Ratcliffe, P R, 1991 Roe deer in Corbet, G B and Harris, S, 518–25

Stead I, 1976 *Excavations at Winterton Roman villa*, DoE Archaeological Rep. **9**. London

Stead, I M, Bourke, J B and Brothwell, D R 1986 *Lindow Man: The body in the bog*, British Museum Press

Stead, I M and Rigby, V, *1986 Baldock. The excavation of a Roman and pre-Roman settlement 1968–72*, Britannia Monograph Series No. **7**, Society for the promotion of Roman studies, Alan Sutton Publishing Ltd, Gloucester

Stead, I M and Rigby V, 1989 *Verulamium: The King Harry Lane Site*. English Heritage Archaeol Rep no. **12**. London

Stockmarr, J, 1971 Tablets with spores used in absolute pollen analysis. *Pollen et Spores* **13**, 614–621

Straker, V, 1998 Charred plant macrofossils, in Parry 77–80

Stuiver, M and Pearson, G W, 1993 *Radiocarbon* **35(1)**, 1

Sunter, N and Woodward, P J, 1987 *Romano-British*

industries in Purbeck, Dorset Nat Hist and Archaeol Soc Mono Ser **6**

Sutherland, D S (ed.), 1982 *Igneous rocks of the British Isles*. Wiley Interscience pub

Swan, V G, 1975 Oare reconsidered and the origins of Savernake ware in Wiltshire, *Britannia* **6**, 36–61

Sylvester-Bradley, P C and Ford, T D (eds), 1968 *The geology of the east Midlands*. Leicester University Press

Tapper, S C, 1991 Brown Hare, in Corbet, G B and Harris, S, 154–61

Taylor, C, 1975 *Fields in the English landscape*, Aldine Press, London

Taylor, C, 1979 *Roads and tracks of Britain*, Dent

Tchernia, A, 1980 Quelques remarques sur le commerce du vin et les amphores, in Arms, J H and Kopff, E C, 305–12

Tester, P J and Bing, H F, 1949 A first century urn-field at Cheriton, near Folkestone, *Archaeologia Cantiana* **62**, 21–36

Thawley, C, 1982 The animal remains, in Wacher, J S and McWhirr, A D, 211–228

Thomas, A and Holbrook, N, 1998 Excavations at the Memorial Hall, Lechlade, in Boyle, A, Jennings, D, Miles, D and Palmer, S, 282–8

Thomas, J, 1991 *Re-thinking the Neolithic*. New Studies in Archaeology. Cambridge University Press, Cambridge

Thomas, J D and Davies, R W 1977 A new military strength report on papyrus, *Journal of Roman Studies* **67**, 50–61

Thomas, R, 1980 A Bronze Age field system at Northfield Farm *Oxoniensia* **45**, 310–11

Thompson, F H, 1954 The excavation of a Roman Barrow at Riseholme, near Lincoln, *Antiquaries Journal* **34**, 28–37

Timby, J, 1990 Severn Valley wares: a reassessment. *Britannia* **21**, 243–51

Timby, J, 1998a *Excavations at Kingscote and Wycomb, Gloucestershire: A Roman Estate Centre and Small Town in the Cotswolds with Notes on Related Settlements*. CAT

Timby, J, 1998b The Beakers, in Thomas, A and Holbrook, N, 286

Timby, J R, 1999 The pottery, in A Bronze Age burnt mound at Sandy Lane, Charlton Kings, Cheltenham, Glos. Excavations in 1971, Cotswold Archaeol Trust, unpublished report No. 991005

Timby, J R, forthcoming The Pottery in E Price, *Frocester: a Romano-British settlement, its antecendents and successors*

Timby, J in prep. a Thornhill Farm

Timby, J, in prep. b The pottery from Huntsman Quarry, Naunton, Report prepared for Archaeological Survey and Evaluation Ltd, Sheffield

Timby, J in prep. C. The pottery from Sherbourne House, Lechlade, Report prepared for Cotswold Archaeological Trust

Timby, J R, unpub. a The pottery from Coppice Corner, Kingsholm, Glos, report prepared for Gloucester Excav Unit, 1989

Timby, J R, unpub. b The pottery from Abbeydale, Glos suburbs, report prepared for Gloucester Excav Unit

Timby, J R, Booth, P and Allen, T G, 1997 A new early Roman fineware industry in the Upper Thames Valley, unpub rep Oxford Archaeol Unit

Tixier, J, Inizan, M L and Roche, H, 1980 *Prehistoire de la pierre taillé: terminologie et technologie.* CREP, Antibes

Todd, M, 1978 *Studies in the Romano-British villa,* Leicester: University Press

Todd, M 1989 *Research on Roman Britain 1960–89,* London: Society for the Promotion of Roman Studies

Tomber, R and Dore, J, 1996 A National Roman Fabric Reference Collection, *Britannia* **27**, 368–82

Torrens, H S, 1982 The geology of Cirencester and district, in Wacher, J S and McWhirr, A, 72–8

Trinder B (ed.), 1992 *The Blackwell Encyclopaedia of Industrial Archaeology.* Blackwell

Trow, S D, 1982 The Bagendon Report 1981–1982: A Brief Interim Report. *Glevensis* **16**, 26–29

Trow, S D, 1985 An interrupted ditch enclosure at Southmore Grove, Rendcomb, Gloucestershire, *Trans Bristol Gloucestershire Archaeol Soc* **102**, 17–22

Trow, S D, 1988 Excavations at Ditches hillfort, North Cerney, Gloucestershire, 1982-3 *Trans Bristol Gloucestershire Archaeol Soc* **106**, 19–85

Trow, S D, 1990 By the northern shores of Ocean; some observations on acculturation process at the edge of the Roman world, in Blagg, T and Millett, M, 101–118

Trow-Smith, R, 1957 *A history of British livestock husbandry to 1700.* London

Tucker, D G, 1971 Millstone Making at Penallt, Monmouthshire, *Indust Archaeol Rev* **8**, 229–239

Turner, G, 1794 *A general view of the agriculture of the county of Gloucester*, London

Turner, J, 1962 The *Tilia* decline: an anthropogenic interpretation. *New Phytologist* **61**, 328–341

Turner, R J and Scaife, R 1995 *Bog Bodies. New Discoveries and New Perspectives*, British Museum Publication

Van der Veen, M, 1989 Charred grain assemblages from Roman Period corn dryers in Britain, *Archaeol J* **146**, 302–319

Van der Werff, J H, 1984 Roman amphorae at Nijmegen - a preliminary report, *Berichten van de Rijksdienst voor het, Oudheidkundig Bodemonderzoek* **34**, 347–87

Vince, A G, 1983 The medieval and post-medieval pottery, in Heighway, C M, 125–165

Viner, D J, 1978 A Palaeolithic implement from Cerney Wick. *Trans Bristol Gloucestershire Archaeol Soc* **96**, 69–70

Von den Driesch, A, 1976 A guide to the measurement of animal bones from archaeological sites *Peabody Mus Bull* **1**

Von den Driesch, A and Boessneck, J, 1974 Kritische Anmerkungen zur Widerristhöhenberechnung aus Längenmaßen vor- und frühgeschichtlicher Tierknochen. *Säugetierkundliche Mitteilungen* **4**, 325–348

Wacher, J S, 1974 *The Towns of Roman Britain,* Batsford

Wacher, J S, 1978 *Roman Britain,*

Wacher, J S and McWhirr, A D, 1982 *Early Roman Occupation at Cirencester.* Cirencester Excavations I, Cirencester Excavation Committee

Wainwright F T, 1959 Ermin Street at Cricklade *Wilts. Archaeol. Nat. Hist. Mag.* Vol. **57** no. 207, 192–200

Wainwright, G J, 1972 The flint, in The excavation of a Neolithic settlement at Broome Heath, Ditchingham, Norfolk (G J Wainwright), *Proc Prehist Soc* **38**, 46–68

Wainwright, G J, 1979 *Gussage All Saints: an Iron Age settlement in Dorset*, DOE Archaeol Rep, **10**, London

Waldén, H W, 1976 A nomenclatural list of land Mollusca of the British Isles, *Journal of Conchology*, London, **29**, 21–5

Walker, I C, 1967 Statistical Methods for Dating Clay Pipe Fragments, *Post-Medieval Archaeol* **1**, 90–101

Waller, M, 1994 Paludification and pollen representation; the influence of wetland size on *Tilia* representation in pollen diagrams. *Holocene* **4**, 430–434

Walters, H B, 1908 *Catalogue of Roman Pottery in the Department of Antiquities in the British Museum,* London

WANHM 1977–78, Evaluation and fieldwork in Wiltshire, *Wilts Archaeol Nat Hist Mag* **72–73**

WANHM 1994 Evaluation and Fieldwork in Wiltshire, *Wilts Archaeol Nat Hist Mag* **87**

WANHM 1995 Evaluation and Fieldwork in Wiltshire 1993, *Wilts Archaeol Nat Hist Mag* **88**.

Webster, G, 1967 Excavations at the Romano-British Villa in Barnsley Park, Cirencester 1961–66, *Trans Bristol Gloucestershire Archaeol Soc* **86**, 74–87

Webster, G, 1981a The Excavation of a Romano-British Rural Establishment at Barnsley Park, Gloucestershire, 1961–1979: Part 1 c. AD 140–360 *Trans Bristol Gloucestershire Archaeol Soc* **99**, 21–78

Webster, G, 1981b Final Report on the Excavations of the Roman Fort at Waddon Hill, Stoke Abbott, 1963–69, *Proc of the Dorset Nat Hist and Archaeol Soc* **101**, 51–90

Webster, G and Smith, L 1982 The excavation of a Romano-British rural establishment at Barnsley Park, Gloucestershire 1961–1979, Part II, c. AD 360–400+, *Trans Bristol and Glos Arch Soc* **100**, 65–189

Webster, J 1992 The objects of bronze, in Evans, D R and Metcalf, V M,

Webster, P V, 1976 Severn Valley ware, *Trans Bristol Gloucestershire Archaeol Soc* **94**, 18–46

Wedlake, W J, 1958 *Excavations at Camerton, Somerset,* privately pub

Wedlake, W J, 1982 *The Excavation of the Shrine of Apollo at Nettleton, Wiltshire, 1956–1971,* Rep of the Res Comm of the Soc of Antiq of London, **40**, Dorking.

Welfare, A, 1995 The milling-stones, in Manning, W

H, Price, J and Webster, J, 214–237

Whimster, R, 1981 *Burial Practices in Iron Age Britain. A Discussion and Gazetteer of the Evidence c. 700 B.C. – A.D. 43,*. BAR Brit Ser **90**, Oxford

White, D A, 1970 The excavation of an Iron Age round barrow near Handley, Dorset, 1969, *Antiq Journal* Vol **L (I)**, 26–36

Whitehead, B J, 1982 The topography and history of North Meadow, Cricklade, *Wilts Archaeol Nat Hist Mag* **76**, 129–140

Whitehead, P F, 1979 An Acheulian handaxe from South Cerney, Gloucestershire, *Trans Bristol Gloucestershire Archaeol Soc* **97**, 117–18

Whittle, A, Atkinson, R J C, Chambers, R and Thomas, N, 1992 Excavations in the Neolithic and Bronze Age complex at Dorchester-on-Thames, Oxfordshire, 1947–1952 and 1981, *Proc Prehist Soc* **58**, 143–202

Wickenden, N P, 1986 Prehistoric settlement and the Romano-British small town at Heybridge, Essex, *Essex Arch and Hist*, 7–68

Williams, A 1947 Excavations at Langford Downs, Oxon., (near Lechlade), *Oxoniensia* **11–12**, 44–62

Williams, D F, 1977 The Romaon-British black burnished industry, in Peacock, D P S, 163–220

Williams, D F 1982 Petrological analysis of the pottery in the Neolithic causewayed enclosure, Abingdon, in Case, H J and Whittle, A W R, 33–5

Williams, D F, 1986 The amphorae, in Foster, J, 124–32

Williams, D F and Peacock, D P S, 1994 Roman amphorae, in Fitzpatrick, A P and Morris, E L, 29–32

Williams, J, 1976 Excavations on a Roman site at Overstone, near Northampton, *Northamptonshire Archaeology* **11**, 100–33

Williams, J H 19 St Peter's Street Northampton; Excavations 1973-1976, Northampton Development Corporation Monograph Series No. **2**, Northampton

Williams, R J, 1993 *Pennyland and Hartigans. Two Iron Age and Saxon sites in Milton Keynes*, Bucks Archaeol Soc Monograph Series, No. **4**, Aylesbury

Williams, R J, 1997 Clay Pipe Assessment, in Lupton, A and Williams, R J

Williams, R J, Hart, P J and Williams, A T L 1996 *Wavendon Gate: a late Iron Age and Roman settlement in Milton Keynes*, Buckinghamshire Archaeol. Soc. Mono. Series **10**

Williams, R J and Zeepvat, R J, 1994   *Bancroft: a late Bronze Age/Iron Age settlement, Roman Villa and Temple-Mausoleum*, (2 Vols.), Buckinghamshire Archaeol. Soc. Monograph. Series **7**

Wilson, B, 1979 The animal bones, in Saville, A, 141–44

Wilson, B, Grigson, C and Payne, S, 1982 *Ageing and sexing animal bones from archaeological sites*, BAR Brit Ser **109**, Oxford

Wilson, C E, 1981 Burials within settlements in southern Britain during the pre-Roman Iron Age *Bulletin Inst. of Archaeol.*, **18**

Wilson, R, 1985 Degraded bones, feature type and spatial patterning on an Iron Age occupation site in Oxfordshire, England, in Fieller, N R J, Gilbertson, D D and Ralph, N G A, 81–94

Wilson, R, 1993, The animal bones, in Allen, T G and Robinson, M A, 123-34 and 168–204

Wilson, R, 1996 *Spatial Patterning Among Animal Bones in Settlement Archaeology: an English Regional Exploration*, BAR Brit Ser **251**, Oxford

Wilson, R in preparation Thornhill Farm

Windell, D, 1983 Clay Lane 1980: Interim Report, in *Northamptonshire Archaeology* **18**, 33–42.

Woodiwiss, S 1992 *Iron Age and Roman salt production and the medieval Town of Droitwich*, CBA Res Rep **81**, London

Woodward, A and Leach, P, 1993 *The Uley Shrines. Excavation of a ritual complex on West Hill, Uley, Gloucestershire: 1977–9*. English Heritage Archaeol Rep **17**, London

Woodward, P J, 1987 The excavation of a late Iron Age settlement and Romano-British industrial site at Ower, Dorset, in Sunter, N and Woodward, A, 45–124

Workshop of European Anthropologists, 1980 Recommendations for age and sex diagnoses of skeletons, *J Hum Evol* **9**, 517–549

Wrathmell, S and Nicholson, A 1990, *Dalton Parlours Iron Age settlement and Roman Villa*, Yorkshire Archaeol **3**, West Yorkshire Archaeological Service, Wakefield,

Yates, D T, 1997 Bronze Age field systems in lowland Britain: The Thames Valley. Unpublished MA thesis, Dept. of Archaeology, University of Reading

Young, C J, 1977 *Oxfordshire Roman Pottery*, BAR Brit Ser **143**, Oxford

Zienkiewicz, J D, 1986 The Legionary Fortress Baths at Caerleon, Cardiff

INDEX

Note 1: Page references in *italics* denote figures and plates. There may also be textual references on these pages.
Note 2: Subheadings are in alphabetical order, except for pottery subheadings which are in chronological order.